UNDERSTANDING AND USING
English Grammar

FIFTH EDITION

Betty S. Azar
Stacy A. Hagen

Understanding and Using English Grammar, Fifth Edition with MyEnglishLab

Azar Associates: Sue Van Etten, Manager

Pearson Education, 221 River Street, Hoboken, NJ 07030

Staff credits: The people who made up the *Understanding and Using English Grammar Fifth Edition* team, representing content creation, design, manufacturing, marketing, multimedia, project management, publishing, rights management, and testing, are Pietro Alongi, Rhea Banker, Elizabeth Barker, Claire Bowers, Stephanie Bullard, Jennifer Castro, Tracey Cataldo, Dave Dickey, Warren Fischbach, Nancy Flaggman, Lester Holmes, Gosia Jaros-White, Barry Katzen, Amy McCormick, Julie Molnar, Brian Panker, Stuart Radcliffe, Jennifer Raspiller, Lindsay Richman, Robert Ruvo, Alexandra Suarez, Paula Van Ells, and Joseph Vella.

Contributing Editors: Barbara Lyons, Janice L. Baillie
Text composition: Aptara

Disclaimer: This work is produced by Pearson Education and is not endorsed by any trademark owner referenced in this publication.

Library of Congress Cataloging-in-Publication Data

A catalog record for the print edition is available from the Library of Congress.

Printed in the United States of America
ISBN 13: 978-0-13-399459-9
ISBN 10: 0-13-399459-7

12 2022

ISBN 13: 978-0-13-427526-0 (International Edition)
ISBN 10: 0-13-427526-8 (International Edition)

To my beautiful grandsons,
Jude and Asa
B.S.A.

For Andy and Julianna
S.H.

Contents

Preface to the Fifth Edition

Understanding and Using English Grammar is a developmental skills text for intermediate to advanced English language learners. It functions principally as a classroom teaching text but also serves as a comprehensive reference text for students and teachers.

Understanding and Using English Grammar takes a time-tested approach that blends direct grammar instruction with carefully sequenced practice to develop all language skills. Grammar is viewed as an organizing system to help students make sense of the language they see and hear, rather than as a mere collection of rules. This perspective provides a natural, logical framework for students to make English their own.

This edition has been extensively revised to keep pace with advances in theory and practice. Every aspect of the previous edition was reviewed, including the charts, exercises, and sequencing of grammar points. We are excited to introduce significant new features and updates:

- **New as well as updated grammar charts based on corpus research** reflect current usage and highlight the differences between written and spoken English in informal and formal contexts.

- **Pretests at the start of chapters** let learners check what they already know and orient themselves to the chapter content.

- **A wide range of thematic exercises** provides opportunities for contextualized language use.

- **A variety of new readings** covers current topics, strategies for student success, study skills, and other academic and practical content.

- **More meaning-based and step-by-step practice** helps learners better grasp concepts underlying the target grammar.

- **Article use (*a, the, an*)** is now the focus of an entire chapter.

- **New guided writing activities** are supported by writing tips and editing tasks.

- **Self-study practice for gerunds and infinitives** has been added, beginning with Chapter 1, so that students can learn at their own pace.

- **A fresh design** includes a generous use of photos to add interest and serve as the basis for fluency practice.

- **A large increase in the number of exercises** supports teachers who would prefer not to supplement.

- **Three topics, absent in the Fourth Edition, are back in the Fifth Edition:** *The Subjunctive in Noun Clauses, Past Forms of Infinitives and Gerunds*, and *Using a Possessive to Modify a Gerund*.

Now more than ever, teachers will find that they can select from an extensive repertoire of presentations, activities, and tasks depending on the specific needs of their classes. To accommodate all of the new material, some Fourth Edition content has been moved to MyEnglishLab.

Components of *Understanding and Using English Grammar*, Fifth Edition:

- **Student Book with Essential Online Resources** includes the access code for audio, video, expanded practice of gerunds and infinitives, self-assessments, and teacher resources with the Student Book answer key.
- **Student Book with MyEnglishLab** includes the access code to MyEnglishLab, an easy-to-use online learning management system that delivers rich online practice to engage and motivate students.
- A comprehensive **Workbook** consists of self-study exercises for independent work.
- A **Teacher's Guide** features step-by-step teaching suggestions for each chart and notes on key grammar structures, vocabulary lists, and expansion activities.
- A revised **Test Bank** with quizzes, chapter tests, and mid-term and final exams.
- A **Chartbook**, a reference book that consists of only the grammar charts.
- *AzarGrammar.com,* a website that provides a variety of supplementary classroom materials as well as a place where teachers can support each other by sharing their knowledge and experience.

MyEnglishLab

MyEnglishLab provides a range of interactive activities that help motivate and engage students. MyEnglishLab for *Understanding and Using English Grammar,* Fifth Edition has been thoroughly revised and includes:

- Rich online practice for all skill areas: grammar, reading, writing, speaking, and listening.
- Instant feedback on incorrect answers.
- Remediation activities.
- Grammar Coach videos.
- Bonus material not included in the Student Book, including expanded practice of gerunds and infinitives.
- Robust assessments that include diagnostic tests, chapter review tests, mid- and end-of-term review tests, and final exams.
- Gradebook and diagnostic tools that allow teachers to monitor student progress and analyze data to determine steps for remediation and support.
- Student Book answer key in the Teacher Resource folder.

The Azar-Hagen Grammar Series consists of

- *Understanding and Using English Grammar* (blue cover), for upper-level students.
- *Fundamentals of English Grammar* (black), for mid-level students.
- *Basic English Grammar* (red), for lower or beginning levels.

Acknowledgments

We are indebted to the reviewers and other outstanding teachers who contributed to this edition by giving us extensive feedback on the Fourth edition and helping us shape the new Fifth edition.

In particular, we would like to thank Maureen S. Andrade, Utah Valley University; Dorothy Avondstondt, Miami Dade College; Judith Campbell, University of Montreal; Holly Cin, Houston Community College; Eileen M. Cotter, Montgomery College, MD; Andrew Donlan, International Language Institute, Washington, D.C.; Gillian L. Durham, Tidewater Community College; Jill M. Fox, University of Nebraska; William Hennessey IV, Florida International University; Clay Hindman, Sierra Community College; Sharla Jones, San Antonio College; Balynda Kelly Foster, Spring International Language Center, CO; June Ohrnberger, Suffolk County Community College, NY; Deniz Ozgorgulu, Bogazici University, Turkey; Jan Peterson, Edmonds Community College; Miriam Pollack, Grossmont College; Carol Siegel, Community College of Baltimore County; Elizabeth Marie Van Amerongen, Community College of Baltimore County; Daniela C. Wagner-Loera, University of Maryland, College Park; Kirsten Windahl, Cuyahoga Community College.

From the start, we have benefited from a first-rate management and editorial team that helped us every step of the way. Gosia Jaros-White, our publisher at Pearson, handled each stage of the process with focus, efficiency, and kindness. We were lucky to once again have Robert Ruvo, our project manager at Pearson, to keep track of a myriad of detail with schedule, production, and delivery. Barbara Lyons, our development editor, brought unparalleled skill and insight to the charts and exercises. Our longtime production editor whiz, Janice Baillie, has an encyclopedic knowledge of the series, and every page benefited from her expertise. We are grateful as always to Sue Van Etten, our steady and savvy business and website manager, for keeping the business side of things running smoothly.

We'd also like to thank the talented writers we are so fortunate to have: Geneva Tesh, Houston Community College, for the new Workbook and MyEnglishLab material; Kelly Roberts Weibel, Edmonds Community College, for the updated Test Bank, and Martha Hall, the New England School of English, for the revised Teacher's Guide.

We are grateful to the Pearson design team of Tracey Cataldo, Warren Fischbach, and Stephanie Bullard for their creativity and patience.

Our gratitude also goes to Pietro Alongi, Director of Content, and Amy McCormick, Category Manager at Pearson. They have been involved with the series for many years now, and we appreciate the dedication they bring to each new edition and their vision for the series.

Our thanks also to our illustrators Don Martinetti and Chris Pavely for their engaging artwork.

Finally, we would like to thank our families for always supporting us and cheering us on.

Betty S. Azar
Stacy A. Hagen

Present and Past; Simple and Progressive

PRETEST: What do I already know?

Write "C" if a sentence has the correct verb form and "I" for incorrect. Check your answers below. After you complete each chart listed, make any necessary corrections.

1. _____ Air is consisting of oxygen, nitrogen, and other gases. (1-1)

2. _____ I am working overtime this week. (1-1)

3. _____ Does the copy machine working right now? (1-2)

4. _____ We aren't knowing Sami's wife. (1-3)

5. _____ My cell phone network is always being slow. (1-3)

6. _____ Gloria canceled her doctor's appointment because she felt better. (1-4)

7. _____ I turned on the stove, am boiling the water, and forget to put in the rice. (1-4)

8. _____ A few children drawed some pictures this morning while the teacher was talking. (1-5)

9. _____ When I turned the key, the car wasn't starting. (1-5)

10. _____ I was going to call you, but my phone died. (1-6)

Incorrect sentences: 1, 3, 4, 5, 7, 8, 9

EXERCISE 1 ▸ Warm-up. (Chart 1-1)

Match the description with the sentence. Which sentences do you agree with?

a. action happening right now

b. general truth

c. habit

1. _____ I look at the stars every night.

2. _____ I'm looking at an astronomy textbook.

3. _____ The earth revolves around the sun.

1-1 Simple Present and Present Progressive

This basic diagram will be used in all tense descriptions.

SIMPLE PRESENT ✳✳✳✳✳✳✳✳✳✳✳	(a) Water *consists* of hydrogen and oxygen. (b) The average person *breathes** 21,600 times a day. (c) The world *is* round.	The simple present says that something was true in the past, is true in the present, and will be true in the future. It expresses *general statements of fact and general truths.*
	(d) I *get* up at seven *every morning.* (e) I *always eat* a salad for lunch.	The simple present is used to express *habitual or everyday activities.*
PRESENT PROGRESSIVE start / now / finish? / in progress	(f) The students *are sitting* at their desks right now. (g) I need an umbrella because it *is raining.* (h) I *am taking* five courses this semester.	The present progressive expresses an activity that is *in progress at the moment of speaking.* The present progressive is a temporary activity that began in the past, is continuing at present, and will probably end at some point in the future.

*See Appendix Chart E-2 for spelling rules for *-ing* verbs and Appendix Chart E-6 for final *-s* pronunciation.

EXERCISE 2 ▶ Let's talk. (Chart 1-1)

Work in small groups. Each member of the group should contribute one sentence for each topic. Share some of your sentences with the class.

1. Tell your group one daily habit you have.
2. Look around the room. Make a sentence about one activity that is happening right now.
3. In one sentence, state a general truth about the world.

EXERCISE 3 ▶ Looking at grammar. (Chart 1-1)

Complete the sentences. Use the simple present or the present progressive of the verbs in parentheses.

1. a. Kristin is in the shower. She (*wash*) _____is washing_____ her hair.

   b. Kristin (*wash*) _____ her hair every other day or so.

2. a. Tony usually (*sit*) _____ in the front row during class.

   b. Today he (*sit*) _____ in the last row.

3. a. Lars (*work*) _____ the night shift on weekends.

   b. He's not home now. He (*work*) _____ a double shift.

4. a. After six days of rain, I'm glad that the sun (*shine*) _____ .

   b. Every morning, the sun (*shine*) _____ in my bedroom window and

   (*wake*) _____ me up.

5. a. Babies (*grow*) _____ very quickly. Newborn babies are very different from three-month olds.

   b. Your baby (*grow*) _____ so fast. She isn't a newborn anymore!

6. a. Please be quiet. I (*try*) _____ to concentrate on my math homework.

   b. Each day, our math teacher (*try*) _____ to explain the material clearly, but I am very confused.

EXERCISE 4 ▸ Let's talk. (Chart 1-1)

With a partner, take turns making a few sentences about each picture. Use the present progressive. You can be imaginative!

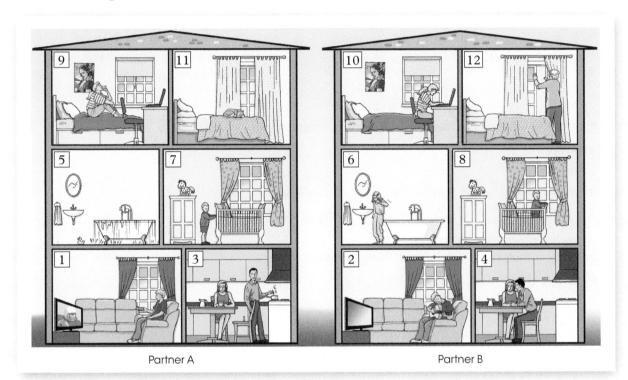

Partner A   Partner B

Examples:

PARTNER A: In picture 1, the boy is watching sports on TV.
He is holding a remote.
He is changing channels.
He is looking for a baseball game. Etc.

PARTNER B: In picture 2, the boy is not watching TV.
He is playing the guitar.
Maybe he is practicing a popular song. Etc.

EXERCISE 5 ▸ Looking at grammar. (Chart 1-1)

Choose the correct completion(s). Discuss your answers with the class.

1. In early summer, the sun ____ around 9:00 P.M. in my hometown.
   a. sets (It's a general statement of fact.)
   b. is setting (It's happening right now.)
   c. Both are possible.

2. It's a beautiful evening. I'm sitting outside. The sun ____ behind the mountains.
   a. sets (It's a general truth.)
   b. is setting (It's happening right now.)
   c. Both are possible.

3. Rice _____ in about 15 minutes.
    a. cooks (It's a general truth.)
    b. is cooking (It's happening right now.)
    c. Both are possible.

4. Hurry! The rice _____ over onto the stove.
    a. boils (It's a general statement of fact.)
    b. is boiling (It's happening right now.)
    c. Both are possible.

5. Dr. Costa _____ his hospital patients before office hours.
    a. visits (It's a habitual activity.)
    b. is visiting (It's happening right now.)
    c. Both are possible.

6. Leo _____ his bike through downtown traffic every day to work.
    a. rides (It's a habitual activity.)
    b. is riding (It's happening right now.)
    c. Both are possible.

7. Jenna _____ for her grandparents at their hotel.
    a. works (It's a habitual activity.)
    b. is working (It's happening right now.)
    c. Both are possible.

8. Francine and Marco _____ each other several times a day.
    a. text (It's a habitual activity.)
    b. are texting (It's happening right now.)
    c. Both are possible.

 EXERCISE 6 ▸ Listening. (Chart 1-1)
Listen to the sentences. Choose <u>all</u> the correct completions.

Outdoors

1. right now.	every day.	in the summer.
2. today.	in the winter.	every April.
3. every year.	right now.	this week.
4. right now.	today.	every winter.
5. every summer.	right now.	in the spring.
6. this week.	every January.	every winter.
7. right now.	every summer.	this month.

EXERCISE 7 ▸ Reading and grammar. (Chart 1-1)
Read the passage. Add the endings **-s/-es** where necessary. You may need to change **-y** to **-ies**. Write **Ø** for no ending.

Do you know these words?
- *amazing*
- *organ*
- *pump*
- *oxygen*
- *waste*
- *tissues*

Our Amazing Heart

The heart is an amazing organ. It beat___ 100,000

times a day and pump___ 2,000 gallons of blood through
                    2

60,000 miles of blood vessels in our bodies. Blood

carry___ fresh oxygen from our lungs to all the parts of
     3

the body. It also remove___ waste from our tissues. Here
                         4

is an interesting fact: when we laugh___, up to 20% more
                                    5

blood go___ through our body, so laughter is good for our
        6

hearts.

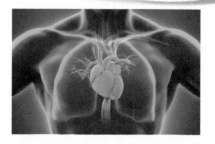

EXERCISE 8 ▶ Warm-up. (Chart 1-2)

Choose the correct completions.

1. Cold air isn't / doesn't rise.
2. What is / does water consist of?
3. Is / Does the earth spinning rapidly or slowly?

1-2	**Simple Present and Present Progressive: Affirmative, Negative, Question Forms**						
	Simple Present			**Present Progressive**			
AFFIRMATIVE		I	help.			I	am	helping.
	You, We, They		help.		You, We, They		are	helping.
	He, She, It		helps.		He, She, It		is	helping.
NEGATIVE		I	do not	help.		I	am not	helping.
	You, We, They		do not	help.		You, We, They		are not	helping.
	He, She, It		does not	help.		He, She, It		is not	helping.
QUESTION	Do	I		help?	Am	I		helping?
	Do	you, we, they		help?	Are	you, we, they		helping?
	Does	he, she, it		help?	Is	he, she, it		helping?
	When do	I		help?	When am	I		helping?

EXERCISE 9 ▶ Looking at grammar. (Chart 1-2)

Complete the sentences with **Do**, **Does**, **Is**, or **Are**.

On an Airplane

1. ___Are___ you ready for takeoff?
2. _____ the plane taking off soon?
3. _____ you nervous?
4. _____ you have your seat belt on?
5. _____ the seats comfortable?
6. _____ your seat comfortable?
7. _____ the seat go back more?

8. _____ they serve food on this flight?
9. _____ the movie beginning?
10. _____ you like to fly?
11. _____ the co-pilot flying the plane?
12. _____ the pilot sleep during the flight?
13. _____ the pilots sleep during the flight?
14. _____ the plane on autopilot?

EXERCISE 10 ▶ Trivia game. (Chart 1-2)

Work in teams. Make true sentences. The team with the most correct answers (factually and grammatically) wins. Use the simple present or present progressive.

1. Ice (*melt*) ___doesn't melt___ at 32°F (0°C).
2. Cold weather (*cause*) _____ fingernails to grow faster.
3. The average person (*fall*) _____ asleep in seven minutes.
4. Salt water (*freeze*) _____ at the same temperature as freshwater.

5. Our noses (*grow*) _____ longer as we age.

6. Our feet (*become*) _____ smaller as we age.

7. Red blood cells in our body (*divide*) _____ right now.

8. On average, a person (*blink*) _____ more than 20,000 times a day.

9. Honey (*spoil*) _____ .

10. A cat (*use*) _____ its whiskers for hunting.

11. The earth (*revolve*) _____ around the moon right now.

12. The earth (*get*) _____ warmer according to scientists.

EXERCISE 11 ▸ Reading and grammar. (Charts 1-1 and 1-2)
Choose the correct completions.

Tornadoes

Tornadoes   occur / are occurring ¹   in most areas of the world. However, the plains of the United States   have / are having ²   the most. (Plains are large areas of flat land with few trees.) Tornado Alley, a frequent area for tornadoes,   stretches / is stretching ³   from Texas to North Dakota. Because tornadoes   form / are forming ⁴   over flat areas of land, they   are not / do not ⁵   so common in the mountains. Cold air   meets / is meeting ⁶   warm air, usually in a thunderstorm. The winds   make / are making ⁷   a spiral or funnel cloud that sometimes reaches 320 miles per hour. They   pick up / are picking up ⁸   cars, trees, and houses. Sometimes this debris   flies / is flying ⁹   for miles. Strong tornadoes   cause / are causing ¹⁰   a lot of damage. Surprisingly, the funnel cloud   doesn't last / isn't lasting ¹¹   long, usually less than ten minutes.

   Right now a tornado   forms / is forming ¹²   over the plains. People   seek / are seeking ¹³   shelter in underground areas such as basements.

Several storm chasers   get / are getting ¹⁴   ready to follow the tornado and collect data. They listen / are listening ¹⁵   to weather radios for storm updates.

   Are you / Do you ¹⁶   familiar with tornadoes?
Are you / Do you ¹⁷   have tornadoes in your area?

EXERCISE 12 ▸ Warm-up. (Chart 1-3)
Choose the correct completions.

1. The chef is in his kitchen right now. He _____.
   a. cooks   b. is cooking

2. He _____ some soup.
   a. tastes   b. is tasting

3. It _____ too salty.
   a. tastes   b. is tasting

4. He _____ it.
   a. doesn't like   b. isn't liking

1-3 Verbs Not Usually Used in the Progressive (Stative Verbs)

(a) I *know* your cousin. (b) *INCORRECT:* ~~I am knowing~~ your cousin.	Some verbs, like ***know***, are *stative* or *non-progressive.* They describe states, not actions, and are rarely used in progressive tenses. ("States" are conditions or situations that exist.)

Common Verbs That Are Usually Non-Progressive (like *know*)

know	like	dislike	belong	consist of	hear	agree
believe	appreciate	fear	possess	contain	sound	disagree
doubt	care about	hate	own			mean
recognize	please	mind		exist	seem	promise
remember	prefer		desire	matter	look like	amaze
suppose			need		resemble	surprise
understand			want			
			wish			

(c) I *think* that your cousin is very nice. (d) I'm *thinking* about my trip to Rome.	Some verbs, like ***think***, have both *non-progressive* meanings and *progressive* meanings. In (c): ***think*** means "believe." In (d): ***am thinking*** means "thoughts are going around in my mind right now."

Common Verbs with Both Non-Progressive and Progressive Meanings (like *think*)

	NON-PROGRESSIVE	PROGRESSIVE
look	It *looks* cold outside.	Olga *is looking* out the window.
appear	Jack *appears* to be tired today.	She's *appearing* on a TV show today.
think	I *think* that Mr. Liu is a good teacher.	I'm *thinking* about my family right now.
feel	I *feel* that Mr. Liu is a good teacher.	I'm *feeling* a little tired today.
have	I *have* a bike.	I'm *having* a good time.
see	*Do* you *see* that bird?	The doctor *is seeing* a patient right now.
taste	The soup *tastes* salty.	The chef *is tasting* the soup.
smell	Something *smells* bad. What is it?	Ann *is smelling* the perfume to see if she wants to buy it.
love	Ken *loves* his baby daughter.	Ken is enjoying parenthood. In fact, he's *loving* it!
be	Mary *is* old and wise.	Al is ill but won't see a doctor. He *is being foolish.**

*****Am/is/are being** + an *adjective* describes temporary behavior. In the example, Al is usually not foolish, but right now he is acting that way.

EXERCISE 13 ▸ Reading, grammar, and speaking. (Charts 1-1 → 1-3)

Part I. Read the paragraph. <u>Underline</u> the verbs that are generally non-progressive. Then write the correct verb endings in the list of benefits: **-s**, **-es**, or **-ies**. Write **Ø** for no ending.

A Summer Internship

Lilly wants to get a job as a restaurant chef. Her culinary arts instructor believes a summer internship at a major restaurant is a good idea. Interns work for free or for a low wage, but they understand that they are receiving valuable experience in return. Some schools offer credit for an internship, and some companies hire their interns when the internship is over. Following are other benefits:

1. An internship apply____ classroom knowledge to real-world work experience.

2. It provide____ on-the-job training.

3. It teach____ important workplace habits (e.g., being on time) and workplace etiquette (how to behave at a company).

4. Interns learn____ about various jobs and opportunities within a company.

5. It give____ students the chance to network with employees.

6. The job experience look____ good on a résumé.

Part II. Find information about a volunteer organization that interests you. It could be a club at your school, a group in your community, a world organization, etc. Make a list of the ways it is helpful. Write 5–7 sentences and present them to the class. Title your list:

Benefits of _____

EXERCISE 14 ▸ Let's talk. (Chart 1-3)

Discuss the differences in meaning of the *italicized* verbs in each group of sentences. Work in pairs, in small groups, or as a class.

At the Park

1. a. These flowers *smell* good.
   b. Jane *is smelling* the flowers.

2. a. I *think* this park is beautiful.
   b. I need to relax. I *am thinking* about all the homework I have.

3. a. You *look* cold. I'll lend you my coat.
   b. I'*m looking* at the sky. A storm is coming.

4. a. I *see* a colorful kite. It's over there.
   b. Alex is coming later. He *is seeing* a doctor about his headaches.
   c. Jack and Ann come here every weekend. They *are seeing* each other.

5. a. I *remember* my first time here. *Do* you *remember* yours?
   b. I'*m remembering* a family picnic here with my cousins. It's a happy memory.

6. a. The children want a snack. They'*re* hungry.
   b. The children *are being* awfully quiet. What are they doing?

7. a. Every weekend there is an outdoor play here. Some of my friends *are appearing* in it.
   b. There is a man coming toward us. He's smiling. He *appears* to know us.

8. a. Gabriel *is being* rude. He's just sitting there, not talking to anyone.
   b. No, he *isn't* rude. He's just shy.

9. a. The baby *is feeling* the grass.
   b. The grass *feels* soft.
   c. I need to sit down. I*'m not feeling* well right now.
   d. I *feel* that it is important to take care of our parks.

EXERCISE 15 ▶ Looking at grammar. (Chart 1-3)

Choose the correct completions.

1. This isn't my book. It _____ to Mai.
   a. belongs   b. is belonging

2. Ask Ahmed for your book. He _____ it.
   a. has   b. is having

3. Your book is over there. Ahmed _____ it.
   a. holds   b. is holding

4. Olga is smiling. She _____ a good time.
   a. has   b. is having

5. Relax. Everything is OK. I _____ you.
   a. believe   b. am believing

6. My computer says my file no longer _____.
   a. exists   b. is existing

EXERCISE 16 ▶ Let's talk. (Charts 1-1 → 1-3)

With a partner, choose one of the pictures and complete the related conversation. Then practice your conversation and perform it for the class. You can look at your book before you speak. When you speak, look at your partner.

1. A: Mmmm. That looks _____.

   B: Thanks. It's fresh out of the oven.

   A: Is it _____?

   B: Yes. And it's my own recipe. Would you

        like to _____?

   A: Wow! It tastes _____.

   B: _____.

2. A: You look _____.

   B: I am.

   A: What's _____?

   B: I _____.

   A: You need to _____.

   B: I know, but I have too much/many _____.

EXERCISE 17 ▸ Looking at grammar. (Charts 1-1 → 1-3)
Choose the correct completions.

1. A: What   are you looking / do you look   at?

   B: You! You   look / are looking   like your father.

   A: Are you thinking / Do you think   so? Many people tell me I   am resembling / resemble
   my mother.

   B: I   see / am seeing   your father's face when I look at you.

2. A: Why   are mosquitos existing / do mosquitos exist?

   B: I   know / am knowing   one reason: they are a food source for other animals.

3. Right now I   sit / am sitting   in the cafeteria. Yoko   texts / is texting.   Ming   is opening / opens
   his lunch. Jae   is taking / takes   a bite of his sandwich. Ali   is staring / stares   off into space.
   He   seems / is seeming   to be daydreaming, but perhaps he   thinks / is thinking   about the test
   next hour. What   do you think / are you thinking   Ali   is doing / does?

EXERCISE 18 ▸ Grammar and listening. (Charts 1-1 → 1-3)
Complete the sentences with the given verbs. Then listen to the forecast and check your answers.

Weather Report

Hello, this is Gayle Givens, your WWKK weather reporter. Well, it certainly (*be*)

_____ a beautiful day today. I (*stand*) _____ here at
                    1   2

City Park and boy,* the sun sure (*shine*) _____. Hundreds of people (*enjoy*)
                                              3

_____ the warmer temperatures today. There (*be*) _____ not
              4   5

a cloud in the sky. We (*look*) _____ at a perfect day right now, but it (*look*)
                                      6

_____ like some clouds (*form*) _____ over the ocean and colder
           7   8

air (*move*) _____ in. We (*forecast*) _____ cooler
                  9   10

temperatures for tomorrow. I (*think*) _____ rain (*be*) _____ unlikely,
                                            11   12

however. Stay tuned for the three-day forecast right after this message.

EXERCISE 19 ▸ Looking at grammar. (Charts 1-1 → 1-3)
Complete the sentences. Use the simple present or the present progressive of the verbs in parentheses.

1. Look! It (*begin*) _____*is beginning*_____ to rain. Unfortunately, I (*have, not***)

   _____ an umbrella with me. I (*own, not*) _____

   an umbrella. Spiro is lucky. He (*wear*) _____ a raincoat. I

   (*wear*) _____ a waterproof hat on rainy days.

---

*Boy is an exclamation to express a strong feeling; similar to *wow*.

A form of **do is usually used in the negative when the main verb is **have**, especially in American English (AmE) but also
commonly in British English (BrE): *I don't have a car.* Using **have** without a form of **do** is also possible but less common:
I haven't a car.

2. Martha is in science class. The chemistry experiment she (*do*) _____
is dangerous, so right now she (*be*) _____ very careful. She
(*want, not*) _____ to spill any of the chemical. She (*be, always*)
_____ careful when she does a chemistry experiment.

3. Right now I (*look*) _____ at Nicole. She (*look*) _____ angry.
I wonder what's the matter. She (*have*) _____ a frown on her face. She certainly
(*have, not*) _____ any fun right now.

4. A: How (*you, like*) _____ the soup? (*it, need*) _____ more garlic?

   B: No, it (*taste*) _____ delicious. It (*remind*) _____ me of my mom's soup.

EXERCISE 20 ▶ Reading and writing. (Charts 1-1 → 1-3)

Part I. Read the review of the movie. <u>Underline</u> the verbs.
What verb tense is used to describe the action?

Do you know these words?
- unjustly
- accuse
- marshall
- vow
- dam
- pharmaceutical
- suspenseful

The Fugitive

The Fugitive is an action-packed, edge-of-your-seat movie. The police unjustly accuse Dr. Richard Kimball, the main character, of his wife's murder. A court finds him guilty and sentences him to death. On the way to jail, the prison bus crashes and Kimball escapes. A U.S. marshall, Samuel Gerard, vows to catch Kimball. Several times he almost succeeds, but Kimball stays one step ahead of Gerard. In one incredible scene, Kimball jumps from the top of a dam into a river to escape.

Kimball doesn't want Gerard to catch him, but he also wants to solve the murder of his wife. His search for answers takes him to Chicago. He finds upsetting information about a friend and the friend's work with a pharmaceutical company. After many suspenseful scenes, Kimball finds the real killers and leads Gerard to them.

Part II. Action in stories (books, movies, TV shows, etc.) is often told in the simple present tense. Find a movie you like. In simple English, tell what happens, give details about the movie, and tell how it ends. Here are some possible ways to begin:

- _____ is an inspiring/exciting/funny/etc., movie. (*The main character*) …
- A dramatic/suspenseful/exciting movie is _____ . In this movie, …
- (*The name of the movie*) is about _____ . In this movie, …

Part III. Edit your paragraph. Underline the verbs. Did you use present tense? Check for the correct use of the third person *-s/-es/-ies* endings.

EXERCISE 21 ▸ Warm-up. (Chart 1-4)

Ask another classmate these questions. Share your answers with the class. Find out the most common answers.

1. In what century did your great-grandparents live? They lived in the _____ century.

2. Where did they grow up? They grew up in (*city/country*) _____ .

1-4 Simple Past Tense	
(a) It *snowed** yesterday. (b) Tom *watched* TV last night.	*At one particular time in the past,* this happened. It began and ended in the past. Most simple past verbs add *-ed*, as in (a) and (b).
(c) Jack *went* to work early. (d) I *came* to work late. (e) We *saw* a great movie last night.	Some verbs have irregular past tense forms, as in (c), (d), and (e). NOTE: See Appendix Chart E-9 for a list of irregular verb forms.
(f) Emily *was* at the office this morning. (g) You *were* tired yesterday.	The simple past forms of *be* are *was* and *were*, as in (f) and (g).
(h) Andrew *caught* the ball, *ran* down the field, and *scored* a point. 	Note that in a series of actions, the verbs are the same tense, as in (h). *INCORRECT:* Andrew caught the ball, ~~is running~~ down the field, and ~~score~~ a point.

Regular Verb Forms

AFFIRMATIVE		NEGATIVE		QUESTION		
I You He, She, It We They	*helped*.	I You He, She, It We They	*did not help*.	*Did* *Did* *Did* *Did* *Did*	I you he, she, it we they	*help?*

Irregular Verb Forms

AFFIRMATIVE		NEGATIVE		QUESTION		
I You He, She, It We They	*ate*.	I You He, She, It We They	*did not eat*.	*Did* *Did* *Did* *Did* *Did*	I you he, she, it we they	*eat?*

***Be* Verb Forms**

AFFIRMATIVE			NEGATIVE			QUESTION		
I, He, She, It You, We, They	*was* *were*	here. here.	I, He, She, It You, We, They	*was not* *were not*	here. here.	*Was* *Were*	I, he, she, it you, we, they	here? here?

*See Appendix Chart E-5 for information about final *-ed* pronunciation.

EXERCISE 22 ▶ Looking at grammar. (Chart 1-4)
Complete the sentences with the correct simple past form of the verb.

An Online Order

1. Anders (*order*) _____ printer ink online last Monday.

2. The next morning he (*realize*) _____ he (*need*) _____ colored ink too.

3. He (*try*) _____ to call the company to add more, but no one (*answer*) _____, and there (*be*) _____ no voicemail.

4. Anders (*worry*) _____ that the website (*be*) _____ fake.

5. He (*email*) _____ the company and (*explain*) _____ his situation.

6. The manager (*respond*) _____ a few hours later and (*fix*) _____ the order quickly.

7. Anders (*relax*) _____ when he (*receive*) _____ a confirmation email from the company.

EXERCISE 23 ▶ Let's talk: pairwork. (Chart 1-4)
Take turns asking and answering questions. You can answer *yes* or *no*.

SITUATION: You just came back from a vacation in Greece. Your friend is asking you questions.

Examples: *fly back last night?*
PARTNER A: Did you fly back last night?
PARTNER B: Yes, I flew back last night.

happy to see your cousins?
PARTNER A: Were you happy to see your cousins?
PARTNER B: Yes, I was happy to see my cousins.

PARTNER A: (*book open*) PARTNER B: (*book closed*)	PARTNER A: (*book closed*) PARTNER B: (*book open*)
1. have a great trip? 2. come back feeling rested? 3. meet all your cousins? 4. hang out with* local people? 5. do a lot of tourist activities? 6. excited to be there? 7. spend time in museums?	8. speak a little Greek? 9. eat in typical Greek restaurants? 10. lie on the beach? 11. buy some Greek sandals? 12. bring me a souvenir? 13. take a lot of photos? 14. sad to leave Greece?

*hang out with = spend time with

EXERCISE 24 ▶ Looking at grammar. (Chart 1-4)

Complete the sentences with the correct forms of verbs that make sense. More than one verb may be appropriate. Some answers are negative.

SITUATION 1: Maria visited a friend at the hospital. A woman in the elevator had a cold and sneezed several times. The next day, ...

ache	feel	leave	schedule	take
eat	have	make	speak to	wake up

1. Maria _____ in the morning with a fever and headache.

2. She _____ well.

3. Her entire* body _____ .

4. She _____ her temperature with a thermometer.

5. She _____ a high fever.

6. She _____ the house all day.

7. She _____ a few spoonfuls of chicken soup.

8. She _____ the nurse at the doctor's office.

9. She _____ an appointment for the following day.

SITUATION 2: Professor Moore is our new math teacher. He is very hard to follow. Yesterday, he ...

confuse	fill	introduce	leave	speak

10. _____ too fast.

11. _____ the material to us quickly.

12. _____ the board with examples.

13. _____ time for questions, unfortunately.

14. _____ everyone in the class.

EXERCISE 25 ▶ Listening. (Chart 1-4)

Listen to the beginning of each sentence. Circle the correct completion(s). More than one completion may be possible.

1. happy.	good about my decision.	on some ice.
2. two classes.	about his wife.	at night.
3. the car with gas?	sick?	OK?
4. with colored pencils.	several faces.	for several hours.
5. in the woods.	some money.	the rain.

---

*entire = whole

6. a picture.	from math class.	some money from the bank.
7. my hand.	some rice.	was cooking.
8. the washing machine?	these jeans?	my shirt?
9. at the sad ending.	the actors.	when the play finished.
10. over the fence.	very quickly.	in a sunny spot.

EXERCISE 26 ▶ Reading and grammar. (Chart 1-4)

Part I. Read the passage. <u>Underline</u> the past tense verbs.

Do you know these words?
- feat
- marathon
- compete
- training
- show up
- session
- retire

AN INCREDIBLE FEAT

In 2011, at the age of 100, Fauja Singh did something incredible: he ran a 26-mile (42 km.) marathon! He was the first 100-year-old to ever run a marathon. Singh decided he wanted to compete in races when he saw a marathon race on TV. He was 89! He didn't know much about training and showed up for his first session in a suit and tie.

Originally from India, Singh moved to England in the 1990s after his wife and son died. At the time, he said he felt more dead than alive. He was very depressed and later believed that long-distance running saved him.

He competed in his first marathon in London at the age of 89. He prepared for it in only ten weeks. His best time was at the 2003 Toronto Waterfront Marathon. He ran it in five hours and 40 minutes. Singh became world-famous and even carried the Olympic torch in 2012. In 2013, he decided to retire from long-distance running and completed his last marathon in Hong Kong.

Running in the London Marathon, 2004

Part II. Complete the sentences with the verbs in the box. Cover the reading.

be	carry	leave	run
✓ become	feel	retire	wear

1. Fauja Singh _____*became*_____ a marathon runner when he was depressed.

2. He _____ a suit and tie to his first training.

3. He _____ India after the death of his wife and son.

4. At the age of 89, he _____ his first marathon.

5. Before he began training, he said he _____ more dead than alive.

6. His best running time _____ five hours and 40 minutes.

7. He _____ the Olympic torch in 2012.

8. He _____ from marathon running in 2013.

EXERCISE 27 ▶ Warm-up. (Chart 1-5)

Write the sentence (a. or b.) that correctly describes each scene.

a. Rita was standing under a tree when it began to rain.
b. Rita stood under a tree when it began to rain.

1st: It began to rain.   **2nd:** Rita stood under a tree.

1. _____

1st: Rita stood under a tree.   **2nd:** It began to rain.

2. _____

1-5 Simple Past vs. Past Progressive

SIMPLE PAST		
X (diagram)	(a) I *walked* to school yesterday. (b) John *lived* in Paris for ten years, but now he lives in Rome. (c) I *bought* a new car three days ago.	The simple past indicates that an activity or situation *began and ended at a particular time in the past.*
	(d) Rita *stood* under a tree *when it began to rain.* (e) *When Mrs. Chu heard a strange noise,* she *got* up to investigate. (f) *When I dropped my cup,* the coffee *spilled* on my lap.	If a sentence contains **when** and has the simple past in both clauses, the action in the *when*-clause happens first. In (d): 1st: The rain began. 2nd: Rita stood under a tree.

PAST PROGRESSIVE	(g) I *was walking* down the street when it began to rain.	In (g): 1st: I was walking down the street. 2nd: It began to rain.
	(h) While I *was walking* down the street, it began to rain.	Both actions occurred at the same time, but *one action began earlier and was in progress when the other action occurred.*
	(i) Rita *was standing* under a tree when it began to rain.	
	(j) At eight o'clock last night, I *was studying.*	In (j): My studying began before 8:00, was in progress at that time, and probably continued.
	(k) While I *was studying* in one room of our apartment, my roommate *was having* a party in the other room.	Sometimes the past progressive is used in both parts of a sentence when two actions are in progress simultaneously.

EXERCISE 28 ▸ Looking at grammar. (Chart 1-5)

Write "1" before the action that started first. Write "2" before the action that started second.

A Stormy Walk Home

1. Hi Mom. I was leaving you a voicemail when you picked up.*

   a. __1__ I was leaving you a voicemail.

   b. __2__ You picked up.

2. I had a terrible walk home. When the storm started, I was coming home from work.

   a. _____ The storm started.

   b. _____ I was coming home.

3. A painter next door was climbing a ladder when lightning hit the house.

   a. _____ A painter was climbing a ladder.

   b. _____ Lightning hit the house.

4. I heard him yell while I was running for cover.

   a. _____ I heard him yell.

   b. _____ I was running for cover.

5. He fell off the ladder when he saw the flash. Fortunately he's OK.

   a. _____ He fell off the ladder.

   b. _____ He saw the flash.

---

pick up (the phone) = answer the phone

EXERCISE 29 ▸ Looking at grammar. (Chart 1-5)

Complete the sentences. Use the simple past or the past progressive of the verbs in parentheses.

Last Night

1. Between 5:00 and 7:00 P.M, I (*sit*) _____was sitting_____ in class. I had a lot of things

   on my mind. I (*think*) _____ about some family issues. I (*listen, not*)

   _____ to the teacher.

2. It was a beautiful evening when I walked home. The moon (*shine*) _____

   over the water, and a warm breeze (*blow*) _____.

3. I (*stop*) _____ by a friend's apartment, but he (*be, not*) _____ home.

   He (*sit*) _____ in heavy traffic. He (*get, not*) _____ home until 10:00.

4. My neighbors (*argue*) _____ about something when I (*walk*)

   _____ by them outside my apartment building.

5. A package (*wait*) _____ for me at home. I (*open*) _____

   it and (*find*) _____ an early birthday present.

6. While I (*read*) _____ to my nephew, he (*fall*) _____ asleep, so

   I (*cover*) _____ him up and (*sneak*) _____ out of the room.

EXERCISE 30 ▸ Let's talk. (Chart 1-5)

Choose the question or statement you would expect the speaker to say. Discuss your answers. Work in pairs, in small groups, or as a class.

1. When I went to bed late last night, I noticed that the light was on in your bedroom.
   a. Were you reading?   b. Did you read?

2. Jane's cousin was at the party last night.
   a. Were you meeting him?   b. Did you meet him?

3. A small airplane flew over our house several times last night.
   a. We were sitting out on the patio, and it made us nervous.
   b. We sat out on the patio, and it made us nervous.

4. I'm not sure if I met Carol Jones at the party last night. Describe her for me.
   a. What was she wearing?   b. What did she wear?

EXERCISE 31 ▸ Looking at grammar. (Chart 1-5)

With a partner, take turns asking and answering the questions. Choose <u>all</u> the expected answers.

1. What were you doing at 5:00 A.M.?	1. (a.) I was sleeping. b. I dreamed. (c.) I was lying in bed.
2. What did you do when you got home last night?	2. a. I was cooking dinner. b. I made dinner. c. I fixed dinner.

3. What were you thinking about?	3. a. I was thinking about all the things I need to do today. b. I was thinking about my family. c. I was remembering my wedding day.
4. What did your mom like best about her vacation?	4. a. She was liking the beach. b. She enjoyed the warm weather. c. She was enjoying the swimming pool.
5. Who were you texting just now?	5. a. I text my mom. b. I am telling my manager I'm sick. c. I was texting a friend.
6. What did your friend make for breakfast?	6. a. He had eggs and coffee. b. He was having rice. c. He was making toast and tea.
7. Where did you live when you were younger?	7. a. We lived in this town for a while. b. We moved around a lot. c. We were moving from town to town.
8. Where were you going when I called you?	8. a. I was walking to the bus. b. I went to the bus stop. c. I was heading* downtown.

*heading = going

EXERCISE 32 ▸ Grammar and speaking. (Chart 1-5)

Work with a partner. Complete the sentences with the given verbs and the words in parentheses. Use the simple past or the past progressive. Practice one of the conversations and perform it for the class or a small group. You can look at your book before you speak. When you speak, look at your partner.

1. *break / cross / slip*

   A: How (*you*) _____ your arm?

   B: I _____ on the ice while I _____ the street in front

   of the dorm.

2. *find / look / park*

   A: You're a half-hour late. Where were you?

   B: I _____ for a place to park.

   A: (*you*) _____ one?

   B: Well, yes and no. I _____ my

   car illegally.

3. *ask / decide / look / see / work*

   A: How did it go? (*you*) _____ the manager for a raise when you

   _____ her yesterday?

   B: No, she _____ on a big presentation for next week. She

   _____ pretty busy. I _____ to wait until later.

4. *want / miss / be / give*

   A: (*you*) _____ in the meeting?

   B: No, I _____ the bus and (*not*) _____ to walk into

   the room while Dr. Romero _____ his speech.

5. *drive / get / happen / keep / pay / see*

   A: I had a bad day yesterday.

   B: Oh? What _____?

   A: I _____ a traffic ticket.

   B: Really? That's too bad. What was it for?

   A: For running a red light. I _____ home and (*not*) _____

   _____ attention to the road. I (*not*) _____ the red light

   and just _____ driving.

🎧 **EXERCISE 33 ▸ Listening.** (Chart 1-5)

Part I. Anna had a scary experience last night. Listen to her story with your book closed. Then open your book and listen to the statements. Circle "T" for true and "F" for false.

   1. T F   2. T F   3. T F   4. T F   5. T F   6. T F

Part II. Listen again. Complete the sentences with the verbs you hear.

A Scary Night

I _____ a terrible experience last night. You won't
        1

believe what happened! A man _____ into my apartment
                      2

while I was asleep. There I was, just sleeping peacefully when someone

_____ the glass in the sliding door!
     3

   The sound _____ me up. I _____ the
             4   5

sliding door open, so I reached for the phone by the bed and called the

police. My voice _____ as I told the operator there was an intruder in my home.
             6

   I _____ in my bedroom closet when the burglar _____ into my
       7   8

room. Soon I _____ sirens as the police _____ to my building.
            9   10

From the crack in the closet door, I _____ the burglar as he _____
                      11   12

outside with my laptop.

   The police jumped out of their cars and followed him, but he managed to get away in a car

that was waiting for him. The police _____ back in their cars and drove after him.
                         13

Later I learned that they _____ him a few miles from my building.
                14

   I _____ really frightened by all this. It really _____ me, as you
      15   16

can imagine. I'm staying at my sister's house for the rest of the week.

EXERCISE 34 ▶ Warm-up. (Chart 1-6)

Circle *yes* if the speaker is expressing an intention or plan; circle *no* if not.

1. I am going to call you at 9:00 tomorrow.	yes	no
2. I was going to call you, but I couldn't find your phone number.	yes	no
3. I was going to class when I ran into a friend from my childhood.	yes	no
4. I was planning to go to college right after high school but then decided to work for a year first.	yes	no

1-6 Unfilled Intentions: *Was / Were Going To*

(a) Jack *was going to go* to the movie last night, but he changed his mind.	*Was / were going to* talk about past intentions. Usually, these are unfulfilled intentions, i.e., activities someone intended to do but did not do. The meaning in (a): *Jack was planning to go to the movie, but he didn't go.*
(b) I *was planning* to go, but I didn't. I *was hoping* to go, but I couldn't. I *was intending* to go, but I didn't. I *was thinking about* going, but I didn't.	Other ways of expressing unfulfilled intentions are to use *plan*, *hope*, *intend*, and *think about* in the past progressive, as in (b).

EXERCISE 35 ▶ Looking at grammar. (Chart 1-6)

Choose <u>all</u> the sentences that are true about the given sentence.

1. I was going to pay you back for the taxi.
   a. I paid you back.
   b. I was planning to pay you back.
   c. I didn't pay you back.

2. I was going to stay home on my day off, but I had too much work at the office.
   a. I was intending to stay home.
   b. I worked at the office.
   c. I had a lot of work, but I stayed home.

3. Jared was going to the hospital to see his mother when he began to feel ill.
   a. Jared was on his way to the hospital.
   b. Jared had plans to see his mother but needed to change them.
   c. Jared didn't go to the hospital.

4. My dad was going to surprise my mom with jewelry for her birthday.
   a. He wanted to give her jewelry.
   b. He gave her some jewelry.
   c. He didn't surprise her with jewelry.

5. I was going to the train station when I remembered your phone call.
   a. I was planning to go to the train station, but I didn't.
   b. I was on my way to the train station.
   c. I didn't go to the train station.

EXERCISE 36 ▸ Writing or speaking. (Chart 1-6)
Take turns completing the sentences. Work in pairs or small groups. Share some of your answers with the class.

1. I was going to get up early this morning, but _____

_____

2. I was planning to visit you this weekend, but _____

_____

3. I was going to call you on your birthday, but _____

_____

4. We were hoping to see that movie in a theater, but _____

_____

5. I was going to text you, but _____

_____

6. We were going to invite Thomas to go out to dinner with us, but _____

_____

7. I was going to replace my computer with a tablet, but _____

_____

EXERCISE 37 ▸ Check your knowledge. (Chapter 1 Review)
Correct the errors.

1. Breakfast is an important meal. I'm always eat a big breakfast.
2. While I was working in my office yesterday, my cousin stops by to visit me.
3. Yuki staied home because she catched a bad cold.
4. My brother is looks like our father, but I am resembling my mother.
5. Jun, are you listen to me? I am talk to you!
6. While I was surfing the Internet yesterday, I was finding a really interesting website.
7. Did you spoke English before you were come here?
8. I am not agree with your opinion.
9. My roommate usually watch television, listen to music, or going out in the evening.
10. Right now Sally in the kitchen eating breakfast.
11. While I'm driving home last night, I heared a strange noise in the engine.
12. Why you talking about me? I'm not appreciate that.
13. Yesterday, while I was sitting at my computer, Shelley was suddenly coming into the room. I wasn't knowing she was there. I was concentrate hard on my work. When she suddenly speak, I am jump. She startle me.

EXERCISE 38 ▸ Reading and writing. (Chapter 1)

Part I. Read the journal entry. <u>Underline</u> the past tense verbs.

Do you know these words?
- somewhat
- embarrassed
- syllabus
- interrupt

A Hopeful Beginning

Today was my first day at the university, and I was late for class. I didn't remember the name of the building and went to the wrong one. After about ten minutes of confusion, I finally found the right class and walked in somewhat embarrassed. A girl with a friendly smile moved her books off the chair next to her. I sat down. The professor was going over the syllabus. I didn't have a copy, but I didn't want to interrupt him. The girl next to me shared hers. The course looked interesting but difficult. I wondered if all my classes had this much work. Then the teacher announced study groups. My new friend and I were in the same group. She introduced herself during the break, and I felt very comfortable when I spoke with her. Maybe the class is going to be OK after all.

Part II. Write a journal entry about your experience in a class on your first day of school.

1. Begin with *It was my first day at the university / in high school / in English class / etc.*
2. What was the teacher doing when you walked in? What were other students doing?
3. Did you notice anyone or anything special?
4. How did you feel?
5. What were your first impressions about the class and what were your thoughts later?

WRITING TIP

It is important to consider your first piece of writing a draft, not your finished copy. When you begin to write, jot down ideas first and then sentences. As you write your paragraph, you can always change, reorder, or delete ideas. After you finish the paragraph, edit it carefully. Correct any errors in your next draft. Then read it again and make additional changes or rewrite if necessary. You might need to do this a few more times. It may sound like a long process, but your writing will be much better.

Part III. Edit your writing. Check for the following:

1. ☐ indented paragraph
2. ☐ use of the simple past for an activity that began and ended at a particular time in the past
3. ☐ use of the past progressive for an activity in progress in the past
4. ☐ correct spelling (use a dictionary or spell-check)

Fluency Practice. Work with a partner. Take three minutes to tell your partner about your experience on the first day of school. Then describe your experience to another student in two minutes. Finally, take one minute to describe your experience to a third student. Did the final time you spoke feel more comfortable and easier than the first time?

SELF-STUDY: Gerunds and Infinitives 1

In Chapters 14 and 15, you will study gerunds and infinitives in depth. However, there are a great many to learn in English. At the end of Chapters 1–12, short self-study lessons are available so that you can begin to practice them. Chapter 1 appears below; Chapters 2–12 are online in MyEnglishLab. You will see this reminder at the end of these chapters:

■■■■■ Go to MyEnglishLab for Self-Study: Gerunds and Infinitives

(a) I *want* **to go**. (b) They *need* **to eat**.	As you know, when one verb follows another, the second verb may take the infinitive form: **to** + simple form of the verb
(c) Please *keep* **going**. (d) They *quit* **asking**.	Sometimes the verb is followed by a gerund: simple form of the verb + **-ing**
(e) It *began* **to rain**. (f) It *began* **raining**.	Some verbs can take either an infinitive or a gerund.

Examples. Study these conversations and then look at the summary chart that follows.

1. A: Would you mind helping me with the dishes?
   B: Sure. I enjoy washing dishes.
   A: Seriously?
   B: Not really. But I like talking/to talk to you.

2. A: Jan and Adam decided to put off their wedding until next summer.
   B: I hope everything's OK.
   A: Jan wants to wait. She just started a new job.

3. A: Do you like those shoes?
   B: Yes, but I can't afford to buy them. Anyway, I buy usually clothes on sale.
      I don't like paying/to pay full price.
   A: I know. I can't stand paying/to pay a lot for clothes.

Infinitive: *to* + verb	Gerund: verb + *-ing*	Infinitive or Gerund
can't afford decide want	enjoy mind miss	can't stand like

Test Yourself. Cover the above chart. Finish with **to go**/**going** or both.

1. She likes _____*to go / going*_____ .
2. I can't afford _____ .
3. Do they mind _____ ?
4. They can't stand _____ .
5. I decided _____ .
6. He wants _____ .
7. We enjoy _____ .
8. They don't like _____ .

PRETEST: What do I already know?

Write "C" if a sentence has the correct verb form and "I" for incorrect. Check your answers below. After you complete each chart listed, make any necessary corrections.

1. _____ How long have you know my sister? (2-1 and 2-2)

2. _____ We have been in this meeting since 7:00 A.M. (2-3)

3. _____ Did you ever seen a ghost? (2-4)

4. _____ How you been? I haven't seen you for a while. (2-5)

5. _____ Jonas owned his home since last year, but his parents helped him buy it. (2-6)

6. _____ How long you have been waiting for me? (2-7)

7. _____ I am watching TV since I got home. (2-7)

8. _____ I had felt sick after dinner, so I went to bed. (2-8)

9. _____ We'd wanted to go out to breakfast, but we overslept. (2-9)

10. _____ Toni's eyes were itchy and red because she had been working in a dusty room. (2-10)

Incorrect sentences: 1, 3, 4, 5, 6, 7

EXERCISE 1 ▶ Warm-up. (Charts 2-1 and 2-2)

Read the conversations. The verbs in blue are in the past participle form. Complete the chart.

1. A: How long have you lived in London?
   B: I've lived in London all my life.

2. A: How long have you spoken English?
   B: I've spoken English for more than a year.

3. A: How long have you done extreme sports?
   B: I've done extreme sports since I was a teenager.

SIMPLE FORM	SIMPLE PAST	PAST PARTICIPLE
1. live	lived	
2. speak	spoke	
3. do	did	

2-1 Regular and Irregular Verbs

Regular Verbs: The simple past and past participle end in -ed.

SIMPLE FORM	SIMPLE PAST	PAST PARTICIPLE	PRESENT PARTICIPLE
hope	hoped	hoped	hoping
stop	stopped	stopped	stopping
listen	listened	listened	listening
study	studied	studied	studying
start	started	started	starting

Irregular Verbs: The simple past and past participle do not end in -ed.

SIMPLE FORM	SIMPLE PAST	PAST PARTICIPLE	PRESENT PARTICIPLE
hit	hit	hit	hitting
find	found	found	finding
swim	swam	swum	swimming
break	broke	broken	breaking
wear	wore	worn	wearing

English verbs have four principal parts:

(1) simple form
(2) simple past
(3) past participle
(4) present participle

Some verbs have irregular past forms.

Most of the irregular verbs in English are given in the alphabetical list in Appendix Chart E-9.

2-2 Irregular Verb List

Group 1: All three forms are the same.

SIMPLE FORM	SIMPLE PAST	PAST PARTICIPLE	SIMPLE FORM	SIMPLE PAST	PAST PARTICIPLE
bet	bet	bet	let	let	let
burst	burst	burst	put	put	put
cost	cost	cost	quit*	quit	quit
cut	cut	cut	shut	shut	shut
fit	fit/fitted	fit/fitted	spread	spread	spread
hit	hit	hit	split	split	split
hurt	hurt	hurt	upset	upset	upset

*Also possible in BrE: *quit-quitted-quitted*.

Group 2: Past participle ends in -en.

SIMPLE FORM	SIMPLE PAST	PAST PARTICIPLE	SIMPLE FORM	SIMPLE PAST	PAST PARTICIPLE
bite	bit	bitten	hide	hid	hidden
break	broke	broken	mistake	mistook	mistaken
choose	chose	chosen	ride	rode	ridden
drive	drove	driven	rise	rose	risen
eat	ate	eaten	shake	shook	shaken
fall	fell	fallen	speak	spoke	spoken
forget	forgot	forgotten	steal	stole	stolen
forgive	forgave	forgiven	swell	swelled	swollen/swelled
freeze	froze	frozen	take	took	taken
get	got	gotten/got*	wake	woke	woken
give	gave	given	write	wrote	written

*In BrE: *get-got-got*. In AmE: *get-got-gotten/got*.

Group 3: Vowel changes from a in the simple past to u in the past participle.

SIMPLE FORM	SIMPLE PAST	PAST PARTICIPLE	SIMPLE FORM	SIMPLE PAST	PAST PARTICIPLE
begin	began	begun	sing	sang	sung
drink	drank	drunk	sink	sank	sunk
ring	rang	rung	stink	stank/stunk	stunk
run	ran	run	swim	swam	swum
shrink	shrank	shrunk			

Group 4: Past tense and past participle forms are the same.

bend	bent	bent	mean	meant	meant
bleed	bled	bled	meet	met	met
bring	brought	brought	pay	paid	paid
build	built	built	read	read	read
buy	bought	bought	say	said	said
catch	caught	caught	sell	sold	sold
dig	dug	dug	send	sent	sent
feed	fed	fed	shoot	shot	shot
feel	felt	felt	sit	sat	sat
fight	fought	fought	sleep	slept	slept
find	found	found	slide	slid	slid
grind	ground	ground	sneak	snuck/sneaked	snuck/sneaked
hang*	hung	hung	speed	sped	sped
have	had	had	spend	spent	spent
hear	heard	heard	spin	spun	spun
hold	held	held	stand	stood	stood
keep	kept	kept	stick	stuck	stuck
lay	laid	laid	sting	stung	stung
lead	led	led	strike	struck	struck
leave	left	left	sweep	swept	swept
lend	lent	lent	swing	swung	swung
light	lit/lighted	lit/lighted	teach	taught	taught
lose	lost	lost	tell	told	told
make	made	made	think	thought	thought
			understand	understood	understood
			weep	wept	wept
			win	won	won

*__Hang__ is a regular verb when it means "to kill someone with a rope around his/her neck." COMPARE: *I hung my clothes in the closet. They __hanged__ the murderer by the neck until he was dead.*

Group 5: Past participle adds final -n to the simple past, with or without a spelling change.

blow	blew	blown	see	saw	seen
do	did	done	swear	swore	sworn
draw	drew	drawn	tear	tore	torn
fly	flew	flown	throw	threw	thrown
grow	grew	grown	wear	wore	worn
know	knew	known	withdraw	withdrew	withdrawn
lie	lay	lain			

Group 6: The first and third forms are the same.

become	became	become
come	came	come
run	ran	run

Group 7: One of the three forms is very different.

be	was, were	been
go	went	gone

Group 8: Both regular and irregular forms are used. (The regular form is more common in AmE, and the irregular form is more common in BrE.)

awake	awakened/awoke	awakened/awoken	prove	proved/proven	proved/proven
burn	burned/burnt	burned/burnt	shine	shined/shone	shined/shone
dream	dreamed/dreamt	dreamed/dreamt	smell	smelled/smelt	smelled/smelt
kneel	kneeled/knelt	kneeled/knelt	spill	spilled/spilt	spilled/spilt
lean	leaned/leant	leaned/leant	spoil	spoiled/spoilt	spoiled/spoilt
learn	learned/learnt	learned/learn			

EXERCISE 2 ▸ Looking at grammar. (Charts 2-1 and 2-2)

Work with a partner. Give the past tense and past participle forms of the verbs, orally or in writing.
Each partner has the answers in italics.

PARTNER A: (*book open;* say the verb) **PARTNER B:** (*book closed;* give the two forms)	**PARTNER B:** (*book open;* say the verb) **PARTNER A:** (*book closed;* give the two forms)
1. go (*went, gone*)	13. begin (*began, begun*)
2. see (*saw, seen*)	14. speak (*spoke, spoken*)
3. sting (*stung, stung*)	15. cut (*cut, cut*)
4. think (*thought, thought*)	16. break (*broke, broken*)
5. lead (*led, led*)	17. catch (*caught, caught*)
6. blow (*blew, blown*)	18. take (*took, taken*)
7. bet (*bet, bet*)	19. make (*made, made*)
8. choose (*chose, chosen*)	20. swim (*swam, swum*)
9. put (*put, put*)	21. grow (*grew, grown*)
10. write (*wrote, written*)	22. let (*let, let*)
11. drive (*drove, driven*)	23. sing (*sang, sung*)
12. feel (*felt, felt*)	24. win (*won, won*)

EXERCISE 3 ▸ Let's talk. (Charts 2-1 and 2-2)

Complete the questions with the past participle form of the verb. Work with a partner. Take turns
asking and answering questions with ***How long have you***.

1. wear glasses → *How long have you worn glasses?*
   → *I've worn glasses for three years.* OR *I don't wear glasses.*
2. speak English
3. know our teacher
4. study English
5. have a passport/visa
6. own (a cell phone, a computer, a tablet, an iPod®, etc.)
7. be awake
8. live in this town
9. participate in sports
10. play (the piano, the guitar, the violin, etc.)

EXERCISE 4 ▸ Warm-up. (Chart 2-3)

Complete the sentences about yourself. What do you notice about the tenses of the verbs in blue?
In which sentences do the situations continue from the past until now?

1. I got up at _____ o'clock today.

2. I have been up since _____ o'clock.

3. I have been up for _____ hours.

2-3 Present Perfect: *Since* and *For*

	(a) Mrs. Oh *has been* a teacher *since* 2002.	The PRESENT PERFECT is often used with *since* and *for* to talk about *situations that began in the past and continue up to now.*
		PRESENT PERFECT FORM = *has/have* + past participle
		In (a): SITUATION = being a teacher TIME FRAME = from 2002 up to now

(b) I *have been* in this city *since* last May.	Notice the use of *since* vs. *for* in the examples:
(c) We *have been* here *since* nine o'clock.	**since** + a specific point in time (e.g., *2002, last May, nine o'clock*)
(d) Rita knows Rob. They met two months ago. She *has known* him *for* two months. I met him three years ago. I *have known* him *for* three years.	**for** + a length of time (e.g., *two months, three years*)
(e) I *have known* Rob *since I was* in high school.	A time clause (i.e., a subject and verb) may follow **since**, as in (e) and (f).* NOTE: The verb before **since** is present
(f) We *have lived* in an apartment *since we moved to* this city.	perfect. The verb in the time clause is simple past.

*See Chart 17-2, p. 373, for more information about time clauses.

EXERCISE 5 ▸ Looking at grammar. (Chart 2-3)

Complete the sentences with appropriate time expressions.

1. Today is ___the 14th of June___ . I bought this book ___two weeks ago___ .

   I have had this book since ___the first of June___ .

   I have had this book for ___two weeks___ .

2. I started learning English in _____ (*year*).

   I've been an English student for _____ .

   I've been an English student since _____ .

3. I met my best friend in _____ .

   I've known her/him for _____ .

   I've known her/him since _____ .

4. I first used _____ (*name of social media*) in _____ .

   I have had a/an _____ account since _____ .

   I have had a/an _____ account for _____ .

5. I have a/an _____ that I bought _____ ago.

   I have had it since _____ .

   I have had it for _____ .

EXERCISE 6 ▶ Let's talk. (Chart 2-3)

Work in small groups. Complete each sentence using **since**. (You may use the Internet.) Then restate your sentence using **for**. Compare your answers with other groups. Answers may vary; discuss the most interesting differences.

Trivia: How Long?

1. Dinosaurs have been extinct since _____ / for _____ years.

2. Humans have used fire since _____ / for _____ years.

3. People have driven cars since _____ / for _____ years.

4. Cars have had airbags since _____ / for _____ years.

5. Doctors have treated infections with penicillin since _____ / for _____ years.

6. People have communicated by email since _____ / for _____ years.

7. Jet airplanes have carried airline passengers since _____ / for _____ years.

8. Satellites have gone into space since _____ / for _____ years.

EXERCISE 7 ▶ Looking at grammar. (Chart 2-3)

Work with a partner. Take turns completing the sentences with the words in the box.

a long time	most of the month	New Year's Day	yesterday
two days	December	days	you got here
the beginning of March	last week	over a week	ages

Snow has been on the ground since ...   *It has been cold for ...*

_____   _____

_____   _____

_____   _____

_____   _____

_____   _____

_____   _____

EXERCISE 8 ▶ Looking at grammar. (Chart 2-3)

Choose the correct verbs.

A House in the Woods

1. Richard and Sylvia   lived / have lived   in a log cabin since they   moved / have moved   to Canada.

2. Since Sylvia   was / has been   a child, she loved / has loved   the outdoors.

3. Richard   wanted / has wanted   to live in the woods since he first   went / has gone   camping with his parents.

4. They   saw / have seen   a lot of wildlife since they   bought / have bought   their property.

5. Since they   left / have left   the city, they   felt / have felt   a lot more relaxed.

EXERCISE 9 ▶ Warm-up. (Chart 2-4)

Check (✓) the statements that are true for you. Then <u>underline</u> the time words in each sentence. Is the time exact or unspecified?

1. _____ I have already had lunch.

2. _____ I haven't finished my homework for this class yet.

3. _____ I have never been late to class.

4. _____ I have felt tired lately.

2-4 Present Perfect: Unspecified Time and Repeated Events

(time? / now)	(a) — *Have* you *ever seen* snow? — No, I *haven't*. I've *never seen* snow. But Anna *has seen* snow. (b) *Have* you *finished* your homework *yet*? I *still haven't finished* mine. Jack *has already finished* his.	The present perfect can talk about *events that have (or haven't) happened before now.* The exact time of the event is unspecified. The adverbs *ever, never, yet, still, already,* and *lately* are often used with the present perfect. In (a): EVENT = seeing snow TIME FRAME = from the beginning of their lives up to now In (b): EVENT = doing homework TIME FRAME = from the time the people started up to now
(just / now)	(c) Sara *has recently finished* her work. (d) Sara *has just finished* her work. (e) Sara *has finished* her work.	Use of the present perfect with *just* or **recently** emphasizes that an action was recently completed. In (c) and (d): EVENT = doing work TIME FRAME = a recent time in the past Sometimes *just* or *recently* is implied by use of the present perfect. For example, in (e), Sara has *recently* or *just* finished her work.
(beginning of term / up to now / now / test 1 test 2 test 3)	(f) We *have had* three tests *so far* this term. (g) I*'ve met* many people *since* I came here.	The present perfect can also express *an event that has occurred repeatedly from a point in the past up to the present time. The event may happen again.* In (f): REPEATED EVENT = taking tests TIME FRAME = from the beginning of the term up to now In (g): REPEATED EVENT = meeting people TIME FRAME = from the time I came here up to now
CONTRACTIONS: (h) *I've* been there. *You've* been there. *We've* been there. *They've* been there. *He's* been there. *She's* been there. *It's* been interesting.		*Have* and *has* are usually contracted with personal pronouns in informal writing, as in (h). NOTE: *He's* there. *He's = He is* *He's* been there. *He's = He has*

EXERCISE 10 ▶ Looking at grammar. (Charts 2-1 → 2-4)

Check (✓) all the correct verbs.

At Work

1. Where have your colleagues _____ so far?

   ✓ been   _____ traveled   _____ presenting

   _____ went   _____ taught   _____ ridden

   ✓ worked   _____ living   _____ flown

   _____ drove   _____ ran   _____ stay

2. We still haven't _____ the project.

   _____ finished   _____ worked on   _____ began

   _____ complete   _____ starting   _____ study

   _____ did   _____ spent time on   _____ viewing

   _____ see   _____ looked at   _____ discussed

3. What hasn't your team _____ yet?

   _____ done   _____ wrote   _____ decided

   _____ saw   _____ gotten   _____ researched

   _____ tried   _____ communicated   _____ understanding

   _____ paid for   _____ bought   _____ spend

EXERCISE 11 ▶ Grammar and speaking. (Charts 2-1 → 2-4)

Complete each sentence with the past participle form of a verb in the box. Some sentences have more than one possibility. Then interview another student and circle *yes* or *no*. If the person answers "yes," ask for more information.

ace*	develop	own	show	teach
become	✓ dream	play	sleep	witness

1. Have you ever _____dreamed / dreamt_____ in English?   yes   no

2. Have you ever _____ in a tent?   yes   no

3. Have you ever _____ someone a skill?   yes   no

4. Have you ever _____ an unusual pet?   yes   no

5. Have you ever _____ a crime?   yes   no

6. Have you ever _____ a test?   yes   no

7. Have you ever _____ in a rock band?   yes   no

8. Have you ever _____ someone around your city?   yes   no

9. Have you ever _____ software?   yes   no

10. Have you ever _____ seasick?   yes   no

---

*ace = do exceptionally well on something

EXERCISE 12 ▶ Looking at grammar. (Charts 2-1 → 2-4)

<u>Underline</u> the present perfect verbs. What is the time frame in each situation?

At a Party

Example: A: I <u>haven't attended</u> many parties since I came to this city. I hardly know anyone here.
B: C'mon. I'll introduce you to some people.
Time frame: from the time the speaker arrived in this city to the present time

1. A: Hi, Judy. Welcome to the party. Have you ever met my cousin, Mark?
   B: No, I haven't. It's nice to meet you.

2. A: How did you like the DVD I lent you?
   B: Gosh, I'm sorry, but I haven't watched it yet. I haven't had time.

3. A: This week has been crazy so far. I've had two tests and a quiz. And it's only Wednesday!
   B: I know. It gets really busy toward the end of the quarter.

4. A: This food looks delicious! I haven't eaten all day.
   B: Try the lobster. It's amazing.
   A: Hmmm. I've never had lobster. I'll try it.

lobster with shrimp around it

EXERCISE 13 ▶ Looking at grammar. (Charts 2-1 → 2-4)

Complete the sentences with the correct form of the present perfect or simple past verb.

An Experience Studying Abroad

Gabriel is the first person in his family to study abroad. He (*be*) _____ a student at

1

Oxford University for the past year. He is studying international relations there on a scholarship.

His parents are very proud. No one in the family (*receive, ever*) _____ a

2

scholarship before. Gabriel (*want*) _____ to study overseas since his family

3

(*take*) _____ a trip to Asia when he was a teenager. He enjoyed meeting people

4

from other cultures and finding out more about them. Since he (*come*) _____

5

to Oxford, he (*meet*) _____ students from around the world. During this

6

time, he (*discover*) _____ common interests among his classmates. He

7

(*hear, also*) _____ a variety of opinions very different from his. He (*learn*)

8

_____ much about the world, both inside and outside the classroom.

9

Oxford University

EXERCISE 14 ▸ Let's talk: game. (Charts 2-1 → 2-4)

Sit in a circle (a maximum of 18 students). If there are more than 18, divide the class into two or more circles as necessary. Student 1 makes a true sentence with the given phrase, using the affirmative with **before** or the negative with **never**.

Example: 1. buy a car → *I've bought a car before.* OR *I've never bought a car.*

Student 2 repeats the sentence using **He/She** and then makes a sentence for item 2.

Example: 2. break a window → *He's bought a car before.* OR *He's never bought a car before.*
              I've never broken a window.

Student 3 repeats the sentences from Students 1 and 2, and then makes a sentence for item 3.
Continue until all students have made sentences. Classmates may help students who are having difficulty.

1. buy a car
2. break a window
3. drive a truck
4. teach a class
5. make a cup of espresso
6. win a contest
7. ride an elephant
8. eat homemade ice cream
9. fall off a ladder
10. swing a baseball bat
11. lose my ID
12. forget to pay a bill
13. grow my own vegetables
14. build a house
15. accidentally tear a page out of a textbook
16. catch a big fish
17. dig up something valuable
18. wear socks that didn't match

EXERCISE 15 ▸ Reading, grammar, and speaking. (Chart 2-4)

Part I. Read the passage. Underline the present perfect verbs.
Discuss their use.

A Bucket List

The phrase "bucket list" has become popular because of a movie of the same name: *The Bucket List*. In the movie, two cancer patients, one a playboy and the other a family man, become roommates in the hospital. Neither has a good prognosis. They spend a lot of time together and talk about what they want to do before they "kick the bucket." *Kick the bucket* is an idiom for "die." So the two friends make "a bucket list": a list of things they want to accomplish before they kick the bucket.

  Now many people have made bucket lists. Activities often include traveling to exotic places and doing exciting sports like skydiving or bungee jumping. There are books and websites with hundreds of suggestions.

  Think about your life. What haven't you done but would like to do?

Do you know these words?
- *cancer patient*
- *prognosis*

Part II. Work with a partner and take turns summarizing what Monica has already done and what she has not yet done. Use these sentences: **She has … already.** OR **She hasn't … yet.**

SITUATION: Monica, an architect, is 65 years old. She has had a bucket list since she was 50. The checkmarks are for the activities she has already done.

1. ✓ ride in a hot-air balloon
2. ___ learn how to write computer code
3. ✓ eat at a 5-star restaurant
4. ___ find a job she never wants to quit
5. ___ sing in front of a live audience
6. ___ discover a cure for her insomnia
7. ___ sleep on a beach under the stars
8. ✓ swim with dolphins
9. ✓ travel to Antarctica
10. ✓ have an interesting conversation with a famous person

Part III. Make your own bucket list of 5–7 items. Share your list with your classmates. Who has the same wishes as you? Who has already accomplished some of them?

EXERCISE 16 ▸ Warm-up: listening. (Chart 2-5)
Listen to these common questions. How are **have** and **has** pronounced?

1. How have you been?
2. How long have you been here?
3. What has happened?
4. What have you done?
5. When have I said that?
6. Where have you been?

2-5 *Have* and *Has* in Spoken English

(a) **How have** you been?
     Spoken: *How/v/ you been?* OR
                 How/əv/ you been?
	In spoken English, the present perfect helping verbs **has** and **have** are often reduced following nouns and question words.*
	 In (a): **have** can sound like /v/ or /əv/.
	 In (b): **has** can sound like /z/ or /əz/.
	 In (c): **has** can sound like /s / or /əs/.**
	 NOTE: "ə" sounds like "uh."

(b) **Jane has** already eaten lunch.
     Spoken: *Jane/z/ already eaten lunch.* OR
                 Jane/əz/ already eaten lunch.	

(c) **Mike has** quit his job.
     Spoken: *Mike/s/ quit his job.* OR
                 Mike/əs/ quit his job.
	Jane/z/ eaten. **Jane's = Jane has**
	 Jane/z/ here. **Jane's = Jane is**
	
	 Mike/s/ quit his job. **Mike's = Mike has**
	 Mike/s/ here. **Mike's = Mike is**

*In very informal writing, **has** is sometimes contracted with nouns (e.g., **Jane's** *already eaten.*) and question words (e.g., **Where's** *he gone?*). **Have** is rarely contracted in writing except with pronouns (e.g., *I've*). See Chart 2-4 for written contractions of **have** and **has** with pronouns. See Appendix Chart C for more information about contractions in general.

**See Appendix Chart E-6 for the pronunciation of final *-s* after voiced and voiceless sounds.

EXERCISE 17 ▸ Listening. (Chart 2-5)
Complete the sentences with *is*, *has*, or *have*. Write the full forms, not the contractions.

At Home with Roommates

Example: You will hear: Finally! The mail's come.
              You will write: Finally! The mail ___*has*___ come.

1. Someone's phone _____ ringing. It's not mine.
2. Your girlfriend _____ just left a message.

3. Her friends _____ canceled, so she's free tonight.

4. The coffee _____ fresh. Have some.

5. It looks like your package _____ arrived.

6. Your sister _____ downstairs. She's borrowing some boxes for her move.

7. Our neighbors _____ planned a party for next weekend.

8. What _____ we told them? Are we going?

EXERCISE 18 ▸ Warm-up. (Chart 2-6)

What do you notice about the verb tenses in blue? Discuss the differences.

I've heard a lot of good things about Professor Stevens, but I haven't taken any of her classes. Have you?

Yes. I took one of her classes last year. I loved it.

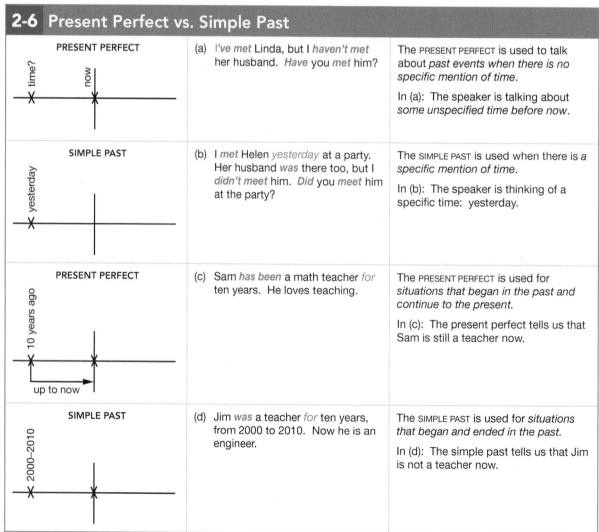

2-6 Present Perfect vs. Simple Past		
PRESENT PERFECT time? / now	(a) *I've met* Linda, but I *haven't met* her husband. *Have* you *met* him?	The PRESENT PERFECT is used to talk about *past events when there is no specific mention of time*. In (a): The speaker is talking about *some unspecified time before now*.
SIMPLE PAST yesterday	(b) I *met* Helen *yesterday* at a party. Her husband *was* there too, but I *didn't meet* him. *Did* you *meet* him at the party?	The SIMPLE PAST is used when there is *a specific mention of time*. In (b): The speaker is thinking of a specific time: yesterday.
PRESENT PERFECT 10 years ago / up to now	(c) Sam *has been* a math teacher *for* ten years. He loves teaching.	The PRESENT PERFECT is used for *situations that began in the past and continue to the present*. In (c): The present perfect tells us that Sam is still a teacher now.
SIMPLE PAST 2000–2010	(d) Jim *was* a teacher *for* ten years, from 2000 to 2010. Now he is an engineer.	The SIMPLE PAST is used for *situations that began and ended in the past*. In (d): The simple past tells us that Jim is not a teacher now.

EXERCISE 19 ▸ Looking at grammar. (Chart 2-6)

Use the information in the timeline to:

   a. make past tense sentences with: **leave, start;**
   b. make present perfect sentences with: **be, live, study, work.**

Jin's Timeline

Example: Jin's parents have been in Australia since 1990.

1990: Jin's parents immigrated to Australia from Hong Kong.
1991: They settled in Sydney, Australia.
1992: They opened a restaurant.
1995: Jin was born.
2013: He entered the University of Melbourne.
2015: He went to Hong Kong to study Chinese.
Now: Jin is studying in Hong Kong.
     His parents are working at their restaurant in Sydney.

EXERCISE 20 ▸ Looking at grammar. (Chart 2-6)

Complete the sentences. Use the simple past or the present perfect form of the verbs in parentheses.

1. Noor is from a hot, dry country. She (*see, never*) _____ snow. Last January,

   I (*see*) _____ snow for the first time in my life.

2. Last night my friend and I (*have*) _____ some free time, so

   we (*go*) _____ to a show. Since classes began, I (*have, not*)

   _____ much free time.

3. Ming Won (*be*) _____ in this class for three months. His English is

   getting better and better. He plans to take this class until the end of May. Mrs. Perez (*be*)

   _____ in our class for three months, but then she left school to get a job.

4. Late-breaking news! A major earthquake (*occur, just*) _____ in

   southern California. It (*occur*) _____ at 9:25 A.M.

5. A: Greg Adams? Yes, I know him. I (*know*) _____ him since college.

   B: Did Natalie just say Joe North passed away? I'm sorry to hear that.

   I (*know*) _____ him well when we were in college together.

6. I admit that I (*get***) _____ older since I last (*see*) _____

   you, but with any luck at all, I (*get, also*) _____ wiser.

---

*Typically, the present perfect is used in sentences with *already, yet,* and *just,* but in some situations the simple past is also commonly used with these adverbs in informal English, especially American English, with no difference in meaning.

**COMPARE:

  (a) ***I have gotten*** or ***have got*** *four letters so far this week.* In this sentence, *have gotten / have got* is present perfect.
    (NOTE: *Got* is used as the past participle of *get* in both American English and British English. *Gotten* occurs only in American English.)

  (b) ***I have got*** *a problem.* In this sentence, *have got* is not present perfect. *I've got a problem = I have a problem.* The expression *have got* means "have" and is common in informal spoken English. Its meaning is present; it has no past form.

EXERCISE 21 ▸ Reading and grammar. (Chart 2-6)

Read the blog entry by author Stacy Hagen. <u>Underline</u> the simple past and present perfect verbs in the paragraphs. Discuss as a class why they are simple past or present perfect.

 BlueBookBlog Using Flashcards with Spaced-Repetition Practice

Have you ever used flashcards to study grammar or vocabulary? Have you made flashcards to study the past participle forms that you saw at the beginning of this chapter? Research has shown that using flashcards with spaced-repetition practice is a very effective way to memorize information.

Spaced repetition means spacing out your practice over a period of time. For example, after you study a list of vocabulary words, you wait a few days to review them. If you get the words correct, you wait longer before you review them again. On the other hand, for words you missed, you practice them over shorter periods of time. There are many apps for spaced-repetition flashcard practice. I personally like AnkiApp because it's very user-friendly. Anki follows your progress and chooses the flashcards for you to study each day.

Why is memorizing this way effective? Think about learning basic math. If you know your times tables (e.g., 5x1, 5x2, 5x3), then your mind is free to do more complex math because you don't have to figure out these basic equations. The answer is right there for you to use. We can think of grammar in a similar way. If you know your past participles automatically, you don't need to think about the form before you try to express your ideas.

For English grammar, I think spaced repetition is especially useful for learning irregular past tense and past participle forms; gerunds and infinitives; prepositions; and two- and three-word verbs. You can try out this technique with the past participles that we have studied in this chapter or with the gerunds and infinitives at the end of Chapter 1. See what you think. You may be pleasantly surprised by your progress. Good luck!

EXERCISE 22 ▸ Let's talk. (Charts 2-1 → 2-6)

Work in groups of 5-7 students. Ask questions with the given words and **Who has**. When someone answers "yes," ask *wh*-questions to get more information. NOTE: The follow-up questions will use past tense.

Example: catch a big fish
STUDENT A: Who has caught a big fish?
STUDENT B: I have.
STUDENT C: What did you catch?
STUDENT D: Where did you catch it? etc.

1. write a blog?
2. lose a credit card?
3. climb to the top of a mountain?
4. give a speech to a large audience?
5. tell a lie?
6. sing in public?
7. ride on a motorcycle?

8. feed a lion?
9. drink Turkish coffee?
10. take a cooking class?
11. shake hands with someone famous?
12. hold a snake?
13. fall on ice?
14. accidentally shrink a shirt?

EXERCISE 23 ▸ Editing. (Chart 2-6)
Help Carolina send an effective job inquiry. Read her letter and correct the 8 errors she makes with past tense and present perfect verbs.

414 3rd Ave.
New York, NY 10026

Dear Mr. Anderson:

I have just learned from my friend Robert Shaw that he has deciding to leave his position as tour guide and that you need to find a summer replacement quickly. I would like to apply for the position.

I have come to this city two years ago to study at Columbia University. I am a student in history and economics since that time. I am a hard worker and have held several part-time jobs at the college: tutor, library researcher, and History Department teaching assistant.

I am originally from Mexico City and speak fluent Spanish and English. My father is an English professor, and I have learned to speak English as a child. When I lived in Mexico, I have worked at my uncle's hotel. I help tourists with their travel arrangements in the city. I also give city tours in both Spanish and English. I have a good sense of humor, and my tours were a lot of fun.

Because of my history background, I am very interested in this city since I arrived. I have done a lot of reading and have discovered many fascinating stories about it.

I think I have the qualifications to make an excellent tour guide. Would it be possible to speak with you about the job at a convenient time? I thank you in advance.

Sincerely,
Carolina Burns
Carolina Burns

EXERCISE 24 ▸ Warm-up. (Chart 2-7)
Check (✓) the two correct sentences in each group.

1. Anita is at the bus stop.
   a. _____ She is waiting for the bus.
   b. _____ She is waiting for the bus for 15 minutes.
   c. _____ She has been waiting for the bus for 15 minutes.

2. Tarik is at the bus stop too.
   a. _____ He is standing beside Anita.
   b. _____ He is standing there since five o'clock.
   c. _____ He has been standing there since five o'clock.

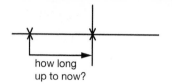

how long
up to now?

(a) Right now I **am sitting** at my desk.	COMPARE:
(b) I **have been sitting** at my desk *since* seven o'clock. I **have been sitting** here *for* two hours.	In (a): The PRESENT PROGRESSIVE expresses *an activity in progress right now*. (See Chart 1-1, p. 2.)
(c) It*'s **been raining*** all day. It*'s* still raining right now.	In (b): The PRESENT PERFECT PROGRESSIVE expresses *how long* an activity has been in progress. In other words, it expresses *the duration of an activity that began in the past and continues in the present*.
	Time expressions often used with this tense are • *since* and *for*, as in (b); • *all day/all morning/all week*, as in (c).
	NOTE: In (c): **It's** *been raining.* **It's** = **It has** **It's** *still raining.* **It's** = **It is**
(d) I**'ve known** Alex *since* he was a child. INCORRECT: ~~I've been knowing~~ Alex since he was a child.	The present perfect progressive is not used with non-progressive or stative verbs such as *know*. To express *the duration of a situation that began in the past and continues to the present*, only the present perfect is used. (See Chart 1-3, p. 7, for a list of non-progressive verbs.)
(e) How long *have* you *been living* here? (f) How long **have** you **lived** here? (g) Ben *has been wearing* glasses since he was ten. (h) Ben **has worn** glasses since he was ten.	For some (not all) verbs, the idea of *how long* can be expressed by either tense — the present perfect progressive or the present perfect. NOTE: (e) and (f) have the same meaning; (g) and (h) have the same meaning. Either tense can be used only when the verb expresses the duration of present activities or situations that happen regularly, usually, habitually: e.g., *live, work, teach, study, wear glasses, play chess, etc.*

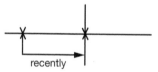

recently

(i) I*'ve been thinking* about looking for a different job. This one doesn't pay enough. (j) All of the students *have been studying* hard. Final exams start next week.	When the tense is used without any mention of time, it expresses a general activity in progress recently, lately. For example, (i) means *I've been thinking about this recently, lately.*

EXERCISE 25 ▸ Looking at grammar. (Chart 2-7)
Complete the sentences with *is, are, has been,* or *have been*.

1. Mr. and Mrs. Jones _____ sitting outside on their porch right now.

   They _____ sitting there since after dinner.

2. The test begins at 1:00. Right now it's 11:00. Sara is at the library. She _____

   reviewing her notes right now. She _____ reviewing her notes all morning.

3. Marco wants to buy a pair of jeans. He _____ waiting for a cashier right now.

   He _____ standing there for over five minutes. He needs to find someone.

EXERCISE 26 ▸ Looking at grammar. (Chart 2-7)
Complete the email with the present perfect progressive form of the verbs in parentheses.

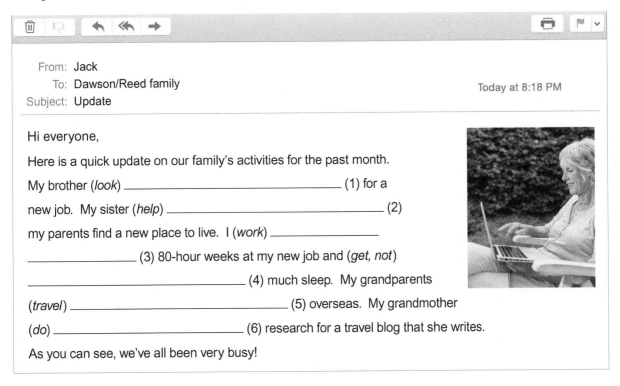

From: Jack
To: Dawson/Reed family
Subject: Update

Today at 8:18 PM

Hi everyone,

Here is a quick update on our family's activities for the past month.

My brother (*look*) _____ (1) for a

new job. My sister (*help*) _____ (2)

my parents find a new place to live. I (*work*) _____

_____ (3) 80-hour weeks at my new job and (*get, not*) _____

_____ (4) much sleep. My grandparents

(*travel*) _____ (5) overseas. My grandmother

(*do*) _____ (6) research for a travel blog that she writes.

As you can see, we've all been very busy!

EXERCISE 27 ▸ Let's talk: pairwork. (Chart 2-7)
With a partner, take turns asking and answering questions. Use the phrases in the box and the present perfect progressive for the answer.

drink a milkshake	stand outside in the cold	swim in the pool
admire your new hairstyle	work for six hours straight	try to fix a leak
drive around the city	listen to music with my headphones on	

1. Why are you shivering?
2. What took you so long? We're late!
3. Do you know you have a milk mustache?

1. I've ...
2. I got lost. I've ...
3. Oops. I've ...

4. When are you going to take a break?
5. Why are you under the kitchen sink?
6. I've been calling you. Didn't you hear me?
7. What?? Why are you looking at me like that?
8. Your eyes are really red. Have you been crying?

4. Soon. I've ...
5. I've ...
6. No, I've ...
7. Nothing's wrong. I've just ...
8. No, I've ...

EXERCISE 28 ▸ Looking at grammar. (Chart 2-7)

Complete the sentences. Use the verb in *italics* in the first sentence to complete the remaining sentence(s). Use the present perfect or the present perfect progressive. In some sentences, either verb form is correct.

1. I'm *trying* to study. I _____*have been trying*_____ to study for the last hour, but something always seems to interrupt me. I think I'd better go to the library.

2. Joe *has* an old bike. He _____*has had*_____ the same bike for 20 years.

3. Matt *works* at ABC Appliances. He ___*has worked / has been working*___ there since 2005.

4. Toshi *is waiting* for his friend. He _____ for her since five o'clock. She's late for their date.

5. I *like* funny TV shows. I _____ comedies ever since I was a child.

6. Susie *is watching* several episodes in a row of her favorite comedy. She _____ _____ them all afternoon without a break.

7. Dr. Chang *teaches* math. He is an excellent teacher. He _____ math at this school for more than 25 years.

8. Don't wake Nora up. She *is sleeping*. She _____ all morning. She isn't feeling well.

9. Sue and Rick *are playing* tennis right now and they're getting tired. They _____ _____ since nine o'clock this morning. Sue's winning. She's the better tennis player. She _____ tennis since she was ten. Rick started playing only last year.

EXERCISE 29 ▸ Listening. (Chart 2-7)

Listen to the conversation one time with your book closed. Then, with your book open, listen again and write the words you hear.

It's been a while!

A: Good to see you! So what _____ up to lately?
                                    1

B: Not too much. _____ it easy.
                        2

A: How nice! Glad to hear you _____ too hard. By the
                                    3

   way, _____ your parents? I _____ them for
            4   5

   a while.

B: _____ great. _____
       6   7
now that they're retired.

A: How long _____ retired?
                     8

B: Gosh, I don't know. _____ a couple of years now.
                              9

A: So _____ a lot*?
              10

B: Yeah. _____ in warm, sunny
                   11
places in the winter and _____ summers here.
                                 12

A: What a great way to spend retirement! I'm glad to hear _____ themselves.
                                                                    13

EXERCISE 30 ▶ Reading and writing. (Chart 2-7)

Part I. Product reviews on websites often use the present perfect and present perfect progressive. Look at the following examples and <u>underline</u> the present perfect and present perfect progressive verbs. Discuss their use.

1. ★★★★☆ **Very Nice Camera!**

   By Sammy P.

   I have had this camera for 8 months now. It takes great pictures. I haven't had any problems with it. It's a little complicated to learn at first, but the instructions help.
   I have ordered other products from this site and have had great service.

2. ★★★★★ **Incredible Product**

   By Vitafan

   I have been taking these vitamins since last year. They're incredible! My memory has improved. I have had more concentration and have been doing better in school. I have lost weight and I haven't even been trying! This product is fantastic!

3. ☆☆☆☆☆ **DO NOT BUY**

   By Adriana J.

   I don't know why this company is in business. I have never been so disappointed with a product in my life. My laptop arrived with a dead battery. The customer service is terrible. I have emailed and called the company numerous times, but they haven't responded. I have asked for a refund and now am waiting for a response. Order from this company only if you want a defective product.

Part II. Find an online product review that uses present perfect and/or present perfect progressive. <u>Underline</u> the verbs in the perfect tenses.

Part III. Write a short product review for an item you own. Use the present perfect and present perfect progressive at least one time each.

---

*Notice: A statement form (not a question form) can sometimes be used to ask a question by using a rising intonation at the end of a sentence.

EXERCISE 31 ▶ Warm-up. (Chart 2-8)

Look at the verbs in blue. Which event happened first?

1. The teacher stood up. Someone had knocked on the classroom door.
2. I looked at the board. The teacher had written my name there.

2-8 Past Perfect

Ann left. Sam came	(a) Sam came at 10:00. Ann left at 9:30. In other words, Ann *had* already *left* when Sam came.	The PAST PERFECT expresses an *activity that was complete before another activity or time in the past.*

(b) *By the time* Sam came, Ann *had* already *left*.	In (a): 1st: Ann left. 　　　　2nd: Sam came. Adverb clauses with *by the time* are frequently used with the past perfect in the main clause, as in (b).*
(c) Sam *had left* before Ann came. (d) Sam *left* before Ann came. (e) *After* the guests *had left,* I went to bed. (f) *After* the guests *left,* I went to bed.	If either *before* or *after* is used in the sentence, the past perfect is often not necessary because the time relationship is already clear. The simple past may be used, as in (d) and (f). NOTE: (c) and (d) have the same meaning; 　　　(e) and (f) have the same meaning.
(g) *Actual spoken words*: I *lost* my keys. (h) *Reported words*: Jenny **said that** she *had lost* her keys.	The past perfect is commonly used in reported speech.** If the actual spoken words use the simple past, the past perfect is often used in reporting those words, as in (h). Common reporting verbs include *tell (someone), say, find out, learn,* and *discover.*
(i) *Written:* Bill *felt* great that evening. Earlier in the day, Annie *had caught* one fish, and he *had caught* three. They *had had* a delicious picnic near the lake and then *had gone* swimming again. It *had been* a nearly perfect vacation day.	The past perfect is often found in more formal writing such as fiction. In (i), the fiction writer uses the simple past to say that an event happened (*Bill felt great*), and then uses the past perfect to explain what had happened before that event.
(j) *I'd* left. *You'd* left. *We'd* left. *They'd* left. *She'd* left. *He'd* left. *It'd* left.	*Had* is often contracted with personal pronouns in informal writing. NOTE: *I'd* left. *I'd = I had* 　　　*I'd* like to leave. *I'd = I would*

*For more information about *by the time,* see Chart 17-2, p. 373.
**For more information about verb form usage in reported speech, see Chart 12-7, p. 262.

EXERCISE 32 ▸ Looking at grammar. (Chart 2-8)

Use the simple past or the past perfect form of the verbs in parentheses to complete the sentences. In some cases, either tense is correct.

How was your day?

1. I woke up with a headache, but I (*feel*) _____ better after I (*take*) _____ some medicine.

2. I was late for my first class. The teacher (*give, already*) _____ a quiz when I (*get*) _____ to class.

3. It was raining really hard when I (*leave*) _____ home this morning. My shoes were soaked when I (*get*) _____ to work. Fortunately, by the time I (*be*) _____ ready to leave, they (*dry, already*) _____ .

4. I (*make*) _____ a fantastic lunch to take to work. I (*put*) _____ it in the staff fridge this morning. I never (*have*) _____ a chance to eat it. When I went to the fridge, someone (*eat, already*) _____ it.

EXERCISE 33 ▸ Looking at grammar. (Chart 2-8)

Complete the sentences with the given verbs and the simple past or past perfect.

1. *feel / forget / look / offer*

   I got ready to pay the bill, but when I _____ in my purse, I discovered that I _____ my wallet. I _____ so embarrassed. My friend generously _____ to pay my part of the bill for me.

2. *lose / recognize / run / talk*

   Yesterday at the airport, I _____ into Rick Collins, an old friend of mine. I (*not*) _____ to him in years. At first, I (*not*) _____ him because he _____ a great deal of weight.

3. *decide / go / see*

   During my lunch break, I _____ to go to the art museum. I (*never*) _____ any of Picasso's paintings before I _____ there.

EXERCISE 34 ▸ Warm-up: listening. (Chart 2-9)

How is **had** pronounced in these sentences?

Excuses

1. I'm sorry I missed the appointment. I had written down the wrong date.
2. We knew we were running late. We had misread the bus schedule.
3. Sorry — I wanted to come to your party, but my family had already made other plans.

2-9 *Had* in Spoken English

(a) **Joe had** already heard the story.
   Spoken: Joe /d/ already heard the story. OR
        Joe /əd/ already heard the story.
	In spoken English, the helping verb **had** in the past perfect is often reduced following nouns and question words. It can be pronounced as /d/ or as /əd/.*
	
	NOTE: "ə" sounds like "uh."

(b) **Who had** been there before you?
   Spoken: Who/d/ been there before you? OR
        Who/əd/ been there before you?	

(c) The dog **had** a bone. *Spoken:* The dog *had* a bone.	**Had** is not reduced when it is a main verb, as in (c).

*See Chart 2-8 for written contractions of **had** with pronouns.

EXERCISE 35 ▶ Grammar and listening. (Charts 2-5, 2-8, and 2-9)

Before listening, complete the sentences with **is, had,** or **would.** Then listen and note the reduced pronunciation for these verbs.

A Base Jumper

1. My friend Tom _____ a base jumper. He jumps off buildings and mountains — for fun. Last year he jumped off a skyscraper. Tom and his team _____ planned it for over a year.

2. Family and friends _____ told him he was crazy, but that didn't change his mind.

3. I wanted to watch, but I _____ gotten sick the day before.

4. Afterward, Tom said it was the most thrilling experience he _____ ever had.

5. I _____ kind of like to try something like that, but I'm afraid of heights.

EXERCISE 36 ▶ Listening. (Charts 2-5, 2-8, and 2-9)

Listen to the sentences. You will hear reduced forms for **had, would, has,** and **have.** Write their non-reduced forms.

Examples: You will hear: The kids'd stayed up too late. They were late for school.
        You will write: The kids ____*had*____ stayed up too late. They were late for school.

        You will hear: The kids'd like to stay up late. There's no school tomorrow.
        You will write: The kids ____*would*____ like to stay up late. There's no school tomorrow.

        You will hear: The kids've stayed up too late. They need to go to bed.
        You will write: The kids ____*have*____ stayed up too late. They need to go to bed.

1. a. You're a new student, aren't you? How long _____ you been in this country?

   b. You left your job? How long _____ you been there?

2. a. You're looking for Jack? Jack _____ left. He isn't here.

   b. We were looking for Sam, but he _____ left by the time we got there.

3. a. Since we're teachers, we have the summers off and do a lot of traveling. We _____ like to travel to Africa next.

   b. We _____ wanted to travel with my parents on our last trip, but they became ill and needed to cancel.

4. a. Unfortunately, my phone died when we were lost. I _____ forgotten to recharge it.

   b. My phone's dead, and I _____ forgotten to bring the charger.

EXERCISE 37 ▶ Warm-up. (Chart 2-10)
Which sentence (a. or b.) logically follows each statement? Discuss the meanings of the verbs in blue.

1. I have been waiting for Jack since 5:00. _____
2. I had been waiting for Jack since 5:00. _____

   a. Then I left.
   b. And I'm still here.

3. I have been working outside for almost an hour. _____
4. I had been working outside for almost an hour. _____

   a. It's hot. I think I'll go inside.
   b. But I got too hot and came inside.

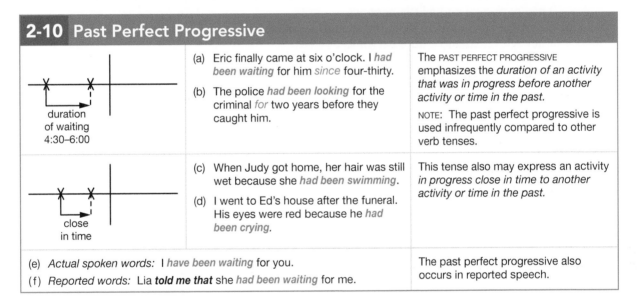

2-10 Past Perfect Progressive		
duration of waiting 4:30–6:00	(a) Eric finally came at six o'clock. I *had been waiting* for him *since* four-thirty. (b) The police *had been looking* for the criminal *for* two years before they caught him.	The PAST PERFECT PROGRESSIVE emphasizes the *duration of an activity that was in progress before another activity or time in the past.* NOTE: The past perfect progressive is used infrequently compared to other verb tenses.
close in time	(c) When Judy got home, her hair was still wet because she *had been swimming.* (d) I went to Ed's house after the funeral. His eyes were red because he *had been crying.*	This tense also may express an activity *in progress close in time to another activity or time in the past.*
(e) *Actual spoken words:* I *have been waiting* for you. (f) *Reported words:* Lia **told me that** she *had been waiting* for me.		The past perfect progressive also occurs in reported speech.

EXERCISE 38 ▶ Looking at grammar. (Chart 2-10)
Read the sentences and answer the questions that follow.

a. Ryan **has been researching** a topic for his thesis since the beginning of the year.
b. Ryan **had been researching** a topic for his thesis when he decided to change majors.
c. Ryan **researched** several different topics for his thesis.
d. Ryan **has researched** several different topics for his thesis.
e. Ryan **had researched** several different topics, but then he decided to change majors.

1. Which sentences emphasize the duration of the activity (research)? _____
2. In which sentences does the activity (research) continue up to now? _____
3. In which sentences is the activity (research) finished? _____
4. Which sentences have two activities in the past, one occurring before the other? _____

EXERCISE 39 ▶ Looking at grammar. (Charts 2-4, 2-7, and 2-10)
Choose the correct sentence in each pair. Explain why the other sentence is incorrect.

Updates on the Family

1. a. My brother Jose has changed majors again. He's not sure what he wants to be.
   b. My brother Jose had changed majors again. He's not sure what he wants to be.

2. a. Until Uncle Rudi went to the doctor, he has not been sleeping well.
   b. Until Uncle Rudi went to the doctor, he had not been sleeping well.

3. a. The twins have been working on a science project all semester. It's taking a lot of time.
   b. The twins had been working on a science project all semester. It's taking a lot of time.

4. a. Jill damaged her knee during a soccer game. She had been having trouble walking, so she had surgery on it. Now she's much better.
   b. Jill damaged her knee during a soccer game. She has been having trouble walking, so she had surgery on it. Now she's much better.

5. a. Our nieces are going to be in the school play next weekend. They had been rehearsing a lot. They're excited and a little nervous.
   b. Our nieces are going to be in the school play next weekend. They've been rehearsing a lot. They're excited and a little nervous.

EXERCISE 40 ▶ Looking at grammar. (Charts 2-7 and 2-10)
Complete the sentences. Use the present perfect progressive or the past perfect progressive form of the verbs in parentheses.

1. a. We (wait) _____*have been waiting*_____ for Nancy for the last two hours, but she

   still hasn't arrived.

   b. We (wait) _____*had been waiting*_____ for Nancy for over three hours before

   she finally arrived yesterday.

2. a. It is midnight. I (study) _____ for five straight hours. No

   wonder I'm getting tired.

   b. It was midnight. I (study) _____ for five straight hours.

   No wonder I was getting tired.

3. a. Jack suddenly realized that the teacher was asking him a question. He couldn't answer

   because he (daydream) _____ for the last ten minutes.

   b. Jack (daydream) _____ a lot. I wonder if he's in love.

4. a. Wake up! You (sleep) _____ long enough. It's time to get up.

   b. When I woke up, I didn't know where I was. I (sleep) _____

   soundly.

5. a. Sofia (work) _____ as a software engineer when her

   company transferred her. Now she's head of the Information Technology department.

   b. Sofia (work) _____ long hours since she got the

   IT position.

EXERCISE 41 ▸ Let's talk. (Chapters 1 and 2 Review)

Answer the questions and discuss the meaning of the verb forms. Work in pairs, in small groups, or as a class.

1. a. When the rain stopped, Gloria was riding her bike to work.
   b. When the rain stopped, Paul jumped on his bike and rode to work.
   QUESTION: Who got wet on the way to work?
   ANSWER: *Gloria.*

2. a. Ms. Lincoln taught at this school for nine years.
   b. Mr. Sanchez has taught at this school for nine years.
   QUESTION: Who is teaching at this school now?

3. a. Alice was opening the door when the doorbell rang.
   b. George walked to the door after the doorbell rang.
   QUESTION: Who had been expecting a visitor?

4. a. Donna lived in Chicago for five years.
   b. Carlos has been living in Chicago for five years.
   QUESTION: Who still lives in Chicago?

5. a. Jane drank some lemonade because she had been working outside.
   b. Sue drank some lemonade because she was working outside.
   QUESTION: Who drank lemonade after she finished working?

6. a. I looked across the street. Mr. Fox was waving at me.
   b. I looked across the street. Mrs. Cook waved at me.
   QUESTION: Who began to wave at me before I looked across the street?

7. a. Dan was leaving the room when I walked in.
   b. Sam had left the room when I walked in.
   QUESTION: Who did I see when I came into the room?

8. a. Ken went to the store because he was running out of food.
   b. Ann went to the store because she had run out of food.
   QUESTION: Who is better at planning ahead?

9. a. Jack had been studying Spanish since he was in elementary school. He spoke it very well by the time he moved to Peru.
   b. Robert has been studying Spanish since he was in elementary school. His Spanish is getting quite good.
   QUESTION: Who is studying Spanish in school?

EXERCISE 42 ▸ Looking at grammar. (Chapters 1 and 2 Review)

Complete the sentences with verbs in the box.

have	has	had	is	was	were

Travel Experiences

1. You need to stay calm now. The plane _____ just hitting some turbulence.

2. Oh, no! I _____ lost my passport! It's not in my bag.

have	has	had	is	was	were

3. While we _____ traveling in Europe last summer on a rail pass, we met people from around the world.

4. I _____ never tried frog legs. Let's try them at this café. The reviews say they're delicious.

5. I _____ never tried frog legs until I visited France.

6. I _____ getting worried when you texted. I was afraid you _____ taken the wrong subway.

7. People are saying that the weather _____ never been so hot and humid. I hope it's not going to stay like this for long.

8. The most amazing thing happened when I was in Tokyo. The very first person I saw when I stepped outside my hotel was a student I _____ taught several years before in New Zealand!

9. William _____ planned to leave for Asia on Tuesday when his sister called with bad news. Their parents _____ been in a car accident.

10. Travel _____ becoming harder for my grandfather now. He _____ lost his ability to walk and needs to use a wheelchair.

11. I _____ just found the tour podcasts you mentioned. Do you want to subscribe?

EXERCISE 43 ▶ Listening. (Chapter 2 Review)
Listen to each situation. Choose the sentence (a. or b.) that correctly describes it.

New Careers?

Example: You will hear: Kristi and her husband have had several conversations in the past few months about changing careers.

　　　　　You will choose: (a.) They have thought about changing careers.
　　　　　　　　　　　　　b. They changed careers a few months ago.

1. a. Kristi knows how to design websites.
   b. Kristi is learning how to design websites.

2. a. Her husband knows how to design websites.
   b. Her husband is learning how to design websites.

3. a. Kristi is working as a nurse but finds it stressful.
   b. Kristi has experience as a nurse.

4. a. Eric is designing websites now.
   b. Eric designed websites when he was in college.

5. a. Eric wants his parents to work for him part-time.
   b. His parents have already done work for Eric part-time.

EXERCISE 44 ▸ Check your knowledge. (Chapters 1 and 2 Review)

Correct the errors in verb tense usage.

1. Since I came to this country, I am learning a lot about the way of life here.

2. I arrive here only a short time ago. I am here since last Friday.

3. How long you are living here? I been here for almost two years.

4. Why you no have been in class for the last couple of days?

5. I am coaching a soccer team for the last two months.

6. When I was a child, I had lived with my aunt instead of my parents. My uncle has die before I am born, so I never knew him. My aunt raised me alone.

7. I'm living in my cousin's apartment since I have arrived here. It very small, and we are sharing the bedroom. I am needing my own place, but I don't find one so far.

8. My grandfather had lived in a small village in Italy when he was a child. At the age of 19, he had moved to Rome, where he had met and had married my grandmother in 1957. My father had been born in Rome in 1960. I am born in Rome in 1989.

EXERCISE 45 ▸ Reading and writing. (Chapter 2)

Part I. How has the world changed since the 1950s? Read the passage. Why does the first paragraph have mostly simple past and the second paragraph have more present perfect?

> Do you know these words?
> - extraordinary
> - dramatically

A Different World

My parents were born in the 1950s.* Since then, the world has gone through extraordinary changes, especially in the areas of communication and electronics. My parents didn't have devices like computers and cell phones. There was no Internet until the 1990s. Students went to the library to do research, and it took them many hours to find information. They typed their papers on typewriters, and when they made a mistake, they began again. They often wrote letters because long-distance phone calls were expensive. They didn't have voicemail, so they had to call people back. Some homes still had party lines: families shared one phone line, and sometimes people picked up the phone and heard their neighbors' conversations. For entertainment, they had just a few channels on the TV, or they watched movies in theaters. They played music on phonographs or listened to the radio.

Since the 1980s, computers and the Internet have changed communication dramatically. People get information instantly online, and they can reach each other quickly through email. Cell phones have been available since the 1990s. Texting has become so popular that for many people it has replaced phone calls. Computers and cell phones have also introduced people to apps for games, social media, music, movie streaming, and photo editing, to name just a few. The world seemed very quiet in my parents' time, but for better or for worse, life today has become digital.

*Note that there is no apostrophe when adding **-s** to *years*.

Part II. Think about the decade when your parents' generation was born. What was different about life in that decade? Here are some areas you can think about to get started: communication, culture, fashion, advertising, entertainment, inventions, transportation, and the environment.

1. Choose one topic and make a list of changes.
2. Write one or two paragraphs based on your list.
3. Think carefully about the use of the simple past and present perfect as you write.

WRITING TIP

If you want your writing to sound more natural, it is important to not translate from your language. There is a good chance that your language expresses ideas very differently. In the beginning, use simple sentence structures that you have learned. You may want to express a complex idea, but if you haven't learned the grammar for this, break the idea down into simpler language. As you learn more advanced grammar, you can begin to express more complex ideas.

Reading English books and listening to English are also very important for good writing. You start to see that particular words go with other words in a specific way. And certain words, phrases, and structures begin to sound familiar as well. At this point, you may find that they start to appear in your writing in a natural way.

Part III. Edit your writing. Check for the following:

1. ☐ indented paragraph(s)
2. ☐ use of the simple past for activities that began and ended at a particular time in the past
3. ☐ use of the present perfect for activities that began in the past and are still in progress, or for unspecified or recent time
4. ☐ correct spelling (use a dictionary or spell-check)

▪▪▪▪▪ Go to MyEnglishLab for Self-Study: Gerunds and Infinitives 2

CHAPTER 2

Future Time

PRETEST: What do I already know?
Write "C" if a sentence has the correct verb form and "I" for incorrect. Check your answers below. After you complete each chart listed, make any necessary corrections.

1. _____ The storm will starts after midnight. It is going to last through the morning. (3-1)

2. _____ Wendy is going to apply to an electrical engineering program. (3-1 and 3-2)

3. _____ Something's wrong. The lights won't turn on. (3-2)

4. _____ As soon as the snow will stop, we will leave. (3-3)

5. _____ The train gets in at midnight tomorrow. (3-4)

6. _____ When you get home, I will be sleeping. (3-5)

7. _____ By the time Violet retires, she will has worked as a nurse for 40 years. (3-6)

Incorrect sentences: 1, 4, 7

EXERCISE 1 ▸ Warm-up. (Chart 3-1)
Complete the sentences with words from the right column.

1. The weather _____ be hot tomorrow.   a. to

2. Athena _____ going to go to the beach.   b. is

3. She will _____ a relaxing day.   c. are

4. Sergio and Yanni _____ going to join her in the afternoon.   d. will

5. They are going _____ come home after sunset.   e. have

3-1 Simple Future: Forms of *Will* and *Be Going To*

⊢———+—×———	(a) It *will* snow tomorrow. (b) It *is going to* snow tomorrow.	*Will* and *be going to* express future time and often have essentially the same meaning. Examples (a) and (b) have the same meaning. See Chart 3-2 for differences in meaning between the two forms.

Will

(c) The weather *will turn* cold tonight. INCORRECT: The weather wills-turn cold. INCORRECT: The weather will turns-cold. INCORRECT: The weather will to-turn cold.	*Will* typically expresses predictions about the future, as in (c). *Will* does not take a final *-s*. *Will* is followed immediately by the simple form of a verb.
(d) It *will not warm* up for several days. (e) The snow *won't melt* soon.	NEGATIVE: *will + not = won't*
(f) *Will* it be icy *tomorrow?* How *will* you get here?	QUESTION: *will + subject + main verb* In (e): The speaker is asking for information about a future event.*
(g) *Spoken* or *written*: *It'll* be cold.	CONTRACTIONS WITH PRONOUNS AND NOUNS:
(h) *Spoken*: *Tom'll* shovel the snow. *Written*: *Tom will* shovel the snow.	*Will* is often contracted with pronouns in both speaking and informal writing: *I'll, you'll, she'll, he'll, it'll, we'll, they'll*.
(i) *Spoken* or *very informal writing*: *Nobody'll* be out. *That'll* be strange. *There'll* probably be some accidents.	*Will* is also often contracted with nouns in speaking but usually not in writing, as in (h). In spoken English and very informal writing, *will* may be contracted with other kinds of pronouns and *there*, as in (i).

Be Going To

(j) Snow *is going to continue* all week. The roads *are going to be* icy.	*Be going to* also commonly expresses predictions about the future. In informal speech, *going to* is often pronounced "gonna."
(k) *Informally spoken*: Snow*'s gonna continue* all week.	
(l) I'm *not going to go* out.	NEGATIVE: *be + not + going to*, as in (l)
(m) *Is* the storm *going to be* dangerous?	QUESTION: *be + subject + going to*, as in (m)

*****Will* can also be used in questions to make polite requests: ***Will** you **open** the door for me, please?* See Chart 9-8, p. 176.

EXERCISE 2 ▶ Looking at grammar. (Chart 3-1)

Check (✓) the sentences that are predictions about the future.

Future Doctors

1. _____ John is going to be a heart surgeon. He wants to work with young children.

2. _____ He is going to be a fantastic doctor.

3. _____ He'll be kind and patient with the kids.

4. _____ He is going to graduate from medical school in June. Then he is going to start his surgical training.

5. _____ John's wife doesn't want to be a surgeon. She is going to specialize in senior care.

6. _____ She will be fantastic. She is so caring.

7. _____ I think they're going to have very busy lives.

EXERCISE 3 ▸ Grammar, speaking, and writing. (Chart 3-1)

Work in small groups. Make predictions by completing each sentence with the words in the box. Give your own opinion, and take turns sharing each of your answers. Then write five predictions about life in the year 2050.

is	are	will	isn't	aren't	won't

In the next decade, ...

1. the climate _____ going to get warmer.

2. cities near the ocean _____ have more flooding.

3. smartphones and tablets _____ going to replace computers.

4. electric cars _____ be more common than gas-powered cars.

5. we _____ going to have flying cars.

6. computers _____ be the main teachers in classrooms.

7. I _____ learn to speak English fluently.

8. my country _____ going to win the World Cup championship.

EXERCISE 4 ▸ Listening. (Chart 3-1)

Complete the sentences about a final exam with the non-contracted forms of the verbs you hear.

1. _____ to turn in all your assignments by tomorrow.

2. _____ for the final exam on Monday.

3. The _____ 50 questions.

4. _____ 50 questions on the exam.

5. _____ the whole hour to complete the test.

6. It's a long exam. Sorry, but _____ early.

7. _____ a lot of work. Study hard!

8. The _____ available in my office the next day.

EXERCISE 5 ▸ Warm-up. (Chart 3-2)

Read the sentences and answer the questions that follow.

a. It's going to rain tomorrow.
b. I'm going to paint the house next week.
c. Here. I'll carry that box. It looks heavy.
d. It will be cloudy this weekend.

1. Which sentence expresses a prior plan? _____

2. Which sentences are predictions? _____ and _____

3. Which sentence expresses an offer to help? _____

3-2 *Will* vs. *Be Going To*

Prediction

(a) According to the weather report, it *will be* cloudy tomorrow. (b) According to the weather report, it *is going to be* cloudy tomorrow.	***Will*** and ***be going to*** mean the same when they make *predictions* about the future (*prediction* = a statement about something the speaker thinks will be true or will occur in the future). Examples (a) and (b) have the same meaning.

Prior Plan

(c) — Why did you buy this paint?
    — I'*m going to paint* my bedroom tomorrow.
 	
 (d) — Are you busy this evening?
    — Well, I really don't have any plans. I'*ll eat*/I'*m going to eat* dinner, of course. And then I'*ll* probably *watch*/I'*m* probably *going to watch* TV for a little while.
 	
 (e) The meeting *will begin* at 10:00 A.M. We *will have* two hours for discussion.
	Be going to is commonly used in speaking to express a *prior plan* (i.e., a plan made before the moment of speaking).
	
	 In (c): The speaker already has a plan to paint his bedroom. He could also say, "I'm planning to paint my bedroom."
	
	 NOTE: In (d), either ***will*** or ***be going to*** is possible. The second speaker has not planned her evening. She is "predicting" her evening (rather than stating any prior plans), so she may use either ***will*** or ***be going to***.
	
	 In writing, ***will*** is more common.

Willingness

(f) — The phone's ringing.
    — I'*ll get* it.
 	
 (g) — How old is Aunt Agnes?
    — I don't know. She *won't tell* me.
 	
 (h) The car *won't start*. Maybe the battery is dead.
	Will (but not ***be going to***) is used to express *willingness* or *offer to help*. In this case, ***will*** expresses a decision the speaker makes at the moment of speaking.
	
	 In (f): The second speaker decides to answer the phone at the immediate present moment; she/he does not have a prior plan.
	
	 Will not / won't can express *refusal*, as in (g) with a person or in (h) with an inanimate object.

EXERCISE 6 ▶ Grammar, speaking, and listening. (Chart 3-2)

Part I. Work with a partner. Read each conversation aloud. Discuss the *italicized* verbs. Are the speakers expressing:

    a. predictions?
    b. decisions they are making at the moment of speaking (willingness)?
    c. plans they made before the moment of speaking?

Casual Conversations

1. A: Are you busy Saturday night? I've got front-row seats for the baseball game.
   B: Oh, sorry. It sounds like a lot of fun, but I'*m going to be* at my cousin's wedding.

2. A: We'*re going to go* out to dinner in a few minutes. Do you want to join us?
   B: Sure. Give me just a minute and I'*ll grab* my coat.

3. A: I heard Sue and David are engaged for the third time!
   B: They *won't* ever *get married*. They fight too much.

4. A: How do you spell "misspell"? One -*s* or two?
   B: Gosh! I forget. I'*ll look* it up.

5. A: That's great news about your new job.
   B: Well, actually, I've changed my mind about it. I*'m not going to take* it after all. I've decided to stay with my old job.

6. A: Sofia's so much fun. And she's very patient with kids.
   B: I know. She*'ll be* great as a camp counselor.

 Part II. Listen to the conversations with your book closed. Notice how *will* and *going to* are pronounced.

EXERCISE 7 ▸ Looking at grammar. (Chart 3-2)
Decide if each *italicized* verb expresses a prediction, a prior plan, or willingness.

Chatting Before Dinner

1. Dinner's almost ready. I*'ll set* the table.	prediction	plan	(willingness)
2. I think you'll *love* this soup. The recipe is from the restaurant we went to.	prediction	plan	willingness
3. Don't worry about the spilled coffee. I*'ll clean* it up.	prediction	plan	willingness
4. Your dad called. He has some vacation time. He *is going to take* next week off.	prediction	plan	willingness
5. Darn! I burned the rice. Someday, there *is going to be* an alarm to prevent that!	prediction	plan	willingness
6. I*'m going to take* some soup to my grandmother tomorrow. She's coming down with* a cold.	prediction	plan	willingness
7. Uh-oh. It looks like the refrigerator light is out. I*'ll pick up* one tomorrow.	prediction	plan	willingness
8. I*'m going to help* the kids with their homework after dinner.	prediction	plan	willingness

EXERCISE 8 ▸ Looking at grammar. (Chart 3-2)
Complete the conversations with **be going to** if you think the speaker is expressing a prior plan. If you think there is no prior plan, use **will**. Use **won't** if the speaker is expressing refusal.

1. A: This letter is in French, and I don't speak French. Can you help me?

   B: Sure. I (*translate*) _____ *will translate* _____ it for you.

2. A: Do you want to go shopping with me? I (*go*) _____ *am going to go* _____ to the mall downtown.

   B: Sure! Thanks.

3. A: How about getting together for dinner tonight?

   B: Sounds good. Where?

   A: How about Alice's Restaurant or the Gateway Café? You decide.

   B: Alice's Restaurant. I (*meet*) _____ you there around six.

   A: Great. I (*see*) _____ you then.

   B: It's a date.

---

*come down with = get (an illness)

4. A: Do you have plans for dinner?

   B: Yes. I (*meet**) _____ a co-worker

   for dinner at Alice's Restaurant. Want to join us?

5. A: Who wants to erase the board? Are there any volunteers?

   B: I (*do*) _____ it!

   C: I (*do*) _____ it!

6. A: Why does he have an eraser in his hand?

   B: He (*erase*) _____ the board.

7. A: Why is that little boy crying?

   B: I don't know. He (*tell, not*) _____ me.

   I wonder where his parents are.

8. A: What's wrong?

   B: The door (*open, not*) _____ . I think the

   lock is broken.

EXERCISE 9 ▶ Grammar and listening. (Chart 3-2)

Choose the expected response (a. or b.). Then listen to the conversations and check your answers.

A Plan or an Offer to Help?

1. A: So, you were talking about your plans for the summer. What are you going to do?
   B: a. I'm going to work at a summer resort in the mountains.
      b. I'll work at a summer resort in the mountains.

2. A: Can you help me out? I need to get this check in the mail by noon.
   B: a. Sure. I'm going to drop it off on my way to work.
      b. Sure. I'll drop it off on my way to work.

3. A: Tell me again. Why are you leaving work early?
   B: a. I'm going to attend my cousin's funeral.
      b. I'll attend my cousin's funeral.

4. A: Darn, this flashlight doesn't work.
   B: a. Here, give it to me. I'm going to fix it for you.
      b. Here, give it to me. I'll fix it for you.

5. A: Here's the broom. What did you want it for?
   B: a. I'm going to sweep the front steps.
      b. I'll sweep the front steps.

---

*When **be going to** expresses a prior plan, it is often also possible to use the present progressive with no change in meaning. There is no difference in meaning between these sentences:

   I am going to meet Larry at Alice's Restaurant at six. OR
   I am meeting Larry at Alice's Restaurant at six.

EXERCISE 10 ▸ Let's talk. (Chart 3-2)

Work with a partner. Imagine you are planning to leave for a wedding in a few minutes. Choose one picture and complete the conversation in your own words. Then practice your conversation and perform it for the class. You can look at your book before you speak. When you speak, look at your partner.

A Fiasco

A: Oh, no. What are we going to do? _____

B: I know. We'll _____

A: How will that help?

B: I don't know. But we need to try something. Let's not panic!

A: Wait! This'll work. We'll _____

B: Perfect.

EXERCISE 11 ▸ Listening and writing. (Chart 3-2)

1. Read the introductory paragraph below and listen to the passage that follows. Then write down as much as you can remember in paragraph form.

2. Work with a partner and share paragraphs. Make any necessary revisions to the content.

3. Work in small groups and compare paragraphs. Edit for correct verb usage, punctuation, and spelling.

A Successful Family Business

The Costa family began their restaurant business five years ago with a small coffee shop. They served coffee, tea, and fresh bakery items. They developed a following, and now they are so popular that they are going to expand their restaurant next month.

EXERCISE 12 ▸ Warm-up. (Chart 3-3)

Complete the sentences with your own words. All the sentences talk about future time. What do you notice about the verbs in blue?

1. After I leave this class, I'm going to _____

2. As soon as I get home tonight, I'll _____

3. Before I do my homework, I'll _____

4. When I finish my English studies, I'm going to _____

3-3 Expressing the Future in Time Clauses

(a) Bob will come soon. *When Bob comes,* we will see him.	In (a): **When Bob comes** is a time clause.* **when** + *subject* + *verb* = *a time clause* When the meaning of the time clause is future, the SIMPLE PRESENT tense is used. *Will* or *be going to* is not used in the time clause.
(b) Linda is going to leave soon. *Before she leaves,* she is going to finish her work.	
(c) I will get home at 5:30. *After I get home,* I will eat dinner.	A time clause begins with such words as *when, before, after, as soon as, until,* and *while* and includes a subject and a verb. The time clause can come either at the beginning of the sentence or in the second part of the sentence: *When he comes,* we'll see him. OR We'll see him *when he comes.* Notice: A comma is used when the time clause comes first in a sentence.
(d) The taxi will arrive soon. *As soon as it arrives,* we'll be able to leave for the airport.	
(e) They are going to come soon. I'll wait here *until they come.*	
(f) *While I am traveling in Europe next year,* I'm going to save money by staying in youth hostels.	Sometimes the PRESENT PROGRESSIVE is used in a time clause to express an activity that will be in progress in the future, as in (f).
(g) I will go to bed *after I finish my work.*	Occasionally, the PRESENT PERFECT is used in a time clause, as in (h). Examples (g) and (h) have the same meaning. The present perfect in the time clause emphasizes the completion of one act before a second act occurs in the future.
(h) I will go to bed *after I have finished my work.*	

*A *time clause* is an adverb clause. See Charts 17-1, p. 371 and 17-2, p. 373 for more information.

EXERCISE 13 ▶ Looking at grammar. (Chart 3-3)
Choose the correct verbs for these sentences.

Chores

1. After the rain   stops / will stop, I am going to wash the car.
2. I'm going to vacuum the inside before I   quit / will quit.
3. Are you going to help me before you   go / will go   to your friend's?
4. My dad   cleans / is going to clean   the garage after he   has / will have   lunch.
5. While he   is cleaning / will clean   the garage later, he   listens / is going to listen   to podcasts.
6. The garage   is / will look   great after he   finishes / will finish   tonight.

EXERCISE 14 ▶ Looking at grammar. (Chart 3-3)
Complete the sentences with the given verbs. Use a form of **be going to,** the simple present, or the present progressive.

1. *listen / sleep*

   I _____ to an English language course while I

   _____ tonight. Do you think it will help me learn English faster?

2. *come / wait*

   Bakir will be here soon. I _____ here until he _____ .

3. *buy / stop / walk*

I'm sure it will stop snowing soon. As soon as the snow _____,

I _____ to the store and _____ some groceries.

4. *enter / get / go / graduate*

Michelle is a junior in college this year. After she _____ with a B.A. next

year, she _____ graduate school and work on an M.A. Then

she _____ on for her Ph.D. after she _____ her master's degree.

EXERCISE 15 ▶ Let's talk: interview. (Chart 3-3)

Make questions using the given words. Ask two students each question. Share some of their answers with the class. Use **be going to** for the future verb.

1. What \ you \ do \ as soon as \ class \ end \ today?
2. Before \ you \ go \ to bed \ tonight \ what \ you \ do?
3. What \ you \ do \ after \ you \ wake up \ tomorrow?
4. What \ you \ do \ when \ you \ have \ free time \ this weekend?
5. After \ you \ complete \ this course \ what \ you \ do?

EXERCISE 16 ▶ Looking at grammar. (Chart 3-3)

Correct the 12 errors in verb forms.

Getting Ready for a Business Trip

Tia need to leave work early. She is going to prepare for her business trip when she will get home. After she is packing her suitcase, she rehearse her PowerPoint® presentation for her clients. Her father is going to come over and watch her presentation after he is finishing dinner. While he watch, Tia is going to ask him to give her honest feedback. After she is practicing several times, she will not feel so nervous about her presentation. She will pays some bills and sending a few work emails before she is going to bed. After she gets into bed, she is going to fall asleep quickly because she is knowing that she is very tired.

EXERCISE 17 ▶ Warm-up. (Chart 3-4)

Decide if each sentence has a present or future meaning. What do you notice about the verb tense in each sentence?

1. I'm having dinner at the airport later tonight.	present meaning	future meaning
2. I'm meeting a friend there.	present meaning	future meaning
3. We're taking a flight at midnight.	present meaning	future meaning

3-4 Using the Present Progressive and the Simple Present to Express Future Time

Present Progressive

(a) My wife has an appointment with a doctor. She *is seeing* Dr. North *next Tuesday*.	The PRESENT PROGRESSIVE may be used to *express future time when the idea of the sentence concerns a planned event or definite intention.*
(b) Sam has already made his plans. He *is leaving* *at noon tomorrow*.	COMPARE: A verb such as *rain* is not used in the present progressive to indicate future time because rain is not a planned event.
(c) — What are you going to do this afternoon? — *After lunch*, I *am meeting* a friend of mine. We *are going* to the mall. Would you like to come along?	A future meaning for the present progressive tense is indicated either by future time words in the sentence or by the context.

Simple Present

(d) The museum *opens* at 10:00 tomorrow morning.	The SIMPLE PRESENT can also be used to *express future time in a sentence concerning events that are on a definite schedule or timetable.* These sentences usually contain future time words. Only a few verbs are used in this way: e.g., *open, close, begin, end, start, finish, arrive, leave, come, return.*
(e) Classes *begin* next week.	
(f) John's plane *arrives* at 6:05 P.M. next Monday.	

EXERCISE 18 ▶ Looking at grammar. (Chart 3-4)
Decide the meaning of each *italicized* verb: ***in the future, now,*** or ***habitually***.

1. A: Students usually *take* four courses each semester. _____habitually_____

   Why *are* you only *taking* three? _____now_____

   B: I have a very demanding internship. But next semester, I *am taking* five courses to make up. _____in the future_____

2. A: What *are* you *doing?* _____

   B: I'*m sending* an email to my parents. It's their anniversary. But they're probably out to dinner. That's how they *celebrate* every year. _____

3. A: What? Our train *leaves* in five minutes? _____

   B: Yes, it *leaves* every hour on the hour. _____

4. A: My brother's birthday is next week. I'*m giving* him a sweater. _____

   B: That's what I usually *give* my brother. Sweaters make a good gift. _____

EXERCISE 19 ▶ Looking at grammar. (Chart 3-4)
Complete each sentence with any present progressive verb.

1. A: How about going across the street for a cup of coffee?

   B: I can't. I _____am meeting_____ Jennifer at the library at 5:00.

2. A: Why are you in such a hurry?

   B: I _____ the four o'clock plane to New York.

3. A: I see you're smoking. I thought you stopped last month.

   B: I did, but I began again. I _____ tomorrow, and this time I mean it.

4. A: Your cough sounds terrible! Are you going to go to the doctor?

    B: Yes. I _____ Dr. Na later this afternoon.

5. A: Where are you and your family going for your vacation this summer?

    B: Ontario, Canada. We're not going to fly. We _____ so we can take our time and enjoy the scenery.

EXERCISE 20 ▶ Reading, writing, and speaking. (Chart 3-4)

Part I. Read the passage. <u>Underline</u> the present verbs and discuss their usage.

My Vacation of a Lifetime

This coming Saturday, I am beginning my "vacation of a lifetime." The first place I'm going to is Bali. My plane leaves at six-thirty Saturday morning. I arrive in Bali late that afternoon. I'm staying at the Nusa Dua Beach Hotel. I leave Bali on the fifteenth and travel to Thailand. While I'm there, I'm staying with some friends. We'll take a boat tour in Bangkok and then travel to the countryside. There is a national park, and we'll do some hiking. Finally we'll finish in Phuket. It'll be nice to relax on the beaches and go windsurfing too. This will be my first trip to these places.

Part II. Imagine that you are going to take your ideal vacation next week. Write a paragraph about your plans, using Part I as a model. Use present tenses where appropriate. Share some of your plans with a partner, in small groups, or with the class.

EXERCISE 21 ▶ Warm-up. (Chart 3-5)

Notice the verbs in blue. What do they have in common?

Right now I am sitting in class. Yesterday at this time, I was sitting in class. Tomorrow at this time, I will be sitting in class.

3-5 Future Progressive

	(a) I will begin to study at seven. You will come at eight. I *will be studying* when you come.	The FUTURE PROGRESSIVE expresses an activity that *will be in progress at a time in the future.*
	(b) Don't call me at nine because I won't be home. I *am going to be studying* at the library.	The progressive form of *be going to:* ***be going to*** + ***be*** + ***-ing***, as in (b)
	(c) I'll be picking Susie up early for a dentist appointment. (d) We'll be contacting you shortly about your inquiry.	***Will*** + the progressive can be used with an activity that is not in progress at a time in the future. It is common in spoken English when the speaker wants to sound more polite or softer. It is an alternative to: 1) the non-progressive form of ***will*** (*I'll pick Susie up early for a dentist appointment.*) OR 2) ***be going to*** (*I'm going to pick Susie up early for a dentist appointment.*)

EXERCISE 22 ▸ Looking at grammar. (Chart 3-5)

Complete the sentences. Use the future progressive form of the given verbs.

1. *finish / sleep / study*   Please don't call our house after 9:00 tonight. The baby

   <u>is going to be sleeping / will be sleeping</u> . My husband _____

   for a test. I _____ a project for work.

2. *talk / do / see*   Dr. Roberts is the town's only medical doctor and works long hours.

   Tomorrow she has an especially busy schedule. From early in the morning until

   lunch, she _____ patients at her clinic. After lunch,

   she _____ research at the hospital. In the evening, she

   _____ to medical students about rural health care.

EXERCISE 23 ▸ Looking at grammar. (Chart 3-5)

Complete the sentences. Use *will* + progressive or the simple present form of the verbs in
parentheses.

1. Tomorrow I'm going to leave for home. When I (*arrive*) _____ at the

   airport, my whole family (*wait*) _____ for me.

2. When I (*get*) _____ up tomorrow morning, the sun (*shine*)

   _____, the birds (*sing*) _____, and my

   roommate (*lie, still*) _____ in bed fast asleep.

3. A: Just think! Two days from now I (*ski*) _____ in the mountains
      in Austria.

   B: Sounds great! I (*think*) _____ about you.

4. A: Are you going to be in town next Saturday?

   B: No. I (*visit*) _____ my aunt in Chicago.

5. A: Where are you going to be this evening?

   B: I (*work*) _____ on my research paper at the library.

EXERCISE 24 ▸ Reading and grammar. (Chart 3-5)

Read the email message from a parent to a high school teacher. <u>Underline</u> the future progressive
verbs. How does the use of future progressive affect the tone of the message?

Subject: Jill Bailey absence   Today at 4:32 PM

Dear Mrs. Rawley,

Jill has some medical tests tomorrow and won't be attending school. Please let me know if there
will be any homework to pick up. I'll be picking up my other children at 3:00 and can get the
assignments then.

Thank you,
Karen Bailey

EXERCISE 25 ▸ Warm-up. (Chart 3-6)
Decide which action in each sentence began first.

1. Leo will work until December 30th, and then he will retire.
2. When Leo retires, he will have worked at the same company for 30 years.
3. When Leo retires, he will have been working at the same company for 30 years.

3-6 Future Perfect and Future Perfect Progressive

NOTE: These two tenses are rarely used compared to the other verb tenses.

FUTURE PERFECT	(a) I will graduate in June. I will see you in July. By the time I see you, *I will have graduated.*	The FUTURE PERFECT expresses an activity that will be *completed before another time or event in the future.* Note the sentence pattern in (a) with *by the time:* ADVERB CLAUSE *by the time* + simple present MAIN CLAUSE future perfect
FUTURE PERFECT PROGRESSIVE	(b) I will go to bed at 10:00 P.M. Ed will get home at midnight. At midnight I will be sleeping. *I will have been sleeping* for two hours by the time Ed gets home.	The FUTURE PERFECT PROGRESSIVE emphasizes the *duration of an activity* that will be *in progress before another time or event in the future.*
	(c) When Professor Jones retires next month, he *will have taught* OR *will have been teaching* for 45 years.	Sometimes the future perfect and the future perfect progressive have the same meaning, as in (c). Also, notice that the activity expressed by either of these two tenses may begin in the past.

EXERCISE 26 ▸ Looking at grammar. (Charts 3-5 and 3-6)
Choose the correct verbs.

A Hospital Stay

1. Roger will get to the hospital early tomorrow morning. He   will stay / will have stayed   there for a week. He is going to have back surgery.
2. When Roger leaves the hospital, he   will stay / will have stayed   there a week.
3. After Roger has back surgery, he   will go / will have gone   to the recovery room.
4. When Roger wakes up, he   will be / will have been   asleep for six hours.
5. When Roger first walks, he   will need / will have needed   assistance.
6. By the time Roger can walk unassisted, he   will have / will have had   many hours of physical therapy.
7. Several specialists   will help / will have helped   Roger by the time he goes home.

EXERCISE 27 ▸ Looking at grammar. (Charts 3-5 and 3-6)
Complete the sentences. Use any appropriate tense of the verbs in parentheses.

1. Ann and Andy got married on June 1st.

   a. Today is June 15th. They (*be*) _____ married for two weeks.

   b. By June 8th, they (*be*) _____ married for one week.

   c. By June 29th, they (*be*) _____ married for four weeks.

June						
Sun	Mon	Tues	Wed	Thurs	Fri	Sat
					①	2
3	4	5	6	7	8	9
10	11	12	13	14	15	16
17	18	19	20	21	22	23
24	25	26	27	28	29	30

2. a. This traffic is terrible. We're going to be late. By the time

   we (*get*) _____ to the airport, Yuri's plane (*arrive, already**)

   _____, and he'll be wondering where we are.

   b. The traffic was terrible. By the time we (*get*) _____ to the airport,

   Yuri's plane (*arrive, already*) _____.

3. a. This morning I came to class at 9:00. Right now it is 10:00, and I am still in

   class. I (*sit*) _____ at this desk for an hour. By 9:30, I

   (*sit*) _____ here for half an hour. By 11:00,

   I (*sit*) _____ here for two hours.

   b. Classes start at 9:00 every day. It's 9:30 and the school bus is late. When the bus

   gets to school, classes (*begin*) _____. The teachers (*teach*)

   _____ since 9:00.

EXERCISE 28 ▸ Looking at grammar. (Charts 3-5 and 3-6)
Look at each pair of sentences. The preferred or correct sentence is checked in each one. Can you explain why the other sentence is not checked?

1. I'm checking airline flights right now.
   ✓ a. By the time you come back from lunch, I will have made our reservation.
   b. By the time you come back from lunch, I will have been making our reservation.

2. This is an incredibly long car ride.
   a. Do you realize that by the time we arrive in Phoenix, we will have driven for 20 hours straight?
   ✓ b. Do you realize that by the time we arrive in Phoenix, we will have been driving for 20 hours straight?

3. Go ahead and leave on your vacation. Don't worry about this work.
   ✓ a. By the time you get back, we will have finished the project.
   b. By the time you get back, we will have been finishing the project.

---

*With the future perfect, **already** has two possible midsentence positions: *I will **already** have finished.* OR
*I will have **already** finished.*

4. I don't understand how those long-distance swimmers do it! The race began more than an hour ago.
   a. By the time they reach the finish line, they will have swum steadily for more than two hours.
   ✓ b. By the time they reach the finish line, they will have been swimming steadily for more than two hours.

EXERCISE 29 ▸ Check your knowledge. (Chapter 3 Review)
Correct the errors in verb tense usage.

1. Marnie will makes a good project manager. She has strong leadership skills.

2. Where you will be after the game finishes?

3. The car no will start. Maybe it has a dead battery.

4. I going to look for a new apartment when my roommate move out.

5. After the movie end, we are going to go out for ice cream.

6. By the time I am 60, my daughter will has finish medical school.

7. Don't worry, honey. Your dad will picking you up soon.

8. My appointment is for 10:15 tomorrow. What time will we be leave here?

9. As soon as the term will be over, I apply for a part-time job.

10. By their next anniversary, my parents will have together for 43 years.

EXERCISE 30 ▸ Reading, speaking, and writing. (Chapter 3)
Part I. Read the three email messages. Discuss the appropriateness of each.

SITUATION 1: College student to professor:

Subject: **Out of town visit**	Today at 7:46 PM

Hey Prof!

How's it going? I need an extension on my project. Maybe an extra week? Some family from out of town are going to arrive tomorrow. No notice. LOL!

Thanx ☺
Janice

SITUATION 2: College student to professor:

Subject: **Jamal Benson absence tomorrow**	Today at 9:04 PM

Dear Professor Wilson,

I'm sorry, but I won't be in class tomorrow. My mother is having surgery, and I'll be taking her to the hospital. I'll get the assignment from my roommate. Thank you for your understanding.

Sincerely,
Jamal Benson
Chem. 101

SITUATION 3: High school student to teacher

| Subject: car accident | Today at 6:31 PM |

Hope ur doing OK. Sorry i missed ur class. I was in a car accident and needed to go to the ER. Everything's OK, but i won't be ready for the test on Tuesday. Also, i lost my study guide, maybe in the accident. I don't know. Please send one ASAP!!!

Later,
Rob

WRITING TIPS

Many students are unsure about how formal or informal an email message to an instructor needs to be. A formal style will come across as more respectful. This means that your message will be more like a business letter and not like a text message or a post on social media. Here are some key points to consider:

- Formal messages do not use texting language, for example, "u" for "you" or "thanx" for "thanks." They do not have smiley faces or other emoticons. Do not even use this: :)
- The subject line needs to be specific.
- At the college level, you can begin your message with *Dear Professor* _____ or *Dear Dr.* _____. If you don't know the title, then you can use *Mr.* or *Ms.* For K–12*, the title will generally be *Mr., Mrs.,* or *Ms.*
- It is better to get class information/assignments online or from a classmate than by contacting the instructor. Only ask the instructor if there are no other options.
- Be sure you have an acceptable reason for your request or excuse. If you don't, don't mention a poor one.
- Sign your first and last name, and begin with one of the following: *Thank you, Sincerely, Regards, Best, Respectfully.*
- Double-check that you have the correct email address. If one letter is wrong, your email will not get to the intended person.
- Keep your message concise and to the point.

Finally, instructors receive a lot of emails in one day. Be sure to proofread for grammar and spelling mistakes. You want your message to be easy to read and you want to convey that you are a conscientious student.

These guidelines will also be useful for writing to other school officials or to people outside of school, such as employers, supervisors, and co-workers. You will probably find that some instructors have a more relaxed style, but until you hear from them, you won't go wrong with a formal style.

*K–12 = kindergarten through 12th grade

Part II. Write two emails to a teacher. In the first, explain why you will be absent for three days. In the second, explain why you will miss an upcoming test. (They do not need to be true.) Share and discuss with one or two classmates.

Part III. Edit your writing. Check for the following:

1. ☐ specific subject line
2. ☐ appropriate form of address and proper signature
3. ☐ complete sentences
4. ☐ formal tone
5. ☐ no texting language or emoticons
6. ☐ correct spelling (use a dictionary or spell-check)

■■■■ Go to MyEnglishLab for Self-Study: Gerunds and Infinitives 3

CHAPTER 4

Review of Verb Tenses

PRETEST: What do I already know?

Write "C" if a sentence has the correct verb form and "I" for incorrect. Check your answers using the answer key below. The chapter numbers are in parentheses. Use them for reference as you make any necessary corrections.

1. _____ It's so noisy right now. Everyone shouting and making a lot of noise in the halls. (Ch. 1)

2. _____ I haven't been in this town very long. I just get here two weeks ago. (Ch. 2)

3. _____ I'm really glad you to come to my hometown next year. (Ch. 3)

4. _____ Why were you deciding to become a nurse? (Ch. 1)

5. _____ I am in Australia for the last four months. During this time, I had done many things and saw many places. (Ch. 2)

6. _____ By the time I graduate from college, I will have taken out several student loans. (Ch. 3)

Incorrect sentences: 1, 2, 3, 4, 5

EXERCISE 1 ▶ Looking at grammar. (Chapters 1 → 3)
Complete the sentences with any appropriate tense of the verbs in parentheses.

Malia's Busy Schedule

1. Malia is in my evening speech class. She (*study*)

   _____ speech this semester. She

   (*take, also*) _____ some other

   night classes. Her classes (*begin*) _____

   at 6:00 every evening.

2. Yesterday Malia woke up at 5:00 A.M. She (*get up, already*) _____

   when her alarm clock (*ring*) _____ .

3. Malia (*work*) _____ at the mall during the day. She (*eat, always*) _____

   _____ a big breakfast before she (*leave*) _____ . She

   (*have, not, usually*) _____ time for a lunch break.

---

4. Malia is in class every evening from 6:00 to 9:00. Yesterday I (*call*) _____
   her at 6:30, but she (*answer, not*) _____ because she
   (*attend*) _____ class at that time.

5. I can't call her tomorrow night because she (*attend*) _____ class then.

6. On Saturday Malia didn't have to work until noon. She took a short nap from 10:00 to 10:30.
   I arrived at 10:15. When I (*get*) _____ there, Malia (*sleep*) _____ .
   She (*sleep*) _____ for 15 minutes by the time I got there.

7. Right now Malia (*sleep*) _____ . She (*fall*) _____
   asleep an hour ago. She (*sleep*) _____ for an hour.

8. Tomorrow is her first day off in weeks. After she (*have*) _____ dinner,
   Malia (*meet*) _____ me and a friend. In other words, she
   (*have*) _____ dinner by the time she (*meet*) _____ us.

EXERCISE 2 ▸ Looking at grammar. (Chapters 1 → 3)
Choose the correct sentence in each group. Explain your choice.

A Stay in Canada

1. a. When I was in my country, I want to come to Canada for my studies.
   b. When I was in my country, I wanted to come to Canada for my studies.
   c. When I was in my country, I have wanted to come to Canada for my studies.

2. a. I wasn't nervous because I had cousins in Canada.
   b. I didn't be nervous because I had cousins in Canada.
   c. I not nervous because I had cousins in Canada.

3. a. I had been here for three months and I like it.
   b. I have been here for three months and I like it.
   c. I am here for three months and I like it.

4. a. I study here for a year.
   b. I will studying here for a year.
   c. I am going to study here for a year.

5. a. When I return to my country, I will have been away for 15 months.
   b. When I return to my country, I am going to be away for 15 months.
   c. When I return to my country, I was away for 15 months.

EXERCISE 3 ▸ Let's talk. (Chapters 1 → 3)
Answer the questions in complete sentences. Work in pairs, small groups, or as a class.

1. What are you doing right now? How long have you been doing that?
2. What were you doing at this time yesterday? What did you do after that?
3. What will you be doing tonight at midnight? What were you doing last night at midnight?
4. What places have you been to since you came to (*this city*)?
5. What are some of the things you have done in your lifetime? When did you do them?
6. What countries/cities have you visited? When did you visit (_____)? Why did you go there?
   What did you like about (_____)? What did you dislike about (_____)? Are you planning to go
   there again someday?

EXERCISE 4 ▶ Looking at grammar. (Chapters 1 → 3)

Complete the sentences with *has*, *have*, *had*, *is*, *am*, *was*, *were*, or *will*.

The Weather

1. It _____ snowing again. The roads _____ be slippery.

2. Billy _____ never seen snow before. He likes trying to catch the flakes.

3. It _____ been raining sideways all morning. When will it stop?

4. Shhh! I _____ trying to listen to the forecast. It sounds like a heat advisory _____ be in effect later this week.

5. When we _____ visiting my in-laws in India last month, there was a heat wave.

6. It was like an oven. I _____ never been in such hot weather before.

7. The lack of rain this month _____ made the smog really bad. My eyes _____ been watering since I got here.

8. When I _____ driving on the freeway, freezing rain _____ just started to fall. It was quite scary.

9. It _____ been a colder than normal winter. I'm ready for spring.

10. I _____ never experienced such violent weather until I came here. The hailstones are huge. Sometimes they _____ the size of baseballs!

EXERCISE 5 ▶ Let's talk. (Chapters 1 → 3)

Work with a partner. Create a story or conversation about the picture. Share it with the class. Pay careful attention to verb tenses.

EXERCISE 6 ▶ Editing. (Chapters 1 and 2)

Rewrite the paragraph on a separate piece of paper and correct the 7 verb errors.

An Immigrant's Wish

In 1985, my parents were emigrating to the United States from Brazil. They have never traveled outside of Brazil and were excited by the challenge of relocating to a foreign country. Eventually, they settle in California. My twin sister and I were born ten years later and are growing up there. Last year, I had gone to Brazil for the first time to meet extended family. I had always want to learn more about my family's background. My dreams finally were coming true.

EXERCISE 7 ▸ Writing. (Chapters 1 and 2)

Write about the picture using the verbs in the box and the given tenses.

cook	memorize
fix	plant
vacuum	wash

1. Tom has had a busy day so far. Right now he's taking a break. What has Tom been doing? Write at least four sentences on another piece of paper. Use the present perfect progressive.
2. Rewrite your sentences using *yesterday*. What verb tense will you use?
3. Rewrite your sentences using *just*. Use the present perfect.
4. Write one sentence about Tom using the past perfect progressive. You can add more verbs to the box.

EXERCISE 8 ▸ Reading and writing. (Chapters 1 → 3)

Read the blog entry by author Stacy Hagen, and respond in writing to the questions at the end.

Do you know these words?
- *challenges*
- *deal with*
- *distractions*
- *tasks*
- *tendency*
- *uninterrupted*
- *overwhelming*
- *daunting*

 **BlueBookBlog**

The Pomodoro Technique

One of the biggest challenges that students face is how to deal with procrastination. Even if you haven't heard of this word, you're probably familiar with it. Procrastination is putting off or delaying something you need to do. Maybe you need to study for a test, but you find lots of other things to do instead. Or perhaps you have a paper due, and you wait until the last minute to begin. With Internet and social media distractions, it's even harder to complete tasks, whether at school, home, or work.

A while ago, I came across a time-management technique I have found very helpful for dealing with my own tendency to procrastinate. It's called the Pomodoro technique. In Italian, *pomodoro* means "tomato." The Italian developer of this idea, Francisco Cirillo, had a food timer in the shape of a tomato, so he named his idea after it.

It's a very simple idea. You take a timer and set it for 25 minutes. Then you work uninterrupted until the timer goes off. Because it's only 25 minutes, it doesn't feel overwhelming. Instead of thinking about all the work you need to do to prepare for a test, for example, (which can seem daunting), you just do a piece of it for 25 minutes.

After the timer goes off, you reward yourself for five minutes. Maybe you look at social media or get a snack. When the five minutes is up, you set the timer again. After you do this four times, you can give yourself a longer reward: a break for maybe 15–30 minutes.

This technique has helped me a lot with procrastination. I have found that it makes tasks at home and work much more doable because you just need to think about 25 minutes of work at a time.

How about you? Do you have problems with procrastination? Have you found helpful techniques? Do you think the Pomodoro technique is something that you want to try?

EXERCISE 9 ▶ Looking at grammar. (Chapters 1 → 3)

Complete the sentences with any appropriate tense of the verbs in parentheses.

Vanessa's Reading List

Three weeks ago, Vanessa (*start*) _____ to read *War and Peace*, a novel by Leo
                                            1

Tolstoy. She (*read*) _____ it because her literature teacher
                                   2

recommended it. It is a very long novel, and it (*have*) _____ many characters.
                                                                   3

She (*finish, not*) _____ reading it yet. Since the beginning
                                  4

of the summer, Vanessa (*finish*) _____ three other books. In
                                            5

her lifetime, she (*read*) _____ many famous novels, but this is the first
                                   6

Tolstoy novel she (*read, ever*) _____. After this book, she
                                          7

(*start*) _____ a popular French detective series.
                   8

EXERCISE 10 ▶ Let's talk. (Chapters 1 → 3)

Answer the questions in complete sentences. Work in pairs, small groups, or as a class.

1. What have we been studying? What is one tense we have studied since the beginning of the term? When, as best as you can remember, did we study it?
2. What else will we have studied in this class by the time the term ends?
3. This class began on (*date*). Had you studied verb tenses before that?
4. We're going to finish studying Chapter 4 on (*day or date*). How long will we have been studying Chapter 4 by that time?
5. Where are you going to be living next year?
6. Think about recent news. What's happening in world affairs? What's happened recently?

EXERCISE 11 ▶ Listening. (Chapters 1 → 3)

Listen to each situation and choose the sentence that comes next (a. or b.).

1. a. Now the passengers are waiting in the baggage claim area.
   b. After the plane lands, the passengers will be waiting in the baggage claim area.
2. a. Then his boss called.
   b. He's finding it very relaxing.
3. a. When did it stop?
   b. When's it going to stop?
4. a. People said "Shhh" as we sat down.
   b. We missed the first half hour.
5. a. Her training is finished.
   b. She's going to take another lesson.
6. a. They never caught him.
   b. They'll never catch him.

EXERCISE 12 ▶ Looking at grammar. (Chapters 1 → 3)

Choose the correct sentence in each group. Explain your choice.

1. a. I am studying here since last January.
   b. I was studying here since last January.
   c. I have been studying here since last January.

2. a. By the time Hassan returned to his country, he had been away from home for more than three years.
   b. By the time Hassan returned to his country, he has been away from home for more than three years.
   c. By the time Hassan returned to his country, he is away from home for more than three years.

3. a. After Neil will graduate, he is going to return to his hometown.
   b. After Neil graduate, he going to return to his hometown.
   c. After Neil graduates, he is going to return to his hometown.

4. a. I want to get married, but I don't meet the right person yet.
   b. I want to get married, but I haven't met the right person yet.
   c. I want to get married, but I hadn't met the right person yet.

5. a. We have been seeing that movie twice, and now we want to see it again.
   b. We have seen that movie twice, and now we are wanting to see it again.
   c. We have seen that movie twice, and now we want to see it again.

6. a. I don't like my job. My brother wants me to quit. I believe he is right.
   b. I am not like my job. My brother wants me to quit. I am believing he is right.
   c. I don't like my job. My brother want me to quit. I believed he is right.

7. a. We cleaned up the kitchen after our dinner guests were leaving.
   b. We cleaned up the kitchen after our dinner guests are going to leave.
   c. We cleaned up the kitchen after our dinner guests left.

8. a. I know my neighbors Mr. and Mrs. Sanchez ever since I was a child.
   b. I have known my neighbors Mr. and Mrs. Sanchez ever since I was a child.
   c. I knew my neighbors Mr. and Mrs. Sanchez ever since I have been a child.

9. a. Many scientists believe there will be a major earthquake in California in the near future.
   b. Many scientists believe there going to be a major earthquake in California in the near future.
   c. Many scientists believe there will to be a major earthquake in California in the near future.

10. a. By the end of the 21st century, man will had discovered the cure for the common cold.
    b. By the end of the 21st century, man will have discovered the cure for the common cold.
    c. By the end of the 21st century, man will discovered the cure for the common cold.

 EXERCISE 13 ▸ Listening. (Chapters 1 and 2)
Part I. Listen to the story with your book closed. Then open your book and read the statements. Write "T" for true and "F" for false.

A Silly Mistake

1. _____ The man broke the lock on the door.

2. _____ The man saw a stranger in his apartment.

3. _____ The man's wife opened the door.

4. _____ The man felt he had done something stupid.

Part II. Listen again. Complete the sentences with the verbs you hear.

When I _____ home to my apartment last night, I _____ out my key to open the
          1   2

door as usual. As always, I _____ it in the lock, but the door _____.
                              3   4

I _____ my key again and again with no luck. So I _____ on the door for
    5   6

my wife to let me in. Finally the door _____, but I _____ my
                                         7   8

wife on the other side. I _____ a stranger. I _____ to get
                           9   10

into the wrong apartment! I quickly _____ and _____ to my own.
                                      11   12

I _____ very stupid about what I _____.
    13   14

EXERCISE 14 ▶ Looking at grammar. (Chapters 1 → 3)

Part I. Choose the correct verb in each pair.

From: Yoko
To: Anna K.
Subject: Hi
3:21 AM

Hi Anna,

I get / got (1) your long email about two weeks ago and was trying / have been trying (2) to find
time to write you back ever since. I am / have been (3) very busy lately. In the past two weeks,
I was having / have had (4) four tests, and I have another one next week. In addition, a friend
stayed / has been staying (5) with me since last Thursday. She wanted to see the city, so we
were spending / have been spending (6) a lot of time visiting some of the interesting places here.
We have been / were going (7) to the zoo, the art museum, and the waterfront.

Yesterday we went / have gone (8) to a park and watch / watched (9) a hot-air balloon race.
Between seeing the city and studying for my exams, I am barely having / have barely had (10)
enough time to breathe.

Right now it is / has been (11) 3:00 A.M., and I am sitting / was sitting (12) at my desk.
I am sitting / have been sitting (13) here for five hours doing my studying. My friend's plane
leaves / leave (14) in a few hours, so I decided / am deciding (15) not to go to bed. That's why
I write / am writing (16) to you at such an early hour in the day. I am getting / get (17) a little
sleepy, but I would rather stay up. I take / am going to take (18) a nap after I get / will get (19)
back from taking her to the airport.

How do you get / are you getting (20) along? How Ø / are (21) your classes going? Please
write soon.

Best,
Yoko

Part II. Write an email to a friend or family member. Discuss your activities, thoughts, feelings, and adventures in the present, past, and future. Use Yoko's email as an example.

Use as many different tenses as seems natural. For example, in the course of your message, tell your reader what you *are doing, do every day, have done since a certain time, have been doing lately, did at some particular time, had done before you did something else, are going to do, etc.*

Part III. <u>Underline</u> the verbs. Exchange papers with another student. Edit your partner's writing by checking all the verbs for correct form and tense. Discuss any suggestions you have.

EXERCISE 15 ▸ Speaking and writing. (Chapters 1 → 3)

Part I. Work with a partner.

PARTNER A: Pretend to be a famous living person. Tell your partner your name. Answer the reporter's questions. You can invent answers.

PARTNER B: You're a nosy reporter. Ask the famous person all kinds of questions about his/her past, present, and future.

Part II. Write an article with your partner about this person for a class newspaper. The newspaper will have articles about all the "famous" people in your class.

EXERCISE 16 ▸ Let's talk. (Chapters 1 → 3)

In a short talk (2 or 3 minutes), summarize a recent news event. Present your talk to a small group or to the class. If necessary, you may speak from brief notes (an outline of only the most important points). Each audience member will write down one or two questions to ask you at the end (as time permits).

▪▪▪▪ Go to MyEnglishLab for Self-Study: Gerunds and Infinitives 4

5

Subject-Verb Agreement

EXERCISE 1 ▸ Warm-up. (Chart 5-1)
Look at the words in blue. Are they singular or plural? Are they nouns or verbs?

	SINGULAR	PLURAL	NOUN	VERB
1. A wedding costs a lot of money.				
2. Weddings cost a lot of money.				
3. Wedding costs are increasing.				
4. The cost of weddings is increasing.				

5-1 Final -s/-es: Use and Spelling

Use

(a) *Noun + -s:* *Friends* are important. *Noun + -es:* I like my *classes*.	A final **-s** or **-es** is added to a noun to make the noun plural. *Friend* and *class* = singular nouns *Friends* and *classes* = plural nouns
(b) *Verb + -s:* Mary *works* at the bank. *Verb + -es:* John *watches* birds.	A final **-s** or **-es** is added to a simple present verb when the subject is a singular noun (e.g., *Mary, my father, the machine*) or third person singular pronoun (*she, he, it*). **Mary works** = singular **She works** = singular **The students work** = plural **They work** = plural

Spelling

(c) sing → *sings* song → *songs*	For most words (whether a verb or a noun), simply add a final **-s** to spell the word correctly.
(d) wash → *washes* watch → *watches* class → *classes* buzz → *buzzes* box → *boxes*	Final **-es** is added to words that end in **-sh, -ch, -s, -z,** and **-x.** NOTE: The pronunciation is /əz/ ("uz").
(e) toy → *toys* buy → *buys* (f) baby → *babies* cry → *cries*	For words that end in **-y:** In (e): If **-y** is preceded by a vowel, only **-s** is added. In (f): If **-y** is preceded by a consonant, the **-y** is changed to **-i** and **-es** is added.

EXERCISE 2 ▸ Spelling (Chart 5-1)
Add **-s** or **-es**.

1. floor*s*
2. tax*es*
3. talk*s*

4. bush___
5. hat___
6. rise___

7. season___
8. develop___
9. touch___

10. cough___
11. method___
12. language___

EXERCISE 3 ▸ Grammar and pronunciation. (Chart 5-1)
Work with a partner. Take turns making sentences. Focus on the **-es** pronunciation.

Example: an alarm clock \ buzz
    → *An alarm clock buzzes.*

1. a teacher \ teach
2. a freezer \ freeze
3. a ball \ bounce
4. a door \ close
5. a boxer \ box

6. a mosquito bite \ itch
7. a boss \ manage
8. a snake \ hiss
9. a soldier \ march
10. a coach \ coach

EXERCISE 4 ▸ Let's talk. (Chart 5-1)

Work in small groups. Take turns reading each sentence a few times. Pay attention to the *-s* endings. Can you figure out the meaning? Do you agree or disagree with the proverb?

Common Proverbs

1. Too many cooks spoil the broth.
2. Tomorrow never comes.
3. Practice makes perfect.
4. Actions speak louder than words.
5. People come in all shapes and sizes.
6. The early bird catches the worm.
7. Good things come in small packages.
8. No news* is good news.

EXERCISE 5 ▸ Warm-up. (Chart 5-2)

Look at the verbs in blue. What words determine if the verbs are singular or plural?

1. a. The fruit in the bowls is fresh.
   b. The apples in the bowl are fresh.

2. a. Vegetables are good for you.
   b. Eating vegetables is good for you.

5-2 Basic Subject-Verb Agreement

Singular Verb	Plural Verb	
(a) My *friend lives* in Boston.	(b) My *friends live* in Boston.	*verb* + *-s/-es* = third person singular in the simple present tense *noun* + *-s/-es* = plural
	(c) My *brother and sister live* in Boston. (d) My *brother, sister, and cousin live* in Boston.	Two or more subjects connected by *and* require a plural verb.
(e) *Every man, woman, and child needs* love. (f) *Everyone is* here. (g) *Everybody is* here. (h) *Each book and magazine is* listed in the bibliography.		EXCEPTION: Expressions with *every* and *each* are always followed immediately by singular nouns. (See Chart 6-10, p. 115.) Even when there are two (or more) nouns connected by *and*, the verb is singular, as in (h).
(i) That *book* on political parties *is* interesting. (k) The *book* that I got from my parents *was* very interesting.	(j) The *ideas* in that book *are* interesting. (l) The *books* I bought at the bookstore *were* expensive.	Sometimes a phrase or clause separates a subject from its verb. These interrupting structures do not affect basic agreement. For example, in (i) the interrupting prepositional phrase **on political parties** does not change the fact that the verb *is* must agree with the subject *book*. In (k) and (l): The subject and verb are separated by an adjective clause. (See Chapter 13.)
(m) *Watching* old movies *is* fun.		A gerund (e.g., *watching*) used as the subject of the sentence requires a singular verb. (See Chart 14-1, p. 303.)

News takes a singular verb. (For more information, see Chart 5-6.)

EXERCISE 6 ▸ Speaking or writing. (Chart 5-2)

Work with a partner or in small groups to complete the sentences, orally or in writing. Use the present tense. Share some of the sentences with the class.

1. Every person in this room …
2. Each student and teacher at this school …
3. Everyone over the age of 18 …
4. Every mother and father …
5. Every parent of teenagers …
6. Everybody born in this country …
7. Every rainbow in the sky …
8. Each galaxy in the universe …

EXERCISE 7 ▸ Looking at grammar. (Chart 5-2)

Choose the correct completions.

1. a. My older brother and sister   is / are   fraternal twins.
   b. My brother   was / were   born on December 31st at 11:55 P.M., and my sister   was / were   born on January 1st at 12:05 A.M.
   c. Everyone in my family   was / were   surprised when this happened.
   d. Being born on different days and in different years   is / are   an interesting topic of conversation.

2. a. The subjects you will be studying in this course   is / are   in the syllabus.
   b. The extent of the knowledge we need to have by the end of the semester really   surprises / surprise   me.
   c. Almost every instructor and student at the university   approves / approve   of the new college president.
   d. Do / Does   Professor Karl and her graduate researchers work closely together?
   e. Getting to know students from all over the world   is / are   one of the best parts of studying at an international university.

3. a. Every man, woman, and child   is / are   protected under the law.
   b. Each man and woman in this country   needs / need   to pay taxes
   c. Every person who buys gas in this state   needs / need   to pay a gas tax.

4. a. Where   does / do   your grandparents live?
   b. Why   was / were   your mom and dad at the retirement home?
   c. Is / Are   taking care of the elderly the responsibility of the family or the government?

5. a. Oranges, tomatoes, fresh strawberries, cabbage, and lettuce   is / are   rich in vitamin C.
   b. Tomatoes   is / are   easy to grow. Growing tomatoes   is / are   especially easy in hot climates.
   c. I like to do the grocery shopping. The produce my roommate buys   isn't / aren't   fresh.
   d. Lettuce   is / are   good for you.
   e. Is / Are   the bag of vegetables still in the car?

EXERCISE 8 ▶ Grammar and listening. (Chart 5-2)

Complete the sentences with the simple present form of the verbs in parentheses. Then listen and check your answers.

Do you know these words?
- thrill
- kayak
- somersault
- have to do with
- hormone
- exhilarating

Thrill Seekers

Going over a waterfall in a kayak (*be*) _____ not
__1__

everyone's idea of a good time. But for some people, the experience

of somersaulting through a curtain of water (*be*) _____
__2__

thrilling, and they (*want*) _____ to keep doing it. It
__3__

(*have*) _____ in part to do with adrenaline. The
__4__

body (*release*) _____ a large amount of this
__5__

hormone in response to danger. For some people, this release

(*produce*) _____ very pleasant feelings, and they
__6__

(*seek out*) _____ activities that will give them
__7__

this feeling. The experience of parachuting from a mountain, for example, (*be*) _____
__8__

exhilarating, not terrifying, for them. Researchers are studying reasons why some people

(*enjoy*) _____ this adrenaline rush and others (*fear*) _____ it.
__9__ __10__

EXERCISE 9 ▶ Warm-up. (Chart 5-3)

Underline the subject in each sentence. Which subjects refer to more than one person? What do you notice about the subject-verb agreement?

A group of people is cheering loudly for the performers. People are clapping excitedly. The audience is asking for an encore.

5-3 Collective Nouns

(a) The *audience is clapping* loudly.	Collective nouns, as in (a)–(d), refer to more than one person.
(b) The *team practices* at noon.	In American English, singular verbs are preferred with collective nouns.
(c) The *faculty has chosen* a new president.	NOTE: British English prefers the plural verb: *The faculty **have** chosen a new president.* OR *The staff **have** been working overtime.*
(d) The *staff has been working* overtime.	
(e) The *faculty are preparing* for classes.	A plural verb can be used to emphasize the individual members. Note the meaning:
(f) The *staff have requested* raises.	(e) = individual faculty members
(g) The *staff members have requested* raises.	(f) = individual staff members
(h) *Members of the staff have requested* raises.	Many speakers rephrase the idea with the word *members,* as in (g) and (h), if they want to emphasize the individual members of the group.

Common collective nouns

audience	committee	faculty	group	staff
choir	crew	family	jury	team
class	crowd	government	public	

EXERCISE 10 ▸ Looking at grammar. (Chart 5-3)
Check (✓) all the correct sentences.

1. a. _____ Members of the audience are leaving early.

   b. _____ The audience sometimes boos the performers.

2. a. _____ The choir practices in the school basement.

   b. _____ The choir members is happy with their progress.

3. a. _____ The team has talked with the coach about the game.

   b. _____ The team is working hard to improve.

   c. _____ Members of the team has spoken with the coach privately about their performance.

EXERCISE 11 ▸ Looking at grammar. (Chart 5-3)
Add the word *members* where possible or write Ø.

Paramedics

1. The ambulance crew _____ has two paramedics.

2. Paramedic staff _____ have the highest level of emergency life-saving training.

3. The crew _____ is the first on the scene to an accident or disaster.

4. The staff _____ work 24-hour shifts.

5. Family _____ are accustomed to their absences.

6. The public _____ pays for ambulance services either privately or through taxes.

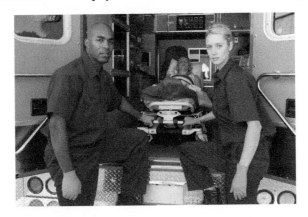

EXERCISE 12 ▸ Warm-up. (Chart 5-4)
Look at the verbs in blue. What words determine if the verbs are singular or plural?

1. Some of this book is interesting.
2. Some of those books are interesting.
3. Most of those books are interesting.
4. Most of the book is interesting.
5. One of those books is Linda's.
6. Each of those books is yours.
7. Fifty percent of the book is photos.
8. Fifty percent of the books are on sale.

5-4 Subject-Verb Agreement: Using Expressions of Quantity

Singular Verb	Plural Verb	
(a) *Some of the **book** is good.*	(b) *Some of the **books** are good.*	With most expressions of quantity, the verb is determined by the noun (or pronoun) that follows *of*.
(c) *A lot of the **equipment** is new.*	(d) *A lot of the **printers** are new.*	For example, in (a) and (b):
(e) *Two-thirds of the **money** belongs to me.*	(f) *Two-thirds of the **coins** belong to me.*	***some of*** + singular noun = singular verb
(g) *Twenty percent of my **income** goes for rent.*	(h) *Twenty percent of my **earnings** go for rent.*	***some of*** + plural noun = plural verb
(i) *Most of our **homework** looks easy.*	(j) *Most of our **assignments** look easy.*	
(k) *All of the **advice** was useful.*	(l) *All of the **suggestions** were useful.*	
(m) ***One** of my friends is here.*		EXCEPTIONS: ***One of**, **each of**,* and ***every one of*** take singular verbs.
(n) ***Each** of my friends is here.*		***one of*** ⎫
(o) ***Every one** of my friends is here.*		***each of*** ⎬ + plural noun = singular verb ***every one of*** ⎭
(p) ***None** of the boys is here.*	(q) ***None** of the boys are here.*	***None of*** is used with a singular verb in formal English, but it is often used with a plural verb in informal spoken and written English.
(r) ***The number** of students in the class is fifteen.*	(s) *A **number** of students are late or absent today.*	COMPARE: In (r): ***The number*** is the subject. In (s): ***A number of*** is an expression of quantity meaning "a lot of." It is followed by a plural noun and a plural verb.

EXERCISE 13 ▸ Looking at grammar. (Chart 5-4)

Part I. <u>Underline</u> the word in each sentence that determines subject-verb agreement.

At a Car Dealership

1. Every one of the cars on the lot is on sale.
2. A number of cars are pre-owned.
3. The number of pre-owned cars is increasing each week.
4. Financing for pre-owned cars is available.
5. Do all of the new cars come with a rear view camera?
6. None of the cars has more than a 5% markup.
7. Have some of the cars been in accidents?
8. One of the best reasons for shopping here is the salesperson's willingness to show the car's actual cost — (the dealer's cost).

Part II. Choose the correct completions.

1. a. Most of the salespeople   was / were   friendly.

   b. Most of the discussion   was / were   about vehicle reliability.

   c. One of the salespeople   was / were   pushy.

2. a. Each car   has / have   a vehicle history report.

   b. Each of the models we looked at   has / have   a good safety record.

3. a. A lot of the safety equipment   is / are   standard in the new models.

   b. A lot of the safety features   isn't / aren't   available in the older cars.

EXERCISE 14 ▸ Reading and writing. (Chart 5-4)
Part I. Read the story and choose the correct verbs.

Do you know these words?
- *exceedingly* - *dawn on*
- *greedy* - *overcome*
- *acquire* - *spell*
- *overjoyed* - *remorse*
- *elaborate* - *humble*
- *dismay*

King Midas

King Midas, an exceedingly greedy king, lives / lives (1) a life of great luxury, but his wealth and fortune is / are (2) not enough to satisfy him. Even the company of his lovely daughter is / are (3) less important to him than money. Acquiring more riches is / are (4) what occupies his thoughts all day long.

One day the king call / calls (5) upon a magician and order / orders (6) him to find more treasures. The magician, however, has something better to offer and give / gives (7) him the power to turn everything he touches / touch (8) into gold. The king, overjoyed with this gift, go / goes (9) out into the forest. Each object he puts / put (10) his finger on turns / turn (11) to gold: a tree, a flower, even a stone in the river. King Midas cannot believe his good fortune.

In the evening the king, alone with his new pieces of gold, sits / sit (12) down to an elaborate feast. To his dismay, the first piece of food he touches / touch (13) turns to gold. He tries a slice of bread, and the same thing happens / happen (14). Slowly it dawns / dawn (15) on him that none of the food is / are (16) edible.

The next morning, his beloved daughter runs / run (17) up to him for a kiss, but the king's embrace turns / turn (18) her into gold. A great sorrow overcomes / overcome (19) him, and he pleads / plead (20) with the magician for help. King Midas tells him that his love for his daughter is / are (21) greater than anything else in the world. He promises to never be greedy again.

The magician waves his wand and the spell disappears / disappear (22). Full of remorse, the king shares his riches and becomes / become (23) a humble and generous ruler. Everyone in the kingdom loves / love (24) him, and he lives a long and contented life among his people.

Part II. Write a story, fairy tale, or folktale from your country. Describe the events in the present tense (present perfect is also OK). Pay special attention to subject-verb agreement with quantity words. Exchange papers with a classmate, and edit for subject-verb agreement.

Fluency Practice. Work with a partner. Take five minutes to tell your partner your story. Then tell your story to another student in four minutes. Finally, take three minutes to tell your story to a third student. The last time you speak should feel more comfortable and easier than the first time.

EXERCISE 15 ▸ Warm-up. (Chart 5-5)

Look around or think about your classroom and complete the statements.

There are _____ in my classroom.

There is _____ in my classroom.

5-5	Subject-Verb Agreement: Using *There + Be*	
(a)	***There is** a fly* in the room.	***There + be*** introduces the idea that something exists in a particular place.
(b)	***There are** three windows* in this room.	***There + be** + subject + expression of place** The subject follows **be** when **there** is used. In (a): The subject is *a fly*. (singular) In (b): The subject is *three windows*. (plural)
(c)	*INFORMAL:* There*'s two sides* to every story.	In informal spoken English, some native speakers use a singular verb even when the subject is plural, as in (c). The use of this form is fairly frequent but is not generally considered to be grammatically correct.

*Sometimes the expression of place is omitted when the meaning is clear. For example, *There are seven continents*. The implied expression of place is clearly *in the world*.

EXERCISE 16 ▸ Grammar and speaking. (Chart 5-5)

Complete the sentences with ***is/isn't/are/aren't***. Take turns sharing your opinions with a classmate.

What do you think?

1. There _____ a good reason for everything that happens to us.

2. There _____ people or beings on other planets.

3. There _____ enough resources (food, water, etc.) in the world for everyone right now.

4. There _____ a lot of problems in the world due to climate change.

5. There _____ too much gun violence in the world.

6. There _____ going to be cures for diseases like cancer and AIDs in the next decade.

7. With enough money, there _____ a solution for every problem in the world.

EXERCISE 17 ▸ Listening. (Chart 5-5)

Choose the words you hear. For many of the sentences, you will hear reductions of the given words.
NOTE: ***Is + there*** can sound like "ih-zehr." For example, *Is there* ("ih-zehr") *a holiday next week?*

At Work

Example: You will hear: There's a receipt for supplies on your desk.
           You will choose: (There is)   There are

1. There is	There are		5. there is	there are
2. There is	There are		6. Is there	Are there
3. Is there	Are there		7. There is	There are
4. Is there	Are there		8. there is	there are

EXERCISE 18 ▶ Grammar and listening. (Charts 5-1 → 5-5)

Underline the words that determine agreement with the verbs. Then choose the correct verb. Listen to the passage and check your answers.

What's the difference?

1. *Rain* vs. *Showers*

Many people   treats / treat   these words as having the same meaning. For people who follow
              1

the weather, however, there   is / are   a difference. Rain is steady and   covers / cover   a
           2   3

larger area. Showers   tends / tend   to be more scattered and   does not last / do not last
                4   5

as long. There   is / are   an easy way to remember the difference: think about taking a
         6

bath vs. taking a shower. Most of us   gets / get   wetter when we take a bath than when we
                    7

stands / stand   in the shower.
  8

    Now, which expression do you think   is /are   correct: *It's raining out* or *It's showering out*? If you
                                9

chose the first one, you are right. We use only *rain,* not *shower,* as a verb to talk about the weather.

2. *Thief* vs. *Robber* vs. *Burglar*

Another set of words with distinct differences   is / are   *thief, robber,* and *burglar.* A thief
                                      1

takes / take   physical property like TVs, computers, or money, but there is no violence or force.
  2

Robbers also   takes / take   property, but the robber   uses / use   force or the threat of force, as
            3   4

with a gun. A burglar illegally   enters / enter   a structure with the intent to commit a crime.
                        5

    If some of this   seems / seem   confusing, you are in good company. Many native speakers
                6

of English   has / have   never learned these subtleties and   doesn't make / don't make
         7   8

distinctions among these words.

EXERCISE 19 ▶ Warm-up. (Chart 5-6)

Look at the subjects and verbs (in blue) in each pair of sentences. Some of them are "exceptions to the rule." For example, nouns that end in *-s* usually take a plural verb, but sometimes not. Look for these irregularities.

1. a. Nations are groups of people who share a common identity.
   b. The United Nations is an international organization.

2. a. Kilometers are measures of distance.
   b. Seven kilometers is too far for me to run.

3. a. English is a language.
   b. The English are concerned about global warming.

4. a. Mix and fix are verbs.
   b. Six and six is twelve.

5. a. Whales are mammals.
   b. People are mammals.

5-6 Subject-Verb Agreement: Some Irregularities

Singular Verb

(a) *The United States is* big. (b) *The Philippines consists* of more than 7,000 islands. (c) *The United Nations has* its headquarters in New York City. (d) *Harrods is* a department store.	Sometimes a proper noun that ends in **-s** is singular. In the examples, if the noun is changed to a pronoun, the singular pronoun *it* is used (not the plural pronoun **they**) because the noun is singular. In (a): **The United States = It** (not **They**)
(e) *The news is* interesting.	**News** is a noncount noun and takes a singular verb.
(f) *Mathematics is* easy for her. *Physics is* easy for her too.	Fields of study that end in **-ics** require singular verbs.
(g) *Diabetes is* an illness.	Certain illnesses that end in **-s** are singular: *diabetes, measles, mumps, rabies, rickets, shingles.*
(h) *Eight hours* of sleep *is* enough. (i) *Ten dollars is* too much to pay. (j) *Five thousand miles is* too far to travel.	Expressions of time, money, and distance usually require a singular verb.
(k) *Two and two is* four. *Two and two **equals** four.* *Two plus two is/**equals** four.* (l) *Five times five is* twenty-five.	Arithmetic expressions require singular verbs.

Plural Verb

(m) *Those people are* from Canada. (n) *The police have* been called. (o) *Cattle are* domestic animals. (p) *Fish live* under water.	*People,* * *police, cattle,* and *fish* do not end in **-s**, but they are plural nouns in the example sentences and require plural verbs.

Singular Verb / Plural Verb

Singular Verb	Plural Verb	
(q) *English is* spoken in many countries. (s) *Chinese is* his native language.	(r) *The English drink* tea. (t) *The Chinese have* an interesting history.	In (q): **English** = language In (r): **The English** = people from England Some nouns of nationality that end in **-sh**, **-ese**, and **-ch** can mean either language or people, e.g., *English, Spanish, Chinese, Japanese, Vietnamese, Portuguese, French.*
	(u) *The poor have* many problems. (v) *The rich get* richer.	A few adjectives can be preceded by **the** and used as a plural noun (without final **-s**) to refer to people who have that quality. Other examples: *the young, the elderly, the living, the dead, the blind, the deaf, the disabled.*

*The word *people* has a final **-s** (*peoples*) only when it is used to refer to ethnic or national groups: *All the **peoples** of the world desire peace.*

EXERCISE 20 ▸ Looking at grammar. (Chart 5-6)
Choose the correct completions.

1. The United States (has)/ have   a population of around 325 million.
2. The *New York Times*   is / are   an established and respected newspaper.
3. Statistics   is / are   a branch of mathematics.
4. The statistics in that report on oil production   is / are   incorrect.*
5. Fifty minutes   is / are   the maximum length of time for the test.
6. Rabies   is / are   an infectious and often fatal disease.
7. The blind   wants / want   us to treat them the same way we treat
   everyone else.
8. French   is / are   somewhat similar to Spanish,   isn't it / aren't they?
9. The French   is / are   proud, independent people.
10. Does / Do   the police have training in mental health issues?
11. Thirty dollars   is / are   an unreasonable price for that T-shirt.
12. Four hours of skiing   provides / provide   plenty of exercise.

EXERCISE 21 ▸ Game. (Chart 5-6)
Work in teams. Choose the correct words (or numbers). Then complete the sentences with *is*
or *are*.

1. The Scots / The Irish /(The English)   ___are___   famous for educational institutions like Oxford
   and Cambridge.
2. Statistics / Linguistics / Physics   _____   the study of the structure and nature of language.
3. Diabetes / Measles / Mumps   _____   a blood-sugar illness.
4. English / French / Afrikaans   _____   the official language of Namibia.
5. People from Canada _____ called   Canadas / Canadians / Canadese.
6. Approximately   60% / 70% / 80%   of the earth _____ covered by water, but
   only   1% / 10% / 20%   of the earth's water _____ drinkable.
7. 312 × .5 + 100 _____   227 / 275 / 256.
8. The United Arab Emirates / The Netherlands / The Philippines   _____   in the Northern
   Hemisphere (i.e., north of the equator).
9. Fish / Whales / Cattle   _____ not mammals.
10. Five hundred thousand + five hundred thousand _____
    ten hundred / one million / one billion.
11. Macy's / Harrods / Hudson's Bay   _____ a department store that began in London.

Statistics is singular when it refers to a field of study (e.g., ***Statistics is*** *an interesting field of study.*). When it refers to
particular numbers, it is used as a count noun: *singular = one statistic* (no final *-s*); *plural = two statistics.* For example, ***This
statistic is*** *correct.* ***Those statistics are*** *incorrect.*

EXERCISE 22 ▸ Let's talk. (Chart 5-6)

Work in small groups. Take turns giving answers.

1. How many hours of sleep is enough for you? What happens if you don't get that amount of sleep?
2. Write one math equation for each answer: 250, 75, 700, and 1,000. Use addition, subtraction, multiplication, or division. Read the equations aloud for others to answer.
3. What do you think is a reasonable amount of money to pay for school supplies and textbooks for one term?
4. What do you think is a manageable distance for a person to commute to and from a job? Give your answer in miles or kilometers.
5. In your opinion, what advantages do the old have over the young? The young over the old?
6. Consider various school subjects: science (biology, chemistry, etc.), mathematics (algebra, geometry, etc.), languages, etc. Which class is easy for you to understand? Which is difficult for you? Which is the most enjoyable?
7. Think of a country that has a history you're familiar with. Share some information about the people (the Chinese, the French, the Egyptians, etc.) of this country. Which country has a history you'd like to know more about?

EXERCISE 23 ▸ Game. (Chapter 5 Review)

Work in teams. Combine the phrases in the left column with phrases on the right. Add punctuation.

Physical Exercise

1. All of the people in the exercise class
2. One of the best ways to prevent injury
3. Recent fitness news
4. Exercise in the water
5. Unfortunately, a lot of people
6. Does
7. Different types of exercise
8. Is
9. Every person at the gym
10. Do
11. Exercising too much

a. 30 minutes of exercise a day enough
b. need to wear athletic shoes.
c. affect the muscles differently
d. the elderly use the gym
e. suggests that exercising with a buddy improves motivation
f. is dangerous
g. is to warm up first
h. needs to wear appropriate clothing
i. is easy on knee and hip joints
j. don't exercise
k. the exercise routine feel comfortable

EXERCISE 24 ▸ Let's talk. (Chapter 5 Review)

Work in small groups. Choose the correct verb in each sentence. Are the sentences true in your opinion? Circle *yes* or *no*. Compare and discuss some of your answers with those of your classmates.

1. The United Nations   has / have   an important role in today's world.   yes   no
2. Mathematics   is / are   an interesting subject.   yes   no
3. Both boys and girls   needs / need   to learn how to do housecleaning.   yes   no

4. Every girl and boy in my country   needs / need   to have immunizations   yes   no
for certain diseases before entering public school.

5. Two hours of homework per day   is / are   too much for elementary   yes   no
school children.

6. Having good computer skills   is / are   necessary if you want to get a   yes   no
high-paying job.

7. One of the biggest problems in the world today   is / are   the lack of   yes   no
suitable housing for significant numbers of people.

8. We may come from different cultures and have different customs, but   yes   no
I believe that people across the world   is / are   more alike than different.

EXERCISE 25 ▸ Check your knowledge. (Chapter 5 Review)

Correct the errors in subject-verb agreement. Some sentences contain no errors.

1. The books in my office ~~is~~ *are* very valuable to me.

2. All of the windows in our house was broken in the earthquake.

3. A lot of the people in my class works during the day and attends class in the evening.

4. The news about the effects of air pollution on the development of children's lungs is disturbing.

5. Studying a foreign language often lead students to learn about other cultures.

6. One of the most common names for dogs in the United States are "Rover."

7. A number of planes were late due to the snowstorm in Chicago.

8. Forty percent of the people in the state of New York lives in New York City.

9. A group of students are waiting for the advising office to open.

10. About 90% of an iceberg is below water.

11. Unless there are a dramatic and comprehensive change in government policies soon, the
economic conditions in that country will continue to worsen.

12. The number of buses in the downtown area has decreased this year due to budget cuts.

13. While I was in Paris, some of my favorite meals was in small out-of-the-way cafés.

14. Most of the mountain peaks in the Himalayan Range has snow year-round.

EXERCISE 26 ▸ Reading and writing. (Chapter 5)

Part I. Read the passage. Then look at the verbs in **bold** and <u>underline</u> the word(s) that determine agreement.

Tipping

Tipping **is** a common practice throughout the world although the custom can differ considerably among countries. Visitors new to a country **are** often unsure about how much to tip in restaurants, hotels, and airports. Technology **has made** the practice easier. There **are** apps that tell how much to tip in each country for various services.

In the United States and Canada, workers in service industries such as restaurants, airports, and taxi driving commonly **receive** tips. In general, customers tip more when they are happy with the service and less when they are not. The amounts generally **range** from 10–20% of the bill, and the tip is based on the pre-tax amount, not the total bill.

In restaurants, 15% **is** average. Many restaurants now **include** suggested amounts at the bottom of the receipt. Some restaurants have a mandatory service charge if there is a large group (typically six or more people). It's important to ask about this charge because it is usually 15–20%. Some carry-out or take-out restaurants and coffee shops **have** tip jars that some customers use.

Skycaps at airports and bellhops at hotels also **expect** tips. Generally the number of bags the traveler has **determines** the tip. The amount per bag **varies**, so it's good to check online before you travel. Tips for a taxi driver **are** usually based on a percentage of the fare, and 10–20% is common.

There **are** other service employees that rely on tip income: housekeeping, valet and concierge staff at hotels; food delivery drivers; hairdressers; and tour guides, to name a few. Many employers base their employees' pay on the belief that most customers will leave tips, and they set the pay lower for that reason. Employees **see** tipping as part of their wages, not as an extra.

Before you visit a country, it's a good idea to research tipping practices so you can make informed decisions about tipping.

Part II. Work with a partner or in a small group. Answer these questions.

1. What are your general thoughts on the practice of tipping?
2. Do people in your country leave tips? If so, for what kinds of services? What is the customary amount for these various services?
3. How do you handle tipping?
4. Is it right for employers to pay workers less because they expect their employees to earn tips?

Part III. Using the information from your discussion in Part II, write about tipping practices in your country or write about your opinion of tipping. Pay special attention to subject-verb agreement.

These expressions will help you express your opinion:

- In my opinion/view, X is ...
- X is a good/bad idea because ...
- I strongly believe that ...
- I believe in X because ...
- I am/am not in favor of X because ...
- In my experience, X is ...

Part IV. Edit your writing. Check for the following:

1. ☐ singular verbs with singular nouns
2. ☐ plural verbs with plural nouns
3. ☐ singular verbs with percentages
4. ☐ singular verbs with *each* and *every*
5. ☐ singular verbs when a gerund is the subject (e.g., *tipping*)
6. ☐ an interrupting structure with a prepositional phrase, *that*-clause, etc., that does not affect subject-verb agreement
7. ☐ correct spelling (use a dictionary or spell-check)

■ ■ ■ ■ ■ Go to MyEnglishLab for Self-Study: Gerunds and Infinitives 5

CHAPTER 6 — Nouns

PRETEST: What do I already know?

Write "C" for the sentences with the correct noun, possessive, and quantifier forms and "I" for incorrect. Check your answers below. After you complete each chart listed, make any necessary corrections.

1. _____ The knifes in the drawer aren't sharp. (6-1)

2. _____ How many potatoes do you need for the soup? (6-1)

3. _____ Their three-years-old son is already reading. (6-2)

4. _____ I live in a bricks house from the 1920s. (6-2)

5. _____ Astrid's mother is moving here from Norway. (6-3)

6. _____ Both my boys beds need new mattresses. (6-3)

7. _____ I'm staying at the house of my brother for the summer. (6-4)

8. _____ Do you have the interview's questions? (6-4)

9. _____ Jeffrey will need a luck on his test. (6-5 → 6-7)

10. _____ A great deal of work went into the project. (6-8)

11. _____ I have little time to relax at home. (6-9)

12. _____ Every employees at this company receives comprehensive health insurance. (6-10)

13. _____ Many of online reviews complained about the quality of the work. (6-11)

Incorrect sentences: 1, 3, 4, 6, 7, 8, 9, 12, 13

EXERCISE 1 ▶ Warm-up. (Chart 6-1)

Read the sentences and give your opinions. Do you know the singular forms for the words in blue? What do you notice about their plural endings?

1. Books belong on bookshelves, not electronic devices.

2. I like to share videos on social media.

3. I prefer to learn from digital rather than print curricula or materials.

6-1 Regular and Irregular Plural Nouns

(a) song—*songs*	The plural of most nouns is formed by adding final **-s.***
(b) box—*boxes*	Final **-es** is added to nouns that end in **-sh, -ch, -s, -z,** and **-x.***
(c) baby—*babies*	The plural of words that end in a consonant + **-y** is spelled **-ies.***
(d) man—*men* ox—*oxen* tooth—*teeth* woman—*women* foot—*feet* mouse—*mice* child—*children* goose—*geese* louse—*lice*	The nouns in (d) have irregular plural forms that do not end in **-s.**
(e) echo—*echoes* potato—*potatoes* hero—*heroes* tomato—*tomatoes*	Some nouns that end in **-o** add **-es** to form the plural.
(f) auto—*autos* photo—*photos* studio—*studios* ghetto—*ghettos* piano—*pianos* tattoo—*tattoos* kangaroo—*kangaroos* radio—*radios* video—*videos* kilo—*kilos* solo—*solos* zoo—*zoos* memo—*memos* soprano—*sopranos*	Some nouns that end in **-o** add only **-s** to form the plural. NOTE: When in doubt, use your dictionary or spell-check.
(g) memento—*mementoes/mementos* volcano—*volcanoes/volcanos* mosquito—*mosquitoes/mosquitos* zero—*zeroes/zeros* tornado—*tornadoes/tornados*	Some nouns that end in **-o** add either **-es** or **-s** to form the plural (with **-es** being the more usual plural form).
(h) calf—*calves* life—*lives* thief—*thieves* half—*halves* loaf—*loaves* wolf—*wolves* knife—*knives* self—*selves* scarf—*scarves/scarfs* leaf—*leaves* shelf—*shelves*	Some nouns that end in **-f** or **-fe** are changed to **-ves** to form the plural.
(i) belief—*beliefs* cliff—*cliffs* chief—*chiefs* roof—*roofs*	Some nouns that end in **-f** simply add **-s** to form the plural.

(j) one deer—*two deer*   one series—*two series*
one fish—*two fish***   one sheep—*two sheep*
one means—*two means*   one shrimp—*two shrimp****
one offspring—*two offspring*   one species—*two species*
	Some nouns have the same singular and plural form: e.g.,
	    One deer is …
	    Two deer are …

(k) criterion—*criteria* (m) analysis—*analyses* phenomenon—*phenomena* basis—*bases* crisis—*crises* (l) bacterium—*bacteria* hypothesis—*hypotheses* curriculum—*curricula* parenthesis—*parentheses* datum—*data* thesis—*theses* medium—*media* memorandum—*memoranda*	Some nouns that English has borrowed from other languages have foreign plurals. In (l), the singular forms *datum* and *medium* are not commonly used. The plural forms *data* and *media* are used informally for both singular and plural.

*For information about the spelling of words ending in **-s/-es**, see Chart 5-1, p. 79.

**Fishes is also possible but rarely used.

***Especially in British English, but also occasionally in American English, the plural of *shrimp* can be *shrimps*.

EXERCISE 2 ▶ Looking at grammar. (Chart 6-1)

Write the plural form of each word in the correct column. Some forms have two spellings.

✓ belief	✓ deer	✓ knife	memo	tomato
box	fish	leaf	photo	video
chief	half	life	mosquito	wolf
class	✓ hero	loaf	scarf	zero
cloud	kilo	match	sheep	zoo

–S	–ES	–VES	NO CHANGE
beliefs	*heroes*	*knives*	*deer*

EXERCISE 3 ▶ Game. (Chart 6-1)

Work in teams of three to five students. Use Chart 6-1 to list plural nouns for each of the four categories. Your teacher will give you a time limit. Choose a leader to write the answers. The team that has the most words wins. Be ready to explain a choice if another team questions it. Your teacher will decide if the word is acceptable.

Example: things in nature that cause people problems
TEAM A LEADER (*writes*): mosquitoes, lice, tornadoes, deer, etc.
TEAM B: How do deer cause problems?
TEAM A: They eat plants.
TEACHER: OK. We'll accept that.

1. things in life that can be dangerous
2. things that you see every day

3. things that you find in nature
4. things that you can hear

EXERCISE 4 ▶ Looking at grammar. (Chart 6-1)

Complete the sentences with the correct forms of the nouns in the box. Use each noun only one time.

attorney	cliff	man	piano
beach	discovery	✓ match	phenomenon
datum	laboratory	medium	✓ tooth

1. The baby has been crying at night because she is getting her first _____ *teeth* _____.

2. I need some _____ *matches* _____ to light the fire.

3. Studies show that _____ process information differently from women.

4. Maria needed some legal advice for her businesses, so she contacted two _____.

5. New scientific _____ occur every day in _____ throughout the world.

6. Online companies collect a lot of _____ about their customers.

7. The north side of the island has no _____ for people to walk on. There are only

   steep _____. No one can climb these steep walls of rock.

8. The music building at the university has 27 _____ for students to practice on.

9. Thunder and lightning are _____ of nature.

10. Many people communicate on the Internet through social _____.

EXERCISE 5 ▸ Listening, grammar, and speaking. (Chart 6-1)

Part I. First listen to the conversation with your book closed. Then listen again and <u>underline</u> the plural nouns.

Ordering Office Supplies

A: Let's see. What do we need?
B: First, we need to order some printer ink cartridges.
A: What quantity?
B: Three combo packages of black and color will do.
A: What about more paper? Do we have enough boxes in stock?
B: No, we don't. Put down four.
A: Anything else?
B: Yes. We need 100 pens and 100 pencils.
A: What else?
B: I think that's it.
A: Great. I'll put in the order right now.

Do you know these words and phrases?
- quantity
- combo packages
- will do
- in stock
- put down
- put in (an order)

Part II. Work with a partner. Imagine you both work for the same company (you choose the company). Make a new conversation and order different supplies. Pay attention to plural endings. Then practice your conversation and perform it for the class. You can look at your notes before you speak. When you speak, look at your partner.

EXERCISE 6 ▸ Looking at grammar. (Chart 6-1)

Choose the correct completions.

1. Bacterium / Bacteria   are very small. They are microscopic (very small)   organism / organisms   that consist of one cell / cells.

2. Bacterium / Bacteria   are in the air, water, and soil* as well as in the bodies of all living   creature / creatures.

3. There are   thousand / thousands   of kinds of bacterium / bacteria.   Most of them are harmless to human being / human beings, but some cause diseases such as tuberculosis and pneumonia.

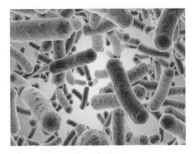

bacteria

---

*Since they are noncount nouns, *air*, *water*, and *soil* have no plural form. See Chart 6-5 for more information.

4. Virus / Viruses   are also microscopic   organism / organisms.
They live in the   cell / cells   of other living   thing / things.
By themselves, they cannot reproduce, but inside a living
cell / cells,   they become active and can multiply hundreds
of   time / times.

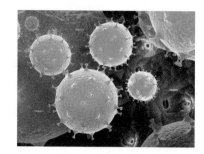

a virus

5. Virus / Viruses   cause many   disease / diseases. They
infect   human / humans   with such illnesses as the common
cold, influenza (the flu), measles, Ebola, and AIDS (Acquired
Immune Deficiency Syndrome).

6. A   virus / viruses   is tiny. The virus that causes AIDS is 230 million* times smaller than
the   period / periods   at the end of this   sentence / sentences.

EXERCISE 7 ▸ Warm-up. (Chart 6-2)
Which nouns in the box commonly follow the nouns **computer** and **airplane**?

passenger	error	pilot	screen	skills	ticket

1. computer _____

   computer _____

   computer _____

2. airplane _____

   airplane _____

   airplane _____

6-2 Nouns as Adjectives

(a) The soup has vegetables in it. It is *vegetable* soup.	When a noun is used as an adjective, it is in its singular form. INCORRECT: vegetable -s- soup
(b) The building has offices in it. It is an *office* building.	NOTE: Adjectives do not take a final **-s**. INCORRECT: *beautiful -s- picture*
(c) The test lasted two hours. It was a *two-hour* test.	When a noun used as a modifier is combined with a number expression, the noun is singular and a hyphen (-) is used.
(d) Her son is five years old. She has a *five-year-old* son.	INCORRECT: She has a five year -s- old son.

EXERCISE 8 ▸ Looking at grammar. (Chart 6-2)
Complete the sentences with the words in *italics*. Use the singular or plural form as appropriate.
Include hyphens (-) as necessary.

1. *shoe*   They sell __*shoes*__ at that store. It is a __*shoe*__ store.

2. *flower*   My garden has _____ in it. It is a _____ garden.

---

*When the words *hundred, thousand, million,* and *billion* are used with numerals, they remain in their singular form:
Six hundred *employees will attend the company picnic this year. There are* **three thousand** *entrants in the photo contest.* When
they are used without numerals to indicate an indefinite but large number of something, they are used in their plural form:
Hundreds *of people came to the concert. There are* **thousands** *of earthquakes in the world every year.*

3. *bean*   This soup is made from black _____. It is black _____

soup.

4. *baby*   People can buy special food in small jars for _____. It is called

_____ food.

5. *child*   Dr. Adams is a psychologist for _____. She is a _____

psychologist.

6. *salad*   At a formal dinner, there are usually two forks on the table. The smaller fork

is for _____. It is a _____ fork.

7. *mosquito*   In tropical climates, sometimes it is necessary

to hang a net over a bed to protect the sleeper

from _____. It is called a

_____ net.

8. *two + hour*   The plane was late. We had a _____

wait. We had to wait for _____.

9. *ten + year + old*   My brother is _____. I have a _____ brother.

10. *three + letter*   *Arm* and *dog* are _____ words. Each word has _____.

EXERCISE 9 ▶ Game. (Chart 6-2)

Work in teams. Think of common expressions with the given noun + another noun. The team that comes up with the most expressions in the given time wins.

Example: flower → *a flower vase, a flower garden, a flower shop, etc.*

1. cotton	5. telephone	9. morning	13. kitchen
2. grammar	6. mountain	10. street	14. baby
3. birthday	7. government	11. newspaper	15. vegetable
4. chicken	8. football	12. hotel	16. bicycle

EXERCISE 10 ▶ Listening. (Chart 6-2)

Complete the sentences with the words you hear. Pay attention to singular/plural endings.

An Assistant Professor

1. Ted is an assistant _____ professor.

2. He worked for two _____ before he got a full-time job.

3. College _____ have a heavy workload.

4. Assistant _____ duties include teaching and research.

5. Ted also supervises the T.A., or teaching _____, program for

his department.

6. Teaching _____ attend his classes and then meet with students in

small groups.

EXERCISE 11 ▶ Looking at grammar. (Chart 6-2)

Complete the sentences with the *italicized* words. Pay attention to singular/plural endings.

1. *airplane / seat*

    a. I don't enjoy flying in _____airplanes_____ anymore.

    The _____seats_____ are getting smaller and smaller.

    b. _____Airplane_____ _____seats_____ are getting

    more and more uncomfortable, don't you think?

2. *taxi / driver*

    a. Joseph and Rob drive _____ for a living.

    b. They are _____ _____ .

3. *manager / office*

    a. _____ of big _____ have a lot of responsibilities.

    b. Maria and her sister have good jobs. They're _____ _____ .

4. *school / activity*

    a. _____ offer a lot of _____ for students.

    b. Anna enjoys _____ _____ such as playing soccer team

    and being on the debate team.

EXERCISE 12 ▶ Editing and writing. (Charts 6-1 and 6-2)

Part I. Read the passage and correct the errors. The number of errors is listed at the end of each paragraph.

Garage Sales

In the U.S. and Canada, a popular way to get rid of used item is through a garage sale. The owner chooses a day or two, usually over a weekend, and sells miscellaneous stuffs from the garage, driveway, or yard.* (2)

Popular items at garage sales include book, old magazine, art, clothes, jewelry, wood furniture, and toy. Usually the price are very low, and often the buyer can bargain with the seller. (4)

Some thing you don't want to buy for safety and health reason include bicycle helmets, child car seat, tire, mattress, upholstered furniture, crib, babies bottles, old cookware, and stuffed animal. The equipment might be outdated, and anything with upholstery or stuffing might have bugs. (8)

Occasionally people find valuable merchandises at garage sales. In 1999, a man in the U.S. paid $29 for a paintings by Martin Heade. It turned out the painting was worth over $800,000! Another man bought a pictures frame for $4.00. Inside was a rare copy of the Declaration of Independence, worth over $2 million! (3)

*Some people call this a "yard sale."

Part II. Do you have garage sales in your country? Do you go to them? What do you do with things you no longer want? Write a paragraph about getting rid of stuff.

EXERCISE 13 ▸ Warm-up. (Chart 6-3)

Decide if the words in blue refer to one person or more than one person.

1. my son's school   one   more than one
2. my sons' school   one   more than one
3. the men's hats   one   more than one
4. the man's hats   one   more than one

6-3 Possessive Nouns

Singular Noun	Possessive Form	
(a) the girl	*the girl's* coat	To express possession — the idea of belonging to someone or something, add an apostrophe (') and **-s** to a singular noun: *The **girl's** coat is in the closet.*
(b) Tom	*Tom's* coat	
(c) my wife	*my wife's* coat	Note in (e): If a singular noun ends in **-s**, there are two possible forms:
(d) a lady	*a lady's* coat	
(e) Thomas	*Thomas's/Thomas'* coat	1. Add an apostrophe and **-s**: ***Thomas's*** *coat.* 2. Add only an apostrophe: ***Thomas'*** *coat.*
		Pronunciation of **'s** as in ***Thomas's***: /əz/

Plural Noun	Possessive Form	
(f) the girls	*the girls'* coats	Add only an apostrophe to a plural noun that ends in **-s**: *The **girls'** coats are in the closet.*
(g) their wives	*their wives'* coats	
(h) the ladies	*the ladies'* coats	Add an apostrophe and **-s** to plural nouns that do not end in **-s**: *The **men's** coats are in the closet.*
(i) the men	*the men's* coats	
(j) my children	*my children's* coats	

(k) *Alan and Lisa's* apartment is on the third floor.	Note the apostrophe usage in (k) and (l):
(l) *Tom's and Joe's* apartments are on the second floor.	In (k), only the final name has an apostrophe. The apartment belongs to both Alan and Lisa. In (l), Tom and Joe have different apartments. Both names have apostrophes.

EXERCISE 14 ▸ Looking at grammar. (Chart 6-3)

Answer the questions.

1. The kids' bedroom is really messy.

   a. What two nouns does the possessive connect? _____*kids*_____ + _____*bedroom*_____

   b. How many kids are there, one or more than one? _____

2. Your manager's offices have a lot of space.

   a. What two nouns does the possessive connect? _____ + _____

   b. How many managers are there, one or more than one? _____

3. My cousin's grandparents are from Iceland.

   a. What two nouns does the possessive connect? _____ + _____

   b. How many cousins are there, one or more than one? _____

4. The judges' decision has been unpopular with the public.

    a. What two nouns does the possessive connect? _____ + _____

    b. How many judges are there, one or more than one? _____

5. The women's restroom is upstairs.

    a. What two nouns does the possessive connect? _____ + _____

    b. How many women are there, one or more than one? _____

EXERCISE 15 ▶ Looking at grammar. (Chart 6-3)

Complete the sentences. Use the possessive form of the nouns in *italics*.

1. a. The (*boy*) _____ names are George and Liam.

    b. The (*boy*) _____ name is Paul.

2. a. The (*children*) _____ toys are all over the floor.

    b. I fixed the (*child*) _____ bike and he rode away.

3. a. The (*baby*) _____ toys fell on the floor. She wants them.

    b. The (*baby*) _____ toys fell on the floor. They want them.

4. a. (*Bess*) _____ last name is Young.

    b. (*Mrs. Thomas*) _____ husband does the dinner dishes when she cooks.

    c. We went to (*Jack and Larry*) _____ house for dinner.

EXERCISE 16 ▶ Let's talk. (Chart 6-3)

Part I. Work with a partner. Make sentences about the family tree. Use possessives.

mother/mom	aunt	niece	sister-in-law	first cousin
father/dad	uncle	nephew	brother-in-law	

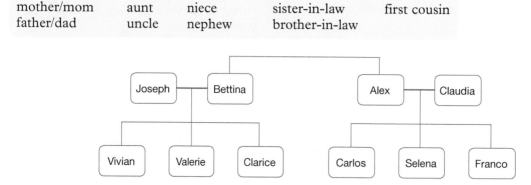

Examples: Bettina is Selena's aunt. Selena is Bettina's niece.

Part II. Draw a tree for your family or a friend's family. Explain the relationships to a classmate using possessives.

EXERCISE 17 ▶ Looking at grammar. (Chart 6-3)

Correct the errors. Add apostrophes to the possessive nouns as necessary.

1. Texas is a leading producer of petroleum and natural gas. It is one of the world's largest storage areas for petroleum.

2. Psychologists have developed many different kinds of tests. A "personality test" is used to evaluate an individuals personal characteristics, such as friendliness or trustworthiness.

3. Many fairy tales tell of heroes encounters with giants or dangerous animals. In one story, the heros encounter with a dragon saves a village from destruction.

4. Play is an important part of childrens lives. It teaches them about their environment while they are having fun. For instance, they learn from playing with miniature boats that boats float, and they can practice ways to make boats move across water.

EXERCISE 18 ▸ Warm-up. (Chart 6-4)
Which phrase sounds better to you in each pair?

1. a. my cousin's home	OR	b. the home of my cousin	
2. a. this week's news	OR	b. the news of this week	
3. a. my country's people	OR	b. people in my country	

6-4 More About Expressing Possession

(a) my *brother's* house (b) the *birds'* feathers (c) *Canada's* borders (d) *UNICEF's* mission	*-'s* is generally used to express possession for the following: • living creatures, as in (a)–(b); • countries, as in (c) • organizations, as in (d)
(e) the *cover of the book* (f) the *start of the race* (g) the *owner of the company*	*Of* is often used to show possession for non-living things, as in (e)–(g). NOTE: The examples in (a)–(g) show the more common usage. With some expressions, either form is acceptable: *the earth's surface* OR *the surface of the earth*. These special occurrences are best learned on a case-by-case basis.
(h) *today's* schedule (i) this *month's* pay (j) last *week's* announcement	Expressions of time do not generally take *of*. INCORRECT: schedule of today pay of this month announcement of last week
(k) *people from my country* (l) *people in my country*	When *country* is combined with *people* to show possession, the prepositions *from* or *in* are used. INCORRECT: *my country's people*
(m) I'll be at the *doctor's*. (n) I was at my *accountant's*. (o) I'm staying at my *cousin's*.	In (m–o), *'s* indicates a business or residence. (m) = doctor's office (n) = accountant's office (o) = cousin's home

(p) I filled out the *application* form.
    INCORRECT: the application's form
 	
(q) Five astronauts were aboard the *space* shuttle.
    INCORRECT: the space's shuttle
	A noun used as an adjective can indicate *type* or *kind*, rather than possession.
	
	In (p), *application* describes the type of form. It does not express possession.
	
	In (q), *space shuttle* indicates the type of shuttle. It does not express possession.

EXERCISE 19 ▶ Looking at grammar. (Chart 6-4)
Choose the more common or correct expression according to Chart 6-4.

1. a. the start of the movie   b. the movie's start
2. a. this year's profits   b. the profits of this year
3. a. the woman's purse   b. the purse of the woman
4. a. the news of yesterday   b. yesterday's news
5. a. the offices of my bosses   b. my bosses' offices
6. a. the women's restroom   b. the restroom of women
7. a. my country's people   b. people from my country
8. a. the U.N.'s funds   b. the funds of the U.N.

EXERCISE 20 ▶ Looking at grammar. (Chart 6-4)
Work with a partner. Choose the correct answer, and explain your reason.

1. a. Wilhelm is a factory's worker.
   b. Wilhelm is a factory worker.

2. a. The astronauts had a wonderful view of the earth.
   b. The astronauts had a wonderful earth's view.

3. a. I have four aunts on my mother's side.
   b. I have four aunts' on my mother's side.

4. a. Let's leave at the show's end.
   b. Let's leave at the end of the show.

5. a. Can you pick me up at the doctors tomorrow?
   b. Can you pick me up at the doctor's tomorrow?

6. a. When I was in Chicago, I stayed at a cousin's apartment.
   b. When I was in Chicago, I stayed at a cousins' apartment.
   c. When I was in Chicago, I stayed at the apartment of cousins.

7. a. I enjoy visiting my friend home.
   b. I enjoy visiting the home of my friend.
   c. I enjoy visiting my friends home.
   d. I enjoy visiting friends' homes.

EXERCISE 21 ▶ Game: Brain Teasers. (Chart 6-4)
Work with a partner to solve these puzzles. The first pair to get all the correct answers wins.

1. Nancy and Jack Hanson's family is large. They have ten sons. If each son has a sister, how many children do the Hansons have?
2. Lucy says, "She's my mother's daughter, but she's not my sister." Who is she?
3. Ricky's mother had four children. The first child's name was April, the second child's name was May, and the third child's name was June. What was her fourth child named?
4. Jake is looking at a photo of someone. His co-worker asks who it is. Jake says, "Sisters and brothers, I have none. But that man's father is my father's son." Who is the person in the photo?
5. A father and son are on a hiking trip in the mountains. They slip and fall down a steep hillside. The father dies on the way to the hospital, and the boy is taken immediately into surgery. The surgeon takes one look at him and says, "I can't operate on this boy. He is my son." Who is the surgeon?

EXERCISE 22 ▸ Warm-up. (Chart 6-5)
Choose all the correct completions.

A: Does the dorm room have much _____?
    a. desk   b. furniture   c. chair   d. bed

B: It has the basics: a _____ for each student.
    a. desk   b. furniture   c. chair   d. bed

6-5 Count and Noncount Nouns

(a) I bought *a chair*. Sam bought *three chairs*.		***Chair*** is called a "count noun." This means you can count chairs: *one chair, two chairs,* etc.
(b) We bought *some furniture*. INCORRECT: We bought some furniture ~~-s-~~. INCORRECT: We bought ~~-a-~~ furniture.		***Furniture*** is called a "noncount noun." You cannot use numbers (*one, two,* etc.) with the word ***furniture***.

	Singular	**Plural**	

COUNT NOUN	*a* chair
	one chair
		two chairs
		some chairs
		many chairs
		Ø chairs*
			A count noun:
			  (1) may be preceded by *a/an* or *one* in the singular.
			  (2) takes a final *-s/-es* in the plural.

NONCOUNT NOUN	*some* furniture
	a lot of furniture
	much furniture
	Ø furniture*
			A noncount noun:
			  (1) is not immediately preceded by *a/an* or *one*.
			  (2) has no plural form, so does not add a final *-s/-es*.

*Ø = nothing (i.e., no article or other determiner)

EXERCISE 23 ▸ Looking at grammar. (Chart 6-5)
Look at the *italicized* nouns. Write "C" above the count nouns and "NC" above the noncount nouns.

1. I bought some *chairs*, *tables*, and *desks*. We needed some new *furniture*.
    (C   C   C   NC)

2. Michiko likes to wear *jewelry*. Today she is wearing four *rings*, six *bracelets*, and a *necklace*.

3. We took pictures of *mountains*, *fields*, and *lakes* on our trip. We saw beautiful *scenery*.

4. The neighbors have a rusty *car* without an *engine*, broken *furniture*, and an old *refrigerator* in their front yard. Their yard is full of *junk*.

5. *Gold* and *iron* are *metals*.

6. I used an *iron* to press my wrinkled shirt.

EXERCISE 24 ▸ Looking at grammar. (Chart 6-5)
Complete the sentences with *a*, *an*, or *some*.

Idioms

1. Every week our instructor gives us _____ new idioms and _____ slang.

2. She told us that _____ teachers find idioms hard to teach, but she enjoys explaining them.

3. To be honest, _____ idiomatic expressions are hard for me to make sense of and remember.

4. _____ phrase that doesn't make a lot of sense to me is "raining cats and dogs."

5. My teacher said to think about it as _____ figure of speech and not worry about the individual words.

6. _____ idiom that is easy for me to picture is "to get up on the wrong side of the bed."

EXERCISE 25 ▶ Game. (Chart 6-5)

Work in teams. The leader has paper and a pen. The teacher will say a noncount noun. As a team, make a list of things that belong to this category until the teacher says "Stop." The team with the most nouns in the list gets a point.

Example:
TEACHER (*book open*): mail
LEADER writes (*book closed*): mail
TEAM to LEADER (*book closed*): letters, postcards, packages, etc.

1. fruit
2. jewelry
3. clothing
4. garbage
5. traffic
6. office equipment

EXERCISE 26 ▶ Grammar and speaking. (Chart 6-5)

Part I. Change the endings to plural with *-es* or *-ies* where necessary. Write **Ø** for no ending.
NOTE: The only noncount noun is *garbage*.

Recycling in Sweden

Imagine a country that recycles 99% of its household garbage____ . For Sweden, that's already
a reality____ . Only 1% of household waste goes into garbage dumps or landfills. How do the
    ‾2‾
Swedes do this? Most separate their garbage____ in their homes. This includes newspaper____ ,
                                               ‾3‾   ‾4‾
plastic container____ , glass bottle____ , light bulb____ , battery____ , and electric appliance____ .
              ‾5‾   ‾6‾   ‾7‾   ‾8‾   ‾9‾
In residential area____ , recycle bin____ are only 300 meter____ (328 yards) away from a home.
                    ‾10‾   ‾11‾   ‾12‾
Fifty percent of the waste is burned or turned into energy. Garbage trucks go
around city____ and pick up electronics and dangerous chemicals. Pharmacy____
        ‾13‾   ‾14‾
take medicines that people don't need. Sweden is a world leader____ in recycling.
                                                             ‾15‾

Part II. Discuss recycling habits for trash, old medicines, chemicals, etc., in your country. Is recycling common? Is it required? Are there different rules for different products?

EXERCISE 27 ▶ Warm-up. (Charts 6-6 and 6-7)

Agree or disagree with the statements. Which nouns in blue are noncount?

1. Sunshine is a good source of vitamin C.	yes	no
2. Smog is a combination of smoke and fog.	yes	no
3. In a storm, we hear thunder before we see lightning.	yes	no

6-6 Noncount Nouns

(a) I bought some chairs, tables, and desks. In other words, I bought some *furniture*.	Many noncount nouns refer to a "whole" that is made up of different parts. In (a): *furniture* represents a whole group of things that is made up of similar but separate items.
(b) I put some *sugar* in my *coffee*.	In (b): *sugar* and *coffee* represent whole masses made up of individual particles or elements.*
(c) I wish you *luck*.	Many noncount nouns are abstractions. In (c): *luck* is an abstract concept, an abstract "whole." It has no physical form; you can't touch it; you can't count it.
(d) *Sunshine* is warm and cheerful.	A phenomenon of nature, such as *sunshine*, is used as a noncount noun, as in (d).

(e) NONCOUNT: Ann has brown *hair*.
    COUNT: Tom has a *hair* on his jacket.
 	
(f) NONCOUNT: I opened the curtains to let in some *light*.
    COUNT: Don't forget to turn off the *light* before you go to bed.
	Many nouns can be used as either noncount or count nouns, but the meaning is different, e.g., *hair* in (e) and *light* in (f).
	
	(Dictionaries written especially for learners of English as a second language are a good source of information on count/noncount usage of nouns.)

*To express a particular quantity, some noncount nouns may be preceded by unit expressions: *a spoonful of sugar, a glass of water, a cup of coffee, a quart of milk, a loaf of bread, a grain of rice, a bowl of soup, a bag of flour, a pound of meat, a piece of furniture, a piece of paper, a piece of jewelry.*

6-7 Some Common Noncount Nouns

This list is a sample of nouns that are commonly used as noncount nouns. Many other nouns can also be used as noncount nouns.

(a) WHOLE GROUPS MADE UP OF SIMILAR ITEMS: baggage, clothing, equipment, food, fruit, furniture, garbage, hardware, jewelry, junk, luggage, machinery, mail, makeup, merchandise, money/cash/change, postage, scenery, stuff, traffic, etc.

(b) FLUIDS: water, coffee, tea, milk, oil, soup, gasoline, blood, etc.
(c) SOLIDS: ice, bread, butter, cheese, meat, gold, iron, silver, glass, paper, wood, cotton, wool, etc.
(d) GASES: steam, air, oxygen, nitrogen, smoke, smog, pollution, etc.
(e) PARTICLES: rice, chalk, corn, dirt, dust, flour, grass, hair, pepper, salt, sand, sugar, wheat, etc.

(f) ABSTRACTIONS:
—beauty, confidence, courage, education, enjoyment, fun, happiness, health, help, honesty, hospitality, importance, intelligence, justice, knowledge, laughter, luck, music, patience, peace, pride, progress, recreation, significance, sleep, truth, violence, wealth, etc.
—advice, information, news, evidence, proof, etc.
—time, space, energy, etc.
—homework, work, etc.
—grammar, slang, vocabulary, etc.
(g) LANGUAGES: Arabic, Chinese, English, Spanish, etc.
(h) FIELDS OF STUDY: chemistry, engineering, history, literature, mathematics, psychology, etc.
(i) RECREATION: baseball, soccer, tennis, chess, bridge, poker, etc.
(j) ACTIVITIES: driving, studying, swimming, traveling, walking (and other gerunds)

(k) NATURAL PHENOMENA: weather, dew, fog, hail, heat, humidity, lightning, rain, sleet, snow, thunder, wind, darkness, light, sunshine, electricity, fire, gravity, etc.

EXERCISE 28 ▶ Looking at grammar. (Charts 6-5 → 6-7)
Use each noun only one time. Add final *-s, -es,* or *-ies* if necessary.

advice	definition	music	symphony
✓ change	equipment	problem	traffic
✓ coin	homework	progress	truck
computer	information	river	vocabulary

1. Yes, I have some money. I have a few _____*coins*_____ in my pocket. In other words, I have

   some _____*change*_____ in my pocket.

2. The Mississippi, the Amazon, and the Nile are well-known _____.

3. I like to listen to operas, _____, and folk songs. I enjoy

   _____ and listen to it often on my iPod®.

4. Look at all the cars, _____, and buses. This city is full of _____.

5. There are _____, phones, copiers, and printers in a typical business office.

   A business office needs a lot of _____.

6. Tonight I have to read 20 pages in my history book, do 30 algebra _____, and

   write a composition. In other words, I have a lot of _____ to do tonight.

7. Antonio is studying the meaning of English words. He learned some new _____

   today. For example, he learned that *fly* has at least two _____.

8. Toronto is Canada's largest city and the fifth largest city in North America. This / These

   _____ didn't surprise me.

9. I didn't feel good. Ann said, "You should see a doctor." Nick said, "You should go to bed."

   Martha said, "You should drink juice and rest." I got _____ from three people.

10. My English is slowly getting better. My vocabulary is increasing. I often understand people

    even when they talk fast. I'm satisfied with the _____ I've made in learning English.

EXERCISE 29 ▶ Trivia game. (Chart 6-7)
Work in teams. Answer the questions. All of the answers are noncount nouns from Chart 6-7.

1. What is one ingredient that is needed to make glass? _____

2. What was Albert Einstein's college major? _____

3. What language does the word *algebra* come from? _____

4. What natural force pulls things to the ground? _____

5. What comes from sheep that we can make into fabric? _____

6. Name one sport in which players score a goal. _____

7. What does boiling water produce? _____

8. What field of study looks at human behavior? _____

9. What substance in our body has red and white cells? _____

10. What does rain turn into at 23°F (–5°C)? _____

EXERCISE 30 ▸ Looking at grammar. (Charts 6-5 → 6-7)
Choose the correct completions.

1. a. It took me a lot of time to finish my   homework / homeworks.
   b. I had a lot of   assignment / assignments.
2. a. I have been to Mexico three   time / times.
   b. I've spent a lot of   time / times   there.
3. a. Abdullah gave me some good   advice / advices.
   b. Nadia also gave me some good   suggestion / suggestions.
4. a. Yoko learned several new   word / words   today.
   b. She is increasing her   vocabulary / vocabularies   quickly.
5. a. I drank two   glass / glasses   of water.
   b. Window / Windows   are made of   glass / glasses.
   c. Mr. Chu wears   glass / glasses   because he has   a poor eyesight / poor eyesight.
   d. Tom put the wrong soap in the dishwasher. What   sight / a sight!

EXERCISE 31 ▸ Grammar and listening. (Charts 6-5 → 6-7)
Add the correct endings (**-s, -es, -ies**) to the nouns where necessary. Write **Ø** for no ending.
Then listen to the passage and check your answers.

Hoarding

Rebecca has a problem. She doesn't have any visitor____. Her family doesn't come to see her
                                                    1
anymore. It's not because they don't like her. It's because no one can get through her front

door. There is too much stuff____ blocking the way. Rebecca is a hoarder.
                              2

Hoarders are unable to throw out or give away thing____ they no longer need such as
                                                     3
newspaper____, magazine____, clothes, and furniture____. Some hoarders have box____ that
           4   5   6   7
reach the ceiling.

Hoarding has just recently come to the attention of the general public____. Hoarding is
                                                                         8
more than having a messy or cluttered home____. Hoarding interferes with a person's ability
                                            9
to function. Occasionally, hoarding can become life-threatening. In one situation, the floor of a

hoarder's house____ collapsed. Sometimes garbage____ builds up in
                10   11
the house and health problem____ arise.
                             12

Scientists believe that an area____ in the brain affects a person's
                              13
ability to make decision____ to get rid of thing____. Researchers
                       14   15
are working on treatments for this condition____.
                                             16

EXERCISE 32 ▸ Warm-up. (Chart 6-8)

Write <u>all</u> the words that can complete each sentence.

two	several	plenty of	a few	a great deal of
a couple of	some	too many	a little	hardly any
both	a lot of	too much	a number of	no

1. I received _____ letters. _____

   _____

2. I received _____ mail. _____

   _____

6-8 Expressions of Quantity Used with Count and Noncount Nouns

Expressions of Quantity	Used with Count Nouns	Used with Noncount Nouns	
(a) one each every	one apple each apple every apple	Ø* Ø Ø	An expression of quantity may precede a noun. Some expressions of quantity are used only with count nouns, as in (a) and (b).
(b) two, etc. both a couple of a few several many a number of	two apples both apples a couple of apples a few apples several apples many apples a number of apples	Ø Ø Ø Ø Ø Ø	
(c) a little much a great deal of	Ø Ø Ø	a little rice much rice a great deal of rice	Some are used only with noncount nouns, as in (c).
(d) no hardly any some/any a lot of / lots of plenty of most all	no apples hardly any apples some/any apples a lot of/lots of apples plenty of apples most apples all apples	no rice hardly any rice some/any rice a lot of/lots of rice plenty of rice most rice all rice	Some are used with both count and noncount nouns, as in (d). In spoken English, **much** and **many** are used in questions and negatives. For affirmative statements, **a lot of** is preferred. However, too + **much/many** is used in affirmative statements. *Do you have **much** time?* *I don't have **much** time.* *I have **a lot of** time.* *I have **too much** time.*

*Ø = not used. For example, **one** is not used with noncount nouns. You can say "I ate one apple" but NOT "I ate one rice."

EXERCISE 33 ▸ Looking at grammar. (Chart 6-8)

Choose <u>all</u> the possible completions for each sentence.

1. A: I bought a number of   thing / items / food / snacks   for our party.

   B: Let me see. Wow! You got a lot of   chocolate / sweets / candy / junk food.

   A: I know. I have no   control / limits.

2. A: How much   homework / assignments / chores / responsibilities   do you have?

B: A lot. Why do you ask?

A: Never mind. I don't want to bother you with too many   problem / questions / requests / concern   right now.

3. A: I sent you a few   text / email / messages / emails   about a new movie that opens today.

B: I know. I'm just reading them.

A: So ... do you want to go with me?

B: Sorry. I have hardly any   time / money / gas in the car / clean clothes.

A: Seriously?

4. A: Miriam is dealing with a great deal of   stress / anxiety / problems / issues.

B: I heard that. She's getting some   help / assistance / advice / support   from a counselor.

EXERCISE 34 ▸ Looking at grammar. (Chart 6-8)

Complete the sentences with *much* or *many*. Write the plural form of the nouns as necessary. Circle the correct verb form where necessary.

Pierre is anxious.

1. There ⦅isn't⦆/ aren't   _____much_____ money in his bank account.

2. He has too _____ medical bill this month.

3. He can't find _____ information for a presentation that's due next week.

4. There   is / are   too _____ long hour at work.

5. He doesn't have _____ time to relax.

6. He hasn't met _____ people since he came here, and he doesn't have _____ friend.

7. There   isn't / aren't   _____ news from his family.

8. There   is / are   too _____ violence in his neighborhood.

EXERCISE 35 ▸ Looking at grammar. (Chart 6-8)

If the given noun can be used to complete the sentence, write it in its correct form (singular or plural). If the given noun cannot be used to complete the sentence, write Ø.

1. *Helen bought several _____.*

   lamp _____lamps_____

   furniture _____Ø_____

   jewelry _____Ø_____

   necklace _____necklaces_____

2. *Sam bought a lot of _____.*

   stamp _____

   rice _____

   stuff _____

   thing _____

3. *I need a little _____.*

   money _____

   advice _____

   time _____

   minute _____

4. *Alice bought a couple of _____.*

   bread _____

   loaf of bread _____

   honey _____

   jar of honey _____

5. *I read a few _____.*

   novel _____

   literature _____

   poem _____

   poetry _____

6. *I needed some _____.*

   orange juice _____

   light bulb _____

   hardware _____

   computer software _____

7. *We need plenty of _____.*

   sleep _____

   information _____

   fact _____

   help _____

8. *I saw both _____.*

   woman _____

   movie _____

   scene _____

   scenery _____

9. *Nick has a number of _____.*

   shirt _____

   homework _____

   pen _____

   chalk _____

10. *The doctor doesn't have a great deal of _____.*

    patience _____

    wealth _____

    patient _____

    pencil _____

11. *The researchers have many _____.*

    idea _____

    theory _____

    hypothesis _____

    knowledge _____

12. *Jack bought too much _____.*

    shoe _____

    salt _____

    equipment _____

    tool _____

EXERCISE 36 ▸ Writing and speaking. (Chart 6-8)

Use the quantity expressions below to state your opinions on the topics in the box. Then share and compare your opinions with a classmate's. How similar or different are your views?

famous celebrities	serious problems in the world
food	TV commercials
movies	teenagers
doctors	cities

1. A great deal of _____

2. A number of _____

3. Too many _____

4. A couple of _____

5. Too few _____

6. Hardly any _____

7. Plenty of _____

8. Most _____

EXERCISE 37 ▸ Warm-up. (Chart 6-9)

Choose the correct answers.

1. Which sentence gives a negative meaning of "not many people"?
   a. Deserts are largely uninhabited. *Very few people* live in the middle of a desert.
   b. We had a good time. We met *a few people* and had some nice conversations.

2. Which sentence gives a negative meaning of "not much water"?
   a. It's hot today. You should drink *a little water*.
   b. A desert is a dry place. There is *little water* in a desert.

6-9 Using *A Few* and *Few*; *A Little* and *Little*

COUNT: (a) We sang *a few* songs. NONCOUNT: (b) We listened to *a little* music.	**A few** and **few** are used with plural count nouns, as in (a). **A little** and **little** are used with noncount nouns, as in (b).
(c) She has been here only two weeks, but she has already made *a few friends*. (Positive idea: She has made some friends.) (d) I'm very pleased. I've been able to save *a little money* this month. (Positive idea: I have saved some money instead of spending all of it.)	**A few** and **a little** give a positive idea; they indicate that something exists, is present, as in (c) and (d).
(e) I feel sorry for her. She has (*very*) *few friends*. (Negative idea: She does not have many friends; she has almost no friends.) (f) I have (*very*) *little money*. I don't even have enough money to buy food for dinner. (Negative idea: I do not have much money; I have almost no money.)	**Few** and **little** (without **a**) give a negative idea; they indicate that something is largely absent, as in (e). **Very** (+ **few**/**little**) makes the negative stronger, the number/amount smaller, as in (f).

EXERCISE 38 ▸ Looking at grammar. (Chart 6-9)

Without changing the meaning of the sentence, replace the *italicized* words with **a few**, **few**, **a little**, or **little**. Which statements are true for you or do you agree with?

1. I like to stream movies on the Internet. Every week I watch ~~two or three~~ *(a few)* movies.

2. I don't watch TV very much because there are ~~hardly any~~ *(few)* programs that I enjoy.

3. There is *almost no* snow in my country.

4. I need *some* sunshine to feel happy.

5. It's good to speak two languages, but *not many* people need more than two.

6. Everyone needs to take *some* vitamins every day to stay healthy.

7. *Not many* things in life are certain.

8. *Some* of the best things in life are free.

EXERCISE 39 ▸ Grammar and listening. (Chart 6-9)
Complete the sentences with *a few*, *few*, *a little*, or *little*. Then listen to the sentences and check your answers.

With Friends

1. A: Do you have ____*a few*____ minutes? I need ____*a little*____ help. I'm having _____ problems with my laptop.

   B: Sure. Now is good. I have _____ time before I need to leave.

2. A: Ben isn't happy at his new high school. He hasn't met many kids, and he has _____ friends.

   B: Give it _____ time. In _____ months, he'll have more.

3. A: I have _____ patience with lazy co-workers. They frustrate me!

   B: Me too. I work with _____ people who do very _____ work but complain about how much they do!

4. A: I'll have _____ coffee with my dessert. Do you want some?

   B: No, thanks. I drink very _____ coffee. It's too bitter.

   A: I love coffee, especially with _____ sugar.

   B: Whoa! You're using more than _____ sugar. Are you drinking coffee with sugar or sugar with coffee?

   A: But it's really good. Do you want to try _____? Maybe you'd drink more coffee this way.

   B: Uh, I don't think so! I have very _____ sugar in my diet. It makes me hyper.*

EXERCISE 40 ▸ Looking at grammar. (Chart 6-9)
Choose the sentence that best describes the situation.

1. Rosie was still hungry. She wanted some more rice.
   a. Rosie wanted a little rice.   b. Rosie wanted little rice.

2. I don't really like much salt on my food.
   a. I add a little salt to my food.   b. I add little salt to my food.

3. I have a long plane ride ahead of me.
   a. I packed a few sandwiches   b. I packed few sandwiches.

4. Mr. Li has never studied English. He only knows how to say "hello."
   a. Mr. Li knows a little English.   b. Mr. Li knows little English.

5. Talk to Mr. Li's daughter. If you speak slowly, you can have a conversation with her.
   a. His daughter knows a little English.   b. His daughter knows little English.

---

*hyper = short for *hyperactive;* having too much energy

6. Mr. Perez doesn't know how to be a good boss. He has a bad temper and yells at people all the time about nothing.
   a. A few people like working for him.   b. Few people like working for him.

EXERCISE 41 ▸ Let's talk. (Charts 6-8 and 6-9)

Read the list of food in Dan and Eva's kitchen. Do they have enough food for the next week? Give your opinion using the expressions of quantity in the box. Work in pairs, in small groups, or as a class.

Example: 36 eggs → *They have too many eggs.*

too much*	too little	(not) enough	just the right amount of
too many	too few	(not) nearly enough	just the right number of

The food in Dan and Eva's kitchen:

40 apples	10 bags of rice	1 kilo of coffee
1 banana	20 cans of tomatoes	2 teabags
6 oranges	0 fresh vegetables	1 box of breakfast cereal
1 quart of orange juice	1 bottle of olive oil	2 slices of bread
4 gallons of ice cream	1 cup of sugar	5 pounds of cheese

EXERCISE 42 ▸ Warm-up. (Chart 6-10)

Notice the words in blue. Complete the sentences with *country* or *countries*.

1. One _____ I would like to visit is Malaysia.

2. One of the _____ my wife would like to visit is Brazil.

3. It would be interesting to visit every _____ in the world. Each
   _____ is unique.

4. I've had wonderful experiences in each of the _____ I've visited during my travels.

6-10 Singular Expressions of Quantity: *One, Each, Every*

(a) *One student* was late to class. (b) *Each student* has a schedule. (c) *Every student* has a schedule.	*One*, *each*, and *every* are followed immediately by singular count nouns (never plural nouns, never noncount nouns).
(d) *One of the students* was late to class. (e) *Each (one) of the students* has a schedule (f) *Every one of the students* has a schedule.	*One of*, *each of*, and *every one of** are followed by specific plural count nouns (never singular nouns; never noncount nouns).

*COMPARE:
> *Every one* (two words) is an expression of quantity (e.g., *I have read **every one** of those books*).
> *Everyone* (one word) is an indefinite pronoun. It has the same meaning as *everybody* (e.g., ***Everyone/Everybody** has a schedule*).

NOTE: *Each* and *every* have essentially the same meaning.
> *Each* is used when the speaker is thinking of one person/thing at a time: *Each student has a schedule.* = *Mary has a schedule. Hiroshi has a schedule. Carlos has a schedule. Sabrina has a schedule. Etc.*
> *Every* is used when the speaker means *all*: *Every student has a schedule.* = *All of the students have schedules.*

---

*In spoken English, *too* is often modified by *way* or *far*: *They have **way/far** too many eggs. They have **way/far** too few teabags.*

EXERCISE 43 ▶ Looking at grammar. (Chart 6-10)

Complete the sentences. Use the singular or plural form of the nouns in parentheses.

A Youth Soccer Team

1. Every (*child*) _____ on the team has some experience.

2. One of the (*child*) _____ has been on the team for two years.

3. There is only one (*goalie*) _____ on the soccer team.

4. Only one of the (*player*) _____ has the skills to play goalie.

5. The coach is very pleased that each of the (*player*) _____ works extremely hard.

6. Every (*child*) _____ gets a certificate of participation.

7. The coach gives a certificate to each of the (*child*) _____.

8. He invites every (*parent*) _____ to the end-of-the-year party.

9. Every one of the (*parent*) _____ tries to attend.

EXERCISE 44 ▶ Game. (Chart 6-10)

Work in teams. Your teacher will randomly call out a sentence number. Correct the error(s). Some of the sentences do not contain any errors. The team that gives the correct answer first wins a point.

1. It's important for every ~~students~~ *student* to have a book.

2. Each of the students in my class has a book. (*no change*)

3. The teacher gave each of students a test paper.

4. Every student in the class did well on the test.

5. Every chairs in that room is uncomfortable.

6. One of the equipment in our office is broken.

7. Each of the woman in the room has an interesting story to tell.

8. One of my favorite place in the world is an island in the Caribbean Sea.

9. Customs officials will check each one of your suitcases.

10. It's impossible for one human being to know every languages in the world.

11. I found each of the error in this exercise.

12. Vietnam is one of the country I want to visit.

EXERCISE 45 ▸ Warm-up. (Chart 6-11)

Complete the sentences with **of** or **Ø**. How do you know when to use **of** in expressions of quantity?

I saw _____

1. some ___Ø___ employees.
2. some ___of___ the employees.
3. some ___of___ them.

4. several _____ employees.
5. several _____ the employees.
6. several _____ your employees.
7. several _____ yours.

6-11 Using *Of* in Expressions of Quantity

(a) *A number of* movies came out today. (b) *A number of the* movies are available online. (c) *None of* my friends are available to watch a movie with me today.	Some expressions of quantity always include **of**: 50% of a number of three-fourths of a great deal of hundreds of a lot of thousands of a majority of millions of none of

(d) *Many* movies are available for free.
(e) *Many of the* movies are free.
 	
(f) *Most of the* movies won awards.
(g) *One of those* movies is really funny.
(h) *Many of my* movies are in Spanish.
 	
(i) *Some of them* have subtitles.
	In the following expressions, **of** is optional:
	
	one, two, etc. (of) some (of)
	each (of) several (of)
	much (of) (a) few (of)
	many (of) (a) little (of)
	most (of) hardly any (of)
	all (of) almost all (of)
	
	Note the difference in meaning:
	
	In (d): movies in general
	In (e): specific movies (e.g., online)
	
	When **of** is used with these expressions, the noun must be modified by
	
	   • an article, as in (e) and (f)
	   • a demonstrative, as in (g)
	   • a possessive, as in (h)*
	
	Or, a pronoun can be used, as in (i).
	
	INCORRECT: most of movies
	                 almost movies

(j) *Every* movie had a review. (k) *No* movie is perfect.	**Every** and **no** are never used with **of**.

*All is an exception. Even when the noun is modified, *all* can be used without *of*: *all the movies, all those movies,* or *all my movies.*

EXERCISE 46 ▸ Looking at grammar. (Chart 6-11)
Complete the sentences with *of* or *Ø*.

Junk Mail

1. I usually get a lot _____ mail.

2. A lot _____ the mail I get is junk mail.

3. I throw most _____ junk mail away.

4. Most _____ people I know don't like getting junk mail.

5. One _____ my neighbors sends it back to the company.

6. My husband got a few _____ catalogs yesterday.

7. Several _____ the catalogs often have coupons or special offers like free shipping.

8. I look at few _____ those.

9. Many _____ companies offer better deals online.

10. Some _____ charitable groups ask for donations via the mail.

11. Most _____ the charitable groups send several _____ requests every year.

12. I respond to some _____ them.

EXERCISE 47 ▸ Let's talk. (Charts 6-10 and 6-11)
Make comments about the situation by using the expressions in the box and the information in the sentences. Work in pairs, in small groups, or as a class.

SITUATION: There are 15 employees taking a basic Chinese language class.

all of	the majority of	several of	a couple of
almost all of	some of	a few of	hardly any of
most of	about half of	very few of	one of

Example: Three have studied Chinese before.
SPEAKER A: A few of them have studied Chinese before.
SPEAKER B: Most of them have never studied Chinese before.

1. Thirteen speak English as their native language.
2. One speaks Thai, and one speaks Arabic.
3. No one speaks Spanish.
4. Two have studied several languages already.
5. Fifteen think Chinese is very difficult.
6. Fourteen are enjoying the class.
7. Five have already bought the textbook.
8. Four are men; eleven are women.

EXERCISE 48 ▸ Grammar and writing. (Charts 6-10 and 6-11)

Part I. Complete the sentences with *of* or Ø.

Junk Food

Junk food is a global phenomenon. Every _____ country offers
          1
snacks that taste delicious but have little _____ nutritional value.
                                              2
Most _____ junk food has these characteristics: a great deal _____
       3   4
fat and a high number _____ calories. It probably contains a lot
                        5
_____ sugar, often high fructose sugar. It has a good deal _____ sodium, and it's somewhat
  6   7
addictive. The sweet and salty ingredients make it difficult for most _____ people to have just
                                                                        8
one bite. Chips, crackers, and soda are a few _____ the most popular junk foods.
                                               9

Part II. Write a paragraph about snacks in your country. What do people like to eat for snacks?
Are the foods healthy or unhealthy? Is there much junk food? What is your opinion of junk food?

EXERCISE 49 ▸ Let's talk: interview. (Charts 6-8 → 6-11)

Conduct a poll among your classmates and report your findings.

Part I. Prepare five *yes/no* questions that ask for opinions or information about your classmates'
likes, dislikes, habits, or experiences. Interview at least five people and record their responses.

Sample questions:

Do you read about the news in English?   Have you ever ridden a camel?
Do you like living in this city?   Are you going to be in bed before 11:00 tonight?
Do you have a car?

Part II. Report your findings to the class. Use expressions of quantity to make generalizations.

Sample report: Only a few of the people in this class read about the news in English.
                 Most of them like living in this city.
                 Three of the people in this class have cars.
                 Very few of them have ridden a camel at some time in their lives.
                 Almost all of them are going to be in bed before 11:00 tonight.

EXERCISE 50 ▸ Let's talk. (Charts 6-8 → 6-11)

Most of the statements are overgeneralizations. Make each statement clearer or more accurate by
adding an expression of quantity. Add other words to the sentences or make any other changes you
wish. Work in pairs, in small groups, or as a class.

Example: My classmates are from Japan.
   → *Most of my classmates are from Japan.*
   → *All (of) my classmates are from Japan.*
   → *One of my classmates is from Japan.*
   → *Hardly any of my classmates are from Japan.*
   → *None of my classmates is from Japan.*

1. Babies are born bald.
2. People are friendly.
3. My classmates speak Arabic.
4. The pages in this book contain illustrations.
5. The students in my class are from South America.
6. People like to live alone.
7. The people I know like to live alone.
8. The countries in the world are in the Northern Hemisphere.
9. The citizens of the United States speak English.
10. Children like to read scary stories.
11. The children in my country go to school.
12. The rivers in the world are polluted.
13. The pollution in the world today is caused by human beings.

EXERCISE 51 ▸ Check your knowledge. (Chapter 6 Review)
Correct the errors.

1. That magazine contain many different kind of story and article.

2. In my country, there is alot of language schools.

3. Alicia is always willing to help her friends in every possible ways.

4. Your country has one of the best-trained army in the world.

5. There are a lot of equipments in the research laboratory.

6. I have a five years old daughter and a three years old son.

7. Most of people in my apartment's building is friendly.

8. Dennis family lives on a sailboat.

9. We had two difficults tests in chemistry last week.

10. Almost students in my class are from Asia.

11. It's difficult for me to understand English when people use a lot of slangs.

12. George works in research and development at an airplane's company.

EXERCISE 52 ▸ Grammar, reading, and writing. (Chapter 6)
Part I. Read the following passage.

Web Design

Websites come in all shapes and sizes. Some are easier to use than others, and some are more attractive than others. Some of this is due to personal preference. Everyone has favorite colors or designs. But there are features that seem to make a website easier to navigate or more visually appealing to us.

For many designers, Apple Inc. is an example of a company with an effective website. The homepage is clean and uncluttered. There isn't much information on the page. It has large photos of its products rather than small ones. It is user-friendly. The links are easy to see and fast. There are many helpful tutorials for products, and they are short. This is important because people want information quickly and don't want to watch long videos. These features have made this company's website attractive and useful.

Part II. In your opinion, what features make a good website? Check (✓) the answers.

1. _____ a lot of photos
2. _____ fast links
3. _____ colorful font
4. _____ a lot of white space
5. _____ contact information
6. _____ user-friendly pages
7. _____ speed: pages that load quickly

8. _____ links to pages (rather than scrolling)
9. _____ music
10. _____ professional art
11. _____ accurate information
12. _____ social media links
13. _____ a few bright colors
14. _____ muted colors

Part III. Choose a website. It can be one you like, dislike, or have mixed feelings about. Write a paragraph and evaluate its effectiveness. Consider your choices in Part II, and give your opinion. Use these sentences as a guide:

- _____ is an example of an effective/helpful/weak, etc. website.
- The opening page is …
- It is/has …
- There is/are/isn't/aren't …
- These features have made/make …

WRITING TIP

It's important to use specific details in your writing and avoid details that are too general or vague. For example, look at the following pairs of sentences.

a. The opening page is interesting.
a. There is a link for a tutorial.

b. The opening page has a colorful logo.
b. There is a tutorial on three additional uses for this product.

In the b. sentences, the writer uses clearer or more specific language. When you write, try to provide this kind of specific information for your reader.

Part IV. Edit your writing. Check for the following:

1. ☐ correct use of *-s/-es-/ies* endings for plural nouns
2. ☐ no *-s/-es-/ies* endings for noncount nouns
3. ☐ no plural endings on adjectives
4. ☐ correct use of expressions of quantity
5. ☐ specific details
6. ☐ correct spelling (use a dictionary or spell-check)

▪▪▪▪▪ Go to MyEnglishLab for Self-Study: Gerunds and Infinitives 6

PRETEST: What do I already know?

Write "C" if a sentence has the correct article usage and "I" for incorrect. Check your answers below. After you complete each chart listed, write any necessary corrections.

1. ____ Here's some coffee. Watch out. It's hot. (7-1)

2. ____ Price of rice and flour is increasing. (7-1)

3. ____ A dolphin is extremely intelligent. (7-2)

4. ____ Carrots and tomatoes are rich in vitamin A. (7-2)

5. ____ Is the wallet on the desk yours? (7-3)

6. ____ An assistant in my office is also a part-time flight instructor. (7-3)

7. ____ Sun sets around 7:00 P.M. tonight (7-4)

8. ____ There's a surprise waiting for you in the kitchen! (7-4)

9. ____ Who is going to clean windows? (7-4)

10. ____ How far is Australia from New Zealand? (7-5)

11. ____ Nile River flows through several countries. (7-5)

Incorrect sentences: 2, 7, 9, 11

EXERCISE 1 ▶ Warm-up. (Chart 7-1)

Match the explanation to the sentence it describes.

a. gifts in general   b. a specific gift   c. one gift, but not specific

1. ____ I received a Valentine's gift.

2. ____ The gift was very thoughtful.

3. ____ Is it better to give or receive gifts?

7-1 Articles (A, An, The) with Indefinite and Definite Nouns

Indefinite Nouns

(a) I had *a banana* for a snack. (b) I had Ø *bananas* for a snack. (c) I had Ø *fruit* for a snack. (d) I had *some bananas* for a snack. (e) I had *some fruit* for a snack.	An indefinite noun is a noun that has not specifically been identified. In (a): The speaker is not referring to "this banana" or "that banana" or "the banana you gave me." The speaker is simply saying that she/he ate one banana. The listener does not know or need to know which specific banana was eaten; it was simply one banana out of all bananas. Because *a** means **one**, it is not used with indefinite plural and noncount nouns, as in (b) and (c). **Some** may be used with indefinite plural count and noncount nouns, as in (d) and (e).

Definite Nouns

(f) Thank you for *the banana*. (g) Thank you for *the bananas*. (h) Thank you for *the fruit*.	A noun is definite when both the speaker and the listener are thinking about the same specific noun. In (f): The speaker uses **the** because the listener knows which specific banana the speaker is talking about, i.e., that particular banana which the listener gave to the speaker. Note that **the** is used with both singular and plural count nouns, as in (f) and (g), and with noncount nouns, as in (h).

Summary of Articles with Indefinite and Definite Nouns

	INDEFINITE	DEFINITE
COUNT (SINGULAR)	a/an*	*the*
COUNT (PLURAL)	Ø, some	*the*
NONCOUNT	Ø, some	*the*

*Before vowels, use **an**: **an** *apple*.

EXERCISE 2 ▸ Looking at grammar. (Chart 7-1)
Decide if the nouns in blue are definite or indefinite.

Nicknames

1. Nicknames are common in my culture. definite indefinite
2. My husband has a nickname. definite indefinite
3. It's "Cowboy." He doesn't like the name. definite indefinite
4. Sometimes cities have nicknames. definite indefinite
5. Chicago is called the "the windy city." definite indefinite

EXERCISE 3 ▸ Looking at grammar. (Chart 7-1)
Add **some** where possible.

To-do

1. We have ^some bills to pay.
2. Here's a bill from the electrician. *no change*
3. Do you have time to pay them?
4. Look at the floors. They're really dirty.

5. There's spilled coffee under the chair.

6. Where's the grocery list? I have things to add.

7. Please make your lunch for tomorrow. There are leftovers in the fridge.

EXERCISE 4 ▸ Looking at grammar. (Chart 7-1)

Complete the sentences with *a, an, the,* or *Ø*. Capitalize where necessary.

1. DEFINITE: Where is ___the___ phone?

   INDEFINITE: Where is ___a___ phone?

2. DEFINITE: Please pick up _____ toys on the floor.

   INDEFINITE: Please pick up _____ toy at the store for Sue's baby.

   INDEFINITE: Sue's baby plays with _____ toys.

3. INDEFINITE: I need _____ onion for dinner.

   DEFINITE: _____ onions I just cut are making me cry.

   DEFINITE: _____ onion looks spoiled.

   INDEFINITE: I need _____ onions for tonight's dinner.

4. INDEFINITE: I smell _____ smoke.

   INDEFINITE: _____ smoke always makes my eyes water.

   DEFINITE: _____ smoke from the fire is bothering my eyes.

EXERCISE 5 ▸ Game. (Chart 7-1)

A popular group game is My Grandfather's Store. Each person begins his/her turn by saying *I went to my grandfather's store and bought.* The first person names something that begins with the letter "A." The second person repeats what the first person said, and then names something that begins with the letter "B." The game continues to the letter "Z." Assume that "grandfather's store" sells just about anything anyone would ever think of. Use *a/an* and *some*.

Example:
SPEAKER A: I went to my grandfather's store and bought **an apple**.
SPEAKER B: I went to my grandfather's store and bought **an apple** and **some bread**.
SPEAKER C: I went to my grandfather's store and bought **an apple, some bread**, and **a camel**.
SPEAKER D: I went to my grandfather's store and bought **an apple, some bread, a camel**, and **some dark socks**. Etc.

EXERCISE 6 ▸ Looking at grammar. (Chart 7-1)

Work with a partner. Check (✓) the incorrect sentences, and explain why they are wrong. Make the necessary corrections.

1. __✓__ We're having a̶ vegetables for dinner. (Reason: *Vegetables* is plural. Do not use *a* with a plural noun.)

2. ____ Flowers make a nice gift.

3. ____ My favorite fruits are an apples and oranges.

4. ____ Do all living things need an oxygen?

5. ____ Rice is a popular dish in my country.

6. ____ I need some coin for the bus fare.

EXERCISE 7 ▸ Listening. (Chart 7-1)

Articles can be hard to hear. Listen to each sentence and choose the word you hear. If you do not hear *a* or *an*, circle **Ø**.

Example: You will hear: That's an excellent idea.
You will choose: a   (an)   Ø

1. a   an   Ø   5. a   an   Ø
2. a   an   Ø   6. a   an   Ø
3. a   an   Ø   7. a   an   Ø
4. a   an   Ø   8. a   an   Ø

EXERCISE 8 ▸ Warm-up. (Chart 7-2)

Complete the sentences with the correct number in the box. Which statements are generalizations rather than comments about specific people or things?

| 12 | 20 | 36 | 52 |

1. A wedge of cantaloupe has about _____ calories.

2. A box has _____ sides (inside and outside).

3. Pianos have _____ white keys and _____ black keys.

7-2 Articles: Generic Nouns

A speaker uses generic nouns to make generalizations. A generic noun represents a whole class of things; it is not a specific, real, concrete thing, but rather a symbol of a whole group.

SINGULAR COUNT NOUN (a) *A banana* is yellow. **PLURAL COUNT NOUN** (b) *Ø Bananas* are yellow. **NONCOUNT NOUN** (c) *Ø Fruit* is good for you.	In (a) and (b): The speaker is talking about any banana, all bananas, bananas in general. In (c): The speaker is talking about any and all fruit, fruit in general. Note in (a): **A** is used with a singular count noun. No article (**Ø**) is used to make generalizations about plural count nouns, as in (b), and noncount nouns, as in (c).
(d) *The blue whale* is the largest mammal on earth. (e) Who invented *the wheel*? *The telephone*? *The airplane*? (f) I'd like to learn to play *the piano*. Do you play *the guitar*?	**The** is sometimes used with a *singular* generic count noun. "Generic *the*" is commonly used with: • species of animals, as in (d). • inventions, as in (e). • musical instruments, as in (f).
(g) Janice works with *the elderly*. (h) Do *the wealthy* have a responsibility to help *the poor*?	**The** is used with nouns that refer to groups of people, as in (g) and (h). Common examples include *the unemployed, the needy, the weak,* and *the sick.* These nouns are plural, and the meaning is generic. (See Chart 5-6, p. 88, for more information.)

EXERCISE 9 ▸ Looking at grammar. (Chart 7-2)

Check (✓) if the noun in blue is singular or plural. Also check (✓) the nouns that have a generic meaning.

	SINGULAR	PLURAL	GENERIC
1. a. The eggs are fresh.			
b. Eggs have cholesterol.			
c. An egg has a lot of protein.			
d. Are the eggs safe to eat?			
2. a. Doctors treat the sick.			
b. A doctor treats sick people.			
c. Doctors treat sick people.			
d. The doctors are waiting outside.			

EXERCISE 10 ▸ Looking at grammar. (Chart 7-2)

Check (✓) the sentences that make generalizations.

1. _____ We need water to survive.
2. _____ Water is becoming scarce in some parts of the world.
3. _____ The water in the river isn't drinkable.
4. _____ Water is expensive in some countries.
5. _____ Don't go in the water. It's not safe for swimming.

EXERCISE 11 ▸ Looking at grammar. (Chart 7-2)

Work in small groups. Choose the sentence (a. or b.) that best describes the given sentence.

1. Lions are magnificent animals.
   a. All lions are magnificent.
   b. Some lions are magnificent.

2. A lion is fierce.
   a. One lion is fierce.
   b. All lions are fierce.

3. I saw a lion at the zoo.
   a. I saw all lions.
   b. I saw one lion.

4. The lion that we saw looked fierce.
   a. One lion looked fierce.
   b. Several lions looked fierce.

5. A lion has a loud roar.
   a. All lions have a loud roar.
   b. One lion has a loud roar.

EXERCISE 12 ▸ Let's talk. (Chart 7-2)

Work in small groups. Follow the instructions.

1. Think about wild animals. Choose three and make general statements. Use **a/an**.
2. Think about inventions. Choose three and make general statements. Use the plural.
3. Think about the rich, the poor, and/or the elderly. Make three general statements.

EXERCISE 13 ▸ Game. (Chart 7-2)
Work in small groups. Complete each sentence with the correct word and an article if necessary. All of the sentences have generic meanings. The team that has the most correct answers wins.

apple	bridge	health	sentence	tennis player
adjectives	✓ food	island	sentences	tennis players
✓ bird	gold	islands	tennis	water

1. _____ A bird _____ has wings.
2. _____ Food _____ contains important vitamins and minerals.
3. _____ is composed of oxygen and hydrogen.
4. _____ is a sport.
5. _____ need to practice long hours.
6. _____ needs to have a strong arm.
7. _____ is a piece of land surrounded by water.
8. _____ are land surrounded by water.
9. _____ is an expensive metal.
10. _____ is a structure that is over a river.
11. _____ is of the most important things in life.
12. _____ describe nouns.
13. _____ usually contain a subject and a verb.
14. _____ needs punctuation.
15. _____ can be red, green, or yellow. Red is the most popular.

EXERCISE 14 ▸ Game: What am I? (Chart 7-2)
Work in pairs. Complete the sentences with *a, the,* or Ø. Then answer each question.

1. I am the biggest bird in the world. I eat just about anything I can reach, including _____ stones, _____ glass, and _____ keys. I can kill _____ person with one kick. What bird am I? _____

2. I produce _____ oxygen and keep the air clean. I provide _____ food and am _____ source of lifesaving medicines. _____ people can use products from me to build _____ houses and to make _____ paper and _____ cloth. What am I? _____

3. About 98% of me contains _____ water. My job is to protect a part of the human body from _____ dust, _____ dirt, and _____ smoke. I help relieve _____ stress. I also keep _____ dryness away. You will see me most often on _____ person's face. I am more common in some people than in others. What am I? _____

EXERCISE 15 ▸ Warm-up. (Chart 7-3)

Read the conversations. In which sentence does **excuse** mean "a specific one"?

1. A: I hope you have an excuse for your absence.
   B: I do.

2. A: Did you think the excuse Mike gave for his absence was believable?
   B: Not really.

7-3 Descriptive Information with Definite and Indefinite Nouns

(a) I'd like *a cup of coffee **from the café*** next door.	Descriptive information may or may not make a noun definite or specific. Study the examples.
(b) *The cup of coffee **I got*** was wonderful.	In (a), **from the café** next door does not make the *cup of coffee* definite. It is one cup of coffee among many.
(c) Do you have *a pen **with red ink***?	In (b), the speaker is referring to a specific cup of coffee — the cup that the speaker got.
(d) *The pen **in my bag*** is leaking.	In (c), the speaker is referring to one of many pens, not a specific one.
	In (d), the speaker is referring to a specific pen.
(e) *The manager **who trained me*** got a promotion.	Descriptive clauses may or may not make a noun specific.
(f) *A manager **who trains workers*** has a lot of responsibility.	(e) = a specific manager (f) = any manager (g) = any managers
(g) *Managers **who train workers*** have a lot of responsibility.	
(h) There is *a piece of the puzzle*.	In general, *there is* and *there are* introduce new topics. Therefore, the noun that follows is usually indefinite. However, in cases where the noun is already known, **the** is used.
(i) There is *the piece you were looking for*.	
(j) There are *Ø pieces on the floor*.	(h) and (j) = not specific (i) and (k) = specific
(k) There are *the pieces you were looking for*.	
(l) Jim works for *a real estate office*.	Adjectives do not automatically make nouns specific.
(m) I stopped at *the real estate office* after work.	(l) = one real estate office of many, not specific (m) = a specific or known real estate office

---

EXERCISE 16 ▸ Reading and grammar. (Chart 7-3)

Look at the nouns in blue. Which ones are specific?

Captive Dolphins

I was listening to the news and heard a sad story. It appears there is evidence that dolphins in captivity suffer. Dolphins that are free in nature live around 40 years. Captive dolphins live an average of 12 years. It is believed that in some cases, captive dolphins even commit suicide. Animal rights activists are working to bring more awareness to the situation of captive dolphins.

EXERCISE 17 ▸ Looking at grammar. (Chart 7-3)

Work with a partner. Look at the nouns in blue. Which ones have the meaning of "one of many?"

1. a. Have you had time to think about the new program that Jackie presented?
   b. William is developing a new computer program for his company.

2. a. Here's a ticket for the new movie.
   b. The ticket that James got for speeding is really expensive.

3. a. A detail that the witness told police was very helpful.
   b. The detail that the witness remembered was very helpful.

4. a. The sport that everyone in my class watches is soccer.
   b. My son is teaching himself a new sport: stand-up paddle boarding.

EXERCISE 18 ▸ Looking at grammar. (Chart 7-3)

Write *a, the,* or Ø according to the given information.

1. SPECIFIC: __the__ ball on the soccer field

   GENERAL: __a__ ball on the soccer field

   GENERAL: __Ø__ balls on the soccer field

2. SPECIFIC: _____ secretary at my school

   GENERAL: _____ secretary at my school

   GENERAL: _____ secretaries at my school

3. GENERAL: _____ fruit in the bowl

   SPECIFIC: _____ fruit in the bowl

4. SPECIFIC: _____ company that makes hats

   GENERAL: _____ company that makes hats

   GENERAL: _____ companies that make hats

5. SPECIFIC: _____ worker who is sick

   GENERAL: _____ workers who are sick

   GENERAL: _____ worker who is sick

   SPECIFIC: _____ workers who are sick

EXERCISE 19 ▸ Grammar and speaking. (Charts 7-1 → 7-3)

Complete the sentences with *a, an, the,* or Ø. Do you agree or disagree with the statements? Circle *yes* or *no*. Share some of your answers with the class. Capitalize as necessary.

1. Everyone needs to have _____ cell phone.   yes   no

2. If you have a cell phone, you don't need to wear _____ watch.   yes   no

3. _____ cell phones are replacing _____ watches.   yes   no

4. One key to _____ healthy life is daily physical exercise.   yes   no

5. I'd like to read a book about _____ life and art of Pablo Picasso.   yes   no

6. _____ jewelry looks good on both _____ men and _____ women.   yes   no

7. English is _____ easy language to learn.   yes   no

8. Listening to _____ loud rock music is fun.   yes   no

9. _____ music I like best is rock 'n roll.   yes   no

10. _____ vocabulary in this exercise is easy.   yes   no

11. _____ golf is _____ exciting sport.   yes   no

EXERCISE 20 ▸ Warm-up. (Chart 7-4)

Which of the two conversations do you think is correct?

1. A: A moon is very bright tonight.
   B: Stars are beautiful too.

2. A: The moon is very bright tonight.
   B: The stars are beautiful too.

7-4 General Guidelines for Article Usage

(a) *The sun* is bright today. Please hand this book to *the teacher*. Please open *the door*. Omar is in *the kitchen*.	GUIDELINE: Use ***the*** when you know or assume that your listener is familiar with and thinking about the same specific thing or person you are talking about.
(b) Yesterday I saw *some dogs*. *The dogs* were chasing *a cat*. *The cat* was chasing *a mouse*. *The mouse* ran into *a hole*. *The hole* was very small.	GUIDELINE: Use ***the*** for the second mention of an indefinite noun.* In (b): first mention = *some dogs, a cat, a mouse, a hole*; second mention = *the dogs, the cat, the mouse, the hole*

(c)   CORRECT: *Apples* are my favorite fruit.
    INCORRECT: ~~The~~ apples are my favorite fruit.
 	
(d)   CORRECT: *Gold* is a metal.
    INCORRECT: ~~The~~ gold is a metal.
	GUIDELINE: Do not use ***the*** with a plural count noun (e.g., *apples*) or a noncount noun (e.g., *gold*) when you are making a generalization.

(e)   CORRECT: (1) I drove *a car*. / I drove *the car*.
            (2) I drove *that car*.
            (3) I drove *his car*.
 	
    INCORRECT: I drove car.
            I drove a that car.
            I drove a his car.
	GUIDELINE: A singular count noun (e.g., *car*) is always preceded by:
	    (1) an article (*a/an* or ***the***); OR
	    (2) ***this/that***; OR
	    (3) a possessive adjective.

*****The*** is NOT used for the second mention of a generic noun. COMPARE:
   (1) *What color is **a banana** (generic noun)?* ***A banana*** (generic noun) *is yellow.*
   (2) *Joe offered me **a banana*** (indefinite noun) *or **an apple**. I chose **the banana*** (definite noun).

EXERCISE 21 ▸ Looking at grammar. (Chart 7-4)

Complete the conversations with ***a, an, the,*** or ***Ø***. Capitalize as necessary.

1. A: I have ___*an*___ idea. Let's go on ___*a*___ picnic Saturday.

   B: OK.

2. A: Did you have fun at ___*the*___ picnic yesterday?

   B: Sure did.

3. A: Where's my blue shirt?

   B: It's in _____ washing machine.

   A: That's OK. I can wear _____ different shirt.

4. A: I wish we had _____ washing machine.

   B: So do I. It would make _____ my life a lot easier.

5. A: Have you seen my boots?

   B: They're in _____ closet in _____ front hallway.

6. A: Wait! Please hold _____ elevator for me.

   B: Hurry. _____ door is closing.

EXERCISE 22 ▸ Grammar, listening, and speaking. (Chart 7-4)

Part I. Complete the conversation with *a*, *an*, or *the*. Capitalize as necessary. Then listen to the conversation and correct your answers.

A Mishap

A: What happened to your bike? $\underset{1}{\rule{2cm}{0.4pt}}$ front wheel is bent.

B: I ran into $\underset{2}{\rule{2cm}{0.4pt}}$ parked car when I swerved to avoid $\underset{3}{\rule{2cm}{0.4pt}}$ big pothole.

A: Did you damage $\underset{4}{\rule{2cm}{0.4pt}}$ car?

B: A little.

A: What did you do?

B: I left $\underset{5}{\rule{2cm}{0.4pt}}$ note for $\underset{6}{\rule{2cm}{0.4pt}}$ owner of $\underset{7}{\rule{2cm}{0.4pt}}$ car.

A: What did you write on $\underset{8}{\rule{2cm}{0.4pt}}$ note?

B: My name and phone number. I also wrote $\underset{9}{\rule{2cm}{0.4pt}}$ apology.

a pothole

Part II. Work with a partner. Choose one of the pictures and create a conversation following the model. Perform it for the class.

A: What happened to the _____? The _____.

B: I _____. Even worse, it doesn't belong to me. It _____.

A: What are you going to do? (Etc.)

EXERCISE 23 ▸ Check your knowledge. (Chart 7-4)

Correct the errors.

What do you like to buy at the grocery store?

1. I always like to have the rice in my cupboard. I eat it every day.

2. I buy the junk food. I know it's not healthy, but I buy it anyway.

3. My a favorite food is the fruit. I have apple or orange every day.

4. I'm on diet, so I don't really enjoy shopping right now!

5. Hmmm. That's interesting question. Probably anything with sugar.

   I have sweet tooth.

EXERCISE 24 ▸ Let's talk. (Chart 7-4)

Work with a partner. Put the sentences below in the correct order to make a story. Be prepared to explain your choices. (It may help to write out the sentences on strips of paper so you can move them around.)

A Brief Encounter with a Shark

_____ The shark didn't fight them and left.

_____ I recently read an interesting article about a long-distance swimmer and an amazing experience he had during a race.

_____ The man survived because of the dolphins' protection.

_____ The dolphins continued to swim with him and guided him for more than an hour.

_____ During the race, he looked down and saw a shark swimming under him.

_____ The man was swimming off the coast of New Zealand

_____ The dolphins made a protective circle around the swimmer.

_____ Fortunately, ten dolphins were swimming nearby.

_____ The area had sharks.

EXERCISE 25 ▸ Looking at grammar. (Chart 7-4)

Complete the sentences with *a, an, the,* or **Ø**. Capitalize as necessary.

1. a. ___Ø___ Caps can protect our heads from the sun.

   b. Bradley is wearing ___a___ baseball cap today.

   c. Bradley likes to wear _____ caps.

   d. _____ cap is _____ piece of clothing.

   e. _____ caps are _____ pieces of clothing.

   f. _____ brown cap on the chair belongs to Sam.

2. a. _____ beef is a kind of meat.

   b. _____ beef we had for dinner last night was excellent.

   c. Vegetarians do not eat _____ beef.

3. a. _____ engineer designed the Brooklyn Bridge in New York City.

   b. John Roebling is _____ name of _____ engineer who designed the Brooklyn Bridge. He died in 1869 from _____ infection.

   c. Roebling's son, Washington, took over the construction of _____ bridge after his father died.

   d. Washington became sick, and his wife, Emily, supervised the completion of _____ bridge. She had studied as _____ engineer.

EXERCISE 26 ▸ Listening. (Charts 7-4)

First, listen to this informal talk with your book closed. Then open your book and listen again. Complete the sentences with *a, an,* or *the*.

Computer Bugs

When there is _____ problem with _____ computer, we often say we
          1   2

have _____ "computer bug." Of course, it's not _____ real insect. It
        3   4

refers to _____ technical difficulty we are having. _____ expression
            5   6

actually goes back to Thomas Edison, who was _____ famous inventor.
                                                  7

When he was working on his first phonograph, he had a lot of problems. He

blamed _____ problems on _____ imaginary insect that had hidden inside _____ machine. He
          8   9   10

was quoted in _____ newspaper as saying there was "_____ bug" in his phonograph. This was in
                11   12

1889, and it is _____ first recorded use of _____ word *bug* in such _____ context.
                  13   14   15

EXERCISE 27 ▸ Interview. (Charts 7-3 and 7-4)

Complete the questions with *a, the,* or *Ø*. Then interview a different classmate for each item. The classmate needs to answer in complete sentences.

1. Do you have _____ siblings? What are _____ names of your brothers and/or sisters?

2. Do you have _____ pet? What is _____ name of your pet?

3. What is _____ your favorite restaurant? Where is _____ restaurant?

4. Think of _____ color. What is _____ color you first thought of?

5. Where is _____ fun place to go on weekends?

6. Imagine you are on _____ plane. Where are you sitting on _____ plane? Why?

7. What is _____ airline you have heard good things about? What have you heard?

8. What is _____ business you have heard complaints about? What are _____ complaints?

9. How is _____ weather in your hometown this time of year?

EXERCISE 28 ▸ Warm-up. (Chart 7-5)

Complete the sentences with words in the box. What do you notice about article usage?

the Gulf Islands	Vancouver Island
the Cascades	Mount Rainier
the Canadian Rockies	Mount Robson

1. _____ and

   _____ are west of Vancouver.

2. _____ are in the provinces of

   Alberta and British Columbia.

the Canadian Rockies

3. _____ is in the Canadian Rockies.

7-5 Using *The* or Ø with Titles and Geographic Names

(a) We met Ø *Mr. Harper*. I go to Ø *Doctor Shue*. Ø *President Costa* is the new leader.	**The** is NOT used with titled names. INCORRECT: We met ~~the~~ Mr. Harper.
(b) They traveled to Ø *Africa*. Ø *Australia* is the smallest continent.	**The** is NOT used with the names of continents. INCORRECT: They traveled to ~~the~~ Africa.
(c) He lives in Ø *Singapore*. Ø *Canada* is a vast country. (d) She's from **the** *United Arab Emirates*. **The** *Czech Republic* is in Europe. Have you ever visited **the** *Philippines*?	**The** is NOT used with the names of most countries. INCORRECT: He lives in ~~the~~ Singapore. **The** is used in the names of only a few countries, as in (d). Others: *the Netherlands, the United States, the Dominican Republic*.
(e) He works in Ø *Tokyo*. I recently traveled to Ø *Kuwait City*.	**The** is NOT used with the names of cities. INCORRECT: He works in ~~the~~ Tokyo.
(f) **The** *Amazon River* is long. They crossed **the** *Atlantic Ocean*. **The** *North Sea* is in Europe. (g) Ø *Lake Baikal* is the deepest lake in the world. Ø *Lake Tanganyika* is the second deepest lake.	**The** is used with the names of oceans, seas, rivers, and canals. **The** is NOT used with the names of lakes. INCORRECT: ~~the~~ Lake Baikal
(h) We hiked in **the** *Rocky Mountains*. **The** *Alps* are in Europe. (i) We climbed Ø *Mount Kilimanjaro*. Ø *Mount Everest* is in **the** *Himalayas*.	**The** is used with the names of mountain ranges. **The** is NOT used with the names of individual mountains. INCORRECT: ~~the~~ Mount Everest
(j) **The** *Hawaiian Islands* and **the** *Canary Islands* are popular with tourists. (k) Ari is from Ø *Tahiti*. (l) Have you ever been to Ø *Vancouver Island*?	**The** is used with groups of islands. **The** is NOT used with the names of individual islands. INCORRECT: ~~the~~ Vancouver Island

EXERCISE 29 ▸ Trivia Game. (Chart 7-5)

Work in teams. Choose the correct place in the box. Complete the sentences with *the* or Ø. The team with the most correct answers wins.

Amazon River	Brazil	Czech Republic	India	Lake Tanganyika
Antarctica	Canary Islands	French Alps	Italy	United Arab Emirates
Australia	Caspian Sea	Indonesia	Kuwait	Yangtze River

1. _____ border Switzerland, Italy, and France.

2. _____ is on the Indian Ocean.

3. _____ is the third longest river in the world.

4. Ten countries border _____.

5. _____ is the biggest salt-water lake in the world.

6. _____ shares a border with Germany

7. Dubai is part of _____.

8. _____ is the driest continent.

EXERCISE 30 ▸ Looking at grammar. (Chart 7-5)
Complete the sentences with **the** or **Ø**.

What part of the world would you like to travel to?

1. I've been looking at brochures of _____ Tahiti and _____ Hawaii.

2. _____ Himalayas are stunning. I'd love to see _____ Mount Everest.

3. _____ Lake Tahoe in California is beautiful, and there's so much to do there. I also want to see _____ Crater Lake in Oregon. It sits on top of a volcano.

4. I do a lot of traveling to major cities like _____ Paris, _____ Shanghai, and _____ Mumbai for business. I would like to see the beaches in _____ Thailand.

5. My husband dreams of sailing to various ports in _____ Mediterranean Sea.

6. I've never been to _____ Eastern Europe. _____ Hungary and _____ Poland interest me.

7. My Japanese teacher, _____ Dr. Kato, says _____ Kyoto and _____ Nara are two of the most scenic cities in _____ Japan.

Crater Lake

EXERCISE 31 ▸ Speaking and writing. (Chart 7-5)
Work in groups or individually. Choose a location you think people would like to visit. Create a brochure for it, using the brochure about Seattle as an example. Include the following information:

- a list of points of interest
- some area facts
- a short description of a place to visit (5–7 sentence paragraph)

Interesting facts:

Seattle is home to Amazon® and Starbucks™.

Boeing® airplanes are built in and around Seattle.

Microsoft® is across the lake from Seattle.

Not to be missed:

Take a side trip to magnificent Mount Rainier. There are tour buses from Seattle, or you can rent a car. It's about a three-hour trip one way. Mount Rainier is the tallest mountain in the Cascades. From the Paradise Visitor Center, you'll have breathtaking views of old-growth forests and wildflower meadows. There are spectacular hikes in every direction. Mount Rainier is a not-to-be-missed destination!

Visit Seattle!

So much to do!

Space Needle ■ Great Wheel ■ Pike Place Market ■ Museum of Flight ■ Downtown Waterfront ■ Experience Music Project ■ Chihuly Garden and Glass ■ International District

EXERCISE 32 ▸ Reading and grammar. (Chapter 7 Review)
Part I. Read the passage.

Do you know these words?
- *freak*
- *petroleum*
- *molecule*
- *ingest*
- *human food chain*
- *toxic*
- *harm*
- *litter*
- *uphill battle*

TOYS IN THE SEA

In 1997, a container ship was traveling from Holland to New York. As it passed the British coastline, a freak wave hit the boat. Sixty-two containers went crashing into the Atlantic Ocean. Inside those containers were LEGO® building bricks, a very popular children's toy. Not just a few went to the bottom of the sea, but millions — 4,756,950 pieces to be exact. Since that time, they have been washing up on beaches around the world.

The BBC has put together a map of the countries and cities where pieces have been found. Some have traveled as far as Australia. Children and collectors have been happy to find them, but they are a problem for wildlife. They are very small, and birds and fish have eaten them.

Another problem is that petroleum-based plastic never goes away. It can degrade, or get smaller and smaller, until it's the size of a molecule, but it never disappears. It's still in the water for sea life and birds to ingest. Eventually it reaches the human food chain. Plastic also releases toxic chemicals as it breaks down, and these chemicals harm sea life.

People are more aware of the problem, and volunteer groups have formed to pick up the pieces along with other plastic litter. However, they face an uphill battle with so much plastic in the oceans and so many little floating pieces.

a container ship

Part II. Answer the questions in complete sentences. Pay special attention to article usage in your sentences.

1. Where did the voyage begin?
2. What was the ship's destination?
3. What caused problems for the boat?
4. What happened to 62 containers?
5. What was inside the containers?
6. Where have people found the plastic pieces?
7. What problems are plastic pieces causing?
8. How small does the plastic become?
9. Why is plastic bad for sea life?
10. Will it be easy to pick up all the plastic litter?

EXERCISE 33 ▸ Check your knowledge. (Chapter 7 Review)
Correct the errors in article usage.

1. ~~The~~ Bali is ∧ very interesting island.
2. I want to live in warm place after I graduate from college.
3. When I was high school student, I took my first airplane ride overseas.
4. Seoul is capital city of South Korea.
5. I had very strange experience at a party last night.
6. Is it good idea to put plastic in microwave oven?

7. At the store, salesperson ignored me. I bought my clothes elsewhere.

8. What are some differences between the men and the women?

9. Is cost of living very high in your country?

10. I need to tell you about very important problem in society today.

11. Photos you took are a very beautiful.

12. The orange juice is on sale at the store.

13. Everyone seeks the happiness in the life.

EXERCISE 34 ▶ Reading, grammar, speaking, and writing. (Chapter 7)
Part I. Read the blog entry by author Stacy Hagen. Look at the words in blue. Work with a partner and explain the article usage (or lack of an article) for each.

 BlueBookBlog An "Aha" Moment in Language Learning

When I was a college student, I went to Austria for a year to study German. I had studied German for two years at a university, but I wanted to learn the language in more authentic surroundings. I was a shy learner at first because my spoken German wasn't very strong. There was a technique I found especially helpful in those early days. I listened to the news on the radio in the morning. Usually I listened for an hour a day while I was doing other things such as getting ready in the morning or cleaning. I didn't listen carefully, and sometimes I just had it on as background noise. But I always had on news or talk radio, not music.

People on the news use a lot of passive sentences. I had studied a lot of complicated German grammar in college, and the passive was especially confusing to me. I really didn't understand the rules, so it wasn't part of my spoken German. But one morning I woke up after about three months, and I knew the passive! I could use all of the forms effortlessly.

This was my "aha" moment. I realized that I had been learning even when I hadn't been studying. The rules I had learned in college helped me, but listening to the radio turned that knowledge into usage. And the radio was an especially effective way to learn because it required listening. There were no clues from the speaker's face or actions to help me. All of this was a powerful lesson for me.

Have you found some especially helpful techniques for learning English? Have you had an "aha" moment?

Part II. Discuss these questions in small groups. Then write about your own experiences as a second language learner.

1. How much English do you speak and read outside the classroom?
2. Is using English in class sufficient for you to meet your language-learning goals?
3. What are some good ways to practice English outside the classroom?
4. Do you avoid certain situations if you have to speak English? For example, speaking on the phone? Attending a party? Participating in class discussion?
5. Are you afraid of making mistakes when you speak? Everyone who is learning a second language makes mistakes. It's part of the process. Do mistakes matter?
6. Are there aspects of English grammar that are especially hard for you?

7. Think about your language-learning experience. What techniques have you found especially helpful for learning English?

8. Have you had an "aha" moment yet while learning English?

WRITING TIP

One way to organize your writing is to begin with more general information. As your writing progresses, give more detailed information. For example, you can begin by describing the type of language learner you are, overall. Then choose one or two specific problems you are having. Give details about these problems. End by describing how you deal with or possibly have solved these problems.

Part III. Edit your writing.

1. Use this list to check your article usage:

   Is the noun specific?

   If *yes*: Use ***the*** for singular count nouns.   If *no*: Use ***a/an*** for singular count nouns.

   Use ***the*** for plural count nouns.   Use **Ø** for plural count nouns.

   Use ***the*** for noncount nouns.   Use **Ø** for noncount nouns.

   Exception: Are you making a general statement about an invention or instrument? Use ***the*** with the singular count form of the noun.

2. Underline any titles and place names in your writing. Review Chart 7-5 for correct use of titles and place names.

3. Check for correct spelling (use a dictionary or spell-check)

▨▨■■■ Go to MyEnglishLab for Self-Study: Gerunds and Infinitives 7

CHAPTER 8 · Pronouns

Write "C" if a sentence has the correct pronoun usage and agreement and "I" for incorrect.
Check your answers below. After you complete each chart listed, make any necessary corrections.

1. _____ The manager asked for a meeting with Bill and I. (8-1)

2. _____ That is your order. This one is ours. (8-1)

3. _____ I enjoy dessert after dinner. Do you enjoy too? (8-1)

4. _____ A student needs to check their work carefully. (8-2)

5. _____ The baseball team is going to win the championship. It has been working hard all year.
   (8-3)

6. _____ Why are you staring at yourself in the mirror? (8-4)

7. _____ How does one apply for early admissions to college? (8-5)

8. _____ Let me tell you other reason I need to borrow some money. (8-6)

9. _____ These vegetables are fresh. The others have been frozen. (8-6)

10. _____ Michael and Reina would rather work with each other on the various projects. (8-7)

11. _____ I'd prefer that you don't tell anyone. In another words, I would like to keep this secret.
    (8-7)

Incorrect sentences: 1, 3, 4, 8, 11

EXERCISE 1 ▸ Warm-up. (Chart 8-1)

Decide if the words in blue are subject or object pronouns. Write "S" for subject and "O" for object.

A: _____ I just finished cleaning. Look at all these remotes.

_____ They were everywhere.

B: _____ That's because the kids never put them away.

A: _____ What about this one? Do we ever use it?

B: _____ I have no idea. I've never seen it before.

8-1 Pronouns and Possessive Adjectives

	Subject Pronoun	Object Pronoun	Possessive Pronoun	Possessive Adjective
SINGULAR	*I* *you* *she, he, it*	*me* *you* *her, him, it*	*mine* *yours* *hers, his, —*	*my* (name) *your* (name) *her, his, its* (name)
PLURAL	*we* *you* *they*	*us* *you* *them*	*ours* *yours* *theirs*	*our* (names) *your* (names) *their* (names)

(a) I read *a book*. *It* was good.	A PRONOUN is used in place of a noun. The noun it refers to is called the "antecedent." In (a): The pronoun *it* refers to the antecedent noun **book**. A singular pronoun is used to refer to a singular noun, as in (a). A plural pronoun is used to refer to a plural noun, as in (b).
(b) I read *some books*. *They* were good.	
(c) *I* like tea. Do *you* like it too?	Sometimes the antecedent noun is understood, not explicitly stated. In (c): *I* refers to the speaker, and *you* refers to the person the speaker is talking to. Note that the direct object cannot be omitted. *INCORRECT:* Do you like too?
(d) John has a car. *He drives* to work. ^S	SUBJECT PRONOUNS are used as subjects of sentences, as *he* in (d).
(e) Bill works in my office. I *know him* well. (f) Will you talk to Bill and *me* about it?	OBJECT PRONOUNS are used as the objects of verbs, as *him* in (e), or as the objects of prepositions, as *me* in (f). *INCORRECT:* talk to Bill and I
(g) That book is *hers.* *Yours* is over there. (h) *INCORRECT:* That book is ~~her's~~. ~~Your's~~ is over there.	POSSESSIVE PRONOUNS stand alone; they are not followed immediately by a noun, as in (g). Possessive pronouns DO NOT take apostrophes, as in (h). (See Chart 6-3, p. 101, for the use of apostrophes with possessive nouns.)
(i) *Her* book is here. *Your* book is over there.	POSSESSIVE ADJECTIVES are followed immediately by a noun; they do not stand alone.
(j) A bird uses *its* wings to fly. (k) *INCORRECT:* A bird uses ~~it's~~ wings to fly. (l) *It's* cold today. (m) The Harbor Inn is my favorite old hotel. *It's been* in business since 1933.	COMPARE: **Its** has NO APOSTROPHE when it is used as a possessive adjective, as in (j). **It's** has an apostrophe when it is used as a contraction of *it is*, as in (l), or *it has* when **has** is part of the present perfect tense, as in (m). NOTE: **It's** vs. **its** is a common source of error for writers of English.

EXERCISE 2 ▸ Looking at grammar. (Chart 8-1)

Draw arrows from the pronouns to their antecedents.

What's new with the family?

1. Robert just received a promotion. He is now assistant manager of the company.

2. Nancy and Thomas have adopted an infant daughter. They have had her for a month.

3. Grandma's cat ran away. She has been sad ever since. I would like to get her a new one, but she says no one can replace him.

4. Emil is applying to several colleges. Because he had high test scores, they are offering him scholarships.

5. Mom's eye surgery was successful. It was just a week ago, but she is reading again.

EXERCISE 3 ▸ Looking at grammar. (Chart 8-1)

Choose the correct completions.

At a Party

1. Let me introduce you to my parents. I've wanted to introduce you to   they / them   for some time.

2. There's Rachel. Come with me. I need to tell both you and   she / her   something.

3. Just between you and   I / me,   I think Sam is in danger of losing his job.

4. Me and Ella / Ella and I   are good friends. Ella needs to know the truth about my meeting with Sam too. I'm going to tell you and   she / her   exactly what happened.

5. Do you need a ride home? Do you want to come with my brother and   I / me?

EXERCISE 4 ▸ Looking at grammar. (Chart 8-1)

Complete the sentences with pronouns/possessive adjectives for the words in blue.

SITUATION 1: There's Sarah.

1. I need to go talk to ___*her*___.

2. _____ and I have been friends since high school.

3. I went to elementary school with _____ brother and _____.

4. _____ parents are best friends with my parents.

5. _____ is getting married next month. Another friend and I are taking _____ on a short trip before _____ wedding.

6. Being with _____ is a lot of fun. We laugh a lot.

SITUATION 2: I'm not feeling well. I think I'd better stay home today.

7. My friends and _____ were planning to volunteer at our local food bank* today.

8. The food bank often asks my friends and _____ to help them with various projects.

---

*food bank = a place that receives donations of food and gives them away to needy people

9. But my friends will have to go without _____ .

10. I'd better call _____ friend Sami to tell him I can't come today.

11. Could I use your cell phone? I forgot _____ .

EXERCISE 5 ▸ Looking at grammar. (Chart 8-1)
Choose the correct completions.

At the Lost-and-Found

1. This is (my)/ mine umbrella. Your /(Yours) is in the box.
2. No, my / mine umbrella is black. That isn't my / mine.
3. Are these Mom's keys? The key ring looks like her / hers, but I don't remember so many keys.
4. I've lost my wallet. It's red and has a hole in it / its.

In the Neighborhood

5. Our / Ours house is almost the same as our / ours neighbor's house. The only difference is that our / ours is gray and their / theirs is beige.
6. Lisa and Michael each have our / their own vegetable garden. Lisa grows tomatoes and peas in her / hers and Michael grows potatoes and carrots in his / its.
7. We have fruit trees in our / ours yard. It / They produce a lot of apples in the fall. We pick it / them in September and make juice from it / them.
8. There are no crosswalks on our / ours streets. It's dangerous for the kids. Some parents walk with they / them to the bus stop.

EXERCISE 6 ▸ Let's talk. (Chart 8-1)
Work with a partner. Complete the conversations with the *italicized* words. Then choose one conversation from each pair to practice. Perform the conversations in small groups without looking at your book.

1. *he's / his / its / it's / mine / my / Ø*

   a. A: My phone bill is really expensive.

   B: I know. _____ is really high too. I'd like to find a cheaper company.

   A: Me too, but _____ difficult.

   b. A: Is this your phone?

   B: No, _____ has a blue case.

   A: Maybe this belongs to Tom.

   B: No, _____ is black.

2. *it / it's / our / ours / them / they're / Ø*

   a. A: Are these the appetizers you and Jae brought?

      B: No, _____ are in the fridge.

      A: Do you want me to take _____ out?

      B: Sure.

   b. A: Your chicken dish is delicious! Is it your own recipe?

      B: No, I got _____ off the Internet. _____ really easy to make.

      A: Our dorm doesn't have a kitchen, so I'm not able to cook much.

      B: We're lucky that _____ does. People on _____ floor cook a lot.

EXERCISE 7 ▶ Looking at grammar. (Chart 8-1)

Choose <u>all</u> the correct answers.

1. A: Do you like living here?
   B: (a.) Yes, I like it a lot.
     b. Yes, I like a lot.
     (c.) Yes, I do.

2. A: Are you enjoying your new job?
   B: a. Yes, I'm enjoying.
     b. Yes, I am.
     c. Yes, I'm enjoying it.

3. A: Nice car! Is it new?
   B: a. Yes, I just got it.
     b. Yes, I just got.
     c. Yes, it is.

4. A: I haven't seen your girlfriend lately.
   B: a. Unfortunately, I haven't seen either.
     b. Unfortunately, I haven't either.
     c. Unfortunately, I haven't seen her either.

5. A: Have you met the new neighbors?
   B: a. Yes, I have. They seem nice.
     b. Yes, I have met them. They seem nice.
     c. Yes, I have met. They seem nice.

6. A: There's Joe over there. You know him, don't you?
   B: a. Sure, I know him.
     b. Sure, I know.
     c. Sure I do.

EXERCISE 8 ▶ Looking at grammar. (Chart 8-1)

Complete the sentences with *its* or *it's*.

A: Beautiful horse. What's _____ name?

B: Thunder.

A: Oh. Is that because _____ noisy?

B: No, _____ named after _____ father, whose name was Lightning.

A: _____ very calm.

B: No, not this horse! _____ anything but calm.

EXERCISE 9 ▶ Looking at grammar. (Chart 8-1)

Complete the sentences with *it, its, it's, they,* or *them*.

1. There is an interesting bird in Florida called an anhinga. _____ a fish eater.

2. _____ dives into the water and spears _____ prey on _____ long, sharp bill.

3. Then _____ tosses the fish into the air, catches _____ in mid-air, and swallows _____ headfirst.

4. _____ interesting to watch these birds in action. I enjoy watching _____ a lot.

EXERCISE 10 ▶ Listening. (Chart 8-1)

Pronouns can be hard to hear in spoken English because they are usually unstressed. Additionally, if the pronoun begins with "h," the /h/ sound is often dropped in rapid, relaxed speech. Complete each conversation with the words you hear.

1. Where's Kim?

   A: I don't know. I haven't seen _____ this morning.

   B: I think _____ in the restroom.

   C: I'm looking for _____ too.

   D: Ask _____ assistant. He'll know.

   E: Have you tried looking in _____ office? I know _____ not there much, but maybe _____ surprise you.

2. The Nelsons are giving their daughter a motorcycle for graduation.

   A: Hmmm. _____ like motorcycles that much?

   B: Really? _____ a motorcycle rider?

   C: That's an odd gift. I wonder what _____ were thinking.

   D: That's what the Smiths gave _____ son. I think _____ already had an accident.

   E: I'm not a fan of motorcycles. Cars just don't see _____ in traffic.

   F: I think _____ a wonderful gift! I've had _____ for years, and _____ been great.

EXERCISE 11 ▶ Warm-up. (Chart 8-2)

Pretend you are writing an article about seat belts. Which sentence would you choose to include? Why? NOTE: All the sentences are grammatically correct.

1. A driver needs to put on his seat belt as soon as he gets in his car.
2. A driver needs to put on her seat belt as soon as she gets in her car.
3. A driver needs to put on his or her seat belt as soon as he or she gets in his or her car.
4. Drivers need to put on their seat belts as soon as they get in their cars.

8-2 Agreement with Generic Nouns and Indefinite Pronouns

(a) *A student* walked into the room. *She* was looking for the teacher. (b) *A student* walked into the room. *He* was looking for the teacher.	In (a) and (b): The pronouns refer to particular individuals whose gender is known. The nouns are not generic.
(c) *A student* needs to complete *his* assignments on time. (d) *A student* needs to complete *his or her* assignments on time. (e) *A student* needs to complete *her* assignments on time.	A GENERIC NOUN is not specific. It does not refer to a particular person or thing. In (c): *A student* is a generic noun; it refers to *anyone who is a student.* With a generic noun, a singular masculine possessive adjective has been used traditionally, but many English speakers now use masculine and/or feminine possessive adjectives to refer to a singular generic noun, as in (d) and (e).
(f) *Students* need to complete *their* assignments on time.	Problems with choosing masculine and/or feminine possessive adjectives can often be avoided by using a plural rather than a singular generic noun, as in (f).

Indefinite pronouns

everyone	someone	anyone	no one*
everybody	somebody	anybody	nobody
everything	something	anything	nothing

(g) *Somebody* left *his* book on the desk. (h) *Everyone* has *his or her* own ideas.	In formal English, the use of a singular possessive adjective to refer to an INDEFINITE PRONOUN is considered to be grammatically correct, as in (g) and (h).
(i) INFORMAL: *Somebody* left *their* book on the desk. *Everyone* has *their* own ideas.	In everyday, informal English (and sometimes even in more formal English), a plural possessive adjective is usually used to refer to an indefinite pronoun, as in (i).

* *No one* can also be written with a hyphen in British English: *No-one* heard me.

EXERCISE 12 ▶ Looking at grammar. (Chart 8-2)

Work with a partner. Change the sentences by using plural instead of singular generic nouns where possible. Change pronouns and verbs as necessary. Discuss the advantages of using plural rather than singular generic nouns.

1. When a student wants to study, he or she should find a quiet place.
   → *When students want to study, they should find a quiet place.*

2. I talked to a student in my chemistry class. I asked to borrow her notes from the class I missed. She kindly gave them to me. (*no change*)

3. Each student in Biology 101 has to spend three hours per week in the laboratory, where he or she does various experiments with his or her lab partners.

4. We heard a really interesting lecture in our government class yesterday. The guest speaker discussed her experiences as a judge.

5. She said a citizen has two primary responsibilities. He should vote in every election, and he should serve willingly on juries.

EXERCISE 13 ▸ Looking at grammar. (Chart 8-2)

Work with a partner. Complete each sentence with the pronoun(s) that seem(s) most appropriate for the situation. Choose the correct verb in blue. Discuss formal vs. informal pronoun usage.

1. *One classmate to another:* Look. Somebody left ____<u>*their*</u>*____ book on my desk. Is it yours?

2. *One friend to another:* Of course you can learn to dance! Anyone can learn how to dance

   if _____ wants / want to.

3. *Business textbook:* An effective manager must be able to motivate _____ employees.

4. *One roommate to another:* If anyone asks where I am, tell _____ you don't know. I want to keep my meeting with Jim a secret.

5. *Son to his mother:* Gosh, Mom, everyone who came to the class picnic was supposed to

   bring _____ own food. I didn't know that. I'm really hungry!

6. *A university lecture:* I will end my lecture today by saying that I believe a teacher needs to

   work in partnership with _____ students.

7. *A magazine article:* People do not always see things the same way. Each person has

   _____ own way of understanding a situation.

EXERCISE 14 ▸ Warm-up. (Chart 8-3)

All the pronouns in blue refer to the noun **team**. Discuss how the pronouns in the two sentences are different. NOTE: Both sentences are correct.

1. When the soccer team won in the closing moments of the game, they ran to the player who had scored the winning goal and lifted him on their shoulders.
2. A basketball team is relatively small. It doesn't have as many members as a baseball team.

8-3 Personal Pronouns: Agreement with Collective Nouns	
(a) My *family* is large. *It* is composed of nine members.	COLLECTIVE NOUNS can be singular or plural. When the speaker wants to refer to a single impersonal unit, a singular pronoun can be used, as in (a).
(b) My *family* is loving and supportive. *They* are always ready to help me. I love *them* very much.	When the speaker wants to refer to the individual members, a plural pronoun can be used for the pronoun, as in (b).*
(c) The *committee* meets once a month. *It* doesn't have a lot of business to take care of. OR *They* don't have a lot of business to take care of.	Choosing a singular or plural pronoun is partly a matter of judgment. In (c), both are possible.

*See Chart 5-3, p. 82, for an explanation of collective nouns.

EXERCISE 15 ▸ Looking at grammar. (Chart 8-3)

Part I. Look at the pronouns in blue in each pair. Which one refers to the individual members of the group? Which one refers to the group as a whole?

1. a. I have a wonderful family. I love them very much, and they love me.
   b. I looked up some information about the average American family. I found out that it consists of 2.3 children.

---

*also possible: *his; his or her; her or his*

2. a. The crowd at the soccer game was huge. It exceeded 100,000 people.

   b. The crowd became more and more excited as the premier's motorcade approached. They began to shout and wave flags in the air.

Part II. Complete the sentences with pronouns. Choose the correct verb in blue. Explain your choices.

1. a. A jury has a great deal of power. _____ decides a person's guilt or innocence.

   b. The jury looked very serious when _____ came back into the courtroom. _____ did not make eye-contact with the defendant.

2. a. The class is planning a party for the last day of school. _____ is / are going to bring many different kinds of food and invite some of their friends to celebrate with _____.

   b. The class is too small. _____ only has / have eight students.

3. a. The faculty wants a bigger lunch room. _____ sits / sit around one small table.

   b. The faculty has a weekly meeting to review curriculum. _____ makes / make ongoing changes.

EXERCISE 16 ▸ Warm-up. (Chart 8-4)

Complete each sentence. Use *herself*, *himself*, or *themselves*.

1. The basketball coach told the players to believe in _____.

2. After the team captain made the winning basket, the coach told her to be proud of _____.

3. The coach plays basketball as a hobby. He's 60 and proud of _____ for staying in good shape.

8-4 Reflexive Pronouns

Singular	Plural
myself *yourself* *herself, himself, itself, oneself*	*ourselves* *yourselves* *themselves*
(a) Larry was in the theater. *I saw him.* I talked *to him.*	Compare (a) and (b): Usually an object pronoun is used as the object of a verb or preposition, as *him* in (a). (See Chart 8-1.)
(b) *I saw myself* in the mirror. *I* looked *at myself* for a long time. (c) INCORRECT: I saw ~~me~~ in the mirror.	A reflexive pronoun is used as the object of a verb or preposition when the subject of the sentence and the object are the same person, as in (b).* *I* and *myself* are the same person.
— Did someone email the report to Mr. Lee? — Yes. — Are you sure? (d) — Yes. *I myself* emailed the report to him. (e) — *I* emailed the report to him *myself.*	Reflexive pronouns are also used for emphasis. In (d): The speaker would say "I myself" strongly, with emphasis. The emphatic reflexive pronoun can immediately follow a noun or pronoun, as in (d), or come at the end of the clause, as in (e).
(f) Anna lives *by herself*.	The expression *by* + *a reflexive pronoun* means "alone."

*Sometimes an object pronoun is used after a preposition even when the subject and object pronoun are the same person. Examples: *I took my books with **me**. **Bob** brought his books with **him**. I looked around **me**. **She** kept her son close to **her**.*

EXERCISE 17 ▸ Grammar and speaking. (Chart 8-4)

Part I. Complete the sentences with appropriate reflexive pronouns.

Selfies

1. I took a picture of _____ *myself* _____.

2. Rosa took a picture of _____.

3. Yusef took a picture of _____.

4. The children took pictures of _____.

5. We took a picture of _____.

6. Olga, you took a picture of _____, didn't you?

7. All of you took pictures of _____, didn't you?

8. When one takes a picture of _____, it is called a selfie.

Part II. Look at the statements about selfies. Do you agree or disagree with any of the statements? Work in pairs, small groups, or as a class.

1. When you take a lot of pictures of yourself, it means you like yourself.
2. People who take a lot of pictures of themselves like themselves too much.
3. In my culture, we don't take pictures of ourselves. It's not appropriate.
4. My parents think it's weird that I like to take so many pictures of myself.
5. They say if you need to take a lot of pictures of yourself, you need a lot of attention.
6. It's healthy to like yourself. There's nothing wrong with taking pictures of yourself.
7. I think women take more pictures of themselves than men.

EXERCISE 18 ▸ Grammar and speaking. (Chart 8-4)

Part I. Complete the conversations with appropriate reflexive pronouns.

1. A: Tommy told a lie. He felt really bad about it.

   B: I know. He was ashamed of _____ *himself* _____.

2. A: William cut _____ badly while he was chopping down a tree. And then

   he drove _____ to the hospital!

   B: My mom did that once after she accidentally cut _____ with a knife.

3. A: I see employees at your company voted to give _____ raises instead of more vacation time.

   B: Yes, but I wanted vacation time. I _____ voted for that.

4. A: Mr. and Mrs. Grayson live by _____.

   B: I know. They're very independent for a couple in their late 90s.

5. A: Should I marry Steve?

   B: No one can make that decision for you, Ann. Only you _____ can make such an important decision about your own life.

6. A: I envy Jacob. He's self-employed. He loves working for _____.

   B: Yeah. I'd like to work for _____ too.

7. A: Jason, you need to eat better and get more exercise. You should take better care

of _____. Your dad takes care of _____, and I take

care of _____. Your dad and I are healthy because we take good care

of _____. People who take care of _____ have a better chance

of staying healthy than those who don't.

B: OK, Mom. Are you done with your speech?

Part II. Work with a partner. Write a short conversation that has one or more reflexive pronouns. Use one of the conversations in Part I as a model. Perform it for the class.

EXERCISE 19 ▶ Reading, grammar, and speaking. (Chart 8-4)

Part I. Read the web article about Amy Cuddy's research on body language. Then <u>underline</u> the reflexive pronouns. Draw an arrow to each antecedent.

Do you know these words?
- stance
- hunch over
- expand
- hormone
- dominant
- measurable

Power Stances

Body language has a powerful influence on how other people see us. But did you know it also affects the way we see ourselves? Amy Cuddy, a Business School professor at Harvard, gave a TED* talk on power stances titled, "Your Body Language Shapes Who You Are." It was so popular that the video has since gone viral.

Cuddy said that when people feel weak, they close up their bodies. They may hunch over or close their arms around themselves. They are trying to avoid taking up space. This is a low-power position.

People who feel strong do the opposite. They try to expand their space. They raise their arms the way runners do when they win a race. They lean back in their chairs and put their hands behind their heads. These are high-power stances. High-power stances project confidence. With these postures, people send the message that they have confidence in themselves.

According to Cuddy, high-power stances affect the chemicals in our bodies. Just holding a power stance for two minutes increases testosterone, a hormone that makes us feel dominant, and decreases cortisol, a hormone that causes stress. It's not just that we appear stronger to others; there are measurable changes in our body chemistry, and we feel differently about ourselves.

*TED = Technology, Education, and Design

Part II. Discuss these questions in small groups.

1. What basic power stances are discussed in the reading?
2. Are these power stances acceptable in your culture?
3. What do people in your culture do to show power?
4. Find Cuddy's TED talk online, and watch it. What do you think of her findings?

EXERCISE 20 ▸ Looking at grammar. (Chart 8-4)

Complete each sentence with a word or expression in the box and an appropriate reflexive pronoun. Use each word/expression only one time.

angry at	feeling sorry for	laugh at	proud of
enjoy	introduced	pat	talking to
entertained	killed	promised	✓ taught

1. Karen Williams never took piano lessons. She _____*taught herself*_____ how to play.

2. Did Roberto have a good time at the party? Did he _____?

3. All of you did a good job. You should be _____.

4. You did a good job, Barbara. You should _____ on the back.

5. A man down the street committed suicide. We were shocked that he had _____

_____.

6. The children played very well without adult supervision. They _____

_____ by playing school.

7. I had always wanted to meet Hong Tran. When I saw her at a party last night, I walked

over and _____ to her.

8. Nothing good ever comes from self-pity. You should stop _____

_____, George, and start doing something to solve your problems.

9. People might think you're a little crazy, but _____ is

one way to practice using English.

10. Humor can ease the problems we encounter in life. Sometimes we have to be able to

_____.

11. Carol made several careless mistakes at work last week, and her boss is getting impatient with

her. Carol has _____ to do better work in the future.

12. Yesterday Fred's car ran out of gas. He had

to walk a long way to a gas station. He is still

_____ for forgetting

to fill the tank.

EXERCISE 21 ▸ Listening. (Chart 8-4)
Listen to the beginning of each sentence. Choose the correct completion.

Example: You will hear: We wanted to save money, so we painted our apartment _____ .
You will circle: myself   (ourselves)   yourselves

1. himself	itself	yourself
2. yourself	myself	ourselves
3. ourselves	themselves	myself
4. themselves	himself	herself
5. ourselves	yourselves	themselves
6. himself	herself	myself

EXERCISE 22 ▸ Warm-up. (Chart 8-5)
Read the conversation. Discuss the pronouns in blue. Who or what do they refer to?

MRS. COOK: Jack Woods bought a used car. Did you hear?
MR. COOK: Yes, I heard all about his car. He paid next to nothing for it.
MRS. COOK: Yes, and now it doesn't run.
MR. COOK: Well, as they say, you get what you pay for.
MRS. COOK: That's right. One gets what one pays for.

8-5 Using *You*, *One*, and *They* as Impersonal Pronouns

(a) *One* should always be polite. (b) How does *one* get to Fifth Avenue from here? (c) *You* should always be polite. (d) How do *you* get to Fifth Avenue from here?	In (a) and (b): *One* means "any person, people in general." In (c) and (d): *You* means "any person, people in general." *One* is much more formal than *you*. Impersonal *you*, rather than *one*, is used more frequently in everyday English. Impersonal *you* is not acceptable in academic writing.
(e) Iowa is an agricultural state. *They* grow a lot of corn there.	*They* is used as an impersonal pronoun in spoken or very informal English to mean "people in general" or "an undefined group of people." Often the antecedent is implied rather than stated. In (e): *They* = farmers in Iowa
(f) Tommy, *we* do not chew with our mouths open.	When talking to children about rules or behavior, parents often use *we*. In (f): *we* = people in general

EXERCISE 23 ▸ Looking at grammar. (Chart 8-5)
Discuss the meanings of the pronouns in *italics*.

1. a. Kyung took his dad's advice and decided to quit his corporate job and go to art school.
    I think *you* need to follow *your* dreams.
      → *The pronouns refer to everyone, anyone, people in general, all of us.*
   b. Jake, if *you* really want my advice, I think *you* should find a new job.
      → *The pronouns refer to Jake specifically.*

2. a. Wool requires special care. If *you* wash wool in hot water, it will shrink. *You* shouldn't throw a wool sweater into a washing machine with *your* cottons.
   b. Alex, I told *you* not to wash *your* sweater in hot water. Now look at it. It's ruined!
   c. Sonya, let's make a deal. If *you* wash the clothes, I'll fold them.

3. a. Memory is selective. *They* say *you* remember only what *you* want to remember.
   b. If *you* ask two people to remember an experience they shared, they might tell *you* two different stories.

4. I've grown to dislike airplane travel. *They* never give *you* enough room for *your* legs. And if the person in front of *you* puts his seat back, *you* can barely move. *You* can't even reach down to pick up something from the floor.

EXERCISE 24 ▸ Let's talk. (Chart 8-5)
Discuss the meanings of these English sayings in pairs, in small groups, or as a class.

1. "You can't teach an old dog new tricks."
2. "You can't win them all."
3. "If you want a job well done, do it yourself."
4. "You can lead a horse to water, but you can't make it drink."

EXERCISE 25 ▸ Reading, writing, and speaking. (Chart 8-5)
Part I. A common problem in academic writing is switching between the pronouns **they** and **you**. Typically, an unskilled writer begins by talking about people in general by using **they**, and then switches to the impersonal and informal **you**. Read the following example from a student paper.

Do you know these words?
- impact
- addiction
- anxious
- interaction
- initiate
- extended
- isolated
- potentially
- monitor

The Negative Impact of Social Media on Children and Teens

Many parents have concerns about the impact of social media on their children. One danger is Internet addiction: kids want to have their phones or computers with them at all times. They become anxious if they can't answer an email or message immediately. They want to do their homework while they are chatting with friends. Teenagers say you can concentrate and still check social media. However, parents worry that their children need constant interaction and cannot handle quiet time.

Another problem is that social media takes away from in-person contact. Children and teenagers are at risk of interacting with screens more than they interact with one another. Texting and chatting online are not the same as actual conversation. You need to learn how to initiate and engage in extended conversations with people. Additionally, when you don't have much human contact, you can become isolated.

A third concern is that social media exposes children and teens to potentially inappropriate content. Parents can monitor their posts, but you can't control other people's posts. There's a good chance your child will see something before you even know about it.

Part II. It is clear that **you** in these paragraphs means "people in general." However, this usage of "you" in academic writing is not acceptable. Correct all the errors in pronoun usage.

Part III. In small groups, discuss the advantages and/or disadvantages of social media. Give your opinion. Then share some of the most common opinions from your group with the class.

EXERCISE 26 ▸ Warm-up. (Chart 8-6)

Match each sentence to the picture it describes.

1. Some of the crows are flying. The others are sitting on a fence. _____

2. Some of the crows are flying. Others are sitting on a fence. _____

A

B

8-6 Forms of *Other*

Singular

(a) One subject that interests me is math. *Another subject is* psychology. OR *Another is* psychology.

another = singular

Meaning in (a): one more in addition to or different from the one(s) already mentioned

ADJECTIVE FORM: *another subject is*

PRONOUN FORM: *another is*

(b) I'm going to take two electives next term. One is sociology. *The other elective is* psychology. OR *The other is* psychology

the other = singular

Meaning in (b): all that remains of a given number; the last one

ADJECTIVE FORM: *the other elective is*

PRONOUN FORM: *the other is*

Plural

(c) There are a lot of interesting movies this weekend. Some are comedies. *Other movies are* dramas. OR *Others are* dramas.

other(s) = plural

Meaning in (c): several more in addition to or different from the one(s) already mentioned

ADJECTIVE FORM: *other movies are*

PRONOUN FORM: *others are*

(d) I've found several movies to watch this weekend. Some are comedies. *The other movies are* dramas. OR *The others are* dramas.

the other(s) = plural

Meaning in (d): the rest; the last ones in a group

ADJECTIVE FORM: *the other movies are*

PRONOUN FORM: *the others are*

(e) I will be here for *another three years*.

(f) I need *another five dollars*.

(g) We drove *another ten miles*.

Another is used as an adjective with expressions of time, money, and distance even if these expressions contain plural nouns. *Another* means "an additional" in examples (e)–(g).

Summary of *Other/Another* Forms

	SINGULAR	PLURAL
ADJECTIVE	*another* book (is)	*other books* (are)
	the other book (is)	*the other books* (are)
PRONOUN	*another* (is)	*others* (are)
	the other (is)	*the others* (are)

EXERCISE 27 ▸ Looking at grammar. (Chart 8-6)
Complete the sentences with a form of *other*.

1. a. Look at your hand. You have five fingers. One is your thumb. _____*Another*_____ is your
   index finger. _____ is your middle finger. _____ finger is your
   ring finger. And _____ finger (the last of the five) is your little finger.

   b. Look at your hands. One is your right hand. _____ is your left hand.

2. a. I have two cell phone chargers. I keep one in the car and _____ next to
   my bed.

   b. I'd like to buy _____ one and leave it in the kitchen.

3. a. I just got three messages. One is from my father. _____ one is from my sister.
   _____ message is from my girlfriend.

   b. I sent Henry a response, but it came back. Does he have _____ email address?

4. a. Some people have red hair. _____
   have brown hair.

   b. Some people have red hair. _____
   people have brown hair.

   c. I have four children. One of them has red hair.
   _____ children have brown hair.

   d. I have four children. One of them has red hair.
   _____ have brown hair.

EXERCISE 28 ▸ Looking at grammar. (Chart 8-6)
Read each pair of sentences and answer the question that follows.

1. a. One North African country Helen plans to visit is Algeria. Another is Morocco.
   b. One North African country Alex plans to visit is Tunisia. The other is Algeria.
   QUESTION: Who is planning to visit more than two countries in North Africa?

2. a. Purple is one of Mai's favorite colors. The others she likes are blue and green.
   b. Purple is one of Elaine's favorite colors. Others she likes are blue and green.
   QUESTION: Who has only three favorite colors?

3. a. Kazuo took a cookie from the cookie jar and ate it. Then he took another one and ate it too.
   b. Susie took a cookie from the cookie jar and ate it. Then she took the other one and ate it too.
   QUESTION: Whose cookie jar had only two cookies?

4. a. Some of the men at the business meeting on Thursday wore dark blue suits. Others wore
   black suits.
   b. Some of the men at the business meeting on Friday wore dark blue suits. The others wore
   black suits.
   QUESTION: Mr. Anton wore a gray suit to the business meeting. Which day did he attend the
   meeting, Thursday or Friday?

EXERCISE 29 ▸ Let's talk. (Chart 8-6)

Work with a partner. Take turns completing the sentences with an appropriate form of *other*.

PARTNER A	PARTNER B
1. I speak two languages. One is …	1. I have two books. One is …
2. I speak three languages. One is …	2. Hawaii is a popular tourist destination. Italy is …
3. I lost my textbook, so I had to buy …	3. Some TV programs are excellent, but …
4. Some people have brown hair, but …	4. There are three colors that I especially like. One is …
5. Some people need at least eight hours of sleep each night, but …	5. Only two of the students failed the quiz. All of …
6. There are three places in particular I would like to see when I visit (*a city/country*). One is …	6. I have two candy bars. I want only one of them. Would you like … ?

EXERCISE 30 ▸ Looking at grammar. (Chart 8-6)

Complete the sentences with a form of *other*.

1. There are two women standing on the corner. One is Helen Jansen, and ___the other___ is Pat Hendricks.

2. My neighbors have three children. One has graduated from college and has a job. _____ is at Yale University. _____ is still living at home.

3. I would like some more books on this subject. Do you have any _____ that you could lend me?

4. I would like to read more about this subject. Do you have any _____ books that you could lend me?

5. Mari reads the *New York Times* every day. She doesn't read any _____ newspapers.

6. Some people prefer jazz, but _____ prefer rock music.

7. I'm almost finished. I just need _____ five minutes.

8. One of the most important inventions in the history of the world was the printing press. _____ was the electric light. _____ were the telephone, the television, and the computer.

9. Some babies begin talking as early as six months; _____ don't speak until they are more than two years old.

10. One common preposition is *from*. _____ common one is *in*. _____ _____ are *by, for,* and *of*. The most frequently used prepositions in English are *at, by, for, from, in, of, to,* and *with*. What are some _____ prepositions?

11. That country has two basic problems. One is inflation, and _____ is the instability of the government.

12. I have been in only three cities since I came to the United States. One is New York, and

_____ are Washington, D.C., and Chicago.

13. When his alarm went off this morning, Toshi shut it off, rolled over, and slept for

_____ hour.

14. It's important to recognize individual differences in children. One child might have a strong

interest in mathematics and science. _____ child might be more artistic.

EXERCISE 31 ▸ Looking at grammar. (Chart 8-6)
Choose the sentence (a. or b.) that best describes the given sentence.

1. I need another hour of sleep, and then I'll feel fine.
   a. I need one more hour.
   b. I need one more hour, maybe more.

2. The #8 bus goes to the mall. The others are the #11 and #15.
   a. Only three buses go to the mall.
   b. More than three buses go to the mall.

3. We're not ready to leave yet. We need another ten minutes.
   a. We need ten more minutes or more.
   b. We can leave in ten minutes.

4. I'm stuck. Do you have any other ideas for our project?
   a. I need just one more idea from you.
   b. Do you have more ideas?

EXERCISE 32 ▸ Listening. (Chart 8-6)
Complete each sentence with the form of *other* that you hear.

1. This coffee is delicious. Could I please have _____ cup?

2. The coffee isn't in this grocery bag, so I'll look in _____ one.

3. There are supposed to be ten chairs in the room, but I count only five. Where are _____ ?

4. No, let's not use this printer. Let's use _____ one.

5. Bill is a short form for William. _____ are Billy and Will.

6. The sky is clearing. It's going to be _____ beautiful day.

EXERCISE 33 ▸ Warm-up. (Chart 8-7)
Read the situation and the statements that follow. Circle "T" for true and "F" for false.

SITUATION: Lisa and Kate talk to each other every other day. Kate saw Lisa the other day at the park. Lisa was with her five children. They were walking behind her, one after the other.

1. Kate talks to Lisa often.	T	F
2. Kate talked to Lisa today. She'll talk to her again tomorrow.	T	F
3. Kate last saw Lisa a few weeks ago.	T	F
4. Lisa's children were walking in a line.	T	F

8-7 Common Expressions with *Other*

(a) Mike and I write to *each other* every week. We write to *one another* every week.	*Each other* and *one another* indicate a reciprocal relationship.* In (a): I write to him every week, and he writes to me every week.

(b) Please write on *every other* line.	*Every other* can give the idea of "alternate."
	The meaning in (b):
	    Write on the first line.
	    Do not write on the second line.
	    Write on the third line.
	    Do not write on the fourth line. (Etc.)

(c) — Have you seen Ali recently? — Yes. I saw him just *the other day*.	*The other* is used in time expressions such as *the other day, the other morning, the other week*, etc., to refer to the recent past. In (c): *the other day* means "a few days ago, not long ago."
(d) The ducklings walked in a line behind the mother duck. Then the mother duck slipped into the pond. The ducklings followed her. They slipped into the water *one after the other*. (e) They slipped into the water *one after another*.	In (d): *one after the other* expresses the idea that separate actions occurred very close in time. In (e): *one after another* has the same meaning as *one after the other*.
(f) No one knows my secret *other than* Rosa. (g) No one knows my secret *except* (*for*) Rosa.	*Other than* is usually used after a negative to mean "except," as in (f). Example (g) has the same meaning as (f).
(h) Fruit and vegetables are full of vitamins and minerals. *In other words*, they are good for you.	In (h): *In other words* is used to explain, usually in simpler or clearer terms, the meaning of the preceding sentence (s).

*In typical usage, *each other* and *one another* are interchangeable; there is no difference between them. Some native speakers, however, use *each other* when they are talking about only two persons or things, and *one another* when there are more than two.

EXERCISE 34 ▶ Looking at grammar. (Charts 8-6 and 8-7)
Complete the sentences with a form of *other*.

1. Two countries border on the United States. One is Canada. ___The other___ is Mexico.

2. One of the countries I would like to visit is Sweden. _____ is Malaysia. Of course,

   besides these two countries, there are many _____ places I would like to see.

3. Louis and I have been friends for a long time. We've known _____ since we

   were children.

4. A: I talked to Sam _____ day.

   B: Oh? How is he? I haven't seen him for ages.

5. In the Southwest, there is a large area of land that has little or no rainfall, no trees, and very

   few plants _____ than cactuses. In _____ words, this area is a desert.

6. Thanks for inviting me to the party. I'd like to go, but I've already made _____

   plans.

7. Some people are tall; _____ are short. Some people are

   nearsighted; _____ people are farsighted. Some people are talkative;

   _____ are shy.

8. Mr. and Mrs. Jay love _____. They support _____.

   They like _____. In _____ words, they are a happily

   married couple.

9. A: How often do you travel to Portland?

   B: Every _____ month I go there to visit my grandmother in a nursing home.

10. Could I borrow your pen? I need to write a check, but I have nothing to write with

    _____ than this pencil.

11. My niece, Kathy, ate one cookie after _____ until

    she finished the whole box. That's why she had a bad stomachache.

12. The baby ducks walked in a line behind their mother one after

    _____ .

EXERCISE 35 ▸ Let's talk. (Charts 8-6 and 8-7)

Work in small groups. Complete the sentences orally with your own words. Use a form of *other* where indicated.

Example: Some people like _____ while (*other*) _____ prefer _____ .
   → *Some people like coffee while others prefer tea.*

1. I have two _____ . One is _____ , and (*other*) _____ is _____ .

2. One of the longest rivers in the world is _____ . (*other*) _____ is _____ .

3. Some people like to _____ in their free time. (*other*) _____ prefer _____ .

4. There are three _____ that I especially like. One is _____ . (*other*) _____ _____

   (*other*) _____ is _____ .

5. There are many kinds of _____ . Some are _____ , (*other*) _____ are _____ , and

   (*other*) _____ are _____ .

EXERCISE 36 ▸ Listening. (Chart 8-7)

Listen to the way *other* and *except* are used. Choose the sentence that is closest in meaning to the one you hear.

Example: You will hear: I spend a lot of time with my grandmother. We enjoy each
                            other's company.
       You will choose: a. My grandmother and I like to spend time with others.
                         (b.) I enjoy spending time with my grandmother.

1. a. All of the students had the wrong answer.
   b. Some students had the wrong answer.

2. a. The Clarks each see others on weekends.
   b. The Clarks spend time together on weekends.

3. a. Susan spoke with him a while ago.
   b. Susan spoke with him recently.

4. a. Three people know about the engagement.
   b. Four people know about the engagement.

5. a. Jan knows about the party.
   b. Jan doesn't know about the party.

EXERCISE 37 ▶ Check your knowledge. (Chapter 8 Review)
Correct the errors.

1. My friends and ~~me~~ I ordered Indian food at the restaurant. I wasn't very hungry at first, but I
   ate most of ~~them.~~ it

2. When we were in school, my brother used to play tennis with my sister and I every day after school.

3. My cousin and her husband moved to other city because they don't like cold weather.

4. If you want to pass your exams, you need to study very hard for it.

5. I like to travel because I like to learn about other country and custom.

6. When I lost my passport, I had to apply for other one.

7. When I got to class, all of the others students were already in his seats.

8. In hot weather, you need to water the plants every other days.

9. I live in a two-room apartment. Its too small for mine family.

10. A child needs to learn how to get along with another people, how to spend their time wisely, and
    how to depend on yourself.

11. Other from Tom, everyone has responded to the wedding invitation.

12. After work, Mr. Gray asked to speak to Mona and I about the company's new policies. He
    explained it to us and asked for ours opinions.

13. My cousins asked to borrow my car because their's was in the garage for repairs.

14. The players were looking at one anothers, trying to find their weakest opponent.

15. The manager introduced Manual and I to the other employees in the new branch office.

16. A hippopotamus spends most of it's time in the water of rivers and lakes.

EXERCISE 38 ▸ Reading and writing. (Chapter 8)

Part I. Read the passage. <u>Underline</u> each sentence that introduces a reason.

Is checking text messages in a meeting appropriate?

Checking text messages in a meeting sends a negative message. First, it is disrespectful. When people check messages, they aren't paying attention to others in the meeting. It is impossible to read messages and listen to the speaker at the same time. Another problem is that the speaker expects the other members to participate in some way. Maybe they are at the meeting because they need to learn new information or perhaps they need to help problem-solve an issue. They can't participate when they are looking at their phone. Finally, when people check messages, they send the message that their lives are more important than the content of the meeting. This superior attitude can make other people resentful.

Part II. Choose one question and give three reasons. Then write a one-paragraph response based on your reasons.

1. Is checking text messages in class appropriate?
2. What are three advantages/disadvantages of social media?
3. What are three advantages/disadvantages of the Internet?
4. What is your opinion of selfies? (You may want to refer to Exercise 17, Part II, for ideas.)

WRITING TIP

To give reasons for something, it is helpful to use the following format:

- First, …
- Another reason/problem/issue/etc. … (Using *another* is very common when adding an additional reason.)
- Finally/Last/Third, …

Part III. Edit your writing. Check for the following:

1. ☐ correct agreement of pronouns
2. ☐ correct forms of *other*
3. ☐ no use of impersonal "you"
4. ☐ use of *it's* for *it is* and *its* for the possessive
5. ☐ correct spelling (use a dictionary or spell-check)

▪▪▪▪▪ Go to MyEnglishLab for Self-Study: Gerunds and Infinitives 8

PRETEST: What do I already know?
Write "C" if a sentence has the correct modal verb in form and meaning and "I" for incorrect.
Check your answers below. After you complete each chart listed, make any necessary corrections.

1. _____ Applicants must to fill in the forms in ink. (9-1)

2. _____ We got to finish this project before we go home tonight. (9-2)

3. _____ The bus doesn't come for a half hour. We don't need to hurry. We must not run. (9-3)

4. _____ I should leave now, and you ought to begin your homework. (9-4)

5. _____ What time we supposed to be at the train station tomorrow? (9-5)

6. _____ The teacher should be back any minute. She just needed to get supplies. (9-5)

7. _____ Are you able to read my handwriting? (9-6)

8. _____ It can snow tomorrow night. There is a 50% chance. (9-7)

9. _____ You may pay the bill online if you prefer. (9-8)

10. _____ May you help me? (9-8)

11. _____ Would you mind turn up the heat? (9-9)

12. _____ Let's not stay home tonight. Shall we go to a movie? (9-10)

Incorrect sentences: 1, 2, 3, 5, 8, 10, 11

EXERCISE 1 ▶ Warm-up. (Chart 9-1)
Check (✓) the grammatically correct sentences. Which sentences do you agree with?

1. _____ School can be stressful.

2. _____ Too much work may be harm a student's health.

3. _____ A teacher doesn't has to give homework.

4. _____ Science and math might be the two most important skills to have for the future.

5. _____ Schools should get rid of grades.

6. _____ Colleges ought to eliminate entrance exams.

9-1 Basic Modal Introduction

Modal auxiliaries generally express speakers' attitudes. For example, modals can express that a speaker feels something is necessary, advisable, permissible, possible, or probable; and, in addition, they can convey the strength of those attitudes. Each modal has more than one meaning or use. See Chart 10-11, pp. 208-209, for a summary of modals.

Modal auxiliaries in English					
can	had better	might	ought (to)	should	would
could	may	must	shall	will	

Modal Auxiliaries

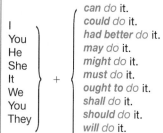

		Modals do not take a final **-s**, even when the subject is *she, he,* or *it*.
	can do it.	CORRECT: **She can** do it.
I	*could do* it.	INCORRECT: She ~~cans~~ do it.
You	*had better do* it.	
He	*may do* it.	Modals are followed immediately by the simple form of a verb.
She	*might do* it.	CORRECT: **She can** do it.
It +	*must do* it.	INCORRECT: She can ~~to~~ do it. / She can ~~does~~ it. / She can ~~did~~ it.
We	*ought to do* it.	
You	*shall do* it.	The only exception is **ought**, which is followed by an infinitive (**to** + *the simple form of a verb*).
They	*should do* it.	CORRECT: He **ought to go** to the meeting.
	will do it.	
	would do it.	See Appendix Chart B-1 for question forms and D-1 for negative forms with modals.

Phrasal Modals

be able to do it	Phrasal modals are common expressions whose meanings are similar to those of some of the modal auxiliaries. For example: **be able to** is similar to **can**; **be going to** is similar to **will**.
be going to do it	
be supposed to do it	
have to do it	An infinitive (**to** + *the simple form of a verb*) is used in these similar expressions.
have got to do it	

EXERCISE 2 ▶ Looking at grammar. (Chart 9-1)

Complete the sentences with **to** or **Ø** as necessary.

An All-Nighter

A: You look exhausted!

B: I know. And I am. I just pulled an all-nighter*. I've got _____ turn in my college applications today.

A: Did you finish?

B: Just barely. You know, applying for college shouldn't _____ be so much work!

A: How many are you applying to?

B: Three right now. I may _____ do a few later. Some have deadlines in a couple of months. What about you?

A: I don't graduate until next year, but I might _____ apply early.

B: You really ought _____. It's pretty stressful waiting until the last minute like I did!

**pull an all-nighter* = stay up all night to finish something

EXERCISE 3 ▸ Warm-up. (Chart 9-2)

Read the statements. Decide the more typical context for the words in blue: everyday conversation or formal writing. Discuss their meanings.

1. Oh, gosh. Look at the time. I've got to go. I have class in five minutes!
2. All applicants must be 18 years of age and must have a valid driver's license.
3. We have to prepare a research paper on climate change in Dr. Chen's seminar this term. I think it'll be an interesting project.

9-2 Expressing Necessity: *Must, Have To, Have Got To*

Must, Have To

(a) All applicants *must take* an entrance exam. (b) All applicants *have to take* an entrance exam.	**Must** and **have to** both express necessity. The meaning is the same in (a) and (b): *It is necessary for every applicant to take an entrance exam. There is no other choice. The exam is required.*
(c) I'm looking for Sue. I *have to talk* to her about our lunch date tomorrow. I can't meet her for lunch because I *have to go* to a business meeting at 1:00. (d) Cell phones *must be* in your backpacks during class. (e) Johnny, you *must stay* away from the stove. It is very hot. (f) *Do* you *have to leave*?	In statements of necessity, **have to** is used more frequently in everyday speech and writing than **must**. The meaning in (c): *I need to do this, and I need to do that.* **Must** is typically stronger than **have to** and indicates urgency or importance. **Must** is usually found in rules, written instructions, or legal information. The meaning in (d): *This is very important!* Adults also use **must** when talking to young children about rules, as in (e). **Have to**, not **must**, is commonly used in questions, as in (f).
(g) I *have to* ("hafta") be home by eight. (h) He *has to* ("hasta") go to a meeting tonight.	NOTE: Native speakers often say "hafta" and "hasta," as in (g) and (h).

Have Got To

(i) I *have got to go* now. I have a class in ten minutes. (j) I *have to go* now. I have a class in ten minutes. (k) *Do* you *have to go* now?	**Have got to** also expresses the idea of necessity: (i) and (j) have the same meaning. **Have got to** is informal and is used primarily in spoken English. **Have to** is used in both formal and informal English. **Have to** is more common in questions, as in (k).
(l) I *have got to go* ("I've gotta go / I gotta go") now.	The usual pronunciation of **got to** is "gotta." Sometimes **have** is dropped in speech: "I gotta do it."

EXERCISE 4 ▸ Looking at grammar. (Chart 9-2)

Work with a partner. In the following sentences, **have to, have got to,** and **must** are all grammatically correct. However, **must** is more often found in the context of rules or legal documents. In each pair, which sentence do you think is more common?

1. a. Your signature on the document has to be legible.
   b. Your signature on the document must be legible.

2. a. We've got to hurry. The movie starts in ten minutes.
   b. We must hurry. The movie starts in ten minutes.

3. a. Charlie and Andy are a few minutes behind us. They have to stop for gas.
   b. Charlie and Andy are a few minutes behind us. They must stop for gas.

4. a. Drivers have got to renew their licenses in person.
   b. Drivers must renew their licenses in person.

EXERCISE 5 ▶ Looking at grammar. (Chart 9-2)

Which verb is best for each sentence? Use the correct form of ***must*** or ***have to***. (Both verbs are grammatically correct.)

1. All passengers _____ show their passports to the customs officer.

2. Mai _____ get up early tomorrow.

3. Sorry. Julie and I _____ leave the party early.

4. Before an operation, all patients _____ sign a consent form, or the surgeon will not perform the surgery.

5. I'll be home a little late. I _____ pick up groceries after work.

6. (*Vicki*) _____ work tomorrow?

7. Drivers _____ pull over when they see a police car's flashing blue lights.

8. (*our neighbor*) _____ play his music so loud every night? It's so noisy.

9. Susie, you _____ put your toys away before you go outside.

10. (*we*) _____ buy our tickets in advance, or are they available at the box office?

EXERCISE 6 ▶ Grammar and speaking. (Chart 9-2)

Write questions for the following. Then ask another student these questions. Share a few of your answers with the class.

1. what \ you \ have to do \ after class today _____

2. what \ you \ have to do \ first thing in the morning

   _____

3. what \ students in this class \ have to pay attention to

   _____

4. what time \ you \ have to be \ in your first class

   _____

5. what \ some rules that students \ must follow _____

6. what \ some requirements that students \ must complete (for this class, for graduation, etc.)

   _____

EXERCISE 7 ▸ Warm-up. (Chart 9-3)
Choose the responses for Speaker B that make sense.

SPEAKER A: The meeting starts in an hour. We have plenty of time.
SPEAKER B: a. We must not hurry.   b. We don't have to hurry.   c. We don't need to hurry

9-3 Lack of Necessity (*Not Have To*) and Prohibition (*Must Not*)

Lack of Necessity

(a) Tomorrow is a holiday. We *don't have to go* to class.	When used in the negative, ***must*** and ***have to*** have different meanings.
(b) I can hear you. You *don't have to shout*.*	Negative form: ***do not have to*** = *not necessary*
	The meaning in (a): *We don't need to go to class tomorrow because it is a holiday.*

Prohibition

(c) You *must not tell* anyone my secret. Do you promise?	***must not*** = prohibition (DO NOT DO THIS!)
	The meaning in (c): *Do not tell anyone my secret. I forbid it. Telling anyone my secret is prohibited.*
(d) *Don't tell* anyone my secret.	***Must not*** is very strong. Speakers generally express prohibition with imperatives, as in (d), or with other modals, as in (e) and (f).
(e) You *can't tell* anyone my secret.	
(f) You'*d better not tell* anyone my secret.	

*Lack of necessity may also be expressed by ***need not*** + *the simple form of a verb: You ***needn't shout***. This is more common in British English.

EXERCISE 8 ▸ Looking at grammar. (Chart 9-3)
Complete the sentences with a verb that makes sense. Then write the negative form.

buy	fill out	offer	wait	work	✓ write

1. College applicants must _____*write*_____ an essay as part of the admissions process.

    NEGATIVE: ____*College applicants don't have to write an essay as part of the admissions process.*____

2. We've got to _____ groceries on the way home.

    NEGATIVE: _____

3. You have to _____ for Martha. She's late.

    NEGATIVE: _____

4. The city has got to _____ more public transportation options.

    NEGATIVE: _____

5. You must _____ the application form by tomorrow.

    NEGATIVE: _____

6. Jin has to _____ overtime this weekend.

    NEGATIVE: _____

EXERCISE 9 ▶ Looking at grammar. (Chart 9-3)

Complete the sentences with **must not** or **do/does not have to**.

1. a. Since you've already finished your homework, you ____*don't have to*____ study tonight.

   b. You _____ skip class. Unexcused absences will lower your grade.

   c. I _____ contact my professor. I found the information I was looking for.

2. a. I _____ go to the doctor. I'm feeling much better.

   b. Patients _____ leave the hospital without their doctor's permission.

   c. You _____ introduce me to your doctor. We've already met.

3. a. Park visitors _____ approach the bears because they can be
   unpredictable and dangerous.

   b. If you encounter a bear, you _____ run. Instead, back away slowly.

4. a. A person _____ get married in order to lead a happy and fulfilling life.

   b. A person _____ become rich and famous in order to live a successful life.

EXERCISE 10 ▶ Let's talk. (Chart 9-3)

What do you look for in a leader? What qualities do you think a leader needs in order to be effective? Complete the sentences with **must, must not, has to,** or **doesn't have to**. Discuss your answers.

An effective leader of a country …

1. _____ be well educated.

2. _____ be flexible and open to new ideas.

3. _____ be wealthy.

4. _____ have a family (spouse and children).

5. _____ be male.

6. _____ have a military background.

7. _____ use his or her power for personal financial gain.

8. _____ ignore the wishes of the majority of the people.

9. _____ be a good public speaker.

EXERCISE 11 ▶ Warm-up. (Chart 9-4)

Amir has a bad toothache. What advice would you give him?

1. He should see a dentist immediately.
2. He should wait and see if the pain goes away.
3. He should call an ambulance.
4. He could put an ice-pack on his cheek.
5. He ought to take some pain medicine.
6. He should get a friend to pull the tooth right away.

9-4 Advisability/Suggestions: *Should, Ought To, Had Better, Could*

(a) You *should study* harder. You *ought to study* harder. (b) Drivers *should obey* the speed limit. Drivers *ought to obey* the speed limit.	**Should** and **ought to** both express advisability. Their meaning ranges in strength from a suggestion (*This is a good idea*) to a statement about responsibility or duty (*This is a very important thing to do*). The meaning in (a): *This is a good idea. This is my advice.* In (b): *This is an important responsibility.*
(c) I *ought to* ("otta") *study* tonight, but I think I'll watch TV instead.	Native speakers often pronounce **ought to** as "otta" in informal speech.
(d) You *shouldn't leave* your keys in the car.	Negative contraction: **shouldn't** NOTE: the /t/ is often hard to hear in relaxed, spoken English. **Ought to** is not commonly used in the negative.
(e) The gas tank is almost empty. We *had better stop* at the next gas station. (f) You *had better take* care of that cut on your hand soon, or it will get infected.	In meaning, **had better** is close to **should** and **ought to**, but **had better** is usually stronger. Often **had better** implies a warning or a threat of possible bad consequences. The meaning in (e): *If we don't stop at a gas station, there will be a bad result. We will run out of gas.* Notes on the use of **had better**: • It has a present or future meaning. • It is followed by the simple form of a verb. • It is more common in speaking than writing.
(g) You*'d better* take care of it.	Contraction: **'d better**, as in (g). In spoken English, you may not hear the "d" in **you'd**. However, "d" is necessary in writing.
(h) You*'d better not* be late.	Negative form: **had better** + **not**
(i) — I'm having trouble in math class. — You *could talk* to your teacher. OR — You *could ask* Ann to help you with your math lessons. OR — I *could try* to help you. (j) You *should talk* to your teacher. (k) *Maybe* you *should talk* to your teacher.	**Could** can also be used to make suggestions. The meaning in (i): *I have some possible suggestions for you. It is possible to do this. Or it is possible to do that.* **Should** is stronger and more definite than **could**. The meaning in (j): *I believe it is important for you to do this. This is what I recommend.* In (k), **maybe** softens the strength of the advice.*

*Two other common ways to give softer suggestions are with the expressions **might want** and **I would**: *You **might want** to talk to your teacher.* OR **I would** *talk to your teacher.* The meaning in the latter is: *If I were you, I would … .* In speaking, this is often shortened to **I would** … . You will study this verb form more in Chapter 20.

EXERCISE 12 ▸ Looking at grammar. (Chart 9-4)

Complete the conversations with your own words. Use **should, ought to, could**, or **had better** to give advice.

1. A: The shoes I bought last week don't fit. When I tried them on in the store, they felt fine, but now they're killing my feet. Fortunately, I've only worn them indoors.

   B: You _____

   _____

2. A: Have you gotten your airplane ticket?

   B: No, not yet.

   A: Flights fill up fast near the holidays. You _____

3. A: Yikes! My class starts in five minutes. I didn't notice the time.

   B: You _____

4. A: I have the hiccups.

   B: You _____

5. A: I bought these expensive apples, and all of them are rotten inside.

   B: You _____

6. A: I have six months to improve my English.

   B: You _____

EXERCISE 13 ▸ Looking at grammar. (Chart 9-4)

Work with a partner. Discuss Speaker B's and C's use of *should* and *could*. What are the differences in meaning?

1. A: Ted doesn't feel good. He has the chills, and he has a flight tomorrow night. What do you think he should do?
   B: He *should go* to urgent care right now.
   C: Well, I don't know. He *could call* his doctor for advice. Or he *could postpone* his trip for a day or two.

2. A: I need to get to the airport in the morning.
   B: You *should take* the airport shuttle. It's cheaper than a taxi.
   C: Well, you *could take* the shuttle, but that's a long ride from here. Maybe you *could ask* Matt to drive you. He works near the airport.

EXERCISE 14 ▸ Let's talk: pairwork. (Chart 9-4)

Work with a partner. Complete the conversations.

PARTNER A	PARTNER B
1. Oops! I spilled _____. → *coffee on my shirt.*	1. You'd better _____ before the stain sets.
2. My _____ is coming for dinner, and I'm a terrible cook.	2. Well, I think you'd better _____.
3. I've been studying for three days straight.	3. I know. You should _____.

PARTNER B	PARTNER A
4. Lately, it's been so hard for me to _____. I'm not getting anything done. I feel _____.	4. Maybe you could _____.
5. My kids are _____ too much.	5. You'd better _____.
6. My apartment is a mess and my _____ is coming to visit tomorrow.	6. You could _____.

EXERCISE 15 ▸ Looking at grammar. (Charts 9-2 → 9-4)

Complete the sentences with **should** or **have to/must**. In some sentences either one is possible, but the meaning is different. Discuss the difference in meanings.

1. a. A person ___*has to / must*___ eat in order to live.

   b. A person ___*should*___ eat a balanced diet.

2. a. The weather is so dark and gloomy right now. Maybe we _____ go somewhere warm for our vacation.

   b. We _____ start looking at places on the Internet.

3. a. According to the college website, an incoming freshman _____ have four years of high school English for acceptance. Three years is not enough.

   b. If you want to become a doctor, you _____ go to medical school for many years.

4. a. I don't have enough money to take the bus, so I _____ walk home.

   b. If you want to get more exercise, you _____ walk to and from work.

5. a. You _____ rinse rice before you cook it.

   b. Rice _____ have water in order to grow.

EXERCISE 16 ▶ Reading, speaking, and writing. (Charts 9-2 → 9-4)

Read the emails. Then work with a partner. Write an email to a friend or relative asking for advice. Make up a personal problem that you need help with. Give your email to another pair, who will write an answer.

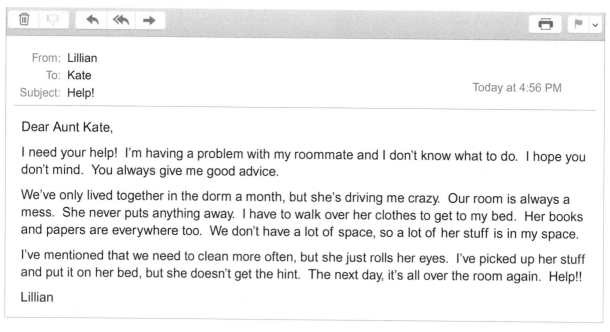

From: Lillian
To: Kate
Subject: Help!

Today at 4:56 PM

Dear Aunt Kate,

I need your help! I'm having a problem with my roommate and I don't know what to do. I hope you don't mind. You always give me good advice.

We've only lived together in the dorm a month, but she's driving me crazy. Our room is always a mess. She never puts anything away. I have to walk over her clothes to get to my bed. Her books and papers are everywhere too. We don't have a lot of space, so a lot of her stuff is in my space.

I've mentioned that we need to clean more often, but she just rolls her eyes. I've picked up her stuff and put it on her bed, but she doesn't get the hint. The next day, it's all over the room again. Help!!

Lillian

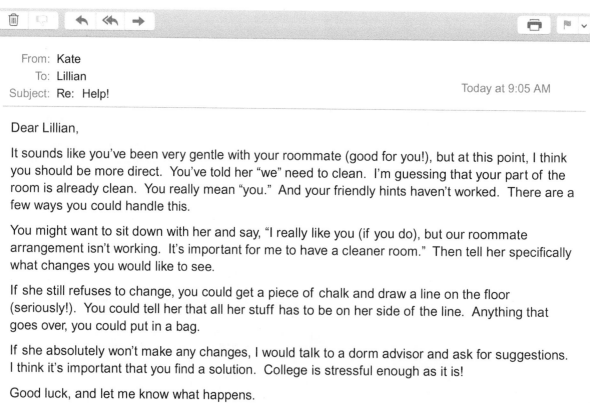

From: Kate
To: Lillian
Subject: Re: Help!

Today at 9:05 AM

Dear Lillian,

It sounds like you've been very gentle with your roommate (good for you!), but at this point, I think you should be more direct. You've told her "we" need to clean. I'm guessing that your part of the room is already clean. You really mean "you." And your friendly hints haven't worked. There are a few ways you could handle this.

You might want to sit down with her and say, "I really like you (if you do), but our roommate arrangement isn't working. It's important for me to have a cleaner room." Then tell her specifically what changes you would like to see.

If she still refuses to change, you could get a piece of chalk and draw a line on the floor (seriously!). You could tell her that all her stuff has to be on her side of the line. Anything that goes over, you could put in a bag.

If she absolutely won't make any changes, I would talk to a dorm advisor and ask for suggestions. I think it's important that you find a solution. College is stressful enough as it is!

Good luck, and let me know what happens.

Aunt Kate

EXERCISE 17 ▸ Looking at grammar. (Charts 9-2 → 9-4)

Choose the answer that has the same meaning as the given sentence. In some cases <u>both</u> answers are correct.

Traveling

1. Don't carry large sums of money with you.
   a. You don't have to carry large sums of money.
   b. You must not carry large sums of money.

2. The guide said it's not necessary to rent a car. There is a bus.
   a. You don't have to rent a car.
   b. You must not rent a car.

3. To apply for a visa, proof of citizenship is necessary.
   a. You must show proof of citizenship.
   b. You have to show proof of citizenship.

4. It will be a good idea to arrive at the train station early tomorrow. It's a holiday weekend.
   a. You ought to arrive early.
   b. You should arrive early.

5. Only airline passengers with boarding passes can go to the gate.
   a. To go to the gate, passengers should have boarding passes.
   b. To go to the gate, passengers must have boarding passes.

EXERCISE 18 ▸ Warm-up. (Chart 9-5)

Check (✓) the sentences you agree with.

In my country, …

1. _____ students are supposed to stand up when a teacher enters the room.
2. _____ people are supposed to take off their shoes before they enter a home.
3. _____ children are supposed to address adults formally, for example, as "Sir" and "Ma'am."
4. _____ students are supposed to knock before they come into a classroom.

9-5	Expectation: *Be Supposed To/Should*
(a) The game *is supposed to begin* at 10:00. (b) The committee *is supposed to vote* by secret ballot.	**Be supposed to** expresses the idea that someone (*I, we, they, the teacher, lots of people, my father, etc.*) expects something to happen. **Be supposed to** often expresses expectations about scheduled events, as in (a), or correct procedures, as in (b).
(c) I *am supposed to go* to the meeting. My boss told me that he wants me to attend. (d) The children *are supposed to put away* their toys before they go to bed.	**Be supposed to** also expresses expectations about behavior. The meaning is the same in (c) and (d): *Someone else expects (requests or requires) certain behavior.* NOTE: **I am supposed to** = *I am expected to* **I suppose** = *I guess, I think, I believe*
(e) The mail *should be* here soon. (f) Amy *should be* back any minute.	**Should** can also express expectation. In (e): The speaker expects the mail to be here soon. In (f): The speaker expects Amy to be back any minute.

EXERCISE 19 ▸ Let's talk. (Chart 9-5)

Answer the questions with **be supposed to**. Work in pairs, in small groups, or as a class.

Example:
SPEAKER A (*book open*):   If you're driving and a traffic light turns red, what are you supposed to do?
SPEAKER B (*book closed*): You're supposed to come to a complete stop.

1. What are you supposed to do if you're involved in a traffic accident?
2. What are you supposed to do before takeoff in an airplane?
3. What are some things athletes in training are supposed to do, and some things they're not supposed to do?
4. If you're driving and an ambulance with flashing lights and blaring sirens comes up behind you, what are you supposed to do?
5. In the place you live or work, who is supposed to do what? In other words, what are the duties or responsibilities of the people who live or work with you?

EXERCISE 20 ▸ Looking at grammar. (Chart 9-5)

Rewrite the sentences with **should**.

1. I expect you to pass your class. It's fairly easy. _____*You should pass your class.*_____
2. It's 10:00. I expect the movie is over now. _____
3. I expect Aja will hear about the job offer soon. _____
4. I expect your advisor will have a solution for you. _____
5. I expect our flight will take off on time. _____

EXERCISE 21 ▸ Speaking or writing. (Charts 9-2 → 9-5)

Make sentences about the occupations listed below. Use the verbs in the box.

should	have got to	do not have to
have to	had better not	had better
be not supposed to	ought to	shouldn't
be supposed to	must	must not

Example: A vet should be very gentle with animals.

1. a tour guide
2. an artist
3. an engineer
4. a nurse
5. a taxi driver
6. a salesclerk
7. a plumber
8. a veterinarian (vet)

EXERCISE 22 ▸ Looking at grammar. (Charts 9-2 → 9-5)

Which sentence in each pair is stronger?

1. a. You *had better wear* a seat belt.
   b. You *have to wear* a seat belt.

2. a. You *must wear* a seat belt.
   b. You *had better wear* a seat belt.

3. a. You *have to wear* a seat belt.
   b. You *are supposed to wear* a seat belt.

4. a. We *are supposed to bring* ID.
   b. We *have to bring* ID.

5. a. We *ought to bring* ID.
   b. We *have got to bring* ID.

6. a. We *should bring* ID.
   b. We *could bring* ID.

EXERCISE 23 ▸ Warm-up. (Chart 9-6)

Decide if the sentence expresses a. a physical ability or b. a learned skill.

1. _____ Isabel knows how to play chess.

2. _____ Jonathan can run really fast. He's a natural.

3. _____ Theodore knows how to use sign language. His mother is deaf and taught him.

4. _____ I won't be able to go swimming on our trip. I have an ear infection.

9-6	Ability: *Can, Know How To,* and *Be Able To*
(a) Tom is strong. He *can lift* that heavy box.	*Can* is used to express physical ability, as in (a).
(b) I *can see* Central Park from my apartment.	*Can* is frequently used with verbs of the five senses: *see, hear, feel, smell, taste,* as in (b).
(c) My husband *cannot stay* awake past 10:00.	The negative form has three options: *cannot, can't,* or *can not. Can not* is becoming unusual in written English.
(d) We *can't wait* any longer for Bill.	In spoken English, *can* is typically unstressed and pronounced /kən/. *Can't* is stressed and is usually pronounced /kænt/ although the "t" is often not heard.
(e) Maria *can play* the piano. She's been taking lessons for many years.	*Can* and *know how to* are used to express a learned skill.
(f) Maria *knows how to play* the piano.	In (f): *knows how to play* = *can play*
(g) I *am able to help* you now.	*Be able to* expresses ability.
(h) *Are you able to help* me I lift this?	In (g): *be able to help* = *can help*
(i) Sorry, I'*m not able to help* you. It's too heavy.	Note the question and negative forms, as in (i) and (j).
(j) Sorry, I'*m unable to help* you.	*Not able* may also be expressed as *unable,* as in (j).

EXERCISE 24 ▸ Looking at grammar. (Chart 9-6)

Part I. Rewrite the sentences using *be able to*.

1. Larry can start a fire without matches. _____

2. I can't send a text. I left my phone at home. _____

3. Can you read the doctor's handwriting? _____

4. Thomas can't drive without glasses. _____

5. I can't remove the stain on your white shirt. _____

6. Every employee can do CPR (cardiopulmonary resuscitation).

_____

_____

Part II. Which three sentences can be rewritten with ***know how to***?
Restate them.

1. _____

2. _____

3. _____

EXERCISE 25 ▶ Let's talk. (Chart 9-6)

Interview your classmates. Ask each person a different question. Share some of their answers with the class.

Sleep Habits

1. In general, are you able to fall asleep easily? About how long does it take you?
2. How many hours can you sleep before waking up?
3. How many hours of sleep do you need every night? Are you able to function well with less sleep?
4. Are you able to sleep with noise (e.g., TV, radio, snoring)?
5. Can you sleep on airplanes? If yes, are you able to sleep during takeoffs and landings?
6. Have you ever had jet lag? Do you know how to recover from it quickly?
7. Are you able to sleep well the night before something stressful, such as a big test?
8. Do you find that reading on a screen before you go to sleep makes it harder for you to fall asleep?

EXERCISE 26 ▶ Listening. (Chart 9-6)

Part I. Listen to the pronunciation of ***can*** and ***can't***.

1. The secretary can help you.
2. My mother can't speak English well.
3. Our friend can meet you at the train station.
4. Scott can't work late tonight.

Part II. Write the words you hear.

1. We _____ to the meeting.

2. Our two-year-old _____ to 50.

3. You _____ that course next term.

4. I _____ complicated dishes.

5. _____ with us?

6. I _____ a semi-truck.

EXERCISE 27 ▸ Warm-up. (Chart 9-7)

Which two sentences mean "It's a general possibility"?

1. This soup may need salt and pepper.
2. Pepper can make people sneeze.
3. Spices can make food taste better.
4. My cooking tonight might be too spicy for you.

9-7 Possibility: *Can, May, Might*

(a) Spices *can be* expensive.	**Can** is used to express a general possibility.
(b) *You can learn* a lot by watching cooking shows.	In (a), this is generally possible, typical, or common.
	In (b), *You can learn* means *It's possible for people in general to learn.* **You** is impersonal. It refers to people in general rather than a specific person.
(c) Spices *may/might be* more expensive at that store.	**May** and **might** express present or future possibility. The idea: *There is a chance.*
(d) Liza *may/might need* your help in the kitchen.	In (c): There is a chance that spices are (or will be) more expensive at that store.
	In (d): There is a chance that Liza needs (or will need) your help.
	Can is not used for this meaning.
	INCORRECT: Liza ~~can~~ need your help in the kitchen.

EXERCISE 28 ▸ Looking at grammar. (Chart 9-7)

Check (✓) all the grammatically correct sentences. Discuss their meanings.

1. a. _____ Physical exercise may improve your mental state.

   b. _____ Physical exercise can improve your mental state.

2. a. _____ The weather may be breezy tomorrow.

   b. _____ The weather can be breezy tomorrow.

3. a. _____ Eating out every day can be expensive.

   b. _____ Eating out every day might be expensive for you.

4. a. _____ The apartment sounds nice, but it can be too far away from my job.

   b. _____ This apartment sounds nice, but it may be too far away from my job.

EXERCISE 29 ▸ Speaking and writing. (Chart 9-7)

Work in small groups or with a partner. Give a few different completions for each sentence orally. Then write your own sentence for each. Share some of your sentences with the class.

1. Students may learn best _____

2. Online courses can be _____

3. Studying all classes online might be _____

4. People can learn a lot about life from _____

5. Music might help us feel _____

6. Psychology can help us understand _____

7. Literature may help us _____

EXERCISE 30 ▶ Warm-up. (Chart 9-8)
Choose <u>all</u> the correct completions.

1. Excuse me, _____ I look at that book?
   a. can
   b. could
   c. would
   d. may
   e. will

2. _____ you hand me that book, please?
   a. Can
   b. Could
   c. Would
   d. May
   e. Will

9-8	Requests and Responses with Modals

"I" as the Subject: May, Could, Can

(a) *May I borrow* your pen (please)? (b) *Could I* (please) *borrow* your pen? (c) *Can I borrow* your pen?	***May I*** and ***could I*** are used to request permission. ***May I*** sounds more formal.* NOTE in (b): In a polite request, ***could*** has a present or future meaning, not a past meaning. ***Can I*** is usually considered less formal than ***may I*** or ***could I***.
TYPICAL RESPONSES Certainly. Yes, certainly. Of course. Yes, of course. Yes, you may. Yes, you can. *INFORMAL:* Sure.	Often the response to a polite request is an action, such as a nod or shake of the head, or a simple "uh-huh," meaning "yes." Both ***may*** and ***can*** express permission. ***May*** is more formal than ***can***.

"You" as the Subject: Would, Could, Will, Can

(d) *Would you pass* the salt (please)? (e) *Will you* (please) *pass* the salt?	***Would you*** and ***will you*** in a polite request have the same meaning. ***Would you*** is more common and is often considered more polite. The degree of politeness, however, is often determined by the speaker's tone of voice.
(f) *Could you pass* the salt (please)?	Basically, ***could you*** and ***would you*** have the same meaning, and they are equally polite. ***Would you*** = Do you want to do this please? ***Could you*** = Do you want to do this please, and is it possible for you to do this?
(g) *Can you* (please) *pass* the salt?	***Can you*** is often used informally. It usually sounds less formal than ***could you*** or ***would you***. ***May*** is not possible in (g). In polite requests, ***may*** is only used with ***I*** or ***we***. INCORRECT: ~~May you pass the salt?~~
TYPICAL RESPONSES Yes, I'd (I would) be happy to / be glad to. Certainly. *INFORMAL:* Sure.	A person usually responds in the affirmative to a polite request. If a negative response is necessary, a person might begin by saying, "I'd like to, but …" (e.g., "I'd like to pass the salt, but I can't reach it.").

Might is also possible: **Might I borrow your pen? **Might I** is quite formal and polite; it is used much less frequently than **may I** or **could I**.*

EXERCISE 31 ▶ Looking at grammar. (Chart 9-8)
Write <u>all</u> the correct verbs: ***Can, Could, May, Will, Would.***

1. _____ you pass the salt, please?

2. Hello. _____ I help you?

EXERCISE 32 ▶ Let's talk. (Chart 9-8)

Take turns asking and answering polite questions with *Would* or *Could*.

Example:

SPEAKER A: You and I are co-workers. We don't know each other well. We're at a lunch table in a cafeteria. You want the pepper.

SPEAKER B: Would/Could you please pass me the pepper? (*Will* is also possible because the speaker uses *please*, but *can* is probably not appropriate in this situation.)

SPEAKER A: Sure. I'd be glad to. Here you are.

1. You and I are good friends. We're in my apartment. You want to use the phone.
2. I'm your instructor. You want to leave class early.
3. I'm your supervisor at work. You knock on my half-open office door. You want to come in.
4. I'm Dr. North's assistant. You want to make an appointment to see Dr. North.
5. You are running toward the elevator. I'm already inside. You ask me to hold the door open.

EXERCISE 33 ▶ Warm-up. (Chart 9-9)

In each conversation, choose the speaker (A or B) who is going to turn on the air-conditioning.

1. A: This car is like an oven! Would you mind turning on the air-conditioning?
   B: No, not at all.

2. A: This car is like an oven! Would you mind if I turned on the air-conditioning?
   B: No, not at all.

9-9 Polite Requests with *Would You Mind*

Asking Permission

(a) *Would you mind if I opened* the window?	Notice in (a): ***Would you mind if I*** is followed by the simple past.*
(b) *Would you mind if I used* the phone?	The meaning in (a): *May I open the window? Is it all right if I open the window? Will it cause you any trouble or discomfort if I open the window?*
(c) *Would you mind if I close* the door?	
(d) ***Mind if I close*** the door?	
	Sometimes, in informal spoken English, the simple present is used, as in (c).
TYPICAL RESPONSES	*Would you mind if I* can be shortened to *Mind if I*, as in (d).
No, not at all.	
No, of course not.	Notice that the typical response is "no." "Yes" means *Yes, I mind.* In other words: *It is a problem for me.* Another typical response might be "unh-uh," meaning "no."
No, that would be fine.	

Asking Someone to Do Something

(e) *Would you mind **opening*** the window?	Notice in (e): ***Would you mind*** is followed by the *-ing* form of a verb (a gerund).
(f) Excuse me. *Would you mind **repeating*** that?	The meaning in (e): *I don't want to cause you any trouble, but would you please open the window? Would that cause you any inconvenience?*
TYPICAL RESPONSES	
No. I'd be happy to.	The informal responses "Sure" and "OK" are common but not logical. The speaker means *No, I wouldn't mind* but seems to be saying the opposite: *Yes, I would mind.*
Not at all. I'd be glad to.	
INFORMAL: No problem. / Sure. / OK.	
	Native speakers understand that the response "Sure" or "OK" in this situation means that the speaker agrees to the request.

*The simple past does not refer to past time after ***would you mind***; it refers to present or future time. See Chart 20-3, p. 430, for more information.

EXERCISE 34 ▶ Looking at grammar. (Chart 9-9)

Make sentences using **Would you mind**.

1. a. I want to turn up the heat. → *Would you mind if I turned up the heat?*
   b. I want you to turn up the heat. → *Would you mind turning up the heat?*

2. a. I want to leave early.
   b. I want you to leave early.

3. a. I want you to talk to Andrew.
   b. I want to talk to Andrew.

EXERCISE 35 ▶ Looking at grammar. (Chart 9-9)

Complete the sentences with the verbs in parentheses. Use *if I* + *the past tense* OR *the -ing form of the verb.* In some of the sentences, either response is possible, but the meaning is different.

1. A: I'm very tired and need to sleep. Would you mind (*go*) _____*if I went*_____ to bed?

   B: I'm sorry. I didn't understand what you said. Would you mind (*repeat*) ____*repeating*____ that?

2. A: Are you coming with us?

   B: I know I promised to go with you, but I'm not feeling very good. Would you mind

   (*stay*) _____ home?

   A: Of course not.

3. A: It's getting hot in here. Would you mind (*open*) _____ the window?

   B: No.

4. A: This is probably none of my business, but would you mind (*ask*) _____
   you a personal question?

   B: It depends.

5. A: Would you mind not (*smoke*) _____?

   B: Oh, sure. Sorry.

6. A: Excuse me. Would you mind (*speak*) _____
   a little more slowly? I didn't catch what you said.

   B: Sure. Of course.

7. A: I don't like this TV program. Would you mind (*change*) _____ the channel?

   B: Unh-uh.

EXERCISE 36 ▶ Listening. (Chart 9-9)

Listen to each request. Choose the expected response (a. or b.). In relaxed speech, **you** in **would you** may sound like "ju" or "juh."

Example: You will hear: This room is stuffy. Would you mind if I opened the door?
          You will choose: ⓐ No, of course not.   b. Yes.

1. a. Yes.   b. Not at all.   4. a. Yes.   b. No, that's fine.
2. a. Yes.   b. No, that would be fine.   5. a. Yes.   b. No problem.
3. a. Yes.   b. No, I'd be happy to.   6. a. Sure.   b. Of course not.

EXERCISE 37 ▸ Let's talk: pairwork. (Charts 9-8 and 9-9)

Work with a partner. Imagine what the speaker might say for each situation, and complete the conversations in your own words.

1.   JACK: What's the trouble, Officer?

    OFFICER: You made an illegal U-turn. May _____ *I see your driver's license?* _____

    JACK: Sure. Here's my wallet.

    OFFICER: Would _____ *you please remove it from your wallet?* _____

    JACK: Here you are.

2.   WAITER: Good evening. Are you ready to order?

    CUSTOMER: No, not quite yet. Would you mind _____

    WAITER: Of course. I'll be back shortly.

3.   SALLY: Are you driving to the meeting tonight?

    SAM: Yes, I am.

    SALLY: Could _____

    SAM: Sure. I'll pick you up at 7:00.

4. MR. PENN: Something's come up, and I can't meet with you Tuesday. Would you mind

    _____

    MS. GRAY: Let me check my calendar.

5. MECHANIC: What seems to be the trouble with your car?

    CUSTOMER: Something's wrong with the brakes, I think. Could _____

    _____

    MECHANIC: Sure. Just pull the car into the garage.

6.   MIKE: Oh, good. The movie hasn't started. How are these seats?

    SHELLEY: Well, the man in front of us is pretty tall. Would you mind _____

    _____

    MIKE: Not at all. There are two seats across the aisle. (*To moviegoer*) Excuse me. May

    _____

  MOVIEGOER: I'm sorry. My kids are sitting here, but it looks like the seats in front of me are free.

EXERCISE 38 ▸ Warm-up. (Chart 9-10)

Imagine that next Tuesday is a holiday. You and your roommate are making plans. Which suggestions below sound good to you?

1. Let's go to a movie.
2. Why don't we study grammar all day?
3. Let's go shopping.
4. Why don't we fly to Rome for lunch?
5. Let's play video games.
6. Why don't we clean and do the laundry?

9-10 Making Suggestions: *Let's, Why Don't, Shall I / We*

(a) *Let's go* to a movie.	**let's = let us** **Let's** means *I have a suggestion for us.* **Let's** is followed by the simple form of a verb.
(b) *Let's not go* to a movie. *Let's stay* home instead.	Negative form: **let's** + **not** + *simple verb*
(c) *Why don't we go* to a movie? (d) *Why don't you come* around seven? (e) *Why don't I give* Mary a call?	**Why don't** is used primarily in spoken English to make a friendly suggestion. The meaning in (c): *Let's go to a movie.* In (d): *I suggest that you come around seven.* In (e): *Should I give Mary a call? Do you agree with my suggestion?*
(f) *Shall I open* the window? Is that OK with you? (g) *Shall we leave* at two? Is that OK?	When **shall** is used with **I** or **we** in a question, the speaker is usually making a suggestion and asking another person if she/he agrees with this suggestion, as in (f) and (g). The use of **shall** + **I/we** is relatively formal and infrequent in American English.
(h) Let's go, *shall we*? (i) Let's go, *OK*?	Sometimes **shall we**? is used as a tag question after **let's**, as in (h). More informally, **OK**? is used as a tag question, as in (i).

EXERCISE 39 ▸ Let's talk. (Chart 9-10)

Complete the conversations with your own words.

1. A: A new Japanese restaurant just opened downtown. Let's _____ *eat there tonight.* _____

   B: Great idea! I'd like some good sushi.

   A: Why don't _____ *you call and make a reservation?* _____ Make it for about 7:30.

   B: No, let's _____ *make it for 8:00.* _____ I'll be working until 7:30 tonight.

2. A: I don't feel like staying home today.

   B: Neither do I. Why don't _____

   A: Hey, that's a great idea! What time shall _____

   B: Let's leave in an hour.

3. A: Shall _____ or _____ first?

   B: Let's _____ first. Then we can take our time over dinner.

   A: Why don't _____

   B: Good idea.

4. A: Let's _____ over the weekend. The fresh air would do us both good.

   B: I agree. Why don't _____

   A: No. Sleeping in a tent is too uncomfortable. Let's _____

EXERCISE 40 ▸ Reading and speaking. (Chapter 9 Review)

Part I. Read the passage from a handbook for incoming freshmen. <u>Underline</u> the modal (or phrasal modal) verbs. With a partner or in small groups, discuss their meaning.

Do you know these words?
- *challenging*
- *stretches (of time)*
- *hefty*
- *extra-curricular*
- *not to mention*
- *evaporate*
- *grades may suffer*

A Challenge for
College Freshmen

Freshman year can turn out to be the most challenging time in college for students. The transition from high school to college or university involves many changes. One of the biggest differences is the amount of freedom you must learn to manage.

In high school, your life is very structured, and you generally can't choose how you spend your day. It begins and ends at the same time. Teachers take attendance and check homework. They tell you (or your parents) about missing assignments and low grades. Many give daily homework so that there is not too much work at one time.

However, college life is much more unstructured. The class schedule might not be the same every day. You can sleep in one morning and have to be up early the next. If you decide to skip a class, there is probably no one there to say you can't do that.

College professors don't have to take attendance or check whether their students have completed assignments. Instructors may have all their assignments on a syllabus and not even mention them in class. They might not remind you about deadlines or missing work. You may hear an instructor say, "I am not your parent." Or even, "I am not a babysitter."

You may find you have large blocks of unscheduled time. There are fewer classes each day than in high school, and you will probably not have every class every day. A two- or three-credit class may meet only once or twice a week. Instructors view these longer stretches of time between classes as valuable opportunities for studying. They often assign hefty amounts of reading, but with so many extra-curricular activities available, not to mention social media and Internet distractions, this study time can quickly evaporate. Your grades may suffer if you can't manage time well. Some students don't realize they are in trouble until it is too late.

With an understanding of the challenges ahead, you can prepare in advance. Most colleges offer programs to help students with their transition, and there are many online resources available. The key is to remember that the responsibility for time management rests with you, not with your parents or teachers.

Part II. In small groups, answer the questions. Then discuss your answers as a class.

1. What are some major distractions for today's student? For you?
2. If you are or were a college freshman, what are/were some of the challenges you had moving from high school to college?
3. Has time management with assignments and studying ever been a problem for you?
4. Do you like to have structure in your day? If so, how do you create it?
5. What recommendations would you give a student who needs to manage time more effectively? Make a list, and use ***should/should not/ought to/had better*** in your sentences. You can check online resources for ideas.

EXERCISE 41 ▸ Writing or speaking. (Chapter 9 Review)

Work with a partner. What would you say for each of the following situations? Use some of the words in the box to come up with at least three possibilities. Share some of your answers with the class.

Example: Imagine that you are an apartment manager. You are talking to a person who is interested in renting an apartment. There is some information about apartment regulations you need to give him/her.

→ *You must not smoke anywhere in the building.*
→ *You have to recycle all paper products and glass.*
→ *Quiet time is 10 P.M. to 7 A.M. You are not supposed to play loud music or make a lot of noise during those hours. …*

should	had better	must	had better not
be supposed to	have to	shouldn't	do not have to
ought to	have got to	be not supposed to	must not

1. Imagine that you are a tour guide and you are helping two students who have arrived for a vacation (choose the place). You want to explain some of the local customs of the places they will be visiting.

2. Imagine that you are the manager of a café and you are talking to two new employees. You want to acquaint them with their jobs and your expectations.

3. Imagine that you are a computer lab instructor and you need to talk to new students about rules for using the computer lab.

EXERCISE 42 ▸ Check your knowledge. (Chapter 9 Review)

Correct the errors.

1. If you have a car, you can traveling around the United States.

2. A film director must has control over every aspect of a movie.

3. I'm sorry. I don't have training in this area. I not able help you.

4. You don't have to have your cell phone on during the test. If you do, you will fail.

5. We supposed to bring our books to class every day.

6. You can having a very good time as a tourist in my country. However, my country has many different climates, so you have better plan ahead before you came.

7. May you please help me with this?

8. The janitor supposed to unlock the building doors.

9. During class the students must to sit quietly.

10. Would I leave a few minutes early today? I have a doctor's appointment.

a janitor

11. I'm suppose to be at the meeting. I suppose I better go.

EXERCISE 43 ▸ Reading and writing. (Chapter 9)

Part I. Read the web article. <u>Underline</u> the verbs with modals (or phrasal modals).

Do you know these words?
- *anxiety*
- *blank mind*
- *racing thoughts*
- *symptoms*
- *retrieve*
- *nausea*
- *cramping*

Test Anxiety

A fast heartbeat, a blank mind, and racing thoughts — these are but a few of the symptoms of test anxiety. It is not unusual for students to feel nervous before tests, but some people become so nervous that they can't think clearly. During the test, they aren't able to understand the questions, and they can't retrieve information they already know. Some students might actually begin to feel physically sick. Nausea, cramping, and headaches are a few of the symptoms that students may have during or even days before a test. In some cases, anxiety can be so severe that otherwise successful students are unable to pass tests.

Part II. Write a paragraph to answer one of the following questions. Use modals in your answer. You may find it helpful to do research on the Internet.

1. What suggestions do you have for a person with test anxiety? Think about what the person can do before the test as well as during it.

2. What can teachers do to help students feel more relaxed when they take a test? Think about test review and preparation as well as the classroom atmosphere.

> **WRITING TIP**
>
> When you write, it is important to avoid excessive repetition of the same words. Instead, try to vary your wording. For example, if you are giving suggestions, you don't want to use *should* for all your sentences. Use other modals that communicate the same idea (*ought to/could/etc.*).

Part III. Edit your writing. Check for the following:

1. ☐ use of modals to express possibility, uncertainty, etc.
2. ☐ correct forms for **be able to**
3. ☐ no **-s** on the main verb after a modal
4. ☐ use of different modals with the same meaning to avoid repetition
5. ☐ correct spelling (use a dictionary or spell-check)

▪▪▪▪ Go to MyEnglishLab for Self-Study: Gerunds and Infinitives 9

Modals, Part 2

1. _____ When I was little, I would carry a blanket with me at all times. (10-1)

2. _____ Nancy's passport has expired. She should have renewed it last month. (10-2)

3. _____ Sorry I'm late. I must drop my mom off at the mall. (10-2)

4. _____ Last night the chef at the restaurant could make our favorite dessert. (10-3)

5. _____ Nadine has missed a week of class. She must be really sick. (10-4)

6. _____ Ryan can't be a doctor! He failed all his exams. (10-5)

7. _____ I can't find my wallet. It may have fell out of my purse. (10-6)

8. _____ You've trained for months for the race. You should do really well. (10-7)

9. _____ Roger jumped when the teacher asked him a question. He must have been daydream. (10-8)

10. _____ We aren't going to be able to catch our plane if we don't get out of this traffic. (10-9)

11. _____ My husband rather cook dinner at home tonight than go out to a restaurant. (10-10)

Incorrect sentences: 3, 4, 7, 9, 11

EXERCISE 1 ▶ Warm-up. (Chart 10-1)
Are the meanings of the two sentences the same or different?

1. When I was a child, I used to build sandcastles at the beach.
2. When I was a child, I would build sandcastles at the beach.

10-1 Using *Would* to Express a Repeated Action in the Past

(a) When I was a child, my father *would read* me a story at night before bedtime.	***Would*** can be used to express *an action that was repeated regularly in the past*. When ***would*** is used to express this idea, it has the same meaning as ***used to*** (*habitual past*). Sentences (a) and (b) have the same meaning. ***Would*** is more common for this purpose than ***used to*** in academic writing.
(b) When I was a child, my father *used to read* me a story at night before bedtime.	
(c) I *used to live* in California. He *used to be* a Boy Scout. They *used to have* a Ford.	To express past situations or states, only ***used to***, not ***would***, is possible, as in (c). *INCORRECT:* They ~~would have~~ a Ford.

EXERCISE 2 ▸ Looking at grammar. (Chart 10-1)

Work with a partner. Choose the correct sentence(s). In some cases, both sentences may be correct.

Visiting My Grandparents

1. a. Every summer, I would visit my grandparents in Mexico for a month.
   b. Every summer, I used to visit my grandparents in Mexico for a month.

2. a. They used to live in the city, but when I was ten, they moved to the coast.
   b. They would live in the city, but when I was ten, they moved to the coast.

3. a. I used to speak Spanish with them, but now my Spanish is a little rusty.
   b. I would speak Spanish with them, but now my Spanish is a little rusty.

4. a. I used to know Spanish pretty well, but I've forgotten a lot of vocabulary.
   b. I would know Spanish pretty well, but I've forgotten a lot of vocabulary.

5. a. I loved visiting them. I would feel really sad each time I said good-bye.
   b. I loved visiting them. I used to feel really sad each time I said good-bye.

EXERCISE 3 ▸ Looking at grammar. (Chart 10-1)

Complete the sentences with the given words. For a repeated action in the past, use ***would*** or ***used to***. For a past state, use ***used to***.

When I was a child …

1. I (*be*) _____ used to be _____ very shy. Whenever a stranger came to our house,

   I (*hide*) _____ would hide / used to hide _____ in a closet.

2. Aunt Ella (*visit*) _____ us often. She (*give*) _____

   _____ me a big kiss and pinch my cheek when she first saw me.

3. I (*like*) _____ junk food, but now I avoid it and eat healthy snacks.

4. I (*be*) _____ afraid of flying. My heart (*start*) _____

   _____ pounding every time I got on a plane. But now I'm used to flying and enjoy it.

5. I got a new bike for my birthday. My friends (*ask*) _____ to ride
   it, but for a long time, I never let anyone else use it.

6. I (*take*) _____ a flashlight to bed with me so that I could read
   comic books without my parents knowing about it.

EXERCISE 4 ▶ Looking at grammar. (Chart 10-1)

Complete the sentences with the correct verb. Use **would** or **used to** and the words in the box to express a repeated action in the past. Use **used to** to express a past state.

hike	live	see	take	wake

My sister _____ in Montana, and when I visited her, we
1
_____ backpacking trips in the mountains for as long as a week.
2
Every morning, we _____
3
up to the sound of singing birds. During the day, we

_____ through meadows and beside
4
mountain lakes. Often we _____
5
deer. Once we saw a bear, but it went off in the opposite direction.

be	find	gather	get	spend

I _____ an anthropology major. Once, I was a member of an
6
archeological expedition. Every morning, we _____ up before
7
sunrise. After breakfast, we _____ our entire day in the field.
8
Sometimes one of us _____ a particularly interesting item, such as
9
a tool or weapon like an arrowhead. When that happened, other members

of the group _____ around to see what had
10

stone arrowhead

been discovered.

EXERCISE 5 ▶ Warm-up. (Chart 10-2)

Choose the correct answer in each pair.

1. A: How was your weekend?
   B: a. Not fun. I had to clean my house.
       b. Not fun. I must have cleaned my house.

2. "We were supposed to have a party last weekend." This means
   a. We had a party.
   b. We didn't have a party.

3. Who said: "I should have studied."
   a. Jason
   b. Jim

Jason

Jim

10-2 Expressing the Past: Necessity, Advisability, Expectation

PRESENT: (a) Julia *has to get* a visa. (b) Julia *has got to get* a visa. (c) Julia *must get* a visa. PAST: (d) Julia *had to get* a visa.	Past necessity: ***had to*** In (d): ***had to*** = *needed to*: *Julia needed to get a visa.* There is no other past form for ***must*** (when it means necessity) or ***have got to***.
PRESENT: (e) I *should study* for the test. I want to pass it. (f) I *ought to study* for the test. (g) I *had better study* for the test. PAST: I failed the test. (h) I *should have studied* for it. (i) I *ought to have studied* for it. (j) I *shouldn't have gone* to the movies the night before.	Past advisability: **should have** **ought to have** } + *past participle* In the past, *should* is more common than *ought to*. The past form of ***had better*** (***had better have***) is almost never used. The meaning in (h) and (i): *Studying was a good idea, but I didn't do it. I made a mistake.* The meaning in (j): *It was a bad idea to go to the movies. I made a mistake.* Usual pronunciation of ***should have***: "should-əv" or "should-ə."
PRESENT: (k) We *are supposed to leave* now. PAST: (l) We *were supposed to leave* last week.	***was/were supposed to***: unfulfilled expectation or obligation in the past
PRESENT: (m) The mail *should be* here. PAST: (n) The mail *should have been* here by now.	***Should have*** + *past participle*: past expectation The speaker expected something to happen; it may or may not have occurred, as in (n).

EXERCISE 6 ▸ Looking at grammar. (Chart 10-2)

Make the sentences express past necessity.

1. I have to leave now
   I must leave now. } I _____ yesterday.
   I've got to leave now.

2. They've got to get new passports.
   They have to get new passports. } They _____ new passports last week.
   They must get new passports.

3. Nelson must have surgery.
   Nelson has got to have surgery. } Nelson _____ surgery last Monday.
   Nelson has to have surgery.

4. Do you have to retake the test? _____ the test this morning?

5. When do we have to register to vote for this election? When _____

   _____ for this election?

6. Why does it have to rain on our vacation? Why _____ on

   our vacation?

EXERCISE 7 ▶ Looking at grammar. (Chart 10-2)
Answer the questions using past necessity.

1. You must pay a late fee if you sign up for the hiking trip after September 1st. John signed up on September 4th. What was the result? ____*He had to pay a late fee.*____

2. Swimmers must take showers before they enter the pool. Susie went swimming. What did she need to do before she got in the pool? _____

3. Sanji agreed to pick up his friend at the airport. The plane was late. Sanji waited at the airport for three hours. What did Sanji have to do last night?

    _____

4. Mila is writing a research paper. She needs a grade of 75% or she has to rewrite it. She got 70%. What did Mila need to do? _____

5. Jacob bought a car, but before he got the car, the dealer gave him a contract to sign. What did Jacob need to do? _____

6. Guests at national parks must make reservations online for campsites. Bob went camping last month at a national park. He stayed at a campsite. What did he need to do before he left home?

    _____

EXERCISE 8 ▶ Looking at grammar. (Chart 10-2)
Make new sentences using ***should/shouldn't have***.

1. You are cold because you didn't wear a coat. ____*I should have worn a coat.*____

2. The room is full of flies because you opened the window.

    _____

3. You don't have any food for dinner because you didn't go to the grocery store.

    _____

4. You bought a friend a box of candy for her birthday. It has peanuts in it, and she's allergic to them.

    _____

5. Your friend is upset because you didn't return his call.

    _____

6. Your friend is upset because you ignored his call.

    _____

EXERCISE 9 ▸ Let's talk. (Chart 10-2)

Work in pairs or small groups. Read the situation and give several answers for each question.

SITUATION: Tom didn't study for the test. During the exam, he panicked and started looking at other students' test papers. He didn't think the teacher saw him, but she did. She warned him once to stop cheating, but he continued. As a result, the teacher took Tom's test paper, told him to leave the room, and failed him on the exam. The teacher told the principal, and the school suspended him for a week.

1. What should/shouldn't Tom have done?
2. What should/shouldn't the teacher have done?
3. What should/shouldn't the school have done?

EXERCISE 10 ▸ Listening. (Chart 10-2)

Choose the sentence that best explains each statement you hear.

Example: You will hear: I should have run a spell-check on my final paper.
　　　　　　　You will choose: a. I ran a spell-check.
　　　　　　　　　　　　　　　　ⓑ I didn't run a spell-check.

1. a. He still needs more coffee.
　　b. He had too much coffee.

2. a. She saved her money.
　　b. She didn't save her money.

3. a. I didn't go to the doctor.
　　b. It was a bad idea to go to the doctor.

4. a. The president shouldn't have been dishonest.
　　b. It's OK for the president to be dishonest.

EXERCISE 11 ▸ Looking at grammar. (Chart 10-2)

Make complete sentences. Use one item from each column.

1. The flight was supposed to be quick, but ____.

2. The hotel was supposed to give us a nonsmoking room, but ____.

3. The weather should have been beautiful for our vacation, but ____.

4. My parents weren't supposed to visit last weekend, but ____.

5. Tyler should have been home at midnight, but ____.

6. The pharmacy should have had a prescription ready for me, but ____.

7. The cafeteria was supposed to begin serving healthier meals, but ____.

8. Tom was supposed to get a promotion to manager, but ____.

a. it rained all week

b. he stayed out until the early morning

c. they put us on the wrong floor

d. we haven't noticed any changes

e. they lost it

f. management chose someone from outside the company

g. they surprised us

h. ice on the runway caused a delay

EXERCISE 12 ▸ Looking at grammar. (Chart 10-2)
Answer the questions with **be supposed to**.

1. Ali's mom told him to get up early, but he overslept. What was Ali supposed to do?

   _____*He was supposed to get up early.*_____

2. Ray's boss expected him to work overtime yesterday, but his wife and kids got sick. What was Ray supposed to do? _____

3. The students expected their teacher, Mr. Robbins, to be absent. He told them he had a doctor's appointment. But he came to class the next day, as usual. What was supposed to happen yesterday? _____

4. The teacher ordered textbooks with exams, but the ones that arrived didn't have them. What were the books supposed to have? _____

5. Vivian set her alarm for 5:00 A.M., but it didn't go off. What time was Vivian supposed to get up? _____

EXERCISE 13 ▸ Looking at grammar. (Chart 10-2)
Restate each situation with **should have** and one of the verbs in the box.

get	finish	land	pick	✓ come

1. My package isn't here. I expected it yesterday. It _*should have come yesterday.*_____

2. The plane's arrival time was 2:00. It's 3:00. The plane _____ by now.

3. We called and asked for a taxi an hour ago. A taxi _____ us up already.

4. I returned an online purchase on the 1st of the month. Now it's the 25th, and my refund hasn't come. I _____ my refund by now.

5. It's 12:30. I expect the race was over at noon. It _____ a half hour ago.

EXERCISE 14 ▸ Warm-up. (Chart 10-3)
Choose <u>all</u> the correct answers.

A: Did you sleep during the flight?

B: a. Yes, I was able to fly business class.
   b. Yes, I could fly business class.
   c. No, I couldn't relax.
   d. No, I wasn't able to relax.

10-3 Expressing Past Ability

PRESENT:	(a)	I *can speak* Farsi.	**Past ability: *could***
PAST:	(b)	I *could speak* Farsi ten years ago.	***was/were able to***
PRESENT:	(c)	I *am able to speak* Farsi.	
PAST:	(d)	I *was able to speak* Farsi ten years ago.	

	(e) Maya *was able to do* well on her exam. OR Maya *did* well on her exam.	For a single action in the past *affirmative*, ***was/were able to*** or the simple past is used, as in (e). ***Could*** is not typically used.*
INCORRECT:	Last week, Maya ~~could do~~ well on her exam.	For the negative, both verbs are possible: Maya *couldn't do* well on the test. Maya *wasn't able to do* well on the test.

*Exception: ***Could*** can be used in the past for one action with these sense verbs: ***hear, feel, see, smell, taste***; and the verbs ***understand, remember, guess***.

EXERCISE 15 ▸ Looking at grammar. (Chart 10-3)

Part I. Check (✓) the sentences that describe one action in the past.

1. _____ Most students were able to finish the test in under an hour.

2. _____ When I was younger, I was able to hold my breath underwater for three minutes.

3. _____ We were able to help take care of our grandkids last weekend.

4. _____ My father is a brilliant mathematician. When he was a child, he was able to do complex problems in his head.

5. _____ I was able to give my speech last night without sounding nervous.

Part II. Rewrite the checked sentences with the simple past. Rewrite the unchecked sentences with ***could***.

EXERCISE 16 ▸ Looking at grammar. (Chart 10-3)

Choose the correct verb. In some cases, both verbs are correct.

1. When I was a child, I _____ spend hours climbing trees, but now I have trouble climbing stairs!
   a. could   b. was able to

2. Jackson's very intelligent. He _____ read by the time he was three.
   a. could   b. was able to

3. I _____ do anything last week! I had the flu.
   a. couldn't   b. wasn't able to

4. I _____ talk briefly with your college advisor. She's very nice.
   a. could   b. was able to

5. We were late, but we _____ catch the train. It was also late.
   a. could   b. were able to

EXERCISE 17 ▸ Warm-up. (Chart 10-4)

Max and his wife had a party last night. The next morning they found a hat on their couch. Max is thinking about whose hat it is. Match Max's thoughts on the right to the statements on the left.

1. Max thinks the hat looks familiar, but he's not certain whose it is.

2. Max thinks he recognizes the hat. He's almost sure he knows the owner.

3. Max knows exactly whose hat it is.

a. "It is Joe Green's hat."

b. "It could belong to Joe Green. It might be Al Goldberg's. Or it may belong to Mr. Perez across the hall."

c. "It must be Joe Green's hat."

10-4 Degrees of Certainty: Present Time

— *Why isn't John in class?* **100% sure**: He *is* sick. **95% sure**: He *must be* sick. **50% sure or less**: { He *may be* sick. He *might be* sick. He *could be* sick. NOTE: These percentages are approximate.	*Degree of certainty* refers to how sure we are — what we think the chances are — that something is true. If we are sure something is true in the present, we don't need to use a modal. For example, if I say, "John is sick," I am sure; I am stating a fact that I am sure is true. My degree of certainty is 100%. NOTE: *Can* does not express degrees of certainty. *INCORRECT:* He ~~can be~~ sick.
— *Why isn't John in class?* (a) He *must be* sick.	*Must* expresses a strong degree of certainty about a present situation, but it is still less than 100%.
(Usually he is in class every day, but when I saw him last night, he wasn't feeling good. So my best guess is that he is sick today. I can't think of another possibility.)	In (a): The speaker is saying, "Probably John is sick. I have evidence to make me believe that he is sick. That is my logical conclusion, but I do not know for certain."
— *Why isn't John in class?* (b) He *may be* sick. (c) He *might be* sick. (d) He *could be* sick. (I don't really know. He may be at home watching TV. He might be at the library. He could be out of town.	*May*, *might*, and *could* express a weak degree of certainty. In (b), (c), and (d): The meanings are all the same. The speaker is saying, "Perhaps, maybe, possibly John is sick. I am only making a guess. I can think of other possibilities."
(e) *Maybe* he is sick.	In (e): *maybe* (one word) is an adverb. In (b): *may be* (two words) is a verb form.

EXERCISE 18 ▸ Looking at grammar. (Chart 10-4)

Complete the sentences by using **must** or **may/might/could** with the expressions in the box or your own words.

✓ be very proud	fit Jimmy	miss them very much
be at a meeting	have the wrong number	

1. A: I've heard that your daughter recently graduated from law school and that your son has

   gotten a scholarship to the state university. You _____*must be very proud*_____ of them.

   B: We are.

2. A: Hello. May I speak to Ron?

   B: I'm sorry. You _____. There's no one here by that name.

3. A: Where's Ms. Adams? She's not in her office.

B: I don't know. She _____, or maybe she's in the staff lounge.

4. A: This jacket is still in good shape, but Brian has outgrown it. Would it fit one of your sons?

B: Well, it's probably too small for Danny too, but it _____.

5. A: How long has it been since you last saw your family?

B: More than a year.

A: You _____.

EXERCISE 19 ▸ Let's talk: pairwork. (Chart 10-4)

Work with a partner. Take turns making guesses. Use **must**.

Example: PARTNER A: Alice always gets the best grades in the class. Why?
PARTNER B: She must study hard. / She must be intelligent.

PARTNER A	PARTNER B
1. The students are yawning. Why? 2. Carol has goose bumps on her arms. Why? 3. Lisa's stomach is growling. Why? 4. Bob is scratching his arm. Why? 5. Yusef is staring off into space. Why?	1. The bride is crying. Why? 2. Katrina is blushing. Why? 3. The fans are jumping up and down and clapping. Why? 4. Don't look at a clock. What time is it? 5. Eliza is sneezing. Why?

EXERCISE 20 ▸ Let's talk: pairwork. (Chart 10-4)

Work with a partner. Take turns answering the questions with *I don't know + may/might/could*.

Example: PARTNER A: Amy's grammar book isn't on her desk. Where is it?
PARTNER B: I don't know. It may/might/could be in her backpack.

1. (*name of a student*) isn't in class today. Where is she/he?
2. What do you think I have in my briefcase/pocket/bag, etc.?
3. What kind of phone does our teacher have?
4. I can't find my wallet. Do you know where it is?
5. What city do you think (*someone famous*) lives in?
6. How old do you think (*someone famous*) is?

EXERCISE 21 ▸ Warm-up. (Chart 10-5)

Answer the questions.

SITUATION: Tim says, "Someone told me that Ed quit his job, sold his house, and moved to a Pacific island."

OPINIONS: **Lucy** says, "That *may not be* true."
Linda says, "That *must not be* true."
Hamid says, "That *can't be* true."
Rob says, "That *isn't* true."

1. Who is absolutely certain?
2. Who is almost certain?
3. Who has an open mind and hasn't decided?

10-5 Degrees of Certainty: Present Time Negative

100% sure:	Sam *isn't* hungry.
99% sure:	{ Sam *couldn't be* hungry. { Sam *can't be* hungry.
95% sure:	Sam *must not be* hungry.
50% sure or less:	{ Sam *may not be* hungry. { Sam *might not be* hungry.

NOTE: These percentages are approximate.

(a) Sam doesn't want anything to eat. He *isn't* hungry. He told me his stomach is full. I heard him say that he isn't hungry. I believe him.	In (a): The speaker is sure that Sam is not hungry.
(b) Sam *couldn't/can't be* hungry. That's impossible. I just saw him eat a huge meal. He has already eaten enough to fill two grown men! Did he really say he'd like something to eat? I don't believe it.	In (b): The speaker believes that there is no possibility that Sam is hungry (but the speaker is not 100% sure). When used in the negative to show degree of certainty, **couldn't** and **can't** forcefully express the idea that the speaker believes something is impossible.
(c) Sam isn't eating his food. He *must not be* hungry. That's the only reason I can think of.	In (c): The speaker is expressing a logical conclusion, a "best guess."
(d) I don't know why Sam isn't eating his food. He *may not/might not be* hungry right now. Or maybe he doesn't feel well. Or perhaps he ate just before he got here. Who knows?	In (d): The speaker uses **may not/might not** to mention a possibility.

EXERCISE 22 ▶ Let's talk: pairwork. (Chart 10-5)

Work with a partner. Give possible reasons for Speaker B's conclusions.

Example: A: Someone is knocking at the door. It might be Lillian.
         B: It couldn't be Lillian. (*Reason? Lillian is in Moscow. / She's at a movie. / Etc.*)

1. A: Someone left this jacket here. I think it belongs to Alex.
   B: It couldn't belong to him. (*Reason?*)

2. A: Someone told me that Karen is in Norway.
   B: That can't be right. She couldn't be in Norway. (*Reason?*)

3. A: Look at that animal. Is it a wolf?
   B: It couldn't be a wolf. (*Reason?*)

4. A: Someone told me that Marie quit her job.
   B: You're kidding! That can't be true. (*Reason?*)

EXERCISE 23 ▶ Looking at grammar. (Chart 10-5)

Make a guess with **not**. Use a modal that corresponds to the percentage.

1. A: Yuko has flunked every test so far this semester.

   B: She (95% sure) _____ *must not study very hard.* _____

2. A: Tarek's been in bed all day.

   B: He (50% sure) _____

3. A: I'm trying to be a good host. I've offered Rosa a glass of water, a cup of coffee, and a soft drink. She doesn't want anything.

   B: She (95% sure) _____

4. A: Daniel hasn't answered my text message.

   B: Hmmm. He (50% sure) _____

5. A: Mrs. Garcia seems very lonely to me.

   B: I agree. She (95% sure) _____

6. A: George almost hit a cat, a dog, and then a tree when he was driving.

   B: His eyesight (50% sure) _____

EXERCISE 24 ▸ Let's talk: pairwork. (Charts 10-4 and 10-5)

Work with a partner. Create a conversation based on the given situation. Perform your conversation for the class or a group of classmates. You can look at your notes before you speak. When you speak, look at your partner.

SITUATION: You and your friend are at home in the evening. The power suddenly goes out. The weather is very calm, and there is no wind. Initially, you feel afraid, but after talking about possibilities, you come up with a logical explanation. What *may / might / could / must / may not / couldn't / must not* be the cause?

EXERCISE 25 ▸ Warm-up. (Chart 10-6)

Decide which past modal in the box best completes each sentence. One of the modals is not appropriate for any of the sentences.

must have left	couldn't have left
should have left	might have left

SITUATION: Jackie can't find her sunglasses.

1. Laura thinks it's possible that Jackie left them on the table at the restaurant. She says, "You _____ them on the table at the restaurant, but I'm just guessing."

2. Sergio disagrees. He looked at everything on the table before they left and doesn't remember seeing her sunglasses there. He thinks it is impossible that Jackie left them there, so he says, "You _____ them there. I'm sure they are somewhere else. Did you check your purse?"

3. Maya disagrees with Sergio. She remembers seeing the sunglasses on the table, so she says, "You _____ them there. That's the only logical explanation I can think of."

10-6 Degrees of Certainty: Past Time

Past Time: Affirmative

— Why wasn't Mary in class?		
(a)	100%:	She *was* sick.
(b)	95%:	She *must have been* sick.
(c) 50% sure or less:		She *may have been* sick.
		She *might have been* sick.
		She *could have been* sick.

In (a): The speaker is sure.

In (b): The speaker is making a logical conclusion, e.g., "I saw Mary yesterday and found out that she was sick. I assume that is the reason why she was absent. I can't think of any other good reason."

In (c): The speaker is mentioning one possibility.

Past Time: Negative

— Why didn't Sam eat?		
(d)	100%:	Sam *wasn't* hungry.
(e)	99%:	Sam *couldn't have been* hungry.
		Sam *can't have been* hungry.
(f)	95%:	Sam *must not have been* hungry.
(g) 50% sure or less:		Sam *may not have been* hungry.
		Sam *might not have been* hungry.

In (d): The speaker is sure.

In (e): The speaker believes that it is impossible for Sam to have been hungry.

In (f): The speaker is making a logical conclusion.

In (g): The speaker is mentioning one possibility.

EXERCISE 26 ▸ Looking at grammar. (Chart 10-6)

Use past modals to restate the sentence in parentheses.

SITUATION 1: The doorbell rang, but I was in bed trying to take a nap. So I didn't get up. I wonder who it was.

1. (*Maybe it was a friend.*) It ___*may / might / could have been*___ a friend.

2. (*It's not possible that it was my next-door neighbor. He was at work.*) It _____

    _____ my next-door neighbor.

3. (*I'm 95% sure it was a delivery person. There was a package outside my door when I got up.*)

    It _____ a delivery person.

SITUATION 2: I sent my best friend a birthday present, but she never responded or thanked me. That's not like her. I wonder why I never heard from her.

4. (*She probably never got it. That's the only reason I can think of for her not responding to me.*) I

    believe she _____ it.

5. (*My mother thinks it's possible that it got lost in the mail, but she's just guessing.*) My mother

    thinks it _____ lost in the mail. I guess that's possible.

EXERCISE 27 ▸ Let's talk. (Chart 10-6)

Make guesses using past modals.

SITUATION: Dan, David, Dylan, Dick, and Doug are all friends. One of them got engaged last night. Who do you think it is?

1. Dan had a huge argument with his girlfriend last night.

    → *It couldn't / must not have been Dan because he fought with his girlfriend last night.*

2. David met with his girlfriend's parents two nights ago.

3. Dylan invited his girlfriend to dinner and took a diamond ring with him.

4. Dick is going to wait to get married until he has a better job.

5. Doug isn't sure if he's ready for marriage. He thinks he's a little young to be a husband.

EXERCISE 28 ▶ Let's talk. (Chart 10-6)

Work with a partner. Partner A asks a question, and Partner B responds with *may have/might have/could have*. Then Partner A disagrees. Partner B responds with a stronger conclusion. Choose one of your conversations to perform for the class. You can look at your book before you speak. When you speak, look at your partner.

Example:
PARTNER A: Larry was absent yesterday afternoon. Where was he?
PARTNER B: I don't know. He may/might/could have skipped class.
PARTNER A: I don't think so. He's not the type.
PARTNER B: He must have had an appointment.

1. A: Beth seems upset.

   B: She _____

   A: I don't think so. _____

   B: Well, she _____

2. A: How did Claudio get to school today?

   B: He _____

   A: I don't think so. _____

   B: Well, he _____

3. A: The subway station is closed.

   B: There _____

   A: I don't think so. _____

   B: Well, there _____

EXERCISE 29 ▶ Looking at grammar. (Charts 10-4 → 10-6)

Complete the conversations with *must* and the verbs in parentheses. Use *not* if necessary.

1. A: Paula fell asleep in class this morning.

   B: She (stay up) _____*must have stayed up*_____ too late last night.

2. A: Jim is eating everything in the salad but the onions. He's pushed all of the onions to the side of his plate.

   B: He (like) _____ onions.

3. A: Marco had to give a speech in front of 500 people.

   B: Whew! That's a big audience. He (be) _____ nervous.

   A: He was, but no one could tell.

4. A: What time is it?

   B: Well, we came at 7:00, and I'm sure we've been here for at least an hour. So it
      (be) _____ around 8:00.

5. A: I met Ayako's husband at the reception. We said hello to each other, but when I asked
      him a question in English, he just smiled and nodded.

   B: He (speak) _____ much English.

6. A: You have a black eye! What happened?

   B: I walked into a door.

   A: Ouch! That (hurt) _____ .

7. A: Who is your teacher?

   B: I think his name is Mr. Rock or something like that.

   A: Mr. Rock? Oh, you (mean) _____ Mr. Stone.

8. A: I grew up in a small town.

   B: That (be) _____ boring.

   A: No, actually it was really fun. There was so much to do outdoors.

9. A: No one's here. Doesn't the party start at 7:00?

   B: No, 8:00.

   A: Oh, I (misunderstand) _____ .

10. A: Listen. Do you hear a buzzing sound in the kitchen?

    B: Yes, it's coming from the fridge. Something (be) _____ wrong with
       the motor.

    A: I hope it's not dying.

EXERCISE 30 ▶ Listening. (Charts 10-2 → 10-6)
The spoken forms of some modals are often reduced. For example, ***may have gone*** may sound
like "may-uv gone" or "may-uh gone." Write the non-reduced forms of the verbs that you hear.

What's wrong? Your parents look upset.

Example: You will hear: You shouldn't have done that.
             You will write: You *shouldn't have done* that.

1. We _____ them.

2. We _____ them.

3. You _____ them.

4. You _____ to find out.

5. Maybe you _____ out so late.

6. You _____ a good excuse for being late.

7. You _____ them what you planned to do.

8. You _____ your behavior would cause problems.

EXERCISE 31 ▸ Warm-up. (Chart 10-7)

Match each sentence to the percentage it best describes.

1. We might get some snow tomorrow.
2. We will get some snow tomorrow.
3. We may get some snow tomorrow.
4. We should get some snow tomorrow.
5. We could get some snow tomorrow.

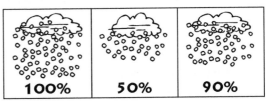

| 100% | 50% | 90% |

10-7	**Degrees of Certainty: Future Time**		
(a)	**100% sure**:	Kay *will do* well on the test.	→ The speaker feels sure.
(b)	**90% sure**:	Kay *should do* well on the test. Kay *ought to do* well on the test.	→ The speaker is almost sure.
(c)	**50% sure or less**:	She *may do* well on the test. She *might do* well on the test. She *could do* well on the test.	→ The speaker is guessing.

EXERCISE 32 ▸ Looking at grammar. (Chart 10-7)

Complete the sentences with the speakers' names based on how certain they are.

SITUATION: Jan asked her roommates, "What time are you going to be home tonight?"

CERTAINTY: **Marco** feels 100% sure.

   Linda is almost sure.

   Ned doesn't know. He's guessing.

1. _____ said, "I might be back by ten."

2. _____ said, "I'll be home by eight."

3. _____ said, "I should be here around nine."

EXERCISE 33 ▸ Looking at grammar. (Charts 10-4 and 10-7)

Complete the sentences with *will, should/ought to,* or *must.* In some cases, more than one modal is possible. Discuss the meanings that the modals convey.

1. A: Lots of people are standing in line to get into that movie.

   B: It _____*must*_____ be good.

2. A: Roberto's going to take care of his niece for the first time tonight. She's only a year old.

   B: That _____*should / ought to / will*_____ be interesting.

3. A: Look. Jack's car is in front of his house. He _____ be at home.

   B: Let's stop and visit him.

4. A: Hello. May I speak to Elena?

   B: She isn't here right now, but she _____ be home around nine or so.

5. A: Which team do you think is going to win the game tomorrow?

   B: Well, we have better players, so we _____ win, but anything can happen.

6. A: It's very important for you to be there on time.

   B: I _____ be there at seven o'clock. I promise!

7. A: Susie is yawning and rubbing her eyes.

   B: She _____ be sleepy. Let's put her to bed early tonight.

8. A: Martha has been working all day. She left for work early this morning.

   B: She _____ be really tired tonight.

9. A: When's dinner?

   B: We're almost ready to eat. The rice _____ be done in five minutes.

10. A: Ed has been acting strangely lately.

    B: He _____ be in love!

EXERCISE 34 ▶ Grammar and speaking. (Charts 10-4 → 10-7)

Work with a partner. Take turns completing the sentences based on the facts of each situation.

SITUATION 1: Someone's knocking at the door. I wonder who it is.
   FACTS: **Ross** is out of town.

   Fred called half an hour ago and said he would stop by this afternoon.

   Alice is a neighbor who sometimes drops by in the middle of the day.

1. It must be _____Fred_____.

2. It couldn't be _____Ross_____.

3. I suppose it might be _____Alice_____.

SITUATION 2: Someone ran into the tree in front of our house. I wonder who did it.
   FACTS: **Stacy** has a car, and she was out driving last night.

   Beth doesn't have a car and doesn't know how to drive.

   Ron has a car, but I'm pretty sure he was at home last night.

   Barb was out driving last night, and today her car has a big dent in the front.

4. It couldn't have been _____.

5. It must not have been _____.

6. It could have been _____.

7. It must have been _____.

SITUATION 3: There is a hole in the bread. It looks like something ate some of the bread. The bread was in a closed drawer until I opened it.
   FACTS: **A mouse** likes to eat bread and often gets into drawers. In fact, we found one last week.

   A cat can't open a drawer. And most cats don't like bread.

   A rat can sometimes get into a drawer, but I've never seen one in our house.

8. It could have been _____.

9. It couldn't have been _____.

10. It must have been _____.

SITUATION 4: My friends Mark and Carol were in the living room with my neighbor. I heard someone playing a very difficult piece on the piano.

     FACTS: **Mark** has no musical ability at all and doesn't play any instrument.

          Carol is an excellent piano player.

          I don't think **my neighbor** plays the piano, but I'm not sure.

11. It couldn't have been _____ .

12. I suppose it could have been _____ .

13. It must have been _____ .

SITUATION 5: The meeting starts in 15 minutes. I wonder who is coming.

     FACTS: I just talked to **Bob** on the phone. He's on his way.

          Stephanie rarely misses a meeting.

          Andre comes to the meetings sometimes, and sometimes he doesn't.

          Janet is out of town.

14. _____ won't be at the meeting.

15. _____ should be at the meeting.

16. _____ will be here.

17. _____ might come.

EXERCISE 35 ▸ Warm-up. (Chart 10-8)

Check (✓) the sentences where the activity is or may be in progress.

1. _____ Grandpa takes a nap every afternoon.

2. _____ Grandpa may take a nap this afternoon.

3. _____ Shhh. Grandpa is taking a nap.

4. _____ Shhh. Grandpa may be taking a nap.

10-8 Progressive Forms of Modals	
(a) Knock on the door lightly. Tom *may be sleeping*. (*right now*) (b) All of the lights in Ann's room are turned off. She *must be sleeping*. (*right now*)	Progressive form, present time: *modal* + ***be*** + ***-ing*** Meaning: *in progress right now*
(c) Sue wasn't home last night when we went to see her. She *might have been studying* at the library. (d) Joe wasn't home last night. He has a lot of exams coming up soon, and he is also working on a term paper. He *must have been studying* at the library.	Progressive form, past time: *modal* + ***have been*** + ***-ing*** Meaning: *in progress at a time in the past*

EXERCISE 36 ▸ Looking at grammar. (Chart 10-8)

Complete the sentences. Use the appropriate progressive forms of ***must, should,*** or ***may/might/could*** and the verbs in parentheses.

1. A: Look. Those people who are coming in the door are carrying wet umbrellas.

   B: It (*rain*) _____ *must be raining* _____ .

2. A: Why is Margaret in her room?

   B: I don't know. She (*do*) _____ *may / might / could be doing* _____ her homework.

3. A: Do you smell smoke?

B: I sure do. Something (*burn*) _____ in the kitchen.

4. A: Julio hasn't answered his text messages all day. What do you suppose he's doing?

B: I don't know. He (*work*) _____ .

5. A: What's all that noise upstairs? It sounds like a herd of elephants.

B: The kids (*play*) _____ some kind of game.

A: That's what it sounds like to me too. I'll go see.

6. A: I need to call Howard. Do you know which hotel he's staying at in Boston?

B: Well, he (*stay*) _____ at the Hilton, but I'm not sure. He

(*stay*) _____ at the Holiday Inn.

7. A: What are you doing?

B: I'm writing an email to a friend, but I (*study*) _____ . I have a test tomorrow.

8. A: Did you know that Majid just quit school and is hitchhiking to Alaska?

B: What? You (*joke*) _____ .

9. A: Did Joe mean what he said about Majid yesterday?

B: I don't know. He (*joke*) _____ when he said that, but who knows?

10. A: Did Joe really mean what he said yesterday?

B: No, I don't think so. I think he (*joke*) _____ .

EXERCISE 37 ▶ Let's talk. (Chart 10-8)

Work in small groups to answer the questions about the drivers in the pictures.

1. In your opinion, which drivers in the pictures are distracted?
2. What should/shouldn't these drivers be doing? Make a list of sentences.
3. Is distracted driving a problem in your country? You may want to support your answer with statistics from the Internet or elsewhere.
4. Have you ever been in the car with a distracted driver? If so, what were you thinking?
5. Does age matter? For example, are adults better able to handle distractions than teens?

EXERCISE 38 ▸ Looking at grammar. (Chart 10-8)
Complete each sentence with the appropriate form of the words in parentheses. Add *not* if necessary.

1. Alex needs to study for a test. He (*should + watch*) _____shouldn't be watching_____ TV right now.

2. There's Mr. Chang. He's standing at the bus stop. He (*must + wait*) _____ _____ for the two o'clock bus.

3. Kathy lost her way while driving to River City. She (*should + leave*) _____ _____ home without directions.

4. My leather jacket isn't in my closet. I think my roommate (*might + borrow*) _____ _____ it. He often borrows my clothes without asking me.

5. When I walked into the room, the TV was on, but the room was empty. Dad (*must + watch*) _____ TV a short while before I came into the room.

   He (*must + forget*) _____ to turn it off before he left the room.

6. A: Why wasn't Mai at the meeting last night?

   B: She (*may + attend*) _____ the lecture at Shaw Hall. I know she really wanted to hear the speaker.

7. A: Where's that cold air coming from?

   B: Someone (*must + leave*) _____ the door open.

8. A: Where's Jessica? I haven't seen her for weeks.

   B: I'm not sure. She (*might + travel*) _____ in Europe. I think I heard her mention something about spending a few weeks in Europe this spring.

9. A: When I arrived, Tarek looked surprised.

   B: He (*must + expect*) _____ you.

10. A: Why didn't Roberto answer the teacher when she asked him a question?

    B: He was too busy staring out the window. He (*must + daydream*) _____ _____. He (*should + pay*) _____ attention.

    He (*should + stare*) _____ out the window during class.

EXERCISE 39 ▶ Let's talk. (Charts 10-2 → 10-8)

A man and woman are sitting at a table having a conversation. In pairs or small groups, use modals to make guesses about the two people and what's happening. What possibilities can you think of? Answer the questions and add your own to the discussion.

MAN: I don't think you should do this alone.

WOMAN: But you don't understand. I have to.

MAN: Let me go with you (*taking out his wallet*). Just give me a minute to pay the bill.

WOMAN: No, I'll be fine.

MAN: You must let me help.

WOMAN: There's nothing you can do (*standing*). This is something I need to do for myself.

MAN: OK. If that's the way you want it.

WOMAN: (*leaving*) I'll call you.

1. Where are the man and woman?
2. Who are they? What is their relationship?
3. Where's the woman going?
4. Why does she want to go alone?
5. Why does the man want to go with her?

EXERCISE 40 ▶ Looking at grammar. (Charts 10-2 → 10-8)

Choose the best completion for each sentence.

1. A: Is Jeff a good student?

   B: He _____. I don't know him well, but I heard he got a scholarship for next year.
   a. must be   b. could be   c. is

2. A: I heard that Eva is visiting. Do you know where she's staying?

   B: She _____ at Barbara's house. Or maybe she's at her sister's.
   a. must be staying   b. could be staying   c. is staying

3. A: I stayed up all night finishing this report for the boss.

   B: You _____ really tired.
   a. must feel   b. might feel   c. feel

4. A: Where's the leftover chicken from dinner last night?

   B: I just saw it when I got some ice cubes. It _____ in the freezer.
   a. must be   b. might be   c. is

5. A: It's supposed to rain tomorrow.

   B: I know, but the forecast _____ wrong. Weather forecasts are far from 100% accurate.
   a. must be   b. could be   c. is

6. A: I heard that Junko has received a scholarship and will be able to attend the university in the fall.

   B: That's great news. She _____ very happy.
   a. must be feeling   b. may be feeling   c. is feeling

7. A: Excuse me. Could you tell me which bus I should take to get to City Hall?

   B: Hmmm. Bus number 63 _____ there. But you'd better ask the driver.
      a. must go   b. might go   c. goes

8. A: Which bus should I take to get to the main post office?

   B: Bus number 39. It _____ right to the post office.
      a. must go   b. could go   c. goes

9. A: Do you suppose Mrs. Chu is sick?

   B: She _____. I can't think of any other reason she isn't at this meeting.
      a. must be   b. may be   c. is

10. A: Is that Adam's brother standing with him in the cafeteria line?

    B: It _____, I suppose. He does look a little like Adam.
       a. must be   b. could be   c. is

11. A: Let's be really quiet when we go into the baby's room. The baby _____, and we don't want to wake her up.

    B: OK.
       a. might sleep   b. might be sleeping   c. might have been sleeping

12. A: I wonder why the TV is on in the family room. No one's in there.

    B: Grandma _____ to turn it off. She was in the family room earlier.
       a. must forget   b. must have forgotten c. must be forgetting

EXERCISE 41 ▶ Warm-up. (Chart 10-9)
Check (✓) the correct sentences.

1. _____ I will can stay late at the office today.

2. _____ I will be able stay late today.

3. _____ I may have to stay late today.

4. _____ I may be able to stay late today.

5. _____ I will have to stay late today.

6. _____ I'm going to have to stay late today.

10-9 Combining Modals with Phrasal Modals	
(a) *INCORRECT:* Janet will ~~can~~ help you tomorrow.	A modal cannot be immediately followed by another modal. In (a): The modal **will** cannot be followed by **can**, which is another modal.
(b) Janet *will be able to* help you tomorrow. (c) You *will have to* pick her up at her home.	A modal can, however, be followed by the phrasal modals **be able to** and **have to**. In (b): The modal **will** is correctly followed by the phrasal modal **be able to**.
(d) Tom *isn't going to be able to* help you tomorrow.	It is also sometimes possible for one phrasal modal to follow another phrasal modal. In (d): **be going to** is followed by **be able to**. This form is more common in negatives and questions than in the affirmative.

EXERCISE 42 ▸ Looking at grammar. (Chart 10-9)
Complete the sentences with the verb phrases in the box. In some cases, more than one completion
may be possible. Discuss the differences in meaning.

have to be able to	must not have been able to
should not have to	would rather not have to
✓ not be going to be able to	

1. My schedule is completely full for the next few weeks. I'm _____*not going to be able to*_____
   meet with you until the end of the month.

2. You need to see a doctor you feel comfortable talking to. It's important that she knows
   how you feel. You _____ tell her exactly how
   you're feeling.

3. Jill just called from work. She sounded upset, but she won't tell me what's wrong.
   She was planning to ask her supervisor for a raise today. I bet that's the problem.
   She _____ get the raise.

4. Let's get to the movie a little late. I don't mind if we miss the previews. It's freezing outside,
   and I _____ stand in a long line outdoors until
   they let us in.

5. Tommy and Jimmy, this room is a mess! I am not going to tell you again to clean it up. Really,
   I _____ tell you this more than once!

EXERCISE 43 ▸ Speaking or writing. (Chart 10-9)
Create a conversation or write a story about the man in the picture using most of the given verb
phrases. If you make a conversation, work with a partner, and perform it for the class.

1. might not be able to
2. is going to have to
3. has to be able to
4. shouldn't have to
5. must not have been able to
6. is not going to be able to
7. may have had to

EXERCISE 44 ▸ Warm-up. (Chart 10-10)
Answer the questions with **would rather**.

1. You are at school right now. Where would you rather be?
2. What would you rather do than go to class?
3. What did you do last night? What would you rather have done?
4. What are you doing right now? What would you rather be doing?

10-10 Expressing Preference: *Would Rather*

(a) I *would rather go* to a movie tonight *than study* grammar.	*Would rather* expresses preference.
(b) I*'d rather study* history *than (study)* biology.	In (a): Notice that the simple form of a verb follows both *would rather* and *than*.
	In (b): If the verb is the same, it usually is not repeated after *than*.
(c) — How much do you weigh? — I*'d rather not tell* you.	Contraction: *I would = I'd* Negative form: *would rather + not*
(d) The movie was OK, but I *would rather have gone* to the concert last night.	The past form: *would rather have* + *past participle* Usual pronunciation: "I'd rather-əv"
(e) I*'d rather be lying* on a beach in India than *(be) sitting* in class right now.	Progressive form: *would rather + be + ing*

EXERCISE 45 ▶ Looking at grammar. (Chart 10-10)

Complete the sentences with *would rather* and your own words.

1. A: Do you want to go to the concert tonight?

   B: Not really. I _____

2. A: Did you go to the concert last night?

   B: Yes, but I _____

3. A: What are you doing right now?

   B: I'm studying grammar, but I _____

4. A: How was the movie last night?

   B: So-so. I _____

5. A: You look really tired.

   B: I am. I still have jet lag from my trip. Instead of working, I _____

   _____ right now.

6. A: I _____ than _____

   B: Not me. I _____ than _____

EXERCISE 46 ▶ Let's talk: interview. (Chart 10-10)

Interview your classmates. Begin each question with *Would you rather*.

Would you rather ...

1. go to Paris, Cairo, or Buenos Aires? Why?
2. see a movie, a play, or an opera? Why?
3. use a bike, a motorcycle, or a car for transportation? Why?
4. prepare your own meals, have someone at home prepare them, or eat out? Why?
5. be playing soccer, shopping for clothes, or taking care of a pet right now? Why?
6. have been born in an earlier century? Why?
7. be swimming at the beach right now or doing this interview? Why?

10-11 Summary Chart of Modals and Similar Expressions

Auxiliary	Uses	Present/Future	Past
may	(1) polite request (only with "I" or "we")	*May* I *borrow* your pen?	
	(2) formal permission	You *may leave* the room.	
	(3) 50% or less certainty	— *Where's John?* He *may be* at the library.	— *Where was John?* He *may have been* at the library.
might	(1) 50% or less certainty	— *Where's John?* He *might be* at the library.	— *Where was John?* He *might have been* at the library.
	(2) polite request (*rare*)	*Might* I *borrow* your pen?	
should	(1) advisability	I *should study* tonight.	I *should have studied* last night, but I didn't.
	(2) expectation	She *should do* well on the test tomorrow.	She *should have done* well on the test.
ought to	(1) advisability	I *ought to study* tonight.	I *ought to have studied* last night, but I didn't.
	(2) expectation	She *ought to do* well on the test tomorrow.	She *ought to have done* well on the test.
had better	(1) advisability with threat of bad result	You *had better be* on time, or we will leave without you.	(*past form uncommon*)
be supposed to	(1) expectation/obligation	Class *is supposed to start* at 10:00.	
	(2) unfulfilled expectation/ obligation		Class *was supposed to start* at 10:00.
must	(1) strong necessity	You *must sign* the forms in ink.	(You *had to sign* the forms in ink.)
	(2) prohibition (*negative*)	You *must not* open that door.	
	(3) 95% certainty	Mary isn't in class. She *must be* sick.	Mary *must have been* sick yesterday.
have to	(1) necessity	I *have to go* to class today.	I *had to go* to class yesterday.
	(2) lack of necessity (*negative*)	I *don't have to go* to class today.	I *didn't have to go* to class yesterday.
have got to	(1) necessity	I *have got to go* to class today.	(I *had to go* to class yesterday.)
will	(1) 100% certainty	He *will be* here at 6:00.	
	(2) willingness	— The phone's ringing. *I'll get it.*	
	(3) polite request	*Will* you please help me?	
be going to	(1) 100% certainty (*prediction*)	He *is going to be* here at 6:00.	
	(2) definite plan (*intention*)	I'm *going to paint* my bedroom.	
	(3) unfulfilled intention		I *was going to paint* my room, but I didn't have time.

Auxiliary	Uses	Present/Future	Past
can	(1) ability	I *can run* fast.	I *could run* fast when I was a child, but now I can't.
	(2) informal permission	You *can use* my car tomorrow.	
	(3) informal polite request	*Can* I *borrow* your pen?	
	(4) possibility	People *can learn* from their mistakes.	
	(5) impossibility (*negative only*)	That *can't be* true!	That *can't have been* true!
could	(1) past ability (*not for a single past event*)		I *could run* fast when I was a child.
	(2) polite request	*Could* I *borrow* your pen? *Could* you *help* me?	
	(3) suggestion (*affirmative only*)	— I need help in math.	You *could have talked* to your teacher.
		You *could talk* to your teacher.	
	(4) 50% or less certainty	— Where's John? He *could be* at home.	He *could have been* at home.
	(5) impossibility (*negative only*)	That *couldn't be* true!	That *couldn't have been* true!
be able to	(1) ability	I *am able to help* you. I *will be able to help* you.	I *was able to help* him.
would	(1) polite request	*Would* you please *help* me? *Would* you *mind* if I left early?	
	(2) preference	I *would rather go* to the park than *stay* home.	I *would rather have gone* to the park.
	(3) repeated action in the past (*not past situations or states*)		When I was a child, I *would visit* my grandparents every weekend.
	(4) polite for "want" (with "like")	I *would like* an apple, please.	
	(5) unfulfilled wish		I *would have liked* a cookie, but there were none in the house.
used to	(1) repeated action in the past		I *used to visit* my grandparents every weekend.
	(2) past situation or state		I *used to live* in Spain. Now I live in Korea.
shall	(1) polite question to make a suggestion	*Shall* I *open* the window?	
	(2) future with *I* or *we* as subject	I *shall arrive* at nine. ("will" = more common)	

NOTE: The use of modals in reported speech is discussed in Chart 12-8, p. 264. The use of modals in conditional sentences is discussed in Chart 20-3, p. 430.

EXERCISE 47 ▸ Let's talk. (Chart 10-11)

Discuss the differences in meaning, if any, in each group of sentences. Describe situations in which these sentences might be used. Work in pairs, in small groups, or as a class.

1. a. May I use your phone?
   b. Could I use your phone?
   c. Can I use your phone?

2. a. You should take an English course.
   b. You ought to take an English course.
   c. You're supposed to take an English course.
   d. You must take an English course.

3. a. You should see a doctor about that cut on your arm.
   b. You had better see a doctor about that cut on your arm.
   c. You have to see a doctor about that cut on your arm.

4. a. You must not use that door.
   b. You don't have to use that door.

5. a. I will be at your house by six o'clock.
   b. I should be at your house by six o'clock.

6. — *There is a knock at the door. Who do you suppose it is?*
   a. It might be Wendy.
   b. It may be Wendy.
   c. It could be Wendy.
   d. It must be Wendy.

7. — *There's a knock at the door. I think it's Ibrahim.*
   a. It may not be Ibrahim.
   b. It couldn't be Ibrahim.
   c. It can't be Ibrahim.

8. — *Where's Jeff?*
   a. He might have gone home.
   b. He must have gone home.
   c. He had to go home.

9. a. Each student should have health insurance.
   b. Each student must have health insurance.

10. a. If you're having a problem, you could talk to Mrs. Ang.
    b. If you're having a problem, you should talk to Mrs. Ang.
    c. If you're having a problem, you should have told Mrs. Ang.
    d. If you're having a problem, you could have told Mrs. Ang.

11. a. The family in the picture must be at a restaurant.
    b. The family in the picture are at a restaurant.

EXERCISE 48 ▶ Looking at grammar. (Chapters 9 and 10 Review)
Use a modal or phrasal modal with each verb in parentheses.

1. It looks like rain. We (*shut*) _____ should / had better / ought to shut _____ the windows.

2. Anya, (*you, hand*) _____ me that dish? Thanks.

3. Spring break starts on the 13th. We (*go, not*) _____ to classes
   again until the 22nd.

4. The baby is only a year old, but she (*say, already*) _____ a few words.

5. In the United States, elementary education is compulsory. All children (*attend*) _____
   _____ six years of elementary school.

6. There was a long line in front of the theater. We (*wait*) _____ almost
   an hour to buy our tickets.

7. A: I'd like to go to a warm, sunny place next winter. Any suggestions?
   B: You (*go*) _____ to Hawaii or Mexico. Or how about Indonesia?

8. A: Mrs. Wilson got a traffic ticket. She didn't stop at a stop sign.
   B: That's surprising. She's a very cautious and safe driver. She (*see, not*) _____
   _____ the sign.

9. A: This is Steve's laptop, isn't it?
   B: It (*be, not*) _____ his. He doesn't have a laptop, at least not that I know
   of. It (*belong*) _____ to Jana or to Mindy. They sometimes bring their
   laptops to class.

10. In my country, a girl and boy (*go, not*) _____ out on a date unless they have
    a chaperone with them.

11. Jimmy was serious when he said he wanted to be a cowboy when he grew up. We (*laugh, not*) _____
    _____ at him. We hurt his feelings.

12. A: Look at all the beautiful flowers! Are those annuals or
    perennials?
    B: I'm not sure. They (*be*) _____ perennials.
    Let's ask.

EXERCISE 49 ▸ Listening. (Chapters 9 and 10 Review)

Listen to each situation and choose the statement (a. or b.) you would most likely say. In some cases, both answers may be possible.

Example: You will hear: It's almost 5:00. Peter's mom will be home soon. She told him to clean his room today, but it's still a mess. She's going to be mad.

        You will choose: a. He might clean it up right away.

                          (b.) He'd better clean it up right away.

1. a. He should have come.
   b. He must have come.

2. a. I am supposed to take a break from studying.
   b. I would rather lie in the sun and listen to music.

3. a. He may have gotten caught in traffic.
   b. He ought to have called by now.

4. a. He's not going to be able to go to work for a few days.
   b. He might not have to go to work today.

5. a. She could have been daydreaming.
   b. She must have been daydreaming.

EXERCISE 50 ▸ Let's talk. (Chapters 9 and 10 Review)

In small groups, debate one or more of the given statements. Do you agree with these statements? Why or why not? At the end of the discussion, choose one member of your group to summarize the main ideas and present them to the class.

1. Violence on television influences people to act violently.
2. Government agencies should censor the Internet.
3. People of different religions should not marry.
4. People shouldn't marry until they are at least 25 years old.
5. All people of the world should speak more than one language.

EXERCISE 51 ▸ Check your knowledge. (Chapter 10 Review)

Correct the errors.

1. I used ⌄ know a lot of Spanish, but I've forgotten a lot.
         to

2. If you can't find your coat, you should to go to the lost-and-found office.

3. When I was a child, I can climb to the roof of my house and saw all the other houses and streets.

4. It may be snow tomorrow. I hope so!

5. We need to reschedule. I won't can see you at the time we scheduled for tomorrow.

6. I could break my leg in a soccer game three months ago.

7. Many students would rather to study on their own than going to classes.

8. Why did Joe must have surgery last week? He looked so healthy.

9. When you visit a big city in my country, you must to be paying attention to your wallet when you are in a crowded place because a thief maybe try to steal it.

10. We supposed to review for the test today, but we ran out of time.

11. Our team could win the soccer championship last week.

EXERCISE 52 ▸ **Reading and writing.** (Chapter 10 Review)
Part I. Read the passage from a student handbook.

> Do you know these words?
> - common practice
> - passive skill
> - effective
> - efficiently
> - headings/ subheadings
> - graphs
> - roadmap
> - high blood pressure

What is the best way to
read a textbook?

Do you use a highlighter pen when you read? For many students, especially at the college level, this has long been a common practice. However, recent research questions the value of highlighting passages in textbooks. In fact, you may want to discard the highlighter pen if you are only marking material instead of actively working with it. Highlighting is a passive skill. Learning is more effective when you can interact with the text. Here are some recommended techniques that can help you read and remember material more efficiently.

A first step is to look at the headings, subheadings, lists, examples, charts, and graphs in the chapter. These can serve as a roadmap for what is important in the reading. For example, if a section has the heading *Salt and High Blood Pressure*, an important question to ask is "What is the connection between *salt and high blood pressure*?" You should write down such questions and try to find the answers in the reading.

Usually you do not have to read every word carefully. Textbooks are written for large populations of students; instructors often have a more specific focus, and they usually don't have the time to cover everything in one course. Instructors specify learning objectives, and you can find them in your syllabus and assignments. You can also pick up on themes from the questions that instructors ask. It's important to connect all this with the information you are reading.

A very important tool for reading more deeply is annotation, or adding notes. One way to annotate is to write notes in the margin. These notes explain or summarize key points. Annotations can be brief. If you need more space, you can write in a separate notebook rather than in the margins. After you annotate, put your notes into a short summary. You only need to mention key ideas.

You may have purchased a used textbook that is already annotated. It is still best if you put the textbook material into your own words. That way your notes will be understandable. Additionally, reading another person's notes is a passive activity, like reading a textbook passage all over again.

Once you identify key concepts, you can write practice test questions based on the textbook material. Some students use online flashcard programs for their questions. Whatever the method, it is important that you quiz yourself repeatedly over many days. Spacing out your practice has proven to be more effective than studying information all at one time. Some researchers recommend that students teach the material to others as a way to learn it really well. Study groups may provide good opportunities for doing this.

Learning needs to be an active process. By taking some or all of these steps, you will interact with the material more and remember it better.

Part II. Reread the passage and annotate each paragraph. Then in small groups, identify the key points. Together, write at least five test questions that you can use for review.

EXERCISE 53 ▶ Reading and writing. (Chapter 10)

Part I. Read the following summary. Does the summary match your ideas of the key points in the previous reading?

Summary: What is the best way to read a textbook?

For students to understand textbook reading material well, they must be active learners. Highlighting is a passive activity. Students instead need to put the ideas into their own words. They should write notes, either in the margin or in a notebook, and then summarize key information. They can use the chapter organization as a guide, for example, and focus on headings, subheadings, and lists. Students should also find out the information the instructor considers important and pay attention to this when they read. After they identify the key information, they ought to make self-study quizzes, so they can test themselves many times in the days before an exam.

Part II. Find a textbook passage or online article that provides advice on how to do something. Your instructor will tell you how long it should be. Annotate the key points. Then write a summary, using modal verbs appropriately.

WRITING TIP

A summary is much shorter than the original passage or article. When you write a summary, you highlight the essential points without repeating ideas, and without bringing in your own conclusions or opinions.

Here is one effective, two-step approach to developing a summary:

1. Write a topic sentence that provides an overview, tying your ideas together.
2. Write one sentence summarizing each paragraph of the passage or article. Make sure your individual summarizing sentences flow together in meaningful paragraphs, as in the example above.

Part III. Edit your writing. Check for the following:

1. ☐ correct forms for present modals
2. ☐ correct forms for past modals
3. ☐ correct meaning of modal verbs
4. ☐ correct forms for phrasal modals
5. ☐ correct spelling (use a dictionary or spell-check)

▪▪▪▪ Go to MyEnglishLab for Self-Study: Gerunds and Infinitives 10

11

The Passive

PRETEST: What do I already know?
Write "C" if a sentence has the correct verb form and "I" for incorrect. Check your answers below. After you complete each chart listed, make any necessary corrections.

1. _____ A car accident was occurred in front of my office yesterday. (11-1)

2. _____ The tax bill checked by the accountant last week. (11-1)

3. _____ A new apartment building is being built next to my house. (11-2)

4. _____ Has the text message been sent already? (11-2)

5. _____ Coffee is best grown in wetter climates. (11-3)

6. _____ The exams will be reading by two different teachers. (11-4)

7. _____ Your homework should have be done before you went to your friend's. (11-4)

8. _____ Sorry, the project isn't quite finish yet. (11-5)

9. _____ Did you know that Alexa is marry to Khalifa? (11-5)

10. _____ What would you like to be remembered for? (11-6)

11. _____ Tomas is two hours late. I'm get nervous. (11-7)

12. _____ The speaker had a monotone voice. We were really boring. (11-8)

Incorrect sentences: 1, 2, 6, 7, 8, 9, 11, 12

EXERCISE 1 ▶ Warm-up. (Chart 11-1)
Match the sentences to the pictures.

1. _____ The girl hit the ball.
2. _____ The ball was hit by the girl.
3. _____ The girl was hit by the ball.
4. _____ The ball hit the girl.
5. _____ The girl was hitting the ball.

Picture A   Picture B

11-1 Active vs. Passive

Active: (a) **Mary** *helped* the boy. *(subject verb object)*	In the passive, *the object* of an active verb becomes *the subject* of the passive verb: *the boy* in (a) becomes the subject of the passive verb in (b).
Passive: (b) **The boy** *was helped* by Mary. *(subject verb)*	Notice that the subject of an active verb follows **by** in a passive sentence. The noun that follows **by** is called the "agent." In (b): **Mary** is the agent. Sentences (a) and (b) have the same meaning.

Passive: (c) He is helped by her.
      He was helped by her.
      He will be helped by her.
*(**be** + past participle)*
	Form of the passive: **be** + *past participle*

Active: (d) An accident *happened*. Passive: (e) (none)	Only transitive verbs (verbs that can be followed by an object) are used in the passive. Here are some common intransitive verbs; they are never passive: *appear, arrive, belong, come, die, fall, happen, look like, occur, resemble, seem, sleep*. (See also Appendix Chart A-1.)

EXERCISE 2 ▸ Looking at grammar. (Chart 11-1)
Identify the **be** verb in each sentence, and identify the past participle if there is one. Then indicate whether or not the sentence is passive.

The Movies

	BE	PAST PARTICIPLE	PASSIVE
1. What movie is playing this week?	is	Ø	no
2. A world premiere movie will be shown tonight.	will be	shown	yes
3. A popular movie was shown last week.			
4. Tickets are sold at the theater and online.			
5. Tickets for the upcoming movie will be sold online soon.			
6. Tickets will be available soon.			
7. Discounts are given for advance purchases.			
8. We are giving tickets to our friends.			
9. The movie will be a blockbuster.			
10. The last ticket was just sold.			

EXERCISE 3 ▸ Looking at grammar. (Chart 11-1)

Decide if the sentences are active (A) or passive (P).

1. a. __A__ Kate made the salad.

   b. __P__ The rice was made by Jamal.

   c. _____ Siri was making the dessert.

   d. _____ Andy has made the tea.

2. a. _____ Anita and Alex came to our apartment for dinner last night.

   b. _____ On their way over, Anita was stopped by the police for speeding.

   c. _____ She was upset, but Alex calmed her down.

3. a. _____ Dinosaurs existed millions of years ago.

   b. _____ The remains of about 14 dinosaurs are discovered every year.

   c. _____ After a discovery, the bones will be studied by paleontologists for years.

EXERCISE 4 ▸ Warm-up. (Chart 11-2)

Complete the passive sentences with the correct verb form of the words in the box.

are	were	have been	will be

ACTIVE		PASSIVE
1. Two instructors will score the tests.	→	The tests _____ scored by two instructors.
2. Two instructors scored the tests.	→	The tests _____ scored by two instructors.
3. Two instructors score the tests.	→	The tests _____ scored by two instructors.
4. Two instructors have scored the tests.	→	The tests _____ scored by two instructors.

11-2 Tense Forms of the Passive

	Active			Passive			
(a) simple present	Mary	*helps*	the boy.	The boy	*is*	*helped*	by Mary.
(b) present progressive	Mary	*is helping*	the boy.	The boy	*is being*	*helped*	by Mary.
(c) present perfect*	Mary	*has helped*	the boy.	The boy	*has been*	*helped*	by Mary.
(d) simple past	Mary	*helped*	the boy.	The boy	*was*	*helped*	by Mary.
(e) past progressive	Mary	*was helping*	the boy.	The boy	*was being*	*helped*	by Mary.
(f) past perfect*	Mary	*had helped*	the boy.	The boy	*had been*	*helped*	by Mary.
(g) simple future	Mary	*will help*	the boy.	The boy	*will be*	*helped*	by Mary.
(h) *be going to*	Mary	*is going to help*	the boy.	The boy	*is going to be*	*helped*	by Mary.
(i) future perfect*	Mary	*will have helped*	the boy.	The boy	*will have been*	*helped*	by Mary.

(j) questions	*Is*	Mary	*helping*	the boy?	*Is*	the boy	*being*	*helped*	by Mary?
	Did	Mary	*help*	the boy?	*Was*	the boy		*helped*	by Mary?
	Has	Mary	*helped*	the boy?	*Has*	the boy	*been*	*helped*	by Mary?
	Will	Mary	*help*	the boy?	*Will*	the boy	*be*	*helped*	by Mary?

*The progressive forms of the *present perfect*, *past perfect*, and *future perfect* are rarely used in the passive.

EXERCISE 5 ▸ Looking at grammar. (Chart 11-2)

Complete the sentences. Change the verbs in *italics* from active to passive.

1. Tom *opens* the door.   The door _____*is opened*_____ by Tom.

2. Tom *is opening* the door.   The door _____ by Tom.

3. Tom *has opened* the door.   The door _____ by Tom.

4. Tom *opened* the door.   The door _____ by Tom.

5. Tom *was opening* the door.   The door _____ by Tom.

6. Tom *had opened* the door.   The door _____ by Tom.

7. Tom *will open* the door.   The door _____ by Tom.

8. Tom *is going to open* the door. The door _____ by Tom.

9. Tom *will have opened* the door. The door _____ by Tom.

10. *Did* Tom *open* the door?   _____ the door _____ by Tom?

11. *Will* Tom *open* the door?   _____ the door _____ by Tom?

12. *Has* Tom *opened* the door?   _____ the door _____ by Tom?

EXERCISE 6 ▸ Let's talk. (Chart 11-2)

Work in small groups or with a partner. Answer the questions with a passive verb.

1. Who designed the Eiffel Tower? The Eiffel tower ...
2. Who collects taxes in your country? Taxes ...
3. Who taught your last English class? My last English class ...
4. Who has helped you a lot in your life? I ...
5. Who sings your favorite music? My favorite music ...
6. Who is supervising this activity? This activity ...
7. Who will pay your next bill? My next bill ...
8. Who is going to decide your future? My future ...

EXERCISE 7 ▸ Looking at grammar. (Charts 11-1 and 11-2)

Work with a partner. Check (✓) all the correct sentences in each group. Explain why the incorrect sentences are wrong.

1. a. __✓__ A surprising thing happened at the game yesterday.

   b. _____ A surprising thing was happened at the game yesterday.

   c. __✓__ Jackie scored the winning goal.

   d. __✓__ The winning goal was scored by Jackie.

2. a. _____ I agree with Dr. Ikeda's theory.

   b. _____ I am agree with Dr. Ikeda's theory.

   c. _____ Dr. Ikeda developed that theory.

   d. _____ That theory was developed by Dr. Ikeda.

3. a. _____ Professor Quirk was given us a difficult math problem.

   b. _____ Professor Quick gave us a difficult math problem.

   c. _____ The answer to the problem appeared to me in a dream.

   d. _____ The answer to the problem was appeared to me in a dream.

4. a. _____ The police are going to arrest the suspect.

   b. _____ The police are going to be arrested the suspect.

   c. _____ The suspect is going to be arrested by the police.

   d. _____ The suspect is going to arrest by the police.

5. a. _____ A hurricane has destroyed much of the town.

   b. _____ Much of the town has been destroyed.

   c. _____ People seem to be in shock.

   d. _____ People are seemed to be in shock.

6. a. _____ What was happened?

   b. _____ What happened?

   c. _____ What was occurred?

   d. _____ What occurred?

7. a. _____ Will our plan be succeed?   c. _____ Will people agree with it?

   b. _____ Will our plan succeed?   d. _____ Will people be agree with it?

EXERCISE 8 ▸ Warm-up. (Chart 11-3)

Tell the class where something that you're wearing or own was made
(e.g., your shoes, shirt, cell phone, etc.). Do you know who made these items?
Is it important to know?

11-3 Using the Passive	
(a) Rice *is grown* in India. (b) Our house *was built* in 1980. (c) This olive oil *was imported* from Crete.	Usually the passive is used without a *by*-phrase. The passive is most frequently used when it is not known or not important to know exactly who performs an action. In (a): Rice is grown in India by people, by farmers, by someone. It is not known or important to know exactly who grows rice in India. Examples (a), (b), and (c) illustrate the most common use of the passive, i.e., without the *by*-phrase.
(d) My aunt *made* this rug. (*active*)	If the speaker knows who performs an action, usually the active is used, as in (d).
(e) This rug *was made* by my aunt. That rug *was made* by my mother. (f) *Huckleberry Finn was written* by Mark Twain.	Sometimes, even when speakers know who performs an action, they choose to use the passive with the *by*-phrase in order to focus attention on the subject of a sentence. In (e): The focus of attention is on two rugs. In (f): The focus is on the book, but the *by*-phrase is included because it contains important information.

EXERCISE 9 ▸ Looking at grammar. (Charts 11-1 → 11-3)

Discuss why passive was chosen for these sentences instead of active.

Tech Age

1. My smartphone *was made* in China.
   → *The speaker or writer probably uses the passive here because he or she doesn't know who made the smartphone. An active sentence (Someone made my smartphone in China) wouldn't add any important information.*
2. The first video *was taken* by Carlos. The second video *was taken* by Natasha.
3. Over 500 websites *are created* every minute.
4. Millions of blog posts *are being written* right now.
5. A self-driving car *is being developed* by a computer company.
6. What new technology *will be designed* next?

EXERCISE 10 ▸ Reading and grammar. (Charts 11-1 → 11-3)

Read the passage. <u>Underline</u> the passive verbs. Discuss why the writer chose to use passive rather than active. Answer the questions in complete sentences.

Do you know these words?
- *papyrus*
- *ancient*
- *substances*
- *soot*
- *tree bark*
- *formulas*

Early Writing Materials

The chief writing material of ancient times was papyrus. It <u>was used</u> in Egypt, Greece, and other Mediterranean lands. Parchment, another writing material that was widely used in ancient times, was made from the skins of animals, such as sheep and goats. After the hair had been removed, the skins were stretched and rubbed smooth to make a writing surface. Paper, the main writing material today, was invented by the Chinese.

Ink has been used for writing and drawing throughout history. No one knows when the first ink was developed. The ancient Egyptians and Chinese made ink from various natural substances such as berries, soot, and tree bark. Through the centuries, thousands of different formulas have been developed for ink. Most ink today is made from chemicals.

1. Before paper was invented, what materials were used for writing?
2. What was parchment made from?
3. What three things were done to animal skins to make writing material?
4. Who first used paper?
5. When was ink first used?
6. In ancient times, what ingredients did the Egyptians and Chinese use for ink?
7. What substances are in ink today?

EXERCISE 11 ▶ Looking at grammar. (Charts 11-1 → 11-3)
Make complete sentences with the given words. Use the simple past. Some are active, and some are passive.

1. a. A package \ deliver \ to our apartment yesterday
   → *A package was delivered to our apartment yesterday.*
   b. It \ send \ to the wrong address
   c. We \ send \ it back

2. a. Maria \ teach \ her son to use the crosswalk for the first time
   b. She \ teach \ by her parents when she was six

3. a. The pickpocket \ almost disappear \ into the crowd
   b. He \ catch \ by an alert police officer

4. a. Tony \ cut down\ a dead tree
   b. The tree \ fall \ to the ground with a crash
   c. Fortunately, no one \ hurt

5. a. Something very sad \ happen \ yesterday
   b. A deer \ hit \ by a truck
   c. It \ kill \ instantly
   d. It \ die \ instantly

6. a. When I was in elementary school, we \ require \ to wear uniforms
   b. Later, my high school \ require \ students to follow a dress code
   c. I \ agree, not \ with the dress code
   d. Now \ my children \ require \ to wear uniforms

EXERCISE 12 ▶ Looking at grammar. (Charts 11-1 → 11-3)
Choose the sentences that have the same meaning as the given sentence.

1. The assistant manager interviewed Mr. Evans for the sales job.
   a. Mr. Evans was interviewed.
   b. Someone interviewed Mr. Evans.
   c. The assistant manager was interviewed.

2. There was a group of noisy kids at the movie theater. They were told to leave.
   a. The kids told others to leave.
   b. The kids were told something.
   c. Someone told the kids to leave.

3. A famous architect has been asked to design the new library.
   a. An architect has asked someone to design the library.
   b. Someone would like the architect to design the new library.
   c. A famous architect would like to design the new library.

4. I was ignored by the salesclerk while she spent five minutes talking on the phone.
   a. The salesclerk ignored me.
   b. I ignored the salesclerk.
   c. Someone ignored me.

5. After the speech, the audience will ask the speaker follow-up questions.
   a. The speaker will ask questions.
   b. The audience will be asked questions.
   c. The speaker will be asked questions.

6. The staff is planning a retirement party for Dr. Wilson.
   a. A party is being planned by Dr. Wilson.
   b. A party is being planned by the staff.
   c. The staff is making plans.

EXERCISE 13 ▶ Looking at grammar. (Charts 11-1 → 11-3)
Change each news headline into a complete sentence. Work in pairs, in small groups, or as a class.

1. 5 PEOPLE KILLED BY TORNADOES

   Five people _____ yesterday.

2. DECISION ON TAX INCREASE TO BE ANNOUNCED SOON

   A decision on a tax increase _____ soon.

3. MORE THAN 2 BILLION CUPS OF COFFEE CONSUMED WORLDWIDE

   More than two billion cups of coffee _____ worldwide each day.

4. 200,000 CARS RECALLED FOR BRAKE DEFECTS SINCE LAST YEAR

   Two hundred thousand cars _____ for brake defects since last year.

5. NEW HIGH-SPEED COMPUTER CHIPS DELAYED

   New high-speed computer chips _____ until next year.

EXERCISE 14 ▶ Looking at grammar. (Charts 11-1 → 11-3)
Work with a partner. Change the sentences to passive if possible, orally or in writing. Use the *by*-phrase only if necessary.

A Contest

1. Someone asked me to be a judge for a design contest at a nearby university.
2. I had taught at the school years before.
3. The school offers many different classes in graphic design.
4. It is a very popular major.
5. A visiting professor is teaching the introductory class.

6. Someone has asked students to submit their best work from the course.

7. Judges will judge applicants on originality and their use of color.

8. Someone is going to announce the winner at the end of the term.

9. Several top students have already submitted designs.

10. Someone will award a scholarship to the winner.

EXERCISE 15 ▶ Game. (Charts 11-1 → 11-3)

Work in teams. Make true sentences by matching the information on the left with the information on the right. Change the verb forms as necessary. Some sentences are passive, and some are active. Three items are questions. Punctuate carefully. The team with the most correct (factually and grammatically) wins.

Example: 1. The electric light bulb was **invented** by Thomas Edison.

1. The electric light bulb was ___h___
2. An island is _____
3. Some forest fires are _____
4. Is ID theft _____
5. The *-ing* form of *sit* is _____
6. Weather satellites orbit _____
7. Coins were first _____
8. Will taxes _____
9. Students have _____
10. People with numerophobia are _____
11. Are wedding rings _____

a. (*spell*) with a double "t."
b. (*grow*) because of poor smartphone security.
c. the earth and (*send*) back images.
d. (*wear*) by more women than men.
e. (*use*) around 1000 B.C.
f. (*cause*) by lightning.
g. (*frighten*) by math.
✓ h. (*invent*) by Thomas Edison.
i. always (*collect*) by governments.
j. (*surround*) by water.
k. long (*confuse*) by English grammar.

EXERCISE 16 ▶ Listening. (Charts 11-1 → 11-3)

Listen to the report about mirrors with your book closed. Then open your book and listen again. Complete the sentences with the verbs you hear.

Do you know these words?
- stone age
- vocano/volcanic
- lava
- grind/ground down
- reflective

Early Mirrors

Mirrors are not a modern invention; they _____

_____ (1) _____

since the stone age. The first mirrors _____ (2) from

rocks. A special type of stone _____ (3): obsidian. This is a volcanic glass

that _____ (4) in lava. To make the mirror, the stone _____ (5)

down on one side with another stone until the surface was flat. Then it

_____ (6) repeatedly until it became extremely shiny. At that point, the

surface was highly reflective, and people were able to see themselves.

obsidian stone

polished obsidian stone

EXERCISE 17 ▶ Looking at grammar. (Charts 11-1 → 11-3)
Complete the sentences with the active or passive form of the verbs in parentheses. Use any appropriate tense.

Did you know ... ?

1. The first antibiotic, penicillin, (*discover*) _____*was discovered*_____ by Alexandar Fleming in 1928.

2. The Amazon valley is extremely important to the ecology of the earth. Forty percent of the world's oxygen (*produce*) _____ there.

3. Frostbite occurs when a person's skin (*expose*) _____ to extreme cold. It most frequently (*affect*) _____ the skin of the cheeks, chin, ears, fingers, nose, and toes.

4. The first cola flavored drink (*introduce*) _____ in 1881. Coca-Cola™ (*invent*) _____ a few years later in 1886. Since that time, many other brands of soft drinks (*develop*) _____ and sold around the world.

5. The first email message (*send*) _____ in 1971. Computer engineer Ray Tomlinson (*send*) _____ messages to himself from one computer to another. Now billions of emails (*send*) _____ every day.

6. Taxes (*collect*) _____ since ancient times. In Mesopotamia, there were no coins, so male citizens (*require*) _____ to pay with a cow or a sheep.

7. Carl Gauss (*recognize*) _____ as a mathematical genius when he was just ten years old. One day a professor gave him an arithmetic problem. Carl (*ask*) _____ to add up all the numbers from 1 to 100 (1 + 2 + 3 + 4 + 5, etc.). It (*take*) _____ him only eight seconds to solve the problem. How could he do it so quickly? Can you do it quickly?

   Carl could do it quickly because he (*know*) _____ that each pair of numbers (1 + 100, 2 + 99, 3 + 98, and so on to 50 + 51) equaled 101. So he (*multiply*) _____ 50 times 101 and (*come*) _____ up with the answer: 5,050.

EXERCISE 18 ▶ Let's talk: interview. (Chart 11-3)
Work in pairs or small groups. Take turns answering the questions. The questions are in the active form, but give answers using the passive.

1. What did your parents expect you to do when you were a child? → *I was expected to ...*
2. What frightens you?
3. What bothers you?
4. What often confuses people?
5. Do you ever deal with insomnia? What causes it?
6. Do you ever get headaches? What causes them?
7. What piece of technology has helped you the most as a student?

EXERCISE 19 ▸ Warm-up. (Chart 11-4)

Complete the sentences in your own words. Are the verbs active or passive?

1. ___Children___ should be taught to be kind to animals.

2. _____ should be expected to be in class on time.

3. _____ can't be grown in a desert.

4. _____ must be treated with kindness.

11-4 The Passive Form of Modals and Phrasal Modals

Passive form:	modal*	+	be	+	past participle	
(a) Tom	will		be		invited	to the picnic.
(b) The window	can't		be		opened.	
(c) Children	should		be		taught	to respect their elders.
(d)	May I		be		excused	from class?
(e) This book	had better		be		returned	to the library before Friday.
(f) This letter	ought to		be		sent	before June 1st.
(g) Mia	has to		be		told	about our change in plans.
(h) Fred	is supposed to		be		told	about the meeting.
Past-passive form:	**modal**	+	**have been**	+	**past participle**	
(i) The letter	should		have been		sent	last week.
(j) This house	must		have been		built	over 200 years ago.
(k) Eric	couldn't		have been		offered	the job.
(l) Jill	ought to		have been		invited	to the party.

*See Chapters 9 and 10 for a discussion of the form and use of modals and phrasal modals.

EXERCISE 20 ▸ Grammar and speaking. (Chart 11-4)

Work with a partner. Check (✓) the sentences that have passive modals. Underline the complete verb in each. Then decide what type of job this is. Is this a good job for you? Why or why not?

Job Requirements

1. _____ You must be able to work in all types of weather.

2. _____ You must be physically strong.

3. _____ You must attend weekly staff meetings.

4. _____ You will be expected to work some weekends.

5. _____ You may be called in for emergencies.

6. _____ You may be subjected to random drug testing.

7. _____ Jewelry may not be worn.

8. _____ The animals must be treated with respect.

9. _____ All safety rules must be strictly observed.

10. _____ You will be expected to interact with the public and answer questions about the animals.

11. _____ You have to truly love animals!

Job: _____

EXERCISE 21 ▸ Looking at grammar. (Chart 11-4)
Complete the sentences with the words in parentheses. Use the appropriate form, active or passive.

1. a. James (*should + tell*) _____should be told_____ the news as soon as possible.

   b. Someone (*should + tell*) _____should tell_____ James the news immediately.

   c. James (*should + tell*) _____should have been told_____ the news a long time ago.

2. a. Meat (*must + keep*) _____ in a refrigerator or it will spoil.

   b. You (*must + keep*) _____ meat in a refrigerator or it will spoil.

3. a. We're trying, but the window (*can't + open*) _____.
   It's painted shut.

   b. I'm trying, but I (*can't + open*) _____ the window.

4. a. The class for next semester is too large. It (*ought to + divide*) _____
   _____ in half, but there's not enough money in the budget to hire another
   teacher.

   b. Last semester's class was too large. It (*ought to + divide*) _____
   _____ in half.

5. a. These books (*have to + return*) _____ to the library by tomorrow.

   b. Polly (*have to + return*) _____ these books by next Friday. If she doesn't
   return them, she (*will + have to + pay*) _____ a fine to the library.

6. a. Good news! I (*may + offer*) _____ a job soon. I had an interview at an
   engineering firm yesterday.

   b. Kristina has good news. The engineering firm where she had an interview yesterday
   (*may + offer*) _____ her a job soon.

   c. I hope Kristina accepts our job offer, but I know she's been interviewing with several
   companies. She (*may + already + offer*)* _____
   a job by a competing firm before we made our offer.

   d. A competing firm (*may + already + offer*) _____
   Kristina a job before we made our offer.

7. a. A: Andy, your chores (*had better + finish*) _____
   by the time I get home, including taking out the garbage.

   B: Don't worry, Mom. I'll do everything you told me to do.

   b. A: Andy, you (*had better + finish*) _____ your chores before
   Mom gets home.

   B: I know. I'll do them in a minute. I'm busy right now.

---

*A midsentence adverb such as **already** may be placed after the first auxiliary (e.g., *might **already** have come*) or after the
second auxiliary (e.g., *might have **already** come*).

8. a. This application (*be supposed to + send*) _____

to the personnel department soon.

b. Ann's birthday was on the 5th, and today is the 8th. Her birthday card (*should + send*)

_____ a week ago. Maybe we'd better give her a call

to wish her a belated happy birthday.

9. a. A: Yoko (*must + surprise*) _____ when she saw her boss

at the movies. He had called in sick.

B: She was.

b. A: Yoko (*must + surprise*) _____ when she runs into her boss

outside of work. He's not very social.

B: She is.

EXERCISE 22 ▸ Let's talk. (Chart 11-4)

Restate the computer lab rules with passive modals. Make at least two sentences for each rule.
Work in pairs or small groups.

Computer Lab Rules

Example: Do not bring food into the lab.   → *Food **cannot** be brought into the lab.*
        → *Food **must not** be brought into the lab.*   → *Food **must** be left outside.*

1. Turn off cell phones.
2. Computers are for school use only.
3. Do not play computer games.
4. Do not download music from the Internet.
5. Use the printer for schoolwork only.

EXERCISE 23 ▸ Looking at grammar. (Chart 11-4)

Make complete sentences with the given words.

Example: must   a. Seat belts \ wear \ during takeoff and landing
                → *Seat belts must be worn during takeoff and landing.*
        b. All passengers \ wear \ their seat belts during takeoff and landing
                → *All passengers must wear their seat belts during takeoff and landing.*

1. will   a. Many lives \ save \ with the new medical procedure
        b. The procedure \ save \ many lives

2. can   a. Shoppers \ look for \ product information on the Internet every day
        b. Product information \ find \ on the Internet

3. should   a. People \ test \ smoke alarms once a month
        b. Smoke alarms \ test \ once a month

4. may   a. The typhoon \ kill \ hundreds of villagers yesterday
        b. Hundreds of villagers \ kill \ in the typhoon yesterday
        c. Hundreds of villagers \ die \ in the typhoon yesterday

5. had better   a. Medical supplies \ deliver \ soon
        b. Villagers \ receive \ medical supplies soon

EXERCISE 24 ▸ Let's talk. (Chart 11-4)

Part I. Work with a partner or in small groups. Complete the sentences with the verbs in parentheses and the modal or phrasal modal that sounds best to you. All of the sentences are passive.

Renting an Apartment

1. A rental application (*fill out*) _____ <u>must be filled out</u> _____.

2. A 1st month's deposit (*require*) _____.

3. A last month's deposit (*require*) _____.

4. A cleaning deposit (*need*) _____.

5. A lease agreement (*sign*) _____.

6. All terms of the agreement (*understand*) _____ by the renter.

7. Any problems with the apartment (*disclose*) _____ by the manager.

8. The renter should ask if the lease (*break*) _____ early.

9. Community rules (*explain*) _____ by the manager.

Part II. What else needs to be considered? Write 3 to 5 more sentences about renting an apartment (or home or car). Use modals or phrasal modals.

EXERCISE 25 ▸ Let's talk. (Chart 11-4)

Work with a partner. Complete each conversation with at least one passive modal. Share a few of your conversations with the class.

Out of the Ordinary

1. A: Who designed this office?

   B: _____ <u>It must have been designed by a robot!</u> _____

   A: _____ <u>I agree. No imagination was used.</u> _____

2. A: Why is this house upside down?

   B: _____

   A: _____

3. A: What is that on the wall?

   B: _____

   A: _____

4. A: There's a pyramid in the parking garage!

   B: _____

   A: _____

 EXERCISE 26 ▸ Listening and grammar. (Charts 11-1 → 11-4)

Part I. Listen to the lecture on the 2004 Indian Ocean tsunami with your book closed.

Do you know these words?
- subsequent
- Richter scale
- due to lack of
- aftershocks
- tragically
- early-warning system
- destruction

Part II. Open your book and choose all the grammatically correct sentences in each group.

1. (a.) An earthquake hit the Indian Ocean.
   (b.) The Indian Ocean was hit by an earthquake.
   c. An earthquake was hit the Indian Ocean.

2. a. Millions of lives were changed forever by the earthquake.
   b. Millions of lives changed forever by the earthquake.

3. a. The quake followed by giant tsunami waves.
   b. The quake was followed by giant tsunami waves.
   c. Giant tsunami waves were followed the earthquake.
   d. Giant tsunami waves followed the earthquake.

4. a. Thousands of people swept out to sea.
   b. Thousands of people were swept out to sea.
   c. The tsunami wave swept thousands of people out to sea.

5. a. Nearly 300,000 people died.
   b. Nearly 300,000 people were died.
   c. Nearly 300,000 people were killed.
   d. Nearly 300,000 people killed.

6. a. The damage could have been lessened by a tsunami early-warning system.
   b. A tsunami early-warning system could have lessened the damage.
   c. A tsunami early-warning system could have been lessened the damage.

7. a. An early-warning system already exists for the Pacific Ocean.
   b. An early-warning system already is existed for the Pacific Ocean.

Part III. Listen again. Complete the sentences with the verbs you hear.

The 2004 Indian Ocean Tsunami

In 2004, several countries that border the Indian Ocean, including Indonesia, Thailand, India,

Malaysia, and Somalia _____ by an earthquake and subsequent tsunami.
                              1

(As you may already know, a tsunami is a giant ocean wave.) In just a few short hours, millions

of lives _____ forever. The earthquake _____
             2   3

at 9.3 on the Richter scale. It was the fourth largest earthquake since 1900 and the second

largest that _____ on the Richter scale.
                  4

The quake _____ by four giant waves as high as 100 feet
                5

(or 30 meters). Whole villages _____. Thousands of people
                                      6

_____ out to sea, and many others _____ due to lack of
        7   8

medical care. In total, almost 300,000 people _____, and 1.3 million
                                                       9

people _____ homeless. Aftershocks from the earthquake _____
            10   11

for several days.

Tragically, the damage _____ if there had been a
                            12

tsunami early-warning system. Such a system already _____ for the Pacific
                                                           13

Ocean, but it _____ to the Indian Ocean. Since the tsunami disaster,
                   14

governments _____ together to develop an early-warning system
                  15

so that Southeast Asia _____ such destruction again from a tsunami.
                            16

EXERCISE 27 ▶ Warm-up. (Chart 11-5)
Look around the room and answer these questions. Notice the words in blue.

1. Are the windows closed?
2. Is the door shut?
3. Are the lights turned on?
4. Is anything broken? If so, what?

11-5 Stative (Non-Progressive) Passive

(a) The door is *old*. (b) The door is *green*. (c) The door is *locked*.	In (a) and (b): **old** and **green** are adjectives. They describe the door. In (c): **locked** is a past participle. It is used as an adjective. It describes the door.
(d) I locked the door five minutes ago. (e) The door was locked by me five minutes ago. (f) Now the door *is locked*.	When the passive form is used to describe an existing situation or state, as in (c), (f), and (i), it is called the "stative" or "non-progressive" passive. In this form: • no action is taking place; the action happened earlier. • there is no *by*-phrase. • the past participle functions as an adjective.
(g) Ann broke the window yesterday. (h) The window was broken by Ann. (i) Now the window *is broken*.	
(j) I *am interested in* Chinese art. (k) He *is satisfied with* his job. (l) Ann *is married to* Alex.	Prepositions other than **by** can follow stative (non-progressive) passive verbs. (See Chart 11-6.)
(m) I don't know where I am. I *am lost*. (n) I can't find my purse. It *is gone*. (o) I *am finished with* my work. (p) I *am done with* my work.	Sentences (m)–(p) are examples of idiomatic usage of the passive form in common, everyday English. These sentences have no equivalent active sentences.

EXERCISE 28 ▸ Looking at grammar. (Chart 11-5)

Complete the sentences with the non-progressive passive of the verbs in parentheses. Use the simple present or simple past.

Problems

1. I had to get new sunglasses. My other ones (*make*) _____*were made*_____ of cheap plastic and broke.

2. The only gas station in town (*close*) _____ right now.

3. The water to the house (*turn*) _____ off yesterday.

4. The room is stifling hot and the window (*lock*) _____.

5. Yesterday it was hot in this room because the window (*lock*) _____.

6. I don't have my final paper. I'm sorry. It (*finish, not*) _____.

7. Hmmm. My dress (*tear*) _____. I wonder how that happened.

8. How can we sit down to dinner? The table (*set, not*) _____,
   the meat and rice (*do, not*) _____, and our guests aren't
   here!

9. I have no idea where we are. We (*lose*) _____!

10. Where's my money? It (*go*) _____! Did someone take it?

EXERCISE 29 ▸ Looking at grammar. (Chart 11-5)

Complete the sentences with the given words. Use the appropriate form.

1. *bear (born)* * / *confuse* / *divorce* / *marry*

   a. My friends Alison and Roger were married to each other for only a year, but now they

      _____*are divorced*_____ .

   b. I'm not sure why they are no longer together. Alison told me one thing and Roger told me

      another. I _____ .

   c. They have one child. He _____ a

      month after the divorce.

   d. I'm lucky. I _____ to a wonderful

      woman. We love each other.

2. *clog* / *qualify* / *plug in* / *schedule* / *spoil* / *stick*

   a. The power was out for two days and now our food _____ . We'll have to

      throw it out.

   b. We're having a problem with our window. It won't open. The latch _____ .

   c. The drain in our sink is very slow. It _____

      _____ with grease.

   d. Our neighbor tried to fix it. He was very nice, but he (*not*)

      _____ for the job.

   e. We've called a plumber. He _____ for

      the day after tomorrow.

   f. We had one other problem. Our TV wasn't working, but that was an easy fix. It (*not*)

      _____ !

3. *cover* / *crowd* / *exhaust* / *locate*

   a. The Grand Bazaar in Istanbul _____ in the Old City.

   b. As many as 400,000 people visit the bazaar every

      day. It _____ very _____ .

   c. There are 60 streets and 5,000 shops. At the end of

      the day, many shoppers _____ .

   d. The bazaar is like a mall. The streets _____

      _____ with domed roofs.

Grand Bazaar in Istanbul, Turkey

---

*In the passive, **born** is used as the past participle of **bear** to mean "given birth to."

232 CHAPTER 11

EXERCISE 30 ▶ Reading and grammar. (Charts 11-1 → 11-5)

Read the blog entry by author Stacy Hagen. <u>Underline</u> the past participles. Which ones are used in the passive? Which past participle functions as an adjective?

🐦 BlueBookBlog The Importance of Context

How important is context to reading? Extremely! In the 1970s, a famous study was conducted by Bransford and Johnson. Participants were asked to listen to a passage and then answer questions. The passage was similar to the following. Take a minute to read it:

> This is a fairly easy process. It can be completed at home or at a different place if the necessary machinery isn't available. First, items are put into different groups. But if there isn't too much to deal with, one group may be enough. It's important to look at everything carefully; a mistake could ruin a group. This first phase doesn't take very long, especially the more times you do it. The next phase goes faster. Once it is taken care of, it won't require your attention until it is finished. At that point, the items will be separated again. These groups will determine where everything goes. Once things are put away, you have finished until the process is repeated the next time.

Did the reading make sense to you? If you were confused, you are not alone. It's difficult to make sense of. Then participants were given the title "Washing Clothes" and asked to read it again. Try this now.

As you can see, context makes a significant difference. That is why you have probably already learned how helpful it is to look at chapter heads and subheads when you are reading a textbook. And don't forget to look at photos and other illustrations even before you start to read — or do an exercise. All of this information will help you read more efficiently.

EXERCISE 31 ▶ Warm-up. (Chart 11-6)

Answer the questions.

What is something that you are ...

1. interested in?
2. annoyed by?
3. concerned about?
4. scared of?
5. excited about?
6. accustomed to?

11-6 Common Stative (Non-Progressive) Passive Verbs + Prepositions

(a) I'm *interested in* Greek culture. (b) He's *worried about* losing his job.	Many stative verbs are followed by prepositions other than *by*.

be concerned be excited be worried	*about*	be composed be made be tired	*of*	be acquainted be associated be cluttered be crowded be done be equipped be filled be finished be pleased be provided be satisfied	*with*		
be discriminated	*against*	be frightened be scared be terrified	*of / by*				
be known be prepared be qualified be remembered be well known	*for*	be accustomed be addicted be committed be connected be dedicated be devoted be engaged be exposed be limited be married be opposed be related	*to*				
be divorced be exhausted be gone be protected	*from*			be annoyed be bored be covered	*with / by*		
be dressed be interested be located	*in*						
be disappointed be involved	*in / with*						

EXERCISE 32 ▶ Looking at grammar. (Chart 11-6)
Complete the sentences with the correct prepositions.

Maya, a Toymaker

1. Maya is excited ___*about*___ creating toys that children enjoy.

2. She is known _____ creating high-quality toys.

3. Her toys are made _____ wood.

4. She is pleased _____ the response to her toys.

5. The materials in her toys are limited _____ wood.

6. She is interested _____ how children play with one another.

7. She is disappointed _____ many of the popular toys in stores today.

8. She worries _____ toys that don't encourage children to use their imagination.

EXERCISE 33 ▸ Listening. (Chart 11-6)

Listen to the sentences. They contain non-progressive passive verbs + prepositions. Write the prepositions you hear.

Example: You will hear: Carol is interested in ancient history.

You will write: _____*in*_____

1. _____   5. _____

2. _____   6. _____

3. _____   7. _____

4. _____   8. _____

EXERCISE 34 ▸ Game. (Chart 11-6)

Work in teams. Complete the sentences by adding the correct prepositions. Then match the person to the sentence. The first team with the most correct sentences (both grammatically and factually) wins.

Juliet Capulet	Florence Nightingale	Marie Curie	Johnny Cash	✓ Mohatma Ghandi
Steve Jobs	Nelson Mandela	Rosa Parks	Robin Williams	Cleopatra

Who am I?

1. He was committed ∧^{to} non-violence in the struggle for independence for India. *Mohatma Ghandi*

2. She was devoted the sick and is known as the founder of modern nursing.

   _____

3. He was discriminated because of the color of his skin and fought for freedom for black people in his country. _____

4. She was married Romeo in Shakespeare's tragedy. _____

5. He was known his comedies, but he was well-acquainted depression. _____

6. She was related King Ptolemy. _____

7. He was associated technological innovation. _____

8. This singer was dressed black so often that he was called "The Man in Black."

   _____

9. She was opposed segregation laws in the American South and refused to give up her seat on the bus to a white person. _____

10. Her life was dedicated science, and she was the first woman to win the Nobel Prize.

    _____

EXERCISE 35 ▸ Let's talk. (Chart 11-6)

Think about changes that modern life has brought in communications, travel, work, school, daily life, etc. Complete the phrases with the correct prepositions and then take turns answering the questions. Work in pairs or small groups.

What changes or innovations are you (or people you know) …

1. excited _____?

2. concerned _____?

3. opposed _____?

4. annoyed _____?

5. addicted _____?

6. not accustomed _____?

solar panels

EXERCISE 36 ▸ Looking at grammar. (Chart 11-6)

Complete each sentence with the non-progressive passive form of the verb and an appropriate preposition. Use the simple present.

With Friends

1. I can't believe it! Derek has come to the party in his work clothes. He's a mechanic, and they

   (*cover*) _____ are covered in _____ grease.

2. Pat (*finish*) _____ her wedding dress. It's stunning. She designed

   it herself.

3. Ann laughingly calls herself a "chocoholic." She says she (*addict*) _____

   chocolate.

4. Leo (*satisfy, not*) _____ his new job. He's looking for another.

5. Hashim (*engage*) _____ Fatima.

6. Elaine (*divorce*) _____ Pierre.

7. Did you know that Rebecca (*relate*) _____ the president?

8. Robin is a pediatric nurse at a children's hospital. She (*dedicate*) _____

   her job.

9. What's going on? Miguel (*dress*) _____ a tuxedo! We're just going to

   a movie.

10. My best friend (*commit*) _____ improving the water quality of lakes

    and rivers in our area.

11. A: Are you (*do*) _____ your preparations for your camping trip?

    B: Yes, we finished packing our sleeping bags, tent, first-aid kit, food, and warm clothes.

    We are finally (*prepare*) _____ our vacation.

EXERCISE 37 ▸ Writing. (Chart 11-6)

Choose an object and write a short paragraph about it. Do NOT include the name of the object in your writing; always use a pronoun to refer to it, not the noun itself.

Describe the object (What does it look like? What is it made of? What does it feel like? Does it make a noise? Does it have a smell? Etc.), and explain why people use it or how it is used. Begin with its general characteristics; then gradually get more specific.

Finally, read your paragraph aloud to the class or to a small group of classmates. They will try to guess what the object is.

Example:

It is usually made of metal. It is hollow. It is round on one end. It can be very small — small enough to fit in your pocket — or large, but not as large as a car. It is used to make noise. It can be used to give a signal. Sometimes it's part of an orchestra. Sometimes it is electric and you push a button to make it ring.

What is it? _____

EXERCISE 38 ▸ Warm-up. (Chart 11-7)

Complete the sentences with the words in the box. Notice the word forms that follow the verb **get**.

dirty	fixed	hurt	wet
dressed	hungry	lost	

1. We didn't have a map or GPS, so we *got* _____ on our way to the airport. We saw a lot of the city, though.

2. Don't go out in the rain without a coat. You*'ll get* _____.

3. I'll be ready to leave as soon as I *get* _____. I just need to throw on a T-shirt and jeans, and I'll be ready.

4. If I skip breakfast, I always *get* _____ during my late morning class.

5. It was a bad accident, but luckily no one *got* seriously _____.

6. The Internet is working again. I don't know why it went out, but somehow it *got* _____.

7. The kids like making clay pots in art class because their hands can *get* _____, and they don't get in trouble.

11-7 The Passive with *Get*

Get + Adjective

(a) I'm *getting hungry*. Let's eat soon. (b) I stopped working because I *got sleepy*.	**Get** may be followed by certain adjectives. **Get** gives the idea of change — the idea of becoming, beginning to be, growing to be. In (a): **I'm getting hungry** = I wasn't hungry before, but now I'm beginning to be hungry.

Common adjectives that follow *get*

angry	cold	fat	hungry	quiet	tall
anxious	comfortable	full	late	ready	thirsty
bald	dark	good	light	rich	warm
better	dizzy	hard	mad	ripe	well
big	easy	healthy	nervous	serious	wet
busy	empty	heavy	noisy	sick	worse
chilly	famous	hot	old	sleepy	

Get + Past Participle

(c) I stopped working because I *got tired*. (d) They *are getting married* next month. (e) You didn't wash the dishes. (f) The dishes *didn't get washed*.	**Get** may also be followed by a past participle. The past participle functions as an adjective; it describes the subject. The passive with **get** can be used to present information more indirectly. Note the difference in tone between (e) and (f). The passive with **get** is common in spoken English, but not in formal writing.

Common past participles with *get*

get accepted (for, into)	get dressed (in)	get invited (to)
get accustomed to	get drunk (on)	get involved (in, with)
get acquainted (with)	get elected (to)	get killed (by, with)
get arrested (for)	get engaged (to)	get lost (in)
get bored (with)	get excited (about)	get married (to)
get confused (about)	get finished (with)	get prepared (for)
get crowded (with)	get fixed (by)	get scared (of)
get divorced (from)	get hurt (by)	get sunburned
get done (with)	get interested (in)	get worried (about)

EXERCISE 39 ▶ Looking at grammar. (Chart 11-7)

Complete the sentences with <u>all</u> the words that make sense.

1. The meeting starts in an hour. I need to get _____ for it.
   a. prepare   (b.) prepared   (c.) ready   d. readying

2. I think I'll stop working for the day. I'm getting _____.
   a. tire   b. tired   c. dark   d. late

3. Sonia stopped working because it was getting _____.
   a. late   b. dark   c. tired   d. sleepy

4. We can leave as soon as you get _____.
   a. pack   b. finish   c. packed   d. finished

5. Sam was supposed to be home an hour ago, but he still isn't here. I'm getting _____.
   a. nervous   b. anxious   c. worry   d. worried

6. I didn't stay for the end of the movie because I got _____.
   a. bore   b. bored   c. interested   d. am bored

7. Are you going to get _____?
   a. marriage   b. marry   c. married   d. engage

EXERCISE 40 ▸ Looking at grammar. (Chart 11-7)
Complete the sentences with any appropriate tense of *get* and the words in the box.

accustom	do	✓ hungry	pay
better	engage	invite	remarry
dark	fire	marry	well
depress	hire	nervous	wet
divorce			

1. What time are we going to eat? I _____*am getting hungry*_____.

2. I didn't have an umbrella, so I _____ while I was waiting for the bus yesterday.

3. Every time I have to give a speech, I _____.

4. Would you mind turning on the light? It _____ in here.

5. Maria's English is improving. It _____.

6. My friend was sick, so I sent him a card. It said, " _____ soon."

7. How long did it take you to _____ to living here?

8. We can leave as soon as I _____ with this work.

9. Chris _____ when she lost her job, so I tried to cheer her up.

10. After Ed graduated, he _____ by an engineering firm.

11. But later he _____ because he didn't do his work.

12. Ben and Sara have had an interesting relationship. First, they _____.
    Then, they _____. Later, they _____.
    Finally, they _____. Today they are a happily married couple.

13. I _____ on Fridays. I'll give you the money I owe you next Friday. OK?

14. I got an invitation. _____ you
    _____ to the party too?

EXERCISE 41 ▶ Let's talk: interview. (Chart 11-7)

Interview your classmates. Share some of their answers with the class.

Example: Have you ever gotten dizzy? Tell me about it.
→ *Yes. I got dizzy when I went on a ride at the fair last summer. But it was a lot of fun!*

1. Tell me about a time you got lost. Where were you and what happened?
2. Do you ever get sleepy during the day? If so, tell me about it. If not, when do you get sleepy?
3. Have you ever gotten really scared? What scared you?
4. Think of the world situation today. What things are getting better, and what things are getting worse?
5. Have you ever gotten hurt in a traffic accident or any kind of accident? What happened?
6. Tell me about a time you got confused about something.
7. Have you or has someone you know ever gotten cheated when you bought something? Tell me about it.
8. Is there an election coming up in this country or another country that interests you? If so, who do you think is going to get elected? Who got elected in the last election in this country?

EXERCISE 42 ▶ Looking at grammar. (Chart 11-7)

Restate the information with **get** to present the information more indirectly.

1. The clothes in the dryer are wet. You didn't turn on the dryer.

   _____*The dryer didn't get turned on.*_____

2. The TV's on. You didn't turn it off. _____

3. The car is still dirty. John didn't wash it. _____

4. Your old photos are on the floor. Susie hasn't put them away.

   _____

5. I know it's raining outside, but you're dripping! You're getting the floor all wet.

   _____

EXERCISE 43 ▶ Warm-up. (Chart 11-8)

Complete the sentences with **movie** and **audience**.

1. The _____ is bored.   2. The _____ is boring.

11-8 -ed/-ing Adjectives

(a) — The problem confuses the students. It is *a confusing problem*.	The *present participle* can serve as an adjective with an active meaning. The noun it modifies performs an action. In (a): The noun **problem** does something; it *confuses*. Thus, it is described as a "confusing problem."
(b) — The students are confused by the problem. They are *confused students*.	The *past participle* can serve as an adjective with a passive meaning. In (b): The students are confused by something. Thus, they are described as "confused students."
(c) — The story amuses the children. It is *an amusing story*. (d) — The children are amused by the story. They are *amused children*.	In (c): The noun **story** performs the action. In (d): The noun **children** receives the action.
(e) It was a *delightful* story. (f) It was a *scary* story.	There are exceptions to these rules. For example, there is no adjective *-ing* form for *delight* and *scare,* as in (e) and (f).

EXERCISE 44 ▸ Looking at grammar. (Chart 11-8)

Match the sentences to the pictures. Some sentences describe <u>neither</u> picture.

Picture A

Picture B

1. _____ The monster is frightened.
2. _____ The monster is frightening.
3. _____ The child is frightened.

4. _____ The child is frightening.
5. _____ The tiger is frightened.
6. _____ The tiger is frightening.

EXERCISE 45 ▸ Looking at grammar. (Chart 11-8)

Complete each sentence with the present or past participle of the verb in *italics*.

1. a. The class *bores* the students. It is a _____*boring*_____ class.

   b. The students *are bored* by the class. They are _____*bored*_____ students.

2. a. The game *excites* the people. It is an _____ game.

   b. The people *are excited* by the game. They are _____ people.

3. a. The news *surprised* the man. It was _____ news.

   b. The man *was surprised* by the news. He was a _____ man.

4. a. The child *was frightened* by the strange noise. The _____ child sought comfort from her father.

   b. The strange noise *frightened* the child. It was a _____ sound.

5. a. The work *exhausted* the men. It was _____ work.

   b. The men *were exhausted*. The _____ men sat down to rest under the shade of a tree.

EXERCISE 46 ▸ Let's talk. (Chart 11-8)

Your teacher will ask you questions. Answer them with a present or past participle. Close your book for this activity.

Example:
TEACHER: If a book confuses you, how would you describe the book?
SPEAKER A: confusing
TEACHER: How would you describe yourself?
SPEAKER B: confused

1. If a story amazes you, how would you describe the story? How would you describe yourself?

2. If a story depresses you, how would you describe yourself? How would you describe the story?

3. If some work tires you, ... ?

4. If a movie bores you, ... ?

5. If a painting interests you, ... ?

6. If a situation embarrasses you, ... ?

7. If a book disappoints you, ... ?

8. If a person fascinates you, ... ?

9. If an assignment frustrates you, ... ?

10. If a noise annoys you, ... ?

11. If an event shocks you, ... ?

12. If an experience thrills you, ... ?

EXERCISE 47 ▸ Listening. (Chart 11-8)

Listen to the sentences. Choose the words you hear.

Example: You will hear: We went on an exciting roller coaster ride.

             You will choose: excite   (exciting)   excited

1. frighten	frightening	frightened
2. scare	scary	scared
3. excite	exciting	excited
4. thrill	thrilling	thrilled
5. finish	finishing	finished
6. thrill	thrilling	thrilled

EXERCISE 48 ▸ Looking at grammar. (Chart 11-8)

Complete the sentences with the present or past participle of the verbs in parentheses.

1. The thief tried to break open the (*lock*) _____*locked*_____ cabinet in the pharmacy.

2. I found myself in an (*embarrass*) _____ situation last night.

3. The (*injure*) _____ woman was put into an ambulance.

4. The teacher gave us a (*challenge*) _____ assignment, but we all enjoyed doing it.

5. The (*expect*) _____ event did not occur.

6. The invention of the (*print*) _____ press was one of the most important events in the history of the world.

7. (*Experience*) _____ travelers pack lightly. They carry only the necessities.

8. A (*grow*) _____ child needs a (*balance*) _____ diet.

9. No one appreciates a (*spoil*) _____ child.

10. There is an old saying: "Let (*sleep*) _____ dogs lie." It means "Don't bring up past problems."

11. We had a (*thrill*) _____ but hair-raising experience on our backpacking trip into the wilderness.

12. The (*abandon*) _____ car was towed away by a tow truck.

13. (*Pollute*) _____ water is not safe for drinking.

14. I don't have any furniture of my own. Do you know where I can rent a (*furnish*) _____ apartment?

15. The equator is the (*divide*) _____ line between the Northern and Southern hemispheres.

16. We all expect our (*elect*) _____ officials to be honest.

17. The psychologist spoke to us about some of the (*amaze*) _____ coincidences in the lives of twins living apart from each other from birth.

EXERCISE 49 ▶ Listening. (Chart 11-8)

Listen to the sentences. Choose the correct completions.

Examples: You will hear: I attended a great lecture last night. It was _____.
You will choose: (fascinating) fascinated

You will hear: The audience listened carefully to the lecture. They were _____.
You will choose: fascinating (fascinated)

1. shocking   shocked
2. shocking   shocked
3. delightful   delighted
4. delightful   delighted
5. confusing   confused
6. confusing   confused

EXERCISE 50 ▶ Let's talk: interview. (Charts 11-5 → 11-8)

Make questions with the given words. Interview two students for each question. Share some of their answers with the class.

1. What \ be \ you \ worried about in today's world?
   → *What are you worried about in today's world?*
2. What \ be \ you \ tired of?
3. What (or who) \ be \ you \ pleased with?
4. What \ you \ get \ really nervous about?
5. What \ you \ want \ to be \ remembered for?
6. What \ be \ excite \ to you?
7. What \ kids \ get excited about?
8. What \ be \ confuse \ to students?
9. What \ be \ you \ confused by?
10. What \ confuse \ to children?

EXERCISE 51 ▶ Listening. (Chapter 11 Review)

Part I. Listen to the lecture about the early Olympic Games with your book closed. Then open your book and read the statements. Circle "T" for true and "F" for false.

Do you know these words?
- showcase
- spectators
- wreath
- olive leaves
- statue
- fame

Gate to the ancient Olympic stadium

1. The Olympic Games were established so that men and   T   F
   women could compete against one another.

2. Greece invited other nations to the games to encourage   T   F
   good relationships among countries.

3. The winning athletes were considered heroes.   T   F

Part II. Listen again. Complete the sentences with the words you hear.

The Early Olympic Games

The Olympic Games _____ more than 2,000 years ago in Olympia, a
                        1

small town in Greece. The games _____ for two purposes. One
                                        2

was to showcase the physical qualities and athletic performances of its young men. At that

time, only Greek males _____ to compete. In fact, women
                              3

_____ to watch the games, and the only spectators were

men. The other goal _____ to encourage good relationships among Greek cities.
5

People of other nationalities _____ to participate.
6

The winner of each event _____ with a wreath made of olive leaves.
7

Additionally, his statue _____ in Olympia for all to see.
8

_____ athletes _____ as heroes when they
9   10

returned to their cities because with their victory, they _____ fame and
11

honor to their hometowns.

EXERCISE 52 ▸ Check your knowledge. (Chapter 11 Review)

Correct the errors.

interested

1. I am ~~interesting~~ in his ideas.

2. Two people got hurted in the accident and were took to the hospital by an ambulance.

3. The show was so bored that we fell asleep after an hour.

4. The students helped by the clear explanation that the teacher gave.

5. The winner of the race hasn't been announcing yet.

6. When and where has the car invented?

7. My brother and I have always been interesting in learning more about our family background.

8. I am not agree with you, so let's agree to disagree.

9. It was late, and I was getting very worry about my mother.

10. Many strange things were happened last night.

11. I didn't go to dinner with them because I had already been eaten.

12. In class yesterday, I was confusing. I didn't understand the lesson.

13. My grandmother was walking on an icy sidewalk and was fallen down.

14. When we were children, we are very afraid of caterpillars. Whenever we saw one of these monsters, we were run to our house before the caterpillars could attack us. I still get scare when I saw a caterpillar close to me.

EXERCISE 53 ▶ Reading, grammar, and writing. (Chapter 11)

Part I. Read the passage. The writer is describing a process. How many verbs are passive?

Do you know these words?
- *liquor*
- *solid*
- *bitter*

How Chocolate Is Made

Chocolate is made from the seeds of roasted cocoa beans. After the seeds have been roasted, the inside of the seed is pressed into a liquid. This liquid is called chocolate liquor. The liquor contains fat, which is separated from the liquor. After this has been done, a solid is left. This solid, which is known as cocoa cake, is ground up and becomes unsweetened cocoa. This is a very bitter chocolate. To make it taste better, other substances such as cocoa butter and sugar are added later.

Part II. Write about a process that you know about. Maybe it's how to make something like a kite, a bookcase, a sweater, or a necklace. Try to use passive verbs where appropriate. Describe what happens first, second, third, etc.

WRITING TIP

The passive is very common (or even preferred) in scientific or technical writing (lab results, reports, etc.). The focus is not on the person, but on the details of the process or the results. The passive makes it easy to focus on this.

The present and present perfect passive are two very common tenses in this type of writing.

Some passive verbs common in writing are *collected, considered, done, found, given, made, measured, seen, shown, tested,* and *used.*

Part III. Edit your writing. Check for the following:

1. ☐ a form of the **be** verb for the passive
2. ☐ the correct past participle forms for the passive
3. ☐ passive only with intransitive verbs
4. ☐ use of **by** only when it is important to know who performed the action
5. ☐ correct spelling (use a dictionary or spell-check)

▪▪▪▪▪ Go to MyEnglishLab for Self-Study: Gerunds and Infinitives 11

PRETEST: What do I already know?
Write "C" if a sentence has the correct form, meaning, and punctuation and "I" for incorrect.
Check your answers below. After you complete each chart listed, make any necessary corrections.

1. _____ At the hotel on the lake where we went for our summer vacation. (12-1)

2. _____ I don't know where does she go after work. (12-2)

3. _____ He didn't understand at all what I did say. (12-2)

4. _____ Can you ask them whether they need help or not? (12-3)

5. _____ Please remind me again how to turn on this machine. (12-4)

6. _____ I wasn't sure where do I look for the information. (12-4)

7. _____ It's interesting that some identical twins can have such different personalities. (12-5)

8. _____ That Ricardo needs to change jobs is clear. (12-5)

9. _____ No cell phone use during class, our teacher said. (12-6)

10. _____ I asked Elias what he was doing. He told me he is waiting for me. (12-7)

11. _____ Roberta said she must have to work late last night. (12-8)

12. _____ It is critical that you be here on time tomorrow. (12-9)

Incorrect sentences: 1, 2, 3, 6, 9, 10, 11

EXERCISE 1 ▶ Warm-up. (Chart 12-1)
Check (✓) all the complete sentences.

1. _____ Are they triplets?

2. _____ They look almost identical.

3. _____ I don't know.

4. _____ How old you think they are?

5. _____ How old are they?

6. _____ I don't know how old they are.

7. _____ how old they are

12-1 Introduction

(a) in the park (b) on a rainy day (c) her grandparents in Turkey	Sentences contain phrases and clauses. A phrase • is a group of words. • does not contain a subject and a verb. • is not a sentence. Examples (a), (b), and (c) are phrases.
(d) He went running in the park. (e) She visited her grandparents in Turkey.	A clause • is a group of words. • contains a subject and a verb. Examples (d) and (e) are clauses.
independent clause (f) ⌜Sue lives in Tokyo.⌝ *independent clause* (g) ⌜Where does Sue live?⌝	Clauses can be independent or dependent. An INDEPENDENT CLAUSE • contains the main subject and verb. • is the main clause of the sentence. • may be a statement or a question. • can stand alone.
dependent clause (h) ⌜where Sue lives⌝	A DEPENDENT CLAUSE • is not a complete sentence. • cannot stand alone. • must be connected to a main clause.
noun clause (i) We don't know ⌜where Sue lives.⌝	Example (i) is a complete sentence. It has • a main subject (**We**). • a main verb (**know**). • a dependent clause (**where Sue lives**). The dependent clause — where Sue lives — is also a noun clause. *It is the object of the verb* **know** *and functions like a noun in the sentence.*

EXERCISE 2 ▶ Looking at grammar. (Chart 12-1)

Underline each clause in the sentences.

1. I couldn't hear what you said.
2. What did you say?
3. No one knows where Tom went.
4. Where did Tom go?
5. I'd like to know where Tom went.
6. How do you know where Tom went?

EXERCISE 3 ▶ Looking at grammar. (Chart 12-1)

Add punctuation and capitalization.

1. Where did Sara go did she go home → *Where did Sara go? Did she go home?*
2. I don't know where Sara went → *I don't know where Sara went.*
3. What does Alex need do you know
4. Do you know what Alex needs
5. We talked about what Alex needs

6. What do you need did you talk to your parents about what you need

7. My parents know what I need

EXERCISE 4 ▸ Warm-up. (Chart 12-2)
Choose the correct sentence in each.

1. Where does Brad live?
    a. I'm not sure where he lives.
    b. I'm not sure where does he live.

2. I'm looking for Brad.
    a. Could you tell me where is Brad?
    b. Could you tell me where Brad is?

12-2 Noun Clauses with Question Words

Question	Noun Clause	
wh + helping + **S** + **V** verb Where does she live? What did he say? When do they go?	*wh* +**S**+ **V** (a) I don't know *where she lives*. (b) I couldn't hear *what he said*. (c) Do you know *when they went?*	Noun clauses can begin with question words. In (a): *where she lives* is a noun clause. It is the object of the verb **know**. In a noun clause, the subject precedes the verb. NOTE: Do not use question word order in a noun clause. Helping verbs **does**, **did**, and **do** are used in questions but not in noun clauses.*
S **V** Who lives there? Who is at the door?	**S** **V** (d) I don't know *who lives there*. (e) I wonder *who is at the door*.	In (d) and (e): The word order is the same in both the question and the noun clause because **who** is the subject in both.
V **S** Who are those men?	**S** **V** (f) I don't know *who those men are*.	In (f): **those men** is the subject of the question, so it is placed in front of the verb **be** in the noun clause. COMPARE: *Who **is** at the door?* = **who** is the subject of the question. *Who **are** those men?* = **those men** is the subject of the question, so **be** is plural.
What did she say? What will they do?	**S** **V** (h) *What she said* surprised me. (i) *What they will do* is obvious.	The noun clause can come at the beginning of the sentence. In (h): **What she said** is the subject of the sentence. Notice in (i): A noun clause subject takes a singular verb (e.g., **is**).

*See Appendix Chart B-2 for more information about question words and question forms.

EXERCISE 5 ▸ Looking at grammar. (Chart 12-2)
Change each question to a noun clause.

Questions from Parents

1. A: How old is your friend Paul?

    B: I don't know _____*how old he is*_____.

2. A: Where does he live?

    B: I'm not sure _____.

3. A: When does the party start?

   B: I'll check _____.

4. A: What time are you leaving?

   B: I need to ask my roommate _____.

5. A: Whose phone numbers are those?

   B: Uh, I'm not sure _____.

6. A: Who left the stove on?

   B: I wasn't the one _____.

7. A: Who are those people?

   B: I don't know _____.

8. A: What happened?

   B: I don't know _____.

9. A: Why did Anna break off her engagement with Thomas?

   B: _____ is a mystery.

10. A: Where did the car keys go?

    B: I don't have any idea _____.

11. A: What are you doing in class?

    B: It's a little confusing. It's not clear yet _____

    _____.

12. A: Do you understand what Mom and I said?

    B: No, I'm sorry but _____

    _____ is still not clear.

EXERCISE 6 ▶ Looking at grammar. (Chart 12-2)

Work with a partner. Take turns making questions with noun clauses. Begin with **Can you tell me**.

School Questions

1. How is this word pronounced? _____ *Can you tell me how this word is pronounced?* _____

2. What does this mean? _____

3. What was my grade? _____

4. Who am I supposed to talk to? _____

5. When is our next assignment due? _____

6. How much time do we have for the test? _____

7. When do classes end for the year? _____

8. Where is our class going to meet? _____

9. What time does the computer lab close? _____

EXERCISE 7 ▸ Looking at grammar. (Chart 12-2)

Make questions with the given sentences. The words in parentheses are the answer to the question you make. Begin with a question word (*who, what, when, where, why*). Then change the question to a noun clause.

A Friend's Visit

1. Tom will be here (*next week*).

   QUESTION: _____When will Tom be here?_____

   NOUN CLAUSE: Please tell me _____when Tom will be here._____

2. He is coming (*because he wants to visit his college friends*).

   QUESTION: _____

   NOUN CLAUSE: Please tell me _____

3. He'll be on flight (*645, not flight 742*).

   QUESTION: _____

   NOUN CLAUSE: Could you tell me _____

4. (*Jim Hunter*) is going to meet him at the airport.

   QUESTION: _____

   NOUN CLAUSE: Do you know _____

5. Jim Hunter is (*his former college roommate*).

   QUESTION: _____

   NOUN CLAUSE: Please tell me _____

6. He lives (*on Riverside Road near the airport*).

   QUESTION: _____

   NOUN CLAUSE: I'd like to know _____

7. Tom is (*in Chicago*) right now.

   QUESTION: _____

   NOUN CLAUSE: Please tell me _____

8. He is there (*for a conference*).

   QUESTION: _____

   NOUN CLAUSE: Do you know _____

9. He works for (*a technology company*).

   QUESTION: _____

   NOUN CLAUSE: Could you tell me _____

10. He has worked for them (*for ten years*).

    QUESTION: _____

    NOUN CLAUSE: Do you know _____

EXERCISE 8 ▸ Let's talk. (Chart 12-2)

Work with a partner. Take turns asking questions and responding with **I don't know** OR **I wonder**. Use the names of your classmates.

Example: Where is (_____)?
PARTNER A: Where is Marco?
PARTNER B: I don't know where Marco is. OR I wonder where Marco is.

PARTNER A	PARTNER B
1. Where does (_____) live?	1. How long has (_____) been married?
2. What country is (_____) from?	2. Why are we doing this exercise?
3. How long has (_____) been living here?	3. Who is looking at their phone?
4. Where are you going to eat lunch/dinner?	4. What is (_____) phone number?
5. Where is (_____) favorite restaurant?	5. Where did (_____) go after class yesterday?
6. What is (_____) favorite color?	6. Why is (_____) smiling?
7. What kind of watch does (_____) have?	7. How often does (_____) go to the library?
8. Whose book is that?	8. Why was (_____) absent yesterday?
9. How far is it to the airport from here?	9. How much did that book cost?

EXERCISE 9 ▸ Let's talk. (Chart 12-2)

<u>Underline</u> the noun clauses. Are these sentences true for you? Circle *yes* or *no*. Discuss your answers.

1. What my family thinks of me is very important to me.	yes	no
2. I always pay attention to what other people think of me.	yes	no
3. Where we live is exciting.	yes	no
4. How we eat is healthy.	yes	no
5. I think how most celebrities behave is admirable.	yes	no
6. I usually don't believe what I read in advertisements.	yes	no

EXERCISE 10 ▸ Looking at grammar. (Chart 12-2)

Complete each sentence with the words in parentheses. Use any appropriate verb tense. Some of the completions contain noun clauses, and some are questions.

1. A: Where (*Ruth, go*) _____*did Ruth go*_____? She's not in her room.

   B: I don't know. Ask her friend Tina. She might know where (*Ruth, go*) _____*Ruth went*_____.

2. A: Oops! I made a mistake. Where (*my eraser, be*) _____? Didn't I lend it to you?

   B: I don't have it. Ask Sally where (*it, be*) _____. I think I saw her using it.

3. A: The door isn't locked! Why (*Franco, lock, not*) _____ it before he left?*

   B: That doesn't sound like Franco. I don't know why (*he, lock, not*) _____ it. Maybe he just forgot.

---

*Word order in negative questions:
   Usual: *Why didn't you call me?* (with *did* + *not* contracted) Very formal: *Why did you not call me?*

4. A: Mr. Lee is a recent immigrant, isn't he? How long (*he, be*) _____ in this country?

   B: I have no idea, but I'll be seeing Mr. Lee this afternoon. Would you like me to ask him how long (*he, be*) _____ here?

5. A: Which road (*we, be supposed*) _____ to take? It's not on the GPS.

   B: I've never been here before. I don't know which road (*we, be supposed*)

   _____ to take.

EXERCISE 11 ▶ Let's talk: interview. (Chart 12-2)

Interview your classmates. Begin with **Do you know** followed by a question word (**who, what, when, where, how many, how long, how far**). If no one in the class knows the answer to a question, research the answer. Share any information you get with the rest of the class.

Trivia

Example: the shortest month of the year
SPEAKER A: Do you know *what* the shortest month of the year is?
SPEAKER B: Yes. It's February. OR No, I don't know what the shortest month is.

1. the number of minutes in 24 hours
2. the winner of the Nobel Peace Prize last year
3. the place (country) Buddha was born
4. the distance from the earth to the sun
5. the year the first man walked on the moon
6. the time it takes for the moon to rotate around the earth

EXERCISE 12 ▶ Warm-up. (Chart 12-3)

Underline the noun clauses. What words are added when a *yes/no* question is changed to a noun clause?

QUESTION: Has the mail arrived?
NOUN CLAUSE: I wonder if the mail has arrived.
I wonder whether the mail has arrived.
I wonder whether or not the mail has arrived.
I wonder whether the mail has arrived or not.
I wonder if the mail has arrived or not.

12-3 Noun Clauses with *Whether or If*

Yes/No Question	Noun Clause	

Will she come?
 	
Does he need help?
	(a) I don't know *whether she will come.*
	    I don't know *if she will come.*
	
	(b) I wonder *whether he needs help.*
	    I wonder *if he needs help.*
		When a *yes/no* question is changed to a noun clause, **whether** or **if** is used to introduce the noun clause.
		
		NOTE: **Whether** is more common in writing and **if** is more common in speaking.

	(c) I wonder *whether or not* she will come. (d) I wonder *whether* she will come *or not.* (e) I wonder *if* she will come **or not.**	In (c), (d), and (e): Notice the patterns when **or not** is used.
	(f) *Whether she comes or not* is unimportant to me.	In (f): The noun clause can be in the subject position with **whether**.

EXERCISE 13 ▸ Looking at grammar. (Chart 12-3)

Complete the sentences by changing the questions to noun clauses.

At the Office

Let me know if ...

1. Is the financial report ready?
2. Will it be ready tomorrow?
3. Does the copy machine need paper?
4. Is someone waiting for me?
5. Do we need anything for the meeting?
6. Are you going to be there?

Please check whether ...

7. Did they get my message?
8. Is the copy machine working?
9. Is there any paper left?
10. Is this information correct?
11. Did the fax come in?
12. Are we going to have Monday off?

EXERCISE 14 ▸ Let's talk. (Chart 12-3)

Work with a partner. Take turns asking questions and restating them with *I wonder*.

Example:
PARTNER A: Does Anna need any help?
PARTNER B: I wonder whether/if Anna needs any help.

PARTNER A	PARTNER B
1. Where is Tom?	1. What causes earthquakes?
2. When is he coming?	2. When was the first book written?
3. Is he having car trouble?	3. Why did dinosaurs become extinct?
4. How long should we wait for him?	4. Is there life on other planets?
5. Did anyone call him?	5. How did life begin?
6. Did he forget?	6. Will people live on the moon someday?

EXERCISE 15 ▸ Let's talk: interview. (Chart 12-3)

Interview students in your class. Ask each one a different question. Begin with *Can/Could you tell me*. Share a few of your answers with the class.

1. Have you ever won a prize? What? → *Can/Could you tell me if you have ever won a prize? What did you win?*
2. Have you ever played a joke on someone? Describe it.
3. Have you ever stayed up all night? Why?
4. Have you ever felt embarrassed? Why?
5. Have you ever been in an earthquake? Where? When?
6. Do you have a talent like singing or dancing (*or something else*)? What?
7. Are you enjoying this interview? Why or why not?

EXERCISE 16 ▸ Let's talk: pairwork. (Charts 12-1 → 12-3)

Work with a partner to create short conversations. Partner A asks a question. Partner B answers the question beginning with the words in *italics*.

Example: When does the next bus come?
              I don't know …
PARTNER A (*book open*):   When does the next bus come?
PARTNER B (*book closed*):   I don't know when the next bus comes.

SITUATION 1: You're at a tourist center.

Let's ask …

1. Where is the bus station?
2. How much does the city bus cost?
3. Is there a bike rack on the bus?
4. Is this bus schedule correct?

We need to figure out …

5. How far is it from here to town?
6. How much does it cost to take a bus from here to downtown?
7. Is there free Wi-Fi anywhere?

Change roles.

SITUATION 2: You're late for work.

I don't know …

8. Where did I leave my keys?
9. Are my keys in my bag?
10. Where is my shoe?
11. What did I do with my briefcase?

SITUATION 3: You have a new neighbor.

I'll find out …

12. Is he single or married?
13. What does he do?
14. Where does he work?
15. Would he like to come to dinner?

EXERCISE 17 ▸ Let's talk. (Charts 12-1 → 12-3)

Work in small groups. What would you say in each situation? Use noun clauses.

Example: Someone asks you about the time the mail comes. You're not sure.
Possible answers: → *I'm not sure what time the mail comes.*
                      → *I don't know when the mail is supposed to be here. (Etc.)*

1. You see a restaurant. You can't tell if it's open yet. You ask a man standing outside.
2. You were absent yesterday. You want to know about homework. You ask another student.
3. Someone asks you the date. You don't know, but you tell them you'll find out.
4. Someone asks you about the weather tomorrow. Is it supposed to be sunny? You haven't heard.
5. You're at a clothing store. You're buying a coat and want to know about the return policy. How many days do you have to return it? You ask a salesperson.
6. Your friend asks you if you want to go to a movie or watch one at home. Both sound good to you. You tell your friend you don't care which you do.
7. You are planning a hiking trip with a friend. This friend wants to bring his dog and asks you if it is OK. It doesn't matter to you.
8. You have a late fee on your bill. You want to know why. You call the company and ask.

EXERCISE 18 ▸ Warm-up. (Chart 12-4)

Complete the second sentence of each pair with
to get or ***to do***. Is the meaning in each pair the
same or different?

What should I do?
I don't have any money
for the bus. How am
I going to get home?

1. a. Susan doesn't know what she should do.

  b. Susan doesn't know what _____.

2. a. She needs to figure out how she will get home.

  b. She needs to figure out how _____ home.

12-4 Question Words Followed by Infinitives

(a) I don't know *what I should do*. (b) I don't know ***what to do***. (c) Pam can't decide *whether she should go or stay home*. (d) Pam can't decide ***whether to go or (to) stay home***. (e) Please tell me *how I can get to the bus station*. (f) Please tell me ***how to get to the bus station***. (g) Jim told us *where we could find it*. (h) Jim told us ***where to find it***.	Question words (***when, where, how, who, whom, whose, what, which***, and ***whether***) may be followed by an infinitive. Each pair of sentences in the examples has the same meaning. Notice that the meaning expressed by the infinitive is either ***should*** or ***can/could***.

EXERCISE 19 ▸ Looking at grammar. (Chart 12-4)

Make sentences with the same meaning by using infinitives.

1. Sally told me when I should come. → *Sally told me when to come.*
2. The plumber told me how I could fix the leak in the sink.
3. Please tell me where I should meet you.
4. Robert had a long excuse for being late for their date, but Sandy didn't know whether she should believe him or not.
5. Jim found two shirts he liked, but he wasn't sure which one he should buy.
6. I've done everything I can think of to help Andy get his life turned around. I don't know what else I can do.

EXERCISE 20 ▸ Looking at grammar. (Chart 12-4)

Complete the sentences with your own words. Use infinitives.

1. A: I can't decide what _____*to wear*_____ to the reception.

  B: How about your green suit?

2. A: Do you know how _____?

  B: No, but I'd like to learn.

3. I don't know what _____ my mom for her birthday. I can't decide

  whether _____ or _____ .

4. Before you leave on your trip, read this tour book. It tells you where

  _____ and what _____ cheaply.

EXERCISE 21 ▸ Warm-up. (Chart 12-5)

Check (✓) the grammatically correct sentences.

1. __✓__ We know that the planets revolve around the sun.

2. _____ Centuries ago, people weren't aware that the planets revolved around the sun.

3. _____ That the planets revolve around the sun is now a well-known fact.

4. _____ Is clear that the planets revolve around the sun.

12-5 Noun Clauses with *That*

Verb + *That*-Clause

(a) I **think** *that Bob will come.* (b) I **think** *Bob will come.*	In (a): *that Bob will come* is a noun clause. It is used as the object of the verb **think**. The word **that** is usually omitted in speaking, as in (b). It is usually included in formal writing. See the list below for verbs commonly followed by a *that*-clause.

agree that	*feel* that	*know* that	*remember* that
believe that	*find out* that	*learn* that	*say* that
decide that	*forget* that	*notice* that	*tell* someone that
discover that	*hear* that	*promise* that	*think* that
explain that	*hope* that	*read* that	*understand* that

Person + *Be* + Adjective + *That*-Clause

(c) **Jan is happy** (*that*) *Bob called.*	*That*-clauses commonly follow certain adjectives, such as *happy* in (c), when the subject refers to a person (or persons). See the list below.

I'm *afraid* that*	Al is *certain* that	We're *happy* that	Jan is *sorry* that
I'm *amazed* that	Al is *confident* that	We're *pleased* that	Jan is *sure* that
I'm *angry* that	Al is *disappointed* that	We're *proud* that	Jan is *surprised* that
I'm *aware* that	Al is *glad* that	We're *relieved* that	Jan is *worried* that

It + *Be* + Adjective + *That*-Clause

(d) **It is clear** (*that*) *Ann likes her new job.*	*That*-clauses commonly follow adjectives in sentences that begin with *it* + *be*, as in (d). See the list below.

It's *amazing* that	It's *interesting* that	It's *obvious* that	It's *true* that
It's *clear* that	It's *likely* that	It's *possible* that	It's *undeniable* that
It's *good* that	It's *lucky* that	It's *strange* that	It's *well known* that
It's *important* that	It's *nice* that	It's *surprising* that	It's *wonderful* that

That-Clause Used as a Subject

(e) *That Ann likes her new job* is clear.	It is possible but uncommon for *that*-clauses to be used as the subject of a sentence, as in (e). The word **that** is not omitted when the *that*-clause is used as a subject.
(f) *The fact* (*that*) *Ann likes her new job* is clear. (g) *It is a fact* (*that*) *Ann likes her new job.*	More often, a *that*-clause in the subject position begins with **the fact that**, as in (f), or is introduced by **it is a fact**, as in (g).

To be afraid has two possible meanings:
   (1) It can express fear: *I'm afraid of dogs. I'm afraid that his dog will bite me.*
   (2) It often expresses a meaning similar to "to be sorry": *I'm afraid you have the wrong number.*

EXERCISE 22 ▶ Let's talk. (Chart 12-5)

Work in pairs, small groups, or as a class. Answer with *that*-clauses.

1. a. What have you recently heard on the news?
   b. What have you recently found out on social media?

2. a. What do scientists know for sure?
   b. What have scientists recently discovered?

3. a. What do parents hope for their children?
   b. What should parents promise their children?

4. a. What do many teenagers think?
   b. What do many adults believe?

EXERCISE 23 ▶ Let's talk: interview. (Chart 12-5)

Interview your classmates. Ask each one a different question. Their answers should follow this pattern: ***I'm*** + *adjective* + *that*-clause.

Example: What is something in your life that you're glad about?
   → *I'm glad that my family is supportive of me.*

1. What is something that disappointed you in the past?
2. What is something that annoys you?
3. What is something about your friends that pleases you?
4. What is something about nature that amazes you?
5. What is something about another culture's traditions that surprises you?
6. What is something that you are afraid will happen in the future?
7. What is something about your future that you are sure of?

EXERCISE 24 ▶ Looking at grammar. (Chart 12-5)

Make noun clauses beginning with ***It*** and any appropriate word(s) in the box. Make another sentence with the same meaning by using a *that*-clause as the subject.

apparent	a pity	surprising	unfair
clear	a shame	too bad	unfortunate
a fact	strange	true	a well-known fact
obvious			

1. The world is round.
   → *It is a fact that the world is round.*
   → *That the world is round is a fact.*
2. Tim hasn't been able to make any friends.
3. The earth revolves around the sun.
4. Exercise can reduce heart disease.
5. Drug abuse can ruin one's health.
6. Some women do not earn equal pay for equal work.
7. Irene, who is an excellent student, failed her entrance examination.
8. English is the principal language of business throughout much of the world.

EXERCISE 25 ▶ Game. (Chart 12-5)

Work in teams. Agree or disagree with the statements. If you think the statement is true, begin with **It's a fact that**. If you think the statement is false, begin with **It isn't true that**. If you're not sure, guess. Choose one person to write your team's statements. The team with the most correct statements wins.

1. _____It's a fact that_____ most spiders have eight eyes.

2. _____It isn't true that_____ some spiders have twelve legs.

3. _____ more men than women are colorblind.

4. _____ 25% of the human body is water.

5. _____ people's main source of vitamin D is fruit.

6. _____ a substance called chlorophyll makes plant leaves green.

7. _____ the World Wide Web went online in 2000.

8. _____ elephants have the longest pregnancy of any land animal.

9. _____ the first wheels were made out of stone.

10. _____ a diamond is the hardest substance found in nature.

11. _____ the Great Wall of China took more than 1,000 years to build.

EXERCISE 26 ▶ Looking at grammar. (Chart 12-5)

Restate the sentences. Begin with **The fact that**.

1. It's understandable that you feel frustrated. → *The fact that you feel frustrated is understandable.*
2. It's undeniable that traffic is getting worse every year.
3. It's unfortunate that the city has no funds for the project.
4. It's obvious that the two leaders don't respect each other.
5. It's a miracle that there were no injuries from the car accident.

EXERCISE 27 ▶ Warm-up. (Chart 12-6)

Look at the quoted speech below. Circle the quotation marks. Is the punctuation inside or outside the quotation marks? In item 3, what do you notice about the punctuation?

> Watch out! Are you OK? You look like you're going to fall off that ladder.

1. "Watch out!" Mrs. Brooks said.
2. "Are you OK?" she asked.
3. "You look like you're going to fall off that ladder," she said.

12-6 Quoted Speech

Quoted speech refers to reproducing words exactly as they were originally spoken or written.* Quotation marks ("…") are used.**

Quoting One Sentence

(a) She said, "My brother is a student."	In (a): Use a comma after **she said**. Capitalize the first word of the quoted sentence. Put the final quotation marks outside the period at the end of the sentence.
(b) "My brother is a student," she said.	In (b): Use a comma, not a period, at the end of the quoted sentence when it precedes **she said**.
(c) "My brother," she said, "is a student."	In (c): If the quoted sentence is divided by **she said**, use a comma after the first part of the quote. Do not capitalize the first word after **she said**.

Quoting More Than One Sentence

(d) "My brother is a student. He is attending a university," she said.	In (d): Quotation marks are placed at the beginning and end of the complete quote. Notice: There are no quotation marks after **student**.
(e) "My brother is a student," she said. *"He is attending a university."*	In (e): Since **she said** comes between two quoted sentences, the second sentence begins with quotation marks and a capital letter.

Quoting a Question or an Exclamation

(f) She asked, "When will you be here?"	In (f): The question mark is inside the closing quotation marks since it is part of the quotation.
(g) "When will you be here?" she asked.	In (g): Since a question mark is used, no comma is used before **she asked**.
(h) She said, "Watch out!"	In (h): The exclamation point is inside the closing quotation marks.
(i) "My brother is a student," *said Anna.* "My brother," *said Anna,* "is a student."	In (i): The noun subject (**Anna**) follows **said**. A noun subject often follows the verb when the subject and verb come in the middle or at the end of a quoted sentence. NOTE: A pronoun subject almost always precedes the verb. *"My brother is a student,"* **she said**. VERY RARE: *"My brother is a student,"* **said she**.
(j) "Let's leave," *whispered* Dave. (k) "Please help me," *begged* the homeless man. (l) "Well," Jack *began,* "it's a long story."	*Say* and *ask* are the most commonly used quote verbs. Some others: *add, agree, announce, answer, beg, begin, comment, complain, confess, continue, explain, inquire, promise, remark, reply, respond, shout, suggest, whisper.*

Quoted speech is also called "direct speech." *Reported speech* (discussed in Chart 12-7) is also called "indirect speech."
**In British English, quotation marks are called "inverted commas" and can consist of either double marks (") or a single mark ('): *She said, 'My brother is a student'*.

EXERCISE 28 ▶ Looking at grammar. (Chart 12-6)
Add punctuation and capitalization.

1. Henry said   there is a phone call for you
2. There is a phone call for you   he said
3. There is   said Henry   a phone call for you

4. There is a phone call for you   it's your sister   said Henry
5. There is a phone call for you   he said   it's your sister
6. I asked him   where is the phone
7. Where is the phone   she asked

EXERCISE 29 ▶ Reading and writing. (Chart 12-6)
Part I. Read the fable. (Fables are stories that teach a lesson.) Then work with a partner and look at the punctuation in each quotation. Explain why some sentences have commas and some have periods. Write the lesson or moral at the end of the story together.

The Grasshopper and the Ant

Once upon a time, there was a lazy grasshopper and an industrious ant. The grasshopper spent his summer days in the sun, chirping and hopping about. It never occurred to him to work. The ant, however, was getting ready for winter. He dragged seeds, leaves, and grains to his nest.

One day the grasshopper visited the ant. "It's such a nice day," he said. "Come out and play with me."

The ant shook his head. "I can't," he replied. "I have too much work to do. I need to get ready for the winter," he added. "You should do the same."

The grasshopper laughed and said, "I have plenty of food. And besides, winter is far away."

Winter came. The ant was snug in his nest, and the grasshopper was starving. There was no food to be found anywhere.

And the moral of the story is _____

summer

winter

Part II. Write a fable that is well known in your country. Use quoted speech. Read your fable to a partner or small group.

EXERCISE 30 ▶ Warm-up. (Chart 12-7)
Look at the words in blue. Do you know why two verbs are present and one is past?

WEATHER REPORTER: "A strong storm is coming."
   a. She just said that a strong storm is coming.
   b. She has said that a strong storm is coming.
   c. She said yesterday that a strong storm was coming.

12-7 Reported Speech

Quoted speech uses a person's exact words, and it is set off by quotation marks. *Reported speech* uses a noun clause to report what someone has said. No quotation marks are used.

NOTE: This chart presents general guidelines to follow. You may encounter variations.

Quoted Speech Reported Speech	
(a) "The world *is* round." → She **said** (that) the world *is* round.	The present tense is used when the reported sentence deals with a general truth, as in (a). **That** is optional; it is more common in writing than speaking.
(b) "I *work* at night." → He **says** he *works* at night. He **has said** that he *works* at night. He **will say** that he *works* at night.	When the reporting verb is simple present, present perfect, or future, the verb in the noun clause does not change.
(c) "I *work* at night." → He **said** he *worked* at night. (d) "I *am working*." → He **said** he *was working*. (e) "I *worked*." → He **said** he *worked/had worked*. (f) "I *have worked*." → He **said** he *had worked*. (g) "I *had worked*." → He **said** he *had worked*.	If the reporting verb (e.g., *said*) is simple past, the verb in the noun clause will *usually* be in a past form. Here are some general guidelines: simple present → simple past present progressive → past progressive simple past → no change or past perfect present perfect → past perfect past perfect → no change
(h) Immediate reporting: — What did the teacher just say? I didn't hear him. — He **said** he *wants* us to read Chapter 6. (i) Later reporting: — I didn't go to class yesterday. Did Mr. Jones give any assignments? — Yes. He **said** he *wanted* us to read Chapter 6.	In spoken English, if the speaker is reporting something immediately or soon after it was said, no change is made in the noun clause verb.
(j) "*Leave*." → She **told** me *to leave*.	In reported speech, an imperative sentence is changed to an infinitive. **Tell** is used instead of **say** as the reporting verb.* See Chart 14-4, p. 308, for other verbs followed by an infinitive that are used to report speech.

*NOTE: **Tell** is immediately followed by a (pro)noun object, but **say** is not: *He told **me** he was late. He said he was late.*
Also possible: *He said **to me** he was late.*

EXERCISE 31 ▶ Looking at grammar. (Chart 12-7)

Change the quoted speech to indirect speech.

Overheard in the Elevator

1. LARRY: "Jason and Liz are engaged."

   a. Larry says _____ *Jason and Liz are engaged* _____.

   b. Larry has said _____.

   c. Larry said _____.

2. TEACHING ASSISTANT: "Not many in the class have a passing grade."

   a. The teaching assistant said _____.

   b. The teaching assistant says _____.

   c. The teaching assistant will say _____.

3. SOMEONE: "There are 1,440 minutes in a day."

   a. Someone said _____.

   b. Someone says _____.

EXERCISE 32 ▸ Let's talk. (Chart 12-7)
Work with a partner. Take turns completing the sentences with noun clauses.

A Restaurant

1. "Your order is ready," said the waiter. → *The waiter said our order was ready.*
2. "I'm having the special," Mustafa said.
3. "We went there for our anniversary," my parents said.
4. "I went to school with the chef," my dad said.
5. I talked to Noor yesterday. She said, "I'm going to join you for lunch."
6. I just talked to Noor. She said, "I'm going to join you for lunch."
7. Mustafa said, "I have never tasted such a delicious dessert."
8. A customer said, "There is a mistake on our bill."

EXERCISE 33 ▸ Looking at grammar. (Charts 12-3 and 12-7)
Change the quoted speech to reported speech.

At a Meeting

1. Talal asked Leo, "Do you want to begin?" → *Talal asked Leo if/whether he wanted to begin.*
2. Maria asked us, "Have you seen my notes?"
3. Oscar asked me, "What are you talking about?"
4. "Does the decision need to be made today?" asked David.
5. Lillian asked, "Is everyone sure this is the right decision?"
6. Ricardo asked me, "Is what you are saying true?"

EXERCISE 34 ▸ Looking at grammar. (Chart 12-7)
Complete the sentences with *said* or *told*.

A TV News Station

1. The owner _____ that he wanted a more interesting newscast.

2. He _____ the TV ratings were dropping.

3. He _____ the director needed to work hard to improve the ratings

4. The director _____ him that she felt the newscast needed more investigative reporting.

5. A reporter _____ he had just finished a report on government corruption.

6. She _____ him to do a longer series on the topic.

EXERCISE 35 ▸ Warm-up. (Chart 12-8)

Complete the description of Alicia and George's conversation.

Where are my glasses? I can't find them and I have to leave.

I know why you can't find them. They're on your head!

Alicia said she _____ find her glasses and that she _____ leave. George told her that they were on her head.

12-8 Reported Speech: Modal Verbs in Noun Clauses

(a) "I *can go.*"	→ She said she *could go.*	The following modal and phrasal modal verbs* change when the reporting verb is in the past:
(b) "I *may go.*"	→ She said she *may/might go.*	
(c) "I *must go.*"	→ She said she *had to go.*	
(d) "I *have to go.*"	→ She said she *had to go.*	
(e) "I *will go.*"	→ She said she *would go.*	
(f) "I *am going to go.*"	→ She said she *was going to go.*	

can	→	could
may	→	may/might
must	→	had to
have to	→	had to
will	→	would
am/is/are going to	→	was/were going to

(g) "I *should go.*"	→ She said she *should go.*	The following modals do not change when the reporting verb is in the past:
(h) "I *ought to go.*"	→ She said she *ought to go.*	
(i) "I *might go.*"	→ She said she *might go.*	should / ought to / might } (no change)

*See Chart 9-1, p. 162, for an explanation of modal and phrasal modal verbs.

EXERCISE 36 ▸ Let's talk. (Chart 12-8)

Students A and B will have a short conversation. Your teacher will ask other students about it.

Example:

STUDENT A: What time can you go?
STUDENT B: Two-thirty.
TEACHER: What did Manuel (*Student A*) want to know?
STUDENT C: He wanted to know what time he could go.
TEACHER: What did Helen (*Student B*) say?
STUDENT D: She told him that he could go at two-thirty.

1. STUDENT A: Can you speak Arabic?
   STUDENT B: _____ .
   TEACHER: What did (*Student A*) ask?
   What did (*Student B*) say?

2. STUDENT A: Where will you be tomorrow at three o'clock?

  STUDENT B: _____.

  TEACHER: What did (*Student A*) ask?

  What did (*Student B*) say?

3. STUDENT A: Will you be on time for your next class?

  STUDENT B: I may _____.

  TEACHER: What did (*Student A*) ask?

  What did (*Student B*) say?

4. STUDENT A: What might happen in the future?

  STUDENT B: _____.

  TEACHER: What did (*Student A*) want to know?

  What did (*Student B*) say?

5. STUDENT A: What should we study after Chapter 12 of this book?

  STUDENT B: _____.

  TEACHER: What did (*Student A*) want to know?

  What did (*Student B*) tell (*Student A*)?

EXERCISE 37 ▸ Looking at grammar. (Charts 12-7 and 12-8)

Complete the conversations with a past form of the verbs in parentheses.

1. A: The test is scheduled for Monday.

   B: Really? I heard it (*schedule*) _____ for Tuesday.

2. A: Mikhail can't come tonight.

   B: Are you sure? I heard he (*can*) _____ come tonight.

3. A: It's raining outside.

   B: Really? I thought it (*snow*) _____.

4. A: Tony has to get a passport.

   B: Are you sure? I heard he (*has*) _____ to get a visa.

5. A: Marita hasn't applied for a job yet.

   B: That's not what I heard. I heard she (*apply*) _____ for work at her

   uncle's company.

6. A: Ms. Alvarez is going to retire.

   B: Really? I thought she (*continue*) _____ in her sales position

   for another year.

EXERCISE 38 ▸ Listening. (Charts 12-7 and 12-8)

Listen to the sentences. Complete them using past verb forms to report the speech that you hear.

1. The speaker said that she _____*wasn't going*_____ to the personnel meeting because she

   _____*had to*_____ finish a report.

2. The speaker said that he _____ Marta any money because his

   wallet _____ in his coat pocket back at home.

3. The speaker said that someone in the room _____ very strong perfume

   and it _____ her a headache.

4. The speaker said that he _____ Emma at the coffee shop at 9:00.

   He said he _____ not to be late.

5. The speaker said she _____ looking for a new job and asked her

   friend what he _____ she _____.

6. The speaker said that they _____ late for the concert

   because his wife _____ a business function after work.

EXERCISE 39 ▸ Looking at grammar. (Charts 12-7 and 12-8)

Change quoted speech to reported speech. Study the example carefully and use the same pattern:
said that ... and that.

1. "My father is a businessman. My mother is an engineer."

   He said that ____*his father was a businessman and that his mother was an engineer.*____

2. "I'm excited about my new job. I've found a nice apartment."

   I got an email from my sister yesterday. She said _____

   _____

3. "I expect you to be in class every day. Unexcused absences may affect your grades."

   Our sociology professor said _____

   _____

4. "Highway 66 will be closed for two months. Commuters should seek alternate routes."

   The newspaper said _____

   _____

5. "Every obstacle is a steppingstone to success. You should view

   problems in your life as opportunities to improve yourself."

   My father often told me _____

   _____

   _____

EXERCISE 40 ▸ Writing. (Charts 12-1 → 12-8)

Read each conversation and write a report about it. Your report should include an accurate idea of
the speaker's words, but it doesn't have to use the exact words.

Example: JACK: I can't go to the game next week.
           TOM: Really? Why not?
           JACK: I don't have enough money for a ticket.

Possible written reports:

→ Jack told Tom that he couldn't go to the game next week because he didn't have enough money for a ticket.

→ When Tom asked Jack why he couldn't go to the game next week, Jack said he didn't have enough money for a ticket.

→ Jack said he couldn't go to the game next week. When Tom asked him why, Jack replied that he didn't have enough money for a ticket.

1. ALEX: What are you doing?
   LEA: I'm drawing a picture.

2. ASAKO: Do you want to go to a movie Sunday night?
   MARTA: I'd like to, but I have to study.

3. JOHNNY: How old are you, Mrs. Robinson?
   MRS. ROBINSON: It's not polite to ask people their age.
   JOHNNY: How much money do you make?
   MRS. ROBINSON: That's impolite too.

EXERCISE 41 ▶ Warm-up. (Chart 12-9)
Choose the correct verb in each sentence.

1. It's important that we   be / are   on time to our own wedding!
2. My brother insists that he   speak / speaks   at our wedding dinner.

12-9 The Subjunctive in Noun Clauses

(a) The teacher *demands* that we *be* on time.	Sentences with subjunctive verbs generally *stress importance or urgency.* A subjunctive verb uses the simple form of a verb. It does not have present, past, or future forms; it is neither singular nor plural. A subjunctive verb is used in *that*-clauses with the verbs and expressions listed at the bottom of this chart.
(b) I *insisted* that he *pay* me the money.	
(c) I *recommended* that she *not go* to the concert.	
(d) *It is important* that they *be told* the truth.	
	In (a): *be* is a subjunctive verb; its subject is *we*.
	In (b): *pay* (not *pays,* not *paid*) is a subjunctive verb; it is in its simple form, even though its subject (*he*) is singular.
	Negative: *not* + *simple form,* as in (c).
	Passive: *simple form of be* + *past participle,* as in (d).
(e) I *suggested/recommended* that she *see* a doctor.	***Should*** is also possible after ***suggest*** and ***recommend.****
(f) I *suggested/recommended* that she *should see* a doctor.	

Common verbs and expressions followed by the subjunctive in a noun clause

advise (that)	propose (that)	it is essential (that)	it is critical (that)
ask (that)	recommend (that)	it is imperative (that)	it is necessary (that)
demand (that)	request (that)	it is important (that)	it is vital (that)
insist (that)	suggest (that)		

*The subjunctive is more common in American English than British English. In British English, ***should*** + *simple form* is more usual than the subjunctive: *The teacher **insists** that we **should be** on time.*

EXERCISE 42 ▶ Looking at grammar. (Chart 12-9)

Complete each sentence with the correct form of the verb in parentheses.

In a Courtroom

1. The court clerk has advised that everyone (*stand up*) ____stand up____ when the judge enters the room.

2. It is essential that people (*turn off*) _____ their cell phones.

3. It is important that everyone (*dress*) _____ appropriately for court.

4. The clerk has asked that the witness (*tell*) _____ the truth and nothing but the truth.

5. The jury has asked that the judge (*explain*) _____ the instructions one more time.

6. The judge insisted that everyone (*be*) _____ quiet when the verdict was read.

EXERCISE 43 ▶ Looking at grammar. (Chart 12-9)

Choose the correct verb. Some are active and some are passive.

Naming a Baby

1. The hospital requested that the parents   provide / be provided   a name for the birth certificate.
2. The grandparents insisted that the baby   give / be given   a traditional name.
3. A sibling asked that the parents   choose / be chosen   a popular name.
4. A cousin suggested that the baby   name / be named   after a great-grandmother.
5. The parents requested that they   allow / be allowed   to choose a name without any outside help.

EXERCISE 44 ▶ Looking at grammar. (Chart 12-9)

Complete each sentence with the correct form of the verb. Use the words in the box. Some are active and some are passive. NOTE: *share* is used twice.

lock	share	show up	turn off	use	wear

Work Rules

1. It is important that everyone _____ for work on time.

2. It is critical that everyone _____ an ID badge while at work.

3. It is vital that employees not _____ computer passwords with other employees.

4. It is vital that computer passwords not _____ by employees.

5. It is important that the heat _____ in offices at the end of the day.

6. It is imperative that the last person out of the office _____ the door.

7. Management has requested that employees not _____ social media for personal purposes during work hours.

EXERCISE 45 ▸ Check your knowledge. (Chapter 12 Review)
Correct the errors.

1. Tell the taxi driver where do you want to go.

2. My roommate came into the room and asked me why aren't you in class? I said I am waiting for a telephone call from my family.

3. It was my first day at the university, and I am on my way to my first class. I wondered who else will be in the class. What the teacher would be like?

4. My professor asked me that what did I intend to do after I graduate?

5. What does a patient tell a doctor it is confidential.

6. What my friend and I did it was our secret. We didn't even tell our parents what did we do.

7. The doctor asked that I felt OK. I told him that I don't feel well.

8. I asked him what kind of movies does he like, he said me, I like romantic movies.

9. Is true you almost drowned? my friend asked me. Yes, I said. I'm really glad to be alive. It was really frightening.

10. It is a fact that I almost drowned makes me very careful about water safety when I go swimming.

11. I didn't know where am I supposed to get off the bus, so I asked the driver where is the science museum. She tell me the name of the street. She said she will tell me when should I get off the bus.

12. My mother did not live with us. When other children asked me where was my mother, I told them she is going to come to visit me very soon.

13. When I asked the taxi driver to drive faster, he said I will drive faster if you pay me more. At that time I didn't care how much would it cost, so I told him to go as fast as he can.

14. My parents told me is essential to know English if I want to study at an American university.

EXERCISE 46 ▸ Reading and writing. (Chapter 12 Review)
Part I. Read the passage. <u>Underline</u> the three noun clauses. Which one has the subjunctive?

Plagiarism

Simon is researching the topic of cell phone radiation for a term paper. He has found extensive information on the Internet. One paragraph in particular gives easy-to-understand information about radiation transmission. Simon is pleased that the information is very clear and pastes it into his paper. However, he changes the font so that it matches the rest of his paper.

What Simon has just done is commit plagiarism — the copying of someone else's work without citing the source. Think of it as the stealing of ideas. In the Internet age, it is very easy to copy and paste information into a paper. Colleges and universities have strict policies regarding plagiarism. In some cases, schools may fail or expel a student for plagiarism.

Generally plagiarism is explained in the student handbook. Many schools have "honor codes" that students agree to follow. It is essential that every student know the school policy regarding plagiarism.

Part II. Research information about the plagiarism policy at your school. If your school doesn't have a policy, choose a university in an English-speaking country to research. Write a paragraph summarizing the information. Use at least one noun clause with the subjunctive in your paragraph.

EXERCISE 47 ▶ Reading and writing. (Chapter 12)

Part I. Read the paragraph from a U.S. government website.*

Cell Phones and the Brain

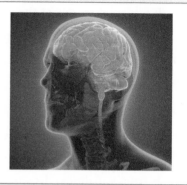

Scientists are looking into a possible link between cell phone use and certain types of tumors. One type is called an acoustic neuroma ("ah-COOS-tik nur-OH-ma"). This type of tumor grows on the nerve that connects the ear to the brain. It doesn't cause cancer, but it may lead to other health problems, like hearing loss. Another type scientists are looking into is called a glioma ("glee-OH-ma"). This is a tumor found in the brain or central nervous system of the body.

*Source: http://www.cdc.gov/nceh/radiation/cell_phones._FAQ.html

Part II. Now read two paraphrases of the paragraph. One way to avoid plagiarism is to paraphrase information — to express an author's ideas in your own words. What differences do you see between the two paraphrases? Which paraphrase seems most appropriate to you? Consider the following questions and discuss your opinions with your classmates:

1. In which paraphrase have the ideas been put into the writer's own words, without copying the sentence structure or the vocabulary of the original?
2. Which paraphrase uses synonyms for key words, while keeping a sentence structure similar to the original?

Paraphrase 1

Scientists are not sure if cell phones cause tumors, but they are looking at two types: an acoustic neuroma and a glioma. The first tumor doesn't cause cancer, but it can cause hearing problems. The second, a glioma, grows in the brain or central nervous system.

Paraphrase 2

Researchers are investigating a potential connection between cell phone usage and different kinds of tumors. One kind is named an acoustic neuroma. This kind of tumor is on the nerve between the ear and the brain. It's not the cause of cancer, but it may be responsible for other health issues, like deafness. Another kind researchers are investigating is a glioma. This is in the brain or central nervous system of the human body.

In the second case, the writer has supplied synonyms for key words, but the sentence structure is the same. It is too similar to the original and is therefore not acceptable.

Part III. Find a paragraph on a topic you are interested in and paraphrase it. Use at least one noun clause in your writing.

A helpful strategy for paraphrasing is to read a passage several times and take notes. Then try not to look at your notes when you write so that you can express the information in your own words. When you are finished, compare your paraphrase with your notes to make sure you have covered everything.

Part IV. Edit your writing. Check for the following:

1. ☐ all sentences contain a subject and a verb
2. ☐ use of one or more noun clauses in your paragraph
3. ☐ use of a singular subject when the noun clause begins the sentence
4. ☐ correct word order in noun clauses (statement word order)
5. ☐ correct spelling (use a dictionary or spell-check)

▪▫▪▪▪ Go to MyEnglishLab for Self-Study: Gerunds and Infinitives 12

PRETEST: What do I already know?

Write "C" if a sentence has the correct sentence structure and "I" for incorrect. Check your answers below. After you complete each chart listed, make any necessary corrections.

1. _____ I enjoyed listening to the tour guide that took us around the city. (13-1)

2. _____ The gift is for you that is on the coffee table. (13-1)

3. _____ A movie a friend recommended it turned out to be very entertaining. (13-2)

4. _____ There is the professor from whom I received the award. (13-3)

5. _____ I spoke with a couple who his son created a popular social media app. (13-4)

6. _____ Each hotel room has a safe which you can keep your valuables. (13-5)

7. _____ I'll never forget the moment when I first met your dad. (13-6)

8. _____ Anyone wants to volunteer is welcome to come. (13-7)

9. _____ Is everything your lawyer says true? (13-7)

10. _____ Indonesia, that consists of thousands of islands, is the fourth most populated country in the world. (13-8)

11. _____ In my chemistry study group, there are eight students, two of whom are repeating the class. (13-9)

12. _____ The apartment building has ten floors and no elevator, which it will be a challenge for me. (13-10)

Incorrect sentences: 2, 3, 5, 6, 8, 10, 12

EXERCISE 1 ▸ Warm-up. (Chart 13-1)

The sentences are all correct. The words in blue are all pronouns. What nouns do they refer to? How does the noun affect the choice of the pronoun?

1. a. A ring floated past a diver. She was exploring some undersea rocks.
   b. A ring floated past a diver who was exploring some undersea rocks.
   c. A ring floated past a diver that was exploring some undersea rocks.

2. a. The diver saw a ring. It was sinking to the bottom of the sea.
   b. The diver saw a ring that was sinking to the bottom of the sea.
   c. The diver saw a ring which was sinking to the bottom of the sea.

13-1 Adjective Clause Pronouns Used as the Subject

I thanked the woman. **She** helped me. ↓ (a) I thanked the woman *who helped me*. (b) I thanked the woman *that helped me*.	In (a): ***I thanked the woman*** = a main clause ***who helped me*** = an adjective clause* An adjective clause modifies a noun. In (a): the adjective clause modifies **woman**.
The book is mine. **It** is on the table. ↓ (c) The book *that* *is on the table* is mine. (d) The book *which* *is on the table* is mine.	In (a): **who** is the subject of the adjective clause. In (b): **that** is the subject of the adjective clause. Examples (a) and (b) have the same meaning. In speaking, **who** and **that** are both commonly used as subject pronouns to describe people. **Who** is more common in writing. Examples (c) and (d) have the same meaning. In contemporary American English, **that** is preferred to **which**.** In British English, **that** and **which** are used interchangeably.

	SUMMARY:
	
	   who = used for people
	   that = used for both people and things
	   which = used for things

(e) CORRECT: The book *that is on the table* is mine. (f) INCORRECT: The book is mine ~~that is on the table~~.	An adjective clause closely follows the noun it modifies.

   *See Chapter 12 for information about clauses.

  Which must be used in nonrestrictive clauses in both American and British English. See Chart 13-8.

EXERCISE 2 ▸ Looking at grammar. (Chart 13-1)

Choose <u>all</u> the possible completions for each sentence. Do not add commas or capital letters.

Identity Theft

1. I read a scary article _____ detailed how easy it is for someone to steal your ID.
   a. who   (b.) that   c. it   d. Ø

2. People _____ own a smartphone have a higher rate of identify theft.
   a. who   b. that   c. which   d. Ø

3. The article mentioned one thief _____ enjoys the challenge of hacking. He does it for fun.
   a. who   b. that   c. he   d. Ø

4. A fact _____ surprised me is that online thieves are rarely caught.
   a. who   b. that   c. it   d. Ø

EXERCISE 3 ▸ Looking at grammar. (Chart 13-1)

Combine the two sentences with **who** or **that**. Use the second sentence as an adjective clause.

On a Subway

1. I know the girl. She is sleeping. → *I know the girl* $\begin{Bmatrix} who \\ that \end{Bmatrix}$ *is sleeping.*

2. The guy is in my math class. He is talking loudly on his phone.

3. The passenger is from Argentina. He is sitting next to me.

4. The students are from Turkey. They are standing behind us.

5. We are going on a route. It is very crowded in the mornings.

6. We are on the train. It often breaks down.

EXERCISE 4 ▶ Let's talk. (Chart 13-1)
Make true sentences by using a word or phrase from each column. Use **who** or **that**.

		work hard.
		like a lot of rules.
		exercise every day.
		are smarter than me.
I like to spend time with	friends classmates co-workers adults people	tell lies.
I don't like to spend time with		are quiet.
		talk a lot.
		talk about themselves a lot.
		like to relax.
		are serious.
		tell a lot of jokes.

EXERCISE 5 ▶ Listening. (Chart 13-1)
Part I. When **who** is contracted with an auxiliary verb, the contraction is often hard to hear.
Listen to the following sentences. What is the full, uncontracted form of the *italicized* verb?

1. He has a friend *who'll* help him.
   (*full form = who will*)
2. He has a friend *who's* helping him.
3. He has a friend *who's* helped him.
4. He has friends *who're* helping him.

5. He has friends *who've* helped him.
6. He has a friend *who'd* helped him.
7. He has a friend *who'd* like to help him.
8. He has a friend *who's* been helping him.

Part II. Complete the sentences with the verbs you hear, but write the full, uncontracted form of
each verb.

Example: You will hear: I work with a man who's lived in 20 different countries.

  You will write: I work with a man who _____*has lived*_____ in 20 different countries.

1. We know a person who _____ great for the job.

2. We know a person who _____ to apply for the job.

3. That's the man who _____ to our department.

4. I know of three people who _____ to transfer to another location.

5. I'd like to talk to the people who _____ to move.

6. There are two people at this company who _____ here all their adult lives.

7. The manager who _____ from the company quit.

EXERCISE 6 ▶ Game. (Chart 13-1)

Work in teams. Make sentences using **who** or **that**. One team member can write them down. The team that finishes first with the most correct answers wins.

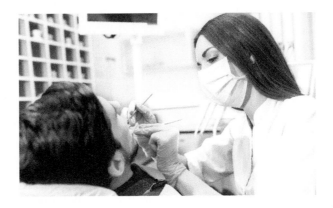

At the Dentist

Example: 1. A dentist is a person who/that treats problems with teeth.

1. A dentist is a person ___e___ .
2. A dental hygienist is a person ____ .
3. A cavity is a part of the tooth ____ .
4. A filling is a material ____ .
5. Novocain is a drug ____ .
6. A crown is an artificial covering ____ .
7. Braces are a device ____ .
8. Orthodontists are dentists ____ .
9. Pediatric dentists are dentists ____ .

a. is decayed
b. straightens teeth
c. is put into a cavity
d. treat children
✓ e. treats problems with teeth
f. put braces on teeth
g. cleans teeth
h. is put around a tooth
i. numbs the tooth area so the patient doesn't feel pain

EXERCISE 7 ▶ Warm-up. (Chart 13-2)

Work with a partner. Read the passage and complete the sentences using the correct verb forms.

William has been a stay-at-home dad for the last seven years, but now both children are in school, and he's going back to work. He's looking for a job that will still allow him to spend time with his children. What kind of job do you think he is looking for?

He is looking for a job that … OR *He is not looking for a job that …*

1. leave him free on weekends
2. require him to work on weekends
3. include a lot of long-distance travel
4. have a long commute
5. be close to home
6. have flexible hours

13-2 Adjective Clause Pronouns Used as the Object of a Verb

	The man was Mr. Jones. I saw **him**. ↓				Notice in the examples: The adjective clause pronouns are placed at the beginning of the clause.
(a)	The man	*who(m)*	*I saw*	was Mr. Jones.	
(b)	The man	*that*	*I saw*	was Mr. Jones.	In (a): **who** is usually used instead of **whom**, especially in speaking. **Whom** is generally used only in very formal English.
(c)	The man	Ø	*I saw*	was Mr. Jones.	

	The movie wasn't very good. We saw **it** last night. ↓			In (c) and (e): An object pronoun is often omitted (**Ø**) from an adjective clause. (A subject pronoun, however, may not be omitted.)
(d)	The movie	*that*	*we saw last night*	wasn't very good.
(e)	The movie	Ø	*we saw last night*	wasn't very good.
(f)	The movie	*which*	*we saw last night*	wasn't very good.

As an object pronoun for people, **that** is more common than **who**, but **Ø** is the most common in speaking and writing.

To describe things, **that** and **Ø** are the most common in speaking. In writing, **that** is the most common, and **Ø** is rare.

SUMMARY:

    who(m) = used for people
    that = used for both people and things
    which = used for things (common in British English but not in contemporary American English)

(g)	*INCORRECT:*	The man who(m) I saw ~~him~~ was Mr. Jones. The man that I saw ~~him~~ was Mr. Jones. The man I saw ~~him~~ was Mr. Jones.	In (g): The pronoun **him** must be removed. It is unnecessary because who(m), that, or Ø functions as the object of the verb **saw**.

EXERCISE 8 ▶ Looking at grammar. (Chart 13-2)

Decide if the word in blue is a subject or object pronoun.

Online Reviews

1. Did you read the online reviews that were written by fake customers?	S	O
2. Every review that I read gave the product five stars.	S	O
3. All the writers that posted this week were paid to write a positive review.	S	O
4. The reviewers that gave five stars used similar vocabulary and sentence structure.	S	O
5. I've decided not to buy products that this particular company makes.	S	O

EXERCISE 9 ▶ Looking at grammar. (Chart 13-2)

Choose all the possible completions for each sentence. Do not add commas or capital letters.

Your Trip

1. Tell me about the people _____ you met when you were in Norway.
   (a.) who   (b.) that   c. they   (d.) whom   (e.) Ø

2. Was the hotel _____ you found on the Internet a nice place to stay?
   a. who   b. that   c. it   d. whom   e. Ø

3. Did you see your Norwegian friend _____ you met in college?
   a. who   b. that   c. he   d. whom   e. Ø

4. Tell me about the other cities _____ you went to.
   a. who   b. that   c. they   d. whom   e. Ø

5. Have you downloaded all the pictures _____ you took yet?
   a. who   b. that   c. they   d. whom   e. Ø

6. Did you find the Norwegian phrases _____ you had learned before you left helpful?
   a. who   b. that   c. they   d. whom   e. Ø

7. I'd like to know more about your cousins _____ you visited in the fishing village.
   a. who   b. that   c. they   d. whom   e. Ø

EXERCISE 10 ▶ Looking at grammar. (Chart 13-2)

Combine the two sentences. Use the second sentence as an adjective clause. Give <u>all</u> the possible patterns, orally or in writing. Use **who, that,** or **Ø**.

Recommendations

1. The book was good. You suggested I read it.
   → *The book that / Ø you suggested I read was good.*
2. I bought the TV. A consumer guide rated it highly.
3. The doctor was very helpful. You advised me to see him.
4. The tour guide recommended a restaurant. His cousin owns it.
5. I didn't like the plumber. My friend told me to call him.

EXERCISE 11 ▶ Warm-up. (Chart 13-3)

Compare the <u>underlined</u> adjective clause in sentence a. with the one in sentence b. What differences do you notice? NOTE: Both sentences are correct.

1. a. I think Lee is a person <u>who you can have fun with</u>.
   b. Do you think Lee is a person <u>with whom you can have fun</u>?

2. a. The art school <u>which Lori applied to</u> is very demanding.
   b. Do you know the name of the art school <u>to which Lori applied</u>?

13-3 Adjective Clause Pronouns Used as the Object of a Preposition

	She is the woman. I told you **about her**. ↓		
(a)	She is the woman	*about whom*	*I told you.*
(b)	She is the woman	*who(m)*	*I told you about.*
(c)	She is the woman	*that*	*I told you about.*
(d)	She is the woman	*Ø*	*I told you about.*

	The music was good. We listened **to it** last night. ↓				
(e)	The music	*to which*	*we listened*	*last night*	*was good.*
(f)	The music	*that*	*we listened to*	*last night*	*was good.*
(g)	The music	*Ø*	*we listened to*	*last night*	*was good.*
(h)	The music	*which*	*we listened to*	*last night*	*was good.*

In very formal English, the preposition comes at the beginning of the adjective clause, as in (a) and (e). Usually, however, in everyday usage, the preposition comes after the subject and verb of the adjective clause, as in the other examples.

NOTE: If the preposition comes at the beginning of the adjective clause, only **whom** or **which** may be used. A preposition is never immediately followed by **that** or **who**.

INCORRECT: She is the woman ~~about who~~ I told you.

INCORRECT: The music ~~to that~~ we listened last night was good.

EXERCISE 12 ▸ Looking at grammar. (Chart 13-3)
Choose all the possible completions for each sentence. Which one seems the most formal?

1. The scholarship _____ requires an essay.

   a. that they are applying for

   b. they are applying for

   c. they are applying

   d. they are applying for it

   e. for which they are applying

2. The counselor _____ had sample essays.

   a. who they spoke to

   b. that they spoke to

   c. who they spoke to her

   d. to whom they spoke

   e. to who they spoke

   f. they spoke to

EXERCISE 13 ▸ Looking at grammar. (Chart 13-3)
Combine the two sentences. Use the second sentence as an adjective clause. Give all the possible patterns, orally or in writing.

1. The man is standing over there. I was telling you about him.
2. I must thank the people. I got a present from them.
3. The meeting was interesting. Omar went to it.

EXERCISE 14 ▸ Looking at grammar. (Charts 13-1 → 13-3)
Give all the possible completions for each sentence. Use *who*, *that*, or *Ø*.

A Party

1. a. Did I tell you about the party _____*that / Ø*_____ I went to last night?

   b. Did I tell you about the party _____*that**_____ lasted until early morning?

2. a. I want to tell you about a woman _____ I met at the party.

   b. I want to tell you about the woman _____ hosted the party.

**Ø cannot be used for the subject position.

3. a. She works for a company _____ is hiring. She told me to apply.

   b. She said the company _____ she works for is excellent.

4. a. A man _____ I was dancing with stepped on my toes.

   b. The man _____ stepped on my toes also tripped and fell down.

5. a. My boyfriend wasn't at the party. He attended an event _____ was

   raising money for an animal shelter.

   b. We should donate to the animal shelter _____ he is supporting.

EXERCISE 15 ▸ Check your knowledge. (Charts 13-1 → 13-3)
Correct the errors in the adjective clauses.

1. In our village, there were many people didn't have much money.

2. I enjoyed the book that you told me to read it.

3. I still remember the man who he taught me to play the guitar when I was a boy.

4. I showed my father a picture of the car I am going to buy it as soon as I save enough money.

5. The man about who I was talking about walked into the room. I hope he didn't hear me.

6. The people appear in the play are amateur actors.

7. I don't like to spend time with people which loses their temper easily.

8. In one corner of the marketplace, an elderly man who was playing a violin.

9. People who works in the hunger program they estimate that 45,000 people worldwide die from starvation and malnutrition-related diseases every single day of the year.

EXERCISE 16 ▸ Let's talk: pairwork. (Charts 13-1 → 13-3)
Work with a partner. Take turns making statements that end in adjective clauses. Use words from each column and *who, that,* or **Ø**. Try to make the sentences true for you.

On Airplanes

Example: I enjoy people who like to have fun.

I enjoy I dislike I like to sit next to I like to talk to I don't like to talk to	flights people friends passengers pilots movies books	are scary. have subtitles. have had interesting experiences. are short. are long. are long-winded.★ make me think. like to have fun. are sleeping. want to know more about me. are talkative. are busy doing other things.

★*long-winded* = boring because they talk too much

EXERCISE 17 ▸ Warm-up. (Chart 13-4)

Check (✓) the sentences that are grammatically correct.

1. _____ I have a friend. His purpose in life is to help others.
2. _____ I have a friend whose purpose in life is to help others.
3. _____ I have a friend who his purpose in life is to help others.
4. _____ I have a friend that his purpose in life is to help others.

13-4 Using *Whose*

I know the man. ***His bike*** was stolen. ↓ (a) I know the man *whose bike was stolen*.	***Whose*** is used to show possession. It carries the same meaning as other possessive pronouns used as adjectives: *his, her, its,* and *their*.

The student writes well.
I read ***her composition***.
↓
(b) The student *whose composition I read* writes well.
	Like *his, her, its,* and *their,* ***whose*** is connected to a noun.
	   his bike → whose bike
	   her composition → whose composition
	Both ***whose*** and the noun it is connected to are placed at the beginning of the adjective clause. ***Whose*** cannot be omitted.

(c) I worked at a ***company*** *whose employees* wanted to form a union.	***Whose*** usually modifies people, but it may also be used to modify things, as in (c).
(d) That's the boy *whose parents* you met. (e) That's the boy *who's* in my math class. (f) That's the boy *who's been living* with our neighbors since his mother became ill.*	***Whose*** and ***who's*** have the same pronunciation. ***Who's*** can mean ***who is,*** as in (e), or ***who has,*** as in (f).

*When ***has*** is a helping verb in the present perfect, it is usually contracted with ***who*** in speaking and sometimes in informal writing, as in (f).
When ***has*** is a main verb, it is NOT contracted with ***who:*** *I know a man **who has** a cook.*

EXERCISE 18 ▸ Looking at grammar. (Chart 13-4)

Change the words in blue to a clause with ***whose***.

1.   A co-worker drives an old taxi to work.
           Her parents own a taxi company.
             ↓

    A co-worker _____ own a taxi company drives an old taxi to work.

2.   The workers got a bonus.
           Their department had the most sales.
            ↓

    The workers _____ had the most sales got a bonus.

3.   The hospital is temporarily closed.
           Its health-care workers are on strike.
            ↓

    The hospital _____ is temporarily closed.

EXERCISE 19 ▶ Looking at grammar. (Chart 13-4)

Complete the sentences with *who* or *whose*.

Acquaintances

1. a. I know a doctor _____ last name is Doctor.

   b. I know a doctor _____ lives on a sailboat.

2. a. The professor _____ teaches art history is excellent.

   b. The professor _____ course I almost dropped is excellent.

3. a. I apologized to the man _____ coffee I spilled.

   b. I made friends with that man _____ is now in my math class.

EXERCISE 20 ▶ Let's talk: pairwork. (Chart 13-4)

Work with a partner. Imagine you are in a room full of people. You and your partner are speaking. Together, take turns identifying various people in the room. Begin with *There is*.

1. That man's wife is your teacher. → PARTNER A: *There is the man whose wife is my teacher.*
2. That woman's husband is a football player. → PARTNER B: *There is the woman whose husband is a football player.*
3. That girl's mother is a surgeon.
4. That person's picture was in the newspaper.
5. That woman's car was stolen.
6. You found that woman's keys.
7. You are in that teacher's class.
8. You read that author's book.

EXERCISE 21 ▶ Looking at grammar. (Chart 13-4)

Combine the two sentences. Use the second sentence as an adjective clause with *whose* or *who*.

College Orientation Day

1. We were taken on a tour by a student. Her major is popular culture.
   → *We were taken on a tour by a student whose major is popular culture.*
2. I have been assigned a roommate. His parents teach at this school.
3. The people seem nice. They live on my dorm floor.
4. I have a professor. She won a prestigious award.
5. I met the man. His wife is the president of the college.

EXERCISE 22 ▶ Listening. (Chart 13-4)

Choose the words you hear: *who's* or *whose*.

Example: You will hear:　　The man who's standing over there is Mr. Smith.

　　　　　　　　You will choose: (who's)　　whose

1. who's	whose		5. who's	whose
2. who's	whose		6. who's	whose
3. who's	whose		7. who's	whose
4. who's	whose		8. who's	whose

EXERCISE 23 ▶ Listening. (Chart 13-4)

Listen to the sentences in normal, contracted speech. You will hear: **whose** or **who's** (meaning **who is** or **who has**). Choose the correct meaning.

Example: You will hear: I know a woman who's a taxi driver.

You will choose: whose   (who is)   who has

1. whose	who is	who has		5. whose	who is	who has
2. whose	who is	who has		6. whose	who is	who has
3. whose	who is	who has		7. whose	who is	who has
4. whose	who is	who has		8. whose	who is	who has

EXERCISE 24 ▶ Warm-up. (Chart 13-5)

All of these sentences have the same meaning, and all of them are grammatically correct. The adjective clauses are in blue. What differences do you notice?

1. The **town** where I grew up is very small.
2. The **town** in which I grew up is very small.
3. The **town** which I grew up in is very small.
4. The **town** that I grew up in is very small.
5. The **town** I grew up in is very small.

13-5 Using *Where* in Adjective Clauses

The building is very old. He lives **there** (**in that building**).				*Where* is used in an adjective clause to modify a place (*city, country, room, house, etc.*).
(a) The building	*where*	*he lives*	is very old.	If *where* is used, as in (a), a preposition is NOT included in the adjective clause.
(b) The building	*in which*	*he lives*	is very old.	If *where* is not used, the preposition must be included, as in (b). *In which* is more common in academic writing.
The building	*which*	*he lives in*	is very old.	
The building	*that*	*he lives in*	is very old.	
The building	Ø	*he lives in*	is very old.	

EXERCISE 25 ▶ Looking at grammar. (Chart 13-5)

Combine the two sentences. Use the second sentence as an adjective clause.

Hiding Places

1. That is the special book. My daughter puts her money there (in that book).

   → *That is the special book where my daughter puts her money.*
   → *That is the special book in which my daughter puts her money.*
   → *That is the special book which/that/Ø my daughter puts her money in.*

2. This is the mattress. My grandmother hid some money there (under the mattress).

3. That is the drawer. Johnny keeps a supply of candy there (in the drawer).

4. Here is the safe. My mom locks up her jewelry there (in that safe).

EXERCISE 26 ▶ Looking at grammar. (Chart 13-5)

Study the examples. Note how the sentences are combined with the words in blue. Then complete the sentences with *where, which,* or *in which.*

Examples: The city is beautiful. I was born there.

The city _____*where*_____ I was born is beautiful.

The city _____*in which*_____ I was born is beautiful.

The city is beautiful. It is next to my hometown.

The city _____*which*_____ is next to my hometown is beautiful.

1. The house is very old. We want to buy it.

   a. The house _____ we want to buy is very old.

   The house is very old. We lived there.

   b. The house _____ we lived is very old.

   c. The house _____ we lived is very old.

2. The town is a nice place to visit. I grew up there.

   a. The town _____ I grew up is a nice place to visit.

   b. The town _____ I grew up is a nice place to visit.

   The town is a nice place to visit. It is near us.

   c. The town _____ is near us is a nice place to visit.

3. The room is empty. It is in the basement.

   a. The room _____ is in the basement is empty.

   The room is unheated. I sleep there.

   b. The room _____ I sleep is unheated.

   c. The room _____ I sleep is unheated.

4. The park is next to the shopping center. It has a nice soccer field.

   a. The park _____ has a nice soccer field is next to the shopping center.

   The park is now a shopping center. I met your dad there.

   b. The park _____ I met your dad is now a shopping center.

   c. The park _____ I met your dad is now a shopping center.

Complete the sentences with *who, that,* or *where*.

Euphemisms

1. A euphemism ("you-fuh-mism") is a word or phrase _____ makes something sound more pleasant.

2. For example, a "used" car is a car _____ has been "pre-owned." "Used" doesn't sound appealing to buyers.

3. A "landfill" is a place _____ people take their garbage. It used to be called a "dump."

4. A person _____ picks up your garbage is a "sanitation engineer."

5. "Pass away" is a phrase _____ sounds more gentle and indirect than "die."

6. People _____ are sick are "under the weather."

7. A guard _____ works at a jail is known as a "corrections officer."

8. The place _____ prisoners stay is a "correctional facility."

9. An employee _____ is fired is "let go."

EXERCISE 28 ▸ Warm-up. (Chart 13-6)

All of these sentences have the same meaning, and all of them are grammatically correct. The adjective clauses are in blue. What differences do you notice?

1. I clearly remember the **day** when I rode a bike for the first time.
2. I clearly remember the **day** on which I rode a bike for the first time.
3. I clearly remember the **day** that I rode a bike for the first time.
4. I clearly remember the **day** I rode a bike for the first time.

13-6 Using *When* in Adjective Clauses

	I'll never forget the day. I met you **then** (**on that day**).	*When* is used in an adjective clause to modify a noun of time (*year, day, time, century, etc.*).
(a) I'll never forget the day	*when* — *I met you.*	The use of a preposition in an adjective clause that modifies a noun of time is somewhat different from that in other adjective clauses: a preposition + *which* is used, as in (b). Otherwise, there is no preposition. The use of a preposition is very formal.
(b) I'll never forget the day	*on which* — *I met you.*	
(c) I'll never forget the day	*that* — *I met you.*	
(d) I'll never forget the day	*Ø* — *I met you.*	

EXERCISE 29 ▸ Looking at grammar. (Chart 13-6)

My Kuwaiti Cousins

Part I. Complete the sentences with the correct preposition.

1. My cousins from Kuwait will come _____ Monday.

2. Their plane arrives _____ 7:05.

3. I last saw them _____ 2010.

4. They asked to visit _____ July.

Part II. Combine the two sentences using ***when*** and ***which***.

1. Monday is the day. My cousins from Kuwait will come then.
   → *Monday is the day when my cousins from Kuwait will come.*
   → *Monday is the day on which my cousins from Kuwait will come.*
2. 7:05 is the time. Their plane arrives then.
3. 2010 is the year. I last saw them then.
4. July is the month. The weather is usually the hottest then.

EXERCISE 30 ▸ Looking at grammar. (Charts 13-5 and 13-6)
Combine the two sentences. Use ***where*** or ***when*** to introduce an adjective clause.

Town Memories

1. That is the building. The fire began there. → *That is the place **where** the fire began*
2. I remember the day. The fire began then. → *I remember the day **when** the fire began.*
3. This used to be a movie theater. I was young then.
4. We liked that restaurant. You could get a good meal for a great price there.
5. The bakery is no longer there. They made the best chocolate cake.
6. There was a time. There were no stoplights then.
7. The house is now an office building. I was born there.

EXERCISE 31 ▸ Let's talk: interview. (Charts 13-1 → 13-6)
For each question, interview two classmates. Encourage them to use adjective clauses in their responses. Share a few of their answers with the class.

Example:

What kind of **food** don't you like? → *I don't like **food** that is too sugary.*

1. What kind of **people** do you like to spend time with?
2. What kind of **people** do you prefer to avoid?
3. What kind of **cities** do you like to visit?
4. What kind of **teachers** do you learn best from?
5. What kind of **place** would you like to live in?
6. What **time of day** do you feel most energetic?

EXERCISE 32 ▸ Listening. (Charts 13-1 → 13-6)
Listen to the sentences. Choose the correct meanings for each sentence.

Example: You will hear: The nurse who gave the medicine to the patients seemed confused.
   You will choose: a. The patients were confused.
                      (b.) The patients received medicine from the nurse.
                      (c.) The nurse was confused.

1. a. A man gave an interview.
   b. The man is the speaker's friend.
   c. The speaker gave an interview.

2. a. Two people were killed in an accident.
   b. Two people blocked all lanes of the highway for two hours.
   c. An accident blocked all lanes of the highway for two hours.

3. a. The speaker lives in a large city.
   b. The speaker was born in a small town.
   c. The speaker was born in a large city.

4. a. The music teacher gives music lessons.
   b. The music teacher is a rock star.
   c. The speaker took music lessons.

5. a. The speaker got a phone from his parents.
   b. The phone takes excellent pictures.
   c. The speaker wants to get a phone that takes excellent pictures.

6. a. The speaker often invites the neighbor to dinner.
   b. The neighbor often visits at dinnertime.
   c. The speaker visits the neighbor at dinnertime.

EXERCISE 33 ▸ Grammar and writing. (Charts 13-1 → 13-6)

On a separate piece of paper, combine the sentences into a paragraph using adjective clauses.

Robert Ballard is an oceanographer.
He made headlines in 1985.
Ballard led a team.
They discovered the remains of the *Titanic*.
The *Titanic* was an "unsinkable" passenger ship.
It has rested on the floor of the Atlantic Ocean since 1912.
It had struck an iceberg in 1912.
After Ballard finished his exploration of the ship, he left a memorial plaque.
It honored all those who died on that terrible night.

EXERCISE 34 ▸ Warm-up. (Chart 13-7)

<u>Underline</u> each adjective clause. Draw an arrow to the word it modifies.

1. A: Management needs someone at the top who understands our jobs.
   B: You can say that again!*

2. A: We're the ones who seem to know everything.
   B: I couldn't agree more!

3. A: Everything they want to do slows us down and costs more.
   B: You said it!

---

*All of the responses are ways to express strong agreement.

13-7 Using Adjective Clauses to Modify Pronouns

(a) There is *someone* I want you to meet.	Adjective clauses can modify indefinite pronouns (e.g., *someone, everybody*).
(b) *Everything* he said was pure nonsense.	Object pronouns (e.g., *who(m), that, which*) are usually omitted in the adjective clause, as in (a) and (b).
(c) *Anybody* who wants to come is welcome.	
(d) Paula was *the only one* I knew at the party.	Adjective clauses can modify **the one(s)** and **those**.*
(e) Scholarships are available for *those* who need financial assistance.	
(f) INCORRECT: ~~I who am a student at this school~~ come from a country in Asia.	Adjective clauses are almost never used to modify personal pronouns. Native English speakers would not say or write the sentence in (f).
(g) It is *I who am responsible*.	Example (g) is possible, but very formal and uncommon.
(h) *He who laughs last* laughs best.	Example (h) is a well-known saying in which **he** is used as an indefinite pronoun (meaning "anyone" or "any person").

*An adjective clause with **which** can also be used to modify the demonstrative pronoun **that**:
We sometimes fear **that which** we do not understand.
The bread my mother makes is much better than **that which** you can buy at a store.

EXERCISE 35 ▶ Looking at grammar. (Chart 13-7)
Complete the sentences with adjective clauses.

Help

1. Ask your mom. She's the one _____ *who can help you.* _____

2. I have a problem. There is something _____

3. This problem is harder than the ones _____

4. Those _____ should stay after class.

5. I'm sorry, but I'm powerless to do anything. There's nothing more _____

6. Could I talk to someone else? I've tried to explain my situation, but I don't think you heard anything _____

7. I did everything _____, but it didn't work.
   We need to find someone _____

8. You are the only one _____

EXERCISE 36 ▶ Let's talk. (Charts 13-1 → 13-7)
Work with a partner or in small groups. Complete this sentence: *The ideal ... is one ....* Use a word in the box and finish it with your own words. Use **who** or **that**.

Examples: The ideal friend is one who(m) you can always trust.
The ideal job is one that has flexible hours.

friend	father	spouse	doctor
student	mother	job	city

EXERCISE 37 ▸ Warm-up. (Chart 13-8)

Listen to your teacher read the sentences aloud. Both are correct. Notice the use of pauses. Then answer the questions for both sentences.

1. I just found out that Lara Johnson, who speaks Russian fluently, has applied for the job at the Russian embassy.

2. That's not the job for you. Only people who speak Russian fluently will be considered for the job at the Russian embassy.

- Which adjective clause can be omitted with no change in the meaning of the noun it modifies?
- What do you notice about the use of commas?

13-8 Punctuating Adjective Clauses

General guidelines for the punctuation of adjective clauses:
(1) **DO NOT USE COMMAS IF** the adjective clause is necessary to identify the noun it modifies.*
(2) **USE COMMAS IF** the adjective clause simply gives additional information and is not necessary to identify the noun it modifies.**

(a) *The professor* who teaches Chemistry 101 is an excellent lecturer.	In (a): No commas are used. The adjective clause is necessary to identify which professor is meant.
(b) *Professor Wilson*, who teaches Chemistry 101, is an excellent lecturer.	In (b): Commas are used. The adjective clause is not necessary to identify Professor Wilson. We already know who he is: he has a name. The adjective clause simply gives additional information.
(c) *Hawaii*, which consists of eight principal islands, is a favorite vacation spot.	GUIDELINE: Use commas, as in (b), (c), and (d), if an adjective clause modifies a proper noun. (A proper noun begins with a capital letter.)
(d) *Mrs. Smith*, who is a retired teacher, does volunteer work at the hospital.	NOTE: A comma reflects a pause in speech.
(e) *The man* { who(m) / that / Ø } I met teaches chemistry.	In (e): If no commas are used, any possible pronoun may be used in the adjective clause. Object pronouns may be omitted.
(f) *Mr. Lee*, whom I met yesterday, teaches chemistry.	In (f): When commas are necessary, the pronoun **that** may not be used (only **who, whom, which, whose, where,** and **when** may be used), and object pronouns cannot be omitted.
	INCORRECT: Mr. Lee, ~~that~~ I met yesterday, teaches chemistry.
COMPARE THE MEANING:	
(g) We took some children on a picnic. *The children, who wanted to play soccer*, ran to an open field as soon as we arrived at the park.	In (g): The use of commas means that *all* of the children wanted to play soccer and *all* of the children ran to an open field. The adjective clause is used only to give additional information about the children.
(h) We took some children on a picnic. *The children who wanted to play soccer* ran to an open field as soon as we arrived at the park. The others played a different game.	In (h): The lack of commas means that *only some* of the children wanted to play soccer. The adjective clause is used to identify which children ran to the open field.

*Adjective clauses that do not require commas are called *essential* or *restrictive* or *identifying*.

**Adjective clauses that require commas are called *nonessential* or *nonrestrictive* or *nonidentifying*.

NOTE: Nonessential adjective clauses are more common in writing than in speaking.

EXERCISE 38 ▸ Looking at grammar. (Chart 13-8)
Read each sentence, first with the adjective clause and then again without it. How does the meaning change? Does the adjective clause identify the noun? If it does not identify the noun, add commas.

1. Mercury which is the nearest planet to the sun is also the smallest planet in our solar system.
2. Research has shown that children who watch violent video games may become more aggressive.
3. People who live in glass houses shouldn't throw stones.
4. In a children's story, Little Red Riding Hood who went out one day to visit her grandmother found a wolf in her grandmother's bed.

EXERCISE 39 ▸ Grammar and listening. (Chart 13-8)
Work with a partner. Read the sentences aloud. Decide if the information in blue is necessary or simply provides additional information. If it is additional, add commas. Then listen to the sentences and correct your answers. Remember, pauses indicate commas.

1. a. Vegetables which are orange have a lot of vitamin A. (*necessary: no commas*)
   b. Vegetables, which come in many shapes and colors, have lots of vitamins.
      (*additional information: commas*)

2. a. Did you hear about the man who rowed a boat across the Atlantic Ocean?
   b. My uncle who loves boating rows his boat across the lake near his house nearly every day.

3. a. Rice which is grown in many countries is a staple food throughout much of the world.
   b. The rice which we had for dinner last night was very good.

4. a. The newspaper article was about a man who died two weeks ago of a rare tropical disease.
   b. The obituary said that Paul O'Grady who died two weeks ago of a sudden heart attack was a kind and loving man.

5. a. Tea which is a common drink throughout the world is made by pouring boiling water onto the dried leaves of certain plants.
   b. Tea which is made from herbs is called herbal tea.

6. a. Toys which contain lead paint are unsafe for children.
   b. Lead which can be found in paint and plastics is known to cause brain damage in children.

EXERCISE 40 ▶ Pronunciation and grammar. (Chart 13-8)
Work with a partner. Read the given sentence aloud. Choose the correct meaning.

1. The teacher thanked the students, who had given her some flowers.
   a. The teacher thanked *only some* of the students.
   (b.) The teacher thanked *all* of the students.

2. The teacher thanked the students who had given her some flowers.
   (a.) The teacher thanked *only some* of the students.
   b. The teacher thanked *all* of the students.

3. There was a terrible flood. The villagers who had received a warning of the flood escaped to safety.
   a. *Only some* of the villagers had been warned; only some escaped.
   b. *All* of the villagers had been warned; all escaped.

4. There was a terrible flood. The villagers, who had received a warning of the impending flood, escaped to safety.
   a. *Only some* of the villagers had been warned; only some escaped.
   b. *All* of the villagers had been warned; all escaped.

5. Natasha reached down and picked up the grammar book, which was lying upside down on the floor.
   a. There was *only one* grammar book near Natasha.
   b. There was *more than one* grammar book near Natasha.

6. Natasha reached down and picked up the grammar book which was lying upside down on the floor.
   a. There was *only one* grammar book near Natasha.
   b. There was *more than one* grammar book near Natasha.

EXERCISE 41 ▶ Looking at grammar. (Chart 13-8)
Add commas where necessary. Read the sentences aloud, paying attention to pauses.

1. a. We enjoyed the city where we spent our honeymoon.
   b. We enjoyed Mexico City where we spent our vacation.

2. a. One of the most useful materials in the world is glass which is made mainly from sand, soda, and lime.
   b. The glass which is used in windows is different from the glass which is used in eyeglasses.

3. a. You don't need to take heavy clothes when you go to Bangkok which has one of the highest average temperatures of any city in the world.
   b. Bangkok where my father was born is known as the Venice of the East.

4. a. Mr. Trang whose son won the spelling contest is very proud of his son's achievement.
   b. The man whose daughter won the science contest is also very pleased and proud.

5. a. I watched some beekeepers collect honey. They told me that beekeepers who wear protective clothing can avoid most bee stings.
   b. A person who doesn't wear protective clothing can get hundreds of bee stings within a minute.

 EXERCISE 42 ▶ Listening. (Chart 13-8)
Listen to the sentences. Choose the correct meaning for each sentence.

1. a. She threw away all of the apples.
   b. She threw away only the rotten apples.

2. a. She threw away all of the apples.
   b. She threw away only the rotten apples.

3. a. Some of the students were excused from class early.
   b. All of the students were excused from class early.

4. a. Some of the students were excused from class early.
   b. All of the students were excused from class early.

EXERCISE 43 ▸ Reading and grammar. (Charts 13-1 → 13-8)

Part I. Answer these questions. Then read the web article. Note the adjective clauses in blue.

1. Do you have a computer?
2. Do you know the name of its operating system?

Do you know these words?
- *computer programmer*
- *acquire the rights*

×

← → C 🔍

Search 🔍

DOS: The First Operating System

As you know, a computer needs to have an operating system in order to run programs. When most people think about the first operating systems that were developed for the personal computer, Microsoft or Bill Gates may come to mind. Actually, the truth is somewhat different.

In the late 1970s, there was a man in Seattle named Tim Paterson, who worked for a company that was called Seattle Computer. He was a computer programmer and needed an operating system for his computer. Paterson got tired of waiting for another company to create one and decided to develop his own program. He called it QDOS, which meant "quick and dirty operating system*." It took him about four months to develop it.

At the same time, Microsoft was quietly looking for an operating system to run a personal computer that IBM was developing. Microsoft saw the program that Paterson had written and in 1980, paid him $25,000 for a license for DOS. A year later they paid another $50,000 to acquire the rights. It became known as the Microsoft disk operating system (MS-DOS), and the rest is history. Microsoft and Bill Gates became very successful using Paterson's operating system.

quick and dirty = something that is done quickly or hastily

Part II. Complete the sentences with information from the article. Use adjective clauses in your completions.

1. Tim Paterson was the person who _____

2. Seattle Computer was the company that _____

3. The abbreviation for the program was QDOS, which _____

   _____

4. IBM was a company that _____

5. Microsoft, which _____

6. Microsoft acquired rights to a program that _____

   _____

EXERCISE 44 ▸ Warm-up. (Chart 13-9)

Choose the correct meaning (a. or b.) for each sentence.

1. The couple has 13 children, only a few of whom live at home.
   a. Ten children live at home.   b. A few of the couple's children live at home.
2. Victoria bought a dozen dresses, most of which she later returned to the store.
   a. Victoria returned a dozen dresses.   b. Victoria kept a few of the dresses.

13-9	Using Expressions of Quantity in Adjective Clauses	
	In my class there are 20 students. *Most of **them**** are from Asia.	An adjective clause may contain an expression of quantity with **of**: *some of, many of, most of, none of, two of, half of, both of,* etc.
(a)	In my class there are 20 students, *most of **whom**** are from Asia.	
(b)	He gave several reasons, *only a few of **which**** were valid.	The expression of quantity precedes the pronoun. Only **whom**, **which**, and **whose** are used in this pattern. This pattern is more common in writing than speaking. Commas are used.
(c)	The teachers discussed Jim, *one of **whose problems**** was poor study habits.	

EXERCISE 45 ▸ Looking at grammar. (Chart 13-9)

Combine the two sentences in each item. Use the second sentence as an adjective clause.

At the Mall

1. The mall has 200 stores. Many of them are having sales this weekend.
   → *The mall has 200 stores, many of which are having sales this weekend.*
2. I went to a few sales. Only one of them had good discounts.
3. There are many clothing stores. The majority of them are for women and teenage girls.
4. I tried on five dresses. I liked two of them.
5. The movie theater is showing four movies. None sound good.
6. There are several ethnic restaurants in the food court. All of them have reasonable prices.
7. There are two cafés side by side. Both of them serve excellent coffee.

EXERCISE 46 ▸ Grammar and writing. (Chart 13-9)

Complete the sentences with your own words. Use adjective clauses.

About Me

1. I have several friends, two of _____*whom grew up with me.*_____

2. I own three _____, one of _____

3. I have many _____, all of _____

4. I bought two _____, neither of _____

5. I am taking _____ courses, one of _____

6. This term I had to buy _____ books, most of _____

7. For this class I need _____, some of _____

EXERCISE 47 ▸ Warm-up. (Chart 13-10)
What does *which* refer to in each sentence?

1. The soccer team worked very hard to win, **which** made their coach very proud.
2. Some of the athletes attended practice during vacation, **which** pleased their coach.

13-10	Using *Which* to Modify a Whole Sentence

(a) Tom was late. **That** surprised me.	The pronouns **that** and **this** can refer to the idea of a whole sentence which comes before.
(b) Tom was late, *which surprised me.*	In (a): The word **that** refers to the whole sentence **Tom was late**.
	Similarly, an adjective clause with **which** may modify the idea of a whole sentence.
(c) The elevator is out of order. **This** is too bad.	In (b): The word **which** refers to the whole sentence **Tom was late**.
(d) The elevator is out of order, *which is too bad.*	Using **which** to modify a whole sentence is informal and occurs most frequently in spoken English. This structure is generally not appropriate in formal writing. Whenever it is written, however, it is preceded by a comma to reflect a pause in speech.

EXERCISE 48 ▸ Looking at grammar. (Chart 13-10)
Combine the two sentences. Use the second sentence as an adjective clause.

Sonya's Challenges

1. Sonya lost her job. That wasn't surprising.
   → *Sonya lost her job, which wasn't surprising.*
2. She usually came to work late. That upset her boss.
3. So her boss fired her. That made her angry.
4. She hadn't saved any money. That was unfortunate.
5. So she had to borrow some money from me. I didn't like that.
6. She has found a new job. That is lucky.
7. So she has repaid the money she borrowed from me. I appreciate that.
8. She has promised herself to be on time to work every day. That is a good idea.

EXERCISE 49 ▸ Looking at grammar. (Charts 13-1 → 13-10)
Combine sentences a. and b. Use b. as an adjective clause. Use formal written English. Punctuate carefully.

1. a. An antecedent is a word.
   b. A pronoun refers to this word.
      → *An antecedent is a word to which a pronoun refers.*

2. a. The blue whale is considered the largest animal that has ever lived.
   b. It can grow to 100 feet and 150 tons.

3. a. The plane was met by a crowd of 300 people.
   b. Some of them had been waiting for more than four hours.

4. a. In this paper, I will describe the basic process.
   b. Raw cotton becomes cotton thread by this process.

5. a. The researchers are doing case studies of people to determine the importance of heredity in health and longevity.
   b. These people's families have a history of high blood pressure and heart disease.

6. a. At the end of this month, scientists at the institute will conclude their AIDS research.
   b. The results of this research will be published within six months.

7. a. According to many education officials, "math phobia" (that is, a fear of mathematics) is a widespread problem.
   b. A solution to this problem can and must be found.

8. a. The art museum hopes to hire a new administrator.
   b. Under this person's direction, it will be able to purchase significant pieces of art.

9. a. The giant anteater licks up ants for its dinner.
   b. Its tongue is longer than 30 centimeters (12 inches).

10. a. The anteater's tongue is sticky.
    b. It can go in and out of its mouth 160 times a minute.

EXERCISE 50 ▶ Reading and grammar. (Charts 13-1 → 13-10)
Read about Ellen and her commute to work. <u>Underline</u> what the words in blue refer to.

Ellen's Commute

Ellen <u>commutes to work by ferry</u>, which (1) means she takes a boat from the island where she lives to the city where (2) she works. She leaves her house at 6:00, which (3) is earlier than she'd like but necessary because the ferry ride takes 30 minutes. Ellen needs 20 minutes to drive to the parking lot where (4) she leaves her car and boards the ferry. Once she's on the other side, she catches a bus that (5) takes her to her office. Traffic is usually heavy at that hour, so she's on the bus for another 30 minutes. On the bus, she usually reads reports that (6) she was too tired to finish the night before. The bus drops her off a few blocks from her office. Sometimes she stops at an espresso stand and picks up coffee for her co-workers, for which (7) they reimburse her later. By the time she gets to her office, she has been commuting for an hour and a half, which (8) she wishes she didn't have to do but isn't going to change because she enjoys her life on the island so much.

EXERCISE 51 ▶ Warm-up. (Chart 13-11)

Look at the words in blue. What differences do you notice between each pair of sentences?

NOTE: Sentences a. and b. have the same meaning.

1. a. I talked to the people who were sitting beside me at the ball game.
   b. I talked to the people sitting beside me at the ball game.

2. a. The notebooks that are on my desk are mine.
   b. The notebooks on my desk are mine.

3. a. I read an article about Gregor Mendel, who is known as the father of genetics.
   b. I read an article about Gregor Mendel, known as the father of genetics.

13-11 Reducing Adjective Clauses to Adjective Phrases

CLAUSE: *A clause* is a group of related words that contains a subject and a verb.
PHRASE: *A phrase* is a group of related words that does not contain a subject and a verb.

(a) CLAUSE: The girl *who is sitting next to me* is Mai. (b) PHRASE: The girl *sitting next to me* is Mai. (c) CLAUSE: The girl *(whom) I saw* was Mai. (d) PHRASE: *(none)*	An adjective phrase is a reduction of an adjective clause. It modifies a noun. It does not contain a subject and verb. Examples (a) and (b) have the same meaning. Only adjective clauses that have a subject pronoun — **who**, **that**, or **which** — can be reduced to modifying adjective phrases. The adjective clause in (c) cannot be reduced to an adjective phrase.
(e) CLAUSE: The man *who is talking* to John is from Korea. PHRASE: The man Ø Ø *talking* to John is from Korea. (f) CLAUSE: The ideas *that are presented* in this book are good. PHRASE: The ideas Ø Ø *presented* in this book are good. (g) CLAUSE: Ann is the woman *that is responsible* for the error. PHRASE: Ann is the woman Ø Ø *responsible* for the error.	There are two ways in which an adjective clause is changed to an adjective phrase. **1.** if the adjective clause contains the **be** form of a verb, omit the subject pronoun and the **be** form, as in (e), (f), and (g).*
(h) CLAUSE: English has an alphabet *that consists* of 26 letters. PHRASE: English has an alphabet Ø *consisting* of 26 letters. (i) CLAUSE: Anyone *who wants* to come with us is welcome. PHRASE: Anyone Ø *wanting* to come with us is welcome.	**2.** If there is no **be** form of a verb in the adjective clause, it is sometimes possible to omit the subject pronoun and change the verb to its **-ing** form, as in (h) and (i).
(j) *Paris,* which is the capital of France, is an exciting city. (k) *Paris,* the capital of France, is an exciting city.	If the adjective clause requires commas, as in (j), the adjective phrase also requires commas, as in (k). An adjective phrase in which a noun follows another noun, as in (k), is called an *appositive*.

*If an adjective clause that contains **be** + *a single adjective* is changed, the adjective is moved to its normal position in front of the noun it modifies.

    CLAUSE: ***Fruit that is fresh*** *tastes better than old, soft, mushy fruit.*
    CORRECT PHRASE: ***Fresh fruit*** *tastes better than old, soft, mushy fruit.*
    INCORRECT PHRASE: Fruit fresh tastes better than old, soft, mushy fruit.

EXERCISE 52 ▶ Looking at grammar. (Chart 13-11)

Change the adjective clauses to adjective phrases.

Early Failures of Famous People

Many famous people did not enjoy immediate success in their early lives:

1. Abraham Lincoln, ~~who was~~ one of the truly great presidents of the United States, ran for public office 26 times and lost 23 of the elections.
2. Walt Disney, who was the creator of Mickey Mouse and the founder of his own movie production company, once was fired by a newspaper editor because he had no good ideas.
3. Thomas Edison, who was the inventor of the light bulb and the phonograph, was believed by his teachers to be too stupid to learn.
4. Albert Einstein, who was one of the greatest scientists of all time, performed badly in almost all of his high school courses and failed his first college entrance exam.

EXERCISE 53 ▶ Looking at grammar. (Chart 13-11)

Change the adjective phrases to adjective clauses.

A Class Trip

1. Our biology class is going to Montreal to see the Biodome, a dome-like structure housing five ecosystems.
   → *Our class is going to Montreal to see the Biodome, which is a dome-like structure that/which houses five ecosystems.*
2. Ecosystems are biological communities containing living and non-living things found in one particular environment.
3. The ecosystems being studied in our class include a tropical rain forest and Antarctic islands.
4. An optional trip to the Montreal Insectarium, considered North America's leading museum of insects, is also being offered.
5. Students not wanting to see insects can spend more time at the Biodome.

tropical rain forest

EXERCISE 54 ▶ Listening. (Chart 13-11)

Listen to the sentences. Choose the correct meaning (a. or b.) for each sentence. In some cases, both are correct.

Example: You will hear: The experiment conducted by the students was successful.
 You will choose: ⓐ The students conducted an experiment.
  ⓑ The experiment was successful.

1. a. There is a fence around our house.
   b. Our house is made of wood.

2. a. All schoolchildren receive a good education.
   b. That school provides a good education.

3. a. The university president will give a speech.
   b. Dr. Stanton will give a speech.

4. a. There is a galaxy called the Milky Way.
   b. Our solar system is called the Milky Way.

the Milky Way

EXERCISE 55 ▶ Game. (Chart 13-11)
Work in teams. Complete the sentences by turning the information in the box into adjective phrases. Use commas as necessary. The team that finishes first with the most correct answers wins.

   a. It is the lowest place on the earth's surface.
 ✓ b. It is the highest mountain in the world.
   c. It is the capital of Iraq.
   d. It is the capital of Argentina.
   e. It is the largest city in the Western Hemisphere.
   f. It is the largest city in the United States.
   g. It is the most populous country in Africa.
   h. It is the northernmost country in Latin America.
   i. They are sensitive instruments that measure the shaking of the ground.
   j. They are devices that produce a powerful beam of light.

1. Mount Everest _____ *, the highest mountain in the world,* _____ is in the Himalayas.

2. One of the largest cities in the Middle East is Baghdad _____

3. Earthquakes are recorded on seismographs _____
   _____

4. The Dead Sea _____
   is located in the Middle East between Jordan and Israel.

5. The newspaper reported an earthquake in Buenos Aires _____

6. Industry and medicine are continually finding new uses for lasers _____
   _____

7. Mexico _____ lies just south of
   the United States.

8. The nation Nigeria _____ consists of
   over 250 different cultural groups even though English is the official language.

9. Both Mexico City _____
   and New York City _____ face challenging futures.

EXERCISE 56 ▸ Reading and grammar. (Charts 13-2 and 13-11)
Read the passage. Find the 7 adjective clauses where *who, that,* or *which* have been omitted. Rewrite them using *who, that,* or *which*.

Do you know these words?
- genius
- unconscious
- sought
- altered
- trauma

An Accidental
Genius

Jason Padgett was not much of a student. A college dropout, he worked for his father at a furniture store in Tacoma, Washington. He thought of himself as a playboy and didn't think that school was important.

In 2002, at the age of 31, Jason's life changed forever. He left a karaoke bar one night, and while he was walking home, two men attacked him. They knocked him to the ground unconscious. After treatment at a hospital, he went home. The next morning he woke up and noticed that his vision was different. He saw geometric designs in the objects he looked at. Water pouring from a faucet had crystal structures. These were details he had never seen before. He began to draw complex patterns, some taking him weeks to finish. Before his injury, Padgett had never studied beyond pre-algebra. Now he saw mathematical structures everywhere.

He sought the help of a doctor, who told Padgett that he had become a math genius because of the injury. Eventually he went to Finland to meet Dr. Berit Brogaard, a specialist in brain injuries. Dr. Brogaard used a special MRI machine* to study Padgett's brain and discovered that the part of the brain used for math was more active. The injury had altered his brain to make it very specialized in math.

Padgett went back to school to study advanced math. Sometimes he knew more than his teachers. He also wrote a book, *Struck by Genius,* in which he described the trauma he went through. He said it has changed his life for the better, and he has no regrets.

*MRI = magnetic resonance imaging; a machine that uses radio waves to take pictures of organs in the body

1. _____
2. _____
3. _____
4. _____
5. _____
6. _____
7. _____

EXERCISE 57 ▸ Looking at grammar. (Chart 13-11)
Change the adjective clauses to adjective phrases. Change the adjective phrases to adjective clauses.

The Diamond Head Hike

1. Diamond Head, a mountain near Waikiki, was formed by a volcano 300,000 years ago.
2. Scientists who study Diamond Head say it is no longer an active volcano.

3. Visitors can hike the Diamond Head Trail, which is located inside the volcano's crater.

Diamond Head Crater

4. The trail leading hikers to a 360-degree view at the top is 2.25 kilometers (1.4 miles) long.
5. Tourists who are planning to hike to the top should bring sunscreen and water because there is no shade on the trail.
6. The path, which ends with 250 steps, is very steep.
7. At the top is an observation point, which overlooks Honolulu and the ocean.
8. Signs posted on the trail warn hikers not to leave the trail.
9. The trails can become very crowded. Some people are asking for changes that allow more access for tourists.
10. Many people wanting to preserve the natural habitats oppose this change.

EXERCISE 58 ▶ Looking at grammar. (Chapter 13 Review)

Combine each group of short, choppy sentences into one sentence. Use the first sentence as the independent clause and build your sentence around it. Use adjective clauses and adjective phrases where possible.

1. Chihuahua is divided into two regions.
   It is the largest Mexican state.
   One region is a mountainous area in the west.
   The other region is a desert basin in the north and east.

   Chihuahua, the largest Mexican state, is divided into two regions, a mountainous area in the west and a desert basin in the north and east.

2. Disney World covers a large area of land.
   It is an amusement park.
   It is located in Orlando, Florida.
   The land includes lakes, golf courses, campsites, hotels, and a wildlife preserve.

   _____

   _____

   _____

3. The Republic of Yemen is an ancient land.
   It is located at the southwestern tip of the Arabian Peninsula.
   This land has been host to many prosperous civilizations.
   These civilizations include the Kingdom of Sheba and various Islamic empires.

   _____

   _____

   _____

EXERCISE 59 ▶ Check your knowledge. (Chapter 13 Review)
Correct the errors.

1. Baseball is the only sport in which I am interested in it.

2. My favorite teacher, Mr. Chu, he was always willing to help me after class.

3. It is important to be polite to people who lives in the same building.

4. My sister has two children, who their names are Ali and Talal.

5. Paulo comes from Venezuela that is a Spanish-speaking country.

6. There are some people in the government who is trying to improve the lives of the poor.

7. A myth is a story expresses traditional beliefs.

8. There is an old legend telling among people in my country about a man lived in the seventeenth century and saved a village from destruction.

9. An old man was fishing next to me on the pier was mumbling to himself.

10. The road that we took it through the forest it was narrow and steep.

11. There are ten universities in Thailand, seven of them are located in Bangkok is the capital city.

12. At the national park, there is a path leads to a spectacular waterfall.

13. At the airport, I was waiting for some relatives which I had never met them before.

14. It is almost impossible to find two persons who their opinions are the same.

15. On the wall, there is a colorful poster which it consists of a group of young people who dancing.

16. The sixth member of our household is Pietro that is my sister's son.

17. Before I came here, I didn't have the opportunity to speak with people who English is their native tongue.

EXERCISE 60 ▸ Grammar and writing. (Chapter 13)

Part I. Some writing assignments require extended definition. This type of writing asks you to explain or describe something, for example, a process, a disease, a device, or perhaps something historical. Read the following example. Underline the adjective clauses and phrases.

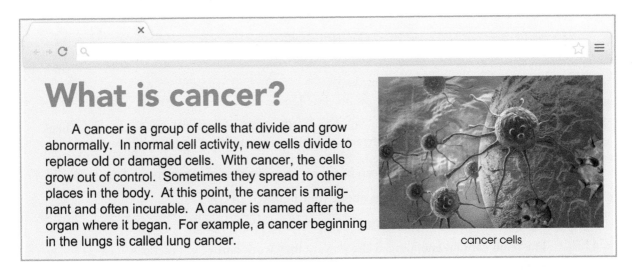

What is cancer?

A cancer is a group of cells that divide and grow abnormally. In normal cell activity, new cells divide to replace old or damaged cells. With cancer, the cells grow out of control. Sometimes they spread to other places in the body. At this point, the cancer is malignant and often incurable. A cancer is named after the organ where it began. For example, a cancer beginning in the lungs is called lung cancer.

cancer cells

Part II. Depending on your topic, it is helpful to address one or more of the following questions when you write an extended definition. Which question(s) does the paragraph above answer?

- What are the different parts? (e.g., the human heart)
- How does it work? (e.g., a seismograph — a machine to measure earthquakes)
- What happens? (e.g., a process like cell division)
- What does it look like? (e.g., an amoeba)
- What is its purpose? (e.g., a political movement)
- Is it similar to or different from anything? (e.g., a historical event)

Part III. Choose something you want to explain or describe. Write an extended definition.

> **WRITING TIP**
>
> Adjective clauses and phrases are useful because they can add interesting and relevant information to your writing in an efficient way. However, you want to be sure that the information is necessary or adds related information. Because adjective clauses can sound "academic" or very impressive, it may be tempting to use them too often. In the second sentence of the example paragraph, if the writer had written *In cell activity which is normal ... ,* the adjective clause is forced. A simple adjective is all that is needed there.

Part IV. Edit your writing. Check for the following:

1. ☐ correct pronoun in adjective clauses (**who, which, that,** *etc.*)
2. ☐ correct use of commas in adjective clauses
3. ☐ if reducing adjective clauses with **be,** delete **be** form and the pronoun
4. ☐ if reducing an adjective clause without **be,** change verb to **-ing** and omit the pronoun
5. ☐ correct spelling (use a dictionary or spell-check)

CHAPTER 14

Gerunds and Infinitives, Part 1

PRETEST: What do I already know?

Write "C" if a sentence has the correct gerund and infinitive form and "I" for incorrect. Check your answers below. After you complete each chart listed, make any necessary corrections.

1. _____ Shopping during the holidays can be more expensive than at other times of the year. (14-1)

2. _____ I appreciated to hear the news about your family. (14-2)

3. _____ The professor decided don't to give a long final exam. (14-3)

4. _____ The team captain encouraged the players they work harder at practices. (14-4)

5. _____ My boyfriend loves holding snakes, but I can't stand to even look at them. (14-5)

6. _____ Who is responsible for to clearing ice from the walkways? (14-6)

7. _____ I'd like to go hiking in the mountains, but I don't have the time right now. (14-7)

8. _____ The security guard caught the thief shoplifting a cell phone from the store. (14-8)

9. _____ It can be deadly driving a car and text at the same time. (14-9)

10. _____ How did you manage to learn four languages fluently? (14-10)

11. _____ Rey mentioned having some difficulty with his boss at work. (14-11)

12. _____ Instead of have a quiet night at home, why don't we invite a few friends over? (14-12)

Incorrect sentences: 2, 3, 4, 6, 9, 12

EXERCISE 1 ▶ Warm-up. (Chart 14-1)

Complete the sentences with the words in the box. Give your own opinion.

| baseball | golf | badminton |
| basketball | soccer | tennis |

1. My friends and I like to play

   _____.

2. I don't know much about playing

   _____.

3. Playing _____

   takes a lot of skill.

14-1 Gerunds and Infinitives: Introduction

(a) $\overset{S}{\text{Playing}}$ tennis $\overset{V}{\text{is}}$ fun.	A *gerund* is the *-ing* form of a verb used as a noun. A gerund is used in the same ways as a noun, i.e., as a subject or as an object.
(b) $\overset{S}{\text{We}}$ $\overset{V}{\text{enjoy}}$ $\overset{O}{\text{playing}}$ tennis.	In (a): *playing* is a gerund. It is used as the subject of the sentence. *Playing tennis* is a *gerund phrase*.
(c) He's excited $\overset{PREP}{\text{about}}$ $\overset{O}{\text{playing}}$ tennis.	In (b): *playing* is a gerund used as the object of the verb *enjoy*.
	In (c): *playing* is a gerund used as the object of the preposition *about*.
(d) $\overset{S}{\text{To play}}$ tennis well $\overset{V}{\text{takes}}$ a lot of practice.	An *infinitive* = *to* + *the simple form of a verb* (*to see, to be, to go,* etc.).
(e) $\overset{S}{\text{He}}$ $\overset{V}{\text{likes}}$ $\overset{O}{\text{to play}}$ tennis.	Like gerunds, infinitives can also be used as the subject of a sentence, as in (d), or as the object, as in (e), but it is more common for the infinitive to be used as the object.

EXERCISE 2 ▸ Looking at grammar. (Chart 14-1)

Work with a partner. Compare the uses of the *-ing* form of verbs in the examples. Then check (✓) the sentences that have gerunds.

Examples:

Walking is good exercise.   (*walking* = a gerund used as the subject of the sentence)

Bob and Ann are playing tennis.   (*playing* = a present participle used as part of the present progressive tense)

That was a surprising win.   (*surprising* = a present participle used as an adjective)

Running

1. a. _____ Running uphill is hard work.

    b. _____ Martin isn't running in the race today.

    c. _____ I need new running shoes.

2. a. _____ I'm scheduling our team practices for the mornings.

    b. _____ Scheduling practices for the afternoons doesn't work.

    c. _____ Would you consider scheduling a practice in the evening?

3. a. _____ Drinking something with electrolytes is important after a race.

    b. _____ Is there any drinking water nearby?

EXERCISE 3 ▸ Looking at grammar. (Chart 14-1)

Work with a partner. Compare the uses of *to* in the examples. Then check (✓) the sentences on page 304 that have infinitives.

Examples:

Marta needs to leave early.   (*to leave* = an infinitive as the object)

To work without breaks is not permitted.   (*to work* = an infinitive as the subject)

Is Elias committed to his job?   (*to* = a preposition)

Co-Workers

1. _____ Franco is engaged to Liz.

2. _____ Danielle is related to the CEO's wife.

3. _____ To become a CEO is Danielle's goal.

4. _____ Viktor has volunteered to mentor new interns.

5. _____ Rachel hasn't been feeling well, but she can't afford to take any sick days right now.

6. _____ Pedro will talk to new employees about texting during meetings.

7. _____ Karl's goal is to speak without any nervousness.

EXERCISE 4 ▶ Warm-up. (Chart 14-2)

Complete the sentences with phrases in the box that are true for you. What do you notice about the form of the verbs in these phrases?

buying things online	talking about politics
posting on social media	watching commercials on TV
surfing the Internet	watching TV news

1. I enjoy _____

2. I don't enjoy _____

3. I avoid _____

14-2 Common Verbs Followed by Gerunds

verb + gerund (a) I *enjoy* *playing* tennis.	Gerunds can be used as the objects of certain verbs. In (a): *enjoy* is followed by a gerund (*playing*). *Enjoy* is not followed by an infinitive. INCORRECT: *I enjoy ~~to play~~ tennis.* Common verbs that are followed by gerunds are listed below.
(b) Joe *quit smoking*. (c) Joe *gave up smoking*.	Some phrasal verbs are followed by gerunds. A *phrasal verb* consists of a verb and a particle (a small word such as a preposition) that together have a special meaning. For example in (c), *give up* means "quit." (Phrasal verbs are in parentheses below.)

Verb + gerund

enjoy	quit (give up)	avoid	consider
appreciate	finish (get through)	postpone (put off)	discuss
mind	stop*	delay	mention
		keep (keep on)	suggest**

*__Stop__ can also be followed by an infinitive of purpose. *He __stopped__ at the station (__in order__) to get some gas.* See Charts 14-5 and 15-1, p. 335.

**__Suggest__ can also be used with a subjunctive noun clause. See Chart 12-9. p. 267.

EXERCISE 5 ▶ Looking at grammar. (Chart 14-2)
Complete the sentences with gerunds. Use the verbs in the box or any appropriate verbs.

be	drop	go	have	make	pay	read

College Plans

A: Aunt Kim, when you're done in the office, would you mind _____*reading*_____ my college
                                               1
    application essay and checking for mistakes?

B: Sure. I just need to get through _____ the bills.
                                             2

    Where are you considering _____ to college?
                                       3

A: I'm still not sure. I've put off _____ where to go.
                                       4

B: Don't you need to decide before you do your essay?

A: No, this is part of the general application. I have to do it for any college I'm interested in.

B: It doesn't seem like you can postpone _____ that decision much longer.
                                       5

A: Here's the problem. I want to study at a big school, but my mom and dad have suggested

    _____ to a smaller one. They said that's what they'll pay for.
              6

B: I went to a college with only about 4,000 students. I appreciated _____ small
                                               7
    classes. That's how I met your uncle.

A: You were a tutor, right? He mentioned _____ your student.
                                       8

B: Yes, for math. He was considering _____ the class, but I convinced him to
                                       9
    stay. It all worked out!

EXERCISE 6 ▶ Looking at grammar. (Chart 14-2)
Complete the sentences with any appropriate gerunds.

Roommates

1. Would you mind ___*opening / closing*___ the door? Thanks.

2. I want to order pizza. Sierra has suggested _____ burgers.

3. What are you considering _____ for dinner?

4. I'm not the best roommate. Sometimes I put off _____ the apartment
   when it's my turn. I know I shouldn't. Actually, when I think about it, all of us avoid
   _____ at some point. None of us enjoy _____.

5. Tony mentioned _____ to a movie later tonight.

6. I have a lot of homework, but I'd still like to go out with you later on. I'll let you know when I
   get through _____ it.

7. No one will be here later. I appreciate _____ able to study in peace and quiet.

EXERCISE 7 ▸ Let's talk. (Chart 14-2)

Work with a partner. Take turns making sentences with the given words. Use any tense and subject.

1. mind \ turn off your phone
2. finish \ eat dinner
3. get through \ eat dinner
4. stop \ rain
5. keep \ work
6. keep on \ work
7. postpone \ do my work
8. put off \ do my work
9. delay \ leave on vacation
10. consider \ get a job
11. talk about \ go to a movie
12. mention \ go out of town

EXERCISE 8 ▸ Listening. (Chart 14-2)

Listen to the conversations. Complete the sentence summaries with appropriate verbs.

1. The speakers enjoy _____*watching*_____ movies on weekends.

2. The speakers have given up _____ for better weather.

3. The speakers are going to keep on _____.

4. The speakers are discussing _____ to a concert in the city.

5. The speakers have put off _____ their homework.

6. The speakers are going to delay _____ the office.

EXERCISE 9 ▸ Warm-up. (Chart 14-3)

Check (✓) the correct sentences.

1. a. _____ We hope winning the game.

   b. _____ We hope to win the game.

   c. _____ We hope win the game.

2. a. _____ The player promised not to react to the referee's decision.

   b. _____ The player promised not getting upset with the referee.

   c. _____ The player promised not yell at the referee.

14-3 Common Verbs Followed by Infinitives

(a) I *hope to see* you again soon.	Some verbs are followed immediately by an infinitive, as in (a) and (b).
(b) He *promised to be* here by ten.	
(c) He *promised not to be* late.	Negative form: ***not*** precedes the infinitive, as in (c).

Common verbs followed by infinitives

hope to (do something)	promise to	seem to	expect to
plan to	agree to	appear to	would like to
intend to*	offer to	pretend to	want to
decide to	refuse to	ask to	need to

*****Intend*** is usually followed by an infinitive (*I **intend to go*** to the meeting.) but sometimes may be followed by a gerund (*I **intend going*** to the meeting.) with no change in meaning.

EXERCISE 10 ▸ Let's talk: interview. (Chart 14-3)

Work with a partner. Take turns asking and answering questions. Share your answers with the class.

1. what \ you \ need \ do \ today?
2. what \ you \ would like \ do \ this weekend?
3. what \ you \ plan \ do \ with English?
4. what \ should people \ refuse \ do?
5. what \ shouldn't people \ pretend \ do?
6. what \ should students \ expect \ do?

EXERCISE 11 ▸ Looking at grammar. (Chart 14-3)

Complete the sentences with your own words. In small groups or with a partner, compare your sentences.

In My Opinion

1. A hard-working employee expects _____
2. A nice teacher sometimes agrees _____
3. A serious student refuses _____
4. An honest police officer promises not _____
5. A lazy employee needs _____
6. A caring doctor offers _____
7. A good actor can appear _____

EXERCISE 12 ▸ Looking at grammar. (Charts 14-2 and 14-3)

Complete each sentence with a gerund or an infinitive.

Small Talk

1. *stop / talk / tell / text / turn off*

   A: How was the movie?

   B: The movie was good, but the guy in back of us

   kept _____*talking*_____ and _____.

   A: Did you ask him _____?

   B: Yes, but it didn't help.

   A: At our theater, the audience is required _____ their electronic devices.

   B: I expected the usher _____ him to stop, but it didn't happen.

2. *have / help / join / lend / pay / see / talk*

   A: We're going out for dinner. Would you like _____ us?

   B: Would you mind _____ me some money?

   A: I thought you just got paid.

   B: I did, but Jens told me he was broke, so I offered _____ him out. I expected

   him _____ me back, but now I'm not sure he's going to. I think he's avoiding

   _____ to me. I saw him at the mall, and he pretended not _____ me.

   A: Good luck! You seem _____ a big problem on your hands.

3. *be / get / hear / take / wait*

A: Joan and David were considering _____ married in June, but they finally

decided _____ until August.

B: They're kind of an odd couple, aren't they? One minute they appear _____
happy, and the next minute they're fighting.

A: Their parents suggested _____ a break from each other, but they didn't

appreciate _____ that!

EXERCISE 13 ▸ Warm-up. (Chart 14-4)
Each sentence in blue is missing a person. Add *you* where appropriate.

1. Why didn't you call us?

We told to call us.

2. Did Sami invite to the party?

He said he was going to.

3. I'm not surprised you had a fender bender.

I warned to drive more slowly.

a fender bender

14-4 Infinitives with Objects

Verb + Object + Infinitive

(a) Mr. Lee *told me to be* here at ten o'clock.	Some verbs are followed by a pronoun or noun object and then an infinitive, as in (a) and (b).
(b) The police *ordered the driver to stop*.	
(c) I *was told to be* here at ten o'clock.	These verbs are followed immediately by an infinitive when they are used in the passive, as in (c) and (d).
(d) The driver *was ordered* to stop.	

Common verbs followed by noun or pronoun + infinitive

tell someone to	invite someone to	require someone to	expect someone to
advise someone to*	permit someone to	order someone to	would like someone to
encourage someone to	allow someone to	force someone to	want someone to
remind someone to	warn someone to	ask someone to	need someone to

Verb + Infinitive / Verb + Object + Infinitive

(e) I *expect to pass* the test.	Some verbs have two patterns:
(f) I *expect Mary to pass* the test.	• *verb + infinitive*, as in (e)
	• *verb + object + infinitive*, as in (f)
	COMPARE:
	In (e): I think I will pass the test.
	In (f): I think Mary will pass the test.

Common verbs followed by infinitives or by objects and then infinitives

ask to OR ask someone to	want to OR want someone to
expect to OR expect someone to	would like to OR would like someone to
need to OR need someone to	

*A gerund is used after ***advise*** (active) if there is no noun or pronoun object.
COMPARE: (1) *He advised buying a Fiat.* (2) *He advised me to buy a Fiat. I was advised to buy a Fiat.*

EXERCISE 14 ▸ Looking at grammar. (Chart 14-4)

Complete the sentences with **to leave** or **me to leave**. In some cases, both are possible.

1. He told _____*me to leave*_____ .

2. He decided _____*to leave*_____ .

3. He asked ___*to leave / me to leave*___ .

4. He offered _____ .

5. She wanted _____ .

6. He agreed _____ .

7. She would like _____ .

8. He warned _____ .

9. She refused _____ .

10. He promised _____ .

11. She hoped _____ .

12. He permitted _____ .

13. She expected _____ .

14. He forced _____ .

15. She allowed _____ .

16. He reminded _____ .

17. She planned _____ .

18. He pretended _____ .

EXERCISE 15 ▸ Looking at grammar. (Chart 14-4)

Complete each sentence with the correct verb.

Advice and Obligations

1. *advised / was advised*

   a. Jack _____ me to get a new apartment.

   b. I _____ to get a new apartment.

2. *forced / was forced*

   a. The driver _____ to stop on the highway.

   b. The police _____ the driver to stop.

3. *encouraged / was encouraged*

   a. I _____ to go to college.

   b. My parents _____ me to go to college.

4. *do not allow / are not allowed*

   a. Residents _____ to have pets.

   b. The building rules _____ pets.

5. *warned / was warned*

   a. Mrs. Jackson _____ her son not

   to touch the hot stove.

   b. He _____ not to touch the

   hot stove.

Summarize each statement by using the verbs in the box to introduce an infinitive phrase. In some cases, more than one verb is appropriate.

allow	expect	permit	require
ask	order	remind	tell

1. The professor said to Alan, "You may leave early."
   → *The professor allowed Alan to leave early.* OR
   → *Alan was allowed to leave early.*
2. Roberto said to me, "Don't forget to take your book back to the library."
3. I am very relieved because the Dean of Admissions said to me, "You may register for school late."
4. The law says, "Every driver must have a valid driver's license."
5. My boss said to me, "Come to the meeting ten minutes early."

EXERCISE 17 ▸ Let's talk: interview. (Chart 14-4)
Interview your classmates. Share some of their answers with the class.

1. What have you been told to do recently?
2. What are you often reminded to do?
3. What have you been asked to do recently?
4. What are you encouraged to do if you want to improve your English?
5. What is something children are warned not to do by their parents?
6. What is something teenagers are expected to do?
7. What is something parents are advised to do?
8. What are citizens in your country required to do?
9. What are citizens in your country not permitted to do?

EXERCISE 18 ▸ Warm-up. (Chart 14-5)
Which pairs have basically the same meaning? Which pairs have different meanings?

1. a. It began to snow.
   b. It began snowing.

2. a. I remembered to wear a warm jacket.
   b. I remembered wearing a warm jacket.

3. a. I forgot to bring gloves.
   b. I forgot bringing gloves.

4. a. We love to walk in the snow.
   b. We love walking in the snow.

5. a. We stopped to throw snowballs.
   b. We stopped throwing snowballs.

14-5 Common Verbs Followed by Either Infinitives or Gerunds

Some verbs can be followed by either an infinitive or a gerund, sometimes with no difference in meaning, as in Group A below, and sometimes with a difference in meaning, as in Group B below.

Group A: Verb + Infinitive or Gerund, with No Difference in Meaning

begin like hate	The verbs in Group A may be followed by either an infinitive or a gerund with little or no difference in meaning.
start love can't stand	
continue prefer can't bear	
(a) It *began to rain.* / It *began raining.*	In (a): There is no difference between ***began to rain*** and ***began raining.***
(b) I *started to work.* / I *started working.*	
(c) It *was beginning to rain.*	If the main verb is progressive, an infinitive (not a gerund) is usually used, as in (c).

Group B: Verb + Infinitive or Gerund, with a Difference in Meaning

remember regret stop	The verbs in Group B may be followed by either an infinitive or a gerund, but the meaning is different.
forget try	
(d) Judy always *remembers to lock* the door.	***remember*** + *infinitive* = remember to perform responsibility, duty, or task, as in (d)
(e) Sam often *forgets to lock* the door.	***forget*** + *infinitive* = forget to perform a responsibility, duty, or task, as in (e)
(f) I *remember seeing* the Alps for the first time. The sight was impressive.	***remember*** + *gerund* = remember (recall) something that happened in the past, as in (f)
(g) I'*ll never forget seeing* the Alps for the first time.	***forget*** + *gerund* = forget something that happened in the past, as in (g)*
(h) I *regret to tell* you that you failed the test.	***regret*** + *infinitive* = regret to say, to tell someone, to inform someone of some bad news, as in (h)
(i) I *regret lending* him some money. He never paid me back.	***regret*** + *gerund* = regret something that happened in the past, as in (i)
(j) I'*m trying to learn* English.	***try*** + *infinitive* = make an effort, as in (j)
(k) The room was hot. I *tried opening* the window, but that didn't help. So I *tried turning* on the fan, but I was still hot. Finally, I turned on the air conditioner.	***try*** + *gerund* = experiment with a new or different approach to see if it works, as in (k)
(l) The students *stopped talking* when the professor entered the room. The room became quiet.	***stop*** + *gerund* = stop an activity
(m) When Ann saw her professor in the hallway, she *stopped (in order) to talk* to him.	Notice that ***stop*** can also be followed immediately by an infinitive of purpose, as in (m): Ann stopped walking in order to talk to her professor. (See Chart 15-1, p. 335.)

*****Forget** followed by a gerund usually occurs in a negative sentence or in a question: e.g., *I'll never forget, I can't forget, Have you ever forgotten,* and *Can you ever forget* are often followed by a gerund phrase.

EXERCISE 19 ▶ Looking at grammar. (Charts 14-3 → 14-5)

Complete each sentence with the correct form of the verb in parentheses.

1. a. Maria loves (*swim*) ____swimming / to swim____ in the ocean.

   b. Her husband likes (*swim*) _____ in freshwater lakes.

2. a. I hate (*see*) _____ any living being suffer.

   b. I can't bear (*watch*) _____ news reports of children who are homeless.

   c. I can't stand (*read*) _____ about animals that have been hurt by people.

3. a. I'm afraid of flying. When a plane begins (*move*) _____ down the runway, my heart starts (*race*) _____ .

   b. Uh-oh! The plane is beginning (*move★*) _____ , and my heart is starting (*race*) _____ .

4. a. After a brief interruption, the professor continued (*lecture*) _____ .

   b. Even though the bell rang, the professor kept on (*talk*) _____ .

5. a. When I travel, I prefer★★ (*drive*) _____ to (*take*) _____ a plane.

   b. I prefer (*drive*) _____ rather than (*take*) _____ a plane.

6. a. I'm so sorry. I regret (*inform*) _____ you that your loan application has not been approved.

   b. I didn't listen to my father. I regret (*follow, not*) _____ his advice. He was right.

7. a. When my four-year-old asks the same question over and over, I try (*remain*) _____ patient as I give the exact same answer each time.

   b. The father tried everything, but his baby still wouldn't stop (*cry*) _____ . He decided to experiment. He tried (*hold*) _____ him, but that didn't help. He tried (*feed*) _____ him, but he refused the food and continued to cry. He tried (*burp*) _____ him. He tried (*change*) _____ his diaper. Nothing worked. His baby wouldn't stop crying.

★If possible, native speakers usually prefer to use an infinitive following a progressive verb instead of using two *-ing* verbs in a row.
    Usual: *The baby is starting **to walk**.* (instead of *walking*)
  If the main verb is not progressive, either form is used:
    *Babies **start to walk** around age one.* OR *Babies **start walking** around age one.*
★★Notice the patterns with **prefer**:
    Prefer + gerund: *I **prefer staying** home to going to the concert.*
    Prefer + infinitive: *I'd **prefer to stay** home rather **than** (to) go to the concert.*

EXERCISE 20 ▸ Looking at grammar. (Chart 14-5)
Match the sentence in the left column with the meaning in the right.

1. _____ I remembered to turn off the lights.

2. _____ I remember playing with dolls when I was a child.

3. _____ What do you remember doing as a teenager?

4. _____ What did you remember to do before you left home?

5. _____ I forgot to pick up my sister.

6. _____ I forgot getting the mail.

7. _____ Stop driving so fast.

8. _____ I stopped to get gas.

9. _____ I stopped driving to work because of the high cost of gas.

a. I stopped one activity to do another.

b. What is your memory of that time?

c. I did something, but I forgot that I did it.

d. I quit the activity. I don't do it anymore.

e. I didn't remember to do something.

f. I have a memory of the event.

g. What didn't you forget?

h. Don't continue.

i. I didn't forget.

EXERCISE 21 ▸ Listening. (Chart 14-5)
Listen to each sentence and choose the sentence with the same meaning.

1. a. Joan thought about her phone call with her husband.
   b. Joan didn't forget to call her husband.

2. a. Rita was thinking about the times she went to the farmers' market with her grandmother.
   b. Rita didn't forget to go to the farmers' market with her grandmother.

3. a. Roger got a cigarette and began to smoke.
   b. Roger quit smoking.

4. a. Mr. and Mrs. Olson finished eating.
   b. Mr. and Mrs. Olson got something to eat before the movie.

5. a. The speaker is sorry about something he did.
   b. The speaker is delivering some bad news.

EXERCISE 22 ▸ Looking at grammar. (Chart 14-5)
Complete each sentence with the correct form of the verb in parentheses.

1. a. I remember (*visit*) _____*visiting*_____ my great-grandparents when I was very young.

   b. What do you remember (*do*) _____ before you leave for class every day?

   c. We almost had a fire. Eric didn't remember (*turn*) _____ off the oven before he went to bed.

   d. What do you remember (*do*) _____ when you were a child?

   e. Did you remember (*lock*) _____ the front door when you left?

   f. Uh-oh. I don't remember (*lock*) _____ it. I'd better go back and check.

2. a. Don't forget (*do*) _____ your homework tonight.

   b. What did Evan forget (*do*) _____ before he went to bed?

   c. I won't ever forget (*watch*) _____ our team score the winning goal in the last seconds of the championship game.

3. a. I want to tell Jeanne to stop (*talk*) _____ so much.

   b. I stopped on the way home (*get*) _____ some groceries.

   c. I stopped (*drink*) _____ coffee at night because it was keeping me awake.

EXERCISE 23 ▶ Let's talk. (Charts 14-1 → 14-5)

Thomas wanted to build a birdhouse for his wife, Eleni. After several hours, she found him like this. Make sentences about the situation. Use the verbs in the box. Work in pairs or small groups.

A Birdhouse Failure

advise	finish	keep on	put off	remind
consider	forgot	look forward to	regret	stop
encourage	intend	offer	remember	suggest

EXERCISE 24 ▶ Looking at grammar. (Charts 14-1 → 14-5)

Complete each sentence by restating the given idea.

1. Don't be late for the meeting.

   a. Nadia reminded ___*me not to be late for the meeting*_____.

   b. Nadia told _____.

   c. Nadia warned _____.

2. Do you need help? I can carry the suitcases.

   a. I volunteered _____.

   b. I offered _____.

3. I have an idea. Let's quit our jobs and open our own business.

    a. We discussed _____.

    b. I suggested _____.

4. I wanted to pay with a check, but the taxi driver only took cash.

    a. The taxi driver refused _____.

    b. The taxi driver told _____.

5. The teacher asked a question. I didn't want to answer, so I didn't look at her.

    a. I avoided _____.

    b. I decided _____.

6. At my last doctor's appointment, the doctor said, "Don't smoke. It causes cancer."

    a. The doctor advised _____.

    b. The doctor reminded _____.

    c. The doctor warned _____.

7. I worked all day on my paper.

    a. I spent the day _____.

    b. I spent most of my time _____.

    c. I spent several hours _____.

8. Sam likes to talk to his friends in class. The teacher asks him to stop, but he doesn't.

    a. He keeps _____.

    b. He keeps on _____.

    c. He continues _____.

9. Roberto bought his wife an anniversary present. He didn't forget this time.

    a. He remembered _____.

    b. He didn't forget _____.

EXERCISE 25 ▸ Warm-up. (Chart 14-6)

Each phrase in blue contains a preposition. What do you notice about the form of the verb that follows each preposition?

1. Sonya is excited about moving to a new city.
2. You'd better have a good excuse for being late.
3. I'm looking forward to going on vacation soon.

14-6 Using Gerunds as the Objects of Prepositions

(a) We talked *about going* to Iceland for our vacation. (b) Sue is in charge *of organizing* the meeting. (c) I'm interested *in learning* more about your work.	A gerund is frequently used as the object of a preposition.
(d) *I'm used to sleeping* with the window open. (e) *I'm accustomed to sleeping** with the window open. (f) I *look forward to going* home next month.	In (d) through (f): *to* is a preposition, not part of an infinitive form, so a gerund follows.
(g) We *talked about not going* to the meeting, but finally decided we should go.	NEGATIVE FORM: *not* precedes a gerund.

Common preposition combinations followed by gerunds

be excited**
be worried } *about doing it*

complain
dream
talk
think
apologize } *about /of doing it*

blame someone
forgive someone
have an excuse
have a reason
be responsible
thank someone } *for doing it*

keep someone
prevent someone
prohibit someone
stop someone } *from doing it*

be interested
believe
participate
succeed } *in doing it*

approve
be accused
be afraid**
be capable
be guilty
be proud**
instead
take advantage
take care } *of doing it*

be tired } *of /from doing it*

count
insist } *on doing* it

be accustomed
in addition
be committed
be devoted
look forward
object
be opposed
be used } *to doing it*

*Possible in British English: *I'm accustomed to sleep with the window open.*

***Be afraid, be excited,* and *be proud* can also be used with an infinitive. See Chart 15-2, page 337.

EXERCISE 26 ▶ Looking at grammar. (Chart 14-6)

Complete each sentence with a preposition and a form of *go*.

A Canceled Trip

1. We thought _____*about going*_____ to the beach for vacation.

2. We talked _____ there.

3. We were interested _____ there.

4. The kids were excited _____ there.

5. They were looking forward _____ there.

6. Heavy rain prevented us _____ there.

7. A windstorm kept us _____ there.

8. So we dreamed _____ there next year.

EXERCISE 27 ▶ Looking at grammar. (Chart 14-6)

Complete each sentence with a preposition and a form of the verb in parentheses.

On an Airplane Flight

1. Two children are excited (*take*) _____*about taking*_____ their first flight.

2. They have been looking forward (*be*) _____ above the clouds.

3. A first-time flyer is worried (*fly*) _____ in stormy weather.

4. One passenger is blaming another passenger (*spill*) _____ his coffee.

5. A man is complaining (*have*) _____ an aisle seat rather than a window seat.

6. The pilot was late, but he had an excuse (*be*) _____ late.

7. The co-pilot will be responsible (*fly*) _____ the plane.

8. A flight attendant is prohibiting a man (*stand*) _____ near the cockpit door.

At a Police Station

9. A teenager has been accused (*steal*) _____ a purse.

10. An elderly woman said he was responsible (*take*) _____ it.

11. The police are blaming him (*do*) _____ it.

12. The teenager said he was trying to prevent someone else (*take*) _____ it.

13. He is upset. The police are listening to the woman instead (*listen*) _____ to his version of the story.

14. He has not yet succeeded (*convince*) _____ the police of his innocence.

EXERCISE 28 ▶ Let's talk. (Chart 14-6)

Work with a partner. Take turns answering the questions on page 318 in complete sentences. Use prepositions followed by gerunds in your answers.

Example:

PARTNER A: People in some countries have their biggest meal at lunch.
Are you used to doing that?

PARTNER B: Yes, I'm used to having my biggest meal at lunch. OR
No, I'm not used to having my biggest meal at lunch.

PARTNER A	PARTNER B
1. Your neighbor helped you carry heavy boxes. Did you thank him/her?	1. Someone broke the window. Do you know who was responsible?
2. You're going to visit friends in another town this weekend. Are you looking forward to that?	2. The weather is hot/cold. What does that prevent you from doing?
3. You didn't come to class on time yesterday. Did you have a good excuse?	3. The advanced students have a lot of homework. Do they complain?
4. You're living in a cold/warm climate. Are you accustomed to that?	4. Your wallet was missing after your friend visited. Do you blame him?
5. You didn't study grammar last night. What did you do instead?	5. A customer interrupted you while you were talking to the store manager. Did she apologize?
6. The students in the class did role-plays. Did all of them participate?	6. You studied last weekend. What did you do in addition?
7. You're going to a deserted island for vacation. Are you excited?	7. Your friend was rude. Did she apologize?

EXERCISE 29 ▶ Looking at grammar. (Chart 14-6)

Complete each sentence with an appropriate preposition and the **-ing** form of the given verb.

At Work

1. Alice is interested (*get*) _____ *in getting* _____ a promotion.

2. You are capable (*do*) _____ better work.

3. I'm accustomed (*get*) _____ to work before everyone else.

4. Thank you (*give*) _____ me an office with windows.

5. Donna insists (*take*) _____ the stairs instead of the elevator to the top floor.

6. Our company believes (*be*) _____ honest at all times with customers.

7. You should take advantage (*work*) _____ with so many experts here.

8. Lexi had a good reason (*come, not*) _____ to work yesterday.

9. Everyone participated (*find*) _____ a new administrative assistant.

10. I apologized (*come*) _____ late to the meeting.

11. Larry isn't used (*wear*) _____ a suit and tie every day.

12. In addition (*work*) _____ full-time, Spiro is going to night school.

13. I stopped the printer (*make*) _____ so much noise.

14. Would you object _____ my (*leave*) _____ early today?

15. Who was opposed to (*have*) _____ employees move offices?

16. Are you committed (*do*) _____ whatever it takes to be successful at this company?

17. Who is responsible (*run*) _____ the office while you are away?

18. Employees are prohibited (*use*) _____ the company email system for personal use.

EXERCISE 30 ▶ Listening. (Chart 14-6)
Listen to each conversation. Summarize it by completing each sentence with a preposition and a gerund phrase.

1. The man apologized ___*for being late*_____.

2. The woman succeeded _____.

3. Both speakers are complaining _____.

4. The man thanked his friend _____.

5. The man didn't have an excuse _____.

6. The woman isn't used _____.

7. The flu kept the man _____.

EXERCISE 31 ▶ Let's talk. (Chart 14-6)
By + a gerund or gerund phrase expresses how something is done. Answer the questions with *by* + *a gerund* or *gerund phrase* to express how something is done. Work in pairs, in small groups, or as a class.

How ... ?

1. How do you turn off a cell phone?
   → *By pushing a button.*
2. How can students improve their listening comprehension?
3. How do people satisfy their hunger?
4. How do people quench their thirst?
5. How did you find out what *quench* means?
6. What are some ways employees get in trouble with their manager?
7. How do dogs show they are happy?
8. How do cats show they are happy?
9. In a restaurant, how do you catch the server's attention?
10. How do you greet a friend you haven't seen in a long time? A family member?
11. How do you remove a blue ink stain from a white shirt?

EXERCISE 32 ▸ **Let's talk: interview.** (Chart 14-6)

Interview your classmates about the different ways people express emotions. Answers can include descriptions of facial expressions, actions, what people say, etc. Try to use **by** + *gerund* in your answers. Share some of the most interesting answers with the class.

Example: excitement
SPEAKER A: How do people show excitement at a sports event?
SPEAKER B: People show excitement at a sports event by clapping their hands, jumping up and down, and yelling.

1. happiness
2. sadness
3. anger
4. frustration
5. confusion
6. disagreement
7. agreement
8. surprise

EXERCISE 33 ▸ **Reading and speaking.** (Chart 14-6)

Part I. Read the passage. What do you notice about the forms in **bold**?

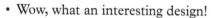

Do you know these words?
- awkward
- loss for words
- souvenir
- knick-knack
- discomfort
- gracefully

The Awkward Gift

Have you ever received a gift that left you at a loss for words? Perhaps it was an item of clothing a distant aunt chose for you, a souvenir a traveler brought back, or some knick-knack that a friend thought was cute. Moments like these can be a little awkward. But with a few generic comments, you can skillfully cover your discomfort. Here are some responses that can be useful when you open your present:

- Wow, what an interesting design!
- Oh, I've never seen one of these before. Where did you find it?
- It's so colorful. The artist/designer/creator must have spent a lot of time on it.
- It looks so warm/soft/comfortable.

The giver might respond **by saying**, "I'm glad you like it." You can finish the exchange with:

- **Thank you for giving** me ... .
- **Thank you for thinking** of me.
- **Thanks for remembering** it was my birthday (or other special day).
- **I appreciate your* thinking** of me.
- It was very **kind of you to think** of me.

Speak enthusiastically — with a smile — and you have gracefully accepted the gift.

*In formal English, the possessive form adjective *your* is necessary. *You* may be used in informal speech.

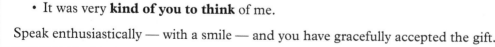

Part II. Work with a partner. Partner A will give a gift to Partner B. You can choose one of the items pictured as a gift, or something you have in your bag or backpack. Complete the conversation. Then practice it and perform it for the class. Remember, you can look at your notes before you speak. When you speak, look at your partner.

A: I have a gift for you. (Pretend to give a wrapped gift to your partner.)

B: Should I open it now?

A: Yes, please. I can't wait to see your reaction!

(*Partner B pretends to open it.*)

B: _____

A: _____

B: _____

A: _____

EXERCISE 34 ▸ Warm-up. (Chart 14-7)

Complete the sentences by circling all the activities that are true for you. All the choices end in *-ing*. What do you notice about the verbs in blue?

1. Last week I went *shopping   running   biking   dancing*.

2. I like to go *hiking   swimming   camping   sightseeing*.

3. I've never gone *fishing   bowling   skiing   skydiving*.

14-7 Go + Gerund

(a) Did you *go shopping*? (b) We *went fishing* yesterday.	**Go** is followed by a gerund in certain idiomatic expressions to express, for the most part, recreational activities.

Go + gerund

go biking	go dancing	go running	go skiing
go birdwatching	go fishing*	go sailing	go skydiving
go boating	go hiking	go shopping	go sledding
go bowling	go hunting	go sightseeing	go snorkeling
go camping	go jogging	go skating	go swimming
go canoeing / kayaking	go mountain climbing	go skateboarding	go window shopping

*Also, in British English: *go angling*.

EXERCISE 35 ▶ Let's talk. (Chart 14-7)

Answer the questions about the activities in Chart 14-7. Work in pairs, in small groups, or as a class.

1. Which activities have you done? When? Briefly describe your experiences.
2. Which activities do you like to do?
3. Which activities do you never want to do?
4. Which activities have you not done but would like to do?

EXERCISE 36 ▶ Reading. (Chart 14-7)

Read the description of Ron's day and complete the sentences with a form of **go** and a verb.

Ron's Busy Saturday

Ron is an active individual. On his days off, he likes to do several activities in one day. His friends can't keep up with him. Last Saturday, for example, he woke up early and went to the lake with his canoe. He finds early mornings on the lake very calm and relaxing. He brought a fishing rod with him so he could catch something for dinner. He saw some friends getting their sailboat ready and thought about joining them but decided instead to take a swim. By that time, it was only noon!

After lunch, he got on his bike and rode in the hills behind his town. Then he cooked a fish that he had caught for dinner, and it was delicious. Later some friends called to invite him out, so he finished the day by going to a dance with them.

1. Early Saturday morning, Ron ___went canoeing on the lake___.
2. He brought a fishing rod so he could _____.
3. He saw some friends on a sailboat but didn't _____ with them.
4. He _____ instead.
5. After lunch, he _____.
6. He finished the day by _____ with some of his friends.

EXERCISE 37 ▶ Let's talk. (Charts 14-2 and 14-7)

Work with a partner. Take turns giving your opinion about the following activities.

Example: I (enjoy, don't enjoy) \ go \ shop \ for clothes
PARTNER A: I don't enjoy going shopping for clothes. How about you?
PARTNER B: No, I don't enjoy it either. OR
　　　　　Actually, I enjoy it.

1. I (go, never go) \ dance \ on weekends
2. I (like to go, don't like to go) \ bowl
3. Go \ hunt \ (sounds, doesn't sound) \ like fun to me

4. I (sometimes postpone, never postpone) \ do \ my homework

5. I (really appreciate, don't appreciate) \ get \ a lot of emails every day

6. I (am considering, am not considering) \ look \ for a new place to live

7. I (used to go, never went) \ fish \ as a child

8. I (go, never go) \ jog \ for exercise

9. I (enjoy, don't enjoy) \ play \ board games

EXERCISE 38 ▸ Warm-up. (Chart 14-8)

Agree or disagree with these statements. What do you notice about the verbs in blue?

1. It's easy to have fun shopping at a mall.	yes	no
2. I have a hard time spending my free time indoors.	yes	no
3. Teenagers spend a lot of time doing important things.	yes	no
4. People waste a lot of money buying unnecessary things.	yes	no

14-8 Special Expressions Followed by -ing

(a) We *had fun* / We *had a good time* } *playing* volleyball.	**-ing** forms follow certain special expressions:
	
	   ***have fun / a good time* + -ing**
	   ***have trouble / difficulty* + -ing**
	   ***have a hard time / a difficult time* + -ing**

(b) I *had trouble* / I *had difficulty* / I *had a hard time* / I *had a difficult time* } *finding* his house.	
(c) Sam *spends most of his time studying*.	***spend* + expression of time or money + -ing**
(d) I *waste a lot of time watching* TV.	***waste* + expression of time or money + -ing**
(e) She *sat at her desk doing* homework.	***sit* + expression of place + -ing**
(f) I *stood there wondering* what to do next.	***stand* + expression of place + -ing**
(g) He *is lying in bed reading* a book.	***lie* + expression of place + -ing**
(h) When I walked into my office, I *found George using* my telephone.	***find* + (pro)noun + -ing** ***catch* + (pro)noun + -ing**
(i) When I walked into my office, I *caught a thief looking* through my desk drawers.	In (h) and (i): Both ***find*** and ***catch*** mean "discover." ***Catch*** often expresses anger or displeasure.

EXERCISE 39 ▸ Looking at grammar. (Charts 14-2, 14-3, 14-6, and 14-8)
Complete the sentences with the correct form of the verb in parentheses.

A Gem in the City

   I had no idea Central Park was so big and had so much to offer! When I was in New York, I

spent a day (*explore*) _____ it, and I didn't even begin to see all of it. The weather

was quite hot, and I enjoyed (*walk*) _____ around the park in the shade. I

found a concert, and I sat on the grass (*listen*) _____ to the music for a

while. I noticed there were a lot of people lying on the ground (*relax*) _____,

(*read*) _____, or (*sleep*) _____. It was so peaceful

that I found myself (*get*) _____ sleepy too. I came across a lake for children to

fish in, and many parents stood nearby (*watch*) _____ their kids catch and

release fish. People told me about another lake that had rowboats for rent. I thought about

(*do*) _____ that, but I had difficulty (*find*) _____ the

boathouse. At the end of the day, I needed (*go*) _____ back to my hotel, but I had

a hard time (*leave*) _____. I definitely plan (*go*) _____ back.

EXERCISE 40 ▸ Grammar and speaking. (Chart 14-8)
Complete the sentences about yourself with appropriate **-ing** verbs. Compare your statements with
a classmate's.

About Me

   1. Sometimes I have trouble _____

   2. On weekends, I have fun _____

   3. In the evenings, I spend my time _____

   4. In the mornings, I stand in front of the mirror _____

   5. At school, I sit in class _____

   6. Sometimes in class I find myself _____

7. Sometimes in the middle of the night, I lie in bed _____

8. I am/am not a decisive person. I have a/an easy/hard time _____

9. You will never catch me _____

EXERCISE 41 ▶ Listening. (Chart 14-8)

Listen to the sentences. Complete the sentences, orally or in writing, using **-ing** verbs.

Example: You will hear: I play soccer every day. I love it!

You will write (or say): The speaker has fun ___*playing soccer*___ .

1. The speaker has trouble _____.

2. The speaker caught his son _____.

3. The speaker stands at the kitchen counter in the mornings _____.

4. The speaker has a hard time _____.

5. The speaker wasted two hours _____.

6. The speaker had a good time _____.

7. The speaker found Tom _____.

8. The speaker spent an hour _____.

EXERCISE 42 ▶ Warm-up. (Chart 14-9)

All of the sentences are grammatically correct. What differences do you notice in their structure?
Do you agree or disagree with the statements? Why or why not?

1. Speaking a second language without an accent is nearly impossible for adult language learners.
2. To speak a second language without an accent is nearly impossible for adult language learners.
3. It is nearly impossible for adult language learners to speak a second language without an accent.

14-9 *It* + Infinitive; Gerunds and Infinitives as Subjects

(a) *It* is difficult *to learn* a second language.	Often an infinitive phrase is used with *it* as the subject of a sentence. The word *it* refers to and has the same meaning as the infinitive phrase at the end of the sentence. In (a): *It* means "to learn a second language."
(b) *Learning* a second language is difficult.	A gerund phrase is frequently used as the subject of a sentence, as in (b).
(c) *To learn* a second language is difficult.	An infinitive can also be used as the subject of a sentence, as in (c), but far more commonly an infinitive phrase is used with *it*, as in (a).
(d) It is easy *for young children* to learn a second language. *Learning* a second language is easy *for young children*. *To learn* a second language is easy *for young children*.	The phrase *for* (*someone*) may be used to specify exactly who the speaker is talking about, as in (d).

EXERCISE 43 ▸ Grammar and speaking. (Chart 14-9)

Work with a partner. Imagine a parent giving advice to a teenager. Make sentences beginning with *it*. Use a form of the given phrase followed by an infinitive phrase for each sentence.

Parent to Teenager

1. be dangerous
   → *It's dangerous to ride a skateboard without wearing a helmet.*
2. be important
3. not be easy
4. be silly
5. be smart
6. not cost much money
7. be necessary
8. take time

EXERCISE 44 ▸ Looking at grammar. (Chart 14-9)

Complete the sentences with the words in the box. Include a person and any other additional information. Make true statements.

be on time	learn English	take advanced math courses
have a visa	speak Spanish	use gerunds and infinitives correctly

1. It is/isn't possible for …
   → *It isn't possible for me to be on time for class when traffic is heavy.*
2. It is/isn't easy for …
3. It is/isn't important for …
4. It is/isn't essential for …
5. It's a good idea for …
6. It is/isn't difficult for …

EXERCISE 45 ▸ Let's talk: pairwork. (Chart 14-9)

Work with a partner. Partner A begins the sentence. Partner B completes it with an infinitive phrase. Partner A restates the sentence using a gerund phrase as the subject. Take turns.

Example:
PARTNER A: It's fun …
PARTNER B: … to ride a horse.
PARTNER A: Riding a horse is fun.

PARTNER A	PARTNER B
1. It's dangerous …	1. It's wrong …
2. It's easy …	2. It takes a lot of time …
3. It's a good idea …	3. It's impolite …
4. It's important …	4. Is it difficult … ?

Verbs with a bullet (•) can also be followed by gerunds. See Chart 14-11.

Verbs Followed Immediately by an Infinitive

1.	agree	They *agreed to help* us.	25.	learn	He *learned to play* the piano.
2.	appear	She *appears to be* tired.	26.	like•	I *like to go* to the movies.
3.	arrange	I'll *arrange to meet* you at the airport.	27.	love•	I *love to go* to operas.
4.	ask	He *asked to come* with us.	28.	manage	She *managed to finish* her work early.
5.	beg	He *begged to come* with us.	29.	mean	I *didn't mean to hurt* your feelings.
6.	begin•	It *began to rain*.	30.	need	I *need to have* your opinion.
7.	can't afford	I *can't afford to buy* it.	31.	offer	They *offered to help* us.
8.	can't bear•	I *can't bear to wait* in long lines.	32.	plan	I'm *planning to have* a party.
9.	can't stand•	I *can't stand to wait* in long lines.	33.	prefer•	Ann *prefers to walk* to work.
10.	can't wait	We *can't wait to see* you.	34.	prepare	We *prepared to welcome* them.
11.	care	I *don't care to see* that show.	35.	pretend	He *pretends not to understand*.
12.	claim	She *claims to know* a famous movie star.	36.	promise	I *promise not to be* late.
			37.	refuse	I *refuse to believe* his story.
13.	consent	She finally *consented to marry* him.	38.	regret•	I *regret to tell* you that you failed.
14.	continue•	He *continued to speak*.	39.	remember•	I *remembered to lock* the door.
15.	decide	I *have decided to leave* on Monday.	40.	seem	That cat *seems to be* friendly.
16.	demand	I *demand to know* who is responsible.	41.	start•	It *started to rain*.
			42.	stop	Let's *stop to get* a snack.
17.	deserve	She *deserves to win* the prize.	43.	struggle	I *struggled to stay* awake.
18.	expect	I *expect to enter* graduate school in the fall.	44.	swear	She *swore to tell* the truth.
			45.	tend	He *tends to talk* too much.
19.	fail	She *failed to return* the book to the library on time.	46.	threaten	She *threatened to tell* my parents.
			47.	try•	I'm *trying to learn* English.
20.	forget•	I *forgot to mail* the letter.	48.	volunteer	He *volunteered to help* us.
21.	hate•	I *hate to make* silly mistakes.	49.	wait	I'll *wait to hear* from you.
22.	hesitate	*Don't hesitate to ask* for my help.	50.	want	I *want to tell* you something.
23.	hope	Jack *hopes to arrive* next week.	51.	wish	She *wishes to come* with us.
24.	intend	He *intends to be* a firefighter.			

Verbs Followed by a (Pro)noun + an Infinitive

1.	advise•	She *advised me to wait* until tomorrow.	15.	invite	Harry *invited the Johnsons to come* to his party.
2.	allow	She *allowed me to use* her car.	16.	need	We *needed Chris to help* us figure out the solution.
3.	ask	I *asked John to help* us.			
4.	beg	They *begged us to come*.	17.	order	The judge *ordered me to pay* a fine.
5.	cause	Her laziness *caused her to fail*.	18.	permit	He *permitted the children to stay* up late.
6.	challenge	She *challenged me to race* her to the corner.			
			19.	persuade	I *persuaded him to come* for a visit.
7.	convince	I couldn't *convince him to accept* our help.	20.	remind	She *reminded me to lock* the door.
			21.	require	Our teacher *requires us to be* on time.
8.	dare	He *dared me to do* better than he had done.			
			22.	teach	My brother *taught me to swim*.
9.	encourage	He *encouraged me to try* again.	23.	tell	The doctor *told me to take* these pills.
10.	expect	I *expect you to be* on time.			
11.	forbid	I *forbid you to tell* him.	24.	urge	I *urged her to apply* for the job.
12.	force	They *forced him to tell* the truth.	25.	want	I *want you to be* happy.
13.	hire	She *hired a boy to mow* the lawn.	26.	warn	I *warned you not to drive* too fast.
14.	instruct	He *instructed them to be* careful.			

Verbs with a bullet (•) can also be followed by infinitives. See Chart 14-10.

1.	admit	He *admitted stealing* the money.
2.	advise•	She *advised waiting* until tomorrow.
3.	anticipate	I *anticipate having* a good time on vacation.
4.	appreciate	I *appreciated hearing* from them.
5.	avoid	He *avoided answering* my question.
6.	begin•	It *began raining*.
7.	can't bear•	I *can't bear waiting* in long lines.
8.	can't help	I *can't help worrying* about it.
9.	can't imagine	I can't *imagine having* no friends.
10.	can't stand•	I *can't stand waiting* in long lines.
11.	complete	I finally *completed writing* my term paper.
12.	consider	I will *consider going* with you.
13.	continue•	He *continued speaking*.
14.	delay	He *delayed leaving* for school.
15.	deny	She *denied committing* the crime.
16.	discuss	They *discussed opening* a new business.
17.	dislike	I *dislike driving* long distances.
18.	enjoy	We *enjoyed visiting* them.
19.	finish	She *finished studying* about ten.
20.	forget•	I'll never *forget visiting* Napoleon's tomb.
21.	hate•	I *hate making* silly mistakes.
22.	imagine	I *imagined getting* a scholarship, and I did.
23.	keep+	I *keep hoping* he will come.
24.	like•	I *like going* to movies.
25.	love•	I *love going* to operas.
26.	mention	She *mentioned going* to a movie.
27.	mind	Would you *mind helping* me with this?
28.	miss	I *miss being* with my family.
29.	postpone	Let's *postpone leaving* until tomorrow.
30.	practice	The athlete *practiced throwing* the ball.
31.	prefer•	Ann *prefers walking* to driving to work.
32.	quit	He *quit trying* to solve the problem.
33.	recall	I don't *recall meeting* him before.
34.	recollect	I don't *recollect meeting* him before.
35.	recommend	She *recommended seeing* the show.
36.	regret•	I *regret telling* him my secret.
37.	remember•	I can *remember meeting* him when I was a child.
38.	resent	I *resent her interfering* in my business.
39.	resist	I couldn't *resist eating* the dessert.
40.	risk	She *risks losing* all of her money.
41.	start•	It *started raining*.
42.	stop	She *stopped going* to classes when she got sick.
43.	suggest	She *suggested going* to a movie.
44.	tolerate	She won't *tolerate cheating* during an examination.
45.	try•	I *tried changing* the light bulb, but the lamp still didn't work.
46.	understand	I don't *understand his leaving* school.
47.	urge	The official *urged using* caution.

Preposition Combinations + Gerunds

1. apologize for — He *apologized for forgetting* his wife's birthday.
2. approve of — The company manager *approved of hiring* me.
3. blame someone for — She *blamed him for stealing* her phone.
4. complain about / of — She *complained about working* too hard.
5. count on — I'*m counting on going* with you.
6. dream about / of — He *dreamed about / of flying* an airplane
7. forgive someone for — She *forgave him for lying*.
8. have a reason for — He *had a reason for being* absent.
9. have an excuse for — Did you *have an excuse for leaving* early?
10. in addition to — *In addition to studying*, I have to work this weekend.
11. insist on — I *insist on coming* with you.
12. instead of — *Instead of sitting* there, why don't you help us?
13. keep someone from — Can a special pillow *keep you from snoring*?

14. look forward to — I'*m looking forward to going* home.
15. object to — The voters *objected to increasing* taxes.
16. participate in — The entire staff *participated in welcoming* students on the first day.
17. prevent someone from — Will the medicine *prevent me from getting* sick?
18. prohibit someone from — The police *prohibited them from leaving*.
19. stop someone from — Security *stopped a passenger from getting* on the subway.
20. succeed in — He *succeeded in getting* the job.
21. take advantage of — I'*m taking advantage of having* a free day tomorrow.
22. take care of — She *took care of filling* out the paperwork.
23. talk about / of — He talked *about / of feeling* homesick.
24. thank someone for — They *thanked him for coming*.
25. think about / of — She *thought about quitting* her job.

Preposition Combinations with *Be* + Gerunds

1. be accused of — He *was accused of stealing*.
2. be accustomed to — She *is accustomed to working* hard.
3. be afraid of — My kids *are afraid of being* alone.
4. be capable of — She *is capable of memorizing* long lists of words.
5. be committed to — Dr. Pak *is committed to improving* medical care in rural areas.
6. be devoted to — They *are devoted to helping* the poor.
7. be excited about — She *is excited about starting* college.
8. be guilty of — He *was guilty of lying* to the judge.

9. be interested in — I *am interested in learning* more about your country.
10. be opposed to — He *is opposed to going* to war.
11. be proud of — She *was proud of knowing* the answer.
12. be responsible for — Who *is responsible for repairing* the roads?
13. be tired of / from — He *was tired of running*. He *was tired from running*.*
14. be used to — She *is used to working* weekends.
15. be worried about — The driver *was worried about getting* a traffic ticket.

He was tired **of running.* = He doesn't want to run anymore.
*He was tired **from** running.* = He was tired because of running.

EXERCISE 46 ▶ Let's talk: pairwork. (Charts 14-10 → 14-12)

Work with a partner. Complete the sentences with *doing it* or *to do it*. Partner A gives the prompt for the first group of ten. Then change roles where indicated. Check Charts 14-10 to 14-12 for the correct verb form if necessary.

Example: I promise
PARTNER A (*book open*): I promise …
PARTNER B (*book closed*): … to do it.

1. We plan …
2. I can't afford …
3. She didn't allow me …
4. I don't care …
5. Please remind me …
6. I am considering …
7. Our director postponed …
8. He persuaded me …
9. I don't mind …
10. Everyone avoided …

Change roles.

11. I refused …
12. I hope …
13. She convinced me …
14. He mentioned …
15. She complained about …
16. I encouraged him …
17. I warned him not …
18. We prepared …
19. I don't recall …
20. Who is responsible for … ?

Change roles.

21. He resented …
22. When will you finish … ?
23. Did you practice … ?
24. She agreed …
25. He was guilty of …

26. Stop …
27. I didn't force him …
28. I couldn't resist …
29. Somehow, the cat managed …
30. Did the little boy admit … ?

Change roles.

31. He denied …
32. I didn't mean …
33. She swore …
34. I volunteered …
35. He suggested …
36. He advised me …
37. He struggled …
38. I don't want to risk …
39. Do you recommend … ?
40. I miss …

Change roles.

41. I can't imagine …
42. She threatened …
43. He seems to dislike …
44. The children begged …
45. She challenged me …
46. Did he deny … ?
47. She taught me …
48. Do you anticipate … ?
49. They are opposed to …
50. I'll arrange …

EXERCISE 47 ▶ Game. (Charts 14-10 → 14-12)

Work in teams. Your teacher will begin a sentence by using any of the verbs in Charts 14-10 to 14-12. Complete the sentence with *to do it* or *doing it,* or with your own words. Each correct answer gets one point.

Example:

TEACHER: I reminded Mario …
STUDENT A: … to do it. OR … to be on time.
TEACHER: Yes. One point!

EXERCISE 48 ▸ Looking at grammar. (Chapter 14 Review)

Work in pairs. Choose <u>all</u> the correct sentences. Explain why each incorrect sentence is wrong.

1. a. Text while you are driving is dangerous.
   b. It is dangerous to text while you are driving.
   c. Texting while you are driving is dangerous.

2. a. We hope visiting them soon.
   b. We hope to visit them soon.
   c. We hope you to visit them soon.

3. a. Jay suggested going to the movies.
   b. Jay suggested that we go to the movies.
   c. Jay suggested me to go the movies.

4. a. Convincing me to take time off it is easy.
   b. It's easy to convince me to take time off.
   c. Convincing me to take time off is easy.

5. a. To run and playing on the beach are two things my kids love to do.
   b. Running and playing on the beach are two things my kids love to do.
   c. Run and play on the beach are two things my kids love to do.

6. a. My grandmother couldn't stand to touch cat fur.
   b. My grandmother couldn't stand to touching cat fur.
   c. My grandmother couldn't stand touching cat fur.

7. a. Roger spends two hours commuting to work.
   b. Roger spends two hours commute to work.
   c. Roger spends two hours for commuting to work.

EXERCISE 49 ▸ Check your knowledge. (Chapter 14 Review)

Correct the errors.

1. I don't mind to have a roommate. *having*

2. Is hard for me understand people who speak very fast. *to*

3. Learning about another country it is very interesting.

4. I tried very hard to don't make any mistakes. *not to*

5. Find an English tutor wasn't difficult. *Finding*

6. All of us needed to went to the ticket office before the game yesterday. *go*

7. I'm looking forward to go to swimming in the ocean. *ing*

8. Ski in the Alps it was a big thrill for me. *Skiing* *Extreme ing*

9. Don't keep to be asking me the same questions over and over. *stop*

10. During a fire drill, everyone is required leaving the building. *to leave*

11. I don't enjoy to play card games. I prefer to spend my time for read or watch movies. *ing*

12. When I entered the room, I found my young son stand on the kitchen table. *ing*

13. Instead of ~~work~~, Katie was lying on her bed think about her fiancé. *ing*

working

EXERCISE 50 ▶ Reading, grammar, and writing. (Chapter 14)

Part I. Read the thank-you note written after a job interview. Then read the tips that follow.

> Dear Mr. Lopez,
>
> Thank you for giving me the opportunity to interview with you. I enjoyed learning more about your business and having the chance to tell you about my skills and experience. Also, it was interesting to find out that you and my uncle went to school together.
>
> As we discussed, I have an associate's degree in automotive technology and two years of on-the-job experience. Combined with my strong work ethic, I believe this background has prepared me well to be an entry-level mechanic with ABC Automotive.
>
> I am excited to be considered for this position. If you have any further questions, please call or email me. I look forward to hearing from you.
>
> Sincerely,
>
> *Gina DeVries*
>
> Gina DeVries

Although there are various ways to write a thank-you note after a job interview, notice the following important points:

- The writer begins by thanking the interviewer and telling him that she enjoyed the experience.
- In the second paragraph, she restates her skills and experience. She adds that she would be a good person for the specific job.
- In the final paragraph, she expresses enthusiasm for the position. She asks the interviewer to contact her if he has any further questions.
- A common way to end this type of letter is to write *I look forward to hearing from you.*
- *Sincerely, Best regards,* or *Kind regards* are polite ways to close.

You might be wondering if the letter should be sent by regular mail or if it can be emailed. It really depends on the culture of the company. For many companies, such as those with a tech or science focus, email is the norm. Also, if the decision is being made quickly, regular mail may be too slow. One rule of thumb is to communicate in the same way as you did previously. If everything has been online, for example, there's a good chance that an email will be preferred.

The thank-you letter is a nice touch. It shows that you are respectful and interested in the position. It may help the interviewer remember you better, especially if you can mention something specific that you talked about. Just be sure that you have someone check it for grammar and spelling! You want to make a good impression.

Part II. Write whether a gerund or infinitive follows each item in the sample letter.

1. Thank you for _____

2. enjoyed _____

3. am excited _____

4. look forward to _____

Part III. Choose one of the following options:

1. Write a thank-you letter to follow up on a job interview that you have had.
2. Write a thank-you letter for the following situation:

   Henry Sanson interviewed with Ms. Azizi for the position of hotel assistant manager.
   He has a recent degree in hotel management and one year's experience as a front desk clerk.

WRITING TIP

Thank-you notes, whether for business or otherwise, often have these key phrases:

- *thank you for* + gerund
- *be interested in* + gerund
- *enjoy* + gerund
- *look forward to* + gerund
- *appreciate your taking the time* + infinitive
- *have the opportunity/chance* + infinitive

When you use these words, be sure to check that you have the correct gerund or infinitive form after them.

Part IV. Edit your writing. Check for the following:

1. ☐ correct use of gerunds
2. ☐ correct use of infinitives
3. ☐ singular verb when a gerund is the subject
4. ☐ correct preposition if one is required
5. ☐ correct spelling (use a dictionary or spell-check)

CHAPTER 15

Gerunds and Infinitives, Part 2

PRETEST: What do I already know?

Write "C" if a sentence has the correct gerund and infinitive form and "I" for incorrect. Check your answers below. After you complete each chart listed, make any necessary corrections.

1. _____ Yasmin is returning home for to complete her medical studies. (15-1)

2. _____ I was sorry to hear that Mila and Pablo are moving away from here. (15-2)

3. _____ Your little puppy seems very eager to pleasing. (15-2)

4. _____ The baby isn't enough tired to sleep right now. (15-3)

5. _____ It's easy to be fool by Jordan's charm. (15-4)

6. _____ Marcus mentioned having lost a large sum of money. (15-5)

7. _____ I was happy to have been invited to the surprise party. (15-5)

8. _____ The car is really dirty. It needs to be wash. (15-6)

9. _____ The walls in our apartment are paper thin, and I could hear my roommate snoring loudly. (15-7)

10. _____ Could you help me to carry the groceries inside? There are several bags. (15-8)

11. _____ Rafael lets his young children to stay up past midnight on weekends. (15-8)

12. _____ Diana makes her kids clean their rooms once a week. (15-9)

13. _____ I appreciate your helping me with the plans for the party. (15-10)

Incorrect sentences: 1, 3, 4, 5, 8, 10, 11

EXERCISE 1 ▸ Warm-up. (Chart 15-1)

Which sentences answer the question "Why"?

1. The baby came to the hospital last week.
2. She has come to the hospital to get special treatment.
3. The doctor wore a clown nose to cheer up his patients.
4. The doctor will check the teddy bear first.
5. The doctor is going to check the teddy bear's heart to relax the baby.

15-1 Infinitive of Purpose: *In Order To*

(a) He came here *in order to study* English. (b) He came here *to study* English.	*In order to* is used to express *purpose*. It answers the question "Why?" *In order* is often omitted, as in (b).
(c) INCORRECT: He came here ~~for studying~~ English. (d) INCORRECT: He came here ~~for to study~~ English. (e) INCORRECT: He came here ~~for study~~ English.	To express purpose, use (*in order*) *to*, not *for*, with a verb.*
(f) I went to the store *for some bread*. (g) I went to the store *to buy some bread*.	*For* can be used to express purpose, but it is a preposition and is followed by a noun object, as in (f).

*Exception: The phrase *be used for* expresses the typical or general purpose of a thing. In this case, the preposition *for* is followed by a gerund: *A saw is used for cutting wood*. Also possible: *A saw is used to cut wood*.

However, to talk about a particular thing and a particular situation, *be used* + *an infinitive* is generally used: *A chain saw was used to cut* (NOT *for cutting*) *down the old oak tree*.

EXERCISE 2 ▶ Looking at grammar. (Chart 15-1)
Complete the sentences with *to* or *for*.

Isabella spent a month in Miami. She went there …

1. ____to____ see her cousins.

2. ____for____ a vacation.

3. _____ business.

4. _____ meet with company executives.

5. _____ discuss long-term plans for the company.

6. _____ spend time with her parents.

7. _____ a visit with childhood friends.

EXERCISE 3 ▶ Looking at grammar. (Chart 15-1)
Complete each sentence with an item from the right column.

Why?

1. Gina went to the grocery store for ____.
2. Gina went to the grocery store to ____.
3. My father swims every day to ____.
4. My mother runs every day for ____.
5. I went to the doctor for ____.
6. I made a doctor's appointment to ____.
7. I went to an ATM to ____.
8. I stopped at an ATM for ____.

a. cash
b. her health
c. get a prescription
d. food
e. make a deposit
f. pick up something for dinner
g. stay in shape
h. a prescription

EXERCISE 4 ▶ Looking at grammar. (Chart 15-1)

Add *in order* wherever possible. If nothing should be added, write **Ø**.

1. a. Lydia went to the dentist _____ to get some relief from her toothache.

   b. She doesn't go often _____ to get checkups.

   c. She's not enthusiastic about going _____ to the dentist.

   d. She's very sensitive _____ to pain, and she's allergic _____ to Novocain.

   e. She also works long hours _____ to support her family and doesn't have time for medical appointments.

2. a. Joe made cookies _____ to take a dessert to the party.

   b. He decorated them _____ to impress his girlfriend.

   c. He likes _____ to bake when he has free time.

   d. He cooks _____ to relax after a stressful day at work.

   e. His father was a pastry chef and taught him how _____ to bake.

EXERCISE 5 ▶ Let's talk: interview. (Chart 15-1)

Ask two classmates each question. Share some of their responses with the class.

What are two reasons why some people …

1. go to Hawaii for vacation?
2. exercise?
3. cheat on exams?
4. meditate?
5. tell white lies?★
6. become actors?

EXERCISE 6 ▶ Warm-up. (Chart 15-2)

Look at the adjectives in blue. What do you notice about the words that come before and after them?

1. Eva *was* sorry *to hear* that the used car she liked had been sold.
2. She *is* certain *to find* another soon.
3. She *was* happy *to find* a helpful dealer.
4. Her friend Kevin had a different experience. He *was* upset *to learn* that the salesperson hadn't given him all the facts.
5. He *is* unlikely *to buy* a car from this dealer.

★*white lies* = lies that aren't considered serious, e.g., telling a friend her dress looks nice when you don't think it does

15-2 Adjectives Followed by Infinitives

(a) We were **sorry to** *hear* the bad news.	Certain adjectives can be immediately followed by infinitives, as in (a) and (b).
(b) I was **surprised to** *see* Ted at the meeting.	In general, these adjectives describe a person (or persons), not a thing. Many of these adjectives describe a person's feelings or attitudes.

Common adjectives followed by infinitives

glad to (do it)	sorry to*	ready to	careful to	surprised to*
happy to	sad to*	prepared to	hesitant to	amazed to*
pleased to*	upset to*	anxious to	reluctant to	astonished to*
delighted to	disappointed to*	eager to	afraid to	shocked to*
content to		willing to		stunned to*
relieved to	embarrassed to	motivated to	certain to	
lucky to	proud to	determined to	likely to	
fortunate to	ashamed to		unlikely to	
excited to				

*The expressions with asterisks are usually followed by infinitive phrases with verbs such as *see, learn, discover, find out, hear.*

EXERCISE 7 ▶ Let's talk. (Chart 15-2)

Work in small groups. Complete the sentences with adjectives from Chart 15-2 that make sense. Discuss your answers.

SITUATION 1: Mr. Wah was offered an excellent job in another country. He sees advantages and disadvantages to moving.

He is …

1. _____*sad to / prepared to / reluctant to*_____ leave his country.

2. _____ move away from his elderly parents.

3. _____ take his wife and children away from family and friends.

4. _____ try a new job.

5. _____ learn a new language.

SITUATION 2: There have been a lot of nighttime burglaries in the town of Viewmont.

The residents have been …

6. _____ leave their homes overnight.

7. _____ lock their doors and windows at night.

8. _____ watch for strangers on the streets.

9. _____ have weekly meetings with the police for updates on their progress.

10. _____ hear that the police suspect neighborhood residents.

EXERCISE 8 ▸ Writing or speaking. (Chart 15-2)

Complete the sentences using the expressions listed in Chart 15-2 and your own words. Use infinitive phrases in your completions.

1. Nicole always speeds on the expressway. She's ...
   → *She's certain to get stopped by the police.*
   → *She's likely to get a ticket.*
2. I've worked hard all day long. Enough! I'm ...
3. Next month, I'm going to a family reunion — the first one in 25 years. I'm very much looking forward to it. I'm ...
4. Some children grow up in unhappy homes. My family, however, has always been loving and supportive. I'm ...
5. Ivan's run out of money again, but he doesn't want anyone to know his situation. He needs money desperately, but he's ...
6. Rosalyn wants to become an astronaut. That has been her dream since she was a little girl. She has been working hard toward her goal and is ...
7. Our neighbors had extra tickets to the baseball game, so they invited us to go with them. Since both of us love baseball, we were ...
8. My sister-in-law recently told me what my brother is up to these days. I couldn't believe my ears! I was ...

EXERCISE 9 ▸ Let's talk: interview. (Chart 15-2)

Make questions using the words in parentheses. Ask two classmates each question. Share some of their answers with the class.

1. What are children sometimes (afraid \ do)?
2. When you're tired in the evening, what are you (content \ do)?
3. What should drivers be (careful \ do) in traffic?
4. If one of your friends has a problem, what are you (willing \ do)?
5. What are people who don't speak English well (reluctant \ do)?
6. What are you (determined \ do) before you are too old?
7. What are things some students are (motivated \ do)?
8. Can you tell me something you were (shocked \ find out)?
9. Can you tell me something you were (sad \ hear)?
10. What are you (eager \ do) in the near future?

EXERCISE 10 ▸ Warm-up. (Chart 15-3)

Complete the sentences with *too, to,* and *enough*.

MARIA: Will these chilies work for your recipe?
ALBERTO: They are too spicy. I don't want to cook with them.
RICARDO: They are spicy enough. I'll cook with them.

1. Alberto says they are _____ spicy

   _____ cook with.

2. Ricardo says they are spicy _____

   _____ cook with.

15-3 Using Infinitives with *Too* and *Enough*

COMPARE:	
(a) That box is *too heavy* for Bob to lift. (b) That box is *very heavy*, but Bob can lift it.	*Too* can be followed by an infinitive, as in (a). In the speaker's mind, the use of *too* implies a negative result. In (a): *too heavy* = It is *impossible* for Bob to lift that box. In (b): *very heavy* = It is *possible but difficult* for Bob to lift that box.
(c) I am *strong enough to lift* that box. I can lift it. (d) I have *enough strength to lift* that box. (e) I have *strength enough to lift* that box.	*Enough* can also be followed by an infinitive. Note the following: • *Enough* follows the adjective, as in (c). • Usually *enough* precedes a noun, as in (d). • In formal English, it may follow a noun, as in (e).

EXERCISE 11 ▶ Looking at grammar. (Chart 15-3)

Complete the sentences with *too* or *enough*.

1. a. It's _____ stormy to go outside. I'll work inside today.

   b. The weather is severe _____ to keep emergency workers indoors.

2. a. Your room needs to be cleaned. You are old _____ to do it yourself.

   b. Please do it now. It's _____ messy to wait another day.

3. a. The conversation occurred _____ long ago to remember any specific details.

   b. It was long _____ ago to make the details seem unimportant.

4. a. It's _____ expensive to fly home on the weekend. We'll need to leave on a weekday.

   b. Jason has money _____ to fly anywhere in the world.

5. a. Rebecca's cold is really contagious. She has sense _____ to stay home.

   b. She has _____ sense to not expose others to her cold.

6. a. When I injure my back, it's often _____ painful to sleep at night.

   b. George's back injury was painful _____ to keep him in bed for a week.

EXERCISE 12 ▶ Let's talk. (Chart 15-3)

Answer the questions. Work in pairs, in small groups, or as a class.

Your Thoughts?

1. What is your backpack/bag big enough to hold? What is it too small to hold?
2. What do you have enough time to do after class today? Are you too busy to do something you'd like to do or should do?
3. Is there enough space in this classroom for 100 people? Or is it too small to hold that many people? How many people is this room big enough to hold comfortably?
4. Do you think it is very important to practice your English? Do you get enough practice? In your opinion, how much practice is enough?
5. Is it very difficult or too difficult to learn English articles (*a, an, the*)?
6. Think of a scientist you have learned about. What was he or she smart enough to do?

Choose the sentence that has the same meaning as the sentence you hear.

Example: You will hear: I didn't fill your cup full enough.
        You will choose: ⓐ You need more.
                     b. You have enough.

1. a. He's old enough to drive.
   b. He shouldn't drive.

2. a. She is too young to stay home alone.
   b. She stays home alone sometimes.

3. a. The test results are excellent.
   b. I'm not sure about the test results.

4. a. The room needs to be bigger.
   b. The room size is OK.

5. a. You will have enough time.
   b. You will need more time.

6. a. I want to eat them.
   b. I don't want to eat them.

EXERCISE 14 ▶ Warm-up. (Chart 15-4)
Choose the correct form of the passive verbs. Reminder: A passive verb has a form of *be* and a past participle, e.g., *the patient **was seen** by a specialist.*

1. The patient was hoping to be given / being given a good diagnosis.
2. He was worried about to be diagnosed / being diagnosed with cancer.
3. The patient appreciated to be seen / being seen by a specialist.
4. It was important for him to be seen / being seen by a specialist.

15-4 Passive Infinitives and Gerunds: Present	
(a) I didn't *expect to be asked* to his party.	PASSIVE INFINITIVE: ***to be*** + *past participle* In (a): ***to be asked*** is a passive infinitive. The understood *by*-phrase is *by him: I didn't expect to be asked to his party (by him).*
(b) I *appreciated being asked* to his party.	PASSIVE GERUND: ***being*** + *past participle* In (b): ***being asked*** is a passive gerund. The understood *by*-phrase is *by him: I appreciated being asked to his party (by him).*

EXERCISE 15 ▶ Looking at grammar. (Chart 15-4)
Complete the sentences with the passive form of ***invite***.

Ann's Party

1. Sam would like _____*to be invited*_____ to Ann's party.

2. Mara also hopes _____ .

3. Maria has no doubts. She expects _____ to it.

4. Omar is looking forward to _____ too.

5. I would enjoy _____ to it, but I probably won't be.

6. Everyone I know wants _____ to Ann's party.

EXERCISE 16 ▸ Looking at grammar. (Chart 15-4)

Complete each sentence with the correct form of the verb in parentheses.

Complaints

1. I don't enjoy (*laugh*) _____*being laughed*_____ at by other people.

2. Ryan lied again. Unfortunately, it's easy (*fool*) _____*to be fooled*_____ by his lies.

3. It's not unusual for teenagers to complain about not (*understand*) _____

   _____ by their parents.

4. Your compositions are not supposed (*handwrite*) _____ . They're

   supposed to (*type*) _____ .

5. Dr. Davis is upset. She doesn't want (*call*) _____ at home unless there

   is an emergency.

6. Please don't lie again. From now on, I insist on (*tell*) _____

   _____ the truth.

7. Lars is hoping (*elect*) _____ to the city

   council, but he's not qualified at all.

8. My sister is a helicopter parent.* Her kids need (*give*) _____

   _____ more independence.

---

a helicopter parent = an overprotective or overinvolved parent

EXERCISE 17 ▸ Reading and listening. (Chart 15-4)
First, read the paragraph and try to complete the sentences using the words in the box.
Then listen to the paragraph and check your answers.

to be understood	to solve	to read
able to read	using	being

An Issue in Health Care: Illiteracy

According to some estimates, well over half of the people in the world are functionally illiterate. This means that they are unable to perform everyday tasks because they can't read, understand, and respond appropriately to information. One of the problems this creates in health care is that millions of people are not _____ directions on
1
medicine bottles or packages. Imagine _____ a parent with a sick child
2
and being unable _____ the directions on a medicine bottle. We all know
3
that it is important for medical directions _____ clearly. One solution
4
is pictures. Many medical professionals are working today _____ this
5
problem by _____ pictures to convey health-care information.
6

EXERCISE 18 ▸ Let's talk. (Chart 15-4)
Agree or disagree with the following statements and give reasons. Work in pairs, in small groups, or as a class.

1. I appreciate *being given* advice by my family and friends.
2. I always expect *to be told* the absolute and complete truth by everyone at all times.
3. I would like *to be invited* to an event where there are a lot of famous people.

EXERCISE 19 ▸ Warm-up. (Chart 15-5)
Look at the sentences. All are correct. Which forms are you most familiar with? What differences do you see between "b." and "c."?

1. a. Liam denied that he cheated on the test.
   b. Liam denied cheating on the test.
   c. Liam denied having cheated on the test.

2. a. He was surprised that he was caught by the teacher.
   b. He was surprised to be caught by the teacher.
   c. He was surprised to have been caught by the teacher.

15-5 Past Forms of Infinitives and Gerunds: Active and Passive

SIMPLE	PAST ACTIVE	PAST PASSIVE	Past infinitives and gerunds use a form of *have* + past participle.
to tell	*to have told*	*to have been told*	
telling	*having told*	*having been told*	

(a) Tim appeared *to have told* his wife about his job promotion.	PAST INFINITIVE: **to have** + *past participle* The event expressed in past phrases happened before the time of the main verb. The meaning in (a): It appeared that Tim had told his wife about his job promotion.
(b) Tim's wife was happy *to have been told* immediately about his job promotion.	PAST PASSIVE INFINITIVE: **to have been** + *past participle* The meaning in (b): Tim's wife was happy that she had been told immediately about his job promotion.
(c) He mentioned *having told* his wife immediately about his job promotion.	PAST GERUND: **having** + *past participle* The meaning in (c): He mentioned that he had told his wife immediately about his job promotion.
(d) She appreciated *having been told* immediately about his job promotion.	PAST PASSIVE GERUND: **having been** + *past participle* The meaning in (d): She appreciated that she had been told immediately about his job promotion.
(e) Tim mentioned *telling* his wife. Tim mentioned *having told* his wife. (f) She was happy *to be told*. She was happy *to have been told*.	Use of the past infinitive or gerund emphasizes that something occurred in the past, prior to another event. In practice, however, there is little difference in meaning between the simple and past forms, as in (e) and (f).

EXERCISE 20 ▸ Looking at grammar. (Chart 15-5)
Rewrite the sentences with the appropriate past infinitive or gerund phrase.

1. It seems that Thomas has received some upsetting news. → *Thomas seems to have received some upsetting news.*
2. The workers mentioned that they lost the contract. → *The workers mentioned having lost the contract.*
3. Mr. and Mrs. Sanchez regret that they missed your wedding.
4. It appears that Nicholas has gotten a new job.
5. The mechanic admitted that he had overcharged for repairs.
6. Mariah claims that she has met several celebrities.

EXERCISE 21 ▸ Looking at grammar. (Chart 15-5)
Complete the sentences with the correct form of the verb in parentheses.

1. I'm not sure I've ever met Billy Williams. (*meet*)

   a. I don't remember that I _____*met*_____ him.

   b. I don't recall having _____*met*_____ him.

   c. I don't recall _____ him.

   d. I don't remember _____ him.

   e. I don't remember having _____ him.

2. Ben was in the army during the war. He was caught by the enemy, but he was able to escape.
   (*survive*)

   a. He was lucky to _____ the war.

   b. He was lucky to have _____ the war.

   c. He was fortunate to _____ the war.

   d. He told us about having _____ the war.

   e. He told us about _____ the war.

   f. It was fortunate that he _____ the war.

EXERCISE 22 ▶ Looking at grammar. (Charts 15-4 and 15-5)
Work with a partner. Choose the correct verbs. Several sentences have more than one correct
answer. Discuss your answers.

1. Carlos looks great! He appears _____ some weight.
   a. losing
   b. to have lost
   c. to losing

2. I don't like _____ by friends.
   a. being lied to
   b. lying to
   c. to lie to

3. Mr. Gow mentioned _____ in an accident as a child.
   a. being injured
   b. having been injured
   c. injured

4. I was expecting _____ to the party, but I wasn't.
   a. being invited
   b. to be invited
   c. to have been invited

5. My husband talked of _____ by his parents.
   a. being misunderstood
   b. having been misunderstood
   c. misunderstood

6. The employees were happy _____
   Mr. Larson as their next president.
   a. to choose
   b. to have chosen
   c. to have been chosen

7. Mr. Larson was happy _____ as the
   next company president.
   a. to choose
   b. to be chosen
   c. to have been chosen

EXERCISE 23 ▶ Warm-up. (Chart 15-6)
Make statements that are true for you. Use the same noun to complete each sentence. Do the
sentences have the same or different meanings?

1. I need to clean my _____ .

2. My _____ needs cleaning.

3. My _____ needs to be cleaned.

15-6 Using Gerunds or Passive Infinitives Following *Need*

(a) I *need to paint* my house.	Usually an infinitive follows *need*, as in (a) and (b).
(b) John *needs to be told* the truth.	
(c) My house *needs painting*.	In certain circumstances, a gerund may follow *need*, as in (c). In this case, the gerund carries a passive meaning. Usually the situations involve fixing or improving something.
(d) My house *needs to be painted*.	Examples (c) and (d) have the same meaning.

EXERCISE 24 ▶ Looking at grammar. (Chart 15-6)

Complete the sentences with the correct form of the verb in parentheses. Some verbs are active, and some are passive.

Farm Chores

1. The tractor is broken. I need (*fix*) _____to fix_____ it. The tractor needs

   (*fix*) _____fixing / to be fixed_____ .

2. The horses are hungry. They need (*feed*) _____ .

3. Their stalls are dirty. We need (*clean*) _____ them.

4. The hens have laid eggs. You need (*gather*) _____

   the eggs.

5. The dog's been digging in the mud. He needs (*wash*) _____ .

6. The vegetable garden is dry. It needs (*water*) _____ .

7. The apples on the tree are ripe. We need (*pick*) _____ them.

8. There is a hole in the fence. The fence needs (*repair*) _____ .

EXERCISE 25 ▶ Let's talk. (Chart 15-6)

Lawrence and Kara have been looking for a house. They've found one on a beautiful piece of land — shown in the photo — but it needs a lot of work. What needs doing or needs to be done? Make sentences using the words in the box or other appropriate vocabulary. Work in pairs or small groups.

A Fixer Upper

fix	paint	replace
foundation	porch	roof
front steps	rebuild	siding*
	repair	windows

Example: The windows need to be replaced. OR
The windows need replacing.

---

*siding = material, often wood, that goes around the outside of the house

EXERCISE 26 ▸ Reading and speaking. (Chapter 14 and Charts 15-1 → 15-6)

Read the blog entry by author Stacy Hagen and answer the questions.

 BlueBookBlog Multitasking

Doing homework, checking text messages, group chatting — these are common activities, but are we capable of doing all of them at the same time and doing them well? According to research, it is impossible to multitask successfully. We either do the tasks more slowly, or we make mistakes. And with each additional task, the mistakes multiply. We make fewer mistakes with one task, more with two, and even more with three.

Our brain functions better when it stays focused on one task. This is why it is more efficient to do things in batches. We have a particular routine or mindset when we pay bills or answer emails, and these routines are different. So we want to pay all our bills or answer all our emails at one time before we move on to something else.

There is a related technique from organizational psychology that can help us stay on task. It is called "OHIO," which stands for "only handle it once." The idea is that once we start a single task like deleting photos from a phone, we should stay with it. We don't put some photos aside to make decisions about later. The result is that instead of looking at something multiple times, we deal with it only once.

Think about what tasks you have that need to be done for school, work, or at home. Maybe there is something that you have started many times but haven't ever finished. You might want to give the OHIO technique a try to see how it works for you.

1. What types of activities are you likely to multitask?
2. Is multitasking an effective approach for you?
3. Have you tried to do things in batches in order to be more efficient?
4. Do you have difficulty completing tasks you have started? Do you have any that still need to be finished?
5. Is OHIO a technique that could be helpful to you?

EXERCISE 27 ▸ Warm-up. (Chart 15-7)

See and *hear* are called "verbs of perception." In other words, they express things that we can perceive (become aware of) through our physical senses. What do you notice about the verb forms following *see* and *hear*?

1. a. CORRECT: I **saw** Mr. Reed give something to the boss.
   b. CORRECT: I **saw** Mr. Reed giving something to the boss.
   c. INCORRECT: I **saw** Mr. Reed ~~to~~ give something to the boss.

2. a. CORRECT: I **heard** Mr. Reed say something to the boss.
   b. CORRECT: I **heard** Mr. Reed saying something to the boss.
   c. INCORRECT: I **heard** Mr. Reed ~~to~~ say something to the boss.

15-7 Using Verbs of Perception

(a) I *saw* my friend *run* down the street. (b) I *saw* my friend *running* down the street. (c) I *heard* the rain *fall* on the roof. (d) I *heard* the rain *falling* on the roof.	Certain verbs of perception are followed by either *the simple form** or *the -ing form*** of a verb. Examples (a) and (b) have essentially the same meaning, except that the *-ing* form emphasizes the idea of "while." In (b): I saw my friend while she was running down the street.
(e) When I walked into the apartment, I *heard* my roommate *singing* in the shower. (f) I *heard* a famous opera star *sing* at the concert last night.	Sometimes (not always) there is a clear difference between using the simple form or the *-ing* form. The use of the *-ing* form gives the idea that an activity is already in progress when it is perceived, as in (e): The singing was in progress when I first heard it. In (f): I heard the singing from beginning to end. It was not in progress when I first heard it.

Verbs of perception followed by the simple form or the *-ing* form

see	look at	hear	feel	smell
notice	observe	listen to		
watch				

*The simple form of a verb = the infinitive form without *to*. INCORRECT: I saw my friend ~~to~~ run down the street.

**The *-ing* form is the present participle of the verb.

EXERCISE 28 ▸ Let's talk. (Chart 15-7)

Work in small groups. Describe what is going on.

1. Ask a classmate to stand up and sit back down. What did you just see him/her do?
2. Close your eyes. What do you hear happening right now?
3. Ask a classmate to go to the board and write something. As he/she does this, describe what you see and hear him/her doing.
4. If possible, find a hotel webcam on the Internet for a vacation spot. What do you see happening?

EXERCISE 29 ▸ Looking at grammar. (Chart 15-7)

Complete the sentences with any appropriate verbs. Both the simple form and the *-ing* form are possible with little or no difference in meaning.

An Earthquake

1. As I stood in the grocery store, I felt the ground _____ *shake / shaking* _____.
2. I heard someone _____ "earthquake."
3. I saw cans of food _____ off shelves.
4. I watched customers in the store _____ outside.
5. I listened to people _____ the size of the earthquake.
6. I observed store staff _____ people outside.

EXERCISE 30 ▸ Looking at grammar. (Chart 15-7)

Read each situation. Complete the sentence below it with the verb form that seems better to you. Remember that the *-ing* form gives the idea that an activity is in progress when it is perceived.

SITUATION 1: I smell smoke. Something must be burning.

Do you smell something _____ *burning* _____? I do.

SITUATION 2: The front door slammed. I got up to see if someone had come in.

When I heard the front door _____, I got up to see if someone had come in.

SITUATION 3: Uncle Ben is in the bedroom. He is snoring.

I know Uncle Ben is in the bedroom because I can hear him _____.

SITUATION 4: When I walked past the park, some children were playing softball.

When I walked past the park, I saw some children _____ softball.

SITUATION 5: It was graduation day in the auditorium. When the school principal called my name, I walked to the front of the room.

When I heard the school principal _____ my name, I walked to the front of the auditorium to receive my diploma.

SITUATION 6: I glanced out the window. Adam was walking toward the house. I was surprised.

I was surprised when I saw Adam _____ toward the house.

SITUATION 7: Someone is calling for help in the distance. I suddenly hear that.

Listen! Do you hear someone _____ for help? I do.

EXERCISE 31 ▸ Warm-up. (Chart 15-8)

Check (✓) the sentences that are grammatically correct.

1. _____ I'm not a morning person. My parents let me sleep late on weekends.
2. _____ My parents let me to sleep late on weekends.
3. _____ After I wake up, I help them do the chores.
4. _____ After I wake up, I help them to do the chores.

15-8 Using the Simple Form After *Let* and *Help*

(a) My father *lets* me *drive* his car.	**Let** is followed by the simple form of a verb, not an infinitive.
(b) I *let* my friend *borrow* my bike.	*INCORRECT:* My father lets me ~~to~~ drive his car.
(c) *Let's go* to a movie.	
(d) My brother *helped* me *wash* my car.	**Help** is often followed by the simple form of a verb, as in (d).
(e) My brother *helped* me *to wash* my car.	Although less common, an infinitive is also possible, as in (e).
	Both (d) and (e) are correct.

EXERCISE 32 ▸ Looking at grammar. (Chart 15-8)

Complete the sentences with the verbs in parentheses.

At Breakfast

1. I forgot to tell you last night. My advisor is letting me (*challenge*) _____ a course. All I need to do is pass the test.

2. Could you help me (*figure*) _____ out my credit card statement before you go?

3. You really shouldn't let the dog (*sit*) _____ under the table.

4. How's our new neighbor, Mrs. Vitale? Did you help her (*move*) _____ her furniture?

5. Don't let me (*forget*) _____ to take my keys with me when I leave.

6. I need to go soon. Could you help me (*clear*) _____ the table?

7. You've been working so hard. Let me (*cook*) _____ dinner tonight.

EXERCISE 33 ▸ Warm-up. (Chart 15-9)
Match each of Andy's statements with the correct meaning.

a. "Weed the dandelions right now! I don't want you to leave until it's done."
b. "You did a good job with the dandelions. I'm glad I asked you to weed."
c. "I told my son I would double his allowance if he weeded the dandelions."

1. Andy got his son to weed the dandelions. _____

2. Andy made his son weed the dandelions. _____

3. Andy had his son weed the dandelions. _____

15-9 Using Causative Verbs: *Make, Have, Get*

(a) I *made* my brother *carry* my suitcase.	*Make*, *have*, and *get* can be used to express the idea that "X" causes "Y" to do something. When they are used as causative verbs, their meanings are similar but not identical.
(b) I *had* my brother *carry* my suitcase.	
(c) I *got* my brother *to carry* my suitcase.	In (a): My brother had no choice. I insisted that he carry my suitcase.
Simple form: X *makes* Y *do something*. Simple form: X *has* Y *do something*. Infinitive: X *gets* Y *to do something*.	In (b): My brother carried my suitcase because I asked him to. In (c): I managed to persuade my brother to carry my suitcase.

Causative *Make*

(d) Mrs. Lee *made* her son *clean* his room. (e) Sad movies *make* me *cry*.	Causative *make* is followed by the simple form of a verb, not an infinitive. *INCORRECT*: She made him ~~to~~ clean his room. *Make* gives the idea that "X" **gives** "Y" **no choice**. In (d): Mrs. Lee's son had no choice.

Causative *Have*

(f) I *had* the plumber *repair* the leak. (g) Jane *had* the waiter *bring* her some tea.	Causative *have* is followed by the simple form of a verb, not an infinitive. *INCORRECT*: I had him ~~to~~ repair the leak. *Have* gives the idea that "X" **requests** "Y" to do something. In (f): The plumber repaired the leak because I asked him to.

Causative *Get*

(h) The students *got* the teacher *to dismiss* class early. (i) Jack *got* his friends *to play* soccer with him after school.	Causative *get* is followed by an infinitive. *Get* gives the idea that "X" **persuades** "Y" to do something. In (h): The students managed to persuade the teacher to let them leave early.

Passive Causatives

(j) I *had* my watch *repaired* (by someone). (k) I *got* my watch *repaired* (by someone).	The past participle is used after *have* and *get* to give a passive meaning. In this case, there is usually little or no difference in meaning between *have* and *get*. In (j) and (k): I caused my watch to be repaired by someone.

EXERCISE 34 ▸ Looking at grammar. (Chart 15-9)

Match each conversation with the correct meaning.

a. ADAM: Mom, can I go out and play?
   MRS. LEE: No, Adam, you cannot go out and play until you clean up your room. I don't know how many times I have to say this. Go clean up your room, and I mean now!
   ADAM: OK, OK!

b. ADAM: Mom, can I go out and play?
   MRS. LEE: Well, let's make a deal. First you clean up your room. Then you can go out and play. How does that sound? It needs to be cleaned before Grandma comes for a visit this evening. And if you do it now, you can stay out and play until dark. You won't have to come home early to clean your room. OK?
   ADAM: OK.

c. ADAM: Mom, can I go out and play?
   MRS. LEE: Sure, but first you need to clean up your room. OK?
   ADAM: OK.

1. Mrs. Lee got Adam to clean up his room. _____

2. Mrs. Lee made Adam clean up his room. _____

3. Mrs. Lee had Adam clean up his room. _____

EXERCISE 35 ▸ Looking at grammar. (Chart 15-9)

Choose the meaning that is closest to the meaning of the verb in blue.

1. The teacher had her class write a composition.
   a. gave them no choice   b. persuaded them   c. requested them to do this

2. Mrs. Wilson made the children wash their hands before dinner.
   a. gave them no choice   b. persuaded them   c. requested them to do this

3. Kostas got some neighborhood kids to help him clean out his garage.
   a. gave them no choice   b. persuaded them   c. requested them to do this

4. My boss made me redo my report because he wasn't satisfied with it.
   a. gave me no choice   b. persuaded me   c. requested me to do this

5. I got Rosa to lend me some lunch money.
   a. gave her no choice   b. persuaded her   c. requested her to do this

6. The police officer had the driver get out of his car.
   a. gave him no choice   b. persuaded him   c. requested him to do this

EXERCISE 36 ▸ Looking at grammar. (Chart 15-9)

Complete the sentences with the correct form of the verbs in parentheses.

Tasks

1. Henry made his son (wash) _____wash_____ the car before he could go outside to play.

2. Mrs. Crane had her house (paint) _____painted_____ .

3. I went to the bank to have a check (cash) _____ .

4. Tom had a bad headache yesterday, so he got his roommate (cook) _____ dinner for him.

5. Scott needed a suit for work. The sleeves were too long, so he had them (*shorten*) _____ .

6. When my laptop stopped working, I took it to the computer store to have it (*fix*) _____ .

7. Benjamin was supposed to wash the windows, but he didn't want to. Somehow he got his little brother (*do*) _____ it for him.

8. We had our cousin (*take*) _____ pictures of everyone at the wedding. We had over 500 pictures (*take*) _____ .

EXERCISE 37 ▸ Let's talk. (Chart 15-9)

Think about the shopping area nearest your home. What can people do there? Make sentences with **can / can't + get**.

At the shopping area nearest my home, people can/can't get their ...

1. car \ fix
2. hair \ cut
3. checks \ cash
4. laundry \ do
5. passport photo \ take
6. blood pressure \ check
7. shoes \ repair
8. clothes \ dry-clean
9. money \ exchange

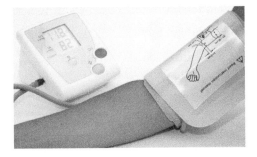

EXERCISE 38 ▸ Let's talk. (Chart 15-9)

Ask and answer the questions. Work in pairs, in small groups, or as a class.

1. What do children sometimes try to **get** their parents **to do** (perhaps at a toy store or grocery store)?
2. What do bosses sometimes **make** their employees **do**?
3. What does our teacher sometimes **have** us **do**?
4. Do teachers usually **let** their students **leave** the classroom whenever they want to? What kinds of things do teachers usually not **let** their students **do** inside a classroom?
5. What do your classmates (or friends) sometimes **help** you **do**?

(Change roles if working in pairs.)

6. What didn't your parents **let** you **do** when you were a child?
7. Will you **let** your children **do** those things? (Or, if you're a parent, do you **let** your children **do** those things?)
8. Did your parents **make** you **do** certain things when you were a child?
9. What do you sometimes **have** the server at a restaurant **do**?
10. What do you sometimes **get** your friends **to do**?

EXERCISE 39 ▸ Warm-up. (Chart 15-10)

Which sentence sounds more like everyday English to you? Which sounds more formal?

1. I appreciate your helping me.   2. I appreciate you helping me.

15-10 Using a Possessive to Modify a Gerund

— We came to class late. Mr. Lee complained about that fact. (a) FORMAL: Mr. Lee complained about *our coming* to class late. (b) INFORMAL: Mr. Lee complained about *us coming* to class late.	In formal English, a possessive adjective (e.g., *our*) is used to modify a gerund, as in (a). In informal English, the object form of a pronoun (e.g., *us*) is frequently used, as in (b).
(c) FORMAL: Mr. Lee complained about *Mary's coming* to class late. (d) INFORMAL: Mr. Lee complained about *Mary coming* to class late.	In formal English, a possessive noun (e.g., *Mary's*) is used to modify a gerund. As in (d), the possessive form is often not used in informal English.

EXERCISE 40 ▸ Looking at grammar. (Chart 15-10)

Complete the sentences with the correct form of the pronoun in parentheses.

Before the Wedding

1. (*I*) a. FORMAL: My parents don't understand _____ wanting a small wedding.

   b. INFORMAL: My parents don't understand _____ wanting a small wedding.

2. (*she*) a. FORMAL: My mom has been too involved. We dislike _____ interfering in the wedding plans.

   b. INFORMAL: We dislike _____ interfering in the wedding plans.

3. (*we*) a. FORMAL: Everyone else understands _____ planning a quiet celebration.

   b. INFORMAL: Everyone else understands _____ planning a quiet celebration.

4. (*they*) a. FORMAL: The Ricardos are coming from out of town. I look forward to _____ coming.

   b. INFORMAL: I look forward to _____ coming.

5. (*you*) a. FORMAL: We appreciate _____ helping us find a restaurant for the reception.

   b. INFORMAL: We appreciate _____ helping us find a restaurant for the reception.

6. (*he*) a. FORMAL: Wait! Uncle Harry doesn't like Aunt Ethel. I insist on _____ being at a different table.

   b. INFORMAL: I insist on _____ being at a different table.

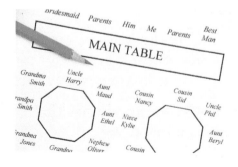

EXERCISE 41 ▸ Looking at grammar. (Chapters 14 and 15 Review)
Choose the correct completions.

1. My cousins helped me _____ into my new apartment.
   a. move   b. to move   c. moving   d. being moved

2. It was a hot day, and the work was hard. I could feel sweat _____ down my back.
   a. run   b. to run   c. running   d. ran

3. He's an amazing soccer player! Did you see him _____ that goal?
   a. make   b. to make   c. makes   d. made

4. We spent the entire class period _____ about the revolution.
   a. talk   b. to talk   c. talking   d. being talked

5. Fifty people applied for the sales job, so Maleek was fortunate _____ for an interview.
   a. chosen   b. being chosen   c. to choose   d. to be chosen

6. If you hear any news, I want _____ immediately.
   a. told   b. being told   c. to be told   d. telling

7. Victor stood in line _____ to buy a movie ticket.
   a. wait   b. waits   c. waiting   d. waited

8. _____ telling Roberto about the party was a mistake.
   a. We   b. My   c. I   d. Ø

9. I was getting sleepy, so I had my friend _____ the car.
   a. drive   b. being driven   c. to be driven   d. to drive

10. The witness to the murder wanted her name kept secret. She asked not _____ in the newspaper.
    a. identify   b. being identified   c. to be identified   d. to identify

EXERCISE 42 ▸ Looking at grammar. (Chapters 14 and 15 Review)
Complete each sentence with an appropriate form of the verb in parentheses.

1. My teenagers enjoy (*allow*) ___*being allowed*___ to stay up later in the summer.

2. I couldn't get to sleep last night, so for a long time I just lay in bed (*think*) _____ about my career and my future.

3. Jacob's at an awkward age. He's old enough (*have*) _____ adult problems but too young (*know*) _____ how (*handle*) _____ them.

4. I don't anticipate (*have*) _____ any difficulties (*adjust*) _____ to a different culture when I go abroad.

5. I was tired, so I just watched my friends (*play*) _____ volleyball instead of (*join*) _____ them.

6. Emily stopped her car (*let*) _____ a cat (*run*) _____ across the street.

7. I'm tired. I wouldn't mind just (*stay*) _____ home tonight and (*get*) _____ to bed early.

8. I don't like (*force*) _____ (*leave*) _____ the living room (*study*) _____ whenever my roommate decides (*have*) _____ a party.

9. Let's (*have*) _____ Ron and Maureen (*join*) _____ us for dinner tonight, OK?

10. Do you know that your co-workers complain about your (*come*) _____ late to work and (*leave*) _____ early?

11. Fish don't use their teeth for (*chew*) _____. They use them for (*grab*) _____, (*hold*) _____, or (*tear*) _____. Most fish (*swallow*) _____ their prey whole.

12. I can't seem (*get*) _____ rid of the cockroaches in my apartment. Every night I see them (*run*) _____ all over my kitchen counters. It drives me crazy. I'm considering (*have*) _____ the whole apartment (*spray*) _____ by a pest control expert.

EXERCISE 43 ▶ Looking at grammar. (Chapters 14 and 15 Review)
Complete each paragraph with the correct form of the given verbs.

1. *be / commute / do / move*

   Traffic has become too heavy for the Steinbergs _____ easily to their jobs in the city. They're considering _____ to an apartment in the city _____ closer to their work. They want to spend more time _____ things they really enjoy rather than being tied up on the highway during rush hour.

2. *ask / cough / feel / get / go / sneeze*

   Last week I was sick with the flu. It made me _____ awful. I didn't have enough energy _____ out of bed. I just lay there. When my father heard me _____ and _____, he opened my bedroom door to see if I needed anything. It was kind of him _____, but there wasn't anything he could do to make the flu _____ away.

EXERCISE 44 ▶ Check your knowledge. (Chapter 15 Review)
Correct the errors.

1. I went to the library ~~for~~ ^{to} study last night.

2. Barbara always makes me laughing. She has a great sense of humor.

3. The teacher opened the window for letting some fresh air into the room.

4. You shouldn't let children playing with matches.

5. I traveled to Osaka for to visit my sister.

6. My parents made me to promise contact them once a week.

7. I asked my roommate to let me borrowed his sleeping bag for my camping trip.

8. I heard a car door to open and closing.

9. I had my friend to lend me his car.

10. I've finally gathered enough information for beginning writing my research paper.

11. My parents want that I marry soon.

12. Lilly deserves to be tell the truth about what happened last night.

13. I went to the pharmacy for having my prescription to be filled.

14. Stop telling me what to do! Let me to make up my own mind.

15. Victoria didn't like her school photo, so she had it taking again.

16. Look at the kitchen windows. They really need to washing. Will you do it?

17. I saw Omar sitting on a park bench look at the ground. The blank expression on his face made me to worry about him.

EXERCISE 45 ▸ Reading and writing. (Chapter 15)

Part I. Read the passage. <u>Underline</u> the gerunds and infinitives. How many gerunds begin sentences? How many infinitives?

Do you know these words?
- *understatement*
- *remedies*
- *foolproof*

Why Do Onions Make Us Cry?

Cutting onions is no fun! Most people end up in tears, and the reason is quite simple. Onions contain a gas: sulfur. When an onion is cut, a very fine spray of sulfur is released into the air. It is an understatement to say that our eyes don't enjoy coming into contact with it. They immediately react by trying to wash the sulfur away with tears.

There are a few remedies that may be helpful to you, though not foolproof. Washing an onion with water can help to keep the sulfur away from your eyes. Refrigerating it weakens its strength. Some people find safety goggles effective. You might look foolish when you put them on, but there's a good chance they will keep you from crying. If you enjoy cooking, it's hard to avoid onions, but one of these simple solutions may be of help.

Part II. Think about an everyday problem that needs a remedy. Describe the problem and provide one or more solutions. Use one of the suggestions below or choose your own. Be sure to include some gerunds and infinitives.

- stopping the itch in a mosquito bite
- removing a stain from fabric
- removing something sticky from a surface
- soothing a sore throat
- soothing a sunburn

Using a gerund as the subject of a sentence rather than an infinitive is more common. In the passage about onions, *cutting onions* or *washing an onion* is preferable to the infinitive forms: *to cut* or *to wash*.

However, if you want to express the idea of *in order to,* use an infinitive: *To cut an onion, use a sharp knife.* The meaning is "In order to cut an onion, use a sharp knife."

Part III. Edit your writing. Check for the following:

1. ☐ correct use of gerunds with the required verbs
2. ☐ correct use of infinitives with the required verbs
3. ☐ correct use of infinitives with the required adjectives
4. ☐ correct use of a gerund if followed by a preposition
5. ☐ singular verb when a gerund is the subject
6. ☐ correct spelling (use a dictionary or spell-check)

CHAPTER 16

Coordinating Conjunctions

EXERCISE 1 ▸ Warm-up. (Chart 16-1)

Identify the parts of speech of the words in blue. Are they nouns, verbs, adjectives, or adverbs? What words connect them?

A Birthday Adventure

1. We hiked to a waterfall and a bridge.
   N   *N*

2. The bridge was extremely high and scary.

3. I felt shaky but excited when I got on it.

4. The bridge rocked and swayed.

5. I tried not to hurry or to look down.

16-1 Parallel Structure

One use of a conjunction is to connect words or phrases that have the same grammatical function in a sentence. This use of conjunctions is called "parallel structure." The conjunctions used in this pattern are **and, but, or,** and **nor.** These words are called "coordinating conjunctions."

(a) *Steve and his friend* are coming to dinner.	In (a): *noun + and + noun*
(b) Susan *raised* her hand *and snapped* her fingers.	In (b): *verb + and + verb*
(c) He *is waving* his arms *and (is) shouting* at us.	In (c): *verb + and + verb* (The second auxiliary may be omitted if it is the same as the first auxiliary.)
(d) These shoes are *old but comfortable*.	In (d): *adjective + but* + adjective
(e) He wants *to watch* TV *or (to) listen* to some music.	In (e): *infinitive + or + infinitive* (The second *to* is usually omitted.)

EXERCISE 2 ▸ Looking at grammar. (Chart 16-1)
Choose all the words that are parallel with the given words.

1. *to watch*	hearing	to listen	saw	to decide	having thought
2. *beautiful*	friendly	nice	honest	happily	goodness
3. *texting*	contacted	to type	chatting	email	sending
4. *rapidly*	difficult	fast	good	slowly	wild

EXERCISE 3 ▸ Looking at grammar. (Chart 16-1)
Choose the correct completions.

My Roommate

1. My roommate, Kate, is friendly and _____.
   (a.) helpful   (b.) kind   c. kindness

2. Friendliness and _____ are admirable qualities in a roommate.
   a. kind   b. kindness   c. kindly

3. We are opposites. She likes to be busy and _____.
   a. actively   b. activity   c. active

4. I'm a quieter type. I prefer to stay home or _____ time with a few friends.
   a. spending   b. spend   c. to spending

5. Kate studies by listening to music and _____ at the same time.
   a. sing   b. singing   c. sings

6. I sit at the library and _____ in silence.
   a. work   b. working   c. worked

7. We get along well, though. We're both very neat and _____.
   a. tidy   b. tidily   c. have tidiness

8. We take turns cleaning our apartment and _____ the cooking.
   a. do   b. to do   c. doing

EXERCISE 4 ▸ Looking at grammar. (Chart 16-1)
Complete each sentence with <u>one</u> word that gives the same idea as the words in parentheses.

Road Rage

1. The driver ran a stop sign and _____*sped*_____ down the street.
   (*he was driving at a high speed*)

2. A pedestrian was shocked and _____ that she was almost hit in the crosswalk.
   (*her feelings were upset*)

3. A police officer stopped him, but the driver spoke impatiently and _____.
   (*his words were rude*)

4. He got out of his car and walked toward the officer. He was tall and _____.
   (*has a lot of strength*)

5. Another police officer arrived and _____ him into custody.
   (*she took*)

EXERCISE 5 ▸ Warm-up. (Chart 16-2)
Check (✓) the sentences that are correctly punctuated with commas.

1. _____ Oranges, and lemons are high in vitamin C. (*not correct*)
2. __✓__ Oranges and lemons are high in vitamin C.
3. _____ Oranges, lemons, and broccoli are high in vitamin C.
4. _____ Oranges, lemons and broccoli are high in vitamin C.
5. _____ Oranges lemons and broccoli are high in vitamin C.
6. _____ Oranges, lemons, and broccoli, are high in vitamin C.

16-2 Parallel Structure: Using Commas

(a) **Steve** and **Joe** are in class.	No commas are used when *and* connects **two** parts of a parallel structure, as in (a).
(b) *INCORRECT PUNCTUATION:* Steve, and Joe are in class.	
(c) **Steve, Joe** and **Rita** are in class.	When *and* connects **three or more** parts of a parallel structure, a comma is used between the first items in the series.
(d) **Steve, Joe,** and **Rita** are in class.	A comma may also be used before *and,* as in (d) and (f). The use of this comma is optional (i.e., the writer can choose).*
(e) **Steve, Joe, Rita, Jan** and **Kim** are in class.	
(f) **Steve, Joe, Rita, Jan,** and **Kim** are in class.	NOTE: A comma often represents a pause in speech.

*The purpose of punctuation is to make writing clear for readers. This chart and others in this chapter describe the usual use of commas in parallel structures. Sometimes commas are required according to convention (i.e., the expected use by educated language users). Sometimes use of commas is a stylistic choice made by the experienced writer.

EXERCISE 6 ▸ Looking at grammar. (Chart 16-2)
Add commas as necessary.

At a Hotel

1. The room includes a king-sized bed, a desk (*optional comma*), and a balcony.
2. The price of the room includes Wi-Fi buffet breakfast and use of the exercise room.
3. The price of the room includes Wi-Fi and buffet breakfast.
4. We got an adjoining room for our son his wife and their daughter.
5. Our son's wife and daughter met us at the rooftop pool.
6. My wife called room service asked about vegetarian options and ordered a meal.
7. We searched for an on-demand movie with action adventure and suspense.
8. We enjoy action and adventure films.
9. The front-desk clerk the bellhop the concierge and the housekeeping staff were very attentive and courteous.

EXERCISE 7 ▸ Looking at grammar. (Charts 16-1 and 16-2)
Parallel structure makes repeating the same words unnecessary. Cross out the words that are unnecessary. Combine the given sentences into one concise sentence. Use parallel structure.

Molly's Party

1. Molly will open the door. ~~Molly will~~ greet her guests.
   → *Molly will open the door **and** greet her guests.*
2. She is opening the door. She is greeting her guests.
3. She is taking their coats. She is hanging them up in the closet.
4. Molly is kind. Molly is generous. Molly is trustworthy.
5. Since she is hard of hearing, please try to speak loudly. Please try to speak clearly.
6. Her boyfriend has come to the party. He has come with flowers. He has come with candy. He has come with a ring.
7. He has knelt down in front of her. He has taken her hand. He has asked her to marry him.
8. Molly is calm enough to listen. Molly is calm enough to say yes.
9. They talked about getting married in June. Or they could get married in August.
10. Molly had expected a surprise. She did not expect a ring.
    → *Molly had expected a surprise **but** not a ring*
11. Molly was surprised. She was not shocked.
12. They had discussed getting married at some point. They had not discussed getting married this year.

EXERCISE 8 ▶ Looking at grammar. (Charts 16-1 and 16-2)
First, complete the unfinished sentence in each group. Second, combine the sentences into one concise sentence that contains parallel structure.

1. The mountain road was curvy.
   The mountain road was steep.

   The mountain road was _____*narrow*_____ .

   The mountain road was curvy, ___*steep, and narrow*___ .

2. I dislike living in a city because of the air pollution.
   I dislike living in a city because of the crime.

   I dislike living in a city because of _____ .

   I dislike living in a city because of the air pollution, _____

   _____ .

3. Hawaii has a warm climate.
   Hawaii has beautiful beaches.
   Hawaii has many interesting tropical trees.

   Hawaii has many interesting tropical _____ .

   Hawaii has a warm climate, beautiful beaches, _____

   _____ .

4. Mary Hart would make a good president because she works effectively with others.
   Mary Hart would make a good president because she has a reputation for integrity.
   Mary Hart would make a good president because she has a reputation for independent thinking.

   Mary Hart would make a good president because she _____ .

   Mary Hart would make a good president because she works effectively with others,

   _____ .

EXERCISE 9 ▶ Let's talk. (Charts 16-1 and 16-2)
Work with a partner. Take turns completing each sentence. Share some of your partner's answers with the class.

1. A good friend needs to be _____ and _____ .

2. English teachers should have these qualities: _____ ,

   _____ , and _____ .

3. _____ , _____ , and _____ are three

   easy ways for me to relax at the end of the day.

4. In my free time, I like to _____ , _____ , and

   _____ .

5. Three activities I don't enjoy are _____ , _____ , and

   _____ .

6. _____ , _____ , and _____ are difficult

   subjects for me.

EXERCISE 10 ▸ Warm-up. (Chart 16-3)

Check (✓) the three sentences with correct punctuation.

1. _____ Thunder clouds rolled by. Flashes of lightning lit the sky.
2. _____ Thunder clouds rolled by, flashes of lightning lit the sky.
3. _____ Thunder clouds rolled by, and flashes of lightning lit the sky.
4. _____ Thunder clouds rolled by. And flashes of lightning lit the sky.

16-3	Punctuation for Independent Clauses; Connecting Them with *And* and *But*	
(a)	It was raining hard. There was a strong wind.	Example (a) contains two *independent clauses* (i.e., two complete sentences).
(b)	*INCORRECT PUNCTUATION:* It was raining hard, there was a strong wind.	PUNCTUATION: A period,* NOT A COMMA, is used to separate two independent clauses.
(c)	It was raining hard; there was a strong wind.	A semicolon may be used in place of a period. Semicolons are used between two *closely related* ideas.
(d)	It was raining hard, *and* there was a strong wind.	***And*** and ***but*** (coordinating conjunctions) are often used to connect two independent clauses.
(e)	It was raining hard. *And* there was a strong wind.	PUNCTUATION: Usually a comma immediately precedes the conjunction, as in (d) and (g).
(f)	It was raining hard *and* there was a strong wind.	
(g)	It was late, *but* he didn't care.	In informal writing, a writer might choose to begin a sentence with a conjunction, as in (e) and (h).
(h)	It was late. *But* he didn't care.	In a very short sentence, a writer might choose to omit the comma in front of ***and***, as in (f). (Omitting the comma in front of ***but*** is rare.)

*In British English, a period is called a "full stop."

EXERCISE 11 ▸ Looking at grammar. (Chart 16-3)

Punctuate the sentences by adding commas and periods. Do not add any words. Capitalize as necessary.

Athletic Conditioning Class

1. Some members did push-ups some members lifted weights.
   → *Some members did push-ups. Some members lifted weights.*

2. Some members did push-ups and some members lifted weights.

3. The teacher demonstrated correct form a group of new members watched.

4. The teacher demonstrated correct form and a group of new members watched.

5. An assistant was available to help but only a few people needed him.

6. An assistant was available to help only a few people needed him.

EXERCISE 12 ▸ Looking at grammar. (Chart 16-3)

Check (✓) the correct sentences. Punctuate the incorrect ones. Do not add any words. Capitalize as necessary.

Email Excerpts

1. _____ I'd like to help, let me know what you need.

2. _____ I'll be happy to come. Thank you for inviting me.

3. _____ It's really hard to know what to do, we don't have much information yet.

4. _____ I'll pay you back. I get paid tomorrow.

5. _____ Let's wait to see what happens, we don't want to make a decision prematurely.

EXERCISE 13 ▸ Looking at grammar. (Chart 16-3)

Rewrite the email with correct punctuation. You may add **and** and **but**.

From: J.B. Leeds	
To: Majda	Today at 2:11 PM
Subject: Update/Thanks	

Dear Majda,

Thank you for offering to drive students to the track meet. We are still hoping we can get a bus, we will know later today. The first race starts at 4:00 the boys will be leaving school around 1:15 the girls can leave at 1:30 since their race is at 4:30. We always appreciate parent volunteers, thanks again for contacting me, I will be back in touch soon.

EXERCISE 14 ▸ Reading and grammar. (Charts 16-1 → 16-3)

Work with a partner. Find and correct the errors with parallel structure and punctuation.

Ziplining

Ziplining began as a way to get people across impassible places like canyons and crossing rivers. But in the 1980s, Costa Rica, with its emphasis on eco-tourism, turned it into a thrilling adventure. The opportunity to soar over spectacular scenery has made ziplining one of Costa Rica's top tourist attractions.

The concept is very simple, a cable is strung across a scenic area, for example, a lush forest or fast-moving river one end of the cable is higher than the other. A harness for the rider hangs from the cable, riders are strapped tightly into the harness. They climb to a platform, jump off, and flying through the air.

Ziplining's popularity has spread worldwide, the longest zipline is in Sun City, South Africa, where one cable is 1.2 miles (2 km) long. Average speeds are 75 miles (120 km) per hour! Not all zipline rides are as hair-raising, companies around the world strive to provide exciting and safety rides that will appeal to a variety of experience levels and age groups.

EXERCISE 15 ▸ Warm-up. (Chart 16-4)

What do you notice about the subject-verb agreement in each pair of sentences?

1. a. Either my brother or my sister is going to tutor me in science.
   b. Either my brother or my sisters are going to tutor me in science.

2. a. Neither my brother nor my sister is a teacher.
   b. Neither my brother nor my sisters are teachers.

3. a. Not only my brother but also my sister has a doctorate in science.
   b. Not only my brother but also my sisters have doctorates in science.

16-4	Paired Conjunctions: *Both ... And; Not Only ... But Also; Either ... Or; Neither ... Nor*
(a) ***Both*** my mother ***and*** my sister *are* here.	Two subjects connected by ***both ... and*** take a plural verb, as in (a).
(b) ***Not only*** my mother ***but also*** *my sister is* here. (c) ***Not only*** my sister ***but also*** *my parents are* here. (d) ***Neither*** my mother ***nor*** *my sister is* here. (e) ***Neither*** my sister ***nor*** *my parents are* here.	When two subjects are connected by ***not only ... but also***, ***either ... or***, or ***neither ... nor***, the subject that is closer to the verb determines whether the verb is singular or plural. ***Not only ... but also*** is used for emphasis or to indicate surprise. It should be used sparingly.
(f) The research project will take *both time and money*. (g) Sue saw *not only a fox in the woods but also a bear*. (h) I'll take *either chemistry or physics* next quarter. (i) That book is *neither interesting nor accurate*.	Notice the parallel structure in the examples. The same grammatical form should follow each part of the paired conjunctions.*
	In (f): ***both*** + noun + ***and*** + noun In (g): ***not only*** + noun + ***but also*** + noun In (h): ***either*** + noun + ***or*** + noun In (i): ***neither*** + adjective + ***nor*** + adjective NOTE: Paired conjunctions are usually used for emphasis; they draw attention to both parts of the parallel structure.

*Paired conjunctions are also called "correlative conjunctions."

EXERCISE 16 ▸ Looking at grammar. (Chart 16-4)

Complete the sentences with *is*/*are*.

1. Both the teacher and the student _____*are*_____ here.

2. Neither the teacher nor the student _____ here.

3. Not only the teacher but also the student _____ here.

4. Not only the teacher but also the students _____ here.

5. Either the students or the teacher _____ planning to come.

6. Either the teacher or the students _____ planning to come.

7. Both the students and the teachers _____ planning to come.

8. Both the students and the teacher _____ planning to come.

EXERCISE 17 ▶ Looking at grammar. (Chart 16-4)

In the News

Part I. Answer the questions with **both ... and**.

1. The homeless received food. Did they receive clothing?
   → *Yes. The homeless received both food and clothing.*

2. Passengers were injured in the bus accident. Was the driver injured in the accident?

3. I know the government is increasing taxes. Is the government increasing spending too?

4. The city suffers from air pollution. Does it suffer from water pollution?

Part II. Answer the questions with **not only ... but also**.

5. I know crime is growing in the cities. Is crime growing in the suburbs?
   → *Yes. Crime is growing not only in the cities but also in the suburbs.*

6. I know our team lost its first game. Did it also lose its second game?

7. I know some tech companies need more workers. Do they need more office space too?

8. I know the city is building a new freeway. Is it also building a new subway too?

EXERCISE 18 ▶ Looking at grammar. (Chart 16-4)

At Our Apartment Building

Part I. Answer the questions with **either ... or**.

1. The manager has my package, or Mrs. Ramirez has my package. Is that right?
   → *Yes. Either the manager or Mrs. Ramirez has your package.*

2. Jonas is going to take care of the neighbor's cat, or William is going to take care of the neighbor's cat. Is that right?

3. Your sister is driving Ms. Androv to the airport, or your brother is driving her. Right?

4. We can use the front stairs, or we can use the back stairs. Is that right?

Part II. Answer the questions with **neither ... nor**.

5. The mail carrier isn't friendly. Is she unfriendly?
   → *No. She is neither friendly nor unfriendly.*

6. Her children don't speak English. Does her husband speak English?

7. They don't have an air conditioner in their apartment. Do they have a fan?

8. The window washers weren't fast. Were they slow?

EXERCISE 19 ▶ Listening. (Chart 16-4)

Choose the sentence (a. or b.) that has the same meaning as the sentence you hear.

Example: You will hear: Sarah is working on both a degree in biology and a degree in chemistry.
You will choose: a. Sarah is working on only one degree.
ⓑ Sarah is working on two degrees.

1. a. Ben will call Mary and Bob.
   b. Ben will call one of them but not both.

2. a. My mother and my father talked to my teacher.
   b. Either my mother or my father talked to my teacher.

3. a. Simon saw both a whale and a dolphin.
   b. Simon didn't see a whale, but he did see a dolphin.

4. a. Our neighborhood had electricity but not water.
   b. Our neighborhood didn't have electricity or water.

5. a. We will have two teachers today.
   b. We will have one teacher today.

EXERCISE 20 ▸ Looking at grammar. (Chart 16-4)

Combine each pair of sentences into one new sentence with parallel structure. Use *both ... and; either ... or; neither ... nor*.

At the Mall

1. I do not have my credit card. I do not have cash.
   → *I have neither my credit card nor cash.*

2. You can get some shoes now, or you can look online more.
   → *You can either get some shoes now or look online more.*

3. Rika enjoys shopping during sales. Bettina enjoys shopping during sales.

   _____

4. Matt is not joining us. Taka is not joining us.

   _____

5. Matt is sick. Taka is sick.

   _____

6. This store doesn't have the size I need. That store doesn't have the size I need.

   _____

7. We can eat lunch here, or we can look for other restaurants.

   _____

8. The manager was helpful. The assistant manager was helpful.

   _____

9. You need your receipt for a return, or you need your credit card.

   _____

10. The stores close at 10:00. The food court closes at 10:00.

    _____

11. We can take the bus home, or we can take the subway.

    _____

EXERCISE 21 ▶ Grammar and listening. (Chapter 16 Review)
Choose the correct completions. Then listen to the passage and
check your answers.

Do you know these words?
- unreasoned
- tangle
- rabies
- pollinating
- overripe
- flourish
- train (a pet)

Bats

What do people in your country think of bats? Are they mean

and scary creatures, or are they symbols of both happiness and

(luck)/ lucky?
    1

In Western countries, many people have an unreasoned fear

of bats. According to scientist Dr. Sharon Horowitz, bats are

not only   harm / harmless   but also   benefit / beneficial
              2   3

mammals. "When I was a child, I believed that a bat would attack

me and   tangle / tangled   itself in my hair. Now I know better,"
              4

said Dr. Horowitz.

Contrary to popular Western myths, bats do not   attack / attacking
                                                     5

humans. Although a few bats may have diseases, they are not major

carriers of rabies or other frightening diseases. Bats help natural plant life by pollinating plants,

spreading seeds, and to   eat / eating   insects. If you get rid of bats that eat overripe fruit, then
                              6

fruit flies can flourish and   destroy / destruction   the fruit industry.
                                   7

According to Dr. Horowitz, bats are both gentle and   train / trainable   pets. Not many
                                                          8

people, however, own or train bats, and bats themselves prefer to avoid people.

EXERCISE 22 ▶ Reading, grammar, and speaking. (Chapter 16 Review)
Part I. Read the paragraph about Dr. Martin Luther King, Jr.

Martin Luther King, Jr., was the leader of the 1960s civil rights
movement in the United States that sought to end segregation and
racial discrimination against African-Americans. In 1964, Dr. King
became the youngest person to receive the Nobel Peace Prize.
He was assassinated in 1968, but his powerful and inspiring
words live on.

Part II. Underline the parallel structures that you find in these quotes from the speeches and
writings of Dr. Martin Luther King, Jr. Discuss the ideas. Work in pairs, in small groups, or as
a class.

1. "The hope of a secure and livable world lies with disciplined nonconformists who are dedicated
   to justice, peace, and brotherhood."

Coordinating Conjunctions   **367**

2. "The ultimate measure of a man is not where he stands in moments of comfort and convenience but where he stands at times of challenge and controversy."

3. "In the end, we will remember not the words of our enemies but the silence of our friends."

4. "Nonviolence is the answer to the crucial political and moral question of our time: the need for mankind to overcome oppression and violence without resorting to oppression and violence. Mankind must evolve for all human conflict a method which rejects revenge, aggression, and retaliation. The foundation of such a method is love."

EXERCISE 23 ▶ Check your knowledge. (Chapter 16 Review)
Correct the errors.

1. Slowly and being cautious, the firefighter climbed the burned staircase.

2. Janice entered the room and looked around she knew no one.

3. Derek made many promises but he had no intention of keeping any of them.

4. The pioneers hoped to clear away the forest and planting crops.

5. When Nadia moved, she had to rent an apartment, make new friends, and to find a job.

6. All plants need light, to have a suitable climate, and an ample supply of water and minerals from the soil.

7. Both the main earthquake and subsequent aftershocks was devastating to the town.

8. With their sharp eyesight, fine hearing, and they have a strong sense of smell, wolves hunt mainly at night.

9. Not only speed but also endurance determine a runner's success in a race.

10. The ancient Egyptians had good dentists archaeologists have found mummies that had gold fillings in their teeth.

EXERCISE 24 ▶ Writing. (Chapter 16)
Part I. Read the post from social media.

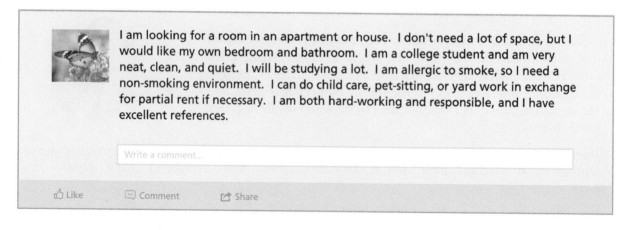

I am looking for a room in an apartment or house. I don't need a lot of space, but I would like my own bedroom and bathroom. I am a college student and am very neat, clean, and quiet. I will be studying a lot. I am allergic to smoke, so I need a non-smoking environment. I can do child care, pet-sitting, or yard work in exchange for partial rent if necessary. I am both hard-working and responsible, and I have excellent references.

Write a comment...

👍 Like   💬 Comment   ↪ Share

Part II. Following the example in Part I, write a social media post about something you are looking for: a place to rent, a car, a pet, etc.

WRITING TIP

When you are writing for social media, your sentences should be clear, uncomplicated, and to the point. Readers like to scroll quickly through posts. If they have to work too hard to follow what you are saying, they may move on to someone else's post.

Emphasize the positive if you are looking for something like a place to rent or a pet, for example. People want to be assured that they will have a good roommate or that they are giving a pet to someone who will take good care of it.

Part III. Edit your writing. Check for the following:

1. ☐ clear, uncomplicated sentences
2. ☐ a period, not a comma, between two complete sentences
3. ☐ parallel structure
4. ☐ correct subject-verb agreement with paired conjunctions, e.g., ***both ... and***
5. ☐ correct spelling (use a dictionary or spell-check)

CHAPTER 17

Adverb Clauses

EXERCISE 1 ▸ Warm-up. (Chart 17-1)
The words in blue are adverb clauses. What do you notice about their placement in the sentence and punctuation?

1. The fireworks display began after it got dark.
2. Because it was New Year's Eve, thousands of people came to watch.
3. Although it was very crowded, everyone had good views.
4. There is a show every year even if the weather is bad.

17-1 Introduction

Adverb clauses are used to show relationships between ideas. They show relationships of *time, cause and effect, contrast,* and *condition.*

adverb clause main clause (a) *When the phone rang,* the baby woke up. (b) The baby woke up *when the phone rang.*	In (a) and (b): ***when the phone rang*** is an adverb clause of time. Examples (a) and (b) have the same meaning. PUNCTUATION: When an adverb clause precedes a main clause, as in (a), a comma is used to separate the clauses. When the adverb clause follows, as in (b), usually no comma is used.
(c) *Because he was sleepy,* he went to bed. (d) He went to bed *because he was sleepy.*	In (c) and (d), ***because*** introduces an adverb clause that shows a cause-and-effect relationship.

(e) *INCORRECT:*
    When we were in New York. We saw several plays.
 	
(f) *INCORRECT:*
    He went to bed. Because he was sleepy.
	Adverb clauses are dependent clauses. They cannot stand alone as a sentence in written English. They must be connected to a main (or independent) clause.*

Summary list of words used to introduce adverb clauses**

TIME		CAUSE AND EFFECT	CONTRAST	CONDITION
after	by the time (that)	because	even though	if
before	once	now that	although	unless
when	as/so long as	since	though	only if
while	whenever			whether or not
as	every time (that)		DIRECT CONTRAST	even if
as soon as	the first time (that)		while	in case
since	the last time (that)			
until	the next time (that)			

*See Chart 12-1, p. 248, for the definition of dependent and independent clauses.
**Words that introduce adverb clauses are called "subordinating conjunctions."

EXERCISE 2 ▸ Looking at grammar. (Chart 17-1)
Check (✓) the sentences that are grammatically complete and contain the correct punctuation.

Annoyances

1. a. ___✓___ The door slammed.

    b. _____ When the door slammed.

    c. _____ I woke up. When the door slammed.

    d. _____ I woke up when the door slammed.

    e. _____ When the door slammed, I woke up.

    f. _____ The door slammed. I woke up.

2. a. _____ After I texted you, my phone died.

    b. _____ The last time I texted you, and you didn't answer.

    c. _____ Every time the phone rings, and no one is there.

    d. _____ Whenever the phone rings, no one is there.

    e. _____ As soon as we sit down to dinner, a telemarketer calls.

EXERCISE 3 ▸ Looking at grammar. (Chart 17-1)

Underline the adverb clauses. Add punctuation and capitalization as necessary. Do not add or delete any words.

A Snowstorm

1. <u>when Adolfo came to Chicago</u>, he planned to stay with his cousins. *(W above "when"; period added)*

2. Adolfo planned to stay with his cousins when he came to Chicago.

3. As soon as the plane landed a blizzard began.

4. A blizzard began as soon as the plane landed.

5. Once the plane landed a blizzard began.

6. Adolfo didn't go outside the airport until it stopped.

7. When it stopped Adolfo went outside.

8. When he went outside there weren't any taxis.

9. He was stranded at the airport until the roads were cleared.

10. As soon as the roads were cleared he left the airport.

EXERCISE 4 ▸ Looking at grammar. (Chapter 16 and Chart 17-1)

Work with a partner. Add punctuation and capitalization as necessary. Do not add or delete any words.

1. Paulo is a member of a championship basketball team he is a wheelchair athlete Paulo's legs are paralyzed when he plays he moves around the basketball court in a wheelchair he has competed in many tournaments, and his team often wins.

2. Fritz is a golden retriever he appears to be a typical dog except he has an important job he is a service dog he has been trained to help a blind person whenever his owner needs to go downtown Fritz assists him Fritz can help him cross streets get on buses go down stairs and avoid obstacles.

3. Sometimes when people speak to someone who is hard of hearing they shout shouting is not necessary it is important to face the person and speak clearly people who are hard of hearing can often read lips my father is hard of hearing, but he can understand me when I look at him and say each word clearly.

EXERCISE 5 ▸ Warm-up. (Chart 17-2)

Add the word(s) in parentheses to the correct place in each sentence. Add commas and capitalization as necessary.

1. Oscar can't catch the meaning *when* people speak English too fast. (*when*)

2. The teacher speaks too fast Oscar is going to ask her to slow down. (*the next time*)

3. Oscar is listening to English he tries not to translate from his language. (*while*)

4. His teacher encourages students to figure out the meaning they check their dictionaries. (*before*)

5. Oscar began studying English he has wanted to speak fluently. (*ever since*)

17-2 Using Adverb Clauses to Show Time Relationships

after *	(a) *After she graduates,* she will get a job. (b) *After she (had) graduated,* she got a job.	A present tense, NOT a future tense, is used in an adverb clause of time, as in (a) and (c). (See Chart 3-3, p. 60, for tense usage in future time clauses.)
before *	(c) I will leave *before he comes.* (d) I (had) left *before he came.*	
when	(e) *When I arrived,* he *was talking* on the phone. (f) *When I got there,* he *had* already *left.* (g) *When it began to rain,* I *stood* under a tree. (h) *When I was in Chicago,* I *visited* the museums. (i) *When I see him tomorrow,* I *will ask* him.	*when* = *at that time* Notice the different time relationships expressed by the tenses.
while as	(j) *While I was walking home,* it began to rain. (k) *As I was walking home,* it began to rain.	*while, as* = *during that time*
by the time	(l) *By the time he arrived,* we *had* already *left.* (m) *By the time he comes,* we *will have* already *left.*	*by the time* = *one event is completed before another event* Notice the use of the past perfect and future perfect in the main clause.
since	(n) I *haven't seen* him *since he left this morning.* (o) I've *known* her *ever since I was a child.*	*since* = *from that time to the present* In (o): *ever* adds emphasis. NOTE: The present perfect is used in the main clause.
until till	(p) We stayed there *until we finished our work.* (q) We stayed there *till we finished our work.*	*until, till* = *to that time and then no longer* (**Till** is used more in speaking than in writing; it is generally not used in formal English.)
as soon as once	(r) *As soon as it stops raining,* we will leave. (s) *Once it stops raining,* we will leave.	*as soon as, once* = *when one event happens, another event happens soon afterward*
as long as so long as	(t) I will never speak to him again *as long as I live.* (u) I will never speak to him again *so long as I live.*	*as long as, so long as* = *during all that time, from beginning to end*
whenever every time	(v) *Whenever I see her,* I say hello. (w) *Every time I see her,* I say hello.	*whenever* = *every time*
the first time the last time the next time	(x) *The first time (that) I went to New York,* I went to a Broadway show. (y) I saw two plays *the last time (that) I went to New York.* (z) *The next time (that) I go to New York,* I'm going to see a ballet.	Adverb clauses can be introduced by: the { first / second / third, etc. / last / next / etc. } time (that)

*After and before are commonly used in the following expressions:

shortly *after*	**shortly** *before*
a short time *after*	**a short time** *before*
a little while *after*	**a little while** *before*
not long *after*	**not long** *before*
soon *after*	

EXERCISE 6 ▶ Looking at grammar. (Charts 17-1 and 17-2)

Complete the sentences with your own words. Add brackets around the adverb clause in each sentence.

1. *Don't worry.*

   a. I will call you [before I _____*come over*_____.]

   b. I will go to bed after I _____ my homework.

   c. I did my chores before I _____ to my friend's house.

   d. By the time you get home, I _____ dinner for you.

2. *Dogs and spiders scare me.*

   a. Ever since I was a child, I _____ of dogs.

   b. One time a small dog bit me when I _____ it.

   c. Whenever I _____ spiders, I scream.

   d. A spider fell out of my shoe as I _____ this morning.

   e. By the time I stopped screaming, the spider _____.

3. *You need to protect your ID.*

   a. The last time I _____ overseas, I lost my passport. The next time I _____, I'm going to bring a photocopy of it.

   b. Whenever I _____ a password for a website, I make it very long.

   c. Ever since I _____ about identity theft, I have been very careful about sharing information online.

EXERCISE 7 ▶ Looking at grammar. (Charts 17-1 and 17-2)

Combine each pair of sentences with the words in parentheses. Add commas as necessary.

On a Flight

1. The baggage will be loaded soon. The plane will take off. (*as soon as*)
   → *As soon as the baggage is loaded, the plane will take off.*
2. The passengers got on the plane. The flight attendant closed the door. (*after*)
3. The passengers got on the plane. The flight attendant closed the door. (*before*)
4. Malea feels nervous. She flies. (*whenever*)
5. The plane was climbing. We hit turbulence. (*while*)
6. I was falling asleep. The pilot made an announcement. (*just as★*)
7. I fell asleep. He finished. (*as soon as*)
8. I stood up to walk to the restroom. The flight attendant told us to fasten our seat belts. (*just after*)
9. We had to stay in our seats. The pilot turned off the seat belt sign. (*until*)
10. We had lunch. The person next to me has been talking non-stop. (*since*)

★*Just* adds the idea of "immediately":
  just as = at that immediate or same moment
  just before = immediately before
  just after = immediately after

11. I fly. I will bring earplugs. (*the next time*)
12. I will text you. We land. (*as soon as*)
13. I get my bags. I will meet you in the passenger-loading zone. (*just as soon as*)
14. I flew this airline. My bags were lost. (*the first time*)
15. I will be happy to stretch my legs. We get off the plane. (*once*)
16. We land. We will have been on the plane for ten hours. (*by the time*)

EXERCISE 8 ▸ Looking at grammar. (Chart 17-2)
Choose the best completion for each sentence.

1. As soon as Martina saw the fire, she _____ the fire department.
   a. was telephoning   c. had telephoned
   (b.) telephoned   d. has telephoned

2. Before Jennifer won the lottery, she _____ any kind of contest.
   a. hasn't entered   c. wasn't entering
   b. doesn't enter   d. hadn't entered

3. Every time Prakash sees a movie made in India, he _____ homesick.
   a. will have felt   c. feels
   b. felt   d. is feeling

4. Since I left Venezuela six years ago, I _____ to visit friends and family several times.
   a. return   c. am returning
   b. will have returned   d. have returned

5. While he was washing his new car, Lawrence _____ some scratches on his front bumper.
   a. has discovered   c. is discovering
   b. was discovering   d. discovered

6. Yesterday while I was attending a sales meeting, Matthew _____ on the company's annual report.
   a. was working   c. has worked
   b. had been working   d. works

7. Tony _____ to have children until his little daughter was born. After she won his heart, he decided he wanted a big family.
   a. doesn't want   c. wasn't wanting
   b. hadn't wanted   d. hasn't wanted

8. After the horse threw her to the ground for the third time, Jennifer picked herself up and said, "I _____ on another horse as long as I live."
   a. never ride   c. will never ride
   b. have never ridden   d. do not ride

9. The next time Paul _____ to New York, he will visit the Metropolitan Museum of Art's famous collection of international musical instruments.
   a. will fly   c. has flown
   b. flies   d. will have flown

10. Ever since Maurice arrived, he _____ quietly in the corner. Is something wrong?
    a. sat   c. had been sitting
    b. has been sitting   d. will have sat

11. After Nela _____ for 20 minutes, she began to feel tired.
    a. jogging   c. has been jogging
    b. had been jogging   d. has jogged

12. Peter, _____ since you got home from football practice?
    a. have you eaten   c. are you eating
    b. will you eat   d. do you eat

13. The last time I _____ in Athens, the weather was hot and humid.
    a. had been   c. am
    b. was   d. will have been

14. By the time the young birds _____ the nest for good, they will have learned how to fly.
    a. will leave   c. are leaving
    b. will have left   d. leave

EXERCISE 9 ▶ Looking at grammar. (Charts 17-1 and 17-2)

Read the description of events. Make sentences using the words in the list.

Example: Just after
    → *Just after Judy parked her car, a thief broke into it.*

4:00   Judy parked her car at the mall and went to buy some jeans.
4:03   A thief broke into her car and stole her radio.
4:30   Judy returned to her car.
4:31   Judy called the police.
4:35   The police arrived.
4:35   Judy began crying in frustration.

1. Just after   3. When   5. By the time
2. Just as   4. While   6. As soon as

EXERCISE 10 ▶ Let's talk. (Charts 17-1 and 17-2)

Work in pairs or small groups. Complete the sentences. Each person should finish each sentence. Share a few things you learned about your classmates.

About Me

Example:
After I left class yesterday, ...
→ *After I left class yesterday, I met my cousin at a café.*

1. After I leave class today, ...
2. Before I go to bed tonight, ...
3. As soon as I get up tomorrow, ...
4. Whenever I feel nervous, ...
5. The first time I came to this class, ...
6. Ever since I was a child, ...
7. As long as I live, ...
8. Just as I was falling asleep last night, ...

EXERCISE 11 ▶ Reading, grammar, and writing. (Charts 17-1 and 17-2)

Part I. Read the passage and then complete the sentences.

Cultural Misunderstandings

Since Marco and Anya came to this country, they've had some memorable misunderstandings due to language and culture. The first time Marco met someone at a party, he was asked, "How's it going?" Marco thought that the person was asking him about leaving, and that seemed very strange.

Once, Anya walked into class, and a native speaker said, "Hi. How are you?" When Anya started to give a long answer, the speaker looked at her rather oddly. This happened several times until Anya learned she was just supposed to say something like "OK" or "Fine, thanks. And you?"

Another time, Marco was at a restaurant and wanted to get the server's attention. He snapped his fingers. The server was not pleased.

Since coming here, Marco and Anya have learned that cultural misunderstandings are a normal part of learning another language. They can be valuable and even entertaining learning experiences. Marco and Anya just smile at these misunderstandings now.

1. The first time Marco was asked, "How's it going?" _____

   _____

2. At first, every time someone asked Anya how she was, _____

   _____

3. The next time Marco wants to get the server's attention at a restaurant, _____

   _____

4. Since Marco and Anya have come to this country, _____

   _____

5. Whenever they have a cultural misunderstanding, _____

   _____

Part II. Write a paragraph about a cultural misunderstanding you have had or experienced.

EXERCISE 12 ▶ Warm-up. (Chart 17-3)
Which adverb clauses give the idea of "because"?

1. Now that I've finished art school, I can focus on finding work as an illustrator.
2. Since I was young, I have been artistic.
3. Since I've had formal training, maybe I can illustrate books.

17-3 Using Adverb Clauses to Show Cause and Effect

because	(a) **Because** he was sleepy, he went to bed. (b) He went to bed **because** he was sleepy.	An adverb clause may precede or follow the independent clause. Notice the punctuation in (a) and (b). Be sure to identify the correct cause and effect. INCORRECT: Because he went to bed, he was sleepy.
now that	(c) **Now that** I've finished the semester, I'm going to rest a few days and then take a trip. (d) Jack lost his job. **Now that** he's unemployed, he can't pay his bills.	**Now that** means "because now." In (c): **Now that I've finished the semester** means "because the semester is now over." NOTE: **Now that** is used with the present, present perfect, or future tenses.
since	(e) **Since** Monday is a holiday, we don't have to go to work. (f) **Since** you're a good cook and I'm not, you should cook the dinner.	When **since** is used to mean "because," it expresses a known cause; it means "because it is a fact that" or "given that it is true that." Cause-and-effect sentences with **since** say, "Given the fact that X is true, Y is the result." In (e): "Given the fact that Monday is a holiday, we don't have to go to work."
	(g) **Since** I came here, I have met many people.	NOTE: **Since** has two meanings. One is "because." It is also used in time clauses, as in (g). See Chart 17-2.

EXERCISE 13 ▸ Looking at grammar. (Chart 17-3)
Combine each pair of sentences with the words in parentheses. Add commas as necessary.

Travel

1. We have a lot of frequent-flier miles. We can visit several countries. (*now that*)
   → *Now that we have a lot of frequent-flier miles, we can visit several countries.*
2. We can compare hotel prices. They are posted online. (*since*)
3. We have read the online hotel reviews. We can choose our hotel. (*now that*)
4. There is little chance we will get lost. We have GPS on our phones. (*because*)
5. People post online reviews instantly. Customer service has improved. (*since*)
6. We won't get so homesick. We can video chat with our families. (*because*)

EXERCISE 14 ▸ Looking at grammar. (Chart 17-3)
Check (✓) the sentences that can be rewritten with **now that**, and then rewrite them.

My Grandmother

1. __✓__ Because my grandfather has died, my mom would like my grandmother to move in with us.
   Now that my grandfather has died, my mom would like my grandmother to move in with us.

2. _____ Because my grandmother lives alone, I visit her more often.

3. _____ Because my grandmother was a nurse, she took good care of her health.

4. _____ Because my grandparents saved for their retirement, she doesn't need to worry about finances.

5. _____ Because she is 90, I have asked her a few times if she should continue driving.

EXERCISE 15 ▶ Warm-up. (Chart 17-4)
Which sentence expresses an unexpected result?

1. Because I was very tired, I went to bed early.
2. Even though I was very tired, I stayed up late.

17-4 Expressing Contrast (Unexpected Result): Using *Even Though*

(a) *Because* the weather was cold, I *didn't go* swimming.	*Because* is used to express expected results.
(b) *Even though* the weather was cold, I *went* swimming.	*Even though* is used to express unexpected results.*
(c) *Because* I wasn't tired, I *didn't go* to bed.	NOTE: Like *because*, *even though* introduces an adverb clause.
(d) *Even though* I wasn't tired, I *went* to bed.	

**Although and *though* have basically the same meaning and use as *even though*. See Chart 19-7, p. 416, for information on the use of *although* and *though*.

EXERCISE 16 ▶ Looking at grammar. (Chart 17-4)
Choose the correct completion for each sentence.

1. Because it was a dark, cloudy day, _____ .
   a. I didn't put on my sunglasses   b. I put on my sunglasses

2. Even though it was a dark, cloudy day, _____ .
   a. I put on my sunglasses   b. I didn't put on my sunglasses

3. Even though Mira was cold, _____ .
   a. she wore a heavy coat outside   b. she wore a light sweater outside

4. Because Mira enjoys the outdoors, _____ .
   a. she goes for walks rain or shine   b. she doesn't go for walks in bad weather

EXERCISE 17 ▶ Looking at grammar. (Chart 17-4)
Complete the sentences with *even though* or *because*.

1. a. Tim's in good shape physically _____*even though*_____ he doesn't get much exercise.

   b. Barry's in good shape physically _____*because*_____ he gets a lot of exercise.

2. a. _____ Yoko has a job, she is able to pay her rent and feed her family.

   b. _____ Melissa has a job, she doesn't make enough money to support her four children.

3. a. Joe speaks Spanish well _____ he lived in Mexico for a year.

   b. Sherry didn't learn Spanish _____ she lived in Mexico for a year.

4. a. Jin jumped into the river to rescue a little girl who was drowning _____ he wasn't a good swimmer.

   b. _____ she was rescued right away, the girl survived.

5. a. _____ the flood washed away
   the bridge, the campers were able to cross the river
   _____ they had a boat.

   b. _____ the bridge was out
   of service for several months, people had to find
   alternate ways to get across the river.

EXERCISE 18 ▶ Let's talk. (Chart 17-4)

Work in pairs, in small groups, or as a class. Speaker A asks the question. Speaker B answers the question beginning with **Yes/No** and followed by **Even though**.

Small Talk

Examples:

SPEAKER A: It was raining. Did you go to the zoo anyway?
SPEAKER B: Yes. Even though it was raining, I went to the zoo.

SPEAKER A: You studied hard. Did you pass the test?
SPEAKER B: No. Even though I studied hard, I didn't pass the test.

1. You stayed up all night. Did you go to work?
2. Your sister has a new baby. Have you met her yet?
3. The food was terrible. Did you eat it anyway?
4. You didn't study. Did you pass the test anyway?
5. The weather is terrible today. Did you stay home?
6. You fell down the stairs. Did you get hurt?
7. You sent in an excellent college application. Did you get accepted?
8. You rehearsed your speech several times. Were you nervous?

(*Change roles if working in pairs.*)

9. You told the truth, but did anyone believe you?
10. You bought a brand-new air conditioner. Does it work?
11. You changed your password. Did your account still get hacked?
12. You have a new cat and dog. Do you have enough pets?
13. Your grandfather is 100 years old. Is he still young at heart?
14. You didn't understand the joke. Did you laugh anyway?
15. Your friends gave you a surprise birthday party. Were you surprised?
16. You backed up your computer files. Could you find all your documents?

EXERCISE 19 ▶ Warm-up. (Chart 17-5)

Check (✓) the sentences that show contrast (i.e., show that "X" is the opposite of "Y").

1. _____ I am a vegetarian, while my husband is a meat-eater.
2. _____ While I was buying vegetables, I remembered that we had leftovers in the fridge.
3. _____ While many vegetarians eat eggs, I don't because they come from chickens.

17-5 Showing Direct Contrast: *While*

(a) Mary is rich, *while John is poor*. (b) John is poor, *while Mary is rich*. (c) *While John is poor*, Mary is rich. (d) *While Mary is rich*, John is poor.	*While* is used to show direct contrast: "this" is exactly the opposite of "that."* Examples (a), (b), (c), and (d) all have the same meaning. Note the use of the comma in (a) and (b): In using *while* for direct contrast, a comma is often used even if the *while*-clause comes second (unlike the punctuation of most other adverb clauses).
COMPARE: (e) The phone rang *while I was studying*.	REMINDER: *While* is also used in time clauses and means "during that time," as in (e). See Chart 17-2.

*__Whereas__ can have the same meaning and use as *__while__*, but it occurs mostly in formal written English and occurs with considerably less frequency than *__while__*: *Mary is rich, __whereas__ John is poor.*

EXERCISE 20 ▶ Looking at grammar. (Chart 17-5)
Choose the best completion for each sentence.

1. Some people are tall, while others are _____.
   a. intelligent   c. short
   b. thin   d. large

2. A box is square, while _____.
   a. a rectangle has four sides   c. we use envelopes for letters
   b. my village has a town square in the center   d. a circle is round

3. While some parts of the world get an abundance of rain, others _____.
   a. are warm and humid   c. get little or none
   b. are cold and wet   d. get a lot

4. In some nations the favorite beverage is coffee, while _____.
   a. I like tea   c. in others it is tea
   b. it has caffeine   d. they drink tea

5. Some people like cream and sugar in their coffee, while _____.
   a. others like it black   c. milk is good in coffee too
   b. others drink hot coffee   d. sugar can cause cavities

6. Steve is an interesting storyteller and conversationalist, while his brother _____.
   a. is a newspaper reporter   c. has four children
   b. bores other people by talking about himself all the time   d. knows a lot of stories too

EXERCISE 21 ▶ Let's talk. (Chart 17-5)
Work in pairs or small groups. Contrast each pair of words using *while*. You may need to research the words. Share some of your answers with the class.

Example: alligators/crocodiles
    → *Alligators are found in the U.S. and China, while crocodiles are found worldwide.*
    → *A crocodile has a V-shaped snout, while an alligator has a rounded snout.*
    → *Alligators can live in freshwater, while crocodiles prefer salt water.*

1. a college/a university
2. an island/a peninsula
3. tap water/filtered water
4. an immigrant/a refugee
5. the word *affect*/the word *effect*
6. a passport/a visa

Check (✓) the sentence with **if** that is grammatically correct.

1. _____ If I will need help, I will ask you.
2. _____ If I need help, I will ask you.
3. _____ If I will need help, I ask you.

17-6 Expressing Conditions in Adverb Clauses: *If*-Clauses

(a) **If it *rains* tomorrow, I *will take*** my umbrella.	*If*-clauses (also called "adverb clauses of condition") present possible conditions. The main clause expresses RESULTS.
	In (a): POSSIBLE CONDITION = *it may rain tomorrow* RESULT = *I will take my umbrella*
	A present tense, not a future tense, is used in an *if*-clause even though the verb in the *if*-clause may refer to a future event or situation, as in (a).*

Words that introduce adverb clauses of condition (*if-clauses*)		
if	even if	unless
whether or not	in case	only if

*See Chapter 20 for uses of other verb forms in sentences with *if*-clauses.

EXERCISE 23 ▸ Looking at grammar. (Chart 17-6)
Make sentences with **if** using the given conditions.

Example: It may be cold tomorrow. → *If it's cold tomorrow, I'm going to stay home.*
→ *We can't go on a picnic if it's cold tomorrow.*

1. I will stay up all night.
2. I may be sick tomorrow.
3. Maybe I will wake up tomorrow and speak English fluently.
4. The power may be out for 24 hours.
5. The government might put a 20% tax on snack food.

EXERCISE 24 ▸ Reading and grammar. (Charts 17-1 → 17-6)
Underline the adverb clauses in the student handbook passage. Correct the errors in punctuation.

Forms of Address
Colleges and Universities

It's your first day of class, and you're not sure what to call your teacher. Is the first name acceptable or too informal? If you use a title, should it be *Dr.* or *Professor*?

At the college level, many teachers actually prefer to use first names, because it feels friendlier and less formal. They prefer not to have the psychological distance that a title creates.

While many teachers prefer first names some would rather use titles. *Dr.* is for someone with a Ph.D. degree. It is important to know that not all instructors have Ph.D.'s. In that case, *Professor* is more appropriate, as long as the teacher has the following job title: *Professor, Associate Professor,* or *Assistant Professor.* Note that the last name, not first name, is used with *Dr.* and *Professor.*

Even though many graduate students teach college courses. They are not professors. One option for addressing them is *Ms.* or *Mr.* + last name. But most prefer first names, since they are still technically students.

You can always ask your teacher: "What would you like to be called?" or "How would you like to be addressed?" Teachers like to have contact with students, and knowing your teacher's preference may make it easier for you to approach him or her.

EXERCISE 25 ▸ Warm-up. (Chart 17-7)

Check (✓) the sentences that logically follow the question and are grammatically correct.

Do you have your cell phone with you?

1. _____ If you do, could I use it?
2. _____ If so, could I use it?
3. _____ If not, I can use someone else's.
4. _____ If you don't, I can use someone else's.
5. _____ If you are, could I use it?

17-7	Shortened *If*-Clauses
(a) Are you a student? 　　*If so / If you are,* the ticket is half-price. 　　*If not / If you aren't,* the ticket is full price. (b) It's a popular concert. Do you have a ticket? 　　*If so / If you do,* you're lucky. 　　*If not / If you don't,* you're out of luck.	When an *if*-clause refers to the idea in the sentence immediately before it, it is sometimes shortened. In (a): **If so / If you are** = If you are a student 　　　　**If not / If you aren't** = If you aren't a student In (b): **If so / If you do** = If you have a ticket 　　　　**If not / If you don't** = If you don't have a ticket

EXERCISE 26 ▸ Looking at grammar. (Chart 17-7)

First, complete the sentences in two ways:
   a. Use **so** or **not**.
   b. Use a helping verb or main verb **be**.
Second, give the full meaning of the shortened *if*-clause.

1. Does Lisa want to go out to dinner with us?

   a. If _____*so*_____, tell her to meet us at 8:00.

   b. If she _____*does*_____, tell her to meet us at 8:00.

   → *Meaning: if Lisa wants to go out to dinner with us*

2. Are you free this weekend?

   a. If _____, do you want to go to a movie?

   b. If you _____, do you want to go to a movie?

3. Do you have a ride to the theater?

   a. If _____, would you like to ride with us?

   b. If you _____, would you like to ride with us?

4. Are you coming to the meeting?

   a. If _____, I'll see you there.

   b. If you _____, I'll see you there.

5. Did you use a spell-check on your email to me?

   a. If _____, it didn't catch all the spelling errors.

   b. If you _____, it didn't catch all the spelling errors.

6. We need some rice. Can you stop at the store on your way home today?

    a. If _____, I'll do it.

    b. If you _____, I'll do it.

EXERCISE 27 ▸ Warm-up. (Chart 17-8)
Check (✓) all the sentences that are true for David.

SITUATION: If David gets married, he will be happy. If he doesn't get married, he will be happy.

1. _____ David will be happy if he doesn't get married.
2. _____ If he gets married, David won't be happy.
3. _____ Even if David gets married, he won't be happy.
4. _____ Even if David doesn't get married, he will be happy.
5. _____ David will be happy whether or not he gets married.
6. _____ Whether or not David gets married, he will be happy.

17-8	Adverb Clauses of Condition: Using *Whether Or Not* and *Even If*
Whether or not	
(a) I'm going to go swimming tomorrow *whether or not it is cold.* OR *whether it is cold or not.*	***Whether or not*** expresses the idea that neither this condition nor that condition matters; the result will be the same. In (a): "If it is cold, I'm going swimming. If it is not cold, I'm going swimming. I don't care about the temperature. It doesn't matter."
Even if	
(b) I have decided to go swimming tomorrow. *Even if the weather is cold,* I'm going to go swimming.	Sentences with ***even if*** are close in meaning to those with ***whether or not.*** ***Even if*** gives the idea that a particular condition does not matter. The result will not change.

EXERCISE 28 ▸ Looking at grammar. (Chart 17-8)
Choose the sentence (a. or b.) that has the same meaning as the given sentence.

1. Even if I get an invitation to the reception, I'm not going to go.
   a. I won't go to the reception without an invitation.
   ⓑ I don't care if I get an invitation. I'm not going.

2. Even if the weather improves, I won't go to the beach.
   a. I'm going to the beach if the weather improves.
   b. I don't care if the weather improves. I'm not going to the beach.

3. Whether or not you want help, I plan to be at your house at 9:00.
   a. I'm going to help you because I think you need help.
   b. I'm going to help you because you want me to.

4. I won't tell even if someone pays me.

   a. I won't tell whether or not someone gives me money.

   b. If someone pays me enough money, I will tell.

5. I have to go to work tomorrow whether I feel better or not.

   a. Whether I go to work or not depends on how I feel.

   b. I'm going to work tomorrow no matter how I feel.

6. Even if John apologizes, I won't forgive him!

   a. John needs to apologize for me to forgive him.

   b. I don't care if John apologizes. It doesn't matter.

EXERCISE 29 ▶ Looking at grammar. (Chart 17-8)

Use the given information to complete sentences a. and b.

SITUATION 1: Usually people need to graduate from school to get a good job. But it's different for Ed. Maybe Ed will graduate from school, and maybe he won't. It doesn't matter because he has a good job waiting for him in his father's business.

   a. Ed will get a good job whether or not …
   → *Ed will get a good job whether or not he graduates.*

   b. Ed will get a good job even if …
   → *Ed will get a good job even if he doesn't graduate.*

SITUATION 2: Cindy's uncle tells a lot of jokes. Sometimes they're funny, and sometimes they're not. It doesn't matter.

   a. Cindy laughs at the jokes whether … or not.

   b. Cindy laughs at the jokes even if …

SITUATION 3: Maybe you are finished with the exam, and maybe you're not. It doesn't matter. The time is up.

   a. You have to hand in your examination paper whether … or not.

   b. You have to hand in your examination paper even if …

SITUATION 4: Max's family doesn't have enough money to send him to college. He would like to get a scholarship, but it doesn't matter because he's saved some money to go to school and has a part-time job.

   a. Max can go to school whether or not …

   b. Max can go to school even if …

SITUATION 5: Sometimes the weather is hot, and sometimes the weather is cold. It doesn't matter. My grandfather always wears his gray sweater.

   a. My grandfather wears his gray sweater whether or not …

   b. My grandfather always wears his gray sweater even if …

SITUATION 6: Your approval doesn't matter to me.

   a. I'm going to marry Harry whether … or not.

   b. I'm going to marry Harry even if …

SITUATION 7: It might snow, or it might not. We don't want to go camping in the snow, but it doesn't matter.

   a. We're going to go camping in the mountains whether … or not.

   b. We're going to go camping in the mountains even if …

EXERCISE 30 ▸ Warm-up. (Chart 17-9)

Choose the sentence (a. or b.) that has the same meaning as the given sentence.

If by chance you have a problem, you can reach me at this number.

    a. In case you have a problem, you can reach me at this number.
    b. When you have a problem, you can reach me at this number.

17-9	Adverb Clauses of Condition: Using *In Case*	
(a)	I'll be at my uncle's house *in case* you *(should) need to reach me.*	*In case* expresses the idea that something probably won't happen, but it might. *In case* means "if by chance this should happen." NOTE: Using *should* in an adverb clause emphasizes the speaker's uncertainty that something will happen.

EXERCISE 31 ▸ Looking at grammar. (Chart 17-9)

Combine each pair of sentences. Begin your new sentence with *In case*.

I'm just letting you know …

1. You probably won't need to get in touch with me, but maybe you will. If so, I'll give you my cell number.
    → *In case you (should) need to get in touch with me, I'll give you my cell number.*
2. You probably won't need to see me, but maybe you will. If so, I'll be in my office tomorrow morning around ten.
3. I don't think you need any more information, but maybe you do. If so, you can call me.
4. You probably don't have any more questions, but maybe you do. If so, ask Dr. Smith.
5. The dentist probably won't call, but maybe she will. If so, come get me. I'll be outside.
6. I hope you're happy with your present, but maybe it won't work. If not, you can return it to the store and get something else.

EXERCISE 32 ▸ Looking at grammar. (Charts 17-7 → 17-9)

Complete the sentences with your own words. Work in pairs, in small groups, or as a class.

Bad Weather

1. Our boss doesn't accept bad weather as an excuse for missing work. We have to go to work even if …
2. The weather is getting worse. I may not be able to make it home tonight. If not, …
3. The trains might not be running. I'd better … in case …
4. I may stay in town tonight. If so, …
5. I packed a change of clothes today in case …

EXERCISE 33 ▸ Warm-up. (Chart 17-10)

Choose the logical completion for each sentence.

1. I'll be at the meeting on time if there   is / isn't   a lot of traffic.
2. I'll be at the meeting on time unless there   is / isn't   a lot of traffic.
3. My manager won't be coming unless she feels   better / worse.
4. My manager won't be coming if she feels   better / worse.

17-10 Adverb Clauses of Condition: Using *Unless*

(a) I'll go swimming tomorrow *unless it's cold*. (b) I'll go swimming tomorrow *if it isn't cold*.	*unless* = *if* ... *not* In (a): *unless it's cold* means "if it isn't cold." Examples (a) and (b) have the same meaning.

EXERCISE 34 ▸ Looking at grammar. (Chart 17-10)
Restate each sentence with **unless**.

FYI (For Your Information)

1. If you don't buy your ticket today, you won't get one.
   → *Unless you buy your ticket today, you won't get one.*
2. You can't travel to that country if you don't have a visa.
3. If you don't sign up for the test by Monday, you can't take it next month.
4. It's difficult to return a product to that store if you don't have a receipt.
5. You can't get a motorcycle license if you haven't passed a special training course.
6. The store won't accept your credit card if you don't have ID with you.
7. Traffic fines increase if you don't pay them right away.

EXERCISE 35 ▸ Looking at grammar. (Chart 17-10)
Complete the sentences with your own words. Work in pairs, in small groups, or as a class.

Sorry, but ...

1. You can't speak to the manager unless ...
   → *You can't speak to the manager unless you have an appointment.*
2. You can't pay with a check unless ...
3. Some students won't be able to pass unless ...
4. ... unless you save more money.
5. Unless you spend more time with your kids, ...
6. Some stores will close permanently unless ...
7. ... unless I get a raise in salary.
8. I'm going to ... unless ...
9. Unless you ...
10. Interest and penalties on your bill will continue to increase unless ...
11. Unless ... , I won't ...

EXERCISE 36 ▸ Warm-up. (Chart 17-11)
Answer the questions about Scott.

SITUATION: Scott closes his bedroom window at night only if it's raining hard.

1. Does Scott close his bedroom window if the temperature is below freezing?
2. Does Scott close his bedroom window if it's windy outside?
3. Does Scott close his bedroom window if there's a light rain?
4. Does Scott close his bedroom window if there is a heavy rain?

17-11 Adverb Clauses of Condition: Using *Only If*

(a) The picnic will be canceled *only if it rains*. If it's windy, we'll go on the picnic. If it's cold, we'll go on the picnic. If it's damp and foggy, we'll go on the picnic. If it's unbearably hot, we'll go on the picnic.	*Only if* expresses the idea that there is only one condition that will cause a particular result.
(b) *Only if* it rains *will the picnic be canceled*.	When **only if** begins a sentence, the subject and verb of the main clause are inverted, as in (b).* This is a less common usage. No commas are used.

*Other subordinating conjunctions and prepositional phrases preceded by **only** at the beginning of a sentence require subject-verb inversion in the main clause:
> **Only when** the teacher dismisses us **can we stand** and **leave** the room.
> **Only after** the phone rang **did I realize** that I had fallen asleep in my chair.
> **Only in** my hometown **do I feel** at ease.

EXERCISE 37 ▸ Looking at grammar. (Chart 17-11)
Check (✓) the sentences that are true for the situation.

SITUATION: You can take Saturday off only if you work Thursday.

1. _____ You must work Thursday if you want Saturday off.

2. _____ You can take Saturday off if you work another day of your choice.

3. _____ If you work Thursday, you don't have to work Saturday.

4. _____ You can work Thursday, but it's not a requirement if you want Saturday off.

EXERCISE 38 ▸ Looking at grammar. (Chart 17-11)
Read the situations and complete the sentences. Work in pairs, in small groups, or as a class.

SITUATION 1: John must take an additional science class in order to graduate. That is the only condition under which he can graduate. If he doesn't take an additional science class, he can't graduate.

> He can graduate only if …
> → *He can graduate only if he takes an additional science class.*

SITUATION 2: You have to have an invitation in order to go to the party. That is the only condition under which you will be admitted. If you don't have an invitation, you can't go.

> You can go to the party only if …

SITUATION 3: You have to have a student visa in order to study here. Unless you have a student visa, you can't go to school here.

> You can attend this school only if …

SITUATION 4: Jimmy's mother doesn't want him to chew gum, but sometimes he chews it anyway.

> Jimmy … only if he's sure his mother won't find out.

SITUATION 5: If you want to go to the movie, we'll go. If you don't want to go, we won't go.

> We … only if you want to.

SITUATION 6: The temperature has to reach 32°F / 0°C before water will freeze.

> Water will freeze only if …

SITUATION 7: You must study hard. Then you will pass the exam.

> Only if you study hard …

SITUATION 8: You have to have a ticket. Then you can get into the soccer stadium.

Only if you have a ticket …

SITUATION 9: His parents make Joseph finish his homework before he can have screen time.

Only if Joseph finishes his homework …

SITUATION 10: I have to get a job. Then I will have enough money to go to school.

Only if I get a job …

EXERCISE 39 ▶ Looking at grammar. (Charts 17-10 and 17-11)

Make sentences with the same meaning as the given sentences. Use ***only if*** and ***unless***.

An Illness

1. If you don't stay in bed and rest, you won't recover quickly from the virus.
    → *You will recover quickly from the virus only if you stay in bed and rest.*
    → *You won't recover quickly from the virus unless you stay in bed and rest.*
2. If you don't see the doctor in person, she won't give you a prescription.
3. If you don't have a fever, you can go back to work.
4. If you don't need my help right now, I will leave for a few hours.
5. If you don't have a doctor's note, you can't take sick time.
6. If you don't call the pharmacy now, your prescription won't be ready on time.
7. If you don't take your medicine, you won't get well quickly.

EXERCISE 40 ▶ Looking at grammar. (Charts 17-6 → 17-11)

Combine these two sentences using the words in the list.

It may or may not rain. The party will be held indoors/outdoors.

Example: If
    → *If it rains, the party will be held indoors.*
    → *If it doesn't rain, the party will be held outdoors.*

1. Even if
2. Whether or not
3. In case
4. Unless
5. Only if

EXERCISE 41 ▸ Check your knowledge. (Chapter 17 Review)

Correct the errors.

1. Once we will pay our bills, we'll have little money left over for the holidays.

2. In the case there is an emergency, call the number on this paper.

3. While my parents live nearby, my siblings don't.

4. Unless you have a doctor's note, you can take sick time from work.

5. If tenants will have any questions about the apartment, they need to contact the manager.

6. Only if you help me I will clean the apartment.

7. When Yusef finished medical school at the age of 21.

8. The last time we were at the theater on a holiday weekend.

9. Even I get a promotion to manager, I won't relocate to another city.

10. I care about you if or not you believe me.

EXERCISE 42 ▸ Reading, grammar, and writing. (Chapter 17)

Part I. <u>Underline</u> the words that introduce adverb clauses. What tense is used in these clauses?

How Do People Learn Best?

How do people learn best? There is not one answer since much depends on individual learning styles and needs. Over 300 years ago, however, the noted inventor Benjamin Franklin made some observations regarding learning that still hold true for a great many learners today: "Tell me and I forget. Teach me and I remember. Involve me and I learn."

Imagine that you are learning how to fold a paper airplane. Before you ever pick up a piece of paper, the person says the following:

- Take a piece of paper.
- Fold it in half.
- Open the paper.
- Look at the crease in the middle.
- Now take one corner and fold it down along the crease.

All of the information is presented verbally. How well are you going to learn how to fold a paper airplane so long as the instructor continues in this manner?

Now imagine that your instructor is standing before you with paper and gives the directions while she folds the paper herself. Will this help you more?

Finally, imagine that both you and your instructor have paper. Every time she gives you instructions, both you and she fold your own papers.

Of the three methods, which one will be the most effective in helping you learn how to fold a paper airplane?

It's interesting to think about Benjamin Franklin's quote in relation to learning English. How do you learn English best? Is "being told" effective for you? What about "being taught"? How about "being involved"?

Part II. Think about your experiences learning English vocabulary and complete the sentences with your own words. Punctuate carefully.

1. I remember new words best when _____

2. I often forget the meanings of new words unless _____

3. Even if I _____
_____

4. I _____ only if _____

5. If students want to increase their vocabulary, _____
_____

6. If teachers want to help their class learn new vocabulary, they _____
_____

7. Although _____
_____

8. When I am involved in my learning, I feel _____
_____

Part III. Write one or more paragraphs about how you learn best. Use the questions in the reading and your statements in Part II to help you develop your ideas. You can also include what does not work for you. Organize the points you want to make and support them with examples.

WRITING TIP

Remember that adverb clauses do not always need to come at the beginning of a sentence. In fact, it can become boring if the writer always puts them in the same place. Try to vary your writing by changing the position of the adverb clauses, putting some at the beginning and some later in your sentences.

Part IV. Edit your writing. Check for the following:

1. ☐ a comma at the end of an adverb clause when it begins a sentence
2. ☐ a period, not a comma, between two complete sentences
3. ☐ correct meaning of adverb clauses
4. ☐ the use of *even though* or *even if* instead of *even*
5. ☐ when *only if* begins a sentence, inversion of the subject and verb in the main clause
6. ☐ placement of adverb clauses: not all at the beginning of sentences
7. ☐ correct spelling (use a dictionary or spell-check)

CHAPTER 18

Reduction of Adverb Clauses to Modifying Adverbial Phrases

PRETEST: What do I already know?

Write "C" if a sentence has the correct sentence structure and "I" for incorrect. Check your answers below. After you complete each chart listed, make any necessary corrections.

1. _____ While checking text messages at the bus stop, Janice dropped her phone in a mud puddle. (18-1)

2. _____ Before accepting the job, the company offered Joseph additional vacation days. (18-1)

3. _____ After having completed two years of medical training, Marisa was ready to begin life as a paramedic. (18-2)

4. _____ Since came to this country, I have experienced some interesting cultural traditions. (18-2)

5. _____ Sitting outdoors in the sun, Jenn realized she had forgotten to put on sunscreen. (18-3)

6. _____ While hotel guests were checking in, they were told about holiday specials. (18-3)

7. _____ Not have spent much time with her grandparents when she was younger, Lauren was happy about their summer visit. (18-4)

8. _____ Needed the package by the weekend, Barry paid for express delivery. (18-4)

9. _____ Upon hearing about the promotion of her assistant, Nela sat down at her desk in surprise. (18-5)

10. _____ On learning about genetics and eye color, Sofia began looking more closely at the eye color of her friends and their parents. (18-5)

Incorrect sentences: 2, 4, 7, 8

EXERCISE 1 ▸ Warm-up. (Charts 18-1 and 18-2)
Check (✓) the sentences that are grammatically correct.

1. _____ While riding the elevator, Zac heard a strange noise.

2. _____ While Zac was riding the elevator, it suddenly stopped.

3. _____ While riding the elevator, it suddenly stopped.

4. _____ While ride the elevator, it suddenly stopped.

18-1 Introduction

(a) Adverb clause:	*While I was walking to class,* I ran into an old friend.	In Chapter 13, we discussed changing adjective clauses to modifying phrases. (See Chart 13-11, p. 295.) Some adverb clauses may also be changed to modifying phrases, and the ways in which the changes are made are the same: • If there is a *be* form of the verb, omit the subject of the dependent clause and *be* verb, as in (b). OR • If there is no *be* form of a verb, omit the subject and change the verb to *-ing*, as in (d).
(b) Modifying phrase:	*While walking to class,* I ran into an old friend.	
(c) Adverb clause:	*Before I left for work,* I ate breakfast.	
(d) Modifying phrase:	*Before leaving for work,* I ate breakfast.	
(e) Change possible:	*While I was sitting in class, I* fell asleep. *While sitting in class, I* fell asleep.	An adverb clause can be changed to a modifying phrase **only when the subject of the adverb clause and the subject of the main clause are the same**.
(f) Change possible:	*While Ann was sitting in class, she* fell asleep. (clause) *While sitting in class, Ann* fell asleep.	A *modifying adverbial phrase* that is the reduction of an adverb clause *modifies the subject* of the main clause.
(g) No change possible:	*While the teacher was lecturing to the class, I* fell asleep.*	No reduction (i.e., change) is possible if the subjects of the adverb clause and the main clause are different, as in (g).
(h) INCORRECT:	~~While watching TV last night,~~ the phone rang.	In (h): *While watching* is called a "dangling modifier" or a "dangling participle," i.e., a modifier that is incorrectly "hanging alone" without an appropriate noun or pronoun subject to modify.

*While lecturing to the class, **I** fell asleep* means "While **I** was lecturing to the class, **I** fell asleep."

EXERCISE 2 ▶ Looking at grammar. (Chart 18-1)
Choose the correct sentence in each pair.

1. a. While sitting at my computer, the fire alarm went off.
   b. While sitting at my computer, I heard the fire alarm go off.

2. a. While standing on the top floor of the building, the crowd below looked like ants.
   b. While standing on the top floor of the building and looking down, Patrick suddenly felt dizzy.

3. a. Before getting up, Mary likes to lie in her warm bed and plan her day.
   b. Before getting up, Mary's alarm clock went off three times by accident.

4. a. While working on his new novel, William found himself telling the story of his childhood.
   b. After finishing his novel, many of William's childhood friends contacted him.

5. a. After standing in line for hours to buy tickets, the manager told us the concert was sold out.
   b. After standing in line for hours to buy tickets, we were told the concert was sold out.

6. a. Before turning in your essay, it is important to check the grammar and spelling.
   b. Before you turn in your essay, it is important to check the grammar and spelling.

18-2 Changing Time Clauses to Modifying Adverbial Phrases

(a) Clause: *Since Maria came* to this country, she has made many friends.	Adverb clauses beginning with **after**, **before**, **when**,* **while**, and **since** can be changed to modifying adverbial phrases.
(b) Phrase: *Since coming* to this country, Maria has made many friends.	
(c) Clause: *When Tyrell cooks*, he uses a lot of spices.	
(d) Phrase: *When cooking*, Tyrell uses a lot of spices.	
(e) Clause: *After he (had) finished* his homework, Peter went to bed.	In (e): There is no difference in meaning between *After he finished* and *After he had finished*. (See Chart 2-8, p. 44.)
(f) Phrase: *After finishing* his homework, Peter went to bed.	In (f) and (g): There is no difference in meaning between *After finishing* and *After having finished*.
(g) Phrase: *After having finished* his homework, Peter went to bed.	
(h) Phrase: Peter went to bed *after finishing* his homework.	The modifying adverbial phrase may follow the main clause, as in (h).

When can also mean "upon." If it has this meaning, it cannot be reduced to a phrase. See Chart 18-5.

EXERCISE 3 ▶ Looking at grammar. (Charts 18-1 and 18-2)
<u>Underline</u> the subject of the adverb clause and the subject of the main clause in each sentence. Change the adverb clauses to modifying adverbial phrases if possible.

1. a. While <u>Joe</u> was driving to school yesterday, <u>he</u> had an accident.
   → *While driving to school yesterday, Joe had an accident.*
   b. While <u>Joe</u> was talking to his insurance company, <u>the police</u> arrived. (*no change*)

2. a. Before I came to class, I stopped in a café for a cup of coffee.
   b. Before the students came to class, they met at a café for lunch.

3. a. Since Alberto moved here, he has been taking business classes.
   b. Since Alberto opened his new business, his family hasn't seen much of him.

4. a. Omar's wife drove Omar to his downtown office after he (had) finished breakfast.
   b. Omar walked up ten flights of stairs to his office after he (had) entered the building.

5. a. When the waiter took my order, I forgot to order a beverage.
   b. When I order coffee, I always ask for extra cream and sugar.

6. a. You should always read a contract carefully before you sign your name.
   b. Before I signed my name, I had a lawyer look over the contract.

7. a. After Karl had been climbing for several hours, his muscles began to ache.
   b. After Karl slipped and lost his footing, he held onto the ledge with all his strength.

EXERCISE 4 ▸ Let's talk: interview. (Chart 18-2)

Ask two classmates each question. Ask them to answer in complete sentences. Share some of their answers with the class.

What do you do ...

1. before going to bed?
2. after waking up?
3. after arriving at school?
4. while sitting in class?
5. before leaving school for the day?
6. while preparing for a difficult exam?

EXERCISE 5 ▸ Warm-up. (Charts 18-3 and 18-4)

Read the sentences and answer the questions.

1. Hiking through the woods yesterday, Alan saw a bear.
   QUESTION: Who was hiking through the woods?

2. Walking through the woods, a bear spotted Alan.
   QUESTION: Who was walking through the woods?

18-3 Expressing the Idea of "During the Same Time" in Modifying Adverbial Phrases

(a) *While I was walking* down the street, *I* ran into an old friend.	Sometimes **while** is omitted, but the **-ing** phrase at the beginning of the sentence gives the same meaning (i.e., "during the same time").
(b) *While walking* down the street, *I* ran into an old friend.	Examples (a), (b), and (c) have the same meaning.
(c) *Walking* down the street, *I* ran into an old friend.	

18-4 Expressing Cause and Effect in Modifying Adverbial Phrases

(a) *Because she needed* some money to buy a book, *Sue* went to a cash machine.	Often an **-ing** phrase at the beginning of a sentence gives the meaning of "because."
(b) *Needing* some money to buy a book, *Sue* went to a cash machine.	Examples (a) and (b) have the same meaning.
(c) *Because he lacked* the necessary qualifications, *he* was not considered for the job.	**Because** is not included in a modifying phrase. It is omitted, but the resulting phrase expresses a cause-and-effect relationship, as in (b) and (d).
(d) *Lacking* the necessary qualifications, *he* was not considered for the job.	
(e) *Having seen* that movie before, *I don't want* to go again.	**Having** + *past participle* gives the meaning not only of "because" but also of "before."
(f) *Having seen* that movie before, *I didn't want* to go again.	
(g) *Because he is* a doctor, Oskar often gets calls in the middle of the night.	A form of **be** in the adverb clause may be changed to **being**. The use of **being** makes the cause-and-effect relationship clear.
(h) *Being* a doctor, Oskar often gets calls in the middle of the night.	Examples (i), (j), and (k) have the same meaning.
(i) *Because she was unable* to afford a car, *she* bought a bike.	
(j) *Being unable* to afford a car, *she* bought a bike.	
(k) *Unable* to afford a car, *she* bought a bike.	

EXERCISE 6 ▸ Looking at grammar. (Charts 18-3 and 18-4)
<u>Underline</u> the modifying adverbial phrases. Which ones have the meaning of "because"? Which ones have the meaning of "while"? Do some of the sentences give the idea of both?

1. a. <u>Driving to my grandparents' house last night</u>, I saw a young woman who was selling flowers. I stopped so that I could buy some for my grandmother. _____*while*_____

   b. Being a young widow with three children, my grandmother had no choice but to go to work. _____

2. a. Sitting on the airplane and watching the clouds pass beneath me, I let my thoughts wander to the new experiences that were in store for me during the next two years of living abroad. _____

   b. Tapping her fingers loudly on the tray table in front of her, the woman next to me talked about her fear of flying. _____

3. a. Having guessed at the answers for most of the test, I did not expect to get a high score. _____

   b. Realizing that I didn't know much, I began to panic. _____

4. a. Walking down the icy steps without using the handrail, Elena slipped and fell.

   _____

   b. Having broken her arm in the fall, Elena had to learn to write with her left hand.

   _____

EXERCISE 7 ▸ Looking at grammar. (Chart 18-4)
Change the adverb clauses to modifying adverbial phrases.

1. Because David didn't want to hurt her feelings, he ate his girlfriend's salty soup.
   → *Not wanting to hurt her feelings, David ate his girlfriend's salty soup.*
2. Because his girlfriend hadn't tasted the soup, she didn't realize how bad it was.
3. Because David thinks that honesty can be hurtful, he doesn't tell her how he really feels.
4. Because David is a better cook, he does most of the cooking for them.

EXERCISE 8 ▸ Looking at grammar. (Charts 18-2 → 18-4)
Choose <u>all</u> the possible answers for each sentence.

1. Before _____ to you, I had never understood that formula.
   a. talked   (b.) talking   (c.) I talked

2. After _____ the chapter four times, I finally understood the author's theory.
   a. I read   b. read   c. reading

3. Since _____ his bachelor's degree, he has had three jobs, each one better than the last.

   a. he completed   b. completing   c. completed

4. _____ across Canada, I could not help being impressed by the great differences in terrain.

   a. Traveling   b. While I was traveling   c. While traveling

5. _____ national fame, the union leader had been an electrician in a small town.

   a. Before gaining   b. He had gained   c. Before he gained

6. _____ in an airplane before, the little girl was surprised and a little frightened when her ears popped.

   a. Had never flown   b. Having never flown   c. Because she had never flown

7. Before _____ vice president of marketing and sales, Peter McKay worked as a sales representative.

   a. became   b. becoming   c. he became

8. _____ the cool evening breeze and listening to the sounds of nature, we lost track of time.

   a. Because enjoying   b. Enjoying   c. We were enjoying

9. _____ to spend any more money this month, Jim decided against going to a café for lunch. He took a sandwich to work instead.

   a. Not wanting   b. Because he didn't want   c. Because not wanting

EXERCISE 9 ▶ Looking at grammar. (Charts 18-3 and 18-4)

Where possible, combine each pair of sentences by making a modifying phrase out of the first sentence.

A Visit Home

   1. a. I am a college student. My family doesn't see me so often now. (*no change*)

       b. I am a freshman in college. I spend most weekends in my dorm room doing homework.

         → *Being a freshman in college, I spend most weekends in my dorm room doing homework.*

   2. a. My younger siblings had made a "Welcome Home" sign. They were excited to see me.

       b. The kids were excited. I offered to play with them right away.

   3. a. My mom lives a long distance from her job. She has to leave early every morning.

       b. My mom spends four hours a day commuting. Her job needs to change.

   4. a. I heard that my cousin was in the hospital. I called my aunt to find out how she was doing.

       b. We decided to visit my cousin. A nurse told us she was resting.

   5. a. My brother was picking blackberries in the garden. A bee stung him.

       b. My brother didn't want to yell. He began taking deep breaths.

   6. a. I recognized my neighbor, but I had forgotten his name. I just smiled and said, "Hi."

       b. He remembered my name as well as my girlfriend's. I felt pretty embarrassed.

   7. a. My little sister was convinced she couldn't learn math. I helped her with some lessons.

       b. I was convinced that she had the ability. I encouraged her to keep trying and not give up.

EXERCISE 10 ▸ Game. (Charts 18-3 and 18-4)

Work in teams. Make sentences by combining the ideas in each column. Use the idea on the left as a modifying adverbial phrase. Show logical relationships. The first group to combine all the ideas correctly is the winner.

Example: 1. They give birth only every five years.
   → *Giving birth only every five years, female elephants do not have many offspring.*

1. They give birth only every five years.

2. She has done very well in her studies.

3. She was born two months early.

4. He had done everything he could for the patient.

5. She had never eaten Thai food before.

6. He had no one to turn to for help.

7. They are extremely hard and nearly indestructible.

8. They are able to crawl into very small places.

a. Marta didn't know what to expect when she went to the restaurant for dinner.

b. Mice can hide in almost any part of a house.

c. Sayid was forced to work out the problem by himself.

d. The doctor left to attend other people.

e. Nancy expects to be hired by a top company after graduation.

f. Diamonds are used extensively in industry to cut other hard minerals.

✓ g. Female elephants do not have many offspring.

h. Monique needed special care for the first few weeks of her life.

EXERCISE 11 ▸ Looking at grammar. (Charts 18-1 → 18-4)

Check (✓) the sentences that are grammatically correct. Rewrite the incorrect sentences.

Out and About

1. _____ After leaving the theater, Tom's car wouldn't start, so we had to take a taxi home.
   → *After we left the theater, Tom's car wouldn't start, so we had to take a taxi home.*
   → *After leaving the theater, we discovered that Tom's car wouldn't start, so we took a taxi home.*

2. _✓_ After leaving work late, we stopped at a coffee shop for a late-night snack.

3. _____ While walking across the street at a busy intersection, a truck nearly hit me.

4. _____ Not wanting to miss the last bus, I yelled for it to wait as I ran along the sidewalk.

5. _____ After arriving at a picnic with my cousins, it began to rain quite hard.

6. _____ While waiting for my husband at the mall, a friend from high school called out my name.

7. _____ When asked for directions by a pair of tourists, I stopped to help them.

8. _____ Being from out of town, two streets that had the exact same name confused visitors.

9. _____ Hearing the siren, drivers pulled over and stopped to let the ambulance pass.

10. _____ Honking the horn, the ambulance driver carefully entered each intersection.

EXERCISE 12 ▸ Reading and grammar. (Charts 18-1 → 18-4)

Read the blog entry by author Stacy Hagen. <u>Underline</u> each modifying adverbial phrase and change it to an adverbial clause.

🐦 BlueBookBlog Learning Strategies

There is a lot of interesting research that addresses how students can become more successful learners. In this blog, I'd like to highlight a few strategies for you to think about. While reading them, ask yourself if these strategies would be helpful to you.

1. **Space your practice**: When deciding whether to cram for a test or spread the review out over several days or weeks, you will benefit more by doing the latter, according to researchers. Cramming is very popular with students, but one problem is that it takes more energy to stay focused as the hours pass by. This energy is better used for learning. More important, cramming uses short-term memory. When you space out the practice over time, you activate your long-term memory and learn the material more deeply.

2. **Take a test**: Before beginning to learn new material, test your existing knowledge. For example, take a pretest like the one that opens each chapter of this book. You may get all the answers wrong, but interestingly enough, this doesn't matter. Many scientists believe that pretests help prepare the brain to take in new information. One theory is that our thinking somehow adjusts so that we better know what to look for when learning new material.

   You can also benefit from self-testing. There are many ways to do this, but here are a few common ones. After reading a passage, try to recall the key points from memory. Or, make your own practice questions to answer. Another helpful technique is to quiz yourself frequently with flashcards that you create. These types of self-quizzing force you to use your long-term memory and help you remember better.

3. **Handwrite, rather than type, your notes**. A study at Princeton and UCLA found that students who wrote out their lecture notes were better able to understand concepts and retain information than students who used a laptop. When writing out notes in longhand, students have to think more. They can't write every single word, so they have to comprehend and summarize as they write. With typing, it can become more of an automatic task, and all the words can be included without students' really thinking about them.

EXERCISE 13 ▸ Warm-up. (Chart 18-5)

Which sentences have the same meaning?

1. When Sharon heard the news of her friend's death, she began to cry.
2. Upon hearing the news of her friend's death, Sharon began to cry.
3. On hearing the news of her friend's death, Sharon began to cry.

18-5 Using *Upon + -ing* in Modifying Adverbial Phrases	
(a) *Upon reaching* the age of 18, I can get my driver's license.	Modifying adverbial phrases beginning with **upon + -ing** can have the same meaning as adverb clauses introduced by **when**.
(b) *When I reach* the age of 18, I can get my driver's license.	Examples (a) and (b) have the same meaning.
(c) *On reaching* the age of 18, I can get my driver's license.	**Upon** can be shortened to **on**. Examples (a), (b), and (c) all have the same meaning.

EXERCISE 14 ▸ Looking at grammar. (Chart 18-5)

Make sentences using *upon + -ing* where possible.

1. a. When Carl saw his wife cross the marathon finish line, he broke into a big smile.
   → *Upon seeing his wife cross the marathon finish line, Carl broke into a big smile.*
   b. When Tina crossed the marathon finish line, she collapsed in exhaustion.

2. a. When I looked in my wallet, I saw I didn't have enough money to pay my restaurant bill.
   b. Sam found that the waiter had made a math error when he brought the bill.

3. a. When you finish the examination, bring your paper to the front of the room.
   b. When I finished the exam, I decided to check all my answers again.

4. a. When the kids heard the good news, they jumped up and down with joy.
   b. The kids couldn't contain their excitement when their mom announced the news.

EXERCISE 15 ▸ Looking at grammar. (Chapter 18 Review)

Change the adverb clause in each sentence to a modifying adverbial phrase if possible. Change punctuation, capitalization, and word order as necessary.

1. a. After it spends some time in a cocoon, a caterpillar will emerge as a butterfly.
   → *After spending some time in a cocoon, a caterpillar will emerge as a butterfly.*
   b. When the butterfly emerged from the cocoon, the children became very quiet. (*no change*)

2. a. When we entered the room for the exam, we showed the teacher our ID.
   → *Upon entering the room for the exam, we showed the teacher our ID.*
   b. Because I was unprepared for the test, I didn't do well.
   → *Being unprepared for the test, I didn't do well.* OR *Unprepared for the test, I didn't do well.*

3. a. Jane's family has only received a few text messages since she arrived in Kenya two weeks ago.
   b. Before Jane left on her trip, she worked two jobs to earn enough money for a three-week stay.

4. a. My parents reluctantly agreed to let me attend the concert after they talked it over.
   b. Because I hadn't checked if I had my ticket with me, I arrived at the concert empty-handed.

5. a. Because the forest area is so dry this summer, it is prohibited to light campfires.
   b. Because the forest campsites are very popular, they are often all taken by mid-morning.

6. a. After we had to wait for more than half an hour, we were finally seated at the restaurant.
   b. When I discovered that I had left my wallet in the car, I told my friends to order without me while I went to get it.

EXERCISE 16 ▸ Let's talk. (Chapter 18 Review)

Work in small groups. Imagine your friend is traveling to a foreign country and has never been abroad before. Give advice by making several suggestions for each item.

Advice Before Going Abroad

1. Before leaving on your trip, …
   → *you'll need to get a visa.*
   → *you should find out if you need immunizations.*
   → *give a friend or family member your itinerary.*
   → *don't forget to have someone pick up your mail.*

2. Upon arriving at the airport, ...
3. After getting to your destination, ...
4. When talking with the local people, ...
5. While visiting tourist sites, ...
6. Before leaving for home, ...
7. In general, when traveling to a foreign country, . . .

 EXERCISE 17 ▸ Listening. (Chapter 18 Review)
Listen to each conversation. Choose the sentence that has the same meaning.

Example: You will hear: A: William, don't forget to pick up some groceries after work.
                 B: Oh yeah, thanks. That's the first thing I'll do when I leave the office.

        You will choose: (a.) After leaving work, William will stop at the grocery store.
                 b. Before leaving work, William will pick up some groceries.

1. a. Fearing people will laugh at her if she plays the piano, Rose doesn't want to play at the family gathering.
   b. Knowing she plays beautifully, Rose is happy to play the piano at the family gathering.

2. a. Not wanting to upset him, Jan isn't going to talk to Thomas this afternoon.
   b. Hoping to change Thomas's work behavior, Jan is going to talk to him this afternoon.

3. a. Upon finding her wedding ring, Susan hid it in a box.
   b. On finding her wedding ring, Susan felt relieved.

4. a. Never having voted in an election, Sam is taking it very seriously.
   b. Having done a lot of research before choosing a candidate, Sam voted in the presidential election.

EXERCISE 18 ▸ Reading and grammar. (Chapter 18 Review)
Modifying adverbial phrases are useful when summarizing information. First, read the passage about the invention of the telephone. It has no modifying adverbial phrases. Then read the summary on the next page and <u>underline</u> the modifying adverbial phrases. How do these phrases allow the ideas to be expressed more briefly yet still clearly?

The First Telephone

Alexander Graham Bell, a teacher of the deaf in Boston, invented the first telephone. One day in 1875, while he was running a test on his latest attempt to create a machine that could carry voices, he accidentally spilled acid on his coat. Naturally, he called for his assistant, Thomas A. Watson, who was in another room. Bell said, "Mr. Watson, come here. I want you." When he heard words coming from the machine, Watson immediately realized that their experiments had at last been successful. He rushed excitedly into the other room to tell Bell that he had heard his words over the machine.

After he successfully tested the new machine again and again, Bell confidently announced his invention to the world. For the most part, scientists appreciated his accomplishment, but the general public did not understand the revolutionary nature of Bell's invention. Most people believed the telephone was a toy with little practical application, and they paid little attention to Bell's announcement.

Summary

A small accident helped Alexandar Graham Bell with his invention of the telephone. While running a test to create a machine for voices, Bell spilled acid on his coat. He called to Mr. Watson, his assistant, who was in a different room. Watson heard Bell's words coming out of their new machine. Upon realizing what had happened, Watson and Bell knew that the invention was successful. Bell told the world about his discovery after testing the machine multiple times. Scientists understood the value of his work, but the general public, believing the phone was more of a toy, paid little attention to his announcement.

EXERCISE 19 ▸ Reading and writing. (Chapter 18)

Part I. Read the passage.

The QWERTY Keyboard

The letters on an English keyboard have a rather strange placement. If you look at the first row of letters on the keyboard shown, you'll notice that Q-W-E-R-T-Y are the first six letters. At first glance, this design doesn't seem to make a lot of sense, but it turns out there is a logical reason for it.

A man named Christopher Sholes, the inventor of the typewriter, came up with this keyboard in the 1860s. He wanted to create a logical design. Sholes first placed the letters in alphabetical order on his typewriter. He put two rows from A to Z on the keyboard. But Sholes found there was a problem. The letters were on typebars — also called keys — and some of these keys crashed into one another. This happened when letters that often occur together in words, like "s" and "l," were near each other on the keyboard. The keys hit each other and got stuck, and the typist had to stop and pull them apart.

Sholes tried to figure out a way to keep the keys from hitting one another. He made a list of letters commonly used together in English, like "s" and "l," or "q" and "u." He then rearranged these letters so they would be on opposite sides of the keyboard. If you look at a keyboard, "q" is on the left side and "u" is on the right side. He put the keys that were most likely to be hit in succession on opposite sides of the keyboard. This keyboard became known as QWERTY.

When we use computers, we don't have to worry about keys crashing into one another, so QWERTY is not necessarily the fastest and most efficient keyboard. People have come up with alternative keyboard patterns, but so far, none has gained much popularity. Since it has survived since the 1860s, QWERTY has demonstrated its longevity. It does not appear that it is going to be replaced any time soon by a faster, more efficient keyboard.

Part II. Write a summary of the passage. You can use the summary in Exercise 17 as a model.*
You may want to work in groups or with a partner first to list the essential information. Include at
least three modifying adverbial phrases in your writing.

Part III. Edit your writing. Check for the following:

1. ☐ only essential information in the summary
2. ☐ use of modifying adverbial phrases in some sentences
3. ☐ subjects of the adverb clause and the main clause are the same when modifying adverbial
   phrases are used
4. ☐ subjects omitted in modifying phrases
5. ☐ a comma used when modifying phrase is first in sentence
6. ☐ correct spelling (use a dictionary or spell-check)

---

*See Chapter 10, Exercise 53, p. 214, for more information on how to write a summary.

CHAPTER 19

Connectives That Express Cause and Effect, Contrast, and Condition

---

PRETEST: What do I already know?

Write "C" if a sentence has the correct connecting words and punctuation. Write "I" for incorrect. Check your answers below. After you complete each chart listed, make any necessary corrections.

1. _____ The clinic received complaints about its care, so it began sending out surveys to its patients. (19-1)

2. _____ Because of the roof was leaking, the living room had water on the floor. (19-2)

3. _____ The restaurant offers delicious Indian food. Consequently, there is often a line out the door. (19-3)

4. _____ Because most large grocery stores have delis we have been cooking less. (19-4)

5. _____ Liza got a raise at work; therefore, she celebrated with her husband. (19-4)

6. _____ The waiter was such helpful that I tipped him extra. (19-5)

7. _____ The color of your shirt is so bright that I need to put on my sunglasses! (19-5)

8. _____ Jill exercises at 5:00 A.M. every day so that she can fit it into her day. (19-6)

9. _____ The weather was sunny and warm. Nevertheless, we went to the beach. (19-7)

10. _____ Despite that Andreas is a hard worker, he can't seem to keep a job for more than a few months. (19-7)

11. _____ Malea is loud and funny; her twin sister, on the other hand, is quiet and reserved. (19-8)

12. _____ We need to hurry. Otherwise, we'll catch our plane. (19-9)

Incorrect sentences: 2, 4, 6, 9, 10, 12

EXERCISE 1 ▶ Warm-up. (Chart 19-1)

<u>Underline</u> the connecting words.

1. Even though Tracey is afraid of heights, she decided to take a ride in a hot-air balloon.
2. Tracey was afraid to go by herself, so she invited a friend.
3. The balloon traveled over mountains; consequently, the passengers had stunning views.

19-1 Introduction

Connectives can express cause/effect, contrast, and condition. They can be adverb-clause words, transitions, conjunctions, or prepositions. In Chapter 17 you studied adverb-clause words to express these ideas. In this chapter you will also look at transitions, conjunctions, and prepositions.

(a) *Because* Julian felt sick, he left work early.	The connectives in (a) and (b) are adverb-clause words.
(b) *Even though* Julian is afraid of doctors, he decided to make an appointment.	
(c) Julian had a rash and fever. *Consequently,* the doctor ran tests.	The connectives in (c) and (d) are transitions.
(d) The doctor ran tests. *However,* she found nothing serious.	
(e) Julian wasn't seriously ill, *but* his doctor told him to rest anyway.	The connectives in (e) and (f) are conjunctions.
(f) Julian wasn't well, *so* his doctor told him to rest.	
(g) *Due to* his illness, Julian missed several days of work.	The connectives in (g) and (h) are prepositions.
(h) He stayed home from work *because of* his illness.	

	Adverb-Clause Words		Transitions	Conjunctions	Prepositions
CAUSE AND EFFECT	because since now that	so (that)	therefore consequently	so	because of due to
CONTRAST	even though although though	while	however nevertheless nonetheless on the other hand	but (… anyway) yet (… still)	despite in spite of
CONDITION	if unless only if even if whether or not	in case	otherwise	or (else)	

EXERCISE 2 ▸ Reading and grammar. (Chart 19-1)

Read the passage and <u>underline</u> the connecting words from Chart 19-1.

A Distracted Driver

Even though Richard was driving the speed limit, he had an accident. The weather was clear; nevertheless, he glanced briefly at a text message. He took his eyes off the road just long enough to lose control and drive over the edge of the road. Fortunately, his car landed upright. Although he wasn't seriously hurt, he was quite shaken up.

   This is Richard's second accident this year, so he knows his insurance rates will go up. Now that he's had two accidents, he's upset with himself. However, he knows his wife will be even more upset. He's not looking forward to telling her.

EXERCISE 3 ▸ Warm-up. (Chart 19-2)

Which sentences express the same meaning as the situation and result?

SITUATION: Monday was a holiday.
RESULT: All schools were closed.

1. All schools were closed on Monday because it was a holiday.
2. Because of the holiday, all schools were closed on Monday.
3. Due to the holiday, all schools were closed on Monday.
4. Due to the fact that it was a holiday, all schools were closed on Monday.
5. Because all schools were closed on Monday, it was a holiday.

19-2 Using *Because Of* and *Due To*	
(a) *Because* the weather was cold, we stayed home.	*Because* introduces an adverb clause; it is followed by a subject and a verb, as in (a).
(b) *Because of* the cold weather, we stayed home. (c) *Due to* the cold weather, we stayed home.	*Because of* and *due to* are phrasal prepositions; they are followed by a noun object, as in (b) and (c).
(d) *Due to the fact that* the weather was cold, we stayed home.	Sometimes (usually in more formal writing) *due to* is followed by a noun clause introduced by *the fact that*.
(e) We stayed home *because of the cold weather*. We stayed home *due to the cold weather*. We stayed home *due to the fact that the weather was cold*.	Like adverb clauses, these phrases can also follow the main clause, as in (e).

EXERCISE 4 ▸ Looking at grammar. (Charts 17-3 and 19-2)

Identify the cause and effect in each pair of sentences. Write "C" for cause and "E" for effect. Then combine the sentences with *because*.

Accomplishments

1.   *E*   *C*
   Jon quit smoking. Jon has breathing problems.
   → *Because Jon has breathing problems, he quit smoking.*

2. Martina feels homesick. Martina moved to a new town.

3. Vivian worked very hard. Vivian won a scholarship.

4. Viktor has lost weight. Viktor reduced his sugar intake.

5. Sanae increased her department's profits. Sanae was promoted to manager.

EXERCISE 5 ▸ Looking at grammar. (Charts 17-3 and 19-2)

Choose all the correct sentences.

1. a. My cell phone doesn't work because the battery is dead.
   b. Because my cell phone doesn't work, the battery is dead.
   c. Because the battery is dead, my cell phone doesn't work.
   d. The battery is dead because my cell phone doesn't work.

2. a. Because Pat doesn't want to return to the Yukon to live, the winters are too severe.
   b. Pat doesn't want to return to the Yukon to live because the winters are too severe.
   c. Because the winters are too severe, Pat doesn't want to return to the Yukon to live.
   d. The winters are too severe because Pat doesn't want to return to the Yukon to live.

EXERCISE 6 ▸ Looking at grammar. (Charts 17-3 and 19-2)

Complete the sentences with *because* or *because of/due to*.

Problems

1. We postponed our trip _____ the bad driving conditions.

2. Sue's eyes were red _____ she had been swimming in a chlorinated pool.

3. We can't visit the museum tomorrow _____ it isn't open.

4. _____ heavy fog at the airport, our plane was delayed for several hours.

5. _____ the elevator was broken, we had to walk up six flights of stairs.

6. Jim had to stop jogging _____ his sprained ankle.

EXERCISE 7 ▸ Looking at grammar. (Chart 19-2)

Complete the sentences with the ideas in parentheses.

News Reports

1. (*The traffic was heavy.*) Due to _____*heavy traffic*_____, alternate routes are advised into the city.

2. (*Students have the flu.*) Many schools in the district have high absentee rates because of

   _____.

3. (*There are loud noises at the beach.*) Police are investigating reports of illegal fireworks because of

   _____.

4. (*Circumstances are beyond their control.*) Due to _____, all City Hall offices are closed today.

5. (*The donors are generous.*) Due to _____, the foods banks have enough food for the holidays.

EXERCISE 8 ▶ Warm-up. (Chart 19-3)
Check (✓) the sentences that logically complete the idea of the given sentence.

Nadia likes fresh vegetables.

1. _____ Therefore, she has a vegetable garden in her yard.
2. _____ As a result, she doesn't grow her own vegetables.
3. _____ Therefore, she buys canned vegetables at the store.
4. _____ As a result, she buys produce from local farmers.
5. _____ She eats a lot of frozen vegetables, therefore.
6. _____ Consequently, she eats produce from her garden.

19-3 Cause and Effect: Using *Therefore, Consequently,* and *So*

(a) Al failed the test because he didn't study. (b) Al didn't study. *Therefore,* he failed the test. (c) Al didn't study. *Consequently,* he failed the test.	Examples (a), (b), and (c) have the same meaning. ***Therefore*** and ***consequently*** mean "as a result." In grammar, they are called *transitions* (or *conjunctive adverbs*). Transitions connect the ideas between two sentences. They are used most commonly in formal written English and rarely in spoken English.

(d) Al didn't study. *Therefore,* he failed the test.
(e) Al didn't study. He, *therefore,* failed the test.
(f) Al didn't study. He failed the test, *therefore.*
 	
POSITIONS OF A TRANSITION:
 	
transition + **S** + **V** (+ rest of sentence)
  S + **transition** + **V** (+ rest of sentence)
  S + **V** (+ rest of sentence) + **transition**
	A transition occurs in the second of two related sentences.
	
	Notice the patterns and punctuation in the examples. A period (NOT a comma) is used at the end of the first sentence.*
	
	The transition has several positions in the second sentence. It is separated from the rest of the sentence by commas.

(g) Al didn't study, *so* he failed the test.	In (g): ***So*** is used as a *conjunction* between two independent clauses. It has the same meaning as ***therefore.*** ***So*** is common in both formal written and spoken English. A comma usually precedes ***so*** when it connects two sentences, as in (g).

*A semicolon is also possible in this situation: *Al didn't study; therefore, he failed the test.* See the footnote to Chart 19-4.

EXERCISE 9 ▶ Looking at grammar. (Chart 19-3)
Rewrite the sentence with the given words. Punctuate carefully.

The runner can compete in races because he wears a special blade attached at his knee.

1. therefore   _____

   _____

2. consequently _____

   _____

3. so   _____

   _____

EXERCISE 10 ▸ Looking at grammar. (Charts 17-3, 19-2, and 19-3)
Punctuate the sentences. Add capital letters as necessary. NOTE: Two sentences need no changes.

1. *adverb clause:* Because it was cold she wore a coat.

2. *adverb clause:* She wore a coat because it was cold.

3. *prepositional phrase:* Because of the cold weather she wore a coat.

4. *prepositional phrase:* She wore a coat because of the cold weather.

5. *transition:* The weather was cold therefore she wore a coat.

6. *transition:* The weather was cold she wore a coat therefore.

7. *conjunction:* The weather was cold so she wore a coat.

EXERCISE 11 ▸ Looking at grammar. (Charts 17-3, 19-2, and 19-3)
Punctuate the sentences. Add capital letters as necessary.

A Storm

1. Freezing rain fell on the city it was unsafe to walk outside because of slippery streets and falling branches.

2. Due to improvements in weather forecasting people knew about the storm well in advance.

3. The storm damaged the power lines consequently the town was without electricity.

4. Due to the snowstorm only two students came to class the teacher therefore canceled the class.

EXERCISE 12 ▸ Warm-up. (Chart 19-4)
Check (✓) the sentences that have the correct punctuation.

1. _____ Some doctors recommend yoga for their patients. Because it can lower stress.

2. _____ Because yoga can lower stress some doctors recommend it for their patients.

3. _____ Yoga can lower stress. Some doctors, therefore, recommend it for their patients.

4. _____ Yoga can lower stress, so some doctors recommend it for their patients.

19-4 Summary of Patterns and Punctuation

ADVERB CLAUSES	(a) *Because* it was hot**,** we went swimming. (b) We went swimming *because* it was hot.	An *adverb clause* may precede or follow an independent clause. PUNCTUATION: A comma is used if the adverb clause comes first.
PREPOSITIONS	(c) *Because of* the hot weather**,** we went swimming. (d) We went swimming *because of* the hot weather.	A *preposition* is followed by a noun object, not by a subject and verb. PUNCTUATION: A comma is usually used if the prepositional phrase precedes the subject and verb of the independent clause.
TRANSITIONS	(e) It was hot. ***Therefore,*** we went swimming. (f) It was hot. We**,** *therefore***,** went swimming. (g) It was hot. We went swimming**,** *therefore*. (h) It was hot**;** *therefore***,** we went swimming.	A *transition* is used with the second sentence of a pair. It shows the relationship of the second idea to the first idea. A transition is movable within the second sentence. PUNCTUATION: A semicolon (;) may be used in place of a period, as in (h).* NOTE: A period is used between the two independent clauses in (e)–(g); a comma is not possible. Commas are usually used to set the transition off from the rest of the sentence.
CONJUNCTIONS	(i) It was hot**,** *so* we went swimming.	A *conjunction* comes between two independent clauses. PUNCTUATION: Usually a comma is used immediately in front of a conjunction.

* In general, a semicolon can be used instead of a period between any two sentences that are closely related in meaning: *Peanuts are not nuts; they are beans.* Notice that a small letter, NOT a capital letter, immediately follows a semicolon.

EXERCISE 13 ▸ Looking at grammar. (Charts 17-3 and 19-4)
Choose all the correct sentences.

1. a. It is important to wear a hat on cold days, since we lose 60% of our body heat through our head.
   b. Since we lose about 60% of our body heat through our head, it is important to wear a hat on cold days.
   c. It is important to wear a hat on cold days since we lose about 60% of our body heat through our head.

2. a. Bill's car wouldn't start; therefore, he couldn't pick us up after the concert.
   b. Bill's car wouldn't start. Therefore, he couldn't pick us up after the concert.
   c. Bill's car wouldn't start, therefore, he couldn't pick us up after the concert.

3. a. When I was in my teens and twenties, it was easy for me to get into an argument with my father because both of us can be stubborn and opinionated.
   b. When I was in my teens and twenties, it was easy for me to get into an argument with my father. Because both of us can be stubborn and opinionated.
   c. When I was in my teens and twenties, it was easy for me to get into an argument with my father, because both of us can be stubborn and opinionated.

4. a. Robert got some new business software that didn't work; so he emailed the software company for technical support.

   b. Robert got some new business software that didn't work, so he emailed the software company for technical support.

   c. Robert got some new business software that didn't work so he emailed the software company for technical support.

EXERCISE 14 ▸ Looking at grammar. (Charts 17-3 and 19-4)

Combine the sentences using the given words. Discuss correct punctuation.

We postponed our trip. The weather was bad.

Example: because → *We postponed our trip **because** the weather was bad.*
→ ***Because** the weather was bad, we postponed our trip.*

1. therefore
2. since
3. so
4. because of
5. consequently
6. due to the fact that

EXERCISE 15 ▸ Looking at grammar. (Charts 17-2 and 19-4)

Combine each pair of ideas with the words in parentheses.

Did you know ... ?

1. A camel can go completely without water for eight to ten days. It is an ideal animal for desert areas. (*due to the fact that*)

2. A tomato is classified as a fruit, but most people consider it a vegetable. It is often eaten in salads along with lettuce, onions, cucumbers, and other vegetables. (*since*)

3. There is a consumer demand for ivory. Many African elephants are being slaughtered ruthlessly. Many people who care about saving these animals from extinction refuse to buy any item made from ivory. (*due to, consequently*)

4. Most 15th-century Europeans believed the world was flat and that a ship could conceivably sail off the end of the earth. Many sailors of the time refused to venture forth with explorers into unknown waters. (*because*)

EXERCISE 16 ▸ Warm-up. (Chart 19-5)

Create humorous sayings by matching a phrase on the left with one on the right.

1. It's such a hot day that I could _____
2. I'm so hungry that I could _____
3. He is such a rich man that he _____
4. She is so sick that she _____

a. buys a new boat when one gets wet.
b. needs two beds.
c. eat a horse.
d. fry an egg on the sidewalk.

19-5 Other Ways of Expressing Cause and Effect: *Such ... That* and *So ... That*

(a) Because the weather was nice, we went to the zoo. (b) It was *such nice weather that* we went to the zoo. (c) The weather was *so nice that* we went to the zoo.	Examples (a), (b), and (c) have the same meaning.
(d) It was *such good coffee that* I had another cup. (e) It was *such a foggy day that* we couldn't see the road.	***Such ... that*** encloses a modified noun: ***such*** + *adjective* + *noun* + ***that***
(f) The coffee is *so hot that* I can't drink it. (g) I'm *so hungry that* I could eat a horse. (h) She speaks *so fast that* I can't understand her. (i) He walked *so quickly that* I couldn't keep up with him.	***So ... that*** encloses an adjective or adverb: ***so*** + { *adjective* or *adverb* } + ***that***
(j) She made *so many mistakes that* she failed the exam. (k) He has *so few friends that* he is always lonely. (l) She has *so much money that* she can buy whatever she wants. (m) He had *so little trouble* with the test *that* he left 20 minutes early.	***So ... that*** is used with ***many, few, much***, and ***little***.
(n) It was *such a good book* (*that*) I couldn't put it down. (o) I was *so hungry* (*that*) I didn't wait for dinner to eat something.	Sometimes, primarily in speaking, ***that*** is omitted.

EXERCISE 17 ▶ Looking at grammar. (Chart 19-5)
Complete the sentences with *so* or *such*.

1. a. It was _____ *such* _____ an enjoyable party that no one wanted to leave.

   b. The party was _____ *so* _____ enjoyable that no one wanted to leave.

   c. We had _____ *so* _____ much fun that no one wanted to leave.

2. a. Leta is _____ afraid of flying that she traveled by train across Canada.

   b. She was gone for _____ a long time that she got homesick.

   c. People on the train were _____ kind that she will always remember them.

3. a. My elderly aunt has _____ few friends that I am beginning to worry about her.

   b. She's not poor, but she spends _____ little money that I'm not sure she's eating right.

   c. I've wanted to visit _____ many times, but she always says no.

4. a. The movie was _____ scary that none of us could sleep last night.

   b. We were _____ scared that we held hands when we walked home.

   c. I was afraid of having _____ bad dreams that I didn't sleep well for a week.

EXERCISE 18 ▶ Let's talk. (Chart 19-5)
Work in small groups. Take turns making sentences using *so/such ... that*. Try to exaggerate your answers. Share your favorite sentences with the class.

Example: I'm hungry. In fact, I'm ... → *I'm **so** hungry (**that**) I could eat a horse.*

Exaggerations

1. I'm really tired. In fact, I'm ....
2. I didn't expect it! I was really surprised. In fact, I was ...
3. I took a very slow bus to town. In fact, it was ...
4. We watched a very exciting movie. In fact, it was ...
5. The weather was really, really hot. In fact, it was ...
6. My wallet fell out of my pocket and I lost a lot of money. In fact, I lost ...
7. I ordered an expensive meal at a restaurant. The server brought a small plate with a tiny amount of food to my table. In fact, it was ...
8. I saw a shark while I was swimming in the ocean. I was frightened. In fact, I was ...

EXERCISE 19 ▸ Looking at grammar. (Chart 19-5)

Make new sentences using **so** or **such** by combining each sentence on the left with the appropriate sentence on the right. Make all necessary changes.

Example: 1. There are many pine cones on that tree.
   → *There are **so** many pine cones on that tree that it is impossible to count them.*

a pine cone

1. There are many pine cones on that tree.
2. The radio was too loud.
3. Olga did poor work.
4. The food was too hot.
5. The wind was strong.
6. The tornado struck with great force.
7. Few students showed up for class.
8. Charles used too much paper when he wrote his report.

a. It burned my tongue.
b. She was fired from her job.
c. It blew my hat off my head.
d. The teacher postponed the test.
✓ e. It is impossible to count them.
f. It lifted cars off the ground.
g. I couldn't hear what Michael was saying.
h. The printer ran out of ink.

EXERCISE 20 ▶ Warm-up. (Chart 19-6)

Check (✓) the sentences that correctly complete the given sentence.

Kay got a new job so that ...

1. _____ she could be closer to home.

2. _____ she is very excited.

3. _____ her husband is taking her out to dinner to celebrate.

4. _____ she could earn more money.

19-6 Expressing Purpose: Using *So That*

(a) I turned off the TV *in order to* enable my roommate to study in peace and quiet.	*In order to* expresses *purpose*. (See Chart 15-1, p. 335.)
(b) I turned off the TV *so (that)* my roommate could study in peace and quiet.	In (a): I turned off the TV for a purpose. The purpose was to make it possible for my roommate to study in peace and quiet. Examples (a) and (b) have the same meaning.

So That + Can or Could

(c) I'm going to cash a check *so that I can* buy my textbooks.	*So that* also expresses *purpose*.* It expresses the same meaning as *in order to*. The word *that* is often omitted, especially in speaking.
(d) I cashed a check *so that I could* buy my textbooks.	*So that* is often used instead of *in order to* when the idea of ability is being expressed. *Can* is used in the adverb clause for a present/future meaning.
	In (c): *so that I can buy* = in order to be able to buy
	Could is used after *so that* in past sentences, as in (d).**

So That + Will / Would or Simple Present

(e) I'll take my umbrella *so that I won't* get wet.	In (e): *so that I won't get wet* = in order to make sure that I won't get wet
(f) Yesterday I took my umbrella *so that I wouldn't* get wet.	*Would* is used in past sentences, as in (f).
(g) I'll take my umbrella *so that I don't* get wet.	In (g): It is sometimes possible to use the simple present after *so that* in place of *will*; the simple present expresses a future meaning.

*NOTE: *In order that* has the same meaning as *so that* but is less commonly used.
    Example: *I turned off the TV in order that my roommate could study in peace and quiet.*
Both *so that* and *in order that* introduce adverb clauses. It is unusual but possible to put these adverb clauses at the beginning of a sentence: *So that my roommate could study in peace and quiet, I turned off the TV.*

**Also possible but less common: the use of *may* or *might* in place of *can* or *could* (e.g., *I cashed a check so that I might buy my textbooks.*).

EXERCISE 21 ▶ Looking at grammar. (Chart 19-6)

Combine the sentences by using *so (that)*.

1. a. Please turn down your music. I want to be able to get to sleep.
    → *Please turn down your music so (that) I can get to sleep.*
   b. My wife turned down her music. I wanted to be able to get to sleep.
    → *My wife turned down her music so (that) I could get to sleep.*

2. a. Put the milk in the refrigerator. We want to make sure it won't/doesn't spoil.
      → *Put the milk in the refrigerator so (that) it won't/doesn't spoil.*
   b. I put the milk in the refrigerator. I wanted to make sure it didn't spoil.
      → *I put the milk in the refrigerator so (that) it wouldn't spoil.*

3. a. Please be quiet. I want to be able to hear what Sharon is saying.
   b. I asked the children to be quiet. I wanted to be able to hear what Sharon was saying.

4. a. I'm going to go to a cash machine. I want to make sure that I have enough money to go to the store.
   b. I went to a cash machine yesterday. I wanted to make sure that I had enough money to go to the store.

5. a. Ann and Larry have a six-year-old child. Tonight they're going to hire a babysitter. They want to be able to go out with some friends.
   b. Last week Ann and Larry hired a babysitter. They wanted to be able to go to a dinner party at the home of Larry's boss.

6. a. Yesterday I put the meat in the oven at 5:00. I wanted it to be ready to eat by 6:30.
   b. Be sure to put the meat in the oven at 5:00. You want to be sure that it will be (OR is) ready to eat by 6:30.

7. a. I'm going to leave the party early. I want to be able to get a good night's sleep tonight.
   b. I'm not going to look at any messages on my phone or computer before I go to sleep. I want to be sure that my mind is free of distractions.

8. a. Tommy pretended to be sick. He wanted to stay home from school.
   b. He held a thermometer under hot water. He wanted it to show a high temperature.

EXERCISE 22 ▸ Looking at grammar. (Charts 19-4 and 19-6)
Add *that* to the sentence if *so* means *in order that*. If *so* means *therefore*, add a comma.

Needs

1. I need to borrow some money so ⌃*that* I can pay my rent.

2. I didn't have enough money for the movie, so I asked my friend to buy my ticket.

3. I need a visa so I can travel overseas.

4. I needed a visa so I went to the embassy to apply for one.

5. Marta is trying to improve her English so she can become a tour guide.

6. Olga wants to improve her English so she has hired a tutor.

7. Tarek borrowed money from his parents so he could start his own business.

8. I turned off my phone so I can concentrate on my paperwork.

EXERCISE 23 ▸ Warm-up. (Chart 19-7)

Usually when someone breaks an arm, he/she goes to a doctor. That is expected behavior. Answer the same question about expected behavior for each statement. Circle *yes* or *no*.

	EXPECTED BEHAVIOR?
1. Ron broke his arm, but he didn't go to the doctor.	yes no
2. Joe went to the doctor because he broke his arm.	yes no
3. Sue broke her arm, so she went to the doctor.	yes no
4. Amy broke her arm; nevertheless, she didn't go to the doctor.	yes no
5. Despite having a broken arm, Rick didn't go to the doctor.	yes no
6. Jeff broke his arm; therefore, he went to the doctor.	yes no

19-7 Showing Contrast (Unexpected Result)

All of these sentences have the same meaning. The idea of cold weather is contrasted with the idea of going swimming. Usually if the weather is cold, one does not go swimming, so going swimming in cold weather is an "unexpected result." It is surprising that the speaker went swimming in cold weather.

ADVERB CLAUSES	*even though*	(a) *Even though* it was cold, I went swimming.
	although	(b) *Although* it was cold, I went swimming.
	though	(c) *Though* it was cold, I went swimming.*
CONJUNCTIONS	*but ... anyway*	(d) It was cold, *but* I went swimming (*anyway*).
	but ... still	(e) It was cold, *but* I (*still*) went swimming.
	yet ... still	(f) It was cold, *yet* I (*still*) went swimming.
TRANSITIONS	*nevertheless*	(g) It was cold. *Nevertheless,* I went swimming.
	nonetheless	(h) It was cold; *nonetheless,* I went swimming.
	however ... still	(i) It was cold. *However,* I (*still*) went swimming.
PREPOSITIONS	*despite*	(j) I went swimming *despite* the cold weather.
	in spite of	(k) I went swimming *in spite of* the cold weather.
	despite the fact that	(l) I went swimming *despite the fact that* the weather was cold.
	in spite of the fact that	(m) I went swimming *in spite of the fact that* the weather was cold.

* Another way to show contrast is to put *though* at the end of the sentence: *It was cold. I went swimming, though.* The meaning is similar to *but* (e.g., *It was cold, but I went swimming.*); however, *though* is softer. This usage is very common in spoken English.

EXERCISE 24 ▸ Looking at grammar. (Charts 19-3 and 19-7)

Complete the sentences with *inside* or *outside* to make logical statements.

1. It rained, but we had our wedding _____ anyway.

2. It rained, so we had our wedding _____.

3. It rained; nevertheless, we had our wedding _____.

4. Though it rained, we had our wedding _____.

5. Even though it rained, we had our wedding _____.

6. Although it rained, we had our wedding _____.

7. Despite the fact that it rained, we had our wedding _____.

8. It rained; therefore, we had our wedding _____.

EXERCISE 25 ▸ Looking at grammar. (Chart 19-7)

Complete the sentences with *was* or *wasn't* to make logical statements.

1. Hans had worked a 24-hour shift; nevertheless, he _____ wide-awake.

2. Though he had worked a 24-hour shift, he _____ sleepy.

3. Even though he had worked a 24-hour shift, he _____ wide-awake.

4. Hans _____ wide-awake although he had worked a 24-hour shift.

5. He had worked a 24-hour shift, yet he _____ wide-awake.

6. Despite the fact that he had worked a 24-hour shift, Hans _____ sleepy.

7. In spite of working a 24-hour shift, Hans _____ wide-awake.

EXERCISE 26 ▸ Looking at grammar. (Chart 19-7)

Part I. Complete the sentences with *but, even though,* or *nevertheless*. Notice the use of punctuation and capitalization.

1. a. Bob ate a large dinner. _____, he is still hungry.

   b. Bob ate a large dinner, _____ he is still hungry.

   c. Bob is still hungry _____ he ate a large dinner.

2. a. I had a lot of studying to do, _____ I went to a movie anyway.

   b. I had a lot of studying to do. _____, I went to a movie.

   c. _____ I had a lot of studying to do, I went to a movie.

3. a. I finished all of my work _____ I was very sleepy.

   b. I was very sleepy, _____ I finished all of my work anyway.

   c. I was very sleepy. _____, I finished all of my work.

Part II. Complete the sentences with *yet, although,* or *however*.

4. a. I washed my hands. _____, they still looked dirty.

   b. I washed my hands, _____ they still looked dirty.

   c. _____ I washed my hands, they still looked dirty.

5. a. Diana didn't know how to swim, _____ she jumped into the pool.

   b. _____ Diana didn't know how to swim, she jumped into the pool.

   c. Diana didn't know how to swim. _____, she jumped into the pool.

EXERCISE 27 ▸ Looking at grammar. (Chart 19-7)

Add commas, periods, and capital letters as necessary. Do not add, omit, or change any words.

1. a. Anna's father gave her some good advice nevertheless she did not follow it.
      → *Anna's father gave her some good advice. Nevertheless, she did not follow it.*

   b. Anna's father gave her some good advice though she didn't follow it.

   c. Even though Anna's father gave her some good advice she didn't follow it.

   d. Anna's father gave her some good advice she did not follow it however.

2. a. Thomas has been broke* for months I offered him some money he refused it.

b. Thomas refused the money although he has been broke for months.

c. Thomas has been broke for months nevertheless he refused the money that I offered him.

d. Thomas has been broke for months yet he still refused the money that I offered him.

EXERCISE 28 ▶ Looking at grammar. (Chart 19-7)

Work in pairs or small groups. Combine the sentences using the given words. Discuss correct punctuation. Use the negative if necessary to make a logical statement.

His grades were low. He was admitted to the university.

1. even though	3. yet … still	5. despite
2. but … anyway	4. nonetheless	6. despite the fact that

EXERCISE 29 ▶ Warm-up. (Chart 19-8)

Read the question and the answers. Which answers express "direct contrast," i.e., the idea that "this" is the opposite of "that"?

What is the difference between hurricanes and tornadoes?

1. Hurricanes develop over warm oceans while tornadoes form over land.
2. Hurricanes develop while they are traveling over warm ocean water.
3. Hurricanes develop over warm oceans, but tornadoes form over land.
4. Hurricanes develop over warm oceans; however, tornadoes form over land.
5. Hurricanes develop over warm oceans; on the other hand, tornadoes form over land.

a hurricane

19-8 Showing Direct Contrast

All of the sentences have the same meaning: "This" is the opposite of "that."

ADVERB CLAUSES	while	(a) Mary is rich, **while** *John is poor*.* (b) John is poor, **while** *Mary is rich*.
CONJUNCTIONS	but	(c) Mary is rich, **but** *John is poor*. (d) John is poor, **but** *Mary is rich*.
TRANSITIONS	however	(e) Mary is rich; **however**, *John is poor*. (f) John is poor; *Mary is rich*, **however**.
	on the other hand	(g) Mary is rich. *John*, **on the other hand**, *is poor*. (h) John is poor. *Mary*, **on the other hand**, *is rich*.

*Sometimes a comma precedes a *while*-clause that shows direct contrast. A comma helps clarify that *while* is being used to express contrast rather than time. The use of a comma in this instance is a stylistic choice by the writer.

---

*be broke = have no money

EXERCISE 30 ▸ Looking at grammar. (Chart 19-8)

For each sentence, make two sentences with the same meaning using **however** and **on the other hand**. Punctuate carefully. Write your sentences on a separate piece of paper.

1. My grandfather is quite active, while my grandmother is often in bed.
2. While my grandmother has a sunny personality, my grandfather is more negative.
3. Elderly people in my country usually live with their children, but the elderly in the United States often live by themselves.

EXERCISE 31 ▸ Looking at grammar. (Chart 19-8)

Complete the sentences with your own words.

Customs

1. In some countries, people greet each other by shaking hands, while in other countries ... *people kiss one another on the cheek.*
2. In the United States, people drive on the right-hand side of the road while people in ...
3. While in Japan people must take off their shoes before entering a house, in some countries ...
4. In some cultures, it is considered impolite to look directly at another person, while in others ...

EXERCISE 32 ▸ Speaking or writing. (Chart 19-8)

Extroverts and Introverts

Part I. Read the information below about extroverts and introverts. Make several sentences with the words in the lists either orally or in writing using the words **but, however, on the other hand,** or **while**.

Examples:
→ *Extroverts like to talk more than listen,* **while** *introverts like to listen more than talk.*
→ *Introverts like to listen more than talk. Extroverts,* **however,** *like to talk more than listen.*

Extroverts ...
    like to be the center of attention.
    like to talk more than listen.
    enjoy meeting people.
    prefer being active.
    like to work in groups.
    don't always think before speaking.
    don't mind noise.
    like crowds.
    are energized by being with others.

Introverts ...
    are uncomfortable being the center of attention.
    like to listen more than talk.
    are reserved when meeting people.
    like to spend time alone.
    don't like to work in groups.
    think carefully before speaking.
    prefer the quiet.
    avoid crowds.
    can find it tiring to spend time with others.

Part II. Are you an extrovert or introvert? Compare yourself to someone you know who is different from you. Make several sentences.

EXERCISE 33 ▸ Let's talk. (Chart 19-8)

Think of two different countries you are familiar with. How are they different? Use **while**, **however**, **on the other hand**, and **but**. Work in pairs, in small groups, or as a class.

1. size
2. population
3. food
4. time of meals
5. economic system
6. educational system
7. role of women
8. language
9. cost of education
10. medical care
11. public transportation
12. dating customs

EXERCISE 34 ▸ Warm-up. (Chart 19-9)

Choose the logical verb for each sentence: **can** or **can't**.

SITUATION: Daniel needs coffee every morning. It wakes him up.

1. If Daniel drinks coffee in the morning, he   can / can't
   wake up quickly.

2. Unless Daniel drinks coffee in the morning, he   can / can't
   wake up quickly.

3. Daniel needs coffee every morning; otherwise, he   can / can't
   wake up quickly.

4. Daniel needs coffee in the morning, or else he   can / can't
   wake up quickly.

19-9 Expressing Conditions: Using *Otherwise* and *Or (Else)*

ADVERB CLAUSES	(a) *If I don't eat breakfast,* I get hungry. (b) You'll be late *if you don't hurry.* (c) You'll get wet *unless you take your umbrella.*	*If* and *unless* state conditions that produce certain results. (See Charts 17-6 and 17-10, pp. 382 and 387.)
TRANSITIONS	(d) I always eat breakfast. *Otherwise,* I get hungry during class. (e) You'd better hurry. *Otherwise,* you'll be late. (f) Take your umbrella. *Otherwise,* you'll get wet.	*Otherwise* expresses the idea "if the opposite is true, then there will be a certain result." In (d): *otherwise = if I don't eat breakfast*
CONJUNCTIONS	(g) I always eat breakfast, *or (else)* I get hungry during class. (h) You'd better hurry, *or (else)* you'll be late. (i) Take your umbrella, *or (else)* you'll get wet.	*Or else* and *otherwise* have the same meaning.

EXERCISE 35 ▸ Looking at grammar. (Chart 19-9)

Make sentences with the same meaning as the given sentence. Use **otherwise**.

Chores

1. If I don't clean the fridge, my roommate will start complaining about how messy I am.
   → *I need to / should / had better / have to / clean the fridge. Otherwise, my roommate will start complaining about how messy I am.*

2. If I don't wash my clothes tonight, I won't have any clean clothes to wear tomorrow.

3. If we don't start cooking dinner now, it won't be ready in time.

4. I won't be able to sleep unless I change my sheets.

5. Only if you help me get ready for the party will I have one.*
6. Unless we clear the snow from the walkway, people could slip and fall.
7. I'll get everything done only if I begin as soon as I get home.
8. If you don't start soon, the weekend will be over!

EXERCISE 36 ▶ Looking at grammar. (Chapter 19 Review)

Using the two ideas of "to study" and "to pass or fail the exam," complete the sentences. Punctuate and capitalize as necessary.

1. Because I did not study _, I failed the exam._____

2. I failed the exam because _____

3. Although I studied _____

4. I did not study therefore _____

5. I did not study however _____

6. I studied nevertheless _____

7. Even though I did not study _____

8. I did not study so _____

9. Since I did not study _____

10. If I study for the exam _____

11. Unless I study for the exam _____

12. I must study otherwise _____

13. Even if I study _____

14. I did not study consequently _____

15. I did not study nonetheless _____

16. I will probably fail the exam whether _____

17. Only if I study _____

18. I studied hard yet _____

19. You'd better study or else _____

 ## EXERCISE 37 ▶ Listening. (Chapter 19 Review)

Listen to each sentence and choose the logical completion.

Example: You will hear: I was exhausted when I got home, but ...
           You will choose: (a.) I didn't take a nap.   b. I took a nap.

1. a. my back gets sore.   b. my back doesn't get sore.
2. a. my old one works fine.   b. my old one doesn't work.

---

*Notice that the subject and verb in the main clause are inverted because the sentence begins with *Only if*. See Chart 17-11, p. 388.

3. a. I hurry.   b. I don't hurry.

4. a. I hurried.   b. I didn't hurry.

5. a. our offices are hot.   b. our offices aren't hot.

6. a. the noise bothers me.   b. the noise doesn't bother me.

7. a. I fell asleep during dinner.   b. I didn't fall asleep during dinner.

EXERCISE 38 ▸ Game. (Chapter 19 Review)

Work in teams. Combine these two ideas using the words below the example. The time is now, so use present and future tenses. The team with the most correct sentences wins.

to go (or not to go) to the beach \ hot, cold, nice weather

Example: because
→ ***Because** the weather is cold, we aren't going to go to the beach.*
→ *We're going to go to the beach **because** the weather is hot.*

1. so ... that
2. so
3. nevertheless
4. despite
5. now that
6. once
7. although

8. because of
9. consequently
10. as soon as
11. such ... that
12. since
13. but ... anyway
14. unless

15. therefore
16. only if
17. nonetheless
18. in spite of
19. even if
20. yet ... still
21. whether ... or not

 EXERCISE 39 ▸ Grammar, reading, and listening. (Chapter 19 Review)

Complete the lecture with the words in the box. Then listen and check your answers. One word is used two times.

however	if	therefore
so that	while	since

Why We Yawn

Have you ever noticed that when a person near you yawns, you may start yawning too? This is called contagious yawning. *Contagious* in this sense means that the behavior spreads: in the case of yawning, when one person yawns, it can cause others to do the same thing.

There are various theories about why people yawn. One popular idea is that yawning brings more oxygen into the brain _____ people will wake up. Is that what you have thought?

_____, in 2007, researchers at a university in New York came up with a new idea: yawning helps cool the brain. When people's brains are warm, they yawn more frequently; yawning brings cooler air into the body and, _____, cools the brain. This is important because cooler brains work better than warmer ones.

This may also help explain why yawning is contagious. People are more awake when their brains are cooler; _____, contagious yawning helps people be more alert. As people evolved, this was important in times of danger. _____ they yawned, they could have been signaling to others to stay awake.

_____ it can be annoying to have a person yawn when you are talking, perhaps you can tell yourself that he or she actually wants to stay awake, not go to sleep.

EXERCISE 40 ▶ Check your knowledge. (Chapter 19 Review)

Correct the errors

1. The hotel had a mistake on its website. The price was very low so that many people wanted rooms.
2. Due to medical care costs a lot in the U.S., people need to have insurance.
3. The dorm room I was assigned to has a broken heater, therefore, I have complained to the office.
4. Because Jamal's visa has expired, he waited too long to renew it.
5. Jenn had surprisingly low test scores. However, the college she chose didn't admit her.
6. Despite the weather is freezing today, I'm going to take a run in the park.
7. It was such a hard test no one finished on time.
8. We should leave now, otherwise, we will get stuck in traffic.
9. The electric bill was months overdue; nevertheless, the power company turned off the power to the home.
10. Please talk more quietly so that we could hear the speaker.
11. You should apply for a scholarship soon unless you don't want to miss the deadline.
12. Since you should change your password, many people know it.
13. My parents bought a house in our neighborhood so that they are going to be closer to their grandchildren.

EXERCISE 41 ▸ Reading, grammar, and writing. (Chapter 19)

Part I. Read the passage comparing optimists and pessimists.

Optimists **vs.** Pessimists

How do you see the glass in the picture? Is it half empty or half full? People who say it is half empty are called pessimists, while people who say it is half full are called optimists. In simple terms, optimists see the best in the world, while pessimists see the worst.

One of the clearest ways to see the differences between the two is to look at the way optimists and pessimists explain events. When something bad happens, optimists tend to see the event as a single occurrence that does not affect other areas of their lives.

For example, Sarah is an optimistic person. When she gets a low grade on a test, she will say something like this to herself: "Oh well, that was one test I didn't do well on. I wasn't feeling well that day. I have another test in a few weeks. I'll do better on that one."

Pessimists, on the other hand, will feel that an event is just one of a string of bad events that affects their lives, and somehow they are the cause of it. Let's take a look at Susan. She is a pessimist. When she gets a low grade on a test, she might say: "I failed again. I never do well on tests. I'm stupid. Why even try?" And when something does go well for Susan, she may say: "I was just lucky that time." She doesn't expect to do well again. While optimists don't see themselves as failures, pessimists do.

Research has shown that optimism can be a learned trait and that, despite their upbringing, people can train themselves to respond to events in more positive terms. For example, Paul has a tendency to react negatively to events. The first thing he has to do is become conscious of that behavior. Once he identifies his reaction, he can reframe his thoughts in more positive terms, as Sarah did when she failed the test. As Paul begins to do more of this, he forms new patterns of responses, and over time these responses become more automatic. Gradually he can develop a more positive outlook on life.

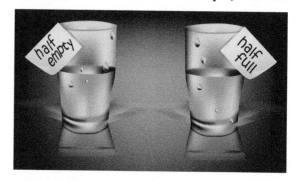

Part II. Complete the sentences with information from the passage.

1. Optimists think positively about life, while …

2. An optimist may do poorly on a test; nevertheless, …

3. Things sometimes go well for a pessimist; however, …

4. Pessimists see themselves as failures; on the other hand, …

5. Optimists see the best in the world; therefore, …

6. Optimists see the best in the world; however, …

7. Although people may have been raised as pessimists, …

8. Optimism can be a learned trait; consequently, …

9. If a pessimist wants to change how he reacts, …

Part III. Are you an optimist, a pessimist, or a combination of both? Write about your personality, and provide some specific examples that support your ideas. Use connecting words from this chapter.

WRITING TIP

Reread the passage "Optimists vs. Pessimists." Note that there is a variety of longer and shorter sentences.

It is important to remember to vary your own sentence style to make your writing more interesting. Good writers use a combination of shorter and longer, more complex sentences. For example, you can use a transition word with a period to create a shorter sentence, but a semicolon to create a longer one.

While it is desirable to use sentence connectors, make sure that not all of your sentences become long and elaborate. Too many connecting words can make your writing seem repetitious. And remember that not all sentences need connecting words!

Part IV. Edit your writing. Check for the following:

1. ☐ a period, not a comma, between two complete sentences
2. ☐ correct meanings of transition words
3. ☐ correct use of adjective and nouns with **so** and **such**:
   > **so**   + *adjective* + **that**
   > **such** + *noun*   + **that**
4. ☐ use of nouns after **because of** and **due to**
5. ☐ use of nouns after **despite** and **in spite of**
6. ☐ correct punctuation (period or semicolon) with transition words
7. ☐ sentence variety by using a combination of shorter and longer sentences
8. ☐ correct spelling (use a dictionary or spell-check)

CHAPTER 20

Conditional Sentences and Wishes

PRETEST: What do I already know?

Write "C" if a sentence has the correct verb forms and "I" for incorrect. Check your answers below. After you complete each chart listed, make any necessary corrections.

1. _____ If I had more money right now, I will lend you some. (20-1)

2. _____ If the lake freezes, neighborhood teens like to skate on it. (20-2)

3. _____ If the plane should take off late, we'll miss our connecting flight. (20-2)

4. _____ I would apply for a scholarship if I was you. (20-3)

5. _____ School would be easy for me if I have your memory. (20-3)

6. _____ If I had taken more math classes, I could have gotten a better job. (20-4)

7. _____ If we had been thinking, we would have picked up your package at the post office on our way home. (20-5)

8. _____ If our team had won the game last night, the town would be celebrating today. (20-6)

9. _____ Had the police known the reason for the decision, would it have made a difference? (20-7)

10. _____ The subway was late. Otherwise, I am here an hour ago. (20-8)

11. _____ Lawrence wishes he had chosen a more interesting college major. (20-9)

12. _____ I wish you will stop complaining. (20-10)

Incorrect sentences: 1, 4, 5, 10, 12

EXERCISE 1 ▶ Warm-up. (Chart 20-1)

Which sentence represents a real or true situation? Which sentence represents an unreal or impossible situation?

1. If I lived underwater, I would see colorful marine life every day.
2. If I am vacationing in the Caribbean, I like to explore coral reefs.

20-1 Overview of Basic Verb Forms Used in Conditional Sentences

Conditional sentences express the idea of *if* … , *then* … . These sentences can talk about real situations — facts, regularly occurring events, etc. — and unreal situations — imaginary or impossible ones.

Situation	*If*-Clause	Result Clause	Examples
REAL IN THE PRESENT	simple present	*simple form of the verb*	If I *have* enough time, I *watch* TV every evening.
REAL IN THE FUTURE		*will* + *simple form*	If I *have* enough time, I *will watch* TV later on tonight.
UNREAL IN THE PRESENT / FUTURE	simple past	*would* + *simple form*	If I *had* enough time, I *would watch* TV now or later on.
UNREAL IN THE PAST	past perfect	*would have* + *past participle*	If I *had had* enough time, I *would have watched* TV yesterday.

EXERCISE 2 ▸ Looking at grammar. (Chart 20-1)

Write "R" next to the sentences that express a real condition and "U" next to the sentences that express an unreal condition.

1. _____ If I have time on weekends, I volunteer at an animal shelter.

2. _____ If I have time, I will volunteer next weekend.

3. _____ If I had time, I would volunteer next weekend.

4. _____ If I had had time, I would have volunteered last weekend.

EXERCISE 3 ▸ Looking at grammar. (Chart 20-1)

Complete the sentences with the words in the box.

would do	will do	would have done

1. Rita believes in hard work and wants her children to work hard. She always tells them, "If you work hard every day, you _____ well."

2. Scott is smart, but he doesn't work very hard. As a result, he is not good at his job. His co-workers often tell him, "If you worked hard every day, you _____ well."

3. Mark planned to study hard for a test yesterday, but some friends called, and he decided to go out with them. He didn't study at all, and he didn't do well on his test the next day. His teacher told him, "If you had studied yesterday, you _____ well on the test."

EXERCISE 4 ▸ Warm-up. (Chart 20-2)

Which sentence expresses a habitual meaning? Which sentence or sentences express a future meaning?

1. If the baby wakes up in the middle of the night, she'll cry.
2. If the baby wakes up in the middle of the night, she cries.
3. Should the baby wake up in the middle of the night, she'll cry.

20-2 Expressing Real Conditions in the Present or Future	
(a) If I *don't eat* breakfast, I always *get* hungry during class. (b) If I *don't eat* breakfast tomorrow morning, I *will get* hungry during class. (c) Water *freezes* if the temperature *reaches* 32°F/0°C. (d) Water *will freeze* if the temperature *reaches* 32°F/0°C.	In conditional sentences that express real or true, factual ideas in the present/future, the *simple present* (not the simple future) is used in the *if*-clause. The result clause has various possible verb forms. A result-clause verb can be: • the *simple present,* to express a habitual activity or situation, as in (a). • the *simple future,* to express a particular activity or situation in the future, as in (b). • the *simple present* or the *simple future,* to express an established, predictable fact or general truth, as in (c) and (d).
(e) If it *rains,* we *should stay* home. If it *rains,* I *might decide* to stay home. If it *rains,* we *can't go.* If it *rains,* we *'re going to stay* home.	The result clause can also include *modals* and *phrasal modals* such as ***should***, ***might***, ***can***, ***be going to***, as in (e).*
(f) If anyone *calls,* please *take* a message. (g) If anyone *should call,* please take a message.	An imperative verb can be used in the result clause, as in (f). Sometimes ***should*** is used in an *if*-clause, as in (g). It indicates a little more uncertainty than the use of the simple present, but basically the meaning of examples (f) and (g) is the same.

*See Chart 9-1, p. 162, for a list of modals and phrasal modals.

EXERCISE 5 ▸ Looking at grammar. (Chart 20-2)

Decide if each sentence expresses a habitual or future meaning.

1. a. If it rains, the streets get wet.   habitual   future
   b. If it rains, the streets will get wet.   habitual   future
2. a. If it should rain, we'll take the bus   habitual   future
   b. If it rains, we take the bus.   habitual   future
3. a. If the meetings run late, I leave early.   habitual   future
   b. Should the meetings run late, I will leave early.   habitual   future

EXERCISE 6 ▸ Looking at grammar. (Chart 20-2)

Choose the correct verb for the result clauses. In some cases, both answers are correct.

1. If there is a bike race, the road   is / will be   closed.
2. If I find out the answer, I   will let / let   you know.
3. If you run up a hill, your heart   beats / will beat   fast.
4. If I have extra time, I   tutor / am going to tutor   students in math.

5. If it should rain tomorrow, we   might change / will change   our plans.

6. If my cell phone battery goes dead, I   will recharge / am recharging   it.

EXERCISE 7 ▸ Let's talk. (Chart 20-2)

Read the three superstitions. Do you agree? Then answer the questions with *if* to express other common superstitions. Work in pairs, groups, or as a class.

Superstitions

- If I cross my fingers, it will bring good luck.
- If I open an umbrella indoors, bad luck will "rain" down on me.
- If I have an itchy palm, I may get or lose money soon.

1. Friday the 13th is an unlucky day in many cultures. What may happen on Friday the 13th?

2. Many hotels don't have a 13th floor. Why do you think this is? What do people think will happen?

3. What happens if you walk under a ladder?

4. What happens if you find the end of a rainbow?

5. What happens if you see a black cat?

6. What happens if you step on a crack in the sidewalk?

7. What happens if you find a four-leaf clover?

EXERCISE 8 ▸ Listening. (Chart 20-2)

If + *pronoun* can be difficult to hear at the beginning of sentences because these words are generally unstressed. Additionally, *if* at the beginning of a sentence is often reduced to /f/. Listen to the sentences spoken in casual, relaxed English. Complete the sentences with the non-reduced forms of the words you hear.

Example: You will hear: If I hear anything, I'll tell you.

You will write: _____*If I hear*_____ anything, I'll tell you.

1. _____ too fast, please tell me.

2. _____ married, everyone will be shocked.

3. _____ OK, I'll ask for some advice.

4. _____ to quit, I hope he lets us know soon.

5. _____, we'll need to try something else.

6. _____ harder, I'm sure she'll succeed.

7. _____ the job, I'll call you right away.

EXERCISE 9 ▸ Warm-up. (Chart 20-3)

Choose the correct completions.

1. If Tom were a teacher, he would teach law.

   a. Tom   is / isn't   a teacher.

   b. Tom   teaches / doesn't teach   law.

2. If he had enough money for tuition, he would be in graduate school.

   a. He   has / doesn't have   enough money.

   b. He   is / isn't   in graduate school.

20-3 Unreal (Contrary to Fact) in the Present or Future

(a) If I *taught* this class, I *wouldn't give* tests.	In (a): Actually, I don't teach this class.
(b) If he *were* here right now, he *would help* us.	In (b): Actually, he is not here right now.
(c) If I *were* you, I *would accept* their invitation.	In (c): Actually, I am not you.
	NOTE: **Were** is used for both singular and plural subjects. **Was** (with *I, he, she, it*) is sometimes used in very informal speech: *If I **was** you, I'd accept their invitation.*
COMPARE:	In (d): The speaker wants a car but doesn't have enough money. **Would** expresses desired or predictable results.
(d) If I had enough money, I *would buy* a car.	
(e) If I had enough money, I *could buy* a car.	In (e): The speaker is expressing one possible result. **could** = would be able to; **could** expresses possible options.

EXERCISE 10 ▶ Looking at grammar. (Charts 20-2 and 20-3)
Decide if each sentence expresses a real or unreal idea.

1. a. If I had more money, I would buy a new car.   real   unreal

    b. If I have enough money, I will buy a car   real   unreal

2. a. If the shirts are on sale, I will get a few.   real   unreal

    b. If the shirt were on sale, I would get a few.   real   unreal

3. a. If you were a teacher, you could help me.   real   unreal

    b. If you are a teacher, you can help me.   real   unreal

EXERCISE 11 ▶ Looking at grammar. (Chart 20-3)
Choose the correct completions by looking at the pictures. Then make sentences with the given words.

1. Grandpa (is)/ isn't   allergic to flowers.

    If Grandpa weren't allergic to flowers, he would bring Grandma flowers more often.

    (if \ Grandpa \ be \ allergic to flowers \ he \ bring \ Grandma flowers more often)

2. Your roommates   spend / don't spend   a lot of time shopping.

    _____

    (If \ they \ spend \ so much time shopping \ they \ save \ a lot of money)

3. The boy   likes / doesn't like   peas.

    _____

    (If \ the boy \ like peas \ he \ eat \ them)

EXERCISE 12 ▶ Looking at grammar. (Charts 20-2 and 20-3)

Complete the sentences with the verbs in parentheses.

1. a. If I have enough apples, I (*bake*) _____will bake_____ an apple pie this afternoon.

   b. If I had enough apples, I (*bake*) ___would bake / could bake___ an apple pie.

2. a. I will fix your bike if I (*have*) _____ the right screwdriver.

   b. I would fix your bike if I (*have*) _____ the right screwdriver.

3. a. I (*go*) _____ to a movie tonight if I don't have any homework to do.

   b. I (*go*) _____ to a movie tonight if I didn't have any homework to do.

4. a. I turn off my phone when I (*be*) _____ in meetings.

   b. I would turn on my phone if I (*be, not*) _____ in a meeting right now.

EXERCISE 13 ▶ Let's talk: interview. (Chart 20-3)

Interview your classmates. Share some of the most interesting answers with the class.

1. If you had the choice of any job in the world, what would it be?
2. If someone famous invited you to dinner, who would you want it to be?
3. If you were in an accident and had to lose one of your five senses*, which one would it be?
4. If you saw someone shoplift something at a jewelry store, what would you do?
5. If you were given a million dollars, what would you do with it?
6. If you knew you only had a week to live, what would you do?
7. If someone were following you on the street at night, what would you do?
8. If you found out that you were going to be the parent of septuplets**, what would you do?
9. If you were lost on a desert island with only three items, what three items would they be?
10. If you spoke five languages fluently, which ones would they be?

EXERCISE 14 ▶ Looking at grammar. (Charts 20-2 and 20-3)

Complete the sentences with the verbs in parentheses.

Science and Nature

1. Oil floats on water. If you pour oil on water, it (*float*) _____.

2. If there (*be*) _____ no trees on earth, there (*be, not*) _____ _____ enough oxygen. Life as we know it (*exist, not*) _____ _____.

3. If you boil water, it (*disappear*) _____ into the atmosphere as vapor.

4. Many animals hibernate in the winter. One reason is because of food. If animals (*hibernate, not*) _____, they (*need*) _____ to find food at a time when food is scarce.

---

*five senses = sight, hearing, feel, touch, smell
**septuplets = seven babies born at the same time

5. If people (*have*) _____ paws instead of hands with fingers and opposable thumbs, the machines we use in everyday life (*have to*) _____ be constructed very differently. We (*be, not*) _____ able to turn knobs, push small buttons, or hold tools and utensils securely.

EXERCISE 15 ▶ Warm-up. (Chart 20-4)
Choose the correct time word.

1. If Ann were available, she would help us.	now	yesterday
2. If Ann had been available, she would have helped us.	now	yesterday

20-4 Unreal (Contrary to Fact) in the Past

(a) If you *had told* me about the problem, I *would have helped* you.	In (a): Actually, you did not tell me about it.
(b) If they *had studied,* they *would have passed* the exam.	In (b): Actually, they did not study. Therefore, they failed the exam.
(c) If I *hadn't slipped* on the stairs, I *wouldn't have broken* my arm.	In (c): Actually, I slipped on the stairs. I broke my arm.
	NOTE: The auxiliary verbs are often reduced in speech. "If you'd told me, I would've helped you (or I-*duv* helped you)."*
COMPARE:	In (d): **would** expresses a desired or predictable result.
(d) If I had had enough money, I **would** have bought a car.	In (e): **could** expresses a possible option. **could have bought** = would have been able to buy
(e) If I had had enough money, I **could** have bought a car.	

*In casual, informal speech, some native speakers sometimes use **would have** in an *if*-clause: *If you **would've told** me about the problem, I would've helped you.* This verb form usage is generally considered to be grammatically incorrect in standard English, but it occurs fairly commonly.

EXERCISE 16 ▶ Looking at grammar. (Chart 20-4)
Write the correct form of the verb in parentheses. Then complete the sentence with a phrase from the right.

1. If Reya had (*go*) _____ to the hospital, she __d__ .

2. If Tim hadn't (*lose*) _____ his passport, he _____ .

3. If you hadn't (*stay*) _____ out all night, you _____ .

4. If you had (*help*) _____ us move, we _____ .

5. If the waiter had (*be*) _____ friendlier, I _____ .

6. If we had (*have*) _____ chains in the car, we _____ .

a. wouldn't have slept all day

b. would have left a bigger tip

c. would have finished already

d. would have gotten better more quickly

e. wouldn't have gotten stuck in the snow

f. wouldn't have missed the flight home

tire chains

EXERCISE 17 ▸ Looking at grammar. (Chart 20-4)

Complete the sentences with past conditionals.

Getting Lost

1. If the map on my phone (*be, not*) ___hadn't been___ wrong, we (*get, not*) ___wouldn't___
   ___have gotten___ lost.

2. If you (*follow*) _____ my directions, we (*spend, not*) _____
   _____ the last two hours driving around.

3. If I (*be, not*) _____ so tired, I (*pay*) _____
   closer attention.

4. If we (*rent*) _____ a car with GPS, we (*find*) _____
   _____ the hotel by now.

5. If you (*listen*) _____ to me, we (*drive, not*) _____
   _____ around in circles.

6. If we (*take*) _____ the train, we (*be*) _____
   there an hour ago.

EXERCISE 18 ▸ Let's talk: pairwork. (Chart 20-4)

Work with a partner. Take turns making statements with *If I had known*.

Example: I didn't know it was your birthday.
   If I had known it was your birthday, I would have brought you a gift.

PARTNER A	PARTNER B
1. I didn't know your dad was in the hospital.	1. I didn't know you were sick for a month.
2. I didn't know you broke your arm and needed help.	2. I didn't know you were broke and couldn't pay your bills.
3. I didn't know you had a graduation party and invited me.	3. I didn't know someone stole your bike and you had trouble getting to school.
4. I didn't know you were allergic to nuts. I put them in the salad.	4. I didn't know you had free tickets to the soccer game and you wanted me to go.

EXERCISE 19 ▸ Listening. (Chart 20-4)

In conditional sentences, /h/ is often dropped in the auxiliary verbs **have** and **had**. **Would have** can sound like "would-a" or "would-uv." Listen to the sentences spoken in casual, relaxed English. Complete the sentences with the non-reduced forms of the words you hear.

SITUATION: Jon told several good friends a lie, and they recently found out. Here are their reactions:

Example: You will hear: If he had been truthful, he wouldn't have lost my trust.
   You will write: ___*If he had been*___ truthful, ___*he wouldn't have lost*___ my trust.

1. _____ the truth sooner, _____ differently.

2. _____ him, _____ so foolish.

3. _____ me what a great guy Jon was, _____

_____ him so easily.

4. _____ another person, _____ so shocked.

5. _____ , _____ more respect for him.

EXERCISE 20 ▸ Looking at grammar. (Charts 20-3 and 20-4)
Answer the questions.

1. If I had gone to the movie with you, I would have enjoyed it.

   a. Did I go with you? _____no_____

   b. Did I enjoy the movie? _____no_____

   c. Is the meaning present or past? _____past_____

2. If I had brought my ID, I could have gotten a student discount.

   a. Did I bring my ID? _____

   b. Did I get a discount? _____

   c. Is the meaning present or past? _____

3. If Dad had his ID, he would get a senior citizen discount.

   a. Does he have his ID? _____

   b. Is he going to get a discount? _____

   c. Is the meaning present or past? _____

4. If I felt better, I would go to work.

   a. Do I feel better? _____

   b. Am I going to work? _____

   c. Is the meaning present or past? _____

5. If I didn't have any friends, I would be lonely.

   a. Am I lonely? _____

   b. Do I have friends? _____

   c. Is the meaning present or past? _____

6. Jackson would have made it to class on time this morning if the bus hadn't been late.

   a. Was the bus late? _____

   b. Did Jackson make it to class on time? _____

   c. Is the meaning present or past? _____

7. If I had more time, I would stay longer and talk.

   a. Do I have more time? _____

   b. Will I stay longer? _____

   c. Is the meaning present or past? _____

EXERCISE 21 ▸ Looking at grammar. (Charts 20-1 → 20-4)
<u>Underline</u> the clause that expresses a condition. Write "R" if the condition is a real condition. Write "U" if the condition is unreal. Then decide if the sentence refers to present/future or past time.

1. a. __R__ <u>If the weather is warm</u>, we'll eat outdoors.   (present/future)   past

   b. __U__ <u>If the weather were warm</u>, we would eat outdoors.   (present/future)   past

   c. _____ If the weather had been warm, we would have eaten   present/future   past
   outdoors.

2. a. _____ If I had more money, I would work less.   present/future   past

   b. _____ If I had had more money, I would have worked less.   present/future   past

3. a. _____ If I don't have to work, I can visit you.   present/future   past

   b. _____ If I hadn't had to work, I could have visited you.   present/future   past

   c. _____ If I didn't have to work, I could visit you.   present/future   past

EXERCISE 22 ▸ Looking at grammar. (Charts 20-1 → 20-4)
Draw a line to each correct completion.

1. a. If I have enough money, ⎯⎯⎯⎯⎯⎯ I would have bought it.
   b. If I had enough money, ⎯⎯⎯⎯⎯⎯ I will buy it.
   c. If I had had enough money,   I would buy it.

2. a. If they arrive early,   they would call.
   b. If they arrived early,   they would have called.
   c. If they had arrived early,   they will call.

3. a. If he had needed help,   he will ask.
   b. If he needs help,   he would have asked.
   c. If he needed help,   he would ask.

4. a. I would buy the coat   if it had fit.
   b. I would have bought the coat   if it fit.
   c. I will buy the coat   if it fits.

5. a. We will stop by   if we had extra time.
   b. We would have stopped by   if we had had extra time.
   c. We would stop by   if we have extra time.

EXERCISE 23 ▸ Looking at grammar. (Charts 20-1 → 20-4)
Complete the sentences with the verbs in parentheses.

1. a. If I (*have*) _____ time, I will go with you.

   b. If I (*have*) _____ time, I would go with you.

   c. If I (*have*) _____ time, I would have gone with you.

2. a. If the weather were nice today, we (*go*) _____ to the zoo.

   b. If the weather had been nice yesterday, we (*go*) _____ to the zoo.

   c. If the weather is nice tomorrow, we (*go*) _____ to the zoo.

3. a. Linda wasn't at home yesterday. If she (*be*) _____ at home yesterday,

   I (*visit*) _____ her.

   b. If Sally (*be*) _____ at home tomorrow, I (*visit*) _____ her.

   c. Jim isn't home right now. If he (*be*) _____ at home right now, I (*visit*)

   _____ him.

EXERCISE 24 ▸ Looking at grammar. (Charts 20-1 → 20-4)

Complete the sentences with the verbs in parentheses.

Conversations

1. A: You should tell your father exactly what happened. If I (*be*) _____

   you, I (*tell*) _____ him the truth as soon as possible.

   B: You're right. I'll do it.

2. A: If I (*have*) _____ my camera with me yesterday, I

   (*take*) _____ a picture of Alex standing on his head.

   B: He's good at yoga. He can do a lot of different poses.

3. A: I'm almost ready to plant my garden. I have a lot of seeds. Maybe

   I have more than I need. If I (*have*) _____ more seeds than I need, I

   (*give*) _____ some to my neighbor.

   B: She would really appreciate it.

4. A: George has only two pairs of socks. If he (*have*) _____ more than two pairs of

   socks, he (*have to, not*) _____ wash his socks so often.

   B: I'm not sure that he washes them that often!

5. A: Since I broke my foot, I haven't been able to clean my apartment.

   B: Why didn't you say something? I (*come*) _____ over and

   (*help*) _____ you if you (*tell*) _____ me.

   A: I know you (*come*) _____ right away if I (*call*) _____

   _____ you, but I didn't want to bother you.

   B: It wouldn't have been a bother. What are friends for?

6. A: It's been a long drought. It hasn't rained for over a month. If it (*rain, not*) _____

   _____ soon, a lot of crops (*die*) _____ . If the crops

   (*die*) _____ , many people (*go*) _____ hungry this coming winter.

   B: I'm very worried about our water supply.

7. A: Shhh! Your father is taking a nap. Uh-oh. You woke him up.

   B: Sorry. If I (*realize*) _____ he was sleeping, I (*make, not*) _____

   _____ so much noise when I came in.

8. A: What (*we, use*) _____ to look at ourselves when we comb our hair if

we (*have, not*) _____ mirrors?

B: It would be very strange to live without mirrors.

🎧 **EXERCISE 25 ▸ Listening.** (Charts 20-1 → 20-4)

Listen to the statements and answer the questions.

Example: You will hear: If Bob had asked me to keep the news about his marriage a secret, I
wouldn't have told anybody. I know how to keep a secret.

You will answer: a. Did I tell anybody the news? ____*yes*____

b. Did Bob ask me to keep it a secret? ____*no*____

1. a. Am I going to go to the art museum? _____

  b. Do I have enough time? _____

2. a. Did Mrs. Jones receive immediate medical attention? _____

  b. Did she die? _____

3. a. Am I a carpenter? _____

  b. Do I want to build my own house? _____

  c. Am I going to build my own house? _____

4. a. Was the hotel built to withstand an earthquake? _____

  b. Did the hotel collapse? _____

EXERCISE 26 ▸ Looking at grammar. (Charts 20-1 → 20-4)

If-clauses can be shortened by the use of an auxiliary verb. Study the examples and then complete
the sentences.

Examples: Ella isn't patient, but if she **were**, she would be a better teacher.
I don't live in the city, but if I **did**, I wouldn't need to take the subway to work.
I didn't go to bed early last night, but if I **had**, I would have gotten up earlier.

1. I don't have a pen, but if I ____*did*____, I would lend it to you.

2. He is busy right now, but if he ____*weren't*____, he would help us.

3. I didn't vote in the election, but if I ____*had*____, I would have voted for Senator Todd.

4. I don't have enough money, but if I _____, I would buy that book.

5. The weather is cold today, but if it _____, I'd go swimming.

6. She didn't come, but if she _____, she would have met my brother.

7. Helium is lighter than air. If it _____, a helium
blimp wouldn't float upward.

8. I'm not a good cook, but if I _____, I would
make all of my own meals.

9. He didn't go to a doctor, but if he _____, the cut
on his hand wouldn't have gotten infected.

10. I always pay my bills. If I _____, I'd get in a lot of trouble.

11. I called my husband to tell him I would be late. If I _____, he would have gotten worried about me.

EXERCISE 27 ▸ Warm-up. (Chart 20-5)
Read the statements and answer the questions.

OLGA: If I hadn't been painting my apartment, I would have gone to a movie with my friends.
YOKO: If I weren't painting my apartment, I would go to a movie with my friends.

1. Who is busy painting her apartment now?
2. Who was busy painting her apartment earlier?

20-5	Using Progressive Verb Forms in Conditional Sentences

Notice the use of progressive verb forms in these examples. Even in conditional sentences, progressive verb forms are used in progressive situations.

(a) Real Situation:	It *is raining* right now, so I *will not go* for a walk.
(b) Conditional Statement:	If it *were not raining* right now, I *would go* for a walk.

(c) Real Situation:	It *was raining* yesterday afternoon, so I *did not go* for a walk.
(d) Conditional Statement:	If it *had not been raining*, I *would have gone* for a walk.

EXERCISE 28 ▸ Looking at grammar. (Chart 20-5)
Make conditional sentences.

1. a. I'm working. If I _____ weren't _____ working, I would be at home.

   b. I'm not working. If I _____ working, I wouldn't be at home.

2. a. Fortunately, the copy machine was working. If it _____ working, we wouldn't have finished our presentation.

   b. The copy machine wasn't working. If it _____ working, we _____ finished our presentation.

3. a. The elevators weren't working. If they _____ working, I _____ walked up to the top floor.

   b. The elevators were working. If they _____ working, I _____ walked up to the top floor.

EXERCISE 29 ▸ Looking at grammar. (Chart 20-5)
Change the statements to conditional sentences.

1. You weren't listening, so you didn't understand the directions. But …
   → *if you had been listening, you would have understood the directions.*
2. You aren't wearing a coat, so you're cold. But …
3. Joe got a ticket because he was driving too fast. But …
4. I'm enjoying myself, so I won't leave. But …
5. You were sleeping, so I didn't tell you the news as soon as I heard it. But …

EXERCISE 30 ▸ Looking at grammar. (Chart 20-5)
Complete the sentences with the verbs in parentheses. Make conditional statements.

1. It's snowing. We can't go to the park.

   If it (*snow*) _____*weren't snowing*_____, we could go to the park.

2. It wasn't snowing. We went to the park.

   If it (*snow*) _____*had been snowing*_____, we wouldn't have gone to the park.

3. Elena just got out of the shower. She's drying her hair with a hair dryer, so she can't hear the doorbell.

   If Elena (*dry*) _____ her hair, she could hear the doorbell.

4. Elena was waiting for a package to come, but as it happened, she was drying her hair when it arrived, and she couldn't hear the doorbell.

   If Elena (*dry*) _____ her hair when the package arrived, she could have heard the doorbell.

5. Max is at a party at his friend's apartment, but he's not having any fun. He wants to leave.

   Max wouldn't want to leave early if he (*have*) _____ fun.

6. My sister was reading a text message while she was driving and wasn't paying enough attention to traffic. When the car in front of her stopped, she rear-ended it.

   If my sister (*read*) _____ a text message, she wouldn't have rear-ended the car in front of her.

7. Simon is vacuuming the car. When he vacuums, he can't hear his phone.

   If Simon (*vacuum*) _____ the car, he could hear his phone ring.

EXERCISE 31 ▸ Warm-up. (Chart 20-6)
Choose the correct time words.

1. If I had done my homework   now / earlier,   I would know the answers   now / earlier.
2. Anita wouldn't be sick   now / earlier   if she had followed the doctor's orders   now / earlier.

20-6 Using "Mixed Time" in Conditional Sentences

Frequently the time in the *if*-clause and the time in the result clause are different: one clause may be in the present and the other in the past. Notice that past and present times are mixed in these sentences.

		past	present
(a)	Real Situation:	I *did not eat* breakfast *several hours ago*,	so I *am* hungry *now*.
		past	present
(b)	Conditional Statement:	If I *had eaten* breakfast *several hours ago*,	I *would not be* hungry *now*.
		present	past
(c)	Real Situation:	He *is not* a good student.	He *did not study* for the test *yesterday*.
		present	past
(d)	Conditional Statement:	If he *were* a good student,	he *would have studied* for the test *yesterday*.

EXERCISE 32 ▸ Looking at grammar. (Chart 20-6)
Choose the correct time frames for each sentence.

1. If I hadn't eaten so much at dinner   now / earlier,   I would feel better   now / earlier.
2. Lynn would be in Egypt   now / earlier   if she had renewed her passport   now / earlier.
3. Professor Azeri would be happier   now / earlier in the semester   if she had been given a different teaching assignment   now / earlier in the semester.
4. Had you told me the truth   now / in the past,   I would trust you more   now / in the past.
5. If you were a more organized person   now / yesterday,   you wouldn't have misplaced your keys, glasses, and phone   now / an hour ago.
6. If my mom weren't in bed with the flu   today / yesterday,   she would have come shopping with us   now / this morning.
7. You wouldn't be paying a fine   right now / yesterday   if you had returned the library book   now / yesterday.

EXERCISE 33 ▸ Looking at grammar. (Chart 20-6)
Put one line under the present clause. Put two lines under the past clause. Then restate the sentences as conditional statements.

1. I'm hungry now because I didn't eat dinner earlier.
   → *If I'd eaten dinner earlier, I wouldn't be hungry now.*
2. The room is full of flies because you left the door open.
3. You are tired this morning because you didn't go to bed at a reasonable hour last night.
4. I didn't finish my report yesterday, so I can't begin a new project today.
5. I'm not you, so I didn't tell him the truth.
6. I don't know anything about plumbing, so I didn't fix the leak in the sink myself.

EXERCISE 34 ▶ Reading and grammar. (Chart 20-4 → 20-6)

Read the passage. Then choose the correct completions in the sentences that follow.

> ## Why Did Dinosaurs Become Extinct?
>
> There are several scientific theories as to why dinosaurs became extinct. One theory has to do with asteroids. Asteroids are rocky objects that orbit the sun. According to this theory, an asteroid collided with the earth millions of years ago, causing disastrous changes in the earth's climate, such as tsunamis, high winds, and dust in the atmosphere that blocked the sun. As a result, dinosaurs could no longer survive. Some scientists believe that if this asteroid had not collided with the earth, dinosaurs would not have become extinct.

1. According to one theory, if an asteroid had collided / hadn't collided with the earth, several disastrous changes in the earth's climate would not have taken place.
2. If an asteroid had hit / hadn't hit the earth, there wouldn't have been catastrophic changes in the earth's climate.
3. If dust had blocked / hadn't blocked the sun, the earth would have been warmer.
4. If an asteroid had collided / hadn't collided with the earth, dinosaurs might still exist.
5. If dinosaurs had survived / hadn't survived, the earth would be a very different place.

EXERCISE 35 ▶ Warm-up. (Chart 20-7)

Check (✓) all the correct sentences.

1. a. _____ Were I more adventurous, I would hike in the Australian Outback.

   b. _____ If I were more adventurous, I would hike in the Australian Outback.

2. a. _____ If my friends had known about my trip, they would have told me to go there.

   b. _____ Had my friends known about my trip, they would have told me to go there.

3. a. _____ Should anyone ask, I'll be gone for another month.

   b. _____ If anyone should ask, I'll be gone for another month.

Pinnacles Desert, Australian Outback

20-7 Omitting *If*

(a) *Were I* you, I wouldn't do that.	With ***were, had*** (past perfect), and ***should***, sometimes ***if*** is omitted, and the subject and verb are inverted.
(b) *Had I known,* I would have told you.	In (a): ***Were I you*** = if I were you
(c) *Should anyone call,* please take a message.	In (b): ***Had I known*** = if I had known
	In (c): ***Should anyone call*** = if anyone should call

EXERCISE 36 ▶ Looking at grammar. (Chart 20-7)

Make sentences with the same meaning by omitting **if**.

FYI (For Your Information)

1. If you should need more money, I'll lend it to you.
   → *Should you need more money, I'll lend it to you.*
2. If I were you, I would let someone know where you'll be.
3. If I were your teacher, I would insist you do more careful work.
4. If I should change my mind, I'll let you know.
5. She would have gotten the job if she had been better prepared.
6. It's just my opinion, but I think your boss is awful. If I had a choice, I would look for another job.
7. I'll be out of the office until June 12th. If you should need to reach me, I'll be at our company headquarters in Seoul.
8. If I had known what would happen, I would have done things differently.

EXERCISE 37 ▶ Looking at grammar. (Charts 20-3 → 20-7)

Work with a partner. Choose <u>all</u> the sentences that best express the meaning of the given sentence.

1. If I hadn't been driving so fast, I wouldn't have gotten a speeding ticket.
   a. I get a lot of speeding tickets.
   b. I was driving too fast. ⟵ circled
   c. I like to drive fast.
   d. I was given a ticket. ⟵ circled

2. Should you need help, I'll be in the room next door.
   a. I'll be helping others in the room.
   b. I'm available to help you.
   c. You shouldn't ask me for help.
   d. Do you need help from me?

3. Had you told us sooner, we could have helped you.
   a. We're glad you told us.
   b. We were happy that we helped you.
   c. We needed to know earlier.
   d. We didn't help you.

4. If there had been a faster way to get to the theater, I would have taken it.
   a. I took the fastest way to the theater.
   b. I didn't take the fastest way.
   c. The theater was too far away.
   d. I took several different routes.

5. Should you have questions, give me a call on my cell.
   a. I'm available by cell phone.
   b. Did you have questions?
   c. Call me soon.
   d. Call me if you have questions.

6. Had anyone warned us about the situation, we would have stayed home.
   a. We stayed home.
   b. We didn't stay home.
   c. No one warned us.
   d. Someone warned us.

7. Were we rich, we would live in a house overlooking the ocean.
   a. Are we rich?
   b. Rich people live in houses overlooking the ocean.
   c. We aren't rich.
   d. We don't live in a house overlooking the ocean.

EXERCISE 38 ▸ Warm-up. (Chart 20-8)
Read the paragraph. Check (✓) the sentences that are true.

One night a fire started in Janet's apartment. A blanket on the sofa got too close to an electric heater. Janet was in a deep sleep and wasn't aware of the fire. Fortunately, her neighbors saw smoke coming out of the window and threw rocks at her bedroom window to wake her up. Janet was very grateful that she hadn't been killed or injured in the fire.

1. _____ Janet would have kept sleeping, but the neighbors woke her up.

2. _____ Janet would have awakened without her neighbors' help.

3. _____ Janet was awakened by her neighbors; otherwise, she wouldn't have woken up.

20-8 Implied Conditions	
(a) I *would have gone* with you, *but I had to study*. (b) I never *would have succeeded* *without your help*.	Often the *if*-clause is implied, not stated. Conditional verbs are still used in the result clause. In (a): the implied condition = *if I hadn't had to study* In (b): the implied condition = *if you hadn't helped me*
(c) She ran; *otherwise*, she *would have missed* her bus.	Conditional verbs are frequently used following **otherwise**. In (c), the implied *if*-clause = *if she had not run*

EXERCISE 39 ▸ Looking at grammar. (Chart 20-8)
Identify the implied conditions by making sentences using *if*-clauses.

Thank goodness!

1. My phone would have died, but Gina had a charger.
   → *My phone would have died if Gina hadn't had a charger.*
2. I couldn't have paid my school tuition without your loan.
   → *I couldn't have paid my school tuition if you hadn't loaned me money.*
3. The fire would have spread quickly, but the fire trucks weren't far away.
4. I stepped on the brakes. Otherwise, I would have hit the little girl on the bike.
5. I couldn't have finished my project on time without your help.
6. My noisy party guests quieted down. Otherwise, the neighbors would have called the police.
7. I would have missed my flight, but my friend called and woke me up.

EXERCISE 40 ▸ Listening. (Chart 20-8)
Choose the statement that is true for each situation. In some cases both answers are correct.

Example: You will hear: I canceled your dentist appointment for Tuesday. Otherwise, you would have had two appointments in one day.
       You will choose: a. I thought you needed two appointments.
                   ⓑ I didn't think you wanted two appointments.

1. a. If I had had your number, I would have called.
   b. I didn't have your number; otherwise, I would have called.

2. a. If my parents hadn't helped me, I wouldn't have gone to college.
   b. If I hadn't gone to college, my parents wouldn't have helped me.

3. a. I picked up your clothes.
   b. I wasn't able to pick up your clothes.

4. a. If someone had told us about the party, we would have come.
   b. We came to the party even though you didn't tell us about it.

5. a. If I'd had your advice, I would have known what to do.
   b. Because of your advice, I knew what to do.

EXERCISE 41 ▶ Looking at grammar. (Charts 20-1 → 20-8)

Complete the sentences with the verbs in parentheses. Some of the verbs are passive.

A Walk Around Town

1. If I could speak better Japanese, I (*try*) _____ to have a conversation with the group of people over there.

2. See that apartment building? We are going to move into it June 1st if it (*finish*) _____ _____ by then.

3. The rent was very reasonable. Otherwise, I (*try*) _____ to find an apartment that was already finished.

4. Thanks for waiting for me. I (*be*) _____ here sooner, but I had car trouble.

5. It's too bad that Nadia can't join us. If she (*work, not*) _____ all the time, we would see her more often.

6. Had I known we were going to walk so far, I (*wear*) _____ more comfortable shoes.

7. A: It's so hot out. It feels suffocating.
   B: I know. If there (*be*) _____ only a breeze, it (*be, not*) _____ quite so bad.

8. A: What would you be doing right now if you (*be, not*) _____ here?
   B: I (*pay*) _____ bills.

9. If I (*turn on, not*) _____ my phone just before you called, I would have missed this chance to be with you.

10. I can't remember if your birthday is this week or next week. Sorry — I have such a bad memory that I (*forget*) _____ my head if it (*be, not*) _____ attached to my body.

11. I try to walk every day. A day without exercise (*be*) _____ _____ unthinkable for me.

12. A: Want to ride the Ferris wheel?
    B: No way! I have a fear of heights. I (*ride, not*) _____ it if you paid me a million dollars!

EXERCISE 42 ▸ Let's talk. (Charts 20-1 → 20-8)

Explain what you would do in these circumstances. Work in pairs or small groups.

Suppose ...

Example:

SPEAKER A (*book open*):   Suppose you find a wallet with money in it in a classroom.
                                            What would you do?

SPEAKER B (*book closed*): I would turn it in to the lost-and-found office.

1. You are at a party. A man starts talking to you, but he is speaking so fast that you can't catch what he is saying. What would you do?

2. Ricardo went to a friend's house for dinner. His friend served a dish that he can't stand/doesn't like at all. What if you were Ricardo?

3. Suppose you went to a cash machine. The amount you got was double what you asked for. What would you do?

4. John was cheating during an exam. Suppose you were the teacher and you saw him. What would you have done?

5. Suppose there were a fire in this building right now. What would you do?

6. Suppose there were a fire in your room or apartment or house. You had time to save only one thing. What would you save?

7. Imagine that one night you were driving your car down a deserted street. You were all alone. In an attempt to avoid a dog in the road, you swerved and hit a parked car. No one saw you. What would you do?

EXERCISE 43 ▸ Warm-up. (Chart 20-9)

Which sentences are true for you? What do you notice about the words in blue?

1. I wish I were someplace else right now.   yes   no

2. I wish I had learned English when I was a child.   yes   no

20-9 Wishes About the Present and Past

Wish is used when the speaker wants reality to be different, to be exactly the opposite, but it isn't.

	"True" Statement	Verb Form Following *Wish*	*Wish* can be followed by a noun clause (see Chart 12-5, p. 257). Past verb forms, similar to those in conditional sentences, are used in the noun clause.
A WISH ABOUT THE PRESENT	(a) I *don't know* French.	I *wish* (that) I *knew* French.	
	(b) It *is raining* right now.	I *wish* it *weren't raining* right now.	
	(c) I *can't speak* Japanese.	I *wish* I *could speak* Japanese.	To make a wish about the present, a past verb form is used, as in (a)–(c).
A WISH ABOUT THE PAST	(d) John *didn't come.*	I *wish* John *had come.**	In (d), the past perfect (**had come**) is used to make a wish about the past.
	(e) Mary *couldn't come.*	I *wish* Mary *could have come.*	
(f) I *wish* I *could* come. (It's not possible. I can't come.)			Note the difference between **wish** and **hope**. **Wish** is used for unreal, contrary-to-fact situations. **Hope** is used for real or possible situations.
(g) I *hope* I *can* come. (It's a possibility. Maybe I can come.)			

*You may hear *I wish Josh would have come.* This is incorrect in formal English.

EXERCISE 44 ▶ Looking at grammar. (Chart 20-9)

Complete the sentences with an appropriate verb form. You may need to add *not*.

1. Our classroom doesn't have any windows. I wish our classroom _____ had _____ windows.

2. The sun isn't shining. I wish the sun _____ right now.

3. I didn't go shopping. I wish I _____ shopping.

4. I don't know how to dance. I wish I _____ how to dance.

5. It's cold today. I'm not wearing a coat. I wish I _____ a coat.

6. I don't have enough money to buy that book. I wish I _____ enough money.

7. You can't meet my parents. I wish you _____ them, but they're out of town.

8. Khalid didn't come to the meeting. I wish he _____ to the meeting.

9. I'm not lying on a sunny beach. I wish I _____ on a sunny beach.

10. Ingrid forgot to get Ernesto's new phone number. She wishes she _____ _____ to get his phone number.

11. I didn't eat breakfast before I came to class. I wasn't hungry, but now I am. I wish I _____ breakfast.

12. Pedro stayed up really late last night. Today he's having trouble staying awake at work. He wishes he _____ stayed up really late last night.

EXERCISE 45 ▶ Looking at grammar. (Chart 20-9)

Complete the sentences with an appropriate auxiliary verb.

1. I'm not at home, but I wish I _____ were _____.

2. I don't know her, but I wish I _____ did _____.

3. I can't sing well, but I wish I _____ could _____.

4. I didn't go, but I wish I _____ had _____.

5. I don't have a bike, but I wish I _____.

6. I didn't read that book, but I wish I _____.

7. I want to go, but I can't. I wish I _____.

8. The city won't add more parks, but I wish it _____.

9. He isn't old enough to drive a car, but he wishes he _____.

10. They didn't go to the movie, but they wish they _____.

11. I don't have a driver's license, but I wish I _____.

12. I'm not living by myself, but I wish I _____.

13. I have roommates, but I wish I _____.

14. You can't come with us, but I wish you _____.

15. He didn't buy a ticket to the game, but he wishes he _____.

EXERCISE 46 ▶ Reading and grammar. (Charts 20-1 → 20-9)

Part I. Read the blog entry by author Stacy Hagen.

Do you know these words?
- wander
- brain scan
- nap
- pop into

 BlueBookBlog Becoming "Unstuck"

If you were trying to write a research paper for a class and couldn't come up with any ideas, what would you do? Would you keep working away or would you stop for a while? Interestingly, research points to stopping so that your mind can wander. Instead of continuing to focus on a task, the best thing to do is to leave the task for a while and do something else that frees up your thinking.

Surprisingly, if we stop concentrating on something, we actually become more creative. Researchers have found by looking at brain scans that our minds are very active during the daydreaming stage. By not focusing on a problem, we are able to look at it in new ways when we come back to it. As our minds wander, they often find the solution.

The company 3M has known this for decades. Since 1948, they have had the 15% rule: 15% of employees' time can be spent on a hobby or project of their choice. On top of that, they are encouraged to take walks, breaks, naps — whatever their minds need to help unlock their creativity.

A Stanford University study found that walking outdoors increased creativity by an average of 60%. I decided to give this a try and was amazed at how quickly I became "unstuck." Possibilities and answers really did pop into my head. To be honest, I was surprised at how effective this was. And, it's not just walking that has helped. Sometimes all I need to do is leave my computer and start another task that lets me daydream — something as simple as getting a snack.

I wish I had known this during my college days. I'm sure it would have helped me be a more efficient and productive student. I certainly know I would have been calmer and more relaxed when I got stuck.

Part II. Identify the time frame of the ideas in the phrases (*now* or *past*). Decide if they express real or unreal conditions.

	NOW/PAST	REAL/UNREAL
1. If you were trying to write a research paper for a class and couldn't come up with any ideas, …	*now*	*unreal*
2. … would you keep working away?		
3. … would you stop for a while?		
4. If we stop concentrating on something, …		
5. It would have helped me …		
6. I would have been calmer and more relaxed …		

Part III. Think about challenges you have when you do homework. What slows you down? Do you ever get stuck? What helps you get unstuck? Would the techniques in this blog work for you if you tried them? Why or why not? Discuss the questions with a partner or in small groups.

Check (✓) all the correct sentences.

1. _____ I wish I were going to visit you next week.   3. _____ I wish I could visit you next week.

2. _____ I wish I visited you next week.   4. _____ I wish I would visit you next week.

20-10	Wishes About the Future; Use of *Wish + Would*
(a) He *isn't going to be* here next week. I *wish* he *were going to be* here next week. (b) She *can't come* tomorrow. I *wish* she *could come* tomorrow. (c) She *won't tell you*. I *wish* she *would tell you*. (d) I *wish* I *could go* with you.	Wishes about the future can be expressed with **were going to**, **could**, or **would**. The speaker wants the situation to be the opposite of what it will be. **Could**, not **would**, is used when the speaker is making a wish with *I*, as in (d). *INCORRECT:* I wish I would go with you.
(e) It is raining. I *wish* it *would stop*.	**Wish + would** can be used when the speaker wants an action or event to change, as in (e). Note that it cannot be used for situations. *INCORRECT:* I wish you would know the answer.
(f) I *wish* you *would leave* now.	**Wish + would** can also be used to make a strong request, as in (f).

EXERCISE 48 ▸ Looking at grammar. (Chart 20-10)
Make future wishes.

1. I can't go with you tomorrow, but I wish I _____ *could go* _____.

2. My friend won't ever lend me his car. I wish he _____ me his car for my date tomorrow night.

3. Mrs. Takasawa isn't coming to dinner with us tonight. I wish she _____ to dinner with us.

4. The teacher is going to give an exam tomorrow. I wish he _____ us an exam tomorrow.

5. Jon won't tell me about his plans, but I wish he _____ me something.

6. It probably won't happen, but I wish it _____.

EXERCISE 49 ▸ Let's talk. (Charts 20-9 and 20-10)
Work with a partner or in small groups. Read the given information. Then answer the questions with **wish + would**.

Example:
TOM: Why are you pacing back and forth?
SUE: I'm waiting to hear from Sam. I want him to call me. I need to talk to him right now. We had an argument. I need to make sure everything's OK.

    (a) What does Sue want to happen?
      → She **wishes** Sam *would call her.*
    (b) What else does Sue wish?
      → She **wishes** she **could** *talk to Sam right now.*
      She probably **wishes** she and Sam **hadn't had** an argument.

1. ANNA: Can't you come to the concert? Please change your mind. I'd really like you to come.
   YOKO: Thanks for the invitation, but I don't see how I can change my work schedule.

   (a) What does Anna want Yoko to do?
   (b) What else does Anna wish?

2. Helen is a neat and orderly person. Judy, her roommate, is messy. Judy never picks up after herself. She leaves dirty dishes in the sink. She drops her clothes all over the apartment. She never makes her bed. Helen nags Judy to pick up after herself.

   (a) What does Helen want Judy to do?
   (b) What does Judy probably wish?

EXERCISE 50 ▸ Looking at grammar. (Charts 20-9 and 20-10)
Make wishes using the verbs in the box.

be	become	come	have to	✓need	tell	wear

1. I need nine hours of sleep. I wish I _____*didn't need*_____ so much sleep. I could get so much more done in a day.

2. Alice doesn't like her job as a nurse. She wishes she _____ a nurse. She wishes she _____ a doctor.

3. We had a good time in the mountains over vacation. I wish you _____ with us.

4. I know that something's bothering you. I wish you _____ me what it is. Maybe I can help.

5. A: I wish I _____ work today.
   B: So do I. I wish it _____ a holiday.

6. A: My feet are killing me! I wish I _____ shoes.
   B: Yeah, me too. I didn't know we were going to be walking on rocks.

EXERCISE 51 ▸ Let's talk: interview. (Charts 20-9 and 20-10)
Ask two classmates each question. Share some of their answers with the class.

1. What is something you can't do but you wish you could do?
2. Where do you wish you were right now? What do you wish you were doing?
3. What is something you don't have but wish you had?
4. What is something that didn't happen yesterday but that you wish had happened?
5. What is something you don't know but wish you knew?
6. What is something you have to do but wish you didn't have to do?
7. What is something you were unable to do yesterday but you wish you could have done?
8. What is something that has never happened in your life but that you wish would happen?
9. What do you wish were different about this city/town?
10. What is something in your life that you wish could be different?

EXERCISE 52 ▶ Check your knowledge. (Chapter 20 Review)

Correct the errors.

1. If I had know more about it, I would have had better advice for you.

2. If were I you, I would spend more time outdoors.

3. Should my manager needs to reach me, I'll be at the bank and post office.

4. Anyone should ask for me, tell them I'm not available.

5. If you continue to drive so fast, I would get out of the car.

6. She wishes she went to the doctor when she first had symptoms.

7. If it were not snow outside, we could walk to the mall.

8. I would have done things differently were I received the correct information.

9. They hurried; otherwise, they wouldn't have missed their train.

10. The team never will have won the game yesterday without your help.

11. I hope I could meet with you tomorrow.

12. We're really late. I wish you hurry.

13. If I had brought a lunch to work, I wouldn't have been hungry now.

14. I wish I would ask more questions when we reviewed for the exam yesterday.

EXERCISE 53 ▶ Reading and writing. (Chapter 20)

Part I. Read the passage. Which words are used to introduce hypothetical situations? <u>Underline</u> them.

Do you know these words?
- *appealing*   - *throbbing*
- *agonizing*   - *untold*
- *suffering*   - *outcomes*

A Life Without Pain

Can you imagine a world where people felt no pain? At first it sounds appealing. You wouldn't know the agonizing suffering that comes from pain. If you had a throbbing headache or toothache, you wouldn't even feel it. But you also wouldn't know to check if the headache or toothache indicated something more serious. Or if you had a different condition, like a broken bone, you wouldn't necessarily know that it needed to be treated.

Some people are born with an inability to feel pain. However, rather than being a positive condition, it causes untold problems. If people can't feel pain, they don't know if they are hurt. For parents of young children, this is a nightmare. How would a child know about the dangers of a hot stove or broken glass? A burn wouldn't be painful and a cut wouldn't hurt.

Parents of these children have to continually watch for injuries. Normal activities like going to the playground aren't at all normal. Suppose a child fell from the top of a slide. He or she might find this fun and try to do it again, risking further injury.

Pain turns out to be lifesaving; it helps us to know if something is wrong and requires treatment. Without it, we would go through life hurting ourselves, possibly with deadly outcomes.

As you have learned, sentence variety (changing the length and structure of your sentences) makes your writing more interesting. Remember that always using *if* to express hypothetical situations can become repetitious. As you saw in the reading passage, there are other words and expressions you can use to introduce hypothetical situations: *without, suppose, imagine, how would.*

Or, as you have learned in Chart 20-7, you can sometimes omit *if* and invert the subject and verb.

Part II. Look at the following topics. Brainstorm ideas with your classmates. Then choose one and write about it. Use conditionals in your writing.

What would life be like without …
- a sense of smell?
- the need for sleep?
- the sun?
- trees?
- schools/education?
- the Internet?
- a cell phone?
- social media?

Part III. Edit your writing. Check for the following:

1. ☐ use of conditional sentences
2. ☐ use of correct verbs with conditional sentences
3. ☐ sentence variety by not always using *if*
4. ☐ correct spelling (use a dictionary or spell-check)

Appendix

Supplementary Grammar Charts

UNIT A: Basic Grammar Terminology

A-1 Subjects, Verbs, and Objects

(a) $\overset{\text{S}}{\overline{Birds}}$ $\overset{\text{V}}{\overline{fly}}$. (noun) (verb)	Almost all English sentences contain a subject (**S**) and a verb (**V**). The verb may or may not be followed by an object (**O**).
(b) The $\overset{\text{S}}{\overline{baby}}$ $\overset{\text{V}}{\overline{cried}}$. (noun) (verb)	VERBS: Verbs that are not followed by an object, as in (a) and (b), are called "intransitive verbs." Common intransitive verbs: *agree, arrive, come, cry, exist, go, happen, live, occur, rain, rise, sleep, stay.*
(c) The $\overset{\text{S}}{\overline{student}}$ $\overset{\text{V}}{\overline{needs}}$ a $\overset{\text{O}}{\overline{pen}}$. (noun) (verb) (noun)	Verbs that are followed by an object, as in (c) and (d), are called "transitive verbs." Common transitive verbs: *build, cut, find, like, make, need, send, use, want.*
(d) My $\overset{\text{S}}{\overline{friend}}$ $\overset{\text{V}}{\overline{enjoyed}}$ the $\overset{\text{O}}{\overline{party}}$. (noun) (verb) (noun)	Some verbs can be either intransitive or transitive. Intransitive: *A student studies.* Transitive: *A student studies books.*
	SUBJECTS AND OBJECTS: The subjects and objects of verbs are nouns (or pronouns). Examples of nouns: *person, place, thing, John, Asia, pen, information, appearance, amusement.*

A-2 Adjectives

(a) Ann is an *intelligent* student. (adjective) (noun) (b) The *hungry* child ate fruit. (adjective) (noun)	Adjectives describe nouns. In grammar, we say that adjectives modify nouns. The word *modify* means "change a little." Adjectives give a little different meaning to a noun: *intelligent student, lazy student, good student.* Examples of adjectives: *young, old, rich, beautiful, brown, French, modern.*
(c) I saw some *beautiful* pictures. INCORRECT: beautiful -s- pictures	An adjective is neither singular nor plural. A final **-s** is never added to an adjective.

A-3 Adverbs

(a) He walks *quickly*. 　　　　　(adverb)	Adverbs modify verbs. Often they answer the question "How?" In (a): *How does he walk?* Answer: *Quickly.*
(b) She opened the door *quietly*. 　　　　　　　　　　(adverb)	Adverbs are often formed by adding **-ly** to an adjective. 　　Adjective: *quick* 　　Adverb:　 *quickly*
(c) I am *extremely happy*. 　　　　(adverb)　(adjective)	Adverbs are also used to modify adjectives, i.e., to give information about adjectives, as in (c).
(d) Ann will come *tomorrow*. 　　　　　　　　(adverb)	Adverbs are also used to express time or frequency. Examples: *tomorrow, today, yesterday, soon, never, usually, always, yet.*
MIDSENTENCE ADVERBS: (e) Ann *always comes* on time. (f) Ann *is always* on time. (g) Ann *has always come* on time. (h) Does *she always come* on time?	Some adverbs may occur in the middle of a sentence. Midsentence adverbs have usual positions; they 　• come in front of simple present and simple past verbs (except **be**), as in (e); 　• follow **be** (simple present and simple past), as in (f); 　• come between a helping verb and a main verb, as in (g). In a question, a midsentence adverb comes directly after the subject, as in (h).

Common midsentence adverbs

ever	usually	generally	seldom	never	already
always	often	sometimes	rarely	not ever	finally
	frequently	occasionally	hardly ever		just
					probably

A-4 Prepositions and Prepositional Phrases

Common prepositions

about	at	beyond	into	since	up
above	before	by	like	through	upon
across	behind	despite	near	throughout	with
after	below	down	of	till	within
against	beneath	during	off	to	without
along	beside	for	on	toward(s)	
among	besides	from	out	under	
around	between	in	over	until	

(a) The <u>student</u> <u>studies</u> <u>in</u> the <u>library</u>. 　　　S　　　V　　PREP　　O of PREP 　　　　　　　　　　　　　　　(noun)	An important element of English sentences is the prepositional phrase. It consists of a preposition (**PREP**) and its object (**O**). The object of a preposition is a noun or pronoun. In (a): ***in the library*** is a prepositional phrase.
(b) <u>We</u> <u>enjoyed</u> the <u>party</u> <u>at</u> your <u>house</u>. 　　S　　V　　　　O　　PREP　　O of PREP 　　　　　　　　　　　　　　　　　　(noun)	
(c) We went *to the zoo* *in the afternoon*. 　　　　　　(Place)　　　　(Time)	In (c): In most English sentences, "place" comes before "time." In (d): Sometimes a prepositional phrase comes at the beginning of a sentence.
(d) *In the afternoon,* we went to the zoo.	

A-5 Preposition Combinations with Adjectives and Verbs

A
be absent from
be accused of
be accustomed to
be acquainted with
be addicted to
be afraid of
    agree with
be angry at, with
be annoyed with, by
    apologize for
    apply to, for
    approve of
    argue with, about
    arrive in, at
be associated with
be aware of

B
    believe in
    blame for
be blessed with
be bored with, by

C
be capable of
    care about, for
be cluttered with
be committed to
    compare to, with
    complain about, of
be composed of
be concerned about
be connected to
    consist of
be content with
    contribute to
be convinced of
be coordinated with
    count (up)on
be covered with
be crowded with

D
    decide (up)on
be dedicated to
    depend (up)on
be devoted to
be disappointed in, with
be discriminated against
    distinguish from
be divorced from
be done with

    dream of, about
be dressed in

E
be engaged in, to
be envious of
be equipped with
    escape from
    excel in, at
be excited about
    excuse for
be exhausted from
be exposed to

F
be faithful to
be familiar with
    feel like
    fight for
be filled with
be finished with
be fond of
    forget about
    forgive for
be friendly to, with
be frightened of, by
be furnished with

G
be gone from
be grateful to, for
be guilty of

H
    hide from
    hope for

I
be innocent of
    insist (up)on
be interested in
    introduce to
be involved in

J
be jealous of

K
    keep from
be known for

L
be limited to
be located in
    look forward to

M
be made of, from
be married to

O
    object to
be opposed to

P
    participate in
be patient with
be pleased with
be polite to
    pray for
be prepared for
    prevent from
    prohibit from
be protected from
be proud of
    provide with

Q
be qualified for

R
    recover from
be related to
be relevant to
    rely (up)on
be remembered for
    rescue from
    respond to
be responsible for

S
be satisfied with
be scared of, by
    stare at
    stop from
    subscribe to
    substitute for
    succeed in

T
    take advantage of
    take care of
    talk about, of
be terrified of, by
    thank for
    think about, of
be tired of, from

U
be upset with
be used to

V
    vote for

W
be worried about

UNIT B: Questions

B-1 Forms of Yes / No and Information Questions

A yes/no question = a question that may be answered by *yes* or *no*

A: Does he live in Chicago?
B: Yes, he does. OR No, he doesn't.

An information question = a question that asks for information by using a question word

A: Where does he live?
B: In Chicago.

Question word order = (*Question word*) + *helping verb* + *subject* + *main verb*

Notice that the same subject-verb order is used in both *yes/no* and information questions.

(Question Word)	Helping Verb	Subject	Main Verb	(Rest of Sentence)	
(a) (b) Where	Does does	she she	live live?	there? 	If the verb is in the simple present, use ***does*** (with *he, she, it*) or ***do*** (with *I, you, we, they*) in the question. If the verb is simple past, use ***did***. Notice: The main verb in the question is in its simple form; there is no final ***-s*** or ***-ed***.
(c) (d) Where	Do do	they they	live live?	there?	
(e) (f) Where	Did did	he he	live live?	there?	
(g) (h) Where	Is is	he he	living living?	there?	If the verb has an auxiliary (a helping verb), the same auxiliary is used in the question. There is no change in the form of the main verb. If the verb has more than one auxiliary, only the first auxiliary precedes the subject, as in (m) and (n).
(i) (j) Where	Have have	they they	lived lived?	there?	
(k) (l) Where	Can can	Mary Mary	live live?	there?	
(m) (n) Where	Will will	he he	be living be living?	there?	
(o) Who (p) Who	Ø can	Ø Ø	lives come?	there?	If the question word is the subject, usual question-word order is not used; ***does, do***, and ***did*** are not used. The verb is in the same form in a question as it is in a statement. Statement: *Tom came.* Question: *Who came?*
(q) (r) Where	Are are	they they?	Ø Ø	there?	Main verb ***be*** in the simple present (*am, is, are*) and simple past (*was, were*) precedes the subject. It has the same position as a helping verb.
(s) (t) Where	Was was	Jim Jim?	Ø Ø	there?	

B-2 Question Words

	Question	Answer	
When	(a) **When** did they arrive? **When** will you come?	Yesterday. Next Monday.	**When** is used to ask questions about *time*.
Where	(b) **Where** is she? **Where** can I find a pen?	At home. In that drawer.	**Where** is used to ask questions about *place*.
Why	(c) **Why** did he leave early? **Why** aren't you coming with us?	Because he's ill. I'm tired.	**Why** is used to ask questions about *reason*.
How	(d) **How** did you come to school? **How** does he drive?	By bus. Carefully.	**How** generally asks about *manner*.
	(e) **How much** money does it cost? **How many** people came?	Ten dollars. Fifteen.	**How** is used with **much** and **many**.
	(f) **How old** are you? **How cold** is it? **How soon** can you get here? **How fast** were you driving?	Twelve. Ten below zero. In ten minutes. 50 miles an hour.	**How** is also used with adjectives and adverbs.
	(g) **How long** has he been here? **How often** do you write home? **How far** is it to Miami from here?	Two years. Every week. 500 miles.	**How long** asks about *length of time*. **How often** asks about *frequency*. **How far** asks about *distance*.
Who	(h) **Who** can answer that question? **Who** came to visit you?	I can. Jane and Eric.	**Who** is used as the subject of a question. It refers to people.
	(i) **Who** is coming to dinner tonight? **Who** wants to come with me?	Ann, Bob, and Al. We do.	**Who** is usually followed by a singular verb even if the speaker is asking about more than one person.
Whom	(j) **Who(m)** did you see? **Who(m)** are you visiting?	I saw George. My relatives.	**Whom** is used as the object of a verb or preposition. In everyday spoken English, **whom** is rarely used; **who** is used instead. **Whom** is used only in formal questions. NOTE: **Whom**, not **who**, is used if preceded by a preposition.
	(k) **Who(m)** should I talk *to*? *To* **whom** should I talk? (formal)	The secretary.	
Whose	(l) **Whose** book did you borrow? **Whose** key is this? (**Whose** is this?)	David's. It's mine.	**Whose** asks questions about *possession*.

	Question	Answer	
What	(m) *What* made you angry? *What* went wrong?	His rudeness. Everything.	*What* is used as the subject of a question. It refers to things.
	(n) *What* do you need? *What* did Alice buy?	I need a pencil. A book.	*What* is also used as an object.
	(o) *What* did he talk *about*? *About what* did he talk? (formal)	His vacation.	
	(p) *What kind of* soup is that? *What kind of* shoes did he buy?	It's bean soup. Sandals.	*What kind of* asks about the particular variety or type of something.
	(q) *What* did you *do* last night? *What* is Mary *doing*?	I studied. Reading a book.	*What + a form of do* is used to ask questions about activities.
	(r) *What countries* did you visit? *What time* did she come? *What color* is his hair?	Italy and Spain. Seven o'clock. Dark brown.	*What* may accompany a noun.
	(s) *What* is Ed *like*?	He's kind and friendly.	*What + be like* asks for a general description of qualities.
	(t) *What* is the weather *like*?	Hot and humid.	
	(u) *What* does Ed *look like*?	He's tall and has dark hair.	*What + look like* asks for a physical description.
	(v) *What* does her house *look like*?	It's a two-story,* red brick house.	
Which	(w) I have two pens. *Which pen* do you want? *Which one* do you want? *Which* do you want?	The blue one.	*Which* is used instead of *what* when a question concerns choosing from a definite, known quantity or group.
	(x) *Which book* should I buy?	That one.	
	(y) *Which countries* did he visit? *What countries* did he visit?	Peru and Chile.	In some cases, there is little difference in meaning between *which* and *what* when they accompany a noun, as in (y) and (z).
	(z) *Which class* are you in? *What class* are you in?	This class.	

*American English: *a two-**story** house.*
British English: *a two-**storey** house.*

B-3 Shortened *Yes / No* Questions

(a) *Going to bed now? = Are you going to bed now?* (b) *Finish your work? = Did you finish your work?* (c) *Want to go to the movie with us? = Do you want to go to the movie with us?*	Sometimes in spoken English, the auxiliary and the subject *you* are dropped from a *yes/no* question, as in (a), (b), and (c).

B-4 Negative Questions

(a) *Doesn't she live* in the dormitory? (b) *Does she not live* in the dormitory? (very formal)	In a *yes/no* question in which the verb is negative, usually a contraction (e.g., *does + not = doesn't*) is used, as in (a). Example (b) is very formal and is usually not used in everyday speech. Negative questions are used to indicate the speaker's idea (i.e., what she/he believes is or is not true) or attitude (e.g., surprise, shock, annoyance, anger).
(c) Bob returns to his dorm room after his nine o'clock class. Matt, his roommate, is there. Bob is surprised. Bob says, *"What are you doing here? Aren't you supposed to be in class now?"*	In (c): Bob believes that Matt is supposed to be in class now. *Expected answer:* **Yes**.
(d) Alice and Mary are at home. Mary is about to leave on a trip, and Alice is going to take her to the airport. Alice says, *"It's already two o'clock. We'd better leave for the airport. Doesn't your plane leave at three?"*	In (d): Alice believes that Mary's plane leaves at three. She is asking the negative question to make sure that her information is correct. *Expected answer:* **Yes**.
(e) The teacher is talking to Jim about a test he failed. The teacher is surprised that Jim failed the test because he usually does very well. The teacher says, *"What happened? Didn't you study?"*	In (e): The teacher believes that Jim did not study. *Expected answer:* **No**.
(f) Barb and Ron are riding in a car. Ron is driving. He comes to a corner where there is a stop sign, but he does not stop the car. Barb is shocked. Barb says, *"What's the matter with you? Didn't you see that stop sign?"*	In (f): Barb believes that Ron did not see the stop sign. *Expected answer:* **No**.

B-5 Tag Questions

(a) Jack *can* come, *can't* he? (b) Fred *can't* come, *can* he?	A tag question is a question added at the end of a sentence. Speakers use tag questions mainly to make sure their information is correct or to seek agreement.*

AFFIRMATIVE SENTENCE + NEGATIVE TAG → AFFIRMATIVE ANSWER EXPECTED

Mary *is* here,	*isn't* she?	Yes, she is.
You *like* tea,	*don't* you?	Yes, I do.
They *have left,*	*haven't* they?	Yes, they have.

NEGATIVE SENTENCE + AFFIRMATIVE TAG → NEGATIVE ANSWER EXPECTED

Mary *isn't* here,	*is* she?	No, she isn't.
You *don't* like tea,	*do* you?	No, I don't.
They *haven't* left,	*have* they?	No, they haven't.

(c) *This / That* is your book, isn't *it?* *These / Those* are yours, aren't *they?*	The tag pronoun for **this / that** = **it**. The tag pronoun for **these / those** = **they**.
(d) *There is* a meeting tonight, *isn't there?*	In sentences with **there + be, there** is used in the tag.
(e) *Everything* is OK, isn't *it?* (f) *Everyone* took the test, didn't *they?*	Personal pronouns are used to refer to indefinite pronouns. **They** is usually used in a tag to refer to **everyone, everybody, someone, somebody, no one, nobody**.
(g) *Nothing is* wrong, *is* it? (h) *Nobody called* on the phone, *did* they? (i) You*'ve never been* there, *have* you?	Sentences with negative words take affirmative tags.
(j) *I am* supposed to be here, *am I not?* (k) *I am* supposed to be here, *aren't I?*	In (j): **am I not?** is formal English. In (k): **aren't I?** is common in spoken English.

*A tag question may be spoken:
   (1) with a rising intonation if the speaker is truly seeking to ascertain that his/her information, idea, belief is correct (e.g., *Ann lives in an apartment, doesn't she?*); OR
   (2) with a falling intonation if the speaker is expressing an idea with which she/he is almost certain the listener will agree (e.g., *It's a nice day today, isn't it?*).

Jim *could* use some help, *couldn't* he?

UNIT C: Contractions

C Contractions

IN SPEAKING: In everyday spoken English, certain forms of **be** and auxiliary verbs are usually contracted with pronouns, nouns, and question words.

IN WRITING: (1) In written English, contractions with pronouns are common in informal writing, but they're not generally acceptable in formal writing.

(2) Contractions with nouns and question words are, for the most part, rarely used in writing. A few of these contractions may be found in quoted dialogue in stories or in very informal writing, such as a chatty letter to a good friend, but most of them are rarely if ever written.

In the following, quotation marks indicate that the contraction is frequently spoken but rarely, if ever, written.

	With Pronouns	**With Nouns**	**With Question Words**
am	*I'm* reading a book.	Ø	*"What'm"* I supposed to do?
is	*She's* studying. *It's* going to rain.	My *"book's"* on the table. *Mary's* at home.	*Where's* Sally? *Who's* that man?
are	*You're* working hard. *They're* waiting for us.	My *"books're"* on the table. The *"teachers're"* at a meeting.	*"What're"* you doing? *"Where're"* they going?
has	*She's* been here for a year. *It's* been cold lately.	My *"book's"* been stolen! *Sally's* never met him.	*Where's* Sally been living? *What's* been going on?
have	*I've* finished my work. *They've* never met you.	The *"books've"* been sold. The *"students've"* finished the test.	*"Where've"* they been? *"How've"* you been?
had	*He'd* been waiting for us. *We'd* forgotten about it.	The *"books'd"* been sold. *"Mary'd"* never met him before.	*"Where'd"* you been before that? *"Who'd"* been there before you?
did	Ø	Ø	*"What'd"* you do last night? *"How'd"* you do on the test?
will	*I'll* come later. *She'll* help us.	The *"weather'll"* be nice tomorrow. *"John'll"* be coming soon.	*"Who'll"* be at the meeting? *"Where'll"* you be at ten?
would	*He'd* like to go there. *They'd* come if they could.	My *"friends'd"* come if they could. *"Mary'd"* like to go there too.	*"Where'd"* you like to go?

UNIT D: Negatives

D-1 Using *Not* and Other Negative Words

(a) AFFIRMATIVE: The earth is round. (b) NEGATIVE: The earth is *not* flat.	*Not* expresses a *negative* idea.

		AUX	+	*NOT*	+	MAIN VERB			*Not* immediately follows an auxiliary verb or *be*.

(c)	I *will* not *go* there. I *have* not *gone* there. I *am* not *going* there. I *was* not there. I *do* not *go* there. He *does* not *go* there. I *did* not *go* there.	*Not* immediately follows an auxiliary verb or *be*. NOTE: If there is more than one auxiliary, *not* comes immediately after the first auxiliary: *I will not be going there.* *Do* or *does* is used with *not* to make a simple present verb (except *be*) negative. *Did* is used with *not* to make a simple past verb (except *be*) negative.

Contractions of auxiliary verbs with *not*

are not = aren't* cannot = can't could not = couldn't did not = didn't does not = doesn't do not = don't	has not = hasn't have not = haven't had not = hadn't is not = isn't must not = mustn't should not = shouldn't	was not = wasn't were not = weren't will not = won't would not = wouldn't

(d) I almost *never* go there. I have *hardly ever* gone there.	In addition to *not*, the following are negative adverbs: *never, rarely, seldom* *hardly (ever), scarcely (ever), barely (ever)*
(e) There's *no* chalk in the drawer.	*No* also expresses a negative idea.

COMPARE: *NOT* VS. *NO* (f) I *do not have* any money. (g) I have *no money*.	*Not* is used to make a verb negative, as in (f). *No* is used as an adjective in front of a noun (e.g., *money*), as in (g). NOTE: Examples (f) and (g) have the same meaning.

*Sometimes in spoken English you will hear "ain't." It means "am not," "isn't," or "aren't." *Ain't* is not considered proper English although it is frequently used for humor.

D-2 Avoiding Double Negatives

(a) INCORRECT: I ~~don't~~ have ~~no~~ money. (b) CORRECT: I *don't* have *any* money. CORRECT: I have *no* money.	Sentence (a) is an example of a "double negative," i.e., a confusing and grammatically incorrect sentence that contains two negatives in the same clause. One clause should contain only one negative.*

*Negatives in two different clauses in the same sentence cause no problems; for example:
   A person who ***doesn't*** *have love* ***can't*** *be truly happy.*
   I ***don't*** *know why he* ***isn't*** *here.*

D-3 Beginning a Sentence with a Negative Word

(a) *Never will I do* that again! (b) *Rarely have I eaten* better food. (c) *Hardly ever does he come* to class on time.	When a negative word begins a sentence, the subject and verb are inverted (i.e., question word order is used).*

*Beginning a sentence with a negative word is relatively uncommon in everyday usage; it is used when the speaker/writer wishes to emphasize the negative element of the sentence and be expressive.

UNIT E: Verbs

E-1 The Verb *Be*

(a)	John	*is* (be)	*a student*. (noun)
(b)	John	*is* (be)	*intelligent*. (adjective)
(c)	John	*was* (be)	*at the library*. (prep. phrase)

A sentence with *be* as the main verb has three basic patterns:

In (a): *be* + a noun
In (b): *be* + an adjective
In (c): *be* + a prepositional phrase

(d) Mary *is* writing a letter.	*Be* is also used as an auxiliary verb in progressive verb tenses and in the passive.
(e) They *were* listening to some music.	
(f) That letter *was* written by Alice.	In (d): *is* = auxiliary; *writing* = main verb

Tense Forms of *Be*

	SIMPLE PRESENT	SIMPLE PAST	PRESENT PERFECT
SINGULAR	I *am* you *are* he, she, it *is*	I *was* you *were* he, she, it *was*	I *have been* you *have been* he, she, it *has been*
PLURAL	we, you, they *are*	we, you, they *were*	we, you, they *have been*

E-2 Spelling of *-ing* and *-ed* Verb Forms

(1) VERBS THAT END IN A CONSONANT AND *-e*	(a) hope date injure	hoping dating injuring	hoped dated injured	*-ING* FORM: If the word ends in *-e*, drop the *-e* and add *-ing*.* *-ED* FORM: If the word ends in a consonant and *-e*, just add *-d*.
(2) VERBS THAT END IN A VOWEL AND A CONSONANT	ONE-SYLLABLE VERBS			
	(b) stop rob	stopping robbing	stopped robbed	1 vowel → 2 consonants**
	(c) rain fool	raining fooling	rained fooled	2 vowels → 1 consonant
	TWO-SYLLABLE VERBS			
	(d) listen offer	listening offering	listened offered	1st syllable stressed → 1 consonant
	(e) begin prefer	beginning preferring	(began) preferred	2nd syllable stressed → 2 consonants
(3) VERBS THAT END IN TWO CONSONANTS	(f) start fold demand	starting folding demanding	started folded demanded	If the word ends in two consonants, just add the ending.
(4) VERBS THAT END IN *-y*	(g) enjoy pray	enjoying praying	enjoyed prayed	If *-y* is preceded by a vowel, keep the *-y*.
	(h) study try reply	studying trying replying	studied tried replied	If *-y* is preceded by a consonant: *-ING* FORM: keep the *-y*; add *-ing*. *-ED* FORM: change *-y* to *-i*; add *-ed*.
(5) VERBS THAT END IN *-ie*	(i) die lie	dying lying	died lied	*-ING* FORM: Change *-ie* to *-y*; add *-ing*. *-ED* FORM: Change *-y* to *-i*; add *-ed*.

*Exception: If a verb ends in *-ee*, the final *-e* is not dropped: *seeing, agreeing, freeing*.
**Exception: *-w* and *-x* are not doubled: *plow → plowed; fix → fixed*.

The Simple Tenses

This basic diagram will be used in all tense descriptions.

SIMPLE PRESENT	(a) It *snows* in Alaska. (b) Tom *watches* TV every day.	In general, the simple present expresses events or situations that exist *always, usually, habitually;* they exist now, have existed in the past, and probably will exist in the future.
SIMPLE PAST	(c) It *snowed* yesterday. (d) Tom *watched* TV last night.	*At one particular time in the past,* this happened. It began and ended in the past.
SIMPLE FUTURE	(e) It *will snow* tomorrow. It *is going to snow* tomorrow. (f) Tom *will watch* TV tonight. Tom *is going to watch* TV tonight.	*At one particular time in the future,* this will happen.

The Progressive Tenses

Form: *be + -ing* (*present participle*)

Meaning: The progressive tenses* give the idea that an action is in progress during a particular time. The tenses say that an action *begins before, is in progress during, and continues after* another time or action.

PRESENT PROGRESSIVE	(a) Tom *is sleeping* right now.	It is now 11:00. Tom went to sleep at 10:00 tonight, and he is still asleep. His sleep began in the past, *is in progress at the present time*, and probably will continue.
PAST PROGRESSIVE 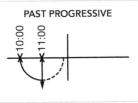	(b) Tom *was sleeping* when I arrived.	Tom went to sleep at 10:00 last night. I arrived at 11:00. He was still asleep. His sleep began before and *was in progress at a particular time in the past.* It continued after I arrived.
FUTURE PROGRESSIVE 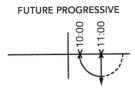	(c) Tom *will be sleeping* when we arrive.	Tom will go to sleep at 10:00 tomorrow night. We will arrive at 11:00. The action of sleeping will begin before we arrive, and it *will be in progress at a particular time in the future*. Probably his sleep will continue.

*The progressive tenses are also called the "continuous" tenses: present continuous, past continuous, and future continuous.

(continued)

The Perfect Tenses

Form: *have + past participle*

Meaning: The perfect tenses all give the idea that one thing *happens before* another time or event.

PRESENT PERFECT 	(a) Tom *has* already *eaten*. 	Tom *finished* eating *sometime before now*. The exact time is not important.
PAST PERFECT 	(b) Tom *had* already *eaten* when his friend arrived.	First Tom finished eating. Later his friend arrived. Tom's eating was completely *finished before another time in the past.*
FUTURE PERFECT	(c) Tom *will* already *have eaten* when his friend arrives.	First Tom will finish eating. Later his friend will arrive. Tom's eating will be completely *finished before another time in the future.*

The Perfect Progressive Tenses

Form: *have + been + -ing (present participle)*

Meaning: The perfect progressive tenses give the idea that one event is *in progress immediately before, up to, until another time or event.* The tenses are used to express the duration of the first event.

PRESENT PERFECT PROGRESSIVE 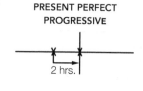	(a) Tom *has been studying* for two hours.	Event in progress: studying. When? *Before now, up to now.* How long? For two hours.
PAST PERFECT PROGRESSIVE 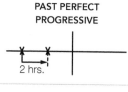	(b) Tom *had been studying* for two hours before his friend came.	Event in progress: studying. When? *Before another event in the past.* How long? For two hours.
FUTURE PERFECT PROGRESSIVE 	(c) Tom *will have been studying* for two hours by the time his friend arrives.	Event in progress: studying. When? *Before another event in the future.* How long? For two hours.

E-4 Summary of Verb Tenses

Simple Present

Tom *studies* every day.

Present Progressive

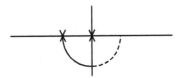

Tom *is studying* right now.

Simple Past

Tom *studied* last night.

Past Progressive

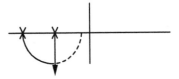

Tom *was studying* when they came.

Simple Future

Tom *will study* tomorrow.
Tom *is going to study* tomorrow.

Future Progressive

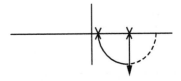

Tom *will be studying* when they come.
Tom *is going to be studying* when they come.

Present Perfect

Tom *has* already *studied* Chapter 1.

Present Perfect Progressive

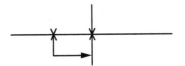

Tom *has been studying* for two hours.

Past Perfect

Tom *had* already *studied* Chapter 1 before he began studying Chapter 2.

Past Perfect Progressive

Tom *had been studying* for two hours before his friends came.

Future Perfect

Tom *will* already *have studied* Chapter 4 before he studies Chapter 5.

Future Perfect Progressive

Tom *will have been studying* for two hours by the time his roommate gets home.

E-5 Regular Verbs: Pronunciation of -ed Endings

Final **-ed** has three different pronunciations: /t/, /d/, and /əd/. The schwa /ə/ is an unstressed vowel sound. It is pronounced like *a* in *alone* in normal, rapid speech (e.g., *She lives alone.*).

(a) looked → look/t/ clapped → clap/t/ missed → miss/t/ watched → watch/t/ finished → finish/t/ laughed → laugh/t/	Final **-ed** is pronounced /t/ after voiceless sounds. Voiceless sounds are made by pushing air through your mouth; no sound comes from your throat. Examples of voiceless sounds: "k," "p," "s," "ch," "sh," "f."	
(b) smelled → smell/d/ saved → save/d/ cleaned → clean/d/ robbed → rob/d/ played → play/d/	Final **-ed** is pronounced /d/ after voiced sounds. Voiced sounds come from your throat. If you touch your neck when you make a voiced sound, you can feel your voice box vibrate. Examples of voiced sounds: "l," "v," "n," "b," and all vowel sounds.	
(c) decided → decide/əd/ needed → need/əd/ wanted → want/əd/ invited → invite/əd/	Final **-ed** is pronounced /əd/ after "t" and "d" sounds. The sound /əd/ adds a whole syllable to a word. COMPARE: looked = one syllable → look/t/ smelled = one syllable → smell/d/ needed = two syllables → need/əd/	

E-6 Pronunciation of Final -s in Verbs and Nouns

Final **-s** has three different pronunciations: /s/, /z/, and /əz/.

(a) seats → seat/s/ ropes → rope/s/ backs → back/s/	Final **-s** is pronounced /s/ after voiceless sounds, as in (a). "t," "p," and "k" are examples of voiceless sounds.	
(b) seeds → seed/z/ robes → robe/z/ bags → bag/z/ sees → see/z/	Final **-s** is pronounced /z/ after voiced sounds, as in (b). "d," "b," "g," and "ee" are examples of voiced sounds.	
(c) dishes → dish/əz/ catches → catch/əz/ kisses → kiss/əz/ mixes → mix/əz/ prizes → prize/əz/ edges → edge/əz/	Final **-s** and **-es** are pronounced /əz/ after "sh," "ch," "s," "x," "z," and "ge"/"dge" sounds. The /əz/ ending adds a syllable. All of the words in (c) are pronounced with two syllables. COMPARE: All of the words in (a) and (b) are pronounced with one syllable.	

E-7 Linking Verbs

(a) The soup *smells* *good*. (linking verb) (adjective)	Other verbs like *be* that may be followed immediately by an adjective are called "linking verbs." An adjective following a linking verb describes the subject of a sentence.*
(b) This food *tastes delicious*.	Common verbs that may be followed by an adjective:
(c) The children *feel happy*.	• *feel, look, smell, sound, taste* • *appear, seem*
(d) The weather *became cold*.	• *become* (and *get, turn, grow* when they mean "become")

*COMPARE:

  (1) *The man looks angry.* → An adjective (**angry**) follows **look**. The adjective describes the subject (**the man**). **Look** has the meaning of "appear."

  (2) *The man looked at me angrily.* → An adverb (**angrily**) follows **look at**. The adverb describes the action of the verb. **Look at** has the meaning of "regard, watch."

Ann *is at the laudromat.*
She *looks* very *busy*.

E-8 Troublesome Verbs: *Raise / Rise, Set / Sit, Lay / Lie*

Transitive	Intransitive	
		Raise, **set**, and **lay** are *transitive* verbs; they are followed by an object.
(a) *raise, raised, raised* Tom **raised** his hand.	(b) *rise, rose, risen* The sun **rises** in the east.	**Rise**, **sit**, and **lie** are intransitive; they are NOT followed by an object.*
(c) *set, set, set* I **will set** the book on the desk.	(d) *sit, sat, sat* I *sit* in the front row.	In (a): **raised** is followed by the object **hand**. In (b): **rises** is not followed by an object.

(e) *lay, laid, laid*
I **am laying** the book on the desk.
	(f) *lie,** lay, lain*
	He *is lying* on his bed.
		NOTE: **Lay** and **lie** are troublesome for native speakers too and are frequently misused.
		    lay = put
		    lie = recline

*See Appendix Chart A-1 for information about transitive and intransitive verbs.

**Lie* is a regular verb (*lie, lied*) when it means "not tell the truth": *He lied to me about his age.*

E-9 Irregular Verbs: An Alphabetical Reference List

NOTE: Verbs followed by a bullet (•) are defined at the end of the this list.

Simple Form	Simple Past	Past Participle	Simple Form	Simple Past	Past Participle
arise	arose	arisen	forbid	forbade	forbidden
awake	awoke	awoken	forecast•	forecast	forecast
be	was, were	been	forget	forgot	forgotten
bear	bore	borne/born	forgive	forgave	forgiven
beat	beat	beaten/beat	forsake•	forsook	forsaken
become	became	become	freeze	froze	frozen
begin	began	begun	get	got	gotten/got*
bend	bent	bent	give	gave	given
bet•	bet	bet	go	went	gone
bid•	bid	bid	grind•	ground	ground
bind•	bound	bound	grow	grew	grown
bite	bit	bitten	hang**	hung	hung
bleed	bled	bled	have	had	had
blow	blew	blown	hear	heard	heard
break	broke	broken	hide	hid	hidden
breed•	bred	bred	hit	hit	hit
bring	brought	brought	hold	held	held
broadcast•	broadcast	broadcast	hurt	hurt	hurt
build	built	built	keep	kept	kept
burn	burned/burnt	burned/burnt	kneel	kneeled/knelt	kneeled/knelt
burst•	burst	burst	know	knew	known
buy	bought	bought	lay	laid	laid
cast•	cast	cast	lead	led	led
catch	caught	caught	lean	leaned/leant	leaned/leant
choose	chose	chosen	leap	leaped/leapt	leaped/leapt
cling•	clung	clung	learn	learned/learnt	learned/learnt
come	came	come	leave	left	left
cost	cost	cost	lend	lent	lent
creep•	crept	crept	let	let	let
cut	cut	cut	lie	lay	lain
deal•	dealt	dealt	light	lighted/lit	lighted/lit
dig	dug	dug	lose	lost	lost
do	did	done	make	made	made
draw	drew	drawn	mean	meant	meant
dream	dreamed/dreamt	dreamed/dreamt	meet	met	met
drink	drank	drunk	mislay	mislaid	mislaid
drive	drove	driven	mistake	mistook	mistaken
eat	ate	eaten	pay	paid	paid
fall	fell	fallen	prove	proved	proven/proved
feed	fed	fed	put	put	put
feel	felt	felt	quit***	quit	quit
fight	fought	fought	read	read	read
find	found	found	rid	rid	rid
fit	fit/fitted	fit/fitted	ride	rode	ridden
flee•	fled	fled	ring	rang	rung
fling•	flung	flung	rise	rose	risen
fly	flew	flown			

*In British English: *get–got–got.* In American English: *get–got–gotten/got.*

**Hang* is a regular verb when it means to kill someone with a rope around his/her neck.

COMPARE: *I **hung** my clothes in the closet. They **hanged** the murderer by the neck until he was dead.*

***Also possible in British English: *quit–quitted–quitted.*

Simple Form	Simple Past	Past Participle	Simple Form	Simple Past	Past Participle
run	ran	run	spring•	sprang/sprung	sprung
say	said	said	stand	stood	stood
see	saw	seen	steal	stole	stolen
seek•	sought	sought	stick	stuck	stuck
sell	sold	sold	sting•	stung	stung
send	sent	sent	stink•	stank/stunk	stunk
set	set	set	strike•	struck	struck/stricken
shake	shook	shaken	strive•	strove/strived	striven/strived
shed•	shed	shed	string	strung	strung
shine	shone/shined	shone/shined	swear	swore	sworn
shoot	shot	shot	sweep	swept	swept
show	showed	shown/showed	swell	swelled	swelled/swollen
shrink•	shrank/shrunk	shrunk	swim	swam	swum
shut	shut	shut	swing•	swung	swung
sing	sang	sung	take	took	taken
sink•	sank	sunk	teach	taught	taught
sit	sat	sat	tear	tore	torn
sleep	slept	slept	tell	told	told
slide•	slid	slid	think	thought	thought
slit•	slit	slit	throw	threw	thrown
smell	smelled/smelt	smelled/smelt	thrust•	thrust	thrust
sneak	sneaked/snuck	sneaked/snuck	understand	understood	understood
speak	spoke	spoken	undertake	undertook	undertaken
speed	sped/speeded	sped/speeded	upset	upset	upset
spell	spelled/spelt	spelled/spelt	wake	woke/waked	woken
spend	spent	spent	wear	wore	worn
spill	spilled/spilt	spilled/spilt	weave•	wove	woven
spin•	spun	spun	weep•	wept	wept
spit	spit/spat	spit/spat	win	won	won
split•	split	split	wind•	wound	wound
spoil	spoiled/spoilt	spoiled/spoilt	withdraw	withdrew	withdrawn
spread•	spread	spread	write	wrote	written

•Definitions of some of the less frequently used irregular verbs:

bet . . . . . wager; offer to pay money if one loses

bid . . . . . make an offer of money, usually at a public sale

bind . . . . . fasten or secure

breed . . . . . bring animals together to produce young

broadcast . . . . . send information by radio waves; announce

burst . . . . . explode; break suddenly

cast . . . . . throw

cling . . . . hold on tightly

creep . . . . . crawl close to the ground; move slowly and quietly

deal . . . . . distribute playing cards to each person; give attention to (deal with)

flee . . . . . escape; run away

fling . . . . . throw with force

forecast . . . . . predict a future occurrence

forsake . . . . . abandon or desert

grind . . . . . crush, reduce to small pieces

seek . . . . . look for

shed . . . . . drop off or get rid of

shrink . . . . . become smaller

sink . . . . . move downward, often under water

slide . . . . . glide smoothly; slip or skid

slit . . . . . cut a narrow opening

spin . . . . . turn rapidly around a central point

split . . . . . divide into two or more parts

spread . . . . . push out in all directions (e.g., butter on bread, news)

spring . . . . . jump or rise suddenly from a still position

sting . . . . . cause pain with a sharp object (e.g., pin) or bite (e.g., by an insect)

stink . . . . . have a bad or foul smell

strike . . . . . hit something with force

strive . . . . . try hard to achieve a goal

swing . . . . . move back and forth

thrust . . . . . push forcibly; shove

weave . . . . . form by passing pieces of material over and under each other (as in making baskets, cloth)

weep . . . . . cry

wind . . . . . (sounds like *find*) turn around and around

Listening Script

Chapter 1: Present and Past; Simple and Progressive

Exercise 6, p. 4.

Outdoors

1. Hey, look out the window! It's raining ...
2. We get a lot of rain here ...
3. Besides the rain, it also snows here a little ...
4. Did you hear? We can go skiing this weekend. It's snowing in the mountains ...
5. We go hiking a lot. We especially like to hike in the mountains ...
6. Our son is spending some time in the mountains ...
7. He works as a mountain guide ...

Exercise 18, p. 10.

Weather Report

Hello, this is Gayle Givens, your WWKK weather reporter. Well, it certainly is a beautiful day today. I am standing here at City Park and boy*, the sun sure is shining. Hundreds of people are enjoying the warmer temperatures today. There is not a cloud in the sky. We are looking at a perfect day right now, but it looks like some clouds are forming over the ocean and colder air is moving in. We are forecasting cooler temperatures for tomorrow. I think rain is unlikely, however. Stay tuned for the three-day forecast right after this message.

Exercise 25, p. 14.

1. Yesterday I felt ...
2. Last week Mr. Jones taught ...
3. Did you fill ...
4. The children drew ...
5. The man hid ...
6. One student withdrew ...
7. When I was cooking dinner, I burned ...
8. Oh, no! Did you shrink ...
9. The audience wept ...
10. The plants in the garden grew ...

Exercise 33, p. 20.

A Scary Night

I had a terrible experience last night. You won't believe what happened! A man burst into my apartment while I was asleep. There I was, just sleeping peacefully, when someone broke the glass in the sliding door!

The sound woke me up. I heard the sliding door open, so I reached for the phone by the bed and called the police. My voice shook as I told the operator there was an intruder in my home.

I hid in my bedroom closet when the burglar came into my room. Soon I heard sirens as the police sped to my building. From the crack in the closet door, I saw the burglar as he ran outside with my laptop.

The police jumped out of their cars and followed him, but he managed to get away in a car that was waiting for him. The police got back in their cars and drove after him. Later I learned that they caught him a few miles from my building.

I felt really frightened by all this. It really upset me, as you can imagine. I'm staying at my sister's house for the rest of the week.

1. The man entered quietly.
2. He opened a window.
3. The woman spoke with the intruder.
4. The woman went into her closet.
5. The police caught the burglar in the woman's apartment.
6. The woman felt relaxed at the end of the story.

Chapter 2: Perfect and Progressive Tenses

Exercise 16, p. 35.

1. How have (*How-uv*) you been?
2. How long have (*long-uv*) you been here?
3. What has (*What-uz*) happened?
4. What have (*What-uv*) you done?
5. When have (*When-uv*) I said that?
6. Where have (*Where-uv*) you been?

Exercise 17, p. 35.

At Home with Roommates

1. Someone's phone's ringing. It's not mine.
2. Your girlfriend's just left a message.
3. Her friends've canceled, so she's free tonight.
4. The coffee's fresh. Have some.
5. It looks like your package has arrived.
6. Your sister's downstairs. She's borrowing some boxes for her move.
7. Our neighbors've planned a party for next weekend.
8. What've we told them? Are we going?

Exercise 29, p. 42.

It's been a while!

A: Good to see you! So, what have you been up to lately?
B: Not too much. I've been taking it easy.
A: How nice! Glad to hear you haven't been working too hard. By the way, how are your parents? I haven't seen them for a while.
B: They're doing great. They're traveling now that they're retired.
A: How long have they been retired?
B: Gosh, I don't know. It's been a couple of years now.
A: So, they've been traveling a lot?
B: Yeah. They've been staying in warm, sunny places in the winter and spending summers here.
A: What a great way to spend retirement! I'm glad to hear they're enjoying themselves.

Exercise 34, p. 45.

Excuses

1. I'm sorry I missed the appointment. I had written down the wrong date.
2. We knew we were running late. We had misread the bus schedule.
3. Sorry — I wanted to come to your party, but my family had already made other plans.

Exercise 35, p. 46.

A Base Jumper

1. My friend Tom's a base jumper. He jumps off buildings and mountains — for fun. Last year he jumped off a skyscraper. Tom and his team had planned it for over a year.
2. Family and friends had told him he was crazy, but that didn't change his mind.
3. I wanted to watch, but I had gotten sick the day before.
4. Afterward, Tom said it was the most thrilling experience he had ever had.
5. I'd kind of like to try something like that, but I'm afraid of heights.

Exercise 36, p. 46.

1. a. You're a new student, aren't you? How long've you been in this country?
   b. You left your job? How long had you been there?
2. a. You're looking for Jack? Jack has left. He isn't here.
   b. We were looking for Sam, but he'd left by the time we got there.
3. a. Since we're teachers, we have the summers off and do a lot of traveling. We'd like to travel to Africa next.
   b. We had wanted to travel with my parents on our last trip, but they became ill and needed to cancel.

4. a. Unfortunately, my phone died when we were lost. I had forgotten to recharge it.
   b. My phone's dead, and I have forgotten to bring the charger.

Exercise 43, p. 50.

New Careers?

1. Kristi has learned how to design websites recently.
2. Her husband, who has an art background, has been learning how to design websites.
3. Kristi had worked as a nurse but found it too stressful.
4. Their son Eric has been designing websites since he left college.
5. Eric started his own company and has asked his parents to work for him part-time.

Chapter 3: Future Time

Exercise 4, p. 55.

1. You'll need to turn in all your assignments by tomorrow.
2. We're going to review for the final exam on Monday.
3. The test'll have 50 questions.
4. There'll be 50 questions on the exam.
5. You'll have the whole hour to complete the test.
6. It's a long exam. Sorry, but nobody'll finish early.
7. It's going to be a lot of work. Study hard!
8. The results'll be available in my office the next day.

Exercise 9, p. 58.

A Plan or an Offer to Help?

1. A: So, you were talking about your plans for the summer. What are you going to do?
   B: I'm going to work at a summer resort in the mountains.
2. A: Can you help me out? I need to get this check in the mail by noon.
   B: Sure. I'll drop it off on my way to work.
3. A: Tell me again. Why are you leaving work early?
   B: I'm going to attend my cousin's funeral.
4. A: Darn, this flashlight doesn't work.
   B: Here, give it to me. I'll fix it for you.
5. A: Here's the broom. What did you want it for?
   B: I'm going to sweep the front steps.

Exercise 11, p. 59.

They're going to move to a building twice as big as their current space. The new restaurant will include a full breakfast and lunch menu. They're going to serve fresh organic fruits and vegetables and offer more vegetarian dishes. The restaurant will have a seating area with couches and comfortable chairs, and it will have double the number of tables. This means the Costas'll need to hire several more employees. It'll be more work for the family, but they're looking forward to it.

Chapter 4: Review of Verb Tenses

Exercise 11, p. 74.
1. Flight 907 landed at 8:06 P.M.
2. It was evening, and Greg was home alone. He was lying on his couch in the living room. He had been listening to classical music for almost an hour.
3. This wet weather is getting very tiresome. It's been raining for days.
4. On the way to the theater, we got stuck in traffic, so we were late. The concert was just starting as we walked in.
5. Janice is interested in learning to fly a small plane. She's had two lessons so far.
6. There was a robbery at the bank ten minutes ago, and the police still haven't come. By the time they get here, the thief'll be far away.

Exercise 13, p. 75.
A Silly Mistake

When I got home to my apartment last night, I took out my key to open the door as usual. As always, I put it in the lock, but the door didn't open. I tried my key again and again with no luck. So I knocked on the door for my wife to let me in. Finally the door opened, but I didn't see my wife on the other side. I saw a stranger. I had been trying to get into the wrong apartment! I quickly apologized and went to my own. I felt very stupid about what I had done.

Chapter 5

Exercise 8, p. 82.
Thrill Seekers

Going over a waterfall in a kayak is not everyone's idea of a good time. But for some people, the experience of somersaulting through a curtain of water is thrilling, and they want to keep doing it. It has in part to do with adrenaline. The body releases a large amount of this hormone in response to danger. For some people, this release produces very pleasant feelings, and they seek out activities that will give them this feeling. The experience of parachuting from a mountain, for example, is exhilarating, not terrifying, for them. Researchers are studying reasons why some people enjoy this adrenaline rush and others fear it.

Exercise 17, p. 86.
At Work

1. Don't leave yet. There're email messages waiting for your response.
2. Excuse me. There's someone on the phone for you.
3. I need your help. Is there a place we could go to talk?
4. Are there chairs for us to sit down?
5. I think there're extra chairs in the hallway.
6. You look tired. Is there anything I can do to help?

7. Still hungry? There're some leftovers from the party in the staff lounge.
8. If you're thirsty, there's juice in the fridge.

Exercise 18, p. 87.
What's the difference?

1. *Rain* vs. *Showers*
   Many people treat these words as having the same meaning. For people who follow the weather, however, there is a difference. Rain is steady and covers a larger area. Showers tend to be more scattered and do not last as long. There is an easy way to remember the difference: think about taking a bath vs. taking a shower. Most of us get wetter when we take a bath than when we stand in the shower.
   Now, which expression do you think is correct: *It's raining out* or *It's showering out*? If you chose the first one, you are right. We use only *rain*, not *shower*, as a verb to talk about the weather.
2. *Thief* vs. *Robber* vs. *Burglar*
   Another set of words with distinct differences is *thief*, *robber*, and *burglar*. A thief takes physical property like TVs, computers, or money, but there is no violence or force. Robbers also take property, but the robber uses force or the threat of force, as with a gun. A burglar illegally enters a structure with the intent to commit a crime.
   If some of this seems confusing, you are in good company. Many native speakers of English have never learned these subtleties and don't make distinctions among these words.

Chapter 6: Nouns

Exercise 10, p. 99.
An Assistant Professor

1. Ted is an assistant college professor.
2. He worked for two colleges before he got a full-time job.
3. College professors have a heavy workload.
4. Assistant professor duties include teaching and research.
5. Ted also supervises the T.A., or teaching assistant program, for his department.
6. Teaching assistants attend his classes and then meet with students in small groups.

Exercise 31, p. 109.
Hoarding

Rebecca has a problem. She doesn't have any visitors. Her family doesn't come to see her anymore. It's not because they don't like her. It's because no one can get through her front door. There is too much stuff blocking the way. Rebecca is a hoarder.

Hoarders are unable to throw out or give away things they no longer need such as newspapers, magazines, clothes, and furniture. Some hoarders have boxes that reach the ceiling.

Hoarding has just recently come to the attention of the general public. Hoarding is more than having a messy or cluttered home. Hoarding interferes with a person's ability to function. Occasionally, hoarding can become life-threatening. In one situation, the floor of a hoarder's house collapsed. Sometimes garbage builds up in the house and health problems arise.

Scientists believe that an area in the brain affects a person's ability to make decisions to get rid of things. Researchers are working on treatments for this condition.

Exercise 39, p. 114.

With Friends

1. A: Do you have a few minutes? I need a little help. I'm having a few problems with my laptop.
   B: Sure. Now is good. I have a little time before I need to leave.
2. A: Ben isn't happy at his new high school. He hasn't met many kids, and he has few friends.
   B: Give it a little time. In a few months, he'll have more.
3. A: I have little patience with lazy co-workers. They frustrate me!
   B: Me too. I work with a few people who do very little work but complain about how much they do!
4. A: I'll have a little coffee with my dessert. Do you want some?
   B: No, thanks. I drink very little coffee. It's too bitter.
   A: I love coffee, especially with a little sugar.
   B: Whoa! You're using more than a little sugar. Are you drinking coffee with sugar or sugar with coffee?
   A: But it's really good. Do you want to try a little? Maybe you'd drink more coffee this way.
   B: Uh, I don't think so! I have very little sugar in my diet. It makes me hyper.

Chapter 7: Articles

Exercise 7, p. 125.

1. My boss has unreasonable expectations.
2. This is not an easy situation to deal with.
3. I feel uneasy about this situation.
4. This is a difficult situation.
5. My manager has made an unreasonable request.
6. The speaker presented a complicated problem.
7. The speaker presented complicated problems.
8. The presentation was uncomplicated.

Exercise 22, p. 131.

A Mishap

A: What happened to your bike? The front wheel is bent.
B: I ran into a parked car when I swerved to avoid a big pothole.
A: Did you damage the car?
B: A little.
A: What did you do?
B: I left a note for the owner of the car.
A: What did you write on the note?
B: My name and phone number. I also wrote an apology.

Exercise 26, p. 133.

Computer Bugs

When there is a problem with a computer, we often say we have a "computer bug." Of course, it's not a real insect. It refers to a technical difficulty we are having. The expression actually goes back to Thomas Edison, who was a famous inventor. When he was working on his first phonograph, he had a lot of problems. He blamed the problems on an imaginary insect that had hidden inside the machine. He was quoted in the newspaper as saying there was "a bug" in his phonograph. This was in 1889, and it is the first recorded use of the word *bug* in such a context.

Chapter 8: Pronouns

Exercise 10, p. 144.

1. Where's Kim?
   A: I don't know. I haven't seen him this morning.
   B: I think he's in the restroom.
   C: I'm looking for him too.
   D: Ask his assistant. He'll know.
   E: Have you tried looking in his office? I know he's not there much, but maybe he'll surprise you.

2. The Nelsons are giving their daughter a motorcycle for graduation.
   A: Hmmm. Does she like motorcycles that much?
   B: Really? Is she a motorcycle rider?
   C: That's an odd gift. I wonder what they were thinking.
   D: That's what the Smiths gave their son. I think he's already had an accident.
   E: I'm not a fan of motorcycles. Cars just don't see them in traffic.
   F: I think it's a wonderful gift! I've had mine for years, and it's been great.

Exercise 21, p. 151.

1. Great photos, Jon! Did you take all of them ...
2. Do you like my dress? I made it ...
3. We were going to take a trip with our cousins, but the plans got so complicated that we finally decided to go by ...
4. My brother has an antique car. He restored it ...
5. Mr. and Mrs. Peterson are planning to sell their house. They are going to put an ad in the paper and sell it ...
6. My sister-in-law is an architect. She designed her office ...

Exercise 32, p. 156.

1. This coffee is delicious. Could I please have another cup?
2. The coffee isn't in this grocery bag, so I'll look in the other one.
3. There are supposed to be ten chairs in the room, but I count only five. Where are the others?

4. No, let's not use this printer. Let's use the other one.
5. Bill is a short form for William. Others are Billy and Will.
6. The sky is clearing. It's going to be another beautiful day.

Exercise 36, p. 158.

1. The teacher asked the students the same question. One after another they gave the wrong answer.
2. Mr. and Mrs. Clark lead such busy lives that they see each other only on weekends.
3. Mr. Perez is doing fine. Susan spoke with him just the other day.
4. A: I have a secret about Danny and me.
   B: Let me guess. You're engaged!
   A: Yes! But it's a secret. We haven't told anyone other than you.
5. A: Have you sent party invitations yet?
   B: Everyone except Jan knows about the surprise party.

Chapter 9: Modals, Part 1

Exercise 26, p. 174.

Part II
1. We can't come to the meeting.
2. Our two-year-old can count to 50.
3. You can take that course next term.
4. I can't cook complicated dishes.
5. Can't you come with us?
6. I can drive a semi-truck.

Exercise 36, p. 178.

1. This is a nonsmoking restaurant. Would you mind putting out your cigarette?
2. The music's awfully loud. Would you mind if I turned it down?
3. It's getting cool in here. Would you mind closing the window?
4. I can't talk now. Mind if I call you back?
5. I can't reach the pepper. Would you mind passing it to me?
6. I'm freezing. Mind if I borrow a sweater?

Chapter 10: Modals, Part 2

Exercise 10, p. 189.

1. Jack shouldn't have had more coffee.
2. My sister should have saved her money.
3. I should have gone to the doctor.
4. The president shouldn't have lied to us.

Exercise 30, p. 198.

What's wrong? Your parents look upset.

1. We should ask them.
2. We shouldn't ask them.
3. You may have upset them.
4. You should try to find out.

5. Maybe you shouldn't have stayed out so late.
6. You'd better have a good excuse for being late.
7. You could have told them what you planned to do.
8. You must have known your behavior would cause problems.

Exercise 49, p. 212.

1. Carlos was planning to come to the party, but he didn't show up. It was a great party. There was delicious food, and we danced until midnight.
2. I have a whole lot of material I need to review before the exam, but I just don't feel like studying this afternoon.
3. Tony's over an hour late for our meeting. That's not like him. I hope nothing bad has happened.
4. Rick was supposed to be at work early today to train his new assistant, but he woke up with a high fever. He can't even get out of bed.
5. The teacher called on Sonya in class yesterday, but she kept looking out the window and didn't respond.

Chapter 11: The Passive

Exercise 16, p. 223.

Early Mirrors

Mirrors are not a modern invention; they have been used since the stone age. The first mirrors were made from rocks. A special type of stone was needed: obsidian. This is a volcanic glass that is found in lava. To make the mirror, the stone was ground down on one side with another stone until the surface was flat. Then it was polished repeatedly until it became extremely shiny. At that point, the surface was highly reflective, and people were able to see themselves.

Exercise 26, p. 229.

The 2004 Indian Ocean Tsunami

In 2004, several countries that border the Indian Ocean, including Indonesia, Thailand, India, Malaysia, and Somalia were hit by an earthquake and subsequent tsunami. (As you may already know, a tsunami is a giant ocean wave.) In just a few short hours, millions of lives were changed forever. The earthquake was measured at 9.3 on the Richter scale. It was the fourth largest earthquake since 1900 and the second largest that has ever been recorded on the Richter scale.

The quake was followed by four giant waves as high as 100 feet (or 30 meters). Whole villages were destroyed. Thousands of people were swept out to sea, and many others died due to lack of medical care. In total, almost 300,000 people were killed, and 1.3 million people were left homeless. Aftershocks from the earthquake continued for several days.

Tragically, the damage could have been lessened if there had been a tsunami early-warning system. Such a system already existed for the Pacific Ocean, but it didn't reach to the Indian Ocean. Since the tsunami disaster, governments have worked together to develop an early-warning system so that Southeast Asia will not experience such destruction again from a tsunami.

Exercise 33, p. 235.
1. Water is composed of hydrogen and oxygen.
2. I am not acquainted with Dr. William's books.
3. I'm finally accustomed to living here.
4. You're so busy. I think you're involved in too many activities.
5. Are you prepared for the next test?
6. Mr. and Mrs. Miller are devoted to each other.
7. I'm concerned about my grandfather's health.
8. Are you satisfied with your progress?

Exercise 47, p. 242.
1. Roller coasters frighten me.
2. Do you like to go on scary roller coasters?
3. Does a roller coaster ride excite you?
4. The ride was a thrilling experience.
5. The ride finished all too soon.
6. A few people weren't thrilled by the ride.

Exercise 49, p. 243.
1. The art museum has an exhibit that people are upset about. People who visit the museum are ...
2. People say that the exhibit is ...
3. My parents enjoy talking with my friend, Maria. They find her ...
4. Maria gets along well with my parents. She thinks they are ...
5. Not one of the students could understand Professor Steven's explanations. Whenever he explains a math problem, the students become more ...
6. His explanations are terribly ...

Exercise 51, p. 244.
The Early Olympic Games
The Olympic Games began more than 2,000 years ago in Olympia, a small town in Greece. The games were established for two purposes. One was to showcase the physical qualities and athletic performances of its young men. At that time, only Greek males were allowed to compete. In fact, women were not even permitted to watch the games, and the only spectators were men. The other goal was to encourage good relationships among Greek cities. People of other nationalities were not invited to participate.

The winner of each event was crowned with a wreath made of olive leaves. Additionally, his statue could be placed in Olympia for all to see. Winning athletes were treated as heroes when they returned to their cities because with their victory, they brought fame and honor to their hometowns.

Chapter 12: Noun Clauses

Exercise 38, p. 265.
1. I'm not going to the personnel meeting because I have to finish a report.
2. I can't lend Marta any money because my wallet is in my coat pocket back at home.

3. Someone in this room is wearing very strong perfume. It's giving me a headache.
4. Hi, Emma. I'll meet you at the coffee shop at 9:00. I promise not to be late.
5. I'm considering looking for a new job. What do you think I should do?
6. We are going to be late for the concert. My wife has to attend a business function after work.

Chapter 13: Adjective Clauses

Exercise 5, p. 274.
Part I
1. He has a friend who'll help him.
2. He has a friend who's helping him.
3. He has a friend who's helped him.
4. He has friends who're helping him.
5. He has friends who've helped him.
6. He has a friend who'd helped him.
7. He has a friend who'd like to help him.
8. He has a friend who's been helping him.

Part II
1. We know a person who'll be great for the job.
2. We know a person who'd like to apply for the job.
3. That's the man who's moving to our department.
4. I know of three people who've asked to transfer to another location.
5. I'd like to talk to the people who're asking to move.
6. There are two people at this company who've worked here all their adult lives.
7. The manager who'd been stealing from the company quit.

Exercise 22, p. 281.
1. I met the professor who's going to be my advisor.
2. I know someone who's famous in the music industry.
3. I talked to the man whose wife was in the car accident on Fifth Street yesterday. She's in the hospital, but she's going to be OK.
4. I forget the name of the woman who's going to call you later — Mrs. Green or Mrs. White or something like that.
5. I need to hurry. The neighbor whose bike I borrowed is waiting for me to return it.
6. I got an email from a friend who's studying in Malaysia. It was really good to hear from her.
7. I recently heard from a friend who's overseas. He finally sent me an email.
8. I'm thinking about getting a pet. There's a woman at work whose dog just had puppies. I might adopt one.

Exercise 23, p. 282.
1. That's the person who's going to help us.
2. That's the person whose help we need.
3. I'd like to introduce you to a teacher who's spent time in Africa.
4. I'd like to introduce you to the teacher whose husband is from Africa.

5. The company is looking for a person who's bilingual.
6. The company is looking for a person whose native language is Arabic.
7. The company is looking for a person who's had a lot of experience in sales.
8. They want to hire a person who's familiar with their sales territory.

Exercise 32, p. 285.
1. The man who gave the news interview is a friend of mine.
2. Two people died in an accident that blocked all lanes of the highway for two hours.
3. The small town where I was born is now a large city.
4. The music teacher who gave me music lessons a long time ago became a rock star.
5. The phone that I got from my parents takes excellent pictures.
6. My neighbor often drops in for a visit about the time when we would like to sit down to dinner.

Exercise 42, p. 290.
1. My mother looked in the fruit basket and threw away the apples that were rotten.
2. My mother looked in the fruit basket and threw away the apples, which were rotten.
3. The students who had done well on the test were excused from class early.
4. The students, who had done well on the test, were excused from class early.

Exercise 54, p. 296.
1. The fence surrounding our house is made of wood.
2. The children attending that school receive a good education.
3. Dr. Stanton, the president of the university, will give a speech at the commencement ceremonies.
4. Our solar system is in a galaxy called the Milky Way.

Chapter 14: Gerunds and Infinitives, Part 1

Exercise 8, p. 306.
1. A: What should we do tomorrow night?
   B: Let's watch a movie. That's what I like doing on weekends.
   A: Same here.
2. A: I was really looking forward to the hike in the mountains this weekend, but I guess we're not going to get there.
   B: It doesn't look like it. I don't think there's any hope. It's supposed to rain for the next two weeks.
3. A: Do you want to take a break?
   B: No, we have to finish this report by 5:00. We don't have time for a break.

4. A: Let's go into the city this weekend. There's a free concert at the park.
   B: That sounds like fun. Who's playing?
5. A: I'd really like to go out this evening, but I have all this work to do. I have three assignments, and I haven't begun to write any of them.
   B: I know how you feel. I'm way behind in my homework too.
6. A: I just heard that there's an accident on the freeway and nothing's moving.
   B: Let's stay here for another couple of hours. We can get caught up on our work.
   A: Good idea. I have so much to do.

Exercise 21, p. 313.
1. Joan remembered to call her husband before she left work yesterday.
2. Rita remembered going to the farmers' market with her grandmother.
3. Roger stopped smoking when the doctor told him he had heart disease.
4. Mr. and Mrs. Olson stopped to eat before the movie.
5. I regret leaving school before I graduated.

Exercise 30, p. 319.
1. A: I'm sorry I'm late.
   B: No problem. We have lots of time.
2. A: I finished the project early.
   B: That's great you got it done so quickly.
3. A: I hate to do housework.
   B: I know. I do too. It's a lot of work.
4. A: You were a big help. Thanks.
   B: Sure. I was happy to help out.
5. A: Your report isn't finished. What's your excuse?
   B: Uh, well, sorry. I don't really have one.
6. A: How do you like the food here?
   B: It's too spicy. I can't eat much of it.
7. A: How was your weekend? Did you go away for the holiday?
   B: No. I got the flu and spent the whole weekend in bed.

Exercise 41, p. 325.
1. I have a terrible memory. I can't even remember my children's birthdays.
2. My teenage son tried to hide his report card, but I caught him.
3. I'm in a hurry in the mornings. I always stand at the kitchen counter and eat my breakfast.
4. Foreign languages are hard for me to learn.
5. I sat in traffic for two hours. It was a waste of time.
6. We sang songs on the bus trip. It was fun.
7. I looked all over for Tom. He was studying in the library.
8. There was a line to buy movie tickets. I had to wait for an hour.

Chapter 15: Gerunds and Infinitives, Part 2

Exercise 13, p. 340.
1. Benjamin is too old to have a driver's license.
2. Our daughter isn't old enough to stay home alone yet.
3. The test results are too good to believe.
4. This room seems big enough for an office.
5. You will have time enough to take a tour of the city.
6. The leftovers look too old to eat.

Exercise 17, p. 342.

An Issue in Health Care: Illiteracy

According to some estimates, well over half of the people in the world are functionally illiterate. This means that they are unable to perform everyday tasks because they can't read, understand, and respond appropriately to information. One of the problems this creates in health care is that millions of people are not able to read directions on medicine bottles or packages. Imagine being a parent with a sick child and being unable to read the directions on a medicine bottle. We all know that it is important for medical directions to be understood clearly. One solution is pictures. Many medical professionals are working today to solve this problem by using pictures to convey health-care information.

Chapter 16: Coordinating Conjunctions

Exercise 19, p. 365.
1. Ben will call either Mary or Bob.
2. Both my mother and father talked to my teacher.
3. Simon saw not only a whale but also a dolphin.
4. Our neighborhood had neither electricity nor water after the storm.
5. Either Mr. Anderson or Ms. Wiggins is going to teach our class today.

Exercise 21, p. 367.

Bats

What do people in your country think of bats? Are they mean and scary creatures, or are they symbols of both happiness and luck?

In Western countries, many people have an unreasoned fear of bats. According to scientist Dr. Sharon Horowitz, bats are not only harmless but also beneficial mammals. "When I was a child, I believed that a bat would attack me and tangle itself in my hair. Now I know better," said Dr. Horowitz.

Contrary to popular Western myths, bats do not attack humans. Although a few bats may have diseases, they are not major carriers of rabies or other frightening diseases. Bats help natural plant life by pollinating plants, spreading seeds, and eating insects. If you get rid of bats that eat overripe fruit, then fruit flies can flourish and destroy the fruit industry.

According to Dr. Horowitz, bats are both gentle and trainable pets. Not many people, however, own or train bats, and bats themselves prefer to avoid people.

Chapter 18: Reduction of Adverb Clauses to Modifying Adverbial Phrases

Exercise 17, p. 401.
1. A: I don't want to play the piano at the family gathering. I don't play well enough. People will laugh at me.
   B: Rose, I know you're nervous, but you play beautifully. Everyone will love hearing you.
2. A: Jan, are you going to tell Thomas that he needs to do more work on the project? He hasn't done his share. He's being really lazy.
   B: Well, he'll probably get upset, but I'm going to talk with him about it this afternoon.
3. A: I'm so relieved that I found my wedding ring. It'd been missing for a month. The next time I take it off, I'm going to put it in a box on top of my dresser.
   B: That sounds like a wise thing to do, Susan. It'd be terrible to lose your wedding ring again.
4. A: This is the first year I'm eligible to vote in the presidential election. I'm going to research all the candidates extensively.
   B: They have very different positions, Sam. It's good to get as much information as you can.

Chapter 19: Connectives That Express Cause and Effect, Contrast, and Condition

Exercise 37, p. 421.
1. Because I lift heavy boxes at work, ...
2. I bought a new TV even though ...
3. Even if I'm late for work, ...
4. I was late for work this morning; nevertheless, ...
5. The air-conditioning has been broken; therefore, ...
6. Although I live in a noisy city, ...
7. I was so tired last night that ...

Exercise 39, p. 422.

Why We Yawn

Have you ever noticed that when a person near you yawns, you may start yawning too? This is called contagious yawning. *Contagious* in this sense means that the behavior spreads: in the case of yawning, when one person yawns, it can cause others to do the same thing.

There are various theories about why people yawn. One popular idea is that yawning brings more oxygen into the brain so that people will wake up. Is that what you have thought?

However, in 2007, researchers at a university in New York came up with a new idea: yawning helps cool the brain. When people's brains are warm, they yawn more frequently; yawning brings cooler air into the body and, therefore, cools the brain. This is important because cooler brains work better than warmer ones.

This may also help explain why yawning is contagious. People are more awake when their brains are cooler; therefore, contagious yawning helps people be more alert. As people evolved, this was important in times of danger. If they yawned, they could have been signaling to others to stay awake.

While it can be annoying to have a person yawn when you are talking, perhaps you can tell yourself that he or she actually wants to stay awake, not go to sleep.

Chapter 20: Conditional Sentences and Wishes

Exercise 8, p. 429.
1. If I'm talking too fast, please tell me.
2. If we get married, everyone will be shocked.
3. If it's OK, I'll ask for some advice.
4. If he's planning to quit, I hope he lets us know soon.
5. If it's not working, we'll need to try something else.
6. If she works harder, I'm sure she'll succeed.
7. If I should get the job, I'll call you right away.

Exercise 19, p. 433.
1. If I had known the truth sooner, I would have acted differently.
2. If we hadn't believed him, we wouldn't have felt so foolish.
3. If you hadn't told me what a great guy Jon was, I wouldn't have believed him so easily.
4. If it had been another person, I wouldn't have been so shocked.
5. If he hadn't lied, I would have had more respect for him.

Exercise 25, p. 437.
1. If I had enough time, I'd go to the art museum this afternoon. I love going to art museums.
2. Mrs. Jones is really lucky. If she hadn't received immediate medical attention, she would have died.
3. If I were a carpenter, I'd build my own house. I'd really enjoy that.
4. So many people died unnecessarily in the earthquake. If the hotel had been built to withstand an earthquake, it wouldn't have collapsed.

Exercise 40, p. 443.
1. I would have called, but I left your number at home.
2. I couldn't have gone to college without my parents' financial help.
3. I ran out of time. Otherwise, I would have picked up your clothes from the cleaners.
4. We would have come to the party, but no one told us about it.
5. Without your advice, I wouldn't have known what to do.

Index

Able to, 202, 205 (*Look on pages 202 and 205.*)	The numbers following the words listed in the index refer to page numbers in the text.
Continuous tenses, 3*fn.* (*Look at the footnote on page 3.*)	The letters *fn.* mean "footnote." Footnotes appear beneath some charts and readings or at the bottom of some pages.

A

A/an, 105, 123, 125, 130, 130*fn.*
Able to, 162, 173, 191
Accustomed to, 316
A couple of, 110
Active verbs, 216
Adjective(s), 452
    after *being* (e.g., *being foolish*), 7*fn.*
    defined, 452
    after *get* (e.g., *get hungry*), 238
    infinitives after (e.g., *happy to meet*), 337
    with linking verbs (e.g., *taste good*), 467
    non-progressive passive verbs used as, 231
    nouns used as (e.g., *vegetable soup*), 98
    participial (e.g., *amusing/amused*), 241
    possessive (*my, your,* etc.), 140, 145, 352
    preposition combinations with, 454
    used as nouns (e.g., *the poor*), 88, 103
Adjective clauses:
    defined, 273
    expressions of quantity in, 292
    object pronouns in (*whom, which, that*), 276
    prepositions in, 278, 282, 284
    pronouns modified by, 287
    punctuation of, 288
    reducing to modifying phrases, 295
    subject pronouns in (*who, which, that*),
        273, 295
    with *when,* 284
    with *where,* 282
    with *which,* 273, 273*fn.,* 276, 287*fn.,* 293
    with *whose,* 280

Adjective phrases, 295, 295*fn.*
Adverb(s), 453
    conjunctive (e.g., *therefore*), 408
    defined, 453
    list of, 453
    midsentence, 453
    with past perfect, 44
    placement in future perfect, 66*fn.*
    with present perfect, 31, 37*fn.*
Adverb clauses, 371
    of cause and effect (*because,* etc.), 371, 378,
        395, 405
    of condition (*if, unless,* etc.), 371, 382, 383,
        384, 386, 387, 388, 405, 420
    as connectives, 405, 410
    of contrast (*although,* etc.), 371, 379,
        405, 416
    defined, 371
    of direct contrast (*whereas, while*), 371,
        381, 418
    punctuation of, 371, 410
    of purpose (*so that*), 414
    reducing to modifying phrases, 393–395,
        399
    of time (*after, before,* etc.), 60, 371, 373
    words used to introduce, 371
Advise, 308*fn.*
A few, 110, 113
Affirmatives, in tag questions, 459
Afraid, 257*fn.*
After, 44, 373, 373*fn.,* 394
A great deal of, 110, 117

Credits

Photo Credits

Page 1: Cameraman/Fotolia; 4: Nerthuz/Fotolia; 6: James Thew/Fotolia; 8 (bottom): George Dolgikh/Fotolia; 8 (top): WavebreakMediaMicro/Fotolia; 9 (left): Pieropoma/Fotolia; 9 (rights): Danilo Rizzuti/Fotolia; 11: Warner Brothers/Everett Collection; 13: Patryk Kosmider/Fotolia; 14: Adam121/Fotolia; 15: REX/Shutterstock; 17: Herrerojorcas/Fotolia; 19: ParisPhoto/Fotolia; 25: Catgrig/Fotolia; 30: Scott Prokop/Fotolia; 33 (bottom): Canadian in Exile/Fotolia; 33 (top): Vpardi/Fotolia; 34: lpstudio/Fotolia; 35: Mariusz Blach/Fotolia; 37: Jiri Foltyn/Fotolia; 41: Contrastwerkstatt/Fotolia; 43: Marcel Mooij/Fotolia; 46: Xof711/Fotolia; 51: Igor Mojzes/Fotolia; 53: Freesurf/Fotolia; 57: Olesia Bilkei/Fotolia; 59 (left): Thomas Perkins/Fotolia; 59 (right): Jstaley4011/Fotolia; 61: Sergey Nivens/Fotolia; 63: Aleksandar Todorovic/Fotolia; 65: Robert Kneschke/Fotolia; 70: Ra2 studio/Fotolia; 72: Rtimages/Fotolia; 73: Mauro Rodrigues/Fotolia; 75: Janis Smits/Fotolia; 78: Wlablack/Fotolia; 79 (left): GVS/Fotolia; 79 (right): Nicholas Piccillo/Fotolia; 81 (bottom): Siro46/Fotolia; 81 (top): Piotr Wawrzyniuk/Fotolia; 82: Galyna Andrushko/Fotolia; 83: Shutterstock; 84: Goodluz/Fotolia; 85: Dreaming Andy/Fotolia; 86: Scvos/Fotolia; 91: Anton Sokolov/Fotolia; 92: Nerthuz/Fotolia; 94: Viperagp/Fotolia; 96 (bottom): Bettys4240/Fotolia; 96 (top): Hinata815/Fotolia; 97: Beawolf/Fotolia; 98: Cutimage/Fotolia; 100 (bottom): Kellis/Shutterstock; 100 (top): Andyh12/Fotolia; 106 (bottom): Real PhotoItaly/Fotolia; 106 (top): Lorelyn Medina/Fotolia; 109: Mantinov/Fotolia; 112: Dashadima/Fotolia; 113: Sborisov/Fotolia; 116 (bottom): 12ee12/Fotolia; 116 (top): Shutterstock; 117: Chagin/Fotolia; 119: Marilyn Barbone/Fotolia; 122: Baibaz/Fotolia; 125: Sommai/Fotolia; 126 (bottom): Daylight Photo/Fotolia; 126 (top): Maxcam/Fotolia; 128 (left): Antonin Spacek/Fotolia; 128 (right): FrankU/Fotolia; 129: Cameramanhamiltn/Fotolia; 130: Alexskopje/Fotolia; 131 (bottom, left): Nikita Kuzmenkov/Fotolia; 131 (bottom, right): Danr13/Fotolia; 131 (center): Chrispo/Fotolia; 131 (top): Hansenn/Fotolia; 132 (bottom): Jörg Hackemann/Fotolia; 132 (top): Andrea Izzotti/Fotolia; 133: NoraDoa/Fotolia; 135 (bottom, left): Tushar Koley/Fotolia; 135 (bottom, right): JFL Photography/Fotolia; 135 (top): Srongkrod/Fotolia; 136: Federico Rostagno/Fotolia; 139: Ksena32/Fotolia; 142: Barbara Helgason/Fotolia; 143: Maridav/Fotolia; 144: Megan Lorenz/Fotolia; 147: Africa Studio/Fotolia; 149: Lightwavemedia/Fotolia; 154: Alexander Kolosov/Fotolia; 158: Nemez210769/Fotolia; 160: Auremar/Fotolia; 161: Auremar/Fotolia; 164: Debbie Torkelson/Fotolia; 166: Pathdoc/Fotolia; 168 (bottom): Robert Wilson/Fotolia; 168 (top): Africa Studio/Fotolia; 169: Acidsulfurik/Fotolia; 172 (center, left): Lisa F. Young/Fotolia; 172 (center, right): Kurhan/Fotolia; 172 (left): Olly/Fotolia; 172 (right): 135pixels/Fotolia; 174 (bottom): Innovated Captures/Fotolia; 174 (top): Kasto/Fotolia; 175: Andriigorulko/Fotolia; 178: Samo Trebizan/Fotolia; 182: Andrey Popov/Fotolia; 183: Alexbrylovhk/Fotolia; 184: Nadezhda1906/Fotolia; 186 (bottom): Johnkepchar/Fotolia; 186 (top): Dfikar/Fotolia; 188: Natalia Bratslavsky/Fotolia; 190: Rebius/Fotolia; 191: Davehanlon/Fotolia; 202 (bottom, left): Dmitry Vereshchagin/Fotolia; 202 (bottom, right): Marc Xavier/Fotolia; 202 (top, center): WavebreakmediaMicro/Fotolia; 202 (top, left): WavebreakmediaMicro/Fotolia; 202 (top, right): Twin Design/Shutterstock; 206: Slasnyi/Fotolia; 211: Malinkaphoto/Fotolia; 213: Nikolai Sorokin/Fotolia; 216: James Steidl/Fotolia; 217: Jackie DeBusk/Fotolia; 218: Dade72/Fotolia; 219: Sergey Andrianov/Fotolia; 220: Freesurf/Fotolia; 221: Shutterstock; 222: Rawpixel/Fotolia; 223 (left): Vvoe/Fotolia; 223 (right): Laks/Fotolia; 225: Jodie777/Fotolia; 228 (left): Photobank/Fotolia; 228 (right): Kingan/Fotolia; 229 (top, left): Victor Zastol'skiy/Fotolia; 229 (bottom): NoraDoa/Fotolia; 229 (top, right): Victor Zastol'skiy/Fotolia; 231: BillionPhotos/Fotolia; 232 (bottom): Luciano Mortula/Fotolia; 232 (center): Ilya Akinshin/Fotolia; 232 (top): Rido/Fotolia; 233: Kenishirotie/Fotolia;

234: Uros Petrovic/Fotolia; 235: Kilala/Fotolia; 236: Mny Jhee/Fotolia; 237: Haveseen/Fotolia; 239: Tiero/ Fotolia; 240: Nejron Photo/Fotolia; 242: Matt Magnone/Fotolia; 243: Annatronova/Fotolia; 244: Gmoulart/ Fotolia; 245: Sapgreen/Fotolia; 246: Iprachenko/Fotolia; 247: Wabkmiami/Fotolia; 250: Flairimages/Fotolia; 253: Romolo Tavani/Fotolia; 255 (bottom): Fotopak/Fotolia; 255 (top): Jim Parkin/Fotolia; 259: Tonyv3112/ Fotolia; 263: Jolopes/Fotolia; 266: Dampoint/Fotolia; 268: WavebreakMediaMicro/Fotolia; 269: Andrey Kuzmin/ Fotolia; 270: Nerthuz/Fotolia; 272: Time House/Alamy Stock Photo; 275 (bottom): Photographee.eu/Fotolia; 275 (top): Xerox123/Fotolia; 277: Elena Suvorova/Fotolia; 280: Burlingham/Fotolia; 282 (bottom): Alswart/ Fotolia; 282 (top): Michael Shake/Fotolia; 283: Pavel Kirichenko/Fotolia; 286: Mariephotos/Fotolia; 291: Mayboro/Fotolia; 292: Yiucheung/Fotolia; 294 (bottom): Iriana Shiyan/Fotolia; 294 (top): Lightpoet/ Fotolia; 296: PackShot/Fotolia; 297: Den Belitsky/Fotolia; 299 (bottom): Takawildcats/Fotolia; 299 (center): Kampanel/Fotolia; 299 (top): Ingusk/Fotolia; 301: Vitanovski/Fotolia; 302: 103tnn/Fotolia; 306: WavebreakMediaMicro/Fotolia; 307: Nyul/Fotolia; 308: Phanuwatnandee/Fotolia; 310: Scherbinator/ Fotolia; 314: Timothy Masters/Fotolia; 315: Syda Productions/Fotolia; 316: Scott Leman/Fotolia; 317: Konstantin Yuganov/Fotolia; 318: BlueSkyImages/Fotolia; 320 (bottom, right): Pixelrobot/Fotolia; 320 (center): Staras/Fotolia; 320 (top, left): Jk1991/Fotolia; 320 (top, right): Kontur Vid/Fotolia; 321: Freefly/ Fotolia; 322: Brian Lasenby/Fotolia; 323: Yommy/Fotolia; 324: Bastos/Fotolia; 326: Yanlev/Fotolia; 334: Halfpoint/Fotolia; 335: WavebreakMediaMicro/Fotolia; 336: Jenifoto/Fotolia; 337 (bottom): Videoeditor4u/ Fotolia; 337 (top): Gamelover/Fotolia; 338: Africa Studio/Fotolia; 341 (bottom): Aleutie/Fotolia; 341 (top): Monkey Business/Fotolia; 342 (bottom): VIPDesign/Fotolia; 342 (top): Jjava/Fotolia; 345 (bottom): Harris Shiffman/Fotolia; 345 (top): Lucian Milasan/Fotolia; 346: Antonioguillem/Fotolia; 348: Piotr Marcinski/Fotolia; 349: Richard Griffin/Fotolia; 350: Strauchburg.de/Fotolia; 351: Paul Maguire/Fotolia; 352: Thinglass/Fotolia; 355: Amyinlondon/Fotolia; 357: Tiero/Fotolia; 359: Alinamd/Fotolia; 360: Destina/Fotolia; 361: Kjersti/Fotolia; 362 (bottom): Mat Hayward/Fotolia; 362 (top): Romolo Tavani/Fotolia; 363: Brocreative/Fotolia; 364: Syda Productions/Fotolia; 366: Dmitry Vereshchagin/Fotolia; 368 (left): Sommai/Fotolia; 368 (right): Jose Ignacio Soto/Fotolia; 370: Sakuraco/Fotolia; 372 (bottom): Michaeljung/Fotolia; 372 (center): Ljupco Smokovski/ Fotolia; 372 (top): Shariff Che'Lah/Fotolia; 375: Photographee.eu/Fotolia; 376: Alexzeer/Fotolia; 377 (bottom, right): Sergey Nivens/Fotolia; 377 (top, left): Rido/Fotolia; 377 (top, right): Creativa Images/Fotolia; 378 (bottom): Suna/Fotolia; 378 (top): Maksym Yemelyanov/Fotolia; 380: Casey E Martin/Fotolia; 385 (bottom): Tomasz Zajda/Fotolia; 385 (top): Ana Blazic Pavlovic/Fotolia; 386: ET1972/Fotolia; 389 (bottom): Mayatnik/ Fotolia; 389 (center, left): Radnatt/Fotolia; 389 (top, right): Mesquitafms/Fotolia; 390: Xavier/Fotolia; 392: Theartofphoto/Fotolia; 394: Therina Groenewald/Fotolia; 395: Kyslynskyy/Fotolia; 396: Sebastian Studio/ Fotolia; 398: Aiisha/Fotolia; 400: Lirtlon/Fotolia; 401 (bottom): Juulijs/Fotolia; 401 (top): Maksym Yemelyanov/ Fotolia; 402 (bottom): Trezvuy/Fotolia; 402 (top): Giuseppe Porzani/Fotolia; 404: Giorgio Pulcini/Fotolia; 405: George Spade/Fotolia; 407 (bottom): 135pixels/Fotolia; 407 (top): Muta/Fotolia; 408 (bottom): Ugrum1/ Fotolia; 408 (top): Hiphoto39/Fotolia; 409 (bottom): Byheaven/Fotolia; 409 (top): Cj2a/Fotolia; 411 (bottom): Steheap/Fotolia; 411 (top): Mariia Pazhyna/Fotolia; 413 (bottom): Mates/Fotolia; 413 (top): Fotomaximum/ Fotolia; 415: Elisabetta Figus/Fotolia; 416: Saharrr/Fotolia; 418: Harvepino/Fotolia; 419 (left): Iordani/Fotolia; 419 (right): Sergey Peterman/Fotolia; 420: Focus Pocus LTD/Fotolia; 422 (bottom): Master1305/Fotolia; 422 (top): Kevron2001/Fotolia; 424: Arkela/Fotolia; 426: Daniele80/Fotolia; 427: Pishkott/Fotolia; 428: Morenovel/Fotolia; 429: Dimakp/Fotolia; 430 (center): Dina777/Fotolia; 430 (left): Ljupco Smokovski/ Fotolia; 430 (right): Esthermm/Fotolia; 432 (bottom): Anatoly Tiplyashin/Fotolia; 432 (top): ksena32/Fotolia; 436: Shotsstudio/Fotolia; 437: Aleciccotelli/Fotolia; 438: Victor zastol'skiy/Fotolia; 439: Osterland/Fotolia; 441 (bottom): Cn0ra/Fotolia; 441 (top): Elenarts/Fotolia; 443: Jeff.b/Fotolia; 444: Vichie81/Fotolia; 446: Pellinni/Fotolia; 449 (bottom): Andy Dean/Fotolia; 449 (top): DragonImages/Fotolia; 450: Dmitry Naumov/Fotolia.

Illustrations: Don Martinetti, pages 7, 16, 20, 28, 44, 58, 66, 73, 99, 105, 118, 133, 150, 153, 159, 178, 193, 199, 241, 260, 289, 312, 463, 464, 459, 467; Chris Pavely, pages 3, 12, 36, 39, 55, 89, 109, 186, 210, 215, 256, 259, 264, 309, 351, 367; Kris Wiltse, page 16

NOTES

NOTES

NOTES

NOTES

NOTES

NOTES